FIFTH EDITION

A PRACTICAL GUIDE TO EARLY CHILDHOOD CURRICULUM

Claudia Eliason
Loa Jenkins

Merrill, an imprint of
Macmillan College Publishing Company
New York

Maxwell Macmillan Canada
Toronto

Maxwell Macmillan International
New York   Oxford   Singapore   Sydney

Editor: Linda Sullivan
Production Supervisor: WordCrafters Editorial Services, Inc.
Production Manager: Francesca Drago
Cover Designer: Robert Vega
Cover photograph: George Ancona/INTERNATIONAL STOCK

This book was set in Electra by Americomp, and was printed and bound by R. R. Donnelley & Sons.
The cover was printed by New England Book Components, Inc.

Macmillan College Publishing Company
866 Third Avenue, New York, New York 10022

Macmillan College Publishing Company is part of the Maxwell Communication Group of Companies.

Maxwell Macmillan Canada, Inc.
1200 Eglinton Avenue East, Suite 200
Don Mills, Ontario M3C 3N1

Be prepared!
With this book
and our encouragement
Go forth . . .
Teach those you reach
and
Reach those you teach.

Library of Congress Cataloging-in-Publication Data
Eliason, Claudia Fuhriman (date)
   A practical guide to early childhood curriculum / Claudia F.
Eliason, Loa T. Jenkins. — 5th ed.
     p.   cm.
   Includes bibliographical references and index.
   ISBN 0-02-332223-3
   1. Early childhood education—Curricula. I. Jenkins, Loa
Thomson (date). II. Title.
LB1140.4.E43   1994
372.19—dc20   93-5646
                              CIP

Printing: 1 2 3 4 5 6 7   Year: 4 5 6 7 8 9 0

Preface

Many are the times
  we will teach;
Many are the times
  we will be taught.
. . . But only once, a child.

While preparing to teach, students become imbued with educational theories but then often find themselves in the classroom as students or professional teachers without practical knowledge of what and how to teach. They understand the process of learning, or at least the theories describing that process, but they often are unable to formulate this information as curricula appropriate for young children. Curriculum books for early childhood and primary grades abound, but they are often general in content, so that it remains difficult for students to combine knowledge and ideas into meaningful units of study.

In this textbook we have not only emphasized the application aspect of teaching but have also given a solid foundation for the theoretical basis of the concepts being applied. We want students and teachers to understand what should be taught to young children, why it is important, and how it can be accomplished. We also emphasize that the child is the center of the curriculum, and the curriculum should encompass the whole child—physical, social, emotional, creative, and cognitive. This book focuses on cognitive areas of the curriculum and effective methods of curriculum implementation. We teach how to present concepts to young children while developing understanding and thinking in the early years.

A Practical Guide to Early Childhood Curriculum is designed for those in the process of preparing to teach young children, as well as for those currently teaching—teachers, teachers' aides, parents, grandparents, church leaders, administrators, and others. The book presents an approach to cognitive development and concept formation in selected areas of early childhood curriculum based on concepts developmentally appropriate for children 3 to 8 years of age. Its purpose is to explore how children learn, what children can learn, and specific avenues for transmitting learning concepts. It is our intent to blend the theory and application of early childhood education.

This book evolved from the constant inquiry and search for meaningful teaching ideas by students and professional teachers. Although our aim is teacher orientation—for we believe that the teacher does indeed set the stage for what is taught and learned—our primary concern is the children being taught. We are concerned that young children have high-quality school experiences. We hope that this book assists in the planning and preparation of exciting, meaningful learning episodes.

A *Practical Guide to Early Childhood Curriculum* has also evolved from our teaching experiences in the primary grades, in Head Start, and in college and university classrooms and laboratories. The concepts selected for inclusion are those that most often meet the needs, interests, and developmental levels of children 3 to 8 years of age. Included are current references and research on each of the specific areas. Also included is an updated section on resources for children's books, records, tapes, cassettes, pictures, multimedia kits, films, filmstrips, videos, and other audiovisual aids.

We have suggested computer software appropriate for specific concept areas. Literally thousands of new works are published each month in early childhood education alone. We therefore suggest that, based on the kind of computer you have and your budget, you evaluate new software choices for your school, classroom, or center on an ongoing basis. We emphasize again that the software selected should be developmentally appropriate for the children, utilize a variety of approaches, and emphasize a variety of concepts. To accomplish this, it may be wise to select materials from several companies. Talk to colleagues, and benefit from their evaluations and experiences. As with all equipment and materials, remember the need to evaluate and update periodically.

The pedagogy has been unified to follow a specific format for each chapter: introductory comments, chapter summary, student learning activities, and suggested resources. The introduction provides an overview of the chapter, and the summary reviews the important notions presented. The student learning activities offer discussion questions and numerous activities to assist students in applying the concepts presented in the chapter. These activities also serve as mainsprings for additional activities. In addition, the references cited in each chapter provide varied ideas and points of view on the specific topics and themes. The full references are listed alphabetically at the end of the book.

A number of major changes have been made in this textbook's fifth edition, including rearrangement of some of the chapters. Multicultural and diversity concepts have been included in Chapter Four, "People and Their Diversity." Information on this important area has been expanded in this current edition. Material on special needs has also been moved to Chapter Four, so that it may act as a foundation concept for students using this text. Also new in this edition are guidelines and information on planning and taking field trips, which are included in Chapter Three, "Planning the Curriculum." A new physical fitness and games section emphasizes the importance of physical fitness as a curriculum area and also gives specific suggestions for physical/motor games. Throughout the text, we encourage cooperative learning and have included specific activities to enhance and provide opportunities for cooperative learning.

The text is divided into eight parts, each presenting a solid theoretical discussion and rationale. Part One, which provides an introduction and framework or structure for the text, includes three chapters. Chapter One is an overview of early childhood education, including a comprehensive look at the historical perspective, as well as where we are today and where we are going in the future. Also included is a section on how children learn. Chapter Two includes an in-depth discussion of the value of play in early childhood education. The types of play experiences appropriate for young children are also discussed, along with the importance of the physical environment in setting the stage for play and learning. In addition to discussing criteria for selecting appropriate toys and equipment, we suggest the use of teacher-made equipment and materials. (Various examples, including line drawings, photographs, and descriptions, are listed throughout the text and in Appendix A.) Teachers should use their own creative resources and expertise to make materials that enrich the environment and provide hands-on practice with manipulatives that are age appropriate and challenging. A detailed discussion of curriculum planning is outlined in Chapter

Three and will prove valuable for the student preparing to teach young children.

Part Two deals with socioemotional skills or competencies and concepts related to understanding and dealing with the self and others. These concepts will be integrated throughout the curriculum, for we constantly strive to help children understand themselves. Every day brings challenges and opportunities for growth in relating more effectively with others, and Chapters Four and Five give specific concepts to teach relating to the self and other people. Although multicultural education is integrated throughout the text, it is considered in greater depth in Chapter Four.

All curriculum development and understanding rest on the child's ability to understand language, and Part Three (Chapter Six) reflects the authors' feelings regarding the importance of language and literacy development. In this revised chapter, theory development is supported by many practical approaches designed to integrate language and literacy across the curriculum. Suggestions are given for creating a literate environment for young children and for stimulating young children's language and literacy learning in developmentally appropriate ways. Particular emphasis is placed on promoting positive habits and attitudes relating to speaking, listening, reading, and writing. Our focus and emphasis are not on skill, techniques, or mechanics, but on meaningful experiences that equip children with the ability to read deeply, hear and understand others, and communicate with depth and understanding by speaking and eventually writing. This chapter is a foundation for all other chapters.

Part Four is divided into two chapters. The recipes in Chapter Seven reflect the need to avoid a high sugar and fat content, as well as to include recipes from various cultures. In writing Chapter Seven, and in suggesting food activities throughout the text, it is our purpose to be especially cognizant of selecting and including high-nutrient foods. To complete this part, the four senses have been combined into one chapter (Chapter Eight).

Part Five includes chapters on music and movement, as well as creativity and art. These are vital parts of the early childhood curriculum and should not be overlooked by teachers. The value of these kinds of experiences is stressed in Chapters Nine and Ten, as well as in the introduction to Part Five.

The focus in Part Six is on science and critical thinking. It is our desire that young children develop competence in critical thinking that will serve them across the curriculum. Children should not be taught only to learn, memorize, and take in facts; more important, they must learn to think deeply—to classify, explain, investigate, wonder, communicate, analyze, compare, and predict. Critical thinking stems from actions, not words, and the knowledge that comes from meaningful experiences is gleaned through the child's activities. However, experiences alone are not enough. In order for learning to be meaningful, children must learn to investigate, question, analyze, solve problems, observe, sort, hypothesize, and come to meaningful conclusions and understandings. This is what critical thinking entails, and it requires sensitive teachers equipped with effective teaching methods. The six chapters included in Part Six all relate to science concepts.

Part Seven includes three chapters relating to math concepts and emphasizes problem-solving skills. Children need to develop an ability to work with math concepts. They should learn to solve problems initially by working with concrete ideas; then, equipped with problem-solving skills, they become able to handle more abstract problems.

Finally, Part Eight deals with an additional teacher skill. Because of the importance of parents in early childhood education, Chapter Twenty explores the importance of working with parents, both inside and outside of the classroom, as curriculum concepts are extended from the school into the home.

We emphasize that we take a developmental approach to teaching young children; that is, experiences are planned in accordance with the developmental needs of the children in the classroom or center. Since lesson plans are a primary focus in the text, our approach to lesson planning is described in detail in Chapter Three. Chapters Four through Eight and Eleven through Nineteen develop specific concepts, such as color, numbers, and texture, that can be taught to young children. Included in each of these chapters is an introduction for that concept, approaches to teaching the concept, a unit plan or web of activities, and, in some cases, a sample lesson plan. We hope that the reader will view these ideas and lesson plans as springboards for infinite possibilities, rather than as structured methods and plans. These activities and suggestions should spark creativity in teachers for adapting ideas to specific localities and situations, and especially to the children who are being taught. The concepts suggested are examples, and they are not meant to be exhaustive or complete.

From our own understandings and observations of young children, we conclude that the best approach to curriculum planning is based on experience. Children's enthusiasm for learning is heightened by concrete experiences with people, places, and things.

In writing this text, our intention has been to provide a different and stimulating approach to teaching in early childhood education. We do not intend to cover the entire gamut of early childhood education, for this text is designed to be used in curriculum courses in early childhood education. We have purposely omitted such topics as safety and health and other general areas that are usually covered in other introductory courses in early childhood education.

The following ideas make this text unique:

1. The approach is thorough. Rather than just addressing broad general areas such as math and science, the text is further divided into specific concepts, approaches, or units that can stand alone as teaching areas for young children. Within each of the chapters on specific topics are well-organized and clearly explained concepts that set the stage for learning. Most texts

with this focus lack the concept development that is included here.
2. There is a wealth and variety of ideas and activities.
3. A unique, detailed, and refreshing approach to planning is presented.
4. The clarity and simplicity of the writing style make it easy for students and teachers to grasp and understand the content.
5. The student learning activities give opportunities for applying what has been learned and provide practical applications for teaching in early childhood classrooms or centers.
6. The references and resource lists are comprehensive, up to date, and varied.
7. Specific unit and lesson plans are presented, and students will find this approach helpful as they learn to develop and implement their own lesson plans.
8. This text will become one students want to keep as a reference and comprehensive resource.

We also encourage teachers and others responsible for selecting children's books to choose literary works carefully, being aware that many excellent nonsexist books are currently being written.

Regarding foods used as art media, we are aware that many areas of the world are affected by starvation, and we caution against the use of foods generally as an art medium. However, when a food item such as macaroni is cheap and abundant, we do not encourage purchasing beads for stringing necklaces from a craft store at many times the cost. We first encourage teachers to seek discarded items; but when a specific art activity is being planned, such as making necklaces, and the macaroni costs less than the craft item, it is wise to use the inexpensive macaroni. In addition, for such creative art activities as orange or potato painting, we encourage teachers to obtain these as discarded items from the produce department of the grocery store. Some of these items are discarded daily because they are no longer fit for human consumption. As children use these foods for art, it should be explained that the foods have been discarded by the grocer because they are perishable and no longer good to eat. The food is not completely wasted when it can still serve as an art medium. We consider it imperative for children to learn early the value of using and preserving, rather than wasting, food.

Writing this book has been an exciting endeavor. Although our aim is to meet the needs of teachers and to support them in carrying out their important stewardship, our efforts are of no avail if the lives of young children are not also influenced positively.

Acknowledgments

We express appreciation to the many people who have assisted, supported, and encouraged us in this project. We are indebted to Paul Jenkins for the photographs throughout the book. We appreciate his sensitivity, skill, time, and effort. We also thank the many children and adults who cooperated in the photography, including the Eastern Idaho Head Start of Human Services Center, Inc., the Lincoln Elementary School, and The Progressive Day School in Idaho Falls, Idaho; in addition, we thank Nina Hansen, director, St. Paul Lutheran School, Child Development Center, Ogden, Utah. We thank Mr. Stephen Felt, principal of Dee School in Ogden, Utah, and the K–2 teachers there. We also thank Mrs. Shirley Bergeson, principal at Wasatch Elementary in Ogden, Utah, and two of her teachers, Connie Jensen and Elizabeth Goff.

A special thanks to Jana Jones for her assistance in providing information on teaching children with special needs. We also express our appreciation to the publisher's reviewers for their valued contributions to the completion of this book: Imelda D'Agostino, Mount St. Mary's College; Christine Bachelder, Black Hawk College; Georgianna Cornelius, New Mexico State University; Sim Lesser, Miami-Dade Community College; Laurie A. Pariseau, University of Texas at San Antonio; and Karen L. Peterson, Washington State University.

Lisa Warner, of Eastern Kentucky University, shared materials with us, and Patrice Liljenquist Borens contributed her graphics and artistic talents.

For editorial assistance, we thank Linda Sullivan and the staff at Macmillan Publishing for their wise direction, patient prodding, and demand for excellence.

We are grateful for our interaction with the children, parents, and students we have taught: Their inspiration, incentive, behavior, and thoughts have influenced whatever understandings we have.

We recognize the contributions of the following early childhood education teachers who have graciously allowed us to publish their lesson plans: Donalee Jones Heaton, Valari Van Valkenburg, Roxann Rothwell, Janet Curtis, Mary Lyn Worley, Julee Ann Hawks, Barbara Scholes, Luci Fowers, Lynette Morris Whalen, Marianne Miller, Karen Clark, Joy Wadley Erekson, Joanne Conrad Anderson, Patsy Thurgood Matthews, Debra Snow, and Adelle Taggart Karren. Special thanks go to Sally Miner for her contributions and assistance. We also are indebted to Dr. Bonita Wise for her help with the chapter on nutrition and food experiences and to Carrie Watt and Joanne Conrad Anderson for their help with the teacher-made materials.

We are indebted to our friends and families, especially to our husbands, Paul and Glen, whose patience, support, interest, and encouragement were vital to the completion of this new edition. We give thanks to our children, Jason, Cathrine, Anne, Matthew, Megan, Eric, Erin, Kyle, Kristen, and Catherine, whose examples have enlightened our understanding of the truths of childhood.

Claudia Fuhriman Eliason
Loa Thomson Jenkins

Brief Contents

Contents

Chapter eight
Smell and Taste, Texture and Touch, Sound and Pitch   227

PART FIVE   AESTHETIC DEVELOPMENT   255

Chapter nine
Music and Movement   259

Chapter ten
Creativity and Art   289

PART SIX   DEVELOPING SCIENCE AND CRITICAL THINKING SKILLS   305

Chapter eleven
Science Experiences   309

Chapter twelve
Weight and Balance   343

Chapter thirteen
Color   353

Chapter fourteen
Animals   364

Chapter fifteen
Plants   385

Chapter sixteen
Temperature, Weather, and Seasons   401

A PRACTICAL GUIDE
TO
EARLY CHILDHOOD
CURRICULUM

INTRODUCTION TO EARLY CHILDHOOD EDUCATION

The three chapters in Part One provide an introduction to and overview of this textbook. Chapter One gives a historical perspective on early childhood education, discusses why it is important, and includes present trends and considerations as well as a look at the future of early childhood education. Although the focus of this book is on children ages 2 to 8 years, most 2-year-olds need a very relaxed curriculum schedule with an emphasis on play. During early childhood, it is suggested that more concepts and structure be added to the curriculum very gradually; however, we wish to emphasize that even though there have been major sociological and technological changes in our society over the past years, developmental rates have not accelerated (Weikart, 1986). Children need environments and learning experiences that are geared to their needs, not focused on highly academic curricula and planned by what adults think children ought to be learning and doing. These children (2- to 8-year-olds) need child-centered environments that encourage learning through play, exploration, and discovery.

Chapter Two stresses the importance of play; it is respected for its value and as an appropriate learning medium during early childhood. The importance of the physical environment is discussed, the value of various areas of the room or play activities is considered, and criteria for selecting materials and toys are given. Teacher-made learning materials are also discussed. Chapter three presents an overview of curriculum planning and gives examples using themes and units. It is hoped that those who use this book will learn what concepts and skills best meet the needs of young children and how to plan in such a way that children have age-appropriate, child-centered educational experiences. We wish to emphasize that different levels of ability and development in each early childhood classroom should be expected, valued, accepted, and planned for.

one

Early Childhood Education

Introduction

The beliefs of many philosophers, psychologists, and educators dating back to the 17th century have greatly influenced early childhood education as it is practiced in the 1990s. The needs and values of early childhood education are many faceted, and caring, qualified early childhood teachers are paramount to the learning of the developing child. In order to implement developmentally appropriate teaching practices in the child's early years, caregivers must be aware of the developmental characteristics of the children with whom they are working. It is also imperative that teachers and other caregivers gain an understanding of just how children learn as they progress toward becoming well-adjusted, confident, and competent individuals.

A Historical Look at Early Childhood Education

Early childhood education has historical roots dating back for centuries, although it has experienced a rediscovery in the past few decades.

Highlights of the 17th and 18th Centuries

Prior to the 1900s, childhood was not looked upon as an important, valuable, and viable part of the total life span. Around 1690, the English philosopher John Locke (1632–1704) was one of the first to emphasize the importance of individual differences, the early years and experiences, and play. Rousseau (1712–1778), a French philosopher, suggested that society has a corrupting influence on children and that children should be treated with sympathy and compassion. The Swiss educator Pestalozzi (1746–1827) maintained that all persons had the right to an education—to develop skills, to learn those things that would help them be successful. He believed that children learn best through self-discovery.

Development of Kindergarten and Nursery School

Friedrich Froebel (1782–1852) originated the first kindergarten, in Germany, around 1837. To achieve his proposed objectives, he designed a curriculum based on play and materials. Froebel believed that children had innate gifts that needed to be developed, and that they would cultivate these gifts by choosing activities that interested them (Osborn & Osborn, 1991). Beginning in 1870 in the United States, and by World War I, kindergarten was incorporated into public schools in large cities. Today, kindergarten education is very close to being as universal as elementary education.

In 1911, Margaret McMillan established the first nursery school in London. In the United States, Patty Smith Hill (1868–1946) was one of the early pioneers in kindergarten education. After observing the McMillan nursery school, she also became a pioneer in nursery or preschool education.

Other Historical Contributors to Early Childhood Education

John Dewey (1859–1952), an American educator and philosopher, developed the idea of pragmatism and maintained that children should experiment and discover. He did not like rote teaching, but believed in natural materials and presumed that children should explore in a free-play environment, with much activity, geared to their own interests.

In the United States following World War I, the ideas of Sigmund Freud affected education. His theory emphasized unconscious motivation, the beginning of sexual development, conflicts between social expectations and spontaneous behaviors, and the impact of emotions on behaviors.

Maria Montessori (1870–1952), the first woman in Italy to be granted a medical degree, is best known for the teaching method that bears her name—the Montessori method. She opened the Casa dei Bambini (children's home) in a tenement area of Rome in 1907. There has been a resurgence of interest in the Montessori method since the reintroduction of her work by Rambusch (1962). Among Montessori's key ideas was her belief that the senses are the source of all intellectual growth and that intellectual development is, therefore, dependent upon the training of the senses. She developed a set of physical materials, autotelic in nature, to be used by the teacher in a prescribed manner. She also emphasized the importance of the school and family working together.

Arnold Gesell(1880–1961), who played a key role in the early childhood movement, is particularly known for his research in establishing norms or indices of the types of behavior likely to occur in children at specific ages. However, he still emphasized the concept of individual differences and cautioned against using the norms literally.

Jean Piaget (1896–1980) is noted for his interest in and theory of children's cognitive development. The impact of his works on present-day education, psychology, and child development is increasingly evident. Piaget's work and writing have generated more interest and research than those of any other person in education or developmental psychology in the last 50 years. His research also radically changed our thinking about the growth of human intelligence. He had great love, empathy, and appreciation for children (Elkind, 1982). Programs that adapt a Piagetian model emphasize that children learn through experimentation and initiative.

The focus in the 1920s and 1930s was on physical and intellectual development. During the 1930s, early education programs were based on the works of Froebel, Montessori, McMillan, Robert Owen, and a few other pioneers of early childhood education (Olmsted, 1992). Between 1940 and 1950, the emphasis was on physical, social, and emotional growth. At the 1950 White House Conference on Youth, Erik Erikson presented his theory on personality development, which was to gain widespread acceptance and favor among educators and swing the emphasis in early childhood education to the social and emotional side.

In the 1960s, research gave evidence that the early environment has a profound effect on the child's development. Suddenly, the poor had greater opportunity for involvement and decision making in the education of their children. Project Head Start, a composite of federally funded preschool programs for children from impoverished backgrounds, was established in 1965. With the organization of Head Start, preschool education moved to the national level and programs became available for all children. It was hoped that by offering an enriched program for lower-income children, this "head start" would reverse the cycle of poverty. This program also emphasized the family and community. Perhaps its foremost accomplishment, however, was awakening in the public a sense of the profound importance of the early years and of education for the young.

The pressures of the 1960s were for openness, humanistic approaches to education, acceptance of individual learning styles, and education for the impoverished. Directions in the 1970s emphasized literacy, discipline, achievement in the "basics," conformity, and demands for accountability. During the late 1960s and the 1970s, many program models received attention. Home-based education focusing on teaching and working with parents was developed by Ira Gordon.

The Ypsilanti, Michigan, Early Training Project is a research study based on Piaget's theorizing, with the aim of promoting total cognitive development. The program developers believe that preventive preschool programs must begin earlier than traditional preschool programs, because the critical years for early learning are age 3 and under. They also maintain that early intervention programs will be much more effective if they involve both the mother and the child. The Ypsilanti research project presents solid evidence that preschool education does make a difference for children (Clement, Schweinhart, Barnett, Epstein, & Weikart, 1984; Schweinhart, Berrueta-Clement, Barnett, Epstein, & Weikart, 1985; Schweinhart & Weikart, 1980). Program models differ in their curriculum emphasis, structure, reinforcement methods, teacher role, activities, and materials, but no program has been found to be the best for all children, and the children in any program show improvements in the areas emphasized in that particular program.

Another significant happening in the 1970s was the enactment of Public Law 94-142, the Education for All Handicapped Children Act of 1975 (renamed the Individuals with Disabilities Education Act in 1990). This law required that all children be given the opportunity to reach their fullest potential and that children with special needs be included in regular public school programs when possible. During the 1970s, much more emphasis was placed on understanding children with special needs or disabilities.

Legislation on behalf of these young children continued in the 1980s with passage of the Education of the Handicapped Act Amendments of 1986 (P.L. 99-457. This legislation represents far-reaching federal policy supporting early childhood intervention for children 3 to 5 years of age.

Early Childhood Education in the 1980s

During the 1980s, we celebrated the International Year of the Child and focus turned toward social changes influencing children. The 1980s were a decade of increased wealth for the affluent and more poverty for America's poor. It was a decade when child abuse became a social disgrace. Perhaps because of our increased awareness more abuse was reported than in the decades before, but the reality of the numbers tells us that child abuse did increase significantly.

Child poverty soared to record levels in the 1980s; it peaked at 22.2% in 1983, following a recession in 1981–1982 (Children's Defense Fund, 1991, p. 23). Now, more and more children from every economic and racial group are being neglected and are in trouble. Their troubles pose a threat to U.S. security, values, and ideals and a prosperous, happy future for every U.S. citizen.

Violence begets violence, and the 1980s saw increased family, gang, and individual violence, often directed toward children. Children were killed as they waited in line at the movie theater, at the park, in their front yards, and in their neighborhoods and schools. Many children and youth went armed to school. Every day in the United States there are 135,000 children who take guns to school (Children's Defense Fund, 1991, p. 5).

The plight of the homeless also invaded our conscience in the 1980s. The homeless are not all middle-aged, single men; many are women and children. In fact, 100,000 American children are homeless each night, and it is estimated that children make up one-third of the nation's homeless population (Children's Defense Fund, 1991, pp. 6, 107). Most homeless families are headed by a single parent, usually the mother. Some researchers estimate that approximately 90% of homeless families are headed by single mothers.

Schools can and should help expand local, state, and national efforts to support homeless children who are victimized by their living situations. As caregivers of these children, we must not single them out, but stress their similarities with others—as we must emphasize that *all* children have more similarities than differences. Remember, too, that parents of children who are homeless *do care* about their families (Linehan, 1992; McCormick & Holden, 1992).

During the 1980s, the trend toward more women working outside the home continued. An increasing number of women found it necessary to enter the workforce because they were the head of the household, because of economic necessity, or because of personal desire. In 1989, 58% of children under 6 years of age had mothers in the workforce (U.S. Dept. of Commerce, 1991, p. 391). With so many women with young children employed outside the home, high-quality, affordable child care became—and still is—a major concern. Wages often decrease, but the cost of

high-quality care increases. When this happens, parents compromise and put children in places that do not meet high standards.

The importance of high standards and excellence in education was a focus in the 1980s in part because of a widely quoted report from the National Commission on Excellence in Education (1983). The report, *A Nation at Risk: The Imperative for Educational Reform*, discusses in detail the "rising tide of mediocrity" in the educational foundations of our country (p. 5).

Other concerns in the 1980s were drug abuse and teenage suicide, and programs were begun with very young children to prevent these social problems from growing. National polls indicated the public's many concerns with education and often focused on the lack of discipline in classrooms as a paramount concern.

The education of the whole child became emphasized in the 1980s, and the need to meet each child's individual needs was again stressed by both the public and educators. A major impetus in sensitizing educators to the needs of *all* children was the understandings gleaned from the multicultural approach to education. Teachers became aware of the direct and subtle things they do that are demeaning to some children.

Children grow in esteem, confidence, and skill as they accomplish new developmental tasks. Accentuating the developmental approach, researchers affirmed the notion that children's developmental rates have not accelerated over time, but we have tried to accelerate their learning (Nebraska State Board of Education, 1986, p. 4). Now we have realized that early childhood programs should be concerned with *all* areas of the child's growth; should be action oriented; and should include educating children in ethics, values, and morals.

Early Childhood Perspective of the 1990s

The challenge in the 1990s is for America's conscience and for its very future—hopefully, a future without poverty, abuse, depression, and child neglect. The 1980s were materialistic and "me" oriented. In the 1990s, it is our hope that people will turn their hearts, minds, and pocketbooks outward and have a desire to share with and strengthen other people, regardless of their gender, race, religion, or economic situation. We must not measure the importance or worth of individuals by what they own or have or by their ethnic background, gender, or social class. The worth of individuals should be measured by what and who they are and the service, support, and help they give to others.

There is a renewal of interest in strengthening the American family, particularly to help families develop a moral orientation and to build stronger values within the family unit. Integrity as a value must be prized. To do this, parents must have a genuine desire to learn, make changes, be committed to their children, and take charge of themselves and their children. They must have their eyes, hearts, and minds focused on high family standards and values. They must put into practice behaviors drawing on traditions, experiences, and expectations that will bring them to a higher ground and enable them to mold and guide children who do better, think better, and *are* better individuals.

Businesses are recognizing the importance of contributing to schools and early childhood programs to ensure a strong and capable workforce for the future as well as provide child-care options for employees. Many agencies and businesses are involved in school partnerships, providing financial help, administrative assistance, or employees' volunteer time as tutors or mentors.

Public schools have expanded the number of safe, affordable child-care options for parents (Strother, 1987). Schools are often used for after-school programs for children who would otherwise be latchkey children. However, when child-care programs are planned in public schools, teachers must be cautioned not to emphasize formal, structured, academic instruction for young children, because when they do, miseducation is the result (Elkind, 1986).

The public, as well as parents, must demand excellence in education of administrators and teachers. The Weikart and Schweinhart studies have equated excellence with the term *high quality*—the key to the lasting effects of their projects. They define a high-quality program as having the following characteristics:

1. It is well managed and monitored.
2. Parents become partners with teachers in educating the child.
3. Competent, committed teachers or caregivers plan and work together in teams to provide mutual support and individual attention to children.
4. A high degree of adult–child interaction is essential.
5. The program is organized around a specific curriculum or set of principles for learning.
6. Teachers or caregivers are trained in the curriculum through ongoing inservice training.
7. The program is regularly assessed to assure that goals for high quality are being met. (High/Scope, 1982, p. 241)

It is our view that early childhood education should provide opportunities that contribute to the development of the whole child, and those working with young children should plan and implement experiences to meet the basic needs of each individual child, no matter the child's gender, social-class, or cultural or ethnic background. Early childhood programs should be open and flexible, while finding innovative ways to involve parents. Early childhood education should be seen as an integrated experience for the child from 2 to 8 years of age. This means that each grade level should be built on the preceding one, with the needs of the child being met at each level.

Goals for Early Childhood Education

Educators and other concerned people need to determine how to best provide for the needs of young children and enable *all* children to reach their full potential. Classrooms must be flexible to allow for the diversity of children being served, and the children must develop self-respect and an understanding of and sensitivity toward all people. Educators must have a sound set of beliefs on which policies, goals, and actions are based. Early childhood professionals must be accountable and keep focused on accomplishing their goals as they relate to the children they serve.

Another priority for the 1990s is to continue the impetus to involve the family more in early childhood programs. The more the family is included, the greater the strides the child makes. Through the increased awareness that comes with involvement, parents can develop better ways of meeting their child's needs.

Still another priority is to improve our professional image, educating the public about the importance of high-quality early childhood programs and seeking to protect and strengthen licensing in states and local communities.

The following are some specific suggestions for early childhood goals for the future:

1. Adopt and enforce state quality assurances for child care and early childhood classrooms. The important consideration is the *quality* of the care or program. We must be committed to excellence, to promoting the optimal development of the child in a safe and healthy environment. Providers should be encouraged to work toward certified degrees or participate in programs that offer such credentials as the Child Development Associate (CDA), which would increase their competencies in providing services for and teaching young children.
2. Increase state support levels for Head Start and other comprehensive and compensatory early childhood programs.
3. Increase state appropriations for child care.
4. Make it absolutely unacceptable for the wealthiest nation in the world to have the poorest children. The United States has the highest child poverty rate when compared to eight other industrialized nations (Children's Defense Fund, 1991). We must pull

out of poverty 5 million children under 6 years of age—children who go without basics of life such as food, clothing, and shelter—by reordering our financial and investment priorities (U.S. Department of Commerce, 1991, p. 463). As expressed by the Children's Defense Fund (1990), "the issue is not money, but national will and values" (p. 18). It is imperative that we realize the great benefits of rich and meaningful early childhood experience as the starting point for *all* of the child's educational experiences. By starting right, the pace is set and the foundation laid for an effective educational experience for life. All children deserve this, but poor children desperately need it.

5. Force the mass media to stop defiling U.S. society with the notion that everything can be as instant as fast food—instant sex without responsibility, instant buying power with a credit card, instant solutions to family and individual problems without hard work and sacrifice.
6. Persuade community, business, and religious leaders, as well as parents and politicians, that child abuse, family violence, drug abuse, neighborhood gangs, and crime are insults to our way of life, pose a threat to our personal security, and prevent us all from having hope for the future.
7. Through immunizations of *all* young children, eradicate childhood diseases such as polio, measles, rubella, and pertussis (whooping cough).
8. Ensure that all children in the United States start kindergarten prepared and ready to learn. Ideally, children from disadvantaged backgrounds and those with special needs will *all* have access to a preschool experience such as Head Start that will prepare them for school and provide them with developmentally appropriate experiences.
9. Empower every parent through access to high-quality parent education programs in

public schools, community agencies, businesses, higher education institutions, and county extension agencies, or through media programs available at local libraries.

10. Reverse the rising trend in child abuse. In 1989, 2.4 million children were reported abused or neglected, a 147% increase from 1979 (Children's Defense Fund, 1991, p. 18).
11. Reduce the number of homeless children. Since there are 100,000 children homeless every day, we should be able to reduce this figure significantly.
12. Provide access to affordable health care for all mothers who are poor and for all children up to the age of 18.
13. Awaken in our citizens the desire to do something for our children—to inculcate positive values; create self-esteem, trust, and confidence in where they are going; to guide, nurture, and defend our hope for the future by *doing* something for them and not just talking about what should be done.

When a child has rich, high-quality early childhood experiences with stimulating activities enhancing his or her development, the effect will likely be lasting. It is exciting, indeed, to envision the results of providing high-quality programs for all children ages 2 to 8 years with excellent, well-trained teachers who enjoy working with children and providing them with first-rate facilities and materials. The vision does not have to stop in the imagination; it can become a reality.

Glasser has used the term *quality* to describe what we are seeking in our classrooms. He points out that, until we change from teachers who are bosses to teachers who are leaders, we will not be able to obtain good work from children. Children work harder and strive more for quality when the work expected of them relates to their lives, is satisfying, and is not boring (Glasser, 1990).

The fabric of our society is woven of strong family values and ideals. The threads are strong individuals who have hope and enthusiasm for opportunities on the horizon and a desire to become educated. Our children must be strong threads—responsible, unselfish, and self-disciplined and holding positive attitudes.

Importance of Early Childhood Education

Factors Influencing the Need for Early Childhood Education

Poor children need the boost of high-quality early childhood education. The work of many psychologists and researchers has influenced both the growth of and the need for early childhood education. Bloom (1964); Clement and colleagues (1984); Elkind (1982); Fowler (1980); Gray, Ramsey, and Klaus (1982); Hunt (1961); and Schweinhart and Weikart (1980), among others, have supported the importance of environmental factors in influencing the early development of the child. Children, especially those from low-income families, need relevant experiences in the preschool environment. Effective preschool experiences help children overcome the influences of poverty (Clement et al., 1984; Schweinhart et al., 1985).

In 1988, 12.8 million families with children under 18 years of age were living below the poverty level (U.S. Department of Commerce, 1991, p. 463). The proportion of children living in poverty in the United States grew by 23% between 1979 and 1988, and one in five American children now lives in poverty (Children's Defense Fund, 1990). If this trend continues, by the year 2000 one in four will be living in poverty. We can and must respond by providing high-quality child care and enriching preschool experiences for our poor children—both for them and for our own future.

Children from single-parent homes or homes where both parents work need child care. The primary factor forcing early childhood education on the national agenda is the number of women in the workforce. Table 1–1 shows the

TABLE 1–1
Percentage of Women in the Labor Force

Description	1970	1980	1989
Married working women	41	50	58
Children aged 3 to 5 years with working mothers	NA	52	64
Married working women with children under 6 years of age	30	45	58
Divorced working women with children under 6 years of age	63	68	71
Married working women with children aged 6 to 17 years	30	45	58
Divorced working women with children aged 6 to 17 years	82	82	85

Statistics from the U.S. Department of Commerce (1991); p. 391.

dramatic changes that have occurred in the last two decades, and it is apparent that the trend toward women entering the labor force has continued. With regard to women who are divorced and have children under 6 years of age, 71% are in the labor force. Well over one-half of all preschool-aged children today have mothers who are employed outside the home (Children's Defense Fund, 1990). By the year 2000, this statistic could rise to 7 in 10 children.

There are currently 9 million children under 5 years of age with mothers in the labor force (U.S. Department of Commerce, 1991; p. 377). Table 1–2 shows how these children are cared for while their mothers are working.

Most of the children ages 3 to 6 years whose mothers are employed are cared for in their own homes or in other homes by relatives, neighbors, or friends. Day-care centers provide for a limited but growing number of children. The trend in the 1980s was toward child care in organized facilities. There is a need not only for more places for child care, but also for upgrading the quality of the care given.

More and more businesses; corporations; and local, state, and federal government agencies are offering day-care services for their employees. This kind of approach allows the parent and child to interact during the day and tends to provide high-quality care. The business is often concerned about the quality of the program and the facility and pays for part of its cost as a benefit to employees.

Another factor contributing to the need for high-quality early childhood programs is the increase in single-parent homes. Table 1–3 shows the changes over the past two decades in children living with both parents compared to children living with their mother only. We should say that there are also more single fathers today who are raising their children, but most children who are in single-parent homes still live with their mothers.

TABLE 1–2
Care of Children Under 5 Years of Age Whose Mothers Are in the Labor Force

Type of Care	Percentage of Children
In own homes	30
In other homes	36
In organized day-care facilities	24
Day-care centers	16
Preschool centers	8
By mother while she works	9

Statistics from the U.S. Department of Commerce (1991); p. 377.

TABLE 1–3
Percentage of Children Living with Both Parents or with Mother Only

Description	1970	1980	1989
White children under 18 years of age living with both parents	90	83	80
Black children under 18 years of age living with both parents	59	42	38
Hispanic children under 18 years of age living with both parents	78	75	67
Children under 18 years of age living with mother only	11	18	22
White children living with mother only	8	14	16
Black children living with mother only	30	44	51
Hispanic children living with mother only	NA	20	28

Statistics from the U.S. Department of Commerce (1991); p. 53.

The developmental need for early childhood education Several aspects of young children's growth point to the need for early childhood education. *Socialization* takes place in the early years, with the family being the first and most important group to which the child belongs. The early childhood group, where children relate to other children of their own age, is an ideal situation for furthering social skill and development. Through their play, they learn to develop friendships that enable them to refine their social behavior. Sharing, listening to others, developing leadership skills, learning to follow others, gaining confidence in dealing with others, and learning to conform to the rules of the group are all examples of by-products of early childhood socialization.

The early childhood experiences of the child also aid in the *development of physical and motor functions*. Materials and apparatus should be provided that enable the child to use and exercise both large and small muscles. Large-muscle apparatus and activities include climbing apparatus, tricycles, wagons, rocking boats, tumble tubs, and locomotor and rhythmic activities. Small-muscle apparatus and activities include puzzles, lacing games and toys, scissors, and crayons, as well as fingerplays and any other activities and materials that encourage the use of the hands

and fingers. There are also many appropriate physical/motor games for children in the early childhood years. They should be simple to play and noncompetitive.

The *emotional development* of the child has long been of paramount concern. This aspect of development relates closely to the development of either a positive or a negative self-image. Children must like themselves. The feelings of being "okay" and important, and of having strengths and direction, make up the positive self-image. They are generated from within but are developed and created from outside the child. It is hoped that in the early years teachers and parents will begin to tap and encourage these kinds of feelings in children and eliminate the opposite kinds of feelings—of no one caring, unimportance, lack of worth and significance. Positive feelings provide motivation and encourage growth, whereas negative feelings stimulate failure and engender bitterness and resentment. One of the goals of early childhood education is to provide children with positive self-images. The significant people in children's early environment reflect back to the children how they are viewed, and the children, in turn, decide how to see themselves. These views of themselves will form their self-concepts, which in turn will determine their behaviors, attitudes, feelings, experiences, and success.

Generally speaking, children who feel good about themselves also feel good about their world; their emotions are characterized by spontaneity, enthusiasm, joy, interest, and happiness. On the other hand, children who do not feel good about themselves view the world with disappointment, anger, resentment, prejudice, and fear. Children cannot be protected from negative emotions and situations, but to be emotionally healthy, they must be equipped to cope with these feelings. Preschool programs offer experiences that help develop this coping ability, which is necessary to emotional health.

Success, accomplishment, trust, belonging, and achievement create positive feelings. The child's early experiences must provide and generate many such feelings in building a framework for healthy emotional development. A basic ingredient in the development of a healthy self-concept and emotional foundation is love.

Arnstein (1975) has proposed that the power of love in the very early years of life is strong enough to make sick children well and that its lack can make well children sick. She states: "This love has such a positive force that it can lessen and shorten the child's inevitable moments of frustration, anger, and hate" (p. 3). Love, according to Arnstein, can change, modify, and channel negative feelings into constructive actions, and later in life toward success and achievement. Katz (1985) suggests that it is important for the child not just to *be* loved but to *feel* loved. The child must feel that "what he [or she] does, or does not do, *really matters* to others" (p. 13).

The term *early childhood education* implies teaching the child. Thus *intellectual development* becomes an ingredient in the growth and development of the young child. It is well documented that the early years are of crucial importance to the child's intellectual growth. Early childhood education opens up a world to young children through experiences with people, events, animals, places, and things. A child cannot have an understanding of what a strawberry is, for example, without some experience with it—either a real experience, or a vicarious experience through a picture or an explanation, in specific detail, of what a strawberry is. The richest and most meaningful experiences for both children and adults are firsthand experiences.

Although young children need opportunities for learning, mastering skills, and thinking, the process must be slow and organized. Young children must be given time "to be as well as become" (Almy, 1975; p. 227). It has been suggested that pressures for early achievement and academic learning have intensified, but the way young children grow and learn has not changed (Seefeldt, 1985b).

For most children, it is believed, elaboration of basic concepts is preferred to rapid and accelerated learning in the cognitive domain (Hanson & Reynolds, 1991). Some cognitively oriented programs focus simply on accelerating development of the child's IQ. However, the individual child should be the focus, and the curriculum should be planned to help each child reach his or her fullest potential. Basic concepts presented in an exciting way are stimulating, fun, interesting, and involving, and they provide the foundations for learning as well as for beginning attitudes toward learning. Teachers of young children thus have the challenge of providing a curriculum that meets their needs and is relevant for them.

Early childhood educators seek to educate children not only to think, but also to feel and act. Teachers should not separate the cognitive from the affective; rather, they should see these domains as integrated parts of the whole and try to gear their instruction to build on this interdependence.

Early childhood education can thus be one of the primary means for meeting and satisfying some of the basic needs of young children: intellectual and linguistic, social, emotional, and physical. The early years are times for the development of language, creativity, thinking, and self-concepts. Therefore, the importance of high-quality education during this period cannot be overestimated.

High quality early childhood education classrooms assist children in feeling comfortable and successful in learning environments.

Early education can also be viewed as the time to alleviate problems by providing special programs: programs focusing on children who are economically disadvantaged and the problems often associated with poverty, programs treating learning disabilities at an early age, programs in special education, or programs reaching children with emotional difficulties at a time when negative behaviors have had little time to become ingrained.

The Early Childhood Teacher

Early childhood education may lose its intellectual thrust and its affirmative status and reputation in our society if it is unable to provide teachers who are specialists and experts in both theory and practice (Almy, 1975). Teachers of young children must be well trained. Teacher training institutions must provide high-quality training from which prospective teachers can gain knowledge of young children, skill in teaching techniques, and a sensitivity to and sense of responsibility for the whole child.

Piaget (1970b) believed that a teacher of young children should be highly intelligent and highly trained. Katz (1984) emphasizes the need for quality training and says that "effective training and education of early childhood teachers can make a significant contribution to children's development and learning" (p. 9). She also points out that professional teachers must "use judgment based on the most reliable knowledge and insight available"

The teacher is the person who implements the model or program. The teacher is also the decision maker and most often determines whether a day is successful or unsuccessful. The attitudes of the teacher and the teaching staff influence every aspect of the program; hopefully, their attitudes will reflect interest, enthusiasm, creativity, empathy, hope, tolerance, understanding, and care. Research on teaching effectiveness indicates that some of the previously mentioned qualities, in addition to flexibility, communication skills, a secure self-image, and ability to involve children actively in learning activities, are the most desirable assets in early childhood education teachers (Evans, 1975).

Early childhood educators must be *learners* who are willing to continually study, grow, and change. They must be able to think and solve problems. Saunders and Bingham-Newman (1984) describe it this way: "Thinking teachers are people who think hard while helping others to think well" (p. 155).

Those who are successful in working with

young children "are likely to have sizeable components of warmth and nurturance in their personalities" (Almy, 1975, p. 27). Children do not tune in or develop a rapport with cold, uncaring teachers; warmth and love are musts for successful early childhood teachers. Children flourish in a classroom where they sense that the teacher deeply *cares* about them—as people, about what they are learning, and about the skills they are developing. When they know the teacher genuinely cares for them, children have a way of living up to the teacher's expectations and striving to do what is expected. In addition, when they see a teacher working very hard to provide good teaching, they, in turn, have a drive to do good work (Glasser, 1990).

Another vital quality for good early childhood teachers is patience, because children make mistakes as they learn. Energy and enthusiasm are also important characteristics. The excellent early childhood teacher must be on the move frequently, and often very quickly, for most of the day. Enthusiasm must highlight the teacher's personality and illuminate every activity, for enthusiasm is caught, not taught. The more excited and enthusiastic the teacher is, the more eager, enthusiastic, and positive the children will be. We should also point out in this discussion that both men and women can be excellent early childhood teachers. The total personality and overall characteristics of the teacher are the critical factors, not the gender.

In this kind of environment—one that is planned to include materials and firsthand expe-

The excellent early childhood teacher is involved with the students all day long, in all kinds of outside and inside activities.

riences, coupled with an atmosphere of teacher warmth and concern—children are apt to flourish and have the groundwork laid for positive educational attitudes, as well as having their needs met in such a way that they can proceed successfully to the next level of development.

Developmentally Appropriate Teaching

Developmentally appropriate teaching means that we approach children from where they are and not from where we think they ought to be (Weikart, 1986). Teachers must understand the developmental needs and characteristics of each age group as well as each individual child. Learning activities and goals must match children's development and provide adequate time for exploring during the various stages of learning. As teachers plan developmentally appropriate activities, they should ask two questions: Is this activity right for a child this age? and Is this activity right for this child? (Bredekamp, 1986). Everything teachers plan and do must focus on the individual child. They must tailor, adjust, and adapt the curriculum to fit each child in the program, rather than expecting children to "fit" the program (Buckner, 1988; Elkind, 1987).

Children should be encouraged "to live each stage of development richly and fully, and make learning a pleasant and interesting journey relevant to their experiences, before they mount the next ladder rung of learning" (Hendrick, 1987; p. 30). As children proceed developmentally, teachers must also be cautious about judging the success of a program or activity solely on the basis of children's performances on standardized tests. The best measure of their success is through careful observations by teachers and professionals who are trained observers and know the children and their developmental characteristics well (Elkind, 1987).

The traditional street-crossing safety reminder, "Stop, look, and listen," can help us iden-tify developmentally appropriate practices in services for young children. Occasionally we must stop what we are doing, look around to see where we and the children are, and listen for feedback, or what is being said. Then, with caution, we can go ahead.

The Inappropriateness of Early Academics

Generally *how* we teach influences success or failure more than *what* we teach. Curriculum content, strategies, or teaching methods that put too much emphasis on intellectual achievement can misuse these early years (Connell, 1987; Elkind, 1987). As a profession, we must stand up for what we know is best for young children and not take them on a road that, based on our research and experience, we know is wrong (Buckner, 1988).

Elkind (1987) believes that the national trend toward pushing young children to achieve academically has led to using inappropriate teaching methods and developing unreasonable expectations for kindergarten and prekindergarten children. The end result has been that many of these children are pressured with too much, too soon, too fast, and they face stress and burnout early in their lives. The kindergarten scene of years gone by, with children building with blocks, painting at the easel, and dressing up has been replaced with workbooks, ditto sheets, and paper and pencil work (Seefeldt, 1985b). Children who are pushed too fast, too far, too soon lose interest in learning, experience failure, are unable to think for themselves, cannot deal with stress, and often find it difficult to relate to peers.

There is a dangerous trend toward teaching skills earlier and earlier in educational settings, increasing the stresses and failures felt by our youth. The college curriculum is being taught in senior high school, the senior high school curriculum in junior high, junior high in later elementary grades, later elementary in early elementary classes, early elementary in kindergarten, and kindergarten in preschool.

Corrie Ten Boom (1971) writes that her father would not allow her to learn too much, too soon, too fast. She had asked him a question, the answer to which he felt she was not yet able to fully understand. He responded by asking her to carry his luggage from the train, which she was unable to do, and she said, "It's too heavy." He answered that it is the same way with knowledge. "Some knowledge is too heavy for children. When you are older and stronger you can bear it. For now you must trust me to carry it for you" (pp. 26–27). In our sometimes faulty evaluations of where children are at a specific stage of development and what they seem capable of handling, we often believe that they can "carry it." We ask you to consider seriously, can they? And if they can carry it right now, how long will they be able to carry it? Is it necessary for them to carry it at this point in time?

Developmentally appropriate practices allow children to learn in ways that are appropriate—through real experiences, exploration, and activity. Young children's curiosity causes them to naturally seek to learn about and make sense of their world. Their learning style is spontaneous and needs to be self-directed rather than teacher- or program-directed. Provided with the appropriate curriculum experiences, children can pace their learning in such a way that it will closely parallel their growth in understanding.

The Excitement of Learning

One need only follow the daily paths of children and experience their enthusiasm for learning to realize that the acquisition of knowledge is exciting. There is a spontaneity in children as they gain new understandings: Their bodies move, their faces smile, their eyes dance with anticipation. This zest for learning is often lost as an individual matures. A new discovery made at any age should stimulate an intrinsic sense of fulfillment within oneself. The challenge is, therefore, to preserve and foster the curiosity and inquisitiveness of the young child.

Much of the learning taking place in today's classrooms and early childhood centers results from planned curriculum experiences and activities based on children's needs. However, oppor-

Curiosity is a very important element of science and discovery, and helps children maintain interest and excitement in learning.

tunities for learning abound in the child's environment beyond that which is teacher prepared. *Incidental learning* is constantly taking place as the child gives to and receives from the existing resources of the world. It is refreshing to observe, as in the following illustration, young children in the process of discovery.

Jalana painted with horizontal strokes of alternating black and white paint that had been placed at the easel. As the two colors ran together, her eyes expressed discovery, and she exclaimed, "I made gray!"

How Children Learn

We propose three main processes by which young children acquire knowledge and thinking skills: (1) experiences and cognition, (2) feedback and cognition, and (3) clarifying misconceptions and extending beyond the original concepts. Through these processes, children can acquire process skills such as observing, inferring, reasoning, rationalizing, questioning, exploring, classifying, and communicating. While reading about these three processes, keep in mind the previous discussion of how children learn and the need to avoid pushing academics, thereby eliminating unnecessary pressure from teaching too much, too soon, too fast.

Experiences and Cognition

It is imperative that children grow up with guided stimulation. One of the major responsibilities of the early childhood teacher is to build and strengthen real experiences for children. They need a variety of experiences around a single notion. One idea must be approached from different angles. Teachers must remember, too, that a single experience is not enough to build a reliable intellectual concept. Children use their experiences to provide the basis for interpreting, conceptualizing, and categorizing into meaningful ideas.

Piaget (1952) asserted that there are four major stages of intellectual growth throughout childhood. The first he described as the sensorimotor stage, which lasts from birth to about 2 years. It is a preverbal stage, and the infant is an active imitator and initiator of behavior. The infant learns, according to Piaget, primarily through the muscles and senses. Even though sensory learning extends into the second stage—the preoperational or representational stage—language becomes a primary tool for learning. Since the child in this stage, from 2 to 7 years, is a concrete, nonevaluative thinker who takes things as they are or as they look, many specific firsthand experiences are needed and teachers should avoid abstract concepts. During this stage, according to Piaget, labels or words become linked to experiences; although they are abstract symbols, they stand for concrete things. Children at this stage of thinking believe what they see and cannot hold an idea in their mind, or *conserve* it.

Children do not think the same way as adults do (Osborn & Osborn, 1983), and they learn in many different ways (Elkind, 1982). They absorb information through concrete experiences involving smelling, tasting, hearing, seeing, and touching. Children are constantly absorbing meaning by observing their environment. As important as the sense of sight is, one must realize that children also need numerous other sensory experiences. Activities involving all the senses provide firsthand experiences from which the child selects and incorporates information into the development of concepts.

Young children learn through many different experiences with the objects, people, and events of the world in which they live. As these odd bits of knowledge collected through this variety of experiences are combined, thinking results. "These are the bits and pieces that make up the child's map of this environment that tells him how to operate in his world. The larger his stock of information, the more detailed is his map, and the clearer his thinking" (Murphy & Leeper, 1970; p. 13).

Participation provides concrete knowledge from which clear understanding evolves, as illustrated in the following anecdote:

Mrs. Harris, in her Head Start center, told the children a story about a donkey. When she asked what a donkey looked like, she realized that the children had never actually seen one. The next day when school began, Mrs. Harris confidently walked into the classroom, leading behind her a reluctant donkey—one which the children could not only see but touch, hear, and even smell.

Input and information must be congruous with what has already been stored (Hunt, 1964). Hunt (1961) referred to this concept as the "problem of the match" (p. 280). Teachers must start where the learner is. When a stimulus is received by the child, it is stored in the mind to be added to the collection of other concepts. In further experiences, the child calls on the material already compiled to help understand and process the new ideas.

Children make generalizations as they build relationships among concepts by relying on information previously accumulated. Without a broad base of direct encounters from which to generalize, children cannot move toward abstract reasoning. Before certain conceptual strategies can be learned, there are specific levels of cognitive development that must be achieved. Learning needs to be continuous; new material encountered must correspond with skills previously assimilated. One "can assimilate only those things which past assimilations have prepared him to assimilate" (Flavell, 1963; p. 50).

Larry often had difficulties keeping his hair combed, face cleaned, shirt tucked in, and shoes on. One day as he entered the room, his appearance was neat, clean, and shiny. He was greeted with a teacher's expression. "You are sharp today, Larry." "No, I'm not sharp—my boots are sharp!" was his retort, as he questioningly looked down at his cowboy boots.

The child's understanding of *sharp* was a product of his limited past experience. Through further learnings, additional meanings of this word will be acquired. As the children in the fol-

lowing example continue to expand their horizons, new meanings will add to their storehouse of knowledge.

As the children were discussing the various kinds and uses of shoes, a soft, furry pair of house slippers was displayed. When asked what these slippers could be called, Margo answered, "We could call them our fuzzy-wuzzy slippers." Michael hurriedly said, "We can't call them, because they won't come!"

Curiosity, another important element in early cognitive development, impels a child to reach out to the environment. An adult can help foster children's curiosity by encouraging them to explore, answering their questions, and being an example of a curious person (Bradbard & Endsley, 1980). Children's surroundings must be kept rich with concrete, sensory, manipulative experiences that allow them to satisfy their curiosity through their senses.

Most people are born with an intrinsic drive to learn about and explore their world. Curiosity is this "push to learn," according to Murphy and Leeper (1970), who describe it further:

To poke, peer, push, and pull at the things around him is the young child's way of finding out. To ask endless "why?" questions of grown-ups is another way. To take apart and put together—to try and fail and try again until he succeeds—all these are ways a child learns through curiosity. (p. 6)

Teachers must accept the individualized approach to education by being cognizant of their responsibility to make the information they teach compatible with what the child already knows. They must provide for each child at each point in development the most stimulating circumstances.

Feedback and Cognition

Through experiences with learning, avenues are constantly being provided that enable the adult to determine the child's level of comprehension. In addition, the adult responds to the child in furthering the development of concept understandings. Therefore, feedback is a two-way process in which there is a constant flow of information and communication between adults and children. Concepts broaden as they are explored in the context of another person's ideas and experiences. This is the great value of cooperative learning.

Simply because an experience has allowed a child to become familiar with an idea, it must not be assumed that the correct information has been assimilated. In the quest for meaning, a child often misunderstands; thus an adult or peer must observe and listen constantly to determine the functioning level of discernment. Through feedback from the teacher, a vital consideration in providing information, the child learns which stimuli should be focused upon.

In the following examples, it is evident that feedback from the child is also an important aspect in the learning process.

A child who had been encouraged to keep her shoes on commented to her teacher at the end of the day: "I wore my shoes all day today, but sometimes I wore my bare feet!"

During an excursion, various drums were shown to the children. It was explained that the kettledrum was so named because of its resemblance to a large pot or kettle that might be used on the stove for cooking. Later, as the concepts were being viewed and reinforced, the children were asked the name of the kettledrum. Peter confidently replied, "Oh, that's a stove drum!"

Feedback, reinforcement, and review are constantly needed to correct, strengthen, and expand a child's understandings. As adults prepare to be receptive to the child's feedback, they must be willing to listen (not just hear) and observe (not just see). Teaching entails much more than disseminating information. It involves listening and observing not only for the obvious, but also for the subtle ways in which the child makes perceptions known.

Questioning is a skill that may be learned, and it should be encouraged as an avenue for feedback. The child asks a question, and the teacher listens to determine whether the input has been correctly interpreted. Then the teacher either reinforces and praises the child for the right information or corrects the misconception.

While Jacob had chicken pox, he asked, "How come my teeth don't itch?"

Listening and responding to a child's questions are accepted as important aspects of feedback. Since children learn through asking questions, their questions should not be stifled but rather seen as an asset to thinking and problem solving. Therefore, questioning has more than a single role in the education of the young child. With respect to questioning, Cazden (1970) suggests that attempts must be made to "(a) . . . teach children to ask more productive questions, and (b) . . . change what happens in classrooms so that more of children's learning will be based on questions which they themselves ask rather than on questions which are asked by the teacher" (p. 217).

Clarifying Misconceptions and Extending Beyond the Original Concepts

Through feedback received from the child, many misconceptions are identified. These misunderstandings must be clarified and corrected. Only then is a child able to obtain further knowledge of concepts in the continuing search for meaningful relationships in the environment. An example of misconceptions that children sometimes acquire follows.

A refrigerator truck for transporting creamery products had a wedge of cheese with a mouse standing near it pictured on the side panel. On the basis of the picture, children often believed that cheese came from mice or that cheese was made for mice.

As another example, from infancy children are encouraged to develop generosity by sharing with those around them. Proudly, adults compliment a child for incorporating this desirable characteristic into his or her personality. As children enter school and become involved with completing assignments, they frequently share their work with friends to assist them in finishing difficult tasks. In this situation, they are said to be *cheating* rather than *sharing*. Certainly young children should develop social morality as they learn the expectations of others; yet it must be remembered that a trait as favorable as this one must be regarded differently as one matures. This misconception is clarified during the child's acquaintance with school and with the responsibilities of students.

Many of the phrases and words in our common language usage are idioms. Until the child has experiences that will clarify meanings, the phrases are interpreted incorrectly and the literal definitions are assumed. Examples include *just pulling your leg, all tied up, on the tip of my tongue, all ears, swing shift, graveyard shift,* and *tongue-tied.* In addition, a word or phrase that has more than one meaning often causes misunderstanding for the child who is familiar with only one definition for that word. Examples include *fork in the road, catching a cold, pinch hitter, broken up, broken down, rat race,* and *wring your neck.*

Children often become needlessly concerned over statements adults make because they interpret them by relying on the information previously stored and understood, as the following two illustrations show:

Two-year-old Christy became upset every time her parents mentioned their forthcoming flight to New York, where they would visit Christy's grandparents. On one of these occasions when they were discussing their plans, Christy exclaimed, "But I don't know how to fly!"

The children had observed a rooster in their classroom for several days, and they anxiously waited for it to crow. Each day just after the children left, the rooster would begin to crow. One day while they were outside playing, the rooster began to crow. One of the teachers then hurried to another teacher and suggested that she take the children inside because the rooster was "crowing its head off." Terrall, who was nearby, asked with alarm, "You mean his head is coming off?"

Children often gain misconceptions through misunderstanding a word, especially when the word is one with which they are unfamiliar, as observed in the following illustrations:

As a group of children was leaving for an excursion to ride an elevator, a passerby asked Mike where they were going. "We're going to ride an alligator," he replied.

After being told that he would be going on an excursion that day, James informed the other children that they would be going on an "explosion."

Kyle unwrapped a birthday present, observed the toy, and said, "I wonder where the 'constructions' are."

Children do not just learn misconceptions as they struggle to derive meaning from their environment, they sometimes are taught these incorrect concepts. The assimilation of incorrect information makes it difficult for the child to develop congruity in the world. Spinach, to a young child, often is a miraculous vegetable that magnifies strength when it is eaten. Popeye, when unable to handle situations, ate cold spinach from a can, and immediately his entire body became strong enough to meet any challenge. Children who are reluctant to eat their spinach might be encouraged by questions such as "Don't you want to be big and strong?" Children are taught concepts concerning the stork and its ability to deliver babies, the sandman and his nightly visit, the Big Rock Candy Mountain they will someday ascend, and many other false conceptions.

Even though pictures offer vicarious experiences for children and teach them many concepts, they often create misconceptions due to their proportions, sizes, textures, and personifications.

Learning opportunities, many of them resulting from formal teaching and planning, are always saturating the child's environment. Much more numerous, however, are the "teachable moments," when a child's curiosity and initial interest in a subject provide fertile ground for the planting and nurturing of clear understandings. Adults must be alert to the ever-questioning and investigating young mind and prepared to assist the child in furthering knowledge and comprehension of the surrounding world. Having correctly interpreted ideas, the child is then prepared and eager to reach toward new galaxies of understanding. An additional challenge for teachers, therefore, is to assist the child in extending beyond the original concepts.

Cooperative Learning Among Peers

Children learn from one another, and this learning includes both cognitive and affective perceptions. When children learn in small groups from their peers, it satisfies their needs more than when they learn alone. (Glasser, 1990) Many academic and prosocial skills are the outcome of cooperative learning. Children's analytical and academic skills are sharpened, and they develop both oral and listening abilities. They learn to be sensitive to others and understand another person's point of view. Because no student in the group succeeds without the cooperation and support of the other group members,

interdependence and bonding result from this type of learning.

Children in today's society will be required to have higher-level thinking skills, technical skills, relationship skills, and communication skills. The most effective way to learn these kinds of skills is in small groups where the focus is on a team effort, on helping and learning from one another, as opposed to a competitive approach.

Cooperative learning fosters higher achievement in children, especially when groups are rewarded for individual achievement (Kagan, 1992). In other words, children achieve the most when their learning is characterized by the team members' having a positive, interdependent goal with individual accountability (Johnson, Johnson, & Holubec, 1987).

Children learn in their cooperative groups when they talk and share with one another and their talk is directed toward academic concepts and achievement. When peers work to support, recognize, and build one another up, enhanced learning occurs and self-esteem is nurtured.

A well-planned outside play area allows for socialization, cooperation, and problem solving—especially when the climbing bars are too high for one child to reach.

Summary

We have looked at early childhood education historically and have found that its roots go back for centuries. The early childhood education perspective dates back to the 17th century, with the beliefs of such people as Locke, Rousseau, Pestalozzi, and Froebel. Others who have influenced early childhood education as it is practiced today include McMillan, Hill, Dewey, Freud, Montessori, Gesell, Piaget, and Erikson. Many early childhood education programs are patterned after the beliefs of particular individuals, while most programs are influenced by many philosophies.

We have examined early childhood education today and have found that, perhaps more than any other aspect of education, it is characterized by variety. Demographics relating to early childhood education have been discussed, as well as some of the sociological and technological influences. By 1980, early childhood concerns focused on such social changes as abuse, poverty, violence, homelessness, working women, suicide, discipline, and education and their changing effects on young children.

We have seen that although early childhood education has made great strides in the past and is moving forward presently, even greater advances are necessary for the future. Only a minority of children is receiving the benefit of preschool education, and an even smaller minority is receiving high-quality preschool education. The challenge in the 1990s is to address these social concerns and direct our efforts toward positive influences on young children. All children should be provided with high-quality child care, regardless of their gender, race, religion, or economic situation. There must be increased support for the strengthening of family values, standards, traditions, experiences, and expectations.

In addition, our concern is for the quality of kindergarten and primary-grade education, which too often have an academic focus, with the main activities each day being completion of worksheets. Early childhood education should be different from other kinds of education. We need to determine how to best provide experiences that contribute to the development of the whole child, and those experiences should be available for *all* children to help them reach their full potential.

Early childhood teachers should be highly trained and reflect enthusiasm, creativity, empathy, hope, tolerance, understanding, warmth, and nurturance. Teachers should be trained to work with children whose needs vary from those of other children. Education must be developmentally appropriate. The developmental needs and characteristics of age groups and individual children must be understood and learning activities and goals must be based on the knowledge that children in early childhood are ready for learning through their senses, utilizing experiences, materials, and concrete activities.

Since this book is concerned with teaching young children, we have looked at the processes by which learning takes place in the young child. We have found that experiences, feedback, and the clarification of misconceptions are the three foremost aspects of learning. At the same time, we have evaluated the results of inappropriate, pressurized early learning. There is an excitement and enthusiasm in learning that should be preserved and fostered throughout an individual's lifetime. Cooperative learning, or learning from each other in small groups, allows children to develop academic, social, communication, relationship, and self-enhancing skills. We propose that children want to learn, and that successful teaching begins with and builds upon concepts and ideas that are developmentally appropriate during the early years of childhood.

Student Learning Activities

1. Describe your own feelings regarding early childhood education. When do you believe children should begin to receive formalized instruction? What kind of program do you prefer at this point? What kinds of early childhood education experiences did you have? Do you have positive memories?

2. Evaluate at least five different early childhood computer software programs. State whether they are appropriate, and explain why or why not. Describe the values of each program: Will the children benefit from it? For what age is each program suitable?

3. From your reading and observation, make a summary chart of the characteristics of children aged 2 to 8 years. Why is it important that teachers of early childhood education be aware of these characteristics in the children they teach? What precautions should be taken in using them?

4. Visit an early childhood classroom or center and write a brief report of your visit. Answer as many of the following questions as possible: In what activities were the children involved? What is the nature of the facilities, both indoors and outdoors? What kind of program is offered by the school? How many children were there? How many teachers were there? Based on your visit, what are your feelings about early childhood education? In terms of your visit, evaluate the program with regard to advantages and/or disadvantages for the young children it serves.

5. If possible, visit a public school that has an after-school program for children who would otherwise have no place to go. Evaluate the program to determine whether it is developmentally appropriate. Does it emphasize formal, academic structure? If you were designing an after-school program, how would you do it?

6. Based on your studies and observations of various programs for young children, describe how you would be able to involve the families of the children in ways that would help meet the needs of the children. What are some kinds of family involvement you have observed in various programs?

CHAPTER
two

Play

Introduction

Both the curriculum and the environment should reflect the teacher's knowledge and acceptance of the value and importance of play in early childhood. Children need time, materials, and a place to explore their ideas and feelings, experience self-initiated problem solving, and experiment in an atmosphere of success. Theoretically, there is widespread acceptance of the idea that play is important—that it is serious business for the young child. However, at the practical level, play is too often being replaced with worksheets and highly structured learning. Children constantly remind us, through their behavior and interest, how compelling and essential play is to them (Nourot & VanHoorn, 1991). The very word *play* is misleading: To some, it suggests frivolous leisure activities, "killing" time, and recreational activities. Play does not provide a concrete, tangible, or academic end product that can be displayed to parents. It is not teacher-directed. However, research verifies that play is a vehicle to enhance children's development (Bordner & Berkley, 1992; NAEYC & NAECS/SDE, 1991).

Good play experiences unite all aspects of development, reaping social, emotional, physical, intellectual, moral, and creative benefits for young children. Good play strengthens skills and deepens understanding of concepts. It gives children opportunities to explore, experiment, create, and imagine (National Association for Education of Young Children and National Association of Early Childhood Specialists in State Departments of Education, 1991). As educators, we must recognize our responsibility to educate parents in the values and purposes of play for young children. This can be done through workshops, orientation meetings, newsletter articles and by providing resource materials that teach the values of play.

Values of Play

Much has been written about the values or purposes of play. Here we discuss various purposes for play to help you recognize its inherent values.

This information will aid you in responding clearly and wisely to such queries as "Is that all my child does? Just play?"

Play Promotes Significant Mental Skills

Play gives the child opportunities to express thoughts and ideas. It provides occasions to organize, plan, discover problems, reason, try out solutions and skills, create, and explore. Play contributes to the child's development of imaginative thinking (Nourot & VanHoorn, 1991). "Play serves as a reinforcer of ideas and patterns of behavior. Play enables the youngster to formulate ideas and then to test them. Much skill development occurs through play" (Osborn & Osborn, 1983, p. 17). During play, children have the opportunity to develop their senses of touch, taste, smell, sound, and sight. In addition, their attention spans are expanded as they stay on task and remain attentive to activities in which they are involved (Rogers & Sawyers, 1988).

Research indicates that play facilitates both divergent thinking (Kogan, 1983) and convergent thinking (Vandenberg, 1981). Convergent tasks have a single answer, while divergent tasks have multiple solutions or approaches. Both kinds of thinking are important, and play provides the opportunity to practice both. Even though it is a vigorous intellectual exercise, play does not create the pressure or tension that is often associated with more structured learning approaches (Rogers & Sawyers, 1988).

Piaget (1973) maintained that play is one of the most important functions of childhood, permitting the child to assimilate reality to self and self to reality. Many researchers feel that communication skills are developed in part through peer play and the need for children to communicate with each other in their play (Chenfeld, 1991; Giffin, 1984; McCune, 1985). Play stretches the vocabulary and expands language development by providing opportunities to use new words, converse with playmates, listen to another's language and point of view, learn new semantics (meanings of words), and hear and subsequently use new syntax (parts of speech). Play synthesizes or brings together previous experiences and thinking, allowing children to piece them together.

"Although play is not a necessary condition for learning language and literacy skills, play is probably the best environment for these abilities to thrive" (Rogers & Sawyers, 1988, p. 64). "Creativity and aesthetic appreciation are developed through play" (Rogers & Sawyers, 1988, p. 58). Developing creativity and aesthetic appreciation can influence the way children think and solve problems.

Play Promotes Physical/Motor Development

"Children cannot be passive recipients of play" (Rogers & Sawyers, 1988, p. 10); play is active. Children use their bodies and increase small-muscle dexterity as they run, climb, skip, and hop.

Play, therefore, provides the exercise and physical activity needed to strengthen and coordinate children's muscles and bodies. Through physical play, children can learn appropriate ways to display aggression and other assertive behaviors without hurting themselves or others (Pellegrini & Perlmutter, 1988).

When a group of kindergarten children were quizzed about their favorite part of school, a large majority stated that they liked recess best of all. During recess, the spontaneous, self-directed activities involve mostly physical/motor play.

Play Encourages Positive Emotional Development

Play is the means for fostering a healthy personality, and it provides the opportunity for each child to discover the self. Play provides the opportunity to express thoughts and ideas and to try out ways of behaving and feeling. Play experiences provide children safe avenues for expressing both positive and negative emotions. As they express thoughts and ideas, children can learn and be directed to the most positive ways of handling their emotions. This will come through support and reinforcement by both peers and teachers.

Children use play to make up for unkindness, defects, and disappointments as well as to play out frustrations, sufferings, and anger. In addition, play allows children to be powerful, in control, and assertive, depending on the choices and decisions made in particular play situations. Play enables children to translate feelings, thoughts, fantasies, and inclinations into action—to literally be in control and in charge of their world and feelings (Rogers & Sawyers, 1988). Perhaps the greatest asset of self-directed, self-discovery, or spontaneous play is the satisfaction it gives children of making choices for themselves, of attaining some control over their own learning, and of being "able to match skills and challenges to their interests" (Rogers & Sawyers, 1988, p. 5).

Freedom to experiment with materials, feelings, words, and ideas gives impetus to the development of creativity. Through carefree, unpressured play, children's imaginations invent new solutions, different approaches, and unique ideas. Even though ideas are "pretend," it is important that the ideas are created; and one day, children will realize that their ideas must be compatible with reality.

Play Allows Children to Develop into Social Human Beings

Piaget (1970a) considered the theoretical relationship between play and socialization. He believed that children are naturally motivated to interact with other children and, as they do so, they become less egocentric and more aware of others. Solitary play is valuable, but in early childhood play usually means people. In play experiences, children learn to be both leaders (telling others what to do) and followers (being told what to do). They learn to try different roles and think of other possibilities (Chenfeld, 1991). They learn to give and take, to put themselves in another's position, to sense another's feelings, to hear another's point of view. Play provides practice in the social skills that society demands for

success. It also provides practice in being less bossy, less selfish, less meek, or less shy. Play encourages a child to be a friend and a contributor, to cooperate, and to be flexible.

As teachers plan the time that children spend in their classrooms, they must remember the inherent values of play for its own sake and for the behaviors it directly affects. We must not structure and arrange so much of the school time that inadequate time is left for spontaneous, self-directed free play periods. In terms of values and benefits, these periods may well be the most important times of the day—and children should not be robbed of them. Every day should have one block or more of time for spontaneous play.

The lesson plans suggested in this book are activity oriented, and the individual activities listed are to be included in the free play or self-directed, spontaneous play period in addition to the centers that are a regular part of the room environment.

Developmental Play Stages

Like other aspects of development, play progresses through stages, with one stage preparing the way for the next. Observing play behavior is an important aspect of gaining an understanding of children's development. Play is a manifestation of the child's social development. As one understands the stage of play in which each child is primarily functioning, appropriate social and group experiences can be determined. For example, if the majority of children in the group are toddlers, and observation determines that their play behavior is primarily solitary, onlooking, and parallel, this indicates a need for most of the classroom play to be spontaneous or free play. Group activities should be short and few in number. (It should be noted that children with disabilities progress through the same stages of play as other children, but at their own rate [Bordner & Berkley, 1992]).

Parten (1932, 1933) suggested dividing play

by the social interaction that takes place among children during their play. During solitary play, the child acts alone and independently of others. Some researchers have indicated that children, as they mature, may still seek solitary play as a means of getting away from it all, or because they are goal directed and have something they desire to accomplish (Rogers & Sawyers, 1988). Onlooking play indicates that the child spends much time watching others play. In parallel play, the child individually plays with toys similar to those used by nearby children. Its purpose may be to allow children to become acquainted with one another or to gain social acceptance, or it may serve as a transition between solitary and more cooperative, interactive play (Rogers & Sawyers, 1988). During associative play, children engage in basically the same activity, but no attempt is made to divide the play tasks or to organize the activity. In cooperative play, children organize in a group for some purpose. In this give-and-take interaction, they share not only materials and equipment, but also ideas and goals. Cooperative play is the ultimate play behavior that parents and early childhood teachers seek. "Solitary and parallel play decline during the preschool years, while associative and cooperative play increase as children approach kindergarten" (Rogers & Sawyers, 1988, p. 10, referring to Partan, 1932).

Play experiences provide an opportunity to try out social behaviors, that is, to put social development and thought into action. They build social skills that allow the child to move to higher levels or stages of play. However, it is still developmentally appropriate for children who have reached the cooperative stage of play to occasionally enjoy solitary, parallel, and associative play.

Fostering Positive and Meaningful Play Experiences

Contact with others, both adults and children, is more important in fostering positive play experiences than the materials and toys. Children de-

Outside play equipment encourages physical activity, cooperation, and turn-taking as children learn to play together and help each other.

velop empathy, understanding, and sensitivity to each other by relating to them. Human relationship skills come from firsthand experiences of learning to give and take, to sense another's feelings and needs, to share kindnesses in words and deeds. Teachers provide models of these human qualities and encourage their development during play situations. The teacher's positive attitude, interest in individual children and groups, and enthusiasm for play experiences will be transferred to the children and influence their attitudes toward play and the meaning they draw from their play experiences.

The Teacher's Role

The teacher's role is to provide, encourage, supervise, and guide the play of young children and to help them reach their potential (Isenberg, Quisenberry, 1988). However, the teacher must not become the object of the play or the center of attraction or dictate what the child can do in the play activity. Teachers should be available to support, assist, observe, interact when appropriate to do so, and indirectly channel misbehavior, as well as direct and encourage positive behaviors. In order for play to be sustained, children do need adult stimulation (Caldwell, 1985; Rubin, Fein, & Vandenberg, 1983), but once limits have been established and children are comfortable with their environment, adults should interfere as little as possible. The teacher can make suggestions for play activity and, through play, expand the children's language development, increase concept understanding, answer questions, and encourage new social interactions and friendships.

During their play, children need many opportunities for making choices. As they make choices, they feel in control, which results in their being able to accept responsibility (Kelman, 1990). However, children's interest will dwindle, and they may even stop playing, if teachers interfere too much or try to structure their play for them (Rogers & Sawyers, 1988). Play is more valuable when children plan, define, shape, and carry out their own play activities (Rogers & Sawyers, 1988). However, the teacher's role must not be diminished. Play should not be used as a reward for children who finish their work. Rather, it has to be planned for by the teacher, expected of all children, and encouraged and understood by parents. Well-planned play during early childhood is more important than adult instruction or formal, structured learning activities (Isenberg & Quisenberry, 1988).

Although the teacher is important, other children provide the greatest source of complex play. It has been found that a toy, regardless of its color, form, or type, cannot encourage sustained play as well as another child (Ellis, 1979).

Providing Developmentally Appropriate Materials

Children do need carefully selected, developmentally appropriate materials that meet the age range of children in the classroom (NAEYC Position Statement, 1986). A particular piece of equipment can be enjoyed by children aged 2 to 8, but the older the child, the more advanced and complex it must be. The structure, as well as the style, of children's play and play materials becomes more diverse and complex as children mature (Fein, 1979). Teachers must be aware of developmental age characteristics and learn to sense what comes next. For example, puzzles and matching materials are enjoyed by a broad age range of children; however, younger children need fewer pieces in order to prevent frustration and foster success. Older children can manage more puzzle or matching pieces. For younger children, simple concepts such as shape and color should be presented, rather than concepts such as time, money, and more complex shapes. Age-appropriate materials, equipment, and toys are suitable for the child's age, interests, and abilities, and children gain most from materials matched to their stage of development.

Preparing a Physical Setting That Is Developmentally Appropriate and Curriculum Supportive

When a teacher recognizes and understands the developmental needs of young children, planning appropriate play experiences and organizing a suitable curriculum are facilitated. This knowledge also positively influences the physical setting, which includes both the outdoor play area and the indoor classroom. These two areas must be planned to focus on the needs of the children while supporting the curriculum and what is being taught. Teachers should know and understand the age characteristics of children so that they can identify developmental changes and needs at different stages in order to select the proper equipment, materials, toys, furniture, and other learning aids. Then, through needs assessment and careful observation, materials can be added or deleted, depending on their appropriateness for the children in the classroom.

The physical setting or environment has a great impact on the child in both an affective and a cognitive way. Feelings engendered in the child by the environment should include a sense of order, enthusiasm, interest, curiosity, cleanliness, and safety. The environment contributes to setting the tone of the school day for both the children and the teacher. An organized, attractive, clean, and cheerful or "warm" setting results in more positive children's behaviors and teachers' attitudes. In addition, the environment should offer opportunities for learning and increasing skill in all developmental areas: physical, social, emotional, cognitive, and language. Children need and deserve an environment conducive to learning, growing, positive behavior, and good play.

Guidelines for Arranging the Early Childhood Classroom

Indoor and outdoor environments should be set up and arranged to avoid situations that naturally frustrate or anger children. For example, toys and materials should not be stored in boxes. If a child desires to play with a soldier that happens to be in the bottom of the box, and dumps out the whole box of toys in order to obtain the soldier, the child may become angry or frustrated when told to pick up all the other toys. The child may honestly say, "But I didn't play with all the toys, only the soldier." Also, toys and equipment should be complete and in good repair. It is frustrating to put a puzzle together only to find that the last piece is missing. Some materials are unsafe when either incomplete or in poor repair. For example, worn, rough wooden blocks can cause slivers; missing vehicle wheels or broken parts can be dangerously sharp.

When the physical setting is arranged with the needs of the children in mind and combined with planning, thought, and purpose, learning opportunities increase and a more orderly and organized environment results. The physical setting strongly influences the behavior and learning activities of children.

The following are suggested guidelines for arranging the physical setting of an early childhood classroom:

1. Equipment and materials must be the correct size and height for children. This means that pictures and bulletin boards should be placed at the child's eye level, not the teacher's. In addition, coat hooks, cupboards, shelves, and other materials or items for children to use must be where the children can reach them. For comfort and availability, chairs and other furniture pieces should be the appropriate size.

2. The room must be organized and uncluttered. A disorderly, cluttered, and disorganized environment frequently ignites similar behavior in children. Classrooms are more orderly and interesting when teachers avoid putting everything out at once. For example, if your classroom has six puzzles, put only one or two out at a time. However, there must be enough toys for all children to have something to play with. Materials for specific areas or learning centers in the room should be kept separate. As a part of cleanup, children should be encouraged to put toys and materials away where they belong.

3. Make certain the room is free of stereotypes. Pictures, toys, materials, dress-up clothes, and other objects should reflect the diversity of people and genders.

4. Consider the traffic flow when planning the room arrangement. Eliminate long corridors or "running spaces" that encourage the children to run. Break up long spaces, for example, with a trough filled with sensory

media. Arrange art areas near a sink for easy access or cleanup (Crosser, 1992). By wisely planning the environment, teachers can manage behavior indirectly; this is referred to as *behavior prevention.*

5. Where possible, keep noisy areas close together and apart from quiet areas. For example, it would not be wise to put a music area with a rhythm band right next to the story area (Crosser, 1992).

6. The classroom and outdoor areas must be clean, neat, and cheerful. The physical environment must be clean for health and sanitary reasons alone. Cheerful, bright touches, combined with carefully selected bulletin board pictures can support the theme. Photographs of the children at work on projects and activities should be placed at a level for them to enjoy. Their pictures and work should also be displayed in the room, and a comment or question a child makes during an activity can be placed alongside the child's work (Katz, 1990). Be careful not to add too many displays; simplicity is a guideline for the entire physical setting, including the bulletin boards.

7. The organization and setup of the room should encourage children to keep the room orderly while developing classifying, categorizing, or matching skills. In the block area, for example, trace a pattern for each size and shape of the small unit blocks on solid-colored, adhesive-backed paper. Then organize and sequence these patterns on the block shelf so that the children can match the blocks to the pattern and, at the same time, organize the block area. Another possibility is to put hooks in your housekeeping area and then place a picture of a hat, dress, or slacks above specific hooks. This encourages children to sense that objects have a place to be put and facilitates matching and classifying. Another idea is to glue pictures of fruits, vegetables, and dairy products in specific locations of the refrigerator. A similar method can be used in the stove and cupboard by gluing pictures that will help children classify and match items to be placed in these areas. Tools can be hung on a pegboard and matched to their shape (Crosser, 1992).

8. Teachers should be able to see and supervise all areas of the room. Place tall cabinets and shelves against the wall, and use shorter cabinets and shelves as area dividers.

9. Consider the care and storage of equipment and materials. For example, to facilitate the cleanup of paint or glue brushes, have some cans or containers of water to put brushes into immediately after use so that the paint or glue will not harden. Ideally, there will be clean, orderly, organized storage areas outside of the classroom, or higher than the children's reach, where some materials can be stored. Other materials and supplies such as paints, paper, pencils, and paint shirts should be accessible to children so they can take responsibility for getting them and putting them away (Casey & Lippman, 1991; Crosser, 1992).

10. Rotating and changing areas and materials often create interest and predictable behavior changes. You may ask, "Will children be secure in an environment that is frequently changed?" The answer is, "Yes." The teacher provides the security, while the environment encourages interest, learning, fun, and interaction among children. Children need variety and become bored with toys that are not rotated (Rogers & Sawyers, 1988).

11. Each area and each piece of equipment and material should have purpose and meaning. In evaluating areas and equipment, ask yourself such questions as "Why am I using this?" and "What am I trying to accomplish?" Remember that the physical setting should serve the needs and interests of the children in the classroom.

Arranging the Environment with Areas to Meet Developmental Needs

The room should be divided into areas, with each area providing opportunities to satisfy the developmental needs of children. If a child avoids a particular area over a period of time, teachers should encourage the child to use that area. Avoidance may be an indication of insecurity or unsureness with that particular area. Kindergarten, first-, and second-grade children may find a contract helpful to promote on-task behavior. "A contract is an agreed-upon individualized activity outline that incorporates teacher direction and guidance with student interests" (Day, 1988, p. 55). Contracts can also effectively guide children to all learning areas. Figure 2–1 includes examples of sample contracts for use with young children. As a child participates in each activity or area, he or she colors in the square or checks in the box. Study of individual contracts for several days alerts teachers to areas or activities the children are not participating in as well as those they are interested in. Contracts also serve as a means of assessment and as a springboard for parent–teacher discussions and conferences. The first example would be used for children 3, 4, and 5 years of age, and the second example would be used for 6-, 7-, and 8-year-old children.

Children can also choose areas or centers by placing pictures or names of the centers on a board and hooks under each that determine how many children can be in that center. When children want to go to a particular center, they put their name or picture on the hook under the name or picture of that center. It has been shown that even preschool children can be effective planners, and approaches such as this help them focus on their choices (Casey & Lippman, 1991).

Because these areas of the room satisfy various needs, they should be organized, orderly, inviting, and on the child's level. Areas can occasionally be changed or modified to maintain motivation and interest. For example, weekly rotation of toys in the manipulative area will stimulate new exploration. Sensory and creative areas can be changed more frequently, depending on the space, the theme, and the balance of planned activities.

The physical setting should support the curriculum whenever possible, with the room setup and outdoor playground correlating with the unit theme being presented. For example, if the current theme is "fish," the block area could be converted into a large fishing pond, with the large hollow blocks set up as the banks of the pond. Fish cutouts with attached paper clips could be caught in the pond, using fishing pole magnets. Also, an aquarium or trough containing live fish could be used as a learning area. Bulletin boards could feature fish and fishing. Another example of adapting a room area to a theme, in this case "mail and the mail carrier," is to convert the jungle gym into a mail truck just by using colored butcher paper and a little imagination.

The following areas are suggested for early childhood classrooms. The size of the room may limit the use of all areas at one time, and the more areas in a classroom, the more complex the physical setting. Teachers in complex settings face greater management challenges (Day, 1988).

Outside play areas will be determined by your facility and what is available. Hopefully, your playground will have appropriate stationary or permanent pieces of equipment such as domes, slides, various climbing apparatus, nesting climbers with boards and bridges, and an adjustable basketball standard/backboard. Items such as barrels, inner tubes, and other salvage pieces can often be purchased inexpensively. Versatile modular gym systems can be set up in a variety of ways for use both indoors and outdoors.

Large-muscle areas include equipment for large-muscle development. Dome climbers or jungle gyms are ideal for large rooms because they can be moved to different areas. Other large-muscle-development equipment includes balance beams, slides, indoor jumping trampolines, and nesting climbers set up in a variety of ways. It is important to plan *how* the equipment will be set up each day and to plan in such a way as to facilitate the physical and motor needs of the

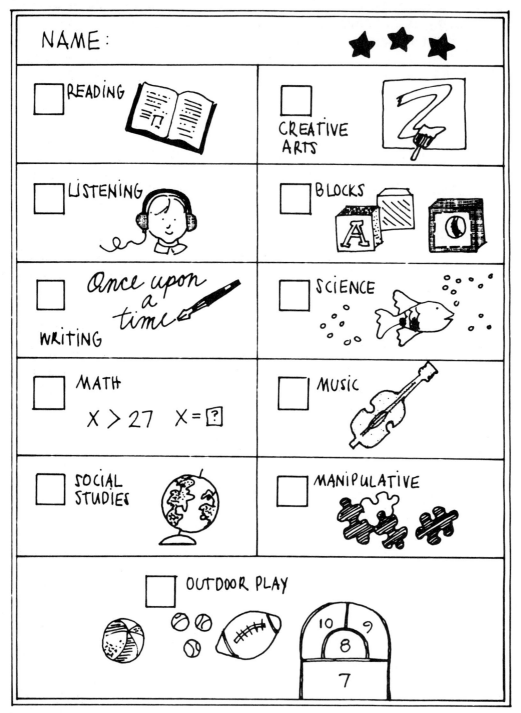

FIGURE 2–1
Sample contracts

NAME:

☆ ☆ ☆

☐ JUNGLE GYM

☐ CREATIVE ARTS

☐ BLOCKS

☐ SCIENCE

DRAMATIC PLAY
☐

☐ READING

☐ SENSORY

☐ MUSIC

☐ MANUPULATIVE

continued

group as well as of individual children (Poest, Williams, Witt, & Atwood, 1990). Some types of smaller jungle gyms fold flat for easy storage and are more appropriate in smaller areas.

Dramatic play areas provide opportunities for role playing, trying out, pretending, and acting out familiar and imaginary experiences. Playing house seems to be the most preferred theme for young children; grocery stores and doctors' offices also spark interest (Griffing, 1983). Additional possibilities are suggested later in the chapter.

Sensory play areas may include a trough, tubs, or other possible methods of setting up media for sensory exploration. Such media might include water, sand, clay, wheat, Styrofoam packing pieces, sawdust, or other available material. Such tools as funnels, bottles, shovels, scoops, cups, beaters, or other utensils and tools also add occasional interest.

Creative arts areas select media from paints,

An abundant supply of hats, shoes, and dress-up clothes encourages dramatic play and supports exploration of various roles in our society.

collage materials, chalk, charcoal, crayons, felt-tipped markers, colored pencils, and other sources to be used with paper on easels, on tables, or on floor or wall murals.

Block areas are often near or part of the large-muscle area. Many classrooms are large enough to accommodate both large and small unit blocks. The block area (especially when it includes large, hollow blocks), the large-muscle area, and sometimes the outdoor play area give children opportunities to develop strength, coordination, and balance. Manipulative and creative toys such as small cars, farm animals, zoo animals, or human figures used together with blocks can stimulate block play and provide variety. If you use human figures, make sure they reflect diverse people.

Science areas or interest centers are often part of the early childhood classroom, especially for supporting science unit themes. For example, during a theme on "color," provide different activities such as color mixing. The science area could be a table with things to explore or displays and simple experiments that focus on helping children explore their environment. Magnifying glasses or microscopes encourage additional exploration and study.

A *"book nook"* or *quiet area* provides a place to explore the world through books. Books should be selected to meet the developmental needs of the children and can support the theme or concepts being taught. The entire book supply should not be displayed at one time; occasional book rotation stimulates renewed interest. When a book is selected, there should always be a rug or table nearby for reading or being read to.

Music areas are places where children listen to music, sing, play musical instruments, or perform creative dances. Additional equipment should include appropriate tapes or records and/or rhythm band instruments.

Manipulative play areas include small blocks, pegboards, puzzles, number games, bead-stringing activities, magnetic games, and other like equipment. Puzzles and other toys should show diversity and should not have any stereotypic images (Derman-Sparks & A.B.C. Task Force, 1989). Display shelves and tables and chairs help to extend interest spans.

Lockers or cubbies may be inside or outside the classroom. Individual children should have a place with their name for storing belongings and hanging outerwear. If these spaces are inside the classroom, they could also serve as places for children to sit for quiet meditation or solitude.

These areas need to be carefully and appropriately selected according to the developmental needs of the children and the concepts being taught and reinforced. Although we have not attempted to list the room areas in the daily plans and lesson plans, we assume that they will be well thought out. Remember to vary these areas and change them often to ensure continued interest and variety. In the plans suggested in this book, we have included individual activities that could be used on specific days and for theme reinforcement. Learning centers can be added according to the needs and developmental abilities of the children. "Learning centers are . . . centers in the classroom . . . that are designed to promote the mastery of skills, the acquisition of knowledge, and the development of concepts, or the formation of generalizations. They are different from interest centers, exploratory centers, or game centers in that they are planned, organized, and developed around the identified learning needs of a specific group of children" (Davidson & Steely, 1978, p. 2). Learning centers are used to emphasize specific cognitive skills and concepts independently (Maxim, 1989). They are most often found in kindergarten and first-grade classrooms.

Interest centers are based on the interests of the children in the classroom. For example, if a child brings in a rock, this may be the stimulus for an interest center on rocks. Books, materials, and rocks brought to the classroom by the children could be put in an interest center on rocks.

Physical Fitness and Motor Development Activities

Each day should provide opportunities for motor development and physical fitness. To be physically fit, children must have cardiovascular endurance; muscle strength, endurance, and agility; and body leanness (Poest et al., 1990). Motor development includes locomotor skills, large-muscle activities, and activities that promote physical fitness or the level of healthy functioning that the body is capable of (Poest et al., 1990). These kinds of activities have many values. They encourage children to be physically fit, to develop a positive attitude toward and habit of daily exercise. Physical fitness leads to better overall health and well-being. Fitness activities and other physical activities give children an occasion to relieve stress and to be active. Teachers ought to start early to develop children's interest in and routines for keeping physically fit and enjoying their lives. Physical games and activities teach coordination and good sportsmanship, and the skills they develop have a positive effect on children's social behavior and self-esteem (Poest et al., 1990). In addition, children often do better in perceptual tasks such as reading when they are well coordinated and inclined toward motor and fitness activities.

The goal of a physical fitness program should be for the children to get exercise and to have fun. Many locomotor and fitness activities can easily be combined with creative movement and music activities.

Fitness and Motor Guidelines

1. To develop their large muscles adequately, young children need teacher or adult guidance in physical activities, not just the opportunity to play on large-muscle equipment (Poest et al., 1990). This is facilitated by planning motor and physical activities and centers.
2. Physical and motor activities should be re-

warding and positive experiences. Children should soon sense that moving and exercising make them feel more energetic and strong.

3. Teachers should emphasize fitness, not competition. Competition must be avoided by early childhood teachers. Competitive pressures lower children's self-esteem, produce rivalry or anger, cause withdrawal or a sense of failure or inadequacy, and decrease the quality of learning (Cartwright, 1991). A child should be taught early to compete with himself or herself, to try to improve and do better.

4. Teachers should observe carefully so that children do not overdo. Gear your guidance and expectations to the needs and abilities of individual children.

5. To provide a positive model for the children, teachers and assistants should participate in physical and motor games and activities whenever it is appropriate to do so (Poest et al., 1990).

Fitness and Motor Activities

Large-Motor Activities. Examples of these are walking, running, galloping, skipping, jogging, balancing, hopping, jumping, sliding, and climbing. Throwing and catching can include bean bag tosses, ball-throwing and -catching games and skills, or ring tosses. Other ball-handling skills include kicking, bouncing, dribbling, and rolling. Riding wheeled equipment is also a good large-motor activity. Balancing skills include walking a beam, stretching, bending, swinging, and twisting. Opportunities to run, walk, or jog should be provided daily to increase cardiovascular fitness.

Small-Motor Activities. These include zipping, lacing, twisting, pouring, cutting, inserting pegs, pounding nails, tracing, and writing. Such activities enhance small-motor skill.

Stunts or Self-Testing Activities. (Note: These must be adapted to the developmental physical and motor abilities of the children in your group. Many are more appropriate for 6- to 8-year-old children. Many can be done to music.)

Tossing a plastic ring back and forth increases eye–hand coordination, improves concentration, and encourages physical development.

Frog Jump. The children assume a squat position with hands on the floor. They move forward with a springy jump, extending their legs and landing first on hands and then on feet.

No Arms. The children lie flat on their backs and fold their arms. The object is to get to a standing position without unfolding the arms.

Crab Walk. The children clutch their ankles with their hands and walk forward step by step.

See Saw. Two children sit on the floor facing one another with their feet together. They clasp hands, and as one leans forward, the other pulls back as far as she or he can. They seesaw back and forth.

Toe Touch. The children stand with their feet astride. They touch the right toe with the left hand and then alternate.

Back to Back. The children are in pairs, standing back to back. They try to sit down and then stand back up while keeping their backs together.

Partner Pull-Up. The children are in pairs, sitting on the ground, facing one another, knees bent, feet flat on the ground, toes touching. With hands grasped, they try to pull each other up, then try to sit back down.

Jumping Jacks

Forward Roll

Backward Roll

Physical Games. During early childhood, games are played much differently than they are when children are school age. Following are some guidelines:

1. Select games on the basis of the developmental characteristics of the children.
2. Keep the games simple, with few rules. The older the children are, the more rules that can be added.

3. Make sure games are noncompetitive. Children cannot tolerate losing before 5 or 6 years of age. Focus on skill development, having fun, and encouraging a sense of fair play.
4. Make sure the children experience accomplishment.
5. When selecting an "It," be impartial. For example, draw from a set of class cards that includes each child's name.
6. When the game has reached its peak of interest, change activities.
7. Be aware of the physical abilities of all children. Plan how you will include children with physical disabilities.
8. Do not match boys against girls.
9. Make sure all children are allowed to participate, but do not force children to take part.
10. Explain how to play the game and then demonstrate how to play.

Examples of Active Games

Following are some games that are appropriate for early childhood. Some are more suitable for younger children; most are more suitable for 5- to 8-year-olds. Some can be adapted to meet the needs of a particular age or group of children. Only a few suggestions are included here. Many other acceptable physical games can be found in game books available at your local library or in book stores.

Hot Potato. Children sit or stand in circle. The ball is a "hot potato" and must be pushed or kicked away when it comes near.

Jump Ball. Players are in circle, with "It" in the center of the circle. Players roll the ball trying to touch "It," who jumps over the ball. If the ball touches "It," she or he changes places with the last child who rolled the ball.

Piglet. All players except Piglet form pairs in a circle. When Piglet says "face to face," the partners face each other. When Piglet says

Active circle games are not only fun, but they encourage socialization, cooperation, and physical development.

"back to back," or "side to side," or "toe to toe," the direction must be followed. If Piglet says "Piglet," everyone tries to find a new partner. The person left without a partner becomes Piglet.

Find the Leader. Players are in circle. "It" is sent from the room, and a leader is designated. After returning to the room, "It" has so many guesses to identify the leader. The leader changes activity, and the players must copy the leader. If the leader is guessed, he or she becomes "It."

Cooperative Musical Chairs. Musical chairs is played the traditional way, except there is a chair for everyone. Another suggestion is to play it so that everyone shares a chair with a partner and no pair is left out (Orlick, 1982).

Freeze Tag. All children are "It" and can freeze other players by touching them and yelling "Freeze!" Players that are frozen must freeze in the positions they are in when touched. When everyone but one person is frozen, that person says "Unfreeze" and the game begins again.

Railroad Cars. Players are in pairs, one behind the other, and each places his or her hands on the waist of the child in front. Put some train music on, and the children try to add other cars onto their train.

Smile if You Love Me. Children are in a circle (if the group is large, make each circle about 6 to 8 children). "It" goes to a player and says, "Smile if you love me." "It" can make faces, sounds, or movements as he or she tries to make the other child smile. If "It" makes the player smile, that child becomes an "It." The object of this game is to try to get everyone in the circle to be an "It" (Kagan, 1992).

Other games of skill include those that require small-muscle coordination such as passing a Lifesaver around a group of 4 to 6 children using a small wooden dowel or a straw. Other examples include bean bag or ball tosses, a ring toss, or coin drops (a coin is dropped into a soda bottle).

In all physical fitness activities and games, children enjoy the opportunity of participating, being active, and having fun. Competition is not a necessary ingredient for success in the activities and games. Physical fitness is great play for young children.

Field Trips

Importance of Field Trips

Field trips must have a purpose in order to have meaning for children. They should not be planned just to have fun, provide variety, or take a trip someplace. Field trips should be tied closely to the curriculum; they are often the means by which children make sense and meaning out of what is being taught in the classroom. They need to be kept simple so they are manageable and developmentally appropriate for young children.

Every school is located in a unique community to explore, and many wonderful field trips can be planned as walking trips. When planning field trips, consider the type of transportation available. Budgets may provide for buses for a monthly field trip or may prevent the frequent use of buses. Some programs have parent volunteers to provide cars.

Values and Benefits of Field Trips

When field trips are planned carefully and with purpose, they provide numerous values and benefits.

1. Children participate in real experiences with people, places, and things; what is seen, heard, smelled, and felt is most often what is remembered. Also, when experiences are first hand, the opportunity for knowledge and understanding is enhanced.
2. Field trips provide excellent opportunities to reinforce and extend concepts and notions.
3. Field trips expand children's knowledge of the world about them, including the diversity of people and cultures.

Planning a Field Trip

As plans are made for field trips, careful consideration must be given to a number of important points.

1. The length of time the trip will take. For half-day programs, the actual bus or car ride to the site should take no more than 20 minutes. For full-day programs, no more than 1 hour of riding time each way should be planned. Young children tire too easily to travel farther. If the zoo is a 90-minute ride one way, wait until the children are older and it will be much more effective for them. Third- or fourth-grade children would still be able to enjoy the zoo even though they had a long ride to get there.
2. The children's safety. Every effort must be made to ensure the safety of the participants. Whether walking or riding, getting to and from the field trip site must be carefully considered. If the children are riding, drivers should be provided with maps so they know exactly where to go and the route to be followed. If parents are driving, the children

must be required to wear seat belts. Arrange for enough vehicles to comply with this rule. Drivers must be properly licensed, and their vehicles must have appropriate insurance.

During the field trip, count the children often. *Never leave a field trip site, or a stop on the way, without making certain every child is accounted for.*

3. The ages, attention spans, and interest levels of the children involved. Field trips must be carefully evaluated with respect for the children you are taking.

4. Adult supervision. Plan for adequate adult supervision based on the number of children going on the field trip. For children ages 2 to 3, there should be one adult for every three to four children; for ages 4 to 6, there should be one adult for every four to five children; for ages 7 to 8, there should be one adult for every five to six children. Supervising adults should be encouraged to ask and answer questions, explain, and extend desired concepts.

5. Permission. Permission must be obtained from parents or guardians. Some schools or programs allow for a single written and signed permission to be obtained from parents at the beginning of the year that covers all field trips during the year. The permission should give legal permission for the child to go on field trips, and it should also release the school from liability in case of accident. Parents must be notified of all field trips the children take and know when and where they are going.

6. Site visit before the actual field trip. The teacher should visit the site of the field trip before the children visit. This provides information regarding the required travel time and route and an estimate of the approximate length of the visit. The teacher should inform the person on site who will be responsible for the discussion what the purpose of the visit is, concepts to be taught, the age level of the children, and the amount of time available. Take note of the availability and locations of restrooms.

7. Need for snacks or lunches. Make preparations for snacks or lunches if warranted by the length of the field trip experience.

8. Preparation of the children. Children need to be adequately prepared for, and introduced to, the field trip. They should be told what to expect and look for, why they are taking the trip, what safety precautions they should follow, and any limits that must be observed. Small groups of children should be assigned to individual adults who will supervise them and with whom they should stay at all times. For safety reasons, children should *not* wear name tags.

Suggestions for Field Trips

Remember, field trips are planned as an extension of the children's experiences and to clarify subjects about which you have heard children express misconceptions or misinformation.

Particular consideration must be given to children with special needs. For example, if you have children in wheelchairs, the transportation, site access, and restroom facilities must accommodate their needs.

Following are 25 suggested field trip ideas. Add other possibilities to this list, especially those unique to your own community.

1. Community nature center
2. Zoo
3. Farm
4. Neighborhood business, park, home
5. Pet store or a home with pets
6. Bus ride
7. Grocery store
8. Park
9. Cemetery
10. Department store
11. A parent's place of work
12. Fire station
13. Post office
14. Police department
15. Library

16. Nursing home
17. Shut-in neighbor
18. Children's museum
19. Field, park, or open space to fly kites
20. High school, college, or university music department
21. Music store
22. Touch, sound, or smell walk
23. Train station
24. Butcher shop or fish market
25. Treasure hunt

Note: Sometimes rather than taking the children on a field trip, site people are willing to visit the center or school. For example, instead of having the children go to the fire station, fire fighters may prefer to bring equipment to the school. Therefore, determine whether it is best to plan for a field trip or a visitor.

Field Trip Follow-Up

Following the field trip, teachers should get feedback to determine comprehension. Use pictures, books and stories, filmstrips and videos, dramatic play, visitors, music, art, and discussions to clarify and enrich the experience as well as to provide outlets for expressions of feeling. As the children recall their experiences, the alert, observant teacher can evaluate the benefit of the field trip and any misconceptions that need to be clarified or concepts that need reinforcement. Language experience charts can be used to record the children's memories, and over time these can be used to recall trips taken. Depending on the age of the children, letters can be written or pictures drawn as a "thank you" to adults who provided transportation and supervision, or to those who guided the children at the field trip site.

Dramatic Play

There are many types of dramatic play activities, and each offers opportunities for all children to talk and listen, thus developing the language arts.

They promote socialization, release of feelings and attitudes, and creative thinking and problem solving. Dramatic play provides opportunities for children to enhance cognitive, emotional, and social skills. It encourages creativity and offers the opportunity for children to play out their own personal culture and world. Because young children love to pretend, and because dramatic play is pretending, that itself is an important value.

Free Dramatic Play

One type of dramatic play activity, often referred to as *free dramatic play,* is set up during individual play for children who choose to participate. An area of the room is set up with desired materials. The children need not be told what to do, since the materials will suggest possibilities to them. Their own experiences and imaginations will be all they need. Dramatic play is especially enjoyed by 3- to 8-year-olds because they like pretending. Playing house seems to be the preferred theme, perhaps because it provides familiar roles for the children to use and expand (Griffing, 1983). It is easy for a child to become a police officer, farmer, mother, father, beautician, or whatever role the materials suggest. Teachers must encourage diversity of roles and watch for stereotyped comments and behaviors. It is suggested that an area of the room be set up for dramatic play, and that this area be changed often to suggest various kinds of dramatic play.

Large, hollow blocks provide a great chance for dramatic play in which children "shape their own learning environments" (Cartwright, 1990). The children choose whether the play is housekeeping, farming, aviation, fishing, boating, or something else. When the accessories are unstructured, even more imagination and creativity can be tapped. For example, fabrics can be furnished for dressing up; small unit blocks for small accessories; paper, tape, and crayons for signs. All are unstructured and leave what they become to the child's imagination (Cartwright, 1990). Following are some suggestions for the dramatic play area to be used during free play.

1. Housekeeping: any housekeeping and domestic tools and equipment, such as brooms, mops, stove, table, refrigerator, dress-up clothes for boys and girls (child sized), hats, purses, shoes, gloves, ties, and eyeglass frames; in addition, towels, washtub, and dolls (of both genders and diverse ethnic and racial backgrounds), along with dishes, cooking utensils, equipment, and pretend foods.
2. Barbershop and beauty shop: actual materials and cosmetics, such as rollers, combs, brushes, hair dryer, mirror, fingernail polish, nail file, cotton balls, old makeup, perfume, lotions, shaving cream, play razor, and aftershave lotion, together with soap and water, as well as cleansing cream, if possible.
3. Camping: sleeping bags, tent, backpacks, canteens, mess kits, compass, hiking boots, rope, flashlight, food, as well as rocks and wood to represent a campfire.
4. Picnic: tablecloth, table, napkins, picnic basket, jug for a drink, sandwiches, cookies, rocks and wood to represent fire, other equipment.
5. Carpentering: hammers, saws, other tools, nails with large heads, scrap lumber, sandpaper, woodworking bench.
6. Plumbing: pipes of all lengths, widths, and shapes; monkey wrenches, plungers, hose and nozzles, and box for tools.
7. Restaurant: small tables set up with matching tablecloths; old menus obtained from restaurants; placemats, napkins, and any other restaurant supplies obtained from local places that might be willing to give you these materials; an area where food is prepared, with both pretend and real foods available to serve customers.
8. Grocery store: foods and empty cartons, as well as empty metal cans with labels; large unit blocks or small tables, with aisles and shelves set up for display of grocery items; cash register, real money (small change), cart or carriage, bags and/or boxes.
9. Hospital: white shirts, stethoscope, adhesive bandages, elastic bandages, cotton balls, cots, pillows and sheets, scales, tongue depressors, flashlight, syringes, masks, rubber gloves, crutches, pill bottles with small candies for medicine, supplies donated from the disposable items used by hospitals and doctor's office (sterilized before using, disposed of or sterilized after using).
10. School: desks, chalk, chalkboard, erasers, paper, pencils, crayons, books, flannel board and flannel figures, any other school supplies.
11. Office: typewriter, paper, pen, pencils, telephone, briefcase, and any other office supplies available.
12. Post office: envelopes, both new and used, rubber stamp and ink pad (perhaps discarded rubber stamps from a post office), scales, used stamps, any kinds of stamps such as trading stamps, mailbag (old newspaper bag or large purse with shoulder strap), mailboxes (small and large shoe boxes), mail sorting box (box with cardboard sections in it).
13. Bakery: bowls, rolling pins, playdough or clay, cookie cutters, muffin tins, cookie sheets, baker's hat, aprons.
14. Gas station: air pumps, boxes, ropes, hoses for pump, tools such as wrench, screwdrivers, oil can, cash register, sponges and paper towels.

Additional possibilities for dramatic play areas include a shoe store (complete with shoeshine area), dentist's office, television station, dress shop, men's clothing store, airport, space station, gardening center, farmhouse, barn, circus play, fashion show, greenhouse, and pet store. Even a few materials will promote dramatic play with children. Another idea is to have a couple of suitcases ready to pack for trips. Line up chairs for an airplane, boat, automobile, bus, train, or whatever means of travel has been chosen. In many early childhood classrooms, the only dramatic play area ever set up is a housekeeping area. After many weeks, the children tire of it and do not use it as often. Try setting up new areas, and you will be amazed at the interest and enthusiasm sparked in both the children and yourself.

Creative Dramatics

Creative dramatics are more sophisticated than free dramatic play. They are planned by the teacher but acted and played out by the children. Creative dramatics have more form than free dramatic play (McCaslin, 1984). However, both free dramatic play and creative dramatics involve the children "in improvised dialogue, identification with a role, and minimal use of props" (Mandelbaum, 1975, p. 88). A great benefit of creative dramatics is the full participation and involvement of all children. As children try out various roles, they learn about others and about themselves. Ideas from all aspects of the curriculum can be used to stimulate creative dramatics.

Dramatizations can be stimulated and motivated in many ways. They must be geared to the ages of the children, and younger children will need more coaching and help from the teacher. Even though these children enjoy dramatizations, they do not often have the know-how to carry them out without guidance and assistance. The teacher may need to participate, or simply give much prompting and assistance. As an example, one kindergarten group was dramatizing "The Three Billy Goats Gruff." The teacher first told them the story and then parts were assigned, with children not having parts being the audience. A plank was set up between two chairs to represent the bridge, the troll wore an old coat and hat, and the three billy goats each wore simple paper-sack masks. As the teacher helped the children with this dramatization, she used such motivating questions as "What happened next?", "What did the first billy goat do then?", and "What did the troll say?" If the children taking the parts could not remember, they were coached by the audience. They enjoyed participating, and it was not important that each "actor" have the part memorized or even remembered it. What was important was that the children were involved in making the story come to life for them. For older children, fewer suggestions, along with the main plot or idea, will enable them to dramatize, or act out, the story. Some suggestions for creative dramatizations include the following activities:

1. Stories: read in class or in a reading group
2. Poems
3. Musical story dramatizations
4. Situations: a friend unwilling to share a toy with you, what to do if a friend gets hurt, being lost
5. Field trips: to the farm, to the zoo, etc.
6. Events: a birthday party, a hike, a hunting expedition, trips to outer space, to Mexico or any other place
7. Dramatizations centered on an object or series of objects: an object or objects put in a bag, with the children making up stories about the object(s)
8. Pretend activities: pretending to be seeds growing or sprouting, a worm crawling along a branch, etc.—especially enjoyed by younger children
9. Plays
10. Role playing: specific role or character for an individual child or a story role played by the entire group to promote understanding of feelings and actions
11. Puppet shows

Puppets

Use of puppets is a kind of dramatic play, and it offers many opportunities for both speaking and listening. "Young children are fascinated by puppets, and readily accept the apparent magic that is responsible for giving them life" (Smith, 1979, p. 4). They are attention getters. Puppets can be used in unstructured situations such as individual play; but sometimes children become aggressive when using them, particularly if animal puppets are being used, and limits and guidelines must be established. Puppets can be used to capture attention in a discussion, tell a story or poem, teach a song, give children directions, or assist in numerous other situations. Puppet skits can be used to help children develop problem-solving skills such as sensitivity to problems or alternative-solution thinking (Smith, 1979). Younger children use puppets in less formal and structured ways. Examples of using puppets include the following:

1. Storytelling
2. Play acting
3. Puppet show
4. Singing songs: puppets used by one or more children when singing songs; often help shy children to sing or speak out more
5. Children in stories: participation by children in parts of stories
6. Stimulation of a dialogue or conversation between two or more children
7. Television shows: television set made out of large box such as a store or refrigerator box; quiz shows, talk shows, movies, or even commercials

Puppets can be made in numerous ways. The puppets that children make should be simple in design and easy to use, such as those made from paper sacks, sticks, felt, socks, vegetables, paper plates, cardboard cylinders, or gloves.

Selecting and Using High-Quality Commercial Toys and Equipment

The market is saturated with toys and early childhood equipment, and it is imperative that educators make wise and careful selections. The following general criteria are suggested for selecting commercial equipment, toys, and other materials.

1. The equipment should be appropriate for the children's ages, levels of development, abilities, needs, and interests.
2. A good piece of equipment encourages par-

ticipation and involvement, not just observation and entertainment. It should stimulate independent activity.
3. The equipment should be versatile, allowing for additional creative and inventive potential.
4. The equipment should be simple and as free of detail as possible. This encourages versatility, imagination, variety, and appeal.
5. The equipment should be durable and safe, sanitary, and repaired immediately when broken. When purchasing equipment, it is wise to find out whether extra pieces or parts are available to replace those that may be lost or broken.

Teacher-Made Learning Materials

In many instances, limited budgets determine the quantity and quality of the equipment and materials that can be purchased. In addition, many commercial toys are restricted in terms of their learning potential. Equipment, materials, and games can easily be made from accessible and inexpensive supplies. This section focuses on materials that contribute to conceptual, perceptual, and language development, in addition to supporting the concepts presented throughout this book.

Equipment and materials are tools for the teacher to use in teaching, and reinforcing learning, as well as for the child to enjoy through play. They provide the child with the opportunity to develop concepts such as color, shape, and number as well as visual perception and eye–hand coordination. Children also use skills that provide the foundation for developing abilities and understanding in reading, writing, and mathematical operations.

When selected wisely, equipment and materials can be used in a variety of ways, including child-initiated and teacher-initiated activities. Frequently when the child initiates the play, it may simply (but importantly) involve explora-

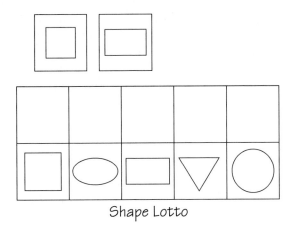

Shape Lotto

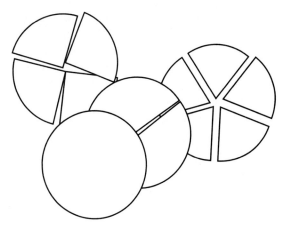

Fraction Pie

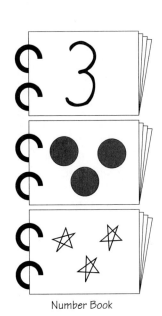

Number Book

Alphabet Board

,tion. Teachers can suggest, model, or prod, but ultimately the children should determine how they want to use equipment and materials (Kuschner & Clark, 1977).

In order to sustain and extend play, a teacher could suggest additional ways of working with a material. The teacher could challenge the child with a question such as "Have you ever thought about how the beads would look on the string if they were strung in a pattern such as two reds and then one blue, two reds and then one yellow, and so on?" In teacher-initiated play, a teacher usually invites the child to play with the equipment and may suggest ways of using the materials or even establish rules for games such as dominoes. Both kinds of play, child initiated and teacher initiated, are valuable, and the selection of either depends on the individual situations and children.

It should be emphasized that although many materials themselves stimulate children's imaginations for use, guided help and teacher assistance are needed in order to focus on the concept being emphasized. A set of shape dominoes may be used as blocks or for building corrals and fences. This is important and of great value. However, as play progresses, show the children how to play shape dominoes with the blocks. Teachers do not always need to play with and near children, but there are both intellectual and emotional advantages in doing so. Positive teacher–child relationships can be strengthened when teachers enjoy focusing on the use of materials and discussing basic concepts with the children.

Teachers need experiences with the materials they provide children. A teacher understands the learning potential and use of manipulative materials by playing with and using the materials. Using and playing with materials and toys is a valuable opportunity for learning about the child's conceptual development. It is also an excellent time for visiting personally with children and becoming better acquainted with their needs, emotions, desires, and interests.

In deciding which equipment to make for enhancing classroom learning, remember that teacher-made materials should be prepared using basically the same criteria that are used in selecting commercial materials and equipment. Be flexible in considering the various ways each material can be used. Many materials adapt to play by one child, many children, child and teacher, or children and teacher.

Many examples of teacher-made materials, including line drawings, photographs, and descriptions, are presented in this chapter and Appendix A. It is hoped that the few suggestions given will ignite your imagination and stimulate interest in further exploration, experimentation, and creation. Following are lists of suggested materials for use in preparing teacher-made learning materials.

Bases

Poster paper	Paneling
Cardboard	Wood
Construction paper	Oilcloth
Masonite	Vinyl
Plywood	Oak tag
Pressed wood	Index cards
Plexiglass	

Covers

Clear adhesive-backed paper	Plastic
Polyurethane	Acetate
Modge-podge	Lamination
	Plexiglass

Attachers

Glue	Tape
Paste	Modge-podge
Staples	

Multipurpose Materials

Felt	Feathers
Pellon	Sequins
Velvet, velour	Wallpaper
Sandpaper	Shelf paper
Beans	Wrapping paper
Buttons	Paper clips
Nuts, bolts, washers	Pop-bottle caps
Macaroni	Styrofoam
Thread spools	Scraps of:
Beads	tile
Paint-chip samples	linoleum
Yarn	Formica
String	wood
Dowels	fabric
Popsicle sticks	carpet
Tongue depressors	fur

Containers

Egg cartons	Jars
Milk cartons cut to desired size	Cans

Small boxes	Bags
Matchboxes	Styrofoam con-
Film cans	tainers for meat
	or pastry

Coloring

Crayons	Colored pencils
Felt-tipped pens	Spray paints
Colored pens	Nontoxic paints
Tempera	Hobby enamels

Picture Sources

Magazines	Greeting cards
Old books	Workbooks
Catalogs	Wrapping paper
Gummed stickers	Advertisements
Photographs	Posters

Properly chosen toys and materials facilitate the child's play (Fein, 1982). Wisely selected teacher-made learning materials contribute to conceptual, perceptual, and language development. Not only do they enrich and reinforce learning, they also provide play enjoyment. The effectiveness of the equipment depends on its arrangement/display/organization, periodic rotation, and care and maintenance. Play is of value whether it is child initiated or teacher initiated when the materials have been selected wisely, with care and understanding of young children's developmental needs.

Summary

Play is an integral part of the early childhood environment and curriculum. Teachers must recognize the inherent values in play, and they must organize an environment that reflects these values and plan a curriculum based on play. Play is developmentally right for children 2 to 8 years of age; it is what they need, based on our understanding of their developmental characteristics.

The physical environment is an important ingredient in determining the feeling tone of the classroom or center. It shows the children what they will learn, how they should behave, and what they should feel about their education. It influences how they act, what they think, and how they feel. Early childhood educators must recognize their responsibility in creating a physical environment that has positive influences on the learning and growth of the children who use that environment. Toys and materials must be properly selected, used, stored, and cared for. They too influence the child's learning, behavior, and feelings.

A variety of play activities are included throughout the text, such as stories, art, music, science, and other kinds of experiences. Three types of play experiences that are not discussed specifically in other parts of the text have been included in this chapter: field trips, physical fitness activities and games, and dramatic play experiences. Examples of these are included in lesson and unit plans throughout this text; however, we felt it necessary in this chapter to explain their value, provide specific guidelines, and give some examples for clarifying and understanding.

The time spent creating an appropriate and inviting environment that offers many opportunities for play will be well worth the effort.

Student Learning Activities

1. Why do you think play is important? Visit an early childhood classroom and evaluate the kinds of and opportunities for play.

2. Using the criteria for room arrangement suggested in this chapter, draw a sample room arrangement. Describe the intended age group. Tell why you included the specific areas. Does the arrangement support a particular curriculum theme?

3. Visit an early childhood classroom and evaluate its physical setup. Are there different areas of play in the room? Describe each section of the room. (You may also wish to draw a plan of the room to facilitate your description.) Describe any interest centers in the room.

4. Create some contracts that are appropriate for children in early childhood classrooms. How would you use them, and what would the benefits be?

5. Visit a toy store and evaluate three early childhood toys, using the criteria suggested in this chapter.

6. Using the criteria suggested in this chapter for selecting appropriate learning materials for young children, visit an early childhood classroom and make a list of the teacher-made learning materials. Then make a checksheet similar to the one that follows:

Equipment	Appro-priate	Not Appro-priate	Reason
Shape stacking cans		X	Sharp edges
Color lotto game	X		
Manipulative boards (lacing, button-ing, zipping)	X		
Dominoes		X	Not durable

7. Develop a list of materials that could be collected from your home and the homes of children in your classroom to be used in an early childhood situation—for example: padlock and keys; old camera; empty spools; materials for counting, sorting, grouping, ordering, and pattern making (e.g., shells, stones, marbles, straws, washers, canceled stamps).

8. Observe in a classroom where a dramatic play area is set up. Describe the area, the play that occurred during your observation, and the benefits for the children from this kind of play.

9. Plan, implement, and evaluate at least one creative dramatics activity for children aged 2 to 8 years.

10. Organize a list of teacher-made materials that you select to begin working on. You may wish to organize your list into areas such as materials for teaching colors, shapes, people, and textures. Also include science, music, and language and literacy materials. Use your list as an action, to-do list!

11. Make at least three teacher-made learning materials.

12. Study the list of field trips given earlier in the chapter and add additional appropriate field trips for your area and community. Is there a particular age level that is appropriate for each field trip, or could it be adapted to suit any early childhood age level? Note this information next to your field trip suggestion.

13. Select two physical games for any early childhood age and prepare a game sheet with directions. Teach class members one of your games.

Suggested Resources

A day at the beach: Barney and the backyard gang (video). The Lyons Group.

Organizing free play (film). Modern Talking Pictures.

CHAPTER
three

Planning the Curriculum

Introduction

The early childhood curriculum should be planned around the developmental needs of the children in the classroom. The goals and objectives of the curriculum are designed to strengthen all aspects of the children's development. Units are based on themes that will be both interesting and developmentally beneficial.

In a position statement by the National Association for the Education of Young Children (NAEYC) and National Association of Early Childhood Specialists in State Departments of Education (NAECS/SDE), curriculum is defined as "an organized framework that delineates the content children are to learn, the processes through which children achieve the identified curricular goals, what teachers do to help children achieve these goals, and the context in which teaching and learning occur" (NAEYC & NAECS/SDE, 1991, p. 21). Curriculum is what happens in the classroom. It must be appropriate to the individual needs and interests of each child

in the program and also be culturally adapted to those involved (NAEYC & NAECS/SDE, 1991).

There is great diversity in children with regard to their experiences, maturation rates, interests, needs, parent support, and learning styles (NAEYC & NAECS/SDE, 1991). A well-planned curriculum takes this diversity into account. This is why it is important to do a needs assessment and to evaluate throughout the program. One source suggests that curriculum development should draw from many sources: "child development knowledge, individual characteristics of children, the knowledge base of various disciplines, the values of our culture, parents' desires, and the knowledge children need to function competently in our society" (NAEYC & NAECS/SDE, 1991, p. 23).

Experiences should be developed to help young children improve their skills in problem solving, thinking, reasoning, and creating—not just their skill in memorizing what is taught by the teacher. Too often the curriculum and the way it is taught encourage children to become expert rote memorizers rather than creative, involved learners. Facts may eventually become outdated, but the skills of thinking and problem solving never will!

Therefore, learning should be a process of active involvement, with rich, meaningful content, using developmentally appropriate practices and approaches—not just focusing on an end result. Learning should be engaging, and it should include many hands-on experiences.

The curriculum will provide opportunities for development in areas besides intellectual or cognitive growth. It should provide encouragement of, and opportunities for, healthy social, emotional, physical, and intellectual development. It should allow adequate time and opportunity for children to express themselves freely through various media: creative materials, large- and small-muscle materials, dramatic or role-playing materials, manipulative toys and materials, books and other literature, sensory media, and resource people.

There is no such thing as a universal curriculum that is appropriate for all. Even the approach we have taken in this text needs to be tailored to fit children, teachers, and program goals. By suggesting a variety of ways to plan and implement curriculum, our intention is to emphasize the need for flexibility and make it easier to accomplish.

Planning Based on Needs

As a teacher answers the questions "What will I do?" "Why will I do it?" and "How will I do it?", the curriculum is determined. The models described in Chapter 1 most often prescribe, in specific terms, the answers to these questions. However, in most classrooms the curriculum is more traditional, and answers to these questions depend on the teacher's training, the materials available, and the purposes or long-range goals—based on the needs of the children. These needs are established for the program by the teacher, administrators, parents, or, ideally, all of these people together. In addition, children should be a part of the planning. They can make suggestions for themes or topics to investigate; or once a theme is selected, they can help select the activ-

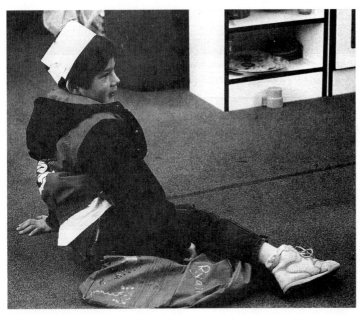

Ryan patiently waits for his ride home after a full day of activity and learning.

ities. As children realize that their ideas result in action, their self-esteem and initiative are enhanced (Nunnelley, 1990).

Goals are absolutely essential to each program. They give something to move toward, some larger framework into which you put your day-to-day activities" (Hatoff, Byram, & Ayson, 1981, p. 84). Every center or program should make a list of purposes or long-range goals: What is the mission of this program? What should a parent expect a child to achieve by attending this school or program for a given length of time? What is the approach, and where is the emphasis? These goals should be posted so that parents, teachers, and administrators can read them—and read them often!

Why?

Goals and objectives constitute the *why* of the curriculum. They provide the reasoning behind the program—the purposes of the teaching. *Why* questions must be asked constantly: Why should we have this particular activity? Why should we have this activity at the time it is planned? Why is it of value to the children? Why will it benefit the child? If there are no purposeful goals or objectives, reevaluation and redirection are needed.

It is necessary to make a distinction between the terms *objectives* and *goals*. Too often the terms *goals, objectives, values,* and *purposes* are used interchangeably. From the long-term goals, the teacher is able to make short-term objectives that will guide the curriculum. When we talk about the long-term desires of a program, we are referring to goals; when we talk about short-term desires, we are referring to objectives. The "specific daily objectives you make *will* add up to the goals you are trying to reach in the long run" (Hatoff et al., 1981, 86).

Objectives should be specific, clearly state the purpose of the activity, and suggest the desired behavior or what should be learned by the child as a result of participation. In some cases, "It may be helpful to make individual plans for a child and write specific *behavioral objectives.* Behavioral objectives are carefully worded statements which describe the behavior expected and the criterion or degree of performance expected" (Hildebrand, 1981, p. 421). There are times when the teacher has specific learning in mind that will result from the child's experiences in the classroom. "A behavioral objective is a description of that learning. It describes the precise way in which the child will demonstrate what he or she has learned" (Hatoff et al., 1981, p. 89). Many educators consider behavioral objectives too rigid and structured, forcing the child to perform certain skills simply to satisfy the goal. We believe that in some cases a behavioral objective is appropriate when a specific behavior is being sought or encouraged. (A more detailed discussion of overall goals and activity objectives in lesson planning is presented later in the chapter.)

What?

What activities and materials are needed to carry out the desired goals and objectives? In effect, what will be done? The curriculum is planned with the themes and activities that are developmentally appropriate and answer the *what* question.

In addition to making a list of the broad program goals or purposes of the center or program, based on children's needs, teachers should plan themes for the entire year to provide direction and meaningful sequencing of themes and concepts. Through careful selection of themes and daily activities (some supporting the theme), days will be balanced with varied experiences, and the question "What will we do?" will be answered.

How?

How will the selected activities (*what*) be presented and carried out for the desired goals and objectives (*why*) to be achieved? Answering this question includes preparing and planning materials and procedures, as well as gathering needed supplies and determining the approach for following through. It encourages the teacher not only to plan the activity but also to organize work. In the approach to lesson planning suggested in this book, the Procedures sections answer this *how* question. With this question answered, the teacher knows the procedures for the activity, from sequence to completion.

As a teacher carefully thinks through these three questions, the curriculum become stronger. We must know *why* we are doing *what* we are doing, and *how*, specifically, we will accomplish our plans.

Assessing Children's Needs

Teacher's Role

The abilities and needs of the children, both individually and collectively, must be assessed by the teacher. Without this preassessment, desired goals of teaching may never be realized. With this objective reached, the teacher is able to plan, set up, and create a learning environment suited to the developing child.

As the curriculum is organized and carried out, a knowledge of what the child needs and is able to do assists the teacher in captivating and motivating the child. In addition, it allows the teacher to promote self-direction and intrinsic rewards in learning. Ultimately, the teacher is accountable for determining what is best for the individual child, as well as the whole class, and then doing it.

Planning Based on Developmental Needs

We know from research that all children pass through stages of growth in the various developmental areas; however, children do not pass through these stages at the same rate. In a classroom of children within a 1-year age range, there may actually be a developmental range of several years in cognitive, social, emotional, and physical areas. Teachers must expect a wide range of in-

dividual differences (NAEYC & NAECS/SDE, 1991). The challenge comes in determining where each child is developmentally, and then matching appropriate learning activities and curriculum to that child's needs. This requires planning, organization, and often help from other professionals.

If all children are asked to do the same things, in the same way, and all at the same time, we are not honoring their distinct, individual learning styles, abilities, and interests (Cartwright, 1991). When programs are geared to individual children, the teacher cannot *control* all the children all of the time; on the contrary, children become self-disciplined as they take responsibility for their own learning. Then they learn from their own initiative and action.

Frequently, we find that teachers have planned the curriculum for an entire school year before they have even met the children they will be teaching. Too often the teaching focus considers only the scope and sequence guides established by state and local administrators and pays little attention to the developmental needs of individual children in the classroom. It is more effective to begin the year with a needs assessment that determines the strengths, developmental levels, and needs of the children; this also identifies the best place to begin and the competencies that should be stressed. Throughout the year, additional observations and assessment determine the child's progress and help select appropriate curricula.

In addition, nearly every classroom has children who have learning difficulties. More and more, schools are utilizing programs for early recognition of children who may be displaying signs of impending special needs. Screening and assessment can alert the school system to the existence of developmental deviations that may be due to physical, psychological, or neurological circumstances. Early diagnosis decreases the possibility of the condition's becoming more severe and increases the opportunity for successful corrective treatment.

As a reminder, we caution you again that

programs should be developmentally appropriate and based on the needs of children. It is far more beneficial and successful to design programs to fit the children than to expect children to fit the program. Therefore, assessment testing should not be a diagnosis for success or failure, advancement or retention, but a means of determining the needs and goals of individual children. Assessment must be based on the goals of the program and be used to benefit children (NAEYC & NAECS/SDE, 1991).

Assessment Tools

Assessment tests. Classroom teachers work with resource teachers or skilled psychologists in selecting and administering appropriate assessment tools. They should involve hands-on activities, rather than pencil-and-paper tests (NAEYC & NAECS/SDE, 1991). One must know the purpose of assessment in order to select the most appropriate test. As the test is evaluated, professionals and classroom teachers work together to determine goals for individual children and to decide whether there is a need for remediation in class or for special education.

It is essential for anyone involved in selecting, administering, and evaluating a test to recognize his or her responsibilities and to be accountable. Those involved in any aspect of testing must have the training required to participate in the selection, administration, and evaluation of the test. In selecting a test, the person must be familiar with the complexity of the test, what skills and abilities are being tested for, and whether the test is age appropriate. Scores on any test should be combined with observational and performance measures to determine appropriate instructional programs for young children.

Screening and assessment results must be utilized carefully, with the needs of the individual child being the primary goal. The child's rights must be protected, and teachers and other staff must realize that test results are confidential. Test results must be interpreted accu-

rately and carefully, and those interpretations must be shared with those working with the child, including the parents, in such a way that they are not misunderstood or misinterpreted. Assessment tools should reflect the diversity of children and be free of biases (NAEYC & NAECS/SDE, 1991).

The kinds of tests given include the following: *Screening* tests are used primarily to identify potential problem areas. They indicate the need for more in-depth assessment of the potential problem. *Assessment* and *achievement* tests are used to find out what the child has learned; they should not be used to judge the child or determine placement. A *norm-referenced achievement test* tells how much a child has learned compared to other children. A *criterion-referenced achievement* or *assessment test* tells what the child knows and does not know.

We must make it very clear that group-administered standardized achievement tests are prohibited before the third grade (Kamii, 1990).

Informal assessment. If you prefer not to use a standardized assessment, the following is a suggested informal assessment to be used in whole or in part. Remember that chronological and developmental age must be taken into consideration. This is a general assessment or inventory and should not be scored. The children should not be judged or placed by the results. It is used to help the teacher learn more about each child—his or her interests, abilities in limited areas, and developmental characteristics. As children are observed and questioned, notes could be taken and specific actions and comments described directly on the assessment sheet. For example, for the item "Knows and recognizes colors," a teacher could write down the colors the child knows and recognizes. For the item "Cries easily," if the child does cry easily, the teacher could note what frequently causes the child to cry. In other words, the degree to which the child accomplishes the task, or the hows and whys of the behaviors and skills, can be noted, based on careful observation, to make this assessment more meaningful to those who work with the child. Indicating words such as *frequently, occasionally,* or *rarely* could be noted on many of the items.

Care should be taken to use this assessment carefully. It should be used to plan how best to meet the needs of individual children and to help determine appropriate learning activities. The observations and notes taken should be regarded as confidential information.

SELF-IMAGE CHECKLIST AND QUESTIONNAIRE

- Knows first and last names _____
- Recognizes first and last names in print _____
- Writes first name _____
- Writes last name _____
- Knows address _____
- Knows phone number _____
- Knows how many brothers and sisters he or she has _____
- Has a favorite color _____
- Has a favorite toy _____
- Has favorite kinds of activities _____
- Draws recognizable pictures _____
- Names right hand and left hand _____
- Names some physical characteristics, such as eye color, hair color _____
- Draws a self-portrait _____

PHYSICAL AND MOTOR CHECKLIST AND QUESTIONNAIRE

- Walks across a balance beam _____
- Hops five times or more on one foot _____
- Balances on either foot _____
- Balances on either foot with eyes blindfolded _____
- Skips _____
- Walks up and down stairs with one foot per step _____
- Jumps using both feet _____

- Throws a ball or bean bag overhand _____
- Kicks a ball _____
- Climbs confidently up and down climbing equipment such as a jungle gym or dome _____
- Catches a ball or bean bag _____
- Dribbles a ball at least three times _____
- Rides wheeled toys confidently _____ What kind? Big wheel _____ Tricycle _____ Bicycle _____
- Easily uses fingers and hands in fingerplays and games _____
- Writes with a pencil _____
- Writes with a crayon or marking pen _____
- Snaps fingers _____
- Uses most cooking utensils, such as knives and peelers _____
- Uses scissors _____
- Has good finger dexterity using manipulative materials and toys such as nuts and bolts, pegs and pegboards, small plastic fit-together units, puzzles, snap beads, etc. _____
- Copies a pattern such as a geometric shape _____
- Traces around shapes such as geometric or animal shapes _____
- Draws various geometric shapes and designs based on chronological age _____
- Ties shoelaces _____
- Fastens snaps _____
- Zips zipper _____
- Builds a tower with cubes _____ How many cubes? _____
- Weaves strips of paper together _____

SOCIAL AND EMOTIONAL CHECKLIST AND QUESTIONNAIRE

- Has one best friend _____
- Is accepted by at least five children _____
- Engages in cooperative play _____
- Initiates play activities with other children _____
- Is primarily friendly with other children _____

- Is primarily assertive with other children _____
- Is primarily shy with other children _____
- Is afraid of _____
- Is overly serious _____
- Cries easily _____
- Is bossy with other children _____
- Manipulates other children _____
- Is sensitive to the needs of other children _____
- Has empathy for other children and their problems _____
- Is learning to share _____
- Has self-confidence _____
- Is able to assume some responsibility _____
- Is trustworthy _____
- Usually has good self-control _____

LANGUAGE CHECKLIST AND QUESTIONNAIRE

- Is bilingual _____
- Enjoys conversation with others _____
- Initiates conversation with others _____
- Articulates most sounds correctly _____
  Sounds the child does not articulate (list) _____
  _____
- Speaks and responds in sentences _____
  Average length of sentences _____
  Repeats a five-to-six-word sentence with correct word order _____
- (Show 10 picture flash cards, such as a watch, for the child to label and tell what they are used for.)
  Number labeled correctly _____
  Can describe the use or function of how many? _____
- Understands questions and communications from others _____
  Answers questions _____
  Follows simple directions _____
- Participates verbally in songs, fingerplays, stories, and games _____
- Uses all parts of speech (i.e., nouns, pronouns, verbs, adverbs, adjectives) _____
- Listening skills are appropriate for age _____

- Can tell a story or rhyme in sequential order _____
- Likes to use new words _____
- Understands puns or plays on words _____

COGNITIVE CHECKLIST AND QUESTIONNAIRE

- Attempts most tasks or projects _____
- Has adequate attention span to stay on task and complete activities _____
- Is curious _____
- Asks thoughtful questions _____
- Enjoys sensory materials and explorations _____
- Understands and follows given directions _____
- Grasps ideas and concepts quickly _____
- Follows spatial directions such as "Draw a circle above the box." _____
- Recognizes and matches colors _____
- Names and recognizes colors _____
- Counts by rote up to _____
- Counts by 2s to _____ by 5s to _____
- Recognizes numbers up to _____
- Does addition up to _____
- Does subtraction up to _____
- Understands basic money concepts _____
- Can tell time _____
- Matches basic geometric shapes _____
- Names basic geometric shapes _____
- Recognizes likenesses and differences, and groups things that belong together _____
- Recognizes alphabet letters (upper and lower case) _____
- Names alphabet letters (upper and lower case) _____
- Knows consonant sounds and can circle pictures representing beginning consonant sounds (e.g., for the "B" sound, can circle pictures such as a ball, bear, or button) _____
- Knows vowel sounds and selects correct vowels in words _____
- Makes comparisons _____
- Classifies things according to similarities _____

- Is willing to make predictions _____
- Analyzes a problem or situation _____
- Is able to hypothesize a problem to approach a solution _____

Scheduling

Planning the curriculum includes scheduling the entire school day—why the program will be what it is and how it will be carried out. Plans are made, encouraging progression toward themes and objectives. Materials assisting in these plans are prepared and organized.

Rigid Scheduling Versus Flexible Scheduling

Curriculum planning in the early childhood years does not mean planning a rigid time schedule. According to Webster and Shroeder, "No timetable can be, or should be, adhered to too rigidly in an early childhood classroom" (1979, p. 66). Too often programs for early learning are geared to the clock, rather than to children. Perhaps the reason young children often become bored, restless, and uninterested in school is not that they are actually tired of school per se, but that they are tired of the daily routines and time schedule. Many routines in early childhood classes waste untold hours, with no real learning taking place (Mugge, 1976). Routines such as greeting, roll taking, and sharing can be changed to foster learning, problem solving, and creativity. The child comes to school knowing that certain things will take place: There will be snack, free play, singing, reading, and a responsive and warm teacher. Knowing that these routines are daily occurrences will provide security, but not knowing exactly how the goals and plans will be carried out or what approaches will be made to the learning activities will create interest, curiosity, and enthusiasm. This does not mean, however, that

Daily schedules of a well-balanced curriculum include a wide range of activities; a housekeeping area is a frequently visited center.

the teacher does not know how the day will proceed. The order of activities must be formulated, whether the day begins with an activity or free play.

The teacher will need to have a general idea of the time activities will begin, what the sequence of activities will be, and so on—but then it is necessary to observe, feel, and determine the needs of the children, allowing for flexibility. For example, free play may be planned for about 30 minutes, but because of the children's involvement and interest, it may be necessary to extend the period to 45 minutes; this, in turn, may make it essential to have another activity shortened or even eliminated during that particular day. Far too often children are rushed from one activity to the next, or an activity is prolonged just because the lesson plan indicates that at 2:00 P.M. music is scheduled. Young children need well-planned units of study that are carried out through activities with objectives, but the amount of time taken by specific activities must be determined by children's interest and involvement (Katz, 1990).

There is great value in a well-structured curriculum of sequential learning plans, but considerable flexibility and skill must be used in following these through (Fowler, 1971). The teacher who has planned activities but has built them on a flexible base is not disturbed when opportunities for taking advantage of teachable moments arise. For example, one day an Angora sheep wandered close to the play yard. The children were fascinated with it and had numerous questions. It was a wise teacher who encouraged the sheep to enter the play yard and allowed the children to smell, romp with, touch, and feed tree blossoms to it. This necessitated eliminating a planned activity, but the advantages were of far greater value than those that would have been obtained through an inflexible time schedule.

Free Play Including Individual Activities

Every day there should be some time for free play—a time when the child individually selects areas of involvement. Weather permitting, the children should have daily opportunities for play both inside and outside. Outside the core of the play will be large-muscle activities: climbing, running, sliding, balancing, jumping, and so on.

Free play should not be a time for teachers to relax and take a break. Guidance from teachers is necessary during free play (Fowler, 1971). They should be nearby to give assistance and encouragement where needed. They should move among the children and engage them in play activities through stimulation and encouragement. Teachers can acknowledge creative and constructive efforts, ask thought-provoking questions that extend and expand children's play, and redirect play that needs changing (Crosser, 1992). The

teacher helps create meaning and purposefulness, then moves to another child or group of children. Much learning, teaching, and interacting should go on between children, between individual children and the teacher, and between small groups of children and the teacher.

Free play should be long enough for children to carry out their play ideas. Research indicates that the length of the play period directly affects the quality and level of play (Christie & Wardle, 1992). To promote both group dramatic and constructive play, it is necessary to provide longer play periods (Christie & Wardle, 1992). It has been suggested that it may be wise to occasionally reduce "the number of activities available during free play in order that there will be less distraction and greater opportunity for involvement in dramatic play" (Griffing, 1983, p. 16).

Whole- and Small-Group Activities

In addition to the free (or individual) activity, the child will participate in small-group and whole-group activities. If all of the children are participating at the same time in the same situation and general location, they are engaged in a whole-group activity. A traditional whole-group activity is *circle time*, when the children sit in a circle and discussions relating to the theme, experiences, music activities, stories, or other activities are presented to the entire group. For small-group activities, the children are divided into groups of three or four.

Many activities are best suited for one of the three approaches—individual, small-group, or whole-group activities. For example, the use of sensory media in the trough or a similar container is generally best suited to individual play. Other activities, such as finger painting, can be carried out as either individual, small-group, or whole-group activities, depending on the desired objectives, available space, and other planned activities for the day.

Effective transitions to move children from one activity to another must be planned carefully. Children can be "enticed" to move to the next activity (Crosser, 1992, p. 26). Signals such as a designated piano chord, a bell, or a word can signal that it is time to clean up or change activities (Crosser, 1992).

Using Cooperative Learning

Cooperative learning is a versatile approach that can be used in small groups, during free play, or in whole groups. When children are in whole groups, they are divided into pairs or teams to solve a problem, discuss a question, or brainstorm an idea. In cooperative learning activities, children work together in small groups or on teams with a common goal in mind (Johnson, Johnson, Holubec, & Roy, 1986). The cooperative learning strategy is not meant to be used exclusively, but rather integrated and used as the teacher feels appropriate. However, research has shown that there are impressive academic and social gains for children who consistently participate in cooperative learning activities (Kagan, 1992).

Cooperative learning emphasizes social skills—learning to work together and helping one another. The children learn that no one in their group succeeds until they all succeed. Even though the focus appears to be on group behavior, the real purpose is to create stronger individuals. Cooperative learning also encourages children to develop friendships with children who are different from themselves (Kagan, 1992). Additional social skills developed in cooperative learning experiences include taking turns, self-direction, positive self-esteem, and the ability to take different roles (Kagan, 1992). Cooperative learning encourages peer tutoring, staying on task, and individual accountability, and it promotes interdependence. There is more motivation, enthusiasm, and participation on the part of all children when cooperative learning is incorporated into the curriculum.

Cooperative learning experiences prepare young children today for the democratic world they will live in tomorrow (Kagan, 1992). Our democratic ideal promotes equal participation by all members; if children have had no experience participating as viable members of a group, they will have difficulty participating as contributing members of society in the future.

Goals of Cooperative Learning

- Build positive interpersonal social skills and habits among students by giving more opportunity for group interaction.
- Give children the opportunity to teach and learn from one another. This builds leadership skills, strengthens self-esteem, and enhances learning.
- Provide experiences that encourage flexibility, cooperation, and problem solving.
- Provide the kind of learning structure that fosters communication skills. In cooperative learning groups, more children have the opportunity to share ideas, exchange information, and talk.

Guidelines for Using Cooperative Learning

- Children need to be shown how to use the cooperative learning strategy, and it must be discussed thoroughly before the children go into their groups.
- The content and objectives of the lesson plan, as well as the developmental level of the children, will determine which particular cooperative learning strategies are used.
- To be an effective member of any group, children need to learn that they will be expected to share ideas (talk) as well as *listen* to what other group members have to say.
- Cooperative learning can be used during free play as children work together on activities, play with manipulatives, paint at the easel, work on a science project, or participate in any variety of cooperative group activities during the free play. The group size may be two, three, four, or more members.

- Cooperative groups can be used to solve a single problem such as a math problem, for more complicated activities, or for a group discussion. Cooperative learning can be used in art, science, language explorations, or virtually any curriculum area. This approach is especially valuable in the language area because all children can then share, discuss, evaluate, write, act out, plan, play a part, have a turn at the game, listen to another, or otherwise participate in whatever the lesson or activity involves.
- Cooperative learning is different from regular small groups in that the focus is on interactive group behavior whereby all children must participate and support the group effort.
- After the groups have worked together, it is wise to "debrief" the children. This means that group members decide what went well and what did not go so well. It is a form of evaluation and feedback as well as an opportunity to bring the activity to an end.

Dividing Children into Groups

- Divide the children into two circles, one inside of the other, and have the circles move in two opposite directions. When a signal is given, the circles stop and the children facing each other are partners.
- Put numbers, colors, animals, shapes, book titles, or songs in four corners or areas of the room (if you want more than four groups, use more than four areas). Have the children go to the corner or area that designates their favorite number, shape, or whatever category has been chosen.
- Put badges or stickers of different colors, animals, numbers, or even different children on class members. The children go with the group that has the same badge as theirs.
- Cut a picture into three, four, or five parts and give a part of the picture to each child. Children are to find the other parts of their picture to form their group (Kagan, 1992).

- Split lines by lining children up, then "folding" the line in half to create a partner for each child. Fold each line again to form groups of four (Curran, 1991).

Cooperative Learning Strategies

- *Numbered Heads Together.* Each of the students in a group has a number. For example, four children in a group would be numbered one through four. The teacher asks a question or gives a problem to solve. The children work on it and agree on their team's answer. When the teacher calls a number, the children with that number share their group's answer (Curran, 1991).
- *Think-Pair-Share.* An idea is given for the children to think about. Each child finds or is assigned a partner, and the two discuss the problem together. Then they report back or share what they have learned.
- *Interviews.* Children are assigned to groups of four. Child 1 interviews child 2, and child 3 interviews child 4. Then they reverse so that child 2 interviews child 1 and child 4 interviews child 3. They share what they have learned. This can be used for a review, for end-of-unit feedback, or for focusing on a particular concept.

For additional suggestions regarding strategies used in cooperative learning, we refer you to Kagan (1992), Johnson and colleagues (1986), and Curran (1991).

Planning Units

Teaching young children requires much preparation. The day must be planned and organized before the children arrive. Several vital components of planning include the following:

- Choosing a theme and the overall goals of the entire unit.
- Brainstorming activities to teach or support the theme (unit plan or web).

- Determining daily activities, ensuring a balance among various kinds of activities (daily activity plan).
- Deciding on a daily schedule of activities (what will be done first, second, etc., and about how long each activity will last).
- Setting objectives for each activity and organizing the lesson plan.
- Preparing materials and resources and organizing each activity.
- Arranging the room's environment. Major room changes may be made each week or less often, and minor room changes made daily to accommodate the activities planned.

Every teacher must plan! The more experienced a teacher becomes, the less this planning will be written and the more it will take place in the mind: "One [teacher] may write more on paper, whereas another relies on memory. The amount of written planning will depend on the experience of the teacher" (Hildebrand, 1981, p. 427). Those with some experience in teaching may be able to think through, instead of writing down, the lesson plan with written objectives; the daily schedule would then serve as the main guide.

A specific part of the scheduling includes planned units, in which activities are coordinated to strengthen and reinforce desired concepts or ideas and to meet the developmental needs of individual children. These are organized plans for accomplishing goal-directed teaching. They ensure that the program is in harmony with the needs and abilities of children in early childhood. The unit approach encourages interest and increases the number of materials to which the children are exposed (Rounds, 1975).

Theme

The curriculum can focus on a topic or theme and at the same time allow for integration of more traditional subject-matter divisions. Using a unit theme, or concept, provides an opportunity for rich and meaningful conceptual development. The unit theme must be selected before

further planning can take place. The possibilities for unit themes are infinite. One author challenged educators, stating that "any subject can be taught effectively in some intellectually honest form to any child at any stage of development" (Bruner 1960, p. 12).

Children at differing stages of development approach a concept from different levels. They first develop an awareness, then explore it, then use inquiry, and finally use the concept or learning (NAEYC & NAECS/SDE, 1991). Thus, any child can benefit and gain something from almost any theme.

The largest portion of this book will deal with specific themes and approaches to teaching them. However, a beginning list of possible themes appropriate for children in the early childhood years follows:

Air	People
Animals	self-concept
specific categories	senses
(farm animals,	body parts
insects)	family
kinds (bees, dogs)	friends
animal houses	other cultures
animal babies	professions
hibernation	Pollution
Boxes	Rocks
Cans	Seeds
Color	Shape
Emotions	Shoes
Fire	Texture
Flowers	Trains
Houses	Trees
Magnets	Water
Numbers	Wheat
Nuts	Wheels
Paper	

Many of these suggestions could be narrowed down further to specific concepts or themes. As suggested, the subject of animals could be broken into categories such as farm animals, animal homes, animal products, hibernation, insects, bees, or caterpillars. Teachers, parents, and children can brainstorm for themes and topics appropriate for their classroom (Nunnelley, 1990).

Unit Plan

Once a theme is selected, the teacher is ready to construct a unit plan. A unit plan includes numerous possible activities for coordinating and carrying out the unit. It results from brainstorming ideas for experiences in various areas of the curriculum (e.g., nutrition or food experiences, science experiences, art activities, field trips, visitors, music experiences, and literary experiences). Usually the unit plan includes far more activities than could be realistically incorporated into a lesson plan. Nevertheless, it provides a rainbow of possibilities and encourages the teacher to plan coordinated activities that support the general theme and meet the needs of the children in the classroom.

For instance, a theme on seeds may be selected. Appropriate subjects for themes are those that strengthen and broaden the young child's understanding of the world. A unit plan on seeds geared to 3- to 8-year-old children could include the following suggested activities.

UNIT PLAN ON SEEDS

Lesson plans on seeds can be effectively planned in the fall, when so many plants, particularly weeds and trees, are shedding seeds, or they can be planned in the spring, which is the planting season for flowers, grains, and vegetables. Activities are selected based on the desired goals, the concepts to be taught, the season of the year, and the needs of the children.

Art

- Seed collages
- Seed shakers (used in rhythm activities)
- Finger painting, with seeds added to mixture
- Screen painting with seeds and pods
- Paint with wheat stems, especially bearded wheat

- Paperweight made with potter's clay with seeds pressed in

Field Trips

- Nature walk, to look for seeds
- Home garden or farm, to plant seeds or to watch gardener or farmer planting seeds
- Seed distributor, to see kinds and varieties of seeds and how they are sold
- Grocery store, to look for foods that are seeds (e.g., sesame seeds, sunflower seeds, peas, beans, corn)
- Granary, to observe storage of seeds (grains)
- Farm, to observe harvesting of grains or use of seeds (corn, barley, wheat) in feeding some animals

Food

- Chili
- Lima bean soup
- Green bean salad, casserole
- Corn casserole or chowder
- Corn on the cob
- Whole-wheat cereal
- Pea salad or casserole
- Food experiences using the seeds of fruits and vegetables that we eat (tomatoes, bananas, beans, peas, corn)
- Some seeds must be cooked before eaten
- Some seeds can be eaten without being cooked
- Breadsticks sprinkled with sesame seeds
- Seed sprouts—may be used in salad
- Popcorn

Science

- Some seeds need the shell removed before eating
- Seeds need water, warmth, food, and air to sprout
- Seeds are different from each other in size, shape, color, and texture
- Avocado seed supported with toothpicks in a jar of water (observation of growth)
- Seeds sprouted and tasted—alfalfa, wheat, and beans work especially well
- Planting of seeds

- Study and tasting of seeds we eat; comparison with inedible seeds
- Study of where the seeds are obtained
- Study of how and why seeds travel
- Comparison of the numbers of seeds produced by various plants
- Study and observation of seedpods
- Observation of the growing stages of seeds—seeds (such as lima beans) placed between glass slabs or between a plastic or glass jar and a wet (and kept wet) paper towel lining the jar; may start new seeds every day for 3 to 5 days so that the day-by-day changes can be observed

Music

- "Musical chairs," in which a seed package is put on the front of each chair (everyone has a chair). When the music has stopped, directions are given, such as "All the carrot seeds stand up and jump around the circle" or "All the petunia seeds change places"
- Songs about seeds
- Decorated seed shakers used as rhythm-band instruments
- Seedpods such as dried honey-locust pods used as shakers; used to accompany a drumbeat or musical selection
- Creative movements relating to seeds, such as milkweed moving and floating through the air, or the growth and sprouting of seeds
- Creative dramatics involving the care of seeds

Visitors

- Gardener
- Farmer
- Seed distributor
- Grocery store clerk
- Seed nursery worker
- Member of child's family to demonstrate seed planting and care
- Forest ranger

Language and Literacy Development

- Stories about seeds
- Poetry

- Seed or package of seeds given to each child, who then describes it, tells whether it is edible or inedible, says what it will grow into and how it is cared for, and so on
- Write, tell, or dictate stories such as "If I were a seed, I would . . ." or "Seeds I like to eat are . . ."

Webbing or Clustering

The process of webbing, or clustering, is similar to doing a unit plan and, although the end product looks different, it actually has the same result. The approach is to pick a theme or concept, then brainstorm activities and ideas for teaching this concept. Figure 3–1 is an example of a web on seeds. Throughout the text you will see examples of other webs. Teachers should not find it necessary to do both a unit plan and a web, since they serve basically the same purpose.

Activity Plan

Once the unit plan or web has been developed, the teacher selects from it the specific experiences to include in teaching. These selections should be made with respect to the goals the teacher desires to accomplish. Most important, the needs and interests of the children must be considered. An activity plan, which is a sketch of the activities planned for each day throughout the duration of the unit, is now formulated. It provides the teacher with an overview and enables the unit to be viewed in perspective.

As you move from a unit plan to an activity plan, take care to balance the day. Have a balance of kinds of activities (art, music, language and literacy, etc.), as well as types of groups.

Some days, you will choose one concept that is a part of the theme to work on and develop, using a variety of activities.

In the construction of this activity plan, activities should be included that correlate, reinforce, and support the theme and desired objectives. However, not all activities during the

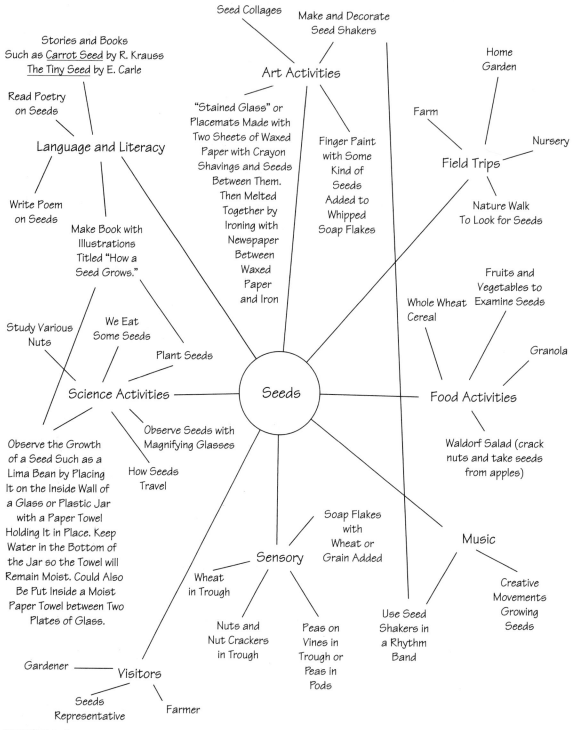

FIGURE 3–1
Web on Seeds

school day need to be, or should be, related to the theme. Too constant exposure to one particular theme results in boredom, lack of interest, and frustration, as in the following illustration:

The children had been studying a unit on the color red. For 4 days the program had been saturated with red objects and items. On the fifth day, 4-year-old Janet happened to wear a red dress and red shoes. Taking advantage of a teaching moment, the teacher inquired, "Janet, what color is your dress?" Janet, obviously frustrated with the constant emphasis on red, answered, "My dress is red, my shoes are red—the whole world is red!"

Following is an example of a 5-day activity plan on seeds. These experiences have been selected from the array of possibilities listed in the unit plan. The activities are designated as individual, small-group, and whole-group, so that a balance of these three kinds of participation can be achieved.

ACTIVITY PLAN ON SEEDS

Day 1

Whole-Group Activity

Science Discussion

• How seeds grow

Small-Group Activity

Field Trip

• Seed walk

Individual Activities

• Bubble blowing
• Seeds in sensory area

Day 2

Whole-Group Activities

Music

• Rhythm experience using seed pods

Science Discussion

• Seeds that travel

Small-Group Activity

Art

• Seed shakers

Individual Activities

• Easel with seed-shaped paper and green paint

Science

• Observe growth of lima bean planted yesterday and plant another bean today

Day 3

Whole-Group Activity

Visitor

• Musician and playing seed shakers

Small-Group Activity

Art

• Seed collages

Individual Activities

• Paper weight made from potter's clay with seeds pressed in

Science

• Observe and explore foods with seeds
• Observe growth of bean plant and plant another bean today

Day 4

Whole-Group Activity

Science Discussion

• We eat some seeds

Small-Group Activity

Food

• Chili

Individual Activities

• Peanuts and other nuts in the sensory area
• Shape tracing and cutting

Science

• Observe growth of bean plants and plant another bean

Day 5

Whole-Group Activity

• Photographs on bulletin board to teach positional words and self-esteem

Small-Group Activity

Art

• Finger painting with seeds added

Individual Activities

• Sorting and classifying seeds

Science

• Observe growth of bean plants and plant another bean

Table 3–1 is included as another example of an activity plan. This one lists the general curriculum areas down the left-hand column so that as each day's activities are planned, you can see how they are balanced in terms of the general curriculum areas.

Daily Schedule of Activities

The daily schedule of activities is an elaboration of the activity plan and a simplification of the lesson plan. For experienced teachers or students who are at an advanced level, the daily schedule of activities may replace both the activity plan and the lesson plan, even though the objectives must be carefully thought through. The daily schedule of activities specifies the order of activ-

TABLE 3–1
Weekly Activity Plan At-a-Glance

Theme: _____ Date: _____				
Planned activity for: Monday	Tuesday	Wednesday	Thursday	Friday
Language development				
Cognitive skills				

Creative expression
  Art
  Music
  Dramatic play
  Other				

Emotional development				
Social development				

Physical development
  Gross motor
  Fine motor				

Source: Lisa G. Warner, M.S., Co-Director, Child Development Center, Eastern Kentucky University, Richmond, Kentucky.

Snack times are routinely looked forward to with eagerness and anticipation, providing a balance between active and quiet activities.

ities, approximate length of time, person responsible (if you are working with several teachers), specific responsibilities of individuals, and materials needed. This plan adapts easily to a chart form with different columns added, depending on the needs of the program (see Table 3–2). Such assignments as setting up outdoor equipment, cleaning, and greeting may be included. Routines of the program, such as snacks, may also be added on the chart, showing the teacher assigned to the preparation and the time it is to be presented. When doing a daily schedule of activities, plan for a full-day program. Include such additional routines as lunch and rest time. The plans presented adapt easily to either half-day or full-day programs. The number of activities remains basically the same because longer programs have additional routines of meals, individual play, and quiet periods. An example of a daily schedule of activities based on the seed plan is shown in Table 3–2.

Lesson Plan

After the unit is seen in broad perspective through the activity plan and the specifics defined in the daily schedule of activities, lesson planning takes place. The lesson plan adds the procedures for the activities and reminds the teacher of the overall goals and specific objectives to be accomplished. The teacher has selected a theme and has determined its benefit and value to the developing child. Through listed objectives, the teacher is able to harmonize the lesson plan's activities with the child's abilities and needs.

As the lesson planning is viewed in perspective, the teacher should keep in mind some general, overall goals to be accomplished during the unit. For example, if the unit plan is on seeds, what will be the general goals and/or concepts to be stressed and taught? In addition to these theme-related goals, child-related goals help to meet the specific needs of the children. For example, a child-oriented goal may be that "the children will be encouraged to put away their own equipment and materials" or that "the children will become more independent in taking off and putting on their own coats." These goals will be valuable if the children need assistance in either of these two areas.

Specific activities for each day should have objectives. Attention can be given to the lesson plan accompanying this chapter; the overall goals are general, and the objectives for the activities are specific. Behavioral objectives—those that describe an observable, desired behavior—are valuable in measuring and evaluating the unit. Behavioral objectives usually include such words or phrases as the following: Each child will be able to *say, write, do,* or *complete.* These words deal with concrete, measurable tasks that can be observed and checked for achievement or completion. However, other valuable goals include words such as *appreciate, understand,* or *acquaint* and deal with more abstract, unmeasurable objectives. Both kinds of objectives are important in lesson planning.

Following is a lesson plan on seeds, including overall goals, activities with specific objectives, and procedures. Keep in mind that as teachers gain experience and insights, the amount of writing in lesson plans will diminish.

TABLE 3–2
Daily Schedule of Activities

Date:		Unit:	Seeds	Head Teacher	Mary

Day 1

Activity	Approximate Time	Type of Group	Person Responsible	Role of the Teacher	Materials and Resources
Greeting and individual play	45 min.	Individual	Dave	Greet	
Bubble blowing			Kerry	Guide children as necessary.	Bubbles, blowers, sponges
Seeds in trough			Mary	Encourage discovery and exploration.	Trough and seeds
Field Trip: seed walk	60 min.	Small group	Everyone will have a group	Encourage questions and discussion on seeds. Encourage each child to collect seeds in a sack.	Name tags color-coded by groups; paper bags for seed collecting
Outside play	30 min.	Individual	Everyone		
Science: how seeds grow	20 min.	Whole group: circle time	Mary	Discuss how seeds grow and describe activity of watching lima beans grow in a jar all week long. Each day prepare new seeds so comparison can be made.	Jar, wet paper towel, soaked lima beans
Individual play	10–30 min.				

TABLE 3–2 (cont.)

Date:		Unit:	Seeds	Head Teacher	Mary
Day 2					
Activity	Approximate Time	Type of Group	Person Responsible	Role of the Teacher	Materials and Resources
Greeting	15 min.		Kerry	Greet	
Children directed to rug for seed stories	15 min.	Whole group	Dave	Read stories.	Books: E. Carle, *The tiny seed.* New York: Crowell, 1970; H. Jordan, *How a seed grows.* New York: Crowell, 1960; R. Krauss, *The carrot seed.* New York: Harper & Row, 1954.
Music rhythm: experience using seedpods; also, several seedpods will be shown and broken open to explore the seeds.	20–30 min.	Whole group	Mary	Discuss seedpods and seeds found within (some are edible and some are not). Dried pods will be available for children to use for music rhythm activity.	Seedpods; musical rhythm record, such as Hap Palmer, *Pretend.*
Children could also sing songs and shake pods to rhythm.					
Individual play	30–45 min.	Individual	Everyone		
Science: observe growth of lima bean planted yesterday			Dave		Lima beans, jar, wet paper towel

TABLE 3-2 (*cont.*)

Activity	Approximate Time	Type of Group	Person Responsible	Role of the Teacher	Materials and Resources
Plant another lima bean.					
Easel			Kerry	Set up easel with seed-shaped paper and green paint; clean up.	Easel, paper and paint
Art: seed shakers Make seed shakers from half-pint cartons or juice cans. Put seeds on inside, and decorate outside of can or carton with seeds.	30 min.	Small group	Everyone		Small juice cans with lids or half-pint milk or cream cartons; seeds, glue, aprons, sponge
Free play outside	20 min.	Individual	Everyone		
Science: seeds that travel	20 min.	Whole group	Mary	Show different kinds of seeds and discuss how they travel.	Many kinds of seeds

TABLE 3–2 (*cont.*)

Date:		Unit:	Seeds	Head Teacher	Mary
Day 3					

Activity	Approximate Time	Type of Group	Person Responsible	Role of the Teacher	Materials and Resources
Greeting	15 min.	Individual	Dave	Greet	
Individual play outside	30 min.	Individual	Everyone	Large parachute will be outside, in addition to regular outside equipment.	Parachute
Art: seed collages	30 min.	Small group	Everyone	Discuss with group of children the seeds collected on the excursion.	Sacks of seeds for children in groups; paper plates, plaster of Paris, aprons, sponge
The children will add water, a small amount at a time, to mix plaster of Paris. Each child will be given a spoonful to smooth out on a paper plate and then encouraged to stick seeds in.					
Individual play inside	45–60 min.	Individual	Everyone		
Science: growth of lima beans			Kerry		Lima beans, jar, and wet paper towel
Observe growth of lima beans already planted and plant another one.					

TABLE 3–2 (*cont.*)

Activity	Approximate Time	Type of Group	Person Responsible	Role of the Teacher	Materials and Resources
Science: foods with seeds			Mary	Help children cut foods open and explore their seeds; discuss and make comparisons.	Foods such as cantaloupe, tomato, orange, cucumber, lemon, cherries, and plums.
Art: potter's clay paperweight			Dave	Help children roll clay into small balls to flatten on one side. Discuss sizes, shapes, colors, and variety of seeds.	Potter's clay or another kind of clay that will harden as it dries; various kinds of seeds; aprons, sponge for cleanup.
Visitor: musician	30 min.	Whole group	Mary	Introduce visitor. If time permits, have children use seed shakers as rhythm instruments.	Seed shakers
Individual play outside	20–30 min.	Individual	Everyone		

TABLE 3–2 (*cont.*)

Date:		Unit:	Seeds	Head Teacher	Mary
Day 4					
Activity	Approximate Time	Type of Group	Person Responsible	Role of the Teacher	Materials and Resources
Greeting	15 min.	Individual	Kerry	Greet	
Food: chili The beans will already be soaked, and the children will chop the onions and add to the hamburger. Brown these two. Seasonings and tomatoes will be added, and then these can be combined into one large pot. Discuss the chili beans as seeds.	30 min.	Small group	Everyone		Soaked chili beans, onion, hamburger, tomato, seasonings, electric frying pans, spoons, knives, large pot
Individual play	45–60 min.	Individual	Everyone		
Science: observe growth of lima bean seeds Observe growth of lima beans previously planted and plant another one.			Dave		Lima beans, jar, wet paper towels

TABLE 3–2 (*cont.*)

Activity	Approximate Time	Type of Group	Person Responsible	Role of the Teacher	Materials and Resources
Sensory area: peanuts and nuts with nut crackers			Mary	Help children open and enjoy eating the seeds.	Nuts, nut crackers
Shape tracing			Kerry	Shape tracing and cutting: Help children trace shapes and cut them out.	Scissors, pencils, cookie cutters, toy pieces that are shapes
			Mary	Chili: Help children stir and observe chili cooking.	
Science: we eat some seeds	20 min.	Whole group	Mary	Show children examples of seeds we eat but caution that we do not eat all seeds. They will also be taught that some seeds have to be cooked before they are eaten, such as the chili bean.	Edible seeds
Outside play	20–30 min.	Individual	Everyone		
Food: eating chili	20–30 min.	Small group	Everyone	Reinforce that the chili beans are seeds. Discuss how chili was prepared and ingredients involved.	Chili, bowls, spoons

TABLE 3–2 *(cont.)*

Date:		Unit:	Seeds	**Head Teacher**	Mary
Day 5					
Activity	Approximate Time	Type of Group	Person Responsible	Role of the Teacher	Materials and Resources
Greeting	15 min.	Individual	Dave	Greet	
Individual play	60 min.	Individual	Everyone		
Science: lima beans			Kerry		Beans, jar, and paper towels
Observe the growth of all lima beans planted, and plant another one.					
Sorting and classifying seeds			Mary		Muffin tins (or egg cartons), seeds
Muffin tins will be used to sort seeds in many different ways—ways they travel, edible versus nonedible, color, size, shape.					
Art: finger painting with seeds added	45 min.	Small group	Everyone	Encourage discovery, creativity, and exploration.	Finger paint, butcher paper, sponges, aprons, seeds such as wheat seeds

TABLE 3–2 (*cont.*)

Activity	Approximate Time	Type of Group	Person Responsible	Role of the Teacher	Materials and Resources
Outside individual play	30 min.	Individual	Everyone		
Photographs and activity relating to bulletin board	30 min.	Whole group	Mary	Teach position words using the bulletin board and children's photographs. Direct children to do particular motor activities by the position of their picture on the bulletin board.	Bulletin board with children's pictures in different positions relating to circles

LESSON PLAN ON SEEDS

Overall Goals

- To motivate, stimulate, and interest the children in learning and developing concepts associated with seeds, specifically the following:
  1. Seeds come from the fruits of plants.
  2. Seeds are different from one another in color, shape, size, and texture.
  3. Seeds need water to grow. (Warmth, food, and air could also be included.)
  4. We eat some seeds.
- To develop a basic understanding of some positional words through concrete, repeated experiences with such words and their meanings.

Day 1

Whole-Group Activity

Science—How Seeds Grow

- On this day, and on each of the 4 following days, put a lima bean seed between glass and moist paper. (By the end of the unit, the children will be able to see the 5-day growth of a particular seed.) Discuss what seeds need to survive during this experience, particularly pointing out their need for water and light.

Objectives

- To teach language labels of *root, sprout, stem,* etc.
- To allow for comparisons of seeds from day to day.
- To explain that seeds need air, light, and water to grow.
- To demonstrate that seeds get larger as they grow.

Small-Group Activity

Field Trip—Seed Walk

- In small groups, have the children walk around the area observing plants, trees, and weeds that are shedding seeds at this time of year. Give a sack to each child for gathering seeds.

Objectives

- To increase observation of nature.

- To encourage noticing differences in seeds, such as texture, shape, size, color, number, and how they travel.
- To teach that seeds come from the fruit of a plant.

Individual Activities

- Bubble blowing
- Seeds in sensory area

Objectives

- To provide for manipulation of different kinds of seeds.
- To look for similarities and differences in seeds, such as color, shape, size, and texture.

Day 2

Whole-Group Activities

Music—Rhythm Experiences Using Seedpods

- Have the children use the seedpods to accompany the rhythm of familiar songs and a record with a definite beat.

Objectives

- To provide an opportunity to see how seeds grow (some seeds grow in pods).
- To allow for creative rhythm expression.

Science—Seeds That Travel

- Raise the question of how a seed goes from one child's house to another child's house. Use a toy town to focus on a demonstration. Then discuss how seeds travel in various ways—burrs cling to animals and people, some seeds fly through the air, some seeds roll.

Objectives

- To teach that seeds travel in various ways.
- To show actual examples of seeds that travel.

Small-Group Activity

Art—Seed Shakers

- Juice cans or half-pint milk cartons will be provided in the art center. Have the children put some seeds on the inside and then glue seeds on the outside. They can secure the lids with tape.

Objectives

- To make comparisons between seeds.
- To allow the children to use some of the seeds gathered on the walk.
- To make an enjoyable musical instrument that can be used as a rhythm instrument.

Individual Activities

- Easel, with seed-shaped paper and green paint

Science

- Observe the growth of a lima bean planted yesterday and plant another today.

Day 3

Whole-Group Activity

Visitor—Musician

- The visitor will play various musical instruments for the children. Then show the children how different kinds of seeds can be used to provide music.

Objectives

- To acquaint children with various musical instruments.
- To show how seeds can contribute to musical enjoyment by using the seed shakers made the previous day.

Small-Group Activity

Art—Seed Collages

- Have the children make seed collages from the seeds they collected on the field trip the first day. They will make plaster of Paris, put the plaster on a paper plate, and then put the seeds in the soft plaster to dry. (If you do not wish to use plaster of Paris, seeds can be glued on the paper plate or stuck into potter's clay.)

Objectives

- To provide for feedback and reinforcement of the field trip.
- To work with a new medium, plaster.
- To look for similarities and differences in seeds.

Individual Activities

Science

- Observe the growth of lima beans planted the 2 previous days and plant another today.
- Take foods for children to explore seeds. Set out a number of the following foods: cantaloupe, tomato, orange, lemon, cucumber, peach, cherry, plum, or others that are in season. Provide plastic, serrated-edge knives and encourage the children to cut the fruits and observe the seeds. Are the seeds edible? Compare sizes, shapes, colors, number of seeds, texture, and other similarities and differences.

Objectives

- To teach that we eat some seeds.
- To compare the similarities and differences among seeds.
- To teach that seeds come from the fruits of plants.

Art—Paperweight Made from Potter's Clay with Seeds Pressed In

- Provide the children with aprons, potter's clay, and a variety of seeds. They will roll the clay into balls, flatten one side, and then push seeds into the clay.

Objectives

- To observe different kinds of seeds.
- To manipulate and work with the potter's clay.

Day 4

Whole-Group Activity

Science—We Eat Some Seeds

- Show the children examples of seeds that we eat, such as peanuts, peas, corn, beans, nuts, squash seeds, cucumber seeds, and potatoes.

Objectives

- To show examples of seeds that we eat.
- To teach names of some seeds that we eat.
- To make sure that children still understand that there are many seeds we do not eat.
- To help children understand that some seeds (chili beans, for example) have to be cooked before being eaten.

Small-Group Activities

Food—Chili

- The beans will already be soaked and cooking. In small groups, have the children watch and help grind the onion. Then they will brown the hamburger and onion and add seasoning and tomatoes. These ingredients will be added to one or two large pots and allowed to cook. The children can, on an individual basis, stir and watch the chili as it cooks.

Objectives

- To teach that we eat some seeds, such as beans.
- To allow children to assist in the preparation of a food.
- To demonstrate how a food grinder works.
- To show differences in raw versus cooked seeds and other products.
- To increase the children's repertoire of language labels for ingredients and measuring.

Food—Eating Chili

- In small groups, serve chili for the children to eat. While the children are eating, reinforce concepts relating to beans being seeds and how the chili was prepared and mixed.

Objectives

- To reinforce that the chili beans are seeds.
- To discuss how chili was prepared and to review the ingredients involved.

Individual Activities

Science

- Observe the growth of lima bean seeds and plant another one.

Sensory Area

- Peanuts and edible nuts, with nutcrackers

Shape Tracing and Cutting

- Various shapes, such as toys and cookie cutters, will be available for the children to trace, and scissors will be provided for them to cut out the shapes.

Day 5

Whole-Group Activity

Photographs on Bulletin Board

- Put pictures of the children on the bulletin board, providing an opportunity to use positional words. Each day, rearrange each child's picture so that the pictures vary in position—beside, under, over, or between circles of a particular color. It will now be easy to divide the children into groups. For example, say, "All those who are beside a blue circle go with (teacher's name) group." Review the positional words by having all the children in particular positions stand, hop around the circle, change places, or perform some other movement.

Objectives

- To increase self-worth as a result of viewing pictures of selves.
- To teach language labels and the meaning of some positional words.

Small-Group Activity

Art—Finger Painting with Seeds Added

- In small groups, have the children finger paint with a mixture to which seeds have been added. When the paint dries, the seeds will stick to the paper. A medium might be whipped soapflakes to which wheat seeds have been added.

Objectives

- To provide a texture experience with seeds.
- To allow for creative expression in finger painting.

Individual Activities

Science

- Observe the growth of lima bean seeds and plant another one.

Sorting and Classifying Seeds

- Muffin tins will be used to sort seeds by various characteristics, such as the way they travel, color, size, kind, and whether they are edible or inedible.

Objectives

- To reinforce concepts associated with seeds.
- To provide for problem solving in sorting and matching seeds on the basis of similarities and differences.

Evaluation

A curriculum is planned to meet the needs of the individual children in the group or classroom, using meaningful goals. The organized teaching units provide avenues for the communication of this curriculum to the children. But the desired achievement of the program for young children depends on continual and effective evaluation. Evaluation is the process of determining the degree to which children's needs are met and desired objectives are achieved (NAEYC & NAECS/

SDE, 1991). It includes evaluating the general curriculum; unit and lesson plans, the activities, procedures, and goals; the performances of the children; and the teacher's role.

Evaluating can be done both formally and informally with written evaluations, check sheets, reports, completed contracts, or anecdotal records and observations. This allows for constant adjustments and redirections in curriculum planning.

Evaluating the Curriculum

When evaluating, observations should be validated and specific comments and insights shared. We should not just share a statement as trite as "The activity was very successful." Why? On what basis do you know? Statements such as "The children stayed with the activity for a long time" or "Each child was absorbed in the activity and anxious to participate" are more specific.

To be effective, evaluation must include both negative and positive aspects, or failures and successes, of the item being evaluated. For example, if an activity turns out much differently from the way it was planned, an objective evaluation may conclude that the activity failed or that it turned out much better than originally planned. Successful and positive evaluations build confidence and ability in the teacher. Failures and negative evaluations show where planning may not have been adequate or follow-through not sufficient. These discoveries, in turn, provide the groundwork for successes in subsequent similar situations.

The curriculum must be evaluated continually if it is to remain in harmony with children's abilities and needs. Because children are constantly changing in development, the curriculum, too, must constantly be adjusted to supplement this development. Is the program challenging, inviting, and exciting for the children? Are they interested and motivated? Is there adequate variation in the scheduling and routines? What are the weaknesses in the curriculum? What are its strengths?

Unit and lesson plans, integral parts of the planned curriculum, should be evaluated often during their presentation and also after the unit is concluded. The in-progress assessment allows any necessary adjustments to be made in the unit so that it can be made more beneficial for the children. It also determines whether the basic concepts have been grasped adequately by the children so that the remainder of the unit can be followed through successfully. At the conclusion of the unit, the entire lesson plan should be evaluated—including not only the objectives and goals achieved but also the activities and their procedures. Did the unit have value for the children? Did it accomplish what was desired? Were the individual activities planned adequately and appropriately for the children's abilities? In what other ways could the procedures have been carried out? Why did a particular activity succeed or not succeed? How would the various activities be carried out another time?

Evaluating Children's Learning and Involvement

The performances of the children are also part of the unit and lesson plan evaluation. Collectively, the group's participation throughout the unit should be assessed. Did the children accomplish the desired objectives? Were there measureable behavior changes when desired? Were the children interested and motivated to participate? Were they actively involved in the experiences, or were activities too difficult or too simple? Individually, the child's performance in the entire classroom program needs constant assessment. Because the teacher keeps abreast of the child's development, goals can be designed to increase or maintain the child's progress. Is the child interested in the program? Is the material too advanced for the child's abilities? Does it provide an adequate challenge? What is the child's relationship with the other children? Is the child socially, physically, and mentally healthy? Does the child have any particular problems that need concentrated guidance and effort? What are the child's strengths?

Figures 3–2 and 3–3 are examples of a checklist and a graph that can be used to evaluate children's participation in various activities. Figure 3–2 is an Activity/Skill Checklist on which the teacher or observer writes down the title of the activity—for example, "Musical Dramatization of 'The Three Bears.'" Then, after each child's name, a + is put for participation or a − for nonparticipation. There is also space to describe the level of activity and skill development for the individual child. Figure 3–3 is a Specific Skill/Activity Graph for a general curriculum area such as art, used over a period of time to illustrate the individual child's involvement in various kinds of activities. It graphically illustrates for teachers each child's participation or nonparticipation in classroom activities in particular curriculum areas.

Evaluating the Child's Development

Evaluation of children's development is imperative. It is a process of continuously appraising the children's development in physical, emotional, social, and academic areas. Knowing how the children you teach are growing and developing is of primary importance in planning what will be taught and how it will be accomplished.

Effective evaluation must take into consideration laws or generalizations of growth and development, which include the following:

- Each child is an individual and grows in his or her own way.
- A child's self-concept affects how he or she learns.
- The child's total development—not just cognitive functioning—must be the focus of the learning environment.
- Children in the early years learn best through concrete, real experiences, by experimenting and discovering.
- The learning experience must take into account the cultural background, needs, interests, and developmental levels of each child in the classroom.

There are different techniques for acquiring evaluation information, such as checklist inventories (like the one described in the assessment section of this chapter); observation notes; and informal, individually given tests of concepts and skills. Anecdotal records should be kept for each child, with notations of growth, achievements, regressions, and concerns. Along with observations, actual child dialogue can be recorded as a means of evaluation. An especially effective evaluation tool is preparing a portfolio of the child's work. Progress in art, writing, math, language, science, and other areas can be assessed through viewing the child's work over time. Also, videotapes, photographs, and tape recordings can be used to capture information about the child's growth and provide evaluation information.

Evaluation yields important information for the teacher, child, and parents. Through evaluation, the teacher can plan learning experiences to match the needs of the child and to challenge the child's abilities. Evaluation information is a must at parent conferences to validate the child's achievements and to give the parents some proof of the child's developmental level. Checklists of developmental skills can be sent home for the child to work on with parents and to give the parents firsthand information on the child's progress. These checklists can be general and include cognitive skills, motor skills, social developments, and emotional characteristics, or they can focus on specific areas, such as math or reading.

A child's own record keeping can be an evaluation tool. "Students should also be encouraged to keep records through their own diaries and activities. This diary will help children understand their own progress; it will help the teacher learn what seems to interest the child most or gives the child the greatest satisfaction" (Day, 1988, p. 589). Journals or diaries also give information on how children feel about themselves and their work (Day, 1988).

In addition, one can develop assessment

STAFF: In the space by the individual child's name, place a + if the child participates or a − for nonparticipation. Use the allotted space to describe the level of activity and skill development.

Title of Activity:_____ Date: _____

(Name)

_____ (   ) _____
_____
_____

_____ (   ) _____
_____
_____

_____ (   ) _____
_____
_____

_____ (   ) _____
_____
_____

_____ (   ) _____
_____
_____

_____ (   ) _____
_____
_____

_____ (   ) _____
_____
_____

_____ (   ) _____
_____
_____

_____ (   ) _____
_____
_____

_____ (   ) _____
_____
_____

FIGURE 3–2
Child Development Center Activity/Skill Checklist
(Lisa G. Warner, M.S., Co-Director. Child Development Center. Eastern Kentucky, Richmond, Kentucky.)

Activity	Finger Paint	Easel Paint	Sawdust Clay	Shape Collages	Straw Paint	Easel Paint	Styrofoam Sculpt.	Shaving Cream	Fabric Collages	Clay
Date	4/3	4/5	4/6	4/7	4/10	4/11	4/14	4/17	4/20	4/21
Name:										
Erin	✓	—	—	✓	✓	✓	—	—	✓	✓

FIGURE 3–3
Specific Skill/Activity Graph
(Lisa G. Warner, M.S., Co-Director, Child Development Center, Eastern Kentucky University, Richmond, Kentucky.)

sheets, even for very young children, to help the teacher and parents determine a child's interests and feelings about many different aspects of the school environment. For example, make a list of activities or draw simple pictures of activities, such as looking at books, drawing pictures, playing with toys, singing songs, listening to a story, playing outside, and having individual play inside. Next to each, draw three faces—one smiling, one with a straight mouth or neutral expression, and one frowning. Read each activity on the list and have the children color the face that represents how they feel about that activity.

Evaluating the Teacher

By means of a continuing evaluation of the curriculum, units and children, the role of the teacher and its fulfillment automatically receive evaluation. Where changes are needed in the program or activities, the teacher makes the alterations. If no changes are needed, the teacher continues to build on the strengths that already exist. The teacher should ask the following questions: What is my relationship with the children individually? Collectively? Am I planning the curriculum to meet the abilities and needs of the children? Are my desired objectives being achieved? Am I providing adequate challenge, guidance, and direction to the children? Am I enjoying what I am doing? What changes do I need to make? What are my strengths?

Summary

The curriculum is everything that takes place in the classroom to meet the needs of the children. This includes the determination of goals and objectives (What? Why? How?), the needs assessment, the scheduling of the program, and the planning of unit and lesson plans. Continual evaluation should take place regarding the curriculum; the children's learning, involvement, and development; and the teacher. Because the teacher actually does the planning, scheduling, and evaluating, the teacher is the key to their combined success. The cooperative learning strategy is a versatile and valuable approach that encourages children to learn from their peers in a cooperative environment. With commitment, responsibility, and dedication, an exciting and meaningful program can be planned and implemented. When this happens, children not only benefit, they reap great rewards!

Student Learning Activities

1. Visit an early childhood classroom and talk with the teacher or teachers about the method or methods of planning used. Compare the approach to those presented in this chapter. Even though the approach will most likely differ from the one in this book, are the basic ingredients and questions (Why? What? How?) still a part of the planning? You may wish to visit with several early childhood teachers to discuss and evaluate various approaches to planning.

2. From visits or observations you have previously made in early childhood classrooms, or from currently planned visits, evaluate the scheduling. How did the scheduling in the

classroom compare to that suggested in this chapter? Were you able to observe some free play during each visit? How do you feel about free play in early childhood classrooms, and what can it accomplish?

3. Select one of the themes suggested in the chapter or one of your own choosing, and complete a unit plan, or web, according to the format suggested in this chapter. Do not select a theme for which a unit plan has already been completed in this book. Follow with preparation of a daily activity plan, daily schedule of activities, lesson plan, or whatever your teacher suggests.

4. Interview three early childhood teachers and ask them what assessment tools or means they use. How often do they use them? How do they evaluate their program, curriculum, children, and themselves? What tools or means do they use for evaluation? As they meet in parent–teacher conferences, what do they share with parents as criteria for evaluation? Make compar-

isons of your findings and draw some conclusions of your own—from your reading and from the interview—as to what you think are the most effective means of assessment and evaluation for early childhood education.

5. If you can find a neighbor or family member who is in the early childhood age range and you have permission from his or her parents, administer the Self-Image Checklist and Questionnaire included in the chapter. What did you learn about the child from this?

6. Do some research on cooperative learning and evaluate this strategy using your research, information in the text, and your own feelings. How will you use cooperative learning as an early childhood teacher?

7. Plan three cooperative learning activities on any theme appropriate for early childhood students. Use at least three different strategies. Present at least one of your activities to class members.

Suggested Resources (Films)

Organizing the school day. Modern Talking Pictures.

Setting the stage for learning. Churchill films.

PART
TWO

SOCIOEMOTIONAL SKILLS

No matter who children are, what they become, or where they live, they all have a need for people skills. We do not live alone, and people everywhere need to learn to relate initially to themselves and then to others around them. The ability to relate to others is dependent on one's attitude toward oneself and toward other people. It is never too early to begin building positive feelings and attitudes. The ability to live effectively within the family and later to function capably within the neighborhood, classroom, and peer group hinges on social skills that begin in early childhood.

Developing social skills is not an easy task. It takes knowledge of correct relationship skills, in addition to time and experience. We must be patient as we provide assistance and guidance to children who struggle to develop positive social and emotional skills. These skills can be taught and learned, but most importantly "caught," as the teacher provides the model for healthy social and emotional skills. A teacher's own attitude toward the self, children, and adults is one of the most powerful forces in this process. If the teacher likes and enjoys others, particularly children, the children receive the message that people are to be liked, respected, and esteemed.

A child must recognize early in life the individual responsibility for learning to like and relate to both the self and people in general. The child must also sense that social and emotional patterns, habits, skills, attitudes, and feelings can be improved if one desires to learn more effective ways of relating.

Chapter Four, "People and Their Diversity," deals with helping children to relate to others effectively and encouraging them to recognize similarities rather than differences among people. The chapter develops children's concepts of other people and outlines many concepts and ideas for teaching children about others. Children are anxious to learn about many people, places, and related concepts in the world around them—family, friends, neighbors, community members, different cultures, and related jobs.

Chapter Four also discusses developing a basic understanding of children with special needs. Included are discussions of the individualized education program (IEP), public laws regarding education of individuals with disabilities, and the special needs in the areas of speech and language; mental retardation; hearing, visual, and physical impairment; emotional, social, and behavioral problems; chronic illness; learning disabilities; and gifted and talented children. Each of the categories of special needs is discussed in terms of particular characteristics, teaching strategies, and available specialists. More and more, we are realizing the benefits of early intervention for children with special needs, and we must tailor our programs and services to meet their individual needs and requirements. Bredekamp (1986) reminds us that "It is the responsibility of the educational system to adjust to the developmental needs and levels of the children it serves; children should not be expected to adapt to an inappropriate system" (p. 13).

Chapter Five, "Myself and My Family," deals with developing children's self-esteem, helping them recognize that everyone is unique, worthwhile, and capable, with special characteristics, feelings, talents, and interests. Children must first believe in themselves before they can care about, believe in, and accept other people. Thus, the basis of a high-quality program in early childhood is promoting and encouraging feelings of dignity and self-esteem in the individual child.

The chapter helps us recognize situations causing stress in children, how they react to stress, and how we can help them cope with stress. The chapter also discusses the influence of the family. The family plays a paramount role in helping children accept and like themselves, and it contributes greatly to the character education of its members.

The world is the only limit in creating socioemotional skills studies for children! During the early childhood years, teachers can select units from areas such as sociology, economics, geography, history, and anthropology. Remember: Gear the units and concepts to the level of the children, and provide social studies activities with concrete learning experiences, such as classroom visitors and field trips. Many of these concepts, elementary as they may seem, remain abstract unless they are made concrete through carefully planned learning.

Within selected units in socioemotional skills, additional areas can be integrated, such as economics, history, and others. For example, you may do a unit on a particular community helper, such as the farmer, and, depending on the ages of the children, discuss various concepts in economics, such as production, distribution, and consumption. A unit on the police officer can include civic concepts that relate to the rights and obligations of responsible citizens. Historical concepts and perspectives can be taught through a unit titled "People—How They Lived 100 Years Ago." After reading and studying the concepts and ideas for teaching presented in Chapters Four and Five, you will become aware of other possibilities for units in the social studies area.

Along with all the cognitive notions about the self and others, we hope that children are taught, by example as well as concept, that people are important and have feelings, and that all of us need to be sensitive and caring about the feelings of others.

CHAPTER
four

People and Their Diversity

Introduction

How children feel about and treat others is influenced by their own regard for themselves, as well as the social skills they have learned from home, school, and other cultural and community groups. From the earliest years, children need help and guidance in developing positive social values and skills—in learning to relate to others effectively. Once again, the teacher provides a model for treating, speaking to, and behaving toward others. Patience is needed by early childhood teachers as they work with children who are often very inexperienced in social behaviors. Teachers should display positive attitudes that serve as models for having friends, learning how to treat others, and understanding their social environment (Allen, Freeman, & Osborne, 1989).

As concepts about people are taught on a daily basis and in specific units, the focus must be on similarities, rather than differences. Recognizing similarities and distinguishing differences are skills learned by preschool-aged children. Learning to identify similarities and accept the nature of differences among peers helps children realize how much we all actually have in common.

In stressing similarities rather than differences, it becomes evident that all children live in some type of family unit, participate in family activities, play games and enjoy toys, learn songs and stories, celebrate holidays, express similar feelings and emotions, and communicate with one another. By discussing differences, children can see that their specific behaviors are simply one way of doing things, not the only or the best way. Children will then be able to understand and appreciate how people are different.

Accepting and understanding similarities and differences is also very important with respect to children who have special needs—those whose learning and behavioral characteristics differ substantially from others and who require special methods of instruction. A basic understanding of particular categories of exceptional-

Learning about culture diversity helps children discover both differences and similarities between people of various cultures.

Teaching and Valuing Diversity

Developing the Perspective of Diversity

The United States, with a broad range of ethnic and cultural groups, is one of the most diverse countries in the world. Recognizing the value and importance of each individual, while respecting and accepting each other's cultures, is essential to maximum growth and development. A person's ethnicity is his or her connection to the past, and it is one of the keys to the individual sense of self: All people have an ethnic heritage! As young children begin maturing and acquiring a positive self-concept, they also being relating to and accepting others. This is the age to start influencing children's basic cultural attitudes, values, and beliefs (Hendrick, 1988). Development and implementation of a diversity perspective is, therefore, imperative.

Culturally diverse classrooms are those that foster genuine respect for all children regardless of race, gender, ethnic orientation, or physical ableness. Children are very aware of gender, language, race, and physical differences early in their lives. They notice observable characteristics such as skin color, language, and dress (Billman, 1992). How they respond to these differences is, to a great extent, determined by the direct and indirect messages and feelings of those around them. Children who are biased consider others to be inferior because of their differences. Teachers must work to overcome ethnocentrism, the attitude that one's own culture is correct, right, or natural. Accepting and respecting diversity should be a way of life, a value that is lived, felt, and woven into all areas of the classroom and curriculum. This means helping children value others and express positive feelings and behaviors toward them. It is an active approach to countering attitudes and behaviors that sustain prejudice, ethnocentrism, racism, stereotyping, sexism, discrimination, and oppression.

During the early childhood years, children develop stereotypic attitudes about gender roles, racial and cultural biases, and negative attitudes about having different abilities. Not only are at-

ity, their characteristics, possible teaching strategies, and available community specialists helps teachers in caring for children and planning programs.

Also of value in planning activities for the classroom are the numerous and detailed ideas and suggestions found later in this chapter in the section titled "Approach to Teaching."

Children's orientation to the social world and their initial development of social skills begin in the family unit and with the formation of early friendships. Early childhood is the time to start preventing children from developing biases and prejudices as their attitudes, values, and beliefs begin to form. Focusing on how lives are similar, yet sometimes different, helps children expand their awareness of others, increase their capacity to accept and cooperate with others, and enhance their own positive self-concepts and esteem.

titudes negatively affected, but experiences become narrow and limited as a result of the stereotyping associated with racism, sexism, and "handicappism." Teachers must, therefore, foster positive attitudes of acceptance and tolerance; children must come to value differences among one another while recognizing that they have many similarities. The similarities, rather than the differences, ought to be the focus (Clark, DeWolf, & Clark, 1992). Children can learn very early that, while individuals may view things differently, they still have many common needs, desires, and hopes (Tye, 1990).

Teaching diversity means modifying the early childhood environment, including the curriculum and the people involved, so that it is more reflective of the diversity within society. Teaching diversity involves helping children to take the perspective of others—to look and see through their hearts, eyes, and minds. Children must understand that all students deserve equal educational opportunities, that all children are equally important to the teacher and others. We live in a complex, global, diverse society today, and this should be reflected in our schools and neighborhoods. If we expect children to function cooperatively in this diverse society, we must teach them attitudes, concepts, and skills that will enable them to do so.

A variety of concepts have emerged as the bases for programs and practices relating to the pluralism of our world. Some of these concepts include multicultural education, multiethnic education, ethnic studies, antibias curriculum, and global education. Each has a somewhat different perspective. We have selected the term *diversity* as our approach, both in this text and as we teach young children, for several reasons. First, young children understand the concept of "different" and can expand this understanding to include the word *diversity*. Also, the term *diversity* is positive, and as we teach diversity, our goal is to help children develop positive feelings and attitudes toward others. Diversity among people encompasses differences in gender, social class, religion, race, ethnic group, and physical or mental abilities. Compatible with our approach and focus, we prefer this broad implication of the term *diversity* as it relates to people, and we feel it is the most appropriate term to use with young children.

We believe that teaching diversity is not just an idea, fad, or educational movement that will pass with time. We hope that it is here to stay—an active process that focuses on the idea that *all* children have a right to learn and to reach their individual potential. Teaching diversity enriches the classroom by providing various ways to solve problems and to view people, events, and situations. When children are able to view the world from the perspective of its diversity, their views of reality are broadened (Banks & Banks, 1993).

The Teacher

Teachers must sense that teaching diversity is a professional and moral responsibility. Teachers set the stage, and they must begin by evaluating their own cultures and eliminating personal biases. They may need to change their attitudes and expectations, realizing that differences in lifestyle and language do not mean ignorance. They may need to be more positive toward children from minority groups and those who are different in any way. A genuine desire to know more about other people is absolutely necessary.

Teachers must affirm their students' diversities, showing and modeling the fact that they value and appreciate differences (Boutte & McCormick, 1992). Early childhood teachers must develop awareness for the feelings of all people and become cognizant of the things they say and do—some very subtle—that demean, oppress, dehumanize, or exclude others. For example, what we say (sit "Indian style"), what we do (make Indian headbands and decorate them with feathers or sing "Ten Little Indians"), or what we don't do (we seldom sing Jewish songs or include symbols of their culture) all affect children and their feelings about who they are and the culture or cultures with which they identify. Teachers must set examples of positive actions and attitudes and use teaching approaches and materials that are sensitive to the backgrounds and experiences of all students.

Teachers must become reeducated and trained in diversity education. They must learn about different ethnic and cultural groups' lifestyles, learn patterns, values, and interests. They must be shown *how* to behave toward, and communicate with, minority children and their parents (Gay, 1989).

Goals of a Classroom Focused on Diversity

Following are the goals we see as important for teaching diversity in the classroom.

All children must be given opportunities to reach their potential regardless of their gender, social class, religion, race, ethnic group, or physical or mental abilities. Each child is different and has unique behaviors, thoughts, and needs. When we teach children from where they are, according to their needs, and help them reach their distinctive potential, we are using developmentally appropriate education and beginning our approach to teaching diversity. In addition, when diversity is taught and practiced within a school, academic achievement improves (Banks & Banks, 1993).

Children's diverse cultural, social, family, and ethnic backgrounds create differences in the ways they think, feel, and behave. It behooves teachers to understand these differences in order to enable them to identify the individual needs of each child.

All children must feel included and valued as worthy members of the class and of society. Our classrooms and centers must become inclusive (Greenberg, 1992), with children developing a sense of dignity and a tolerance for all people.

Children must be helped to clarify and feel positive toward their own identity, including their sex, ethnic background, race, and physical abilities. Children need to understand who they are and why they behave, feel, and value the things they

do. Until they accept their own differences, they will surely have difficulty accepting the differences in other people. Teachers should help all children gain greater self-esteem and self-understanding as they view themselves from the perspective of differences and similarities. Children need information on their culture and need to develop pride in their heritage (Hale-Benson, 1986). This will be followed by greater self-esteem and respect for, understanding of, and sensitivity to other people.

Children will learn to take the perspective of children who are different from themselves. Children can develop an empathy for many other children, not just those in their own class. They can do this only through positive exposure to, and experiences with, other children. They must see how they are alike and how they are different and be taught to value the differences. Diversity education that focuses on respect for and love of our fellow human beings will be well worth the effort (Phenice & Hildebrand, 1988).

The diversity perspective must be integrated into all aspects of the school or program. If, as teachers, we only do "other people" units of study or an occasional multicultural activity, we are not solving the problem. These activities do not allow adequate time for exploring or developing concepts, and they often misrepresent various aspects of a particular culture. Separate units of study also tend to perpetuate stereotypes and emphasize differences.

When the curriculum includes a particular ethnic group only in a specific unit of study on that group, children do not learn to view the group as an inherent part of our total society. They view it as being separate, and this separateness is often assumed by children to mean inferiority. One author (Derman-Sparks & A.B.C. Task Force, 1989) refers to this curriculum approach as the "tourist" approach. By this she means that we "tour" a country and provide a sampling of that country—its foods, holidays, and traditions, for instance. We look at "things" from that country. When we do this, we teach on the surface but do not build or teach understanding

The teacher enjoys spending a few minutes engaged in conversation with this student, who has a hearing impairment.

of other people (Derman-Sparks & A.B.C. Task Force, 1989). Another danger of this approach is that we tend to select units on some groups of people and leave others out completely.

If we are really going to solve the problem, the concept of diversity must be infused into our materials, environment, and curriculum, and it must be reflected in *all* staff attitudes and beliefs. Content from diverse groups of people must be integrated into all parts of the curriculum. For example, one Native American teacher said that teachers should "mingle" Native Americans into all of the curriculum instead of confining them to one unit (Greenberg, 1992). It has been suggested that instead of one-week units, "everyday attitudes, discussions, and activities are more respectful and effective" (Billman, 1992, p. 24).

Diversity is not a separate subject that should be added to the curriculum, nor is it the study of isolated facts, cultures, or countries. It is not teaching isolated lessons such as cooking ethnic foods or discussing achievements of African Americans during Black History month. While these activities have purpose, by themselves they are inadequate. Rather, there need to be both planned and spontaneous integrated learning activities that build positive and reliable concepts

about all people (Boutte & McCormick, 1992). Children need to understand other people's feelings and beliefs and comprehend their daily experiences and ways of life (Clark, DeWolf, & Clark, 1992). Notions and feelings must be "caught" and not just "taught" (Boutte & McCormick, 1992).

Children must understand the classroom rule that discriminatory or insulting actions, language, or attitudes toward others will not be tolerated (Greenberg, 1992). When children know that adults expect particular behaviors, they will seek to live up to those expectations. Our classroom norms must reflect respect and tolerance for all differences in people.

These goals must be tailored to fit your specific needs; however, it is important to recognize the need for some foundation goals that provide direction in teaching diversity. We believe it is also important for you to discuss these goals with the children in your classroom at the beginning of the school year. If children can read, the goals should be posted and reviewed as needed.

Teaching diversity helps children to develop an awareness of our culturally diverse society. In doing so, they gain understanding and acceptance of both their own culture and the cultures of others. We must strive to create an equitable society and commit to building a world for our children in which they can all flourish and be accepted (Ramsey & Derman-Sparks, 1992).

Gender Bias

Overt stereotyping relating to gender bias is not as common as it was 20 years ago, but subtler bias persists, and it hurts both males and females—especially those from minority cultural backgrounds. The ways teachers treat students sometimes reflect these biases. Gender bias is found in curriculum materials, in the learning environment, and in teacher expectations and interactions. Teachers must diligently strive to overcome intentional or unintentional gender bias in classrooms so that *all* their students will feel important, respected, and equal to their peers. Once again, teachers set the stage, and their attitudes either overcome or reinforce biases.

Gender bias takes many forms. Several of these are described in the following paragraphs.

Stereotyping

When teachers assign traditional and rigid roles or attributes based on sex, the abilities and potentials of each gender are limited. Stereotyping denies students an understanding of the diversity and variation of genders. Children who see themselves portrayed only in stereotypic ways may internalize these stereotypes and fail to develop their own unique abilities and interests and their full potential. One common gender stereotype assumes that boys are better in math and science and girls are better in language skills. We expect qualities of caring and sharing in girls and qualities of assertiveness, competitiveness, and critical thinking in boys. Girls are expected to be more courteous and kind than boys. Girls are rewarded for appreciative, dependable, considerate, and dependent behavior, while boys are rewarded

for active, curious, and questioning behavior. Interests are stereotyped by expecting boys to prefer carpentry, cars, sports, and science, for example, while we expect girls to be interested in such things as housekeeping, cooking, and quiet activities. Stereotyping is damaging and debilitating to young children and does not promote equity.

Inequitable Attention

Research shows that, too often, boys are given more attention by the teacher in the classroom (Conroy, 1988). Girls frequently form a quiet background to the active role of boys. Teachers interact more frequently with boys, reward them for their academic work more often, and talk to and question them more often than they do girls. Females are often omitted or included less frequently than males on bulletin boards and in discussions of famous people, books, and displays. One author found that in the Caldecott Medal books, "ten boys are pictured for every girl (Conroy, 1988, p. 44). Girls are not called on as often as boys, and they are not rewarded as frequently for their academic achievements. Too often females are left out of our culture, creating the impression that the male experience is the norm. Making someone "invisible" is a way of demeaning that person or gender (Sheldon, 1990).

Dividing Students by Sex

By arbitrarily separating boys and girls in the classroom procedures such as lining up, forming groups, and organizing sports or recreational activities, teachers promote isolation and division of the sexes. Teachers ought to take measures to ensure mixed grouping.

Linguistic Bias

Curriculum materials, teacher conversation, and other forms of communication often reflect the discriminatory nature of our language. Masculine terms and pronouns such as "forefathers," "mankind," or even the generic "he" all exclude women. In addition, masculine labels such as "fireman," "mailman," or "chairman" deny the legitimacy of women working in various fields or in different capacities. Other forms of biased language sometimes include reference to all doctors, construction workers, or lawyers as "he" or all secretaries or nurses as "she." In conversation and in books, our use of the pronoun "he" when we refer to something or someone whose gender is unknown reinforces the notion that females do not exist or are invisible (Sheldon, 1990). Teachers must carefully monitor what they say and realize the impact of their words on young children. For instance, when reading a book that refers to an animal as a "he," substitute "she" part of the time.

Behavior Expectations

Too often teachers expect certain kinds of behavior from one sex or the other. For example, boys are expected to behave in a courageous and chivalrous way, swearing is tolerated from them, and more boisterous behavior is acceptable. Girls, on the other hand, are expected to be neat and clean, submissive, gentle, and kind, and they should not take the lead on any activity. Even duties and chores within the classroom are too often assigned on the basis of sex. The same behavior should be expected from all students, and the same behavior not tolerated from all students.

All activities in the early childhood classroom should be available to all children. As both girls and boys hammer nails, construct buildings, shovel dirt, pilot boats, drive road graders, tend babies, cook dinner, sweep floors, paint pictures, kick balls, repair tricycles, sing, dance, follow ants, carve pumpkins, extinguish fires, plant seeds, dress up, and play in the beauty shop, avenues of learning and exploration become limitless.

Teachers must assess their areas of responsibility, review materials for content and form, evaluate their learning environments, and become aware of their interaction patterns with others, particularly young children. The total learning environment must foster integrity, equality, and initiative in all children—boys and girls—in order to prepare them for sound and vigorous futures. By establishing a nonsexist educational atmosphere, we allow young children to explore freely and identify gradually the roles that they find most comfortable and fulfilling.

Religious Bias

There is great diversity in religious preferences in our society today, and children's religious preferences will considerably impact how they behave, the traditions they share from their homes, and their beliefs, values, and moral standards. Religious beliefs about human events such as birth and death and the very purpose of life all influence what children think, say, and do in the classroom. The degree of religious influence in the school varies from one community to another; however, if a school has a dominant religious group, the perspective of that group may be reflected in the school and its curriculum. A family's religious belief will influence what parents expect from the school, the teacher, and the child (Gollnick & Chinn, 1986).

Children are aware of religious diversity early, and they can describe their own religious identity by the time they are 5 years of age. By the time they are 9 years old, they know whether someone is religious or nonreligious and they can tell you what religion some people are by some of the things they do (Gollnick & Chinn, 1986).

Most parents (98%, according to a 1984 Gallup Poll) believe that their children should have religious training at home in order to build character, give security, and promote family unity; however, the majority of families in the United States do not attend weekly church services on a regular basis (Gollnick & Chinn, 1986).

Teachers must be sensitive to the religious beliefs of all of the children in the classroom. Again, the teacher's example of respect and tolerance for different beliefs helps children to build this same regard and consideration for another person's way of life and belief system. Teachers can better understand their students if they know the children's religious identifications. Sometimes religious identity is combined with ethnic identity, as it is for the Russian Jew, the Irish Catholic, and others. A child's membership in two microcultures can help a teacher better understand the child's behavior and self-concept, and the teacher can then assist other children in gaining the same understanding.

Religious perspective affects children's friendships, dress standards, social activities, customs, and dietary habits (Gollnick & Chinn, 1986), and teachers must not tolerate criticism from the children's peers with regard to these obvious differences. Rather, teachers can openly teach and model patience, tolerance, and respect for habits and behaviors that reflect a child's religious beliefs and teachings.

Exceptional Children

Beyond genders, cultures, and ethnic groups, the concept of recognizing similarities and differences among peers includes exceptional children. Those who have severe disabilities as well as children who are gifted are considered exceptional or special-needs children. Exceptional children are those who have learning or behavioral characteristics that differ substantially from others and require special methods of instruction. Although exceptional children have differences, they are actually more like other children than unlike them, and they must be treated as individuals, not labeled as members of particular groups (Heward & Orlansky, 1989). We must treat them first as children, and then as children with special needs.

A disability becomes a handicap only when the condition limits or stops the person's ability to function normally (Shaver & Curtis, 1981). We must have an attitude of openness and acceptance, and realize that exceptional children

New experiences can sometimes cause feelings of fear and insecurity; these feelings are more easily handled when one is accompanied by a friend (such as a doll).

are members of our society and can make valuable contributions. Of children who have disabilities, 90% have only mild impairments (Heward & Orlansky, 1989). Some of these children do require specialized attention.

With these individual needs in mind, Congress passed Public Law 94-142 (the Education for All Handicapped Children Act) in 1975. This law mandated that a free and appropriate education be provided for all children with disabilities aged 5 through 18 years in an environment closest to that of a "normal" child. Schools implemented an approach whereby children who need special services are identified and then assessed or evaluated to determine their degree of impairment. Then intervention is planned to best meet their needs. An individualized education program (IEP) is developed with the child's teacher, qualified school personnel and, most important, the child's parents.

There is also an amendment to Public Law 94-142 that has significantly influenced and enhanced early intervention with young children who have special needs. Public Law 99-457, the Education of the Handicapped Amendments of 1986, did not mandate universal service for children under 5 years of age, but it strengthened incentives for states to serve 3- to 6-year-old children and established a new discretionary program for services to children from birth to 3 years of age.

How does this affect the early childhood teacher? Children with varying disabilities may be mainstreamed into regular classrooms. To prepare for these children, teachers should learn as much as possible about normal child development, research the disabilities they will be dealing with, seek help from specialists who work with the children, attend workshops or inservice training sessions, and talk with the children's parents. Teachers need extra skill, flexibility, and tolerance to work effectively with children who have special needs.

It is important for teachers to understand the conditions that children in their classrooms may have. Following are general categories, with characteristics, possible teaching strategies, and specialists in the community whom teachers may consult. Keep in mind that these are generalizations; not every exceptional child will exhibit the same set of characteristics, but some of the most persistent features are included. Although each child is unique, good strategies can be adapted to meet his or her needs.

Speech and Language Impairments

Characteristics. Many problems can occur in a young child with a speech and/or language deficiency. Knowing the normal development of language and speech sounds will help a teacher to determine whether there is a problem. Some signs include omissions, substitutions, distortions, or additions of speech sounds. Use of single words and/or gestures, along with difficulty in following directions, are indications of a developmental problem. An early childhood teacher may also have children in the classroom who are bilingual (learning two languages).

Reaching a child by using his or her first language is also very important. This language is the familiar vehicle of oral communication, and the student needs acceptance of and understanding in the use of that language in any program. If a child in an early childhood setting is bilingual, that is, learning and using two languages, someone should be available to communicate with the child in both languages.

Teaching Strategies. There are many things a teacher can do to assist a child in speech and language development. Give simple directions, using phrases or short sentences. When addressing the child, do not talk down or use baby talk. Provide daily oral experiences, such as singing, language activities, or answering questions. Always listen and respond to the child. Provide good models for the child to listen to. If the problem persists or does not appear to be developmental, refer the child for testing. If the child is bilingual, have an interpreter seek to understand the culture, and keep the vocabulary as basic as possible.

Specialists. Communication disorder specialists or itinerant migrant education teachers are among the community specialists in the area of speech and language development who can assist or consult with the early childhood teacher.

Mental Retardation

Characteristics. For many years, levels of retardation were measured by intelligence testing. Other factors to consider and evaluate when assessing a child's potential in the classroom include the child's developmental gains in motor, language, social, and self-help skills for his or her age; physical difficulties or illnesses; and the length of the child's attention span. Teachers should observe the rate of learning and comprehension of abstract concepts.

Teaching Strategies. If a child is delayed in two or more of the previously mentioned areas, the teacher should refer the child for developmental testing. Adjustments can be made in the classroom that will assist the teacher and child. Low child–staff ratios are necessary to provide the individualized attention that the child will need. Tasks that are being taught should be broken into small components, and these should be repeated often and reinforced. The presentation should be consistent and the directions brief and simple.

Specialists. The following specialists can help in evaluating and programming for children who have mental retardation: psychologist, special education teacher, developmental specialists, communicative disorder specialist, occupational therapist, and physical therapist.

Hearing Impairments

Characteristics. The following characteristics may indicate a hearing problem: limited communication skills, inability to understand or respond to the speech of others, misbehavior, inattentiveness, watching the speaker's face and lips, and complaints of earaches. If a hearing test has been given, a loss of 20 to 60 decibels (measurement of sound density) is considered hard of hearing, and a loss of 60 decibels or more is considered deaf.

Teaching Strategies. In the classroom, seat a child with a hearing impairment near the source of instruction and where there is good visibility. Articulate clearly, do not exaggerate, and face the child when speaking. If the child is using hearing aids, be familiar with them, check to see whether they are operating, know how to put them in the child's ear, and be prepared to charge the battery. Provide constant language stimulation. The teacher may need to learn some sign language.

Specialists. Specialists to be consulted in case of a hearing impairment are the audiologist, communicative disorder specialist, and itinerant teacher for students who are hard of hearing. The parents should also be consulted.

Visual Impairments

Characteristics. A child who has been diagnosed as having a severe vision problem falls into one of two categories: partially sighted or blind. Children who are partially sighted have a field of vision that is 20/200 (that is, they can see at 20 feet what a normally sighted person can see at 200 feet) or better in the corrected eye, but not greater than 20/70. Children who are blind have a field of vision of 20/200 or less in the corrected better eye. Characteristics of children with visual impairments are excessive blinking; rubbing, crossing, and squinting of the eyes; holding things close or far away; tilting the head when trying to focus; and dizziness or headaches.

Teaching Strategies. To adjust materials and activities to meet the needs of a child with a visual impairment, rely on the use of the other senses. Orient the child to the classroom and make sure that he or she knows of any changes. Assign a buddy to help the child orient quickly and develop social interactions.

Specialists. The teacher may consult with the child's ophthalmologist or an itinerant teacher of children with visual impairments to find materials and adjust the program for the child.

Physical Impairments

Characteristics. Indications of a physical problem include poor coordination or control of fine or gross motor skills, poor balance, and frustration and discouragement when attempting motor skills. Children with a physical disability may have normal intelligence. Common physical disabilities that can be identified in young children at birth or shortly afterward include cerebral palsy, epilepsy, and spina bifida. In addition to congenital impairments, there are impairments caused by diseases and accidents.

Teaching Strategies. One of the major changes necessary when a child with a physical disability is in a regular classroom is the building of appropriate structures and equipment (i.e., ramps, walkers). Learn as much as possible about the physical problems and what limitations they may have on the child. Help the child develop motor, language, speech, and social skills to the fullest potential. Be sensitive to the child's feelings about the disability.

Specialists. To develop a program that is appropriate for a child with physical problems, the teacher should consult with an occupational therapist, a physical therapist, the child's physician, and the child's parents. In extreme cases, a neurologist should be consulted.

Emotional, Social, or Behavioral Problems

Characteristics. Children with emotional, social, or behavioral problems may exhibit them to a marked degree in two different ways: passively or aggressively. A passive child may stare for long periods of time, seldom communicate; be withdrawn, afraid, sensitive, or shy; and have poor eye contact. An aggressive child may be overcompetitive, rebellious, easily distracted, disruptive, hostile, assaultive, and defiant of authority. These children have difficulty building positive relationships with others and often experience depression. Children with autism also fit into this category.

Teaching Strategies. A child with behavioral problems may need a change in environment to provide the individualized attention needed to verbalize his or her feelings. Children with these problems need love, patience, and understanding. Most of all, they need consistency in expectations of them and positive reinforcement for appropriate behaviors. Teachers may need to draw information from specialists in the field to assist them in the class.

Specialists. Early childhood teachers may need to consult with a psychologist, social worker, counselor, or special education teacher when working with children with emotional, social, or behavioral problems.

Chronic Illness

Characteristics. Children who are chronically ill usually have a disorder that is always present and that may limit their physical activity. Some examples are asthma, cystic fibrosis, diabetes, tuberculosis, arthritis, muscular dystrophy, and hemophilia. Children who are chronically ill usually have normal intelligence.

Teaching Strategies. Consult with the child's physician to find out about his or her disease and limitations, and formulate expectations and responsibilities accordingly. Learn about medications and what to do in case of an emergency.

Specialists. The child's parents, physicians, and the school nurse are the best consultants for teachers when dealing with children who are chronically ill.

Learning Disabilities

Characteristics. The category known as *learning disabilities* has existed for 25 years. It refers to a disorder in one or more basic psychological processes associated with either understanding or using language (Maxim, 1989). Some characteristics include motor disinhibition (being unable to refrain from responding), disassociation (responding to the elements of a stimulus rather than to the whole stimulus), figure-ground disturbance (confusing a figure with its background), perseveration (not changing from one task to another), and absence of a well-developed self-concept and body image (Broman, 1989). Other characteristics are poor gross and fine motor skills and lack of established handedness.

Teaching Strategies. Children with learning disabilities often need one-on-one teaching with simple tasks and simple instructions. Proceed slowly, making sure the child is paying attention.

Be sure the child has mastered skills at one level before proceeding to the next. Use positive reinforcement when a child is learning each task.

Specialists. Specialists in the area of learning disabilities include psychologists, special education teachers, developmental specialists, and social workers.

Gifted and Talented Children

Characteristics. Gifted children are the most underserved group of exceptional children. Children who are gifted show above-average ability or potential in one or more of the following areas: "(1) general intellectual ability, (2) specific academic aptitude, (3) leadership ability, (4) creative or productive thinking, (5) visual and performing arts, and (6) psychomotor ability" (Lupkowski & Lupkowski, 1985, p. 10). Children who are gifted may peak in some areas at particular times, but not necessarily in all cognitive areas. Karnes and Johnson (1989) agree that "Giftedness comes in many forms. Is the child an unusually creative thinker? Artistic? Musical? Mentally sharp? Good grades and giftedness are not the same thing" (p. 56). However, isolated incidents do not indicate giftedness. Also, gifted children may not necessarily score high on all parts of intelligence tests. Professionals and those involved in evaluating should look at what children can do instead of what they cannot do. Parent reports and teacher observations should also be used in describing children's strengths, talents, and capabilities. Children who are gifted and talented are creative and observant, ask numerous questions, and learn quickly and easily. They are attentive, have a capacity for seeing relationships and patterns, enjoy problem solving, exhibit an early interest in printed material, and have exceptional memory. They also have in-depth interests, a high energy level, and good reasoning and insight ability (Lupkowski & Lupkowski, 1985). They are sensitive and have high expectations. These children usually have large, accurate vocabularies and use expanded language. It is difficult for children from minority groups to be identified and served by programs for gifted children.

Teaching Strategies. Provide stimulating, challenging, and varied enrichment opportunities to develop knowledge, talents, and work habits. Provide extra assignments. Build on language skills. Independence and self-direction need to be encouraged. Older children (5–8 years) often need academic acceleration and enrichment (extending the regular curriculum), whereas younger children (2–5 years) benefit from individualization, discovery learning, and encouragement of talents.

Specialists. Itinerant teachers of children who are gifted and talented or psychologists or resource teachers can assist the early childhood teacher in planning activities to enhance the child's program in the regular classroom setting.

Programs for Meeting Special Needs

The needs of children who have multiple disabilities—children with more than one of the preceding disabling conditions—must be met according to each child's disabilities and abilities. Consultants from all areas can be used to provide appropriate programs for the children to achieve their greatest potential.

After the teacher comes to an understanding of a child's disabling condition, his or her acceptance of that child as a whole child, not just one who has a disability, is critical. The teacher becomes a model for the other children in showing acceptance for the child who has a disability in the classroom. Through the teacher, the other children will come to understand and accept this child. Research suggests that social integration of children, both with and without disabilities, does not occur automatically; it develops only when sensitive teachers structure experiences for social integration (Odom & McEvoy, 1988). Morgan and York (1981, p. 21) quote Napier, Kappen, and Tuttle (1974): "All children can learn from their relationships with those who are handicapped. It is the able teacher who makes the presence of a blind child an advantage rather than a disadvantage as he works with his students through the year." This applies to all other disabling conditions as well.

A comprehensive program for exceptional children includes the following:

1. A teacher knowledgeable in child development who accepts children at their level of development
2. A teacher who understands that children need consistency, a dependable schedule, and gentle but firm limits
3. A curriculum that has a multisensory approach
4. A curriculum that enhances growth in all areas of development
5. A curriculum that provides various hands-on experiences
6. Many opportunities for play
7. A natural, appropriate setting in which learning may be directly applied, with no need for delayed generalization from a highly structured and isolated lesson. (Morgan & York, 1981, p. 20)

Forming a basic understanding of normal child development is necessary if a teacher is to work effectively among children with special needs. This understanding provides the teacher with a guideline to devise developmental instructional activities, a basis to modify the activities to meet the individual needs of the children in the classroom, and a guideline to form realistic expectations for all the children. The secret of good instruction is knowing what learning should occur, when it should occur, and the most appropriate method to ensure that it does occur (Bailey & Wolery, 1984). Understanding child development is essential for this to happen (Bredekamp, 1986; Honig, 1983).

With knowledge of normal child development, early childhood teachers can adapt and individualize their programs to meet the needs of the children in their classroom. This individual-ization process involves breaking down tasks into small enough steps so that the child can progress successfully, providing appropriate models for the child to follow, maintaining accurate records of the child's progress, and altering the physical makeup of the building and equipment to meet the child's special needs. Consulting with specialists and following through with the programs outlined also assist the teacher in developing individual plans and directions.

Mainstreaming can be a positive experience for all children in the classroom. The values of mainstreaming for the normal child are learning to accept differences in people; learning to be helpful, caring people; and learning how and when to help. The values of mainstreaming for the child with special needs are the opportunity to choose friends with whom to play, to realize potential skills more fully, and to learn from normal peers (Morgan & York, 1981).

The potentials of special children inherent in heterogeneous groups, including mainstreaming, are greater for language and social development than for academic achievement (Jenkins, Odom, & Speltz, 1989). Educational services should be individually planned to best serve the needs of each child. According to research by Danielson and Bellamy (1989), 94% of children with disabilities are educated in regular school buildings and 6% in segregated schools or facilities. Their research also indicates that of the 94% in regular schools, 24% receive education in special classrooms. It is our hope that each child will be evaluated carefully to determine how the school and community can best serve individual special needs. Again, educational services for children with special needs ought to be individually planned.

Once a child has been placed, ongoing evaluation and observation should be done to determine whether or not the program is providing optimal education for the child. To determine whether a program or service is effective, the student needs to demonstrate that he or she is progressing successfully (Danielson & Bellamy, 1989).

Creating a Diverse Curriculum and Classroom

Creating a classroom environment, curriculum, and atmosphere that focus on diversity is challenging. In addition to broadly incorporating the goals stated earlier in the chapter, there are specific things that can be done to create and teach diversity in the classroom. The following suggestions are not inclusive; add your own ideas to this list. In addition, each chapter of this text contains specific ideas for including and teaching diversity within the framework of various concepts.

Teachers must change their attitudes and practices. Perhaps most important of all is that teachers do not just add the component of diversity to their curriculum; rather, the entire classroom and curriculum must be revised to reflect a change in attitude and practice that indicates genuine acceptance of all people. Teachers can do much by helping children rid themselves of the we/they attitude and replace it with the we/us attitude.

Books, materials, and resources must be selected carefully. Diversity materials need to be consistently available (Derman-Sparks & A.B.C. Task Force, 1989), and teachers must consciously evaluate the messages that are contained in these materials. "Only when we are deliberately selecting and evaluating can we hope that the messages children receive while in our care are consistent with the philosophy and goals of our programs" (Neugebauer, 1992, p. 160). Teachers must be cautious and careful in selecting materials such as books, pictures, tests, games, and toys that are free of biases and stereotypes. Select materials that show diversity of culture, ethnic, gender, and racial groups and take the perspective of various minorities (Saracho & Spodek, 1983). Images of the elderly and people with disabilities should also appear in materials in the environment.

Books and materials that have no ethnic minorities pictured may give the impression that these people are either invisible or inferior (Spencer & Markstrom-Adams, 1990). We must work to provide all children with the experience of seeing themselves in their books and then learning to care for the others they see. Children also need to be able to identify with heroes and heroines of their own culture (Harris, 1991). Avoid the practice of tokenism—selecting one book, picture, or doll that includes an ethnic minority. Throughout the year pictures, toys, and books should reflect the diversity of people. Books should be chosen that are written by minority authors about their minority groups; all children need to experience authentic literature from other cultures (Harris, 1991).

Bulletin boards, films and videos, visitors, and field trips to visit people or places should constantly confirm the diversity of our world and present the minority perspective. During the year, invite several visitors from the same culture so that children may capture the variability that exists within a culture (Boutte & McCormick, 1992). As materials and resources are selected, remember that *sameness* of resources for diverse children should not be the rule (Gay, 1989). Calendars should include dates of ethnic holidays and note outstanding citizens of diverse ethnic origins.

Dolls in the classroom should reflect different ethnic identities, physical abilities, and genders. "Persona" dolls can be used to introduce differences, particularly some of the differences not found among children in the classroom (Derman-Sparks & A.B.C. Task Force, 1989). These dolls have names, and the children personally identify with them through playing, interacting, associating, and listening to stories about their lives. For example, one doll might be named Jenny, and Jenny might be blind and live with her mother and grandmother. Throughout the year, the teacher can build on Jenny's story and help the children understand not only Jenny, but that her blindness is a way she is different.

Games from other cultures are enjoyed by children and help broaden their perspectives. Music and art from other cultures can be included as a natural part of the early childhood environment.

Dramatic play offers ready opportunities to share clothing and items that reflect such diversities as the different physical abilities, different genders, and various ages of people.

If available materials are screened and found to be biased or presenting obvious stereotypes, the materials may need to be disregarded or altered. If this is the case, teachers should be honest with the children, pointing out biases and discussing them in ways that children can understand. Teachers can develop or make supplementary materials that help to correct some of the misconceptions or biases found in materials.

Teachers must expose children to the diversity of cultures. There are more than 100 ethnic groups in the United States. Teachers cannot include curriculum content about each one, but they can focus on different groups that have a variety of customs, values, and traditions. Children should be acquainted with art, music, literature, and foods from various ethnic groups. Musical instruments, songs, dances, and stories can be presented and taught by people from various cultures. These should not be presented in ways that suggest tokenism, but rather so that children gain the perspective of, and feel respect toward, other people.

As diversity is integrated into the curriculum, teachers must be mindful that the differences found among people are not to be interpreted as deficiencies or inferiorities. Cultures should not be described in terms of how they deviate from the mainstream culture. Diversity must be recognized as a strength and not considered a weakness (Tiedt & Tiedt, 1986). Young children should understand the value of differences. People have different beliefs, eat many different foods, live in different ways, practice different religions, and have different names—and that is the way it should be!

The classroom focus should be on similarities among all people. Throughout the classroom and the curriculum, a notion that might be referred to as the "common thread idea" should be integrated, discussed, and felt by all children. We acknowledge the commonality of all people: We are all alike in that we are all people with feelings and hopes, and we are all more alike than differ-

ent (Wardle, 1990). Yes, we are of different genders, social classes, religions; from a variety of ethnic backgrounds; and have various physical abilities; but we share many similarities.

Teachers must accept language and dialect diversity. Teachers must support language and dialect diversity, including sign language, and even teach words in other languages. If there are bilingual children in the classroom, they should often teach words or phrases relating to topics that are being discussed. Preferably in bilingual classes, children should use their native languages about half of the time, and the teacher should be fluent in the language of the majority of the students from minority groups. If there are no bilingual children in the classroom, the teacher could teach words or phrases from another language. For example, numbers, shapes, colors, units of money or time, the alphabet, songs, and fingerplays can all be taught in many languages.

All people speak different dialects, which includes both vocabulary and word pronunciation. Children have the right to their own language, and no dialect should be considered unacceptable.

Teachers can use the daily news as a springboard for cultural awareness. As news and current events are discussed, other countries or states can be located on maps and brief dialogues about people in those areas can be included.

Differences in occupations and lifestyles can be taught. Children should become familiar with not only the obvious differences among people, but also the varieties of people's occupations and lifestyles. These varieties can be included in pictures, books, visitors, and field trips. Teachers must connect the classroom with the diversities in the community and neighborhood. Parents and extended family members are great resources; they can share their interests, leisure pursuits, and professions. To overcome sexism, be sure to include women and men doing nontraditional jobs and having hobbies or interests that are nontraditional for a particular sex. This can help children overcome the biases and stereotypes regarding sex roles and occupations.

A field trip to the farm gives children first-hand experiences with a farmer, animals, gardens, and farm equipment. A follow-up experience story written by the children will become a favorite book in the reading center.

Visits to or from elderly people and people with different physical abilities help children overcome stereotypes for these people. Books and stories also help to develop accurate concepts relating to these groups.

Diversity in family lifestyles needs to be taught, valued, and accepted. Some families have a single mom or dad; some have a mom who works and a dad at home; some have a dad who works and a mom who is at home; some have both parents who work; some have two moms and two dads (stepparents); some families are headed by grandparents or foster parents; some have interracial parents; some families have members with special needs.

Cooperative learning should be used as a strategy. Cooperative learning is a strategy that was discussed previously, but teachers should know that this approach to teaching and learning can promote integration of children from minority groups. As children come to know one another through working together, they naturally develop the respect, tolerance, and sensitivity we are trying to achieve.

Specific Curriculum Activities

Once we have adopted the diversity perspective, many ways of integrating it with our educational goals and implementing it in the classroom become obvious. All aspects of the curriculum should include the diversity approach through experiences and materials that accurately reflect all cultural groups and avoid stereotypes. Activities should be concrete, comprehensible, and linked to experiences in which the children can become involved. These activities will enrich and expand their overall experiences. As teachers, it is important that we make comparisons of similarities and differences among cultures whenever possible, focusing on the ways they are alike.

Following are some activities that can be incorporated into general areas of the basic curriculum. Additional activities are found in this chapter under the heading "Activities and Experiences." Also, each chapter in the text includes specific ways of integrating diversity into the teaching of specific concepts.

Communication Skills

Listed here are suggestions for increasing acceptance and understanding of children's primary languages.

- Listen to records and tapes, and practice singing a variety of songs in different languages.
- Have the children learn many words and phrases in languages other than their native language, and especially in the languages of children in their class. Use names, foods, greetings, and other appropriate words and phrases.
- Translate children's names into other languages.
- Expose the children to sign language, the fourth most frequently used language in the United States.
- Talk to the children using words from different languages. Ask them whether they can understand the words. How does it make them feel when they are unable to understand the words?
- Have the children share and describe objects that are important to their culture.
- Interview parents and people in your community about their culture, jobs, traditions, be-

liefs, or other things that will help the children capture a feeling of diversity.
- Share human interest stories from news programs and photographs from the newspaper; locate on a map or globe where the stories take place.
- Have parents, staff members, or community members make tapes reading the children's favorite stories in different languages. These can be enjoyed as a group or with earphones, individually.

Literacy Skills

Stories and poetry have been used for many years to transmit values, traditions, skills, and practices important to various cultures. Listed here are some activities that can point out similarities in language and literacy experiences.

- Use open-ended and problem-solving situations about children from different backgrounds and of different abilities to help increase sensitivity to others. End with such questions as "How would you feel if. . . ?"
- Have the children observe and discuss pictures from ethnic magazines, calendars, cards, or professional journals so that they can learn about people who are different from themselves. Include a variety of cultures, children or adults doing nontraditional activities for their gender, and children of different physical abilities.
- Provide blank books for the children to dictate and illustrate stories about their families.
- Make a comparison of how alphabets are written in different cultures. Let the children experiment by writing their own.
- During the year, share books, stories, poetry, and folktales that represent the cultures of each child in your class.

Motor and Physical Skills

The following are some skills for increasing awareness that children everywhere develop and enjoy similar motor and physical activities.

- Acquire books, tapes, or records that describe in detail traditional games played by children of different cultures.
- Identify and play such games as "Hopscotch" and "Tag" that may be found in all cultures. Describe specific culture variations.
- Teach the children how to play various card or board games using toys and manipulatives from different cultures.
- Teach authentic dances from other cultures, especially dances that offer cultural insights. Also listen to music and sing songs from that culture.

Creative Arts

Music and art offer many opportunities for providing cultural experiences for young children.

- Frequently listen to music from other countries, even as background music while the children are working or playing.
- Have pieces of art from different cultures displayed in the classroom.
- Invite artists and musicians from different cultures to visit and perform; discuss what feelings or messages they might be trying to portray.
- Have children share music they listen to in their homes, or art their family appreciates.
- Provide paints or marking pens in such skin colors as brown, black, or peach (Derman-Sparks, 1989).

Dramatic Play

The following dramatic play activities offer opportunities to explore various aspects of culture diversity.

- Provide dress-up clothes and objects from different cultures in the housekeeping area, allowing both sexes to try out a variety of roles. Teachers may need to intervene if they hear stereotypic comments such as, "You can't wear the mail carrier's hat because you are a girl."

- Provide equipment that is used by people with disabilities. Allow the children to explore such things as crutches, wheelchairs, glasses, even a prosthesis.
- Cut from magazines, old sewing pattern books, and other sources pictures of children from various ethnic backgrounds and abilities. Laminate the pictures, mount them to sticks, and use them for telling stories, exploring language, or dramatizing.

Food Activities

Snacks and food activities from various cultures can often be added to the curriculum. Be careful of stereotyping by saying, for example, "This is Mexican food." Instead say, "This is a snack enjoyed by some Mexican Americans." Do not allow children to comment negatively about a food from another culture and do not force any child to eat a particular food (Derman-Sparks & A.B.C. Task Force, 1989). The following are a few examples of food activities:

- Share a particular culture's differences between daily foods and holiday foods.
- Visit ethnic restaurants to capture feelings, smells, and flavors.
- Make a recipe book of families' favorite recipes.

Math Skills

Children can learn about and compare counting systems used by various cultures by participating in some of the following activities:

- Teach the children to count in a different language.
- Study the development of calendar and time systems from different cultures.
- Compare money systems from different cultures. Compare coins and their sizes and values. Convert a dollar into rubles, liras, yen, and marks.
- Compare how numerals are written in other cultures.

Social Skills

Children's self-concepts grow when they feel they are an important part of their environment. Some activities that may enhance the child's self-concept as well as build acceptance of diversity follow.

- Names are basic to a person's identity. Explore this concept by asking such questions as "Where did your name come from?" "Does your surname (last) or first name have an ethnic origin?" "Who named you?" "How do you pronounce your full name correctly?" "Can you say your name in other languages?"
- Make a friendship tree by hanging objects from many cultures on branches of a tree. Have the children identify each object, talk about it, tell whether it has a meaning, and match it with children from that heritage in the class.
- Have the children bring photos of themselves to compile into a book or make a bulletin board in the classroom. Let each child know that he or she is an important part of the class.
- Explore a variety of jobs—in the home and outside of the home—that are nontraditional for either sex.
- Do a bulletin board on the variety of families in the class.

Cultural Comparisons

The study of all cultures should be based on the premise that all people share the same basic needs for food, clothing, and families. Provide activities demonstrating that these and other needs are met in varied ways by different people.

- Use films, videos, and resource people to acquaint children with diverse people.
- Use maps and a globe to show geographic locations.
- Provide dolls from both sexes and various cultures for the children to play with.
- Have children bring in real objects used by their families that may be historical or typical of the child's cultural group (e.g., rice steamer, fish trap, Krumkake iron).
- Collect ways the families and children recognize special days, seasons, rituals, holidays. Make a scrapbook or display to share with the class.

Social Skills

There are many social skills that young children learn and develop competence in. Those skills that we are anxious to help children develop are called *prosocial* skills or behaviors. Most prosocial skills come with experience and maturation. All children need guidance and correct modeling; many are aided by that spirit of self-confidence we call self-esteem. Many prosocial skills depend on the child's attitude; therefore, the teacher's goal in helping the child develop prosocial behavior is to encourage the development of more positive attitudes among the children. Rogers and Ross (1986) caution that "Although children need adult guidance to promote prosocial development, they also need opportunities to interact with peers with minimal adult intervention (p. 13).

The following are some of the prosocial skills encouraged by early childhood teachers:

- Following classroom or center rules.
- Learning to cope with social conflicts such as name calling or teasing.
- Treating others politely and courteously, and learning to use words such as *please* and *thank you.*
- Being able to share the attention of others, including the teacher.
- Developing eye-to-eye contact with peers and adults.
- Learning to smile at others.
- Being helpful to others.
- Showing empathy for another's feelings or situation, and giving or expressing sympathy to others when they experience difficulties.

- Being comfortable talking with others and learning to be a good listener.
- Learning to follow simple rules of games, to take turns, and to cooperate.
- Learning to gain attention from friends in positive and constructive ways.
- Developing responsible behaviors such as taking care of one's own possessions.
- Learning to compliment, rather than criticize, others.
- Showing tolerance for others and their differences.
- Being able to share and cooperate with others in play situations.
- Being able to express sorrow when actions or words have hurt another.
- Being able to accept the consequences of behavior and actions.

Although these skills will be taught daily, the teacher's modeling is critical to learning.

Another important concept for children to learn is that people have all kinds of jobs. Your challenge as a teacher of young children is to expose them to a variety of jobs. Be careful not to stereotype jobs so that the children develop misconceptions, such as that only boys can be fire fighters or police officers. Early childhood teachers should expose children to various kinds of jobs that people do, acquainting them with the necessary tools or machinery involved. As a caution: If you begin discussing the jobs of some of the children's parents, in some way address the jobs of all of the parents so that no child is left out.

Visitors with all kinds of talents, skills, and hobbies should be invited into the classroom. Field trips for the same purpose of exposure could be arranged. Borden (1987) refers to the *community connection*: "Every school is located in a community. Every community has members who care about the well-being of its children. Every community is filled with people with talents, hobbies, and resources that can enrich the pupils' educational experiences. Reach out! Ask them!" (p. 23). Borden also discusses the importance of the

educator's attitude toward field trips. They must not be considered as extra events to be squeezed in, but as valuable opportunities for firsthand experiences.

One relevant notion to explore is that people have feelings and that what we do and say can affect these feelings. Occasionally ask, "How would you feel if . . . ?" This question helps sensitize children to others' feelings. However, we need to emphasize that individuals are unique and have different feelings, so the same situation or event can result in different responses among people of various ages. Open-ended stories help to stimulate thinking about how other people feel in particular situations. Reading stories from children's literature also allows opportunities to stop and discuss how children would respond in a similar situation and how they feel about a particular happening. It is our "responsibility to select books of great worth that provide rich metaphors and help children understand themselves and others, books that teach, books that touch the heart. . . . Storytime can nurture a sense of compassion in children" (Smith, 1986, p. 49). Trying to take the place of characters in the story will help children to become more sensitive to the feelings of others in real life. "The development of empathy and other positive social interactions will be encouraged when children engage in activities such as block play, water and sand play, dramatic play, or similar activities with limited adult intervention" (Rogers & Ross, 1986, p. 13).

Approach to Teaching

Concepts and Ideas for Teaching

1. People are born (all people are babies at one time).
   a. Characteristics and needs of infants.
   b. Differences and likenesses among babies, young children, and adults.
   c. The day a person is born is called his or her *birthday*, and it is celebrated each year.

2. People die (all people will die at some time).

3. People do different things at different times.

    a. People generally sleep during the night.

    b. Sometimes people sleep in the daytime.

    c. Children are in school part of the day and at home part of the day.

4. People have different capabilities.

    a. Most can see, touch, hear, taste, and smell.

    b. Some cannot do one or more of these things.

    c. Some are athletic.

    d. Different people have different talents.

5. Different people have the same capabilities.

    a. A barber and a parent can both cut hair.

    b. A teacher and an orchestra member can both play the clarinet.

    c. A sibling and a friend can both play ball.

    d. A parent and a mechanic can both repair cars.

6. People are different sizes.

    a. Babies are smaller, adults bigger.

    b. Not all babies are the same size.

    c. Some parents are tall, some short.

7. People are different shapes.

    a. Some people are thin.

    b. Some people are fat.

8. People are of different races and nationalities. (Concepts included here could be differences in homes, foods, clothes, and physical characteristics of respective groups.)

9. People have different thoughts and ideas, and each person's ideas are important.

10. People have various religious beliefs.

11. People have various likes and dislikes.

    a. Some like spinach, some do not.

    b. Some like winter weather, some do not.

12. People have jobs. (Concepts include what these people do; how their jobs help; what equipment, machinery, and materials they use; and that they are important for more than the job they fill. Be sensitive to children who have a parent or parents who are unemployed.)

    a. Doctor
    b. Mechanic
    c. Musician
    d. Carpenter
    e. Telephone operator
    f. Parent
    g. Engineer
    h. Teacher
    i. Secretary
    j. Upholsterer
    k. Salesperson
    l. Gardener
    m. Accountant
    n. Janitor
    o. Photographer
    p. Author
    q. Electrician
    r. Server
    s. Pilot
    t. Police officer
    u. Jeweler
    v. Artist
    w. Dentist
    x. Clerk
    y. Farmer
    z. Other

13. People change.

    a. Growth and age (new skills may be learned as person grows older; sometimes older age curtails activity).

    b. Makeup, cosmetics, clothes, costumes, jewelry, wigs, hairstyles (alter appearance).

    c. Voice (changes from infancy through old age; the same voice can sing, talk, and cry).

    d. Exposure to sun (may cause suntan or sunburn).

    e. Accidents or injuries (physical or emotional change).

    f. Increase in knowledge and learning (following directions, learn to read, walk, drive, tie shoelaces, delay gratification).

14. People eat food.

    a. Kinds of food.

    b. Variations because of the time of day or season of the year.

c. Likes and dislikes in foods.

d. Cultural variations.

15. People wear clothes.

    a. Names of particular clothing items; how they are worn.

    b. When specific articles are worn (seasons, professions, occasions).

    c. Sequences of putting on clothing.

    d. Fasteners on clothing.

    e. Care of clothing.

16. People live in homes. (Be sensitive to families who may be homeless.)

    a. Different kinds of homes.

    b. Different buildings materials used: brick, lumber, rock, adobe, canvas.

    c. Inside and outside of homes.

    d. Separate rooms, furnishings of rooms.

    e. Different activities in different rooms.

    f. Grounds surrounding homes.

17. People travel

    a. Place people travel.

      (1) To other homes

      (2) On rides

      (3) To stores

      (4) To church

      (5) For recreation and sports

      (6) To work or business

      (7) To school

    b. Ways people travel.

      (1) Automobile

      (2) Airplane

      (3) Train

      (4) Taxi

      (5) Van

      (6) Bus

      (7) Boat, ship

      (8) Truck

      (9) Motorcycle

      (10) Bicycle, tricycle

      (11) Tractor

      (12) Caterpillar and other heavy equipment

      (13) Snowplow

      (14) Ice skates, roller skates, roller blades

      (15) Skis

      (16) On foot

      (17) Wagon, cart

      (18) Horse

      (19) Snowmobile

      (20) Emergency vehicles (fire truck, ambulance)

      (21) Other animals (camels, elephants)

      (22) Wheelchair

      (23) Skateboard

    c. Various methods of transportation have particular characteristics and related concepts (make selections appropriate to your specific curriculum plans).

      (1) Speed and distance (miles per hour, time)

      (2) Size and shape (dimensions, number of passengers, tires)

      (3) Color (owner's choice, no choice, specifically designated)

      (4) Sound (starting, running, stopping, horn/siren, wipers)

      (5) Texture (inside, outside)

      (6) Smell (fuel, engines, upholstery, paint, wood)

      (7) Kind (models, company, use)

      (8) Number (passengers, wheels, prices, speed, fuel, tickets)

      (9) Shelters (garages, hangers, stations)

      (10) Related jobs (mechanic, salesperson, attendant, driver, pilot)

      (11) Parts (mechanical, physical)

      (12) Purpose and use (recreation, business, education, shopping)

18. People have feelings and emotions.

    a. Sadness

    b. Anger

    c. Fear

    d. Happiness

    e. Excitement

    f. Loneliness

19. People have names.
    a. Personal names.
        (1) Child's own name, first and last
        (2) Names of others
        (3) Others may have the same name
    b. Sex-related names.
        (1) Boy/girl
        (2) Male/female
        (3) Man/woman
        (4) Father/mother
        (5) Husband/wife
        (6) Uncle/aunt
        (7) Brother/sister
        (8) Gentleman/lady
        (9) Fellow/gal
       (10) Grandfather/grandmother
    c. Other names (may also be roles, and people have more than one name or role).
        (1) Relative (cousin, etc.)
        (2) Family
        (3) People
        (4) Person
        (5) Child, children
        (6) Boss
        (7) Neighbor
        (8) Friend
        (9) Baby
       (10) Adult
       (11) Teenager, adolescent
       (12) Names of professions
       (13) Employer, employee
       (14) Other

20. People have friends.
    a. Friends can be the same sex or the opposite sex.
    b. Friends can be the same age or different ages.
    c. Friendship takes effort and kindness.

Activities and Experiences

1. Provide hammers, nails, blocks, lumber, canvas, and boxes for building different sizes, shapes, and kinds of houses, businesses, and transportation.

2. Make a neighborhood or community map, including schools, churches, homes, and businesses. Lay this map out flat, and provide small human figures and vehicles for the children to play with.

3. Make a game by cutting out a house or apartment representing the dwelling of each child. Put the child's address on his or her "house." Make cards and letters for each child, and put them in a bag. The children will enjoy playing mailperson and delivering the mail to the proper homes.

4. Obtain an old camera, or make pretend cameras. Give the children the opportunity of pretending to take each other's picture. They may wish to draw pictures to represent those they "take."

5. Make a set of flashcards or similar cards with pictures of community helpers. The children could be encouraged to bring pictures of their parents at their jobs or wearing clothing appropriate for those jobs. Another game could be added by collecting pictures of tools or items related to various jobs and having the children sort them. For example: for a hairdresser, one can use pictures of a comb, brush, scissors, and hairdryer. (Refer to item 12 on p. 111 for additional suggestions.)

6. Interviews with community helpers could be taped on a recorder if these persons cannot visit the classroom. Children will be especially proud to hear their parents tell about their jobs.

7. Make up riddles for different jobs or careers and have the children guess the answer to each riddle. For example: "I work with animals. I ride on a tractor. I grow wheat to make bread, and I grow other things that you eat. Who am I?"

8. The children can study briefly the history of their country, state, or community, becoming acquainted with significant people in that history and the part they played in making the nation, state, or community

great. Children can create and illustrate storybooks about their study.

9. Lotto or matching games can be made using pictures or words, depending on the skills of the children. The pictures or names of the community helpers can be matched with tools or items relating to their job. For example, a picture or the words *fire fighter* are matched with such pictures or words as hydrant, fire engine, fire hat, or other related tools.

10. Use maps whenever you go on a field trip, helping children to understand that maps give directions and help us know how to get to a particular destination.

11. The children can interview their parents about their jobs, asking questions about what they are and why, how, and where they are done. Charts or stories can be compiled; plan visits on-site or invite parents into the classroom.

12. The children can read or study the classified section of the newspaper where jobs are advertised. They can draw pictures of the persons doing particular jobs and then print the information about the jobs underneath.

13. The children can draw or make a collage of a large poster of their community and title it "Why (name of community) Is a Good Place to Live." Encourage children to contact community resources and agencies for information brochures that can also supply pictures for collages.

14. The children can tell and/or illustrate stories about their own roots or histories. They can tell about an ancestor, show a pedigree chart, or show family histories, journals, or scrapbooks; they can even invite a grandparent or great-grandparent to visit the class. Some children may have clothing or other antique items to share and discuss with the class.

15. The children can become acquainted with different sections of the newspaper and decide what their favorite section is.

16. With tape to designate roads, design a community on the floor. Include methods of transportation, people, animals, and blocks for buildings.

17. Make up transportation riddles about methods of travel and related jobs.

18. Play the "How many ways can you travel?" game. The game keeps going as long as the children think of different ways to travel.

19. Collect picture cards of different means of transportation for the children to name and describe. Add other pictures of things associated with transportation, such as people dressed in uniforms or clothing that represent jobs related to transporting, as well as buildings such as roundhouses, airports, and garages. Then let the children sort the cards into categories or groups.

20. From a paint store, obtain paint chips that resemble skin colors, eye colors, and hair colors. Have the children find the colors that are closest to their skin color, eye color, and hair color. Either mount a snapshot of each child on paper or have each child draw a picture of himself or herself. Write or have the child write his or her name and "My skin color is _____" (write the color name) and then put the paint chip next to it. "My hair color is _____" (write the color name) and then put the paint chip next to it. "My eyes are _____" (write the color name) and then put the paint chip next to it. These can be put in a class book or on a bulletin board. (Adapted from Derman-Sparks & A.B.C. Task Force, 1989)

UNIT PLAN ON PEOPLE

(This could most effectively be broken down into more specific units.)

Field Trips

- Hospital
- Doctor's office
- Grocery store
- Barbershop
- Beauty shop
- Service station
- Fire station
- Police station
- Dentist's office
- Clothing store
- Basketball court
- Landmark buildings or historical sites
- Skating rink
- Another school
- Livestock auction
- Eye doctor's office
- Airport
- Train depot
- Bus station
- Water's edge, with boat dock
- Farm
- Care center
- Court of law
- Museums

Visitors

- Doctor
- Nurse
- Barber
- Beautician
- Grocery store clerk
- Grandparent
- Baby
- Mechanic
- Musician
- Train engineer
- Fire fighter
- Dentist
- Clothing store clerk
- Pilot
- Farmer
- Auctioneer
- Garbage truck operator
- Janitor or custodian
- Athlete
- Soldier
- Clown

Music

- Creative movements of various professions, as well as children growing, traveling different ways, dressing up, and so on
- Music from many cultures

Art

- Decoration of handmade musical instrument
- Houses built from large cardboard boxes, poles, canvas, and so on, and decorated
- Boats, trains, cars, wagons built from large cardboard boxes and then decorated
- Collage of pictures of people and objects relating to people, cut from catalogs or magazines
- Make litter bags

Food (Any Food Activity)

- Common foods, unusual foods
- Foods specific to season
- Foods specific to holiday
- Foods for breakfast, lunch, dinner
- Foods from various cultures

Science

- Study of how bricks, canvas, lumber, adobe, etc., are prepared for use in building; bricks made of straw and mud and then dried
- Study germs under a microscope
- Study effects of aging
- Study effects of land, water, and air pollution

Literacy and Diversity Activities

- Make a book titled "Our Families Are Different." All children will have a page to draw or put photographs of their families, then write or dictate a few sentences about their families.
- Make a book titled "Families Do Different Things." All children will have a page to put drawings, photographs, and sentences that describe things their families do. They may wish to include parents' or guardians' jobs, hobbies, or things the family does together.
- Make a book or bulletin board titled "How My Family Celebrates Holidays." The children can share through words, pictures, and photographs how they celebrate particular holidays. Be sure to point out the variations that exist even within a particular culture.
- Discuss and/or write about how families worship in a variety of ways. Point out that individuals and families have their own beliefs.
- Make a book on your community titled "Our Neighborhood." Visit, take pictures, and write a few sentences about a variety of neighbors. You may want to visit an elderly person, a person with special needs, or businesses such as the grocery store, service station, restaurant, bank, or other business. Put each neighbor or business on a separate sheet of paper, laminate the

Do any food activity as a cooperative learning experience.

Tell or read story of <u>A Friend Is Someone Who Likes You</u>.

Tell or read book <u>Charlotte's Web</u> and/or watch video. Discuss characters' friendship traits.

Food

Language and Literacy

Write or dictate letter to a friend.

Do fingerprints and compare similarities and differences among class members.

Each child completes page for booklet titled "How to Be a Friend."

Discuss and share how friends can have similarities and differences.

Science

In cooperative learning groups do an activity such as planting a seed.

In cooperative learning groups, make a collage of a picture titled "I Can Have Many Different Friends." Pictures can be cut from magazines and pattern books from fabric stores.

Art

Friends

Mail a letter to a friend.

Field Trips

Make a friendship braclet or necklace to share with a friend.

Do a picture or simple craft for a friend.

Visit a dentist at a dental clinic.

Elderly person

Visitors

Music

Make a "pretend" camera using a small jewelry box. "Take" pictures of friends. Put magazine pictures inside. Using a rubber band around the box, the children can "snap" pictures.

Librarian to tell about a book that focuses on friends. Example: Tell about friends in <u>Indian in the Cupboard</u>.

Police Officer

Learn a dance for which each child needs a partner.

Do a rhythm band and focus on sharing instruments.

Teach songs such as "I Have a Friend" that focus on friendships.

Suggested Books
(Note: Complete references are provided in "Suggested Resources" at the end of the chapter.)

A Friend Is Someone Who Likes You (Anglund, 1983)
Indian in the Cupboard (Banks, 1981)
Do You Want to Be My Friend? (Carle, 1971)
Will I Have a Friend? (Cohen, 1967)
Best Friends (Cohen, 1971)

May I Bring a Friend? (DeRegniers, 1971)
Best Friends (Hopkins, 1986)
Best Friends (Kellogg, 1990)
Frog and Toad Are Friends (Lobel, 1970)
Charlotte's Web (White, 1952)

FIGURE 4–1

sheets, combine them into a book, and allow the children to read it during the year.
- Discuss stereotypes of certain holidays such as Thanksgiving. Share and critique pictures and books. Ask, "How would you feel if you were a Native American and you saw this pictures?" (Derman-Sparks & A.B.C. Task Force, 1989)

UNIT PLAN ON AUTOMOBILES

Visitors

- Auto mechanic
- Service station attendant
- New-car dealer
- Person from auto body shop who paints cars
- Automobile seat upholsterer
- Parent showing how to care for car, wash car exterior, and change tire
- Police officer with police car
- Taxicab driver
- Chauffeur
- Race car driver
- Older child with model car display

Field Trips

- Auto mechanic shop
- Used-car lot
- Business where cars are sold
- Auto seat upholstery shop
- Automatic car wash
- Manual car wash
- Service station
- Junkyard for useless cars
- Self-service gas pump
- Parking lot where numerous cars are parked (shopping center, school parking lot, golf course, etc.)—notice colors, sizes, shapes, sounds
- Auto body and paint shop

Science

- Repair a flat tire
- Discussion of value of keeping car's interior and exterior clean; vacuuming, washing, and drying inside and outside of car

- Demonstration of how wax finish repels water and other agents
- Discussion of parts of auto (depending on ages and understandings of children); allow children to experiment with no-longer-used engine parts

Food

- Food items commonly eaten in cars—hamburgers, milkshakes, floats, sundaes, french fries, sandwiches, cookies, carrot and celery sticks, candy, ice cream cones

Art

- Tires, windows, doors, etc., pasted-on car shape
- Shapes of cars used for easel painting
- Cardboard-box cars painted and decorated
- Decoration of shakers made from juice cans, then filled with screws, nuts, and bolts from cars

Music

- Musical cars—played as musical chairs, but with decorated cardboard boxes
- Drums made from empty gallon cans and rubber from inner tubes—both ends cut from can; rubber circles cut larger than can ends; rubber circles placed over ends and laced together
- Shakers made from cans and filled with screws, nuts, and bolts of various sizes used in cars
- Creative movements—pretending to be a car going fast or slow, having a flat tire, running out of gas, getting stuck in snow or mud

"Webbing" provides a visual picture for brainstorming and developing unit plans. See Figures 4–1 and 4–2 for examples of web drawings; refer back to Chapter 3 for a more in-depth description of webbing procedure.

LESSON PLAN ON COMMUNITY HELPERS (4-DAY)

Overall Goals

- To encourage involvement in the functions of a community so that a realistic understanding of community helpers will be gained.

FIGURE 4–2

The diagram shows "Neighborhood" at the center connected to the following branches:

Science
- Study air or water purity or pollution.
- Find out what happens to garbage.
- Explore how neighborhood is changing.

Field Trips
- Visit an elderly person at home or at a nursing home.
- Visit someone in the neighborhood who has an interesting hobby.
- Visit someone in the neighborhood who has a flower or vegetable garden.

Visitors
- Business owner
- Store owner
- Public service employee to share what he or she does..

Literacy
- Read books and poetry about community helpers, stores and businesses, names, ways to travel.
- Each child completes page for book titled "What I Can Do to Be a Good Neighbor?"
- Each child completes a page of booklet titled "What I can do to Make our Neighborhood Great?"

Projects
- Each child can make a map of his or her neighborhood.
- Do a three-dimensional map of the neighborhood immediately around the school.

Food Activities
- Make a snack or treat to take to a lonely neighbor.
- Make a treat to use and share in "Spreading Love in The Neighborhood" activity.

Art
- "Spreading Love in The Neighborhood." Each child designs a heart or love poster. Do a class letter that tells recipient that this is from someone in the neighborhood who loves him or her. The letter will also challenge the recipient to make a treat, make a letter and poster, and pass on the goodwill to another family. Let each child share the poster, and the treat made as a food activity, along with letter.

- To increase the children's awareness of how these people help us, and the necessity of the skills they possess.
- To learn ways of assisting the community helpers.
- To increase familiarity with a variety of tools and equipment used by community helpers.
- To help the children learn to appreciate each occupation and respect the worker for the job that is done, eliminating fears and misconceptions. *Note:* Activities in this lesson plan are listed in order of schedule.

Day 1—Farm Day (Food Sources)

Small-Group Activity

Food—Making Bread. As the children come in, greet them and give each one a name tag in the shape of either stalks of grain, a loaf of bread, a sack of flour, or a grocery store. Set up four centers in the room, and instruct the children to go to any one of them and see what the teacher is doing. At the tables are small amounts of bread dough—one for each child—and the teachers instruct the children to knead and fold it. Give the children adequate time to work the dough until all the children have arrived; then show them how to shape the dough into a small loaf and place it in their own individual small bread pans. Each group will take its bread to a warm place to rise, and then go over to the rug and sit down.

Objectives

- To allow the children an experience of working with their tactile sense.
- To have the bread ready when the other activities call for it.

Whole-Group Activity

Farm Discussion. Begin singing the song "Old MacDonald Had a Farm" as the children begin coming over to the rug, and encourage them to join in. When everyone gets to the rug, tell a story about a vegetable and then lead into a discussion of farms. Talk about what is grown on farms and why they are important. Emphasize that wheat is grown on the farm and is later made into bread.

Objectives

- To give the children the chance to voice their opinions on what they think farms are like.
- To promote awareness of a variety of foods that are furnished by the farm, including wheat, which is made into bread.

Transition. Tell the children to look at their name tags. In the classroom, there is a table with some stalks of grain on it, a table with a flour sack on it, a table with a loaf of bread on it, and a table with a miniature grocery store on it. Encourage the children to go to the table that corresponds to their name tags.

Small-Group Activity

Art—Puppets. Spread out on the table materials with which the children can make sack puppets of farm animals, including pigs, cows, chickens, and horses. They can have their choice, and creativity is the key. The basic patterns are there for them to cut out and use; what they do is up to them. Also make available construction paper, blunt-end scissors, and glue. As the children finish, they will assist in cleaning up.

Objectives

- To give an opportunity for free expression and creativity through cutting, pasting, and manipulating puppets.
- To provide a chance for the children to make their own choices among a variety of options.

Individual Activities

- Stage on which to play with puppets
- Table with seeds, grains, feathers, and eggshells for making a collage
- Cups, dirt, and seeds that can be worked and planted
- Playhouse

Objectives

- To give an opportunity for making use of the puppets.
- To experiment with farm items in making a collage.
- To plant seeds and watch their progress throughout the unit.

Whole-Group Activity

Farm Record. Put on a record of farm animal sounds while children clean up and come to the rug. Then read stories and sing songs about cows. (By the way, the bread is now baking in the oven.) Talk about how the cream in the milk turns into butter, and show the children how it is done by bringing out a churn. Let them all take a turn at churning for a little while. When everyone has had a chance and the butter is all churned, add some salt for flavor. Then all the children will be able to eat their small loaf of bread with some of the churned butter on it and have a small glass of milk. After finishing, they will go outside to play until it is time to go home.

Objectives

- To help the children learn that butter comes from milk, which comes from the cow.
- To help them see that the farmer is important because of food production.

Day 2—Our Health Helpers

When the children arrive, give them name tags that are like little Red Cross badges. Ask them to hang up their coats and explore the different areas in the room.

Individual Activities

- Area with collections of books about community helpers
- Housekeeping area with hospital arrangement (bandages, small pillows, adhesive bandages, empty spray cans, gauze, syringes, and tape)
- Art area, constructing nurses' or doctors' hats from available materials
- Dentist's office complete with magazines, reception desk, phone, office chair, teeth models, white coats, cloth to go over patients, and tongue depressors

Objectives

- To enable the children to examine tools used by medical helpers and to experience some role playing.
- To enable them to examine books that have safety ideas and hints
- To provide an opportunity for constructing a nurse's hat or a doctor's hat.

Whole-Group Activity

Discussion on Checking and Maintaining Health. Take a large freezer box and decorate it so that it looks like an ambulance. Make a siren noise and have the children hook onto the teacher's back like a train. Go around the room for everyone, and then go to the rug. After watching a filmstrip about community helpers and safety, have a discussion about the ambulance, doctors, nurses, and dentists. Stress the point that they are available to help us, not to harm us. Pull out a satchel and begin taking items out of it. Discuss what each item is and how it is used. Also explain how to make microscope slides. The items in the satchel should include a microscope, slides, and instructions for use; measuring tape; an elastic bandage, a reflex hammer; tongue blades; stethoscopes; sphygmomanometer; balloons; thermometers; and a dental hygiene kit. As soon as everyone knows what the items are and how to use them, send an even number of students to each of the four different areas for the science experience.

Objectives

- To explain and understand the use of various pieces of equipment, identifying them by their proper names.
- To enable children to identify safety helpers and their responsibilities.
- To develop a secure feeling in regard to doctors and dentists.

Small-Group Activities

Science Experiences. Each group will spend about 10 minutes in each interest center, and the signal to change will be a siren. (1) Set up microscopes with certain prepared slides, and provide materials for the children to make their own slides showing such items as salt, pond water, sugar, and others. They will be able to see the slides under the microscopes. (2) Place a long piece of butcher paper along one wall. Set up a scale to weigh each child, mark the child's height by a line on the butcher paper. On that line, write the child's name, height, and weight. These measurements are not mandatory, and children who are reluctant and do not want to participate should be allowed that choice. During this process, the others can occupy themselves with wrapping each other up in elastic bandages, checking each other's reflexes, and looking at each other's tonsils with the tongue blades. (3) Provide several stethoscopes so that the children can hear each other's heartbeats. Set up a sphygmomanometer to take blood pressures. Have the children blow up balloons so that they can see what their lungs do, and provide thermometers so that they can take their own temperatures. (Properly sterilize or provide disposable plastic sheaths or covers for thermometers.) (4) By the sinks provide a toothbrushing kit for each child, and set up mirrors. Have the children brush once and then chew the little red tablets to see where they have brushed their teeth adequately; then have them brush again. Show them how to brush their teeth properly.

Objectives

- To learn how to use the microscope and discover its ability to enlarge objects through the use of slides.
- To see how the children compare to their peers in weight and height.
- To learn about normal body temperature and discover the sound of a heartbeat.
- To watch balloons expand as air is passed out of the lungs.
- To see what a sphygmomanometer is and how it works to determine blood pressure.
- To learn how to brush the teeth properly and see where tooth decay hides during brushing. *Note:* When the siren is heard for the fifth time, everyone will clean up and go to the rug.

Art—Mobiles or Ambulances. In a large group, discuss the doctor, dentist, and first-aid kit. Make sure the children understand that both males and females can be doctors and dentists. Then divide into smaller groups. At the tables, the children have materials before them from which to choose one or two activities: (1) making mobiles of teeth out of string, paper, cardboard, crayons, sticks, tape, pictures of teeth and mouths, glue, and marking pens; or (2) making ambulances out of matchboxes and white paper by adding details such as wheels with black construction paper,

doors, a red beacon light, stripes, headlights, and so on. (Ambulances could also be made out of rectangular-shaped pieces of Styrofoam, with red gumdrops for the sirens and black circles for wheels.)

Objectives

- To enhance the concept of balance by means of the mobiles.
- To encourage role playing of concepts learned by means of the ambulances. *Note:* When the children have finished their work and have cleaned up, they are welcome to play indoors or outside until it is time to go home.

Day 3—The Mail Carrier

The children's name tags today will be in the shapes of business envelopes, letter envelopes, packages, or stamps. As the children come in, direct them to tables where there is cookie dough. They may all help put the cookies on cookie sheets and bake them in the oven while waiting for everyone to arrive.

Whole-Group Activity

Introduction to the Mail Carrier. Have everyone gather on the rug. Read a story about the mail carrier, and talk about the forthcoming field trip to the post office and some of the things to observe. Explain that both males and females can be mail carriers and postal workers. Assign the children to cars and teachers according to their name tags. Before going, they will first go over to tables where there are certain materials.

Objectives

- To orient the children to the activities of the day.
- To let the children know what will be expected at the post office and what to observe.

Small-Group Activity

Wrapping Cookies and Field Trip to the Post Office. At the tables, each child finds a small box, some brown wrapping paper, and some string.

Give the children two of the chocolate chip cookies to put in their boxes and wrap like presents. Then put the children's names on their boxes. When they are finished, have each group get into a car for the field trip. When they are all out of the room, put the "packages" in a big bag to be used later, after returning.

Objectives

- To provide practice in small-muscle coordination (cutting, wrapping, and tying string).
- To discover how the post office functions.
- To see the work that goes on in delivering the mail.
- To meet some postal workers and learn about their jobs.
- To see letters being stamped and processed, and to observe the large amount of mail.

Note: After returning from the post office, go to the rug and have the juice passed out. Discuss the day and the mail carrier. Then have another teacher bring out the bag and pass out the packages of cookies to each child; the cookies are eaten with the juice.

Day 4—The Fire Fighter

This morning welcome the children and encourage them to explore freely the different areas in the room.

Individual Activities

- Trough filled with wood and twigs
- Housekeeping
- Easel for painting
- In one area, a tape playing a story about a fire fighter
- Blocks for constructing a fire station; ladders and trucks, along with striped overalls, bell, fire hats, and long hose

Whole-Group Activity

Visitor—Fire Fighter. When the sound of the siren begins, gather all the children in the center of the room and ask them what they think it is. Then go to see that it is a fire fighter who has come to visit and has brought the truck. The fire fighter will tell the children all about the truck, show them all its parts, and then come in to talk to them. The fire fighter will discuss safety measures and how to prevent forest fires, house fires, and accidents. Emphasis will be placed on the fact that although some fire is good for heat and cooking, it is harmful when it gets out of hand. Emphasize that fire fighters can be women or men. When the visitor has gone, make a long fire engine and drop off "fire fighters" at the different tables.

Objectives

- To enable the children to come in contact with a real fire fighter.
- To give an opportunity to inspect a fire engine.
- To promote awareness that fire can be helpful as well as harmful; also to discuss safety measures.
- To foster an understanding that the fire fighter is not only a fire fighter but a lifesaver, a protector of people, and in charge of many things.

Small-Group Activity

Food—Fondue. At the tables are fondue pots over small sterno fires. Each child will prepare several kinds of fondue and have juice.

Objectives

- To enable the children to see that fire (heat) can cook foods.
- To promote the understanding that fire should be contained to be useful.
- To provide experimentation with this unusual type of cooking and an acquaintance with a fondue pick.

Whole-Group Activity

Dramatization. Have the children pretend that they are on fire and must find a way to extinguish the fire. The fire fighter comes to the rescue and saves the people. The fire fighter explains the ways to put out fires. This should include these three main ways: (1) put a blanket around you,

(2) lie down on the rug and roll, (3) find some dirt or just get on the ground and roll. Emphasize the phrase "Stop, drop, and roll." Stress walking, rather than running. Talk about how water is important in putting out fires. Then tell the children the story of "Smokey Bear."*

After the fire fighter is finished, the three groups who were involved in dramatic play will be ready for the art activity.

Objectives

- To give the children chances to develop ideas for extinguishing fires.
- To teach the children three main safety rules if their hair or clothing catches fire.
- To have the children see the need to help others who are in trouble.

* Teacher's Forest Fire Prevention and Conservation Kit, Forest Service. U.S. Department of Agriculture and your State Forestry Department.

Small-Group Activity—Working Cooperatively

Art—Making Smokey Bear. Place art supplies at the tables for the children to construct a Smokey Bear on a piece of contact board. Materials available will include fuzzy fur for the body, which will be cut in the proper shape, and construction paper, string, yarn, and glue for the features. Have each group work together on one Smokey Bear. After the children finish, have them go over to the rug, where someone will be reading stories until all groups have finished the art project.

Objectives

- To provide an opportunity to use small muscles in the creation of the individual child's image of Smokey Bear.
- To encourage discussion of the fire fighter, fire engine, and safety measures.

Summary

Children need to begin to develop social values and skills in their earliest years. As children become aware of similarities and differences among people, emphasis should *always* be on the ways people are more alike than different. This also helps to prevent the development of biases and prejudices.

As teachers strive to incorporate the perspective of diversity, they must successfully foster genuine respect for *all* children regardless of gender, race, physical abilities, or ethnic orientation. Teachers must also promote attitudes of tolerance and acceptance in order to prevent the acquisition of stereotypes relating to racism, sexism, "handicappism," and other forms of discrimination. Children must be taught positive attitudes, concepts, and skills that enable them to function cooperatively in this diverse society.

It is the professional and moral responsibility of teachers to evaluate their own philosophies regarding diversity, then demonstrate and model how differences are valued and appreciated.

All children must be given opportunities to reach their potential, encouraged to feel valued as members of society, and taught to understand differences among people. They must be taught that discriminatory actions and attitudes are not acceptable; and helped to feel positive identification toward their own gender, race, physical abilities, and ethnic backgrounds.

Teachers must be aware of biases and stereotyping with regard to race, gender, religion, and special needs. Public Laws 94-142 and 99-457 provide direction for identifying and providing educational programs for children who have disabilities. This chapter includes characteristics, teaching strategies, and specialists in such special needs areas as speech and language impairments; mental retardation; hearing impairments; visual impairments; emotional, social, or behavioral problems; chronic illness; learning disabilities; and gifted and talented children.

In creating a diverse curriculum and classroom, teachers must change their attitudes and practices; carefully select books, materials, and resources; expose children to cultural diversities; accept dialect and language diversity; teach differences in occupations and lifestyles; and use cooperative learning as a strategy.

Suggestions for incorporating unit plans and lesson plans into the diversified curriculum have been presented, along with the valuable tool of "webbing" for brainstorming and developing unit ideas.

Student Learning Activities

1. Describe yourself in terms of your own culture. Using professional journals or books, find at least two sources that help you define and understand your own culture. Remember, your culture includes your ethnicity, religion, social class, physical abilities, and gender.

2. Examine and describe some of your own biases. What do you specifically plan to do to overcome these biases?

3. After you have read and studied this chapter, can you think of any additional goals that need to be added to the ones the authors present for developing the perspective of diversity?

4. If you were just setting up a classroom for the first time in your present community, what would be the first five things you would do to begin to develop a diversity perspective?

5. Suppose you are preparing a unit on one of the seasons. How might you include the diversity perspective in your teaching?

6. There are many more activities and experiences appropriate for teaching children concepts relating to other people. Think of at least 10 ideas to add to the list in this chapter.

7. Prepare a unit plan, or web, on one or more of the following: a specific community helper, a type of transportation, homes, similarities among class members, differences among class members. Evaluate your work to see whether you included the diversity perspective.

8. Using one unit plan or web prepared in item 7, prepare a 5-day activity plan following the format suggested on page 67.

9. Observe in a classroom of young children and describe how the diversity perspective was woven into the curriculum, the environment, and discussions or conversations. What changes would you suggest?

10. Evaluate how you think social skills can best be taught. List five things you will do as a teacher to encourage the development of prosocial skills in young children.

11. Observe in a classroom of young children and describe how the teacher assisted the children in developing social skills such as those discussed in this chapter.

12. Prepare a list of possible teacher-made learning materials that focus on teaching children concepts related to other people. Can you think of some that would specifically teach appreciation of people's diversity and respect for other people?

13. Prepare and make at least two of the materials you listed in item 12.

14. Review children's books related to people and their diversities. Add at least five books to

the book list included in this chapter. Bring one book to share in class.

15. With a group of children, implement at least one of the activities and experiences suggested in this chapter or from the list you made in item 6. Evaluate the experience. Did you enjoy the activity? How did the children respond? Would you change your approach another time?

Suggested Resources

Children's Books

Aardema, V. (1991). *Pedro and the padre: A Tale from Jalisco, Mexico.* New York: Dial.

Adoff, A. (1973). *Black is white is tan.* New York: Harper & Row.

Albert, D. (1991). *Where does the trail lead?* New York: Simon & Schuster.

Aliki. (1986). *Corn is maize: The gift of the Indians.* New York: Harper Collins.

Anglund, J. W. (1983). *A friend is someone who likes you.* New York: Harcourt Brace Jovanovich.

Aseltine, L., & Mueller, E. (1986). *I'm deaf and it's okay.* Niles, IL: Whitman.

Bailey, D. (1990). *Cities.* Austin, TX: Steck-Vaughn.

Bailey, D. (1990). *Nomads.* Austin, TX: Steck-Vaughn.

Bailey, D. (1990). *Where we live series: Australia.* Madison, NJ: Steck-Vaughn. (Also included in series: *Hong Kong, India, Trinidad.*)

Balgerman, L. (1991). *Girders and cranes: A skyscraper is built.* Morton Grove, IL: Whitman.

Bang, M. (1983). *Ten, nine, eight.* New York: Greenwillow.

Banks, L. R. (1981). *Indian in the cupboard.* New York: Doubleday.

Baylor, B. (1986). *Hawk, I'm your brother.* New York: Macmillan.

Bellet, J. (1984). *A-B-C-ing: An action alphabet.* New York: Crown.

Birdseye, T. (1990). *A song of stars.* New York: Holiday House.

Bourke, L. (1981) *Handmade ABC reading.* Reading, MA: Addison-Wesley.

Bradman, T. (1992). *It came from outer space.* New York: Dial.

Brown, M. W. (1948) *The little farmer.* New York: Young Scott Books.

Brown, M. W. (1952). *The little fireman.* New York: Young Scott Books.

Brown, M. W. (1979). *The dead bird.* New York: Dell.

Brown, R. (1988). *100 words about working.* San Diego: Gulliver.

Brown, T. (1984). *Someone special, just like you.* New York: Holt, Rinehart & Winston.

Burton, V. L. (1937). *Choo, choo.* Boston: Houghton Mifflin.

Burton, V. L. (1974). *Kate and the big snow.* Boston: Houghton Mifflin.

Burton, V. L. (1977). *Mike Milligan and his steam shovel.* Boston: Houghton Mifflin.

Caines, J. (1982). *Just us women.* New York: Harper & Row.

Cairo, S. (1985). *Our brother has Down's syndrome.* Buffalo, NY: Firefly Books.

Cameron, A. (1981). *The stories Julian tells.* New York: Pantheon.

Carle, E. (1971). *Do you want to be my friend?* New York: Harper Collins.

Children's Television Workshop. (1980). *Sign language fun.* New York: Random House.

Christiansen, C. B. (1989). *My mother's house, my father's house.* New York: Atheneum.

Clifton, L. (1970). *The black ABCs.* New York: Holt.

Clifton, L. (1980). *My friend Jacob.* New York: Elsevier/Dutton.

Clifton, L. (1983). *Everett Anderson's goodbye.* New York: Holt.

Cohen, M. (1967). *Will I have a friend?* New York: Macmillan.

Cohen, M. (1971). *Best friends.* New York: Macmillan.

Cohen, M. (1974). *The new teacher.* New York: Macmillan.

Crews, D. (1991). *Big Mama's.* New York: Greenwillow.

Daly, N. (1985). *Not so fast songololo*. New York: Atheneum.

De Paola, T. (1981). *Now one foot, now the other*. New York: Putnam.

DePoix, C. (1973). *Jo, Flo, and Yolanda*. Carrboro, NC: Lollipop Power.

DeRegniers, B. S. (1971). *May I bring a friend?* New York: Macmillan.

Dorros, A. (1991). *Abuela*. New York: Dutton.

Fassler, J. (1975). *Howie helps himself*. Niles, IL: Whitman.

Fassler, J. (1983). *My grandpa died today*. New York: Human Sciences Press.

Feelings, M. (1971). *Moja means one*. New York: Dial.

Feeney, S. (1985). *Hawaii is a rainbow*. Honolulu: University of Hawaii Press.

Florian, D. (1991). *A carpenter*. New York: Greenwillow.

Florian, D. (1991). *A potter*. New York: Greenwillow.

Florian, D. (1991). *An auto mechanic*. New York: Greenwillow.

Frank, D. (1974). *About handicaps: An open family book for parents and children together*. New York: Walker.

Gibbons, G. (1985). *Fill it up! All about service stations*. New York: Crowell.

Gill, S. (1987). *The Alaska Mother Goose and other north country nursery rhymes*. Homer, AK: Paws IV.

Greenberg, P. (1954). *People aren't potatoes*. Washington, DC: Growth Program Press.

Greenfield, E. (1974). *She come bringing me that little baby girl*. New York: Lippincott.

Greenfield, E. (1975). *Me and Nessie*. New York: Harper & Row.

Greenfield, E. (1978). *Honey, I love*. New York: Harper & Row.

Greenfield, E. (1980). *Darlene*. New York: Methuen.

Greenfield, E. (1981). *Daydreamers*. New York: Dial.

Greenfield, E. (1991). *Night on Neighborhood Street*. New York: Dial.

Hamilton, V. (1974). *M. C. Higgins, the great*. New York: Macmillan.

Hamilton, V. (1988). *In the beginning: Creative stories from around the world*. New York: Harcourt Brace Jovanovich.

Henroid, L. (1982). *Grandma's wheelchair*. Niles, IL: Whitman.

Highwater, J. (1981). *Moonsong lullaby*. New York: Lee & Shepard.

Hopkins, L. B. (Ed.). (1986). *Best friends*. New York: Harper Collins.

Howard, E. (1988). *The train to Lulu's*. New York: Bradbury.

Hoyt-Goldsmith, D. (1990). *Totem pole*. New York: Holiday House.

Isadora, R. (1990). *Babies*. New York: Greenwillow.

Isadora, R. (1990). *Friends*. New York: Greenwillow.

Jeffers, S. (1991). *Brother Eagle, Sister Sky*. New York: Dial.

Jensen, V. A. (1983). *Catching*. New York: Putnam.

Johnson, A. (1989). *Tell me a story, Mama*. New York: Orchard.

Johnson, A. (1990). *Do like Kyla*. New York: Orchard.

Joseph, L. (1990). *Coconut kind of day*. New York: Lothrop, Lee & Shepard.

Josse, B. M. (1991). *Mama, do you love me?* San Francisco: Chronicle Books.

Kellogg, S. (1990). *Best friends*. New York: Dial.

Koss, A. G. (1991). *City critters around the world*. Los Angeles: Price Stern Sloan.

Larch, D. W. (1986). *Father Gander nursery rhymes*. Santa Barbara, CA: Advocacy.

Larson, H. (1978). *Don't forget Tom*. New York: Crowell.

Lasker, J. (1974). *He's my brother*. Niles, IL: Whitman.

Lenski, L. (1937). *The little sailboat*. New York: McKay.

Lenski, L. (1938). *Little airplane*. New York: McKay.

Lenski, L. (1940). *The little train*. New York: McKay.

Lenski, L. (1942). *The little auto*. New York: McKay.

Lenski, L. (1946). *The little fire engine*. New York: Oxford University Press.

Lerner, M. R. (1960). *Red man, white man, African chief: The story of skin color*. Minneapolis: Lerner Co.

Litchfield, A. (1976). *A button in her ear*. Niles, IL: Whitman.

Litchfield, A. (1977). *A cane in her hand*. Niles, IL: Whitman.

Litchfield, A. (1980). *Words in our hands*. Niles, IL: Whitman.

Littledale, F. (1984). *The elves and the shoemaker*. New York: Scholastic.

Lobel, A. (1970). *Frog and Toad are friends*. New York: Harper Collins.

Locker, T. (1991). *The land of the gray wolf*. New York: Dial.

Macdonald, M. (1992). *Little hippo gets glasses*. New York: Dial.

Mandelbaum, P. (1990). *You be me, I'll be you*. New York: Kane/Miller.

Martin, B., Jr., & Archambault, J. (1987). *Knots on a counting rope*. New York: Holt.

McDermott, G. (1977). *Arrow to the sun: A Pueblo Indian tale*. New York: Puffin.

McKissack, P. C. (1986). *Flossie and the fox*. New York: Dial.

Merriam, E. (1989). *Mommies at work*. New York: Simon & Schuster.

Miller, M. (1990). *Who uses this?* New York: Greenwillow.

Musgrove, M. (1976). *Ashanti to Zulu*. New York: Dial.

Nomura, T. (1991). *Grandpa's town*. New York: Kane/Miller.

Ortiz, S. (1988). *The people shall continue*. San Francisco: Children's Book Press.

Peterson, J. (1977). *I have a sister, my sister is deaf*. New York: Harper & Row.

Piper, W. (1980). *The little engine that could*. New York: Platt & Munk.

Porte, B. A. (1991). *Harry gets an uncle*. New York: Greenwillow.

Powers, M. E. (1986). *Our teacher's in a wheelchair*. Niles: IL: Whitman.

Provensen, A., & Provensen, M. (1983). *The glorious flight*. New York: Viking.

Quinsey, M. B. (1986). *Why does that man have such a big nose?* Seattle: Parenting Press.

Rabe, B. (1981). *The balancing girl*. New York: Dutton.

Rockwell, A. (1986). *Fire engines*. New York: Dutton.

Rockwell, A. (1988). *Trains*. New York: Dutton.

Rogers, J. (1988). *Runaway Mittens*. New York: Greenwillow.

Romanova, N. (1985). *Once there was a tree*. New York: Dial.

Rosenberg, M. (1983). *My friend Leslie*. New York: Lothrop, Lee & Shepard.

Ross, L. H. (1991). *Buba Leah and her paper children*. Philadelphia: Jewish Publication Society.

San Souci, R. D. (1987). *The enchanted tapestry*. New York: Dial.

Sargent, S., & Wirt, D. A. (1983). *My favorite place*. New York: Abingdon.

Scarry, R. (1972). *Richard Scarry's hop aboard, here we go*. New York: Western.

Scarry, R. (1974). *Richard Scarry's cars and trucks and things that go*. New York: Western.

Schlank, C. H., & Metzker, B. (1989). *Martin Luther King, Jr.: A biography for young children*. Henrietta, NY: Rochester Association of Young Children.

Sierra, J., & Kaminski, R. (1991). *Multiculture folktales: Stories to tell young children*. Phoenix, AZ: Oryx.

Stein, S. B. (1974). *About handicaps*. New York: Walker.

Steiner, B. (1988). *Whale brother*. New York: Walker.

Steptoe, J. (1971). *Train ride*. New York: Harper & Row.

Steptoe, J. (1987). *Mulfaro's beautiful daughters*. New York: Lothrop, Lee & Shepard.

Steptoe, J. (1988). *Baby says*. New York: Lothrop, Lee & Shepard.

Stolz, M. (1991). *Go fish*. New York: Harper Collins.

Torre, B. L. (1990). *The luminous pearl*. New York: Orchard.

Udry, J. (1966). *What Mary Jo shared*. New York: Scholastic.

Vaughn, J. (1990) *Where we live series: Greece*. Madison, NJ: Steck-Vaughn. (Also included in series: *Russia*.)

Viorst, J. (1971). *The tenth good thing about Barney*. New York: Atheneum.

Wall, L. M. (1991). *Judge Rabbit and the tree spirit*. San Francisco: Children's Book Press.

Walter, M. P. (1989). *Habari gani?* New York: Lothrop, Lee & Shepard Books.

Weissman, J. (1981). *All about me/Let's be friends*. Mt. Rainier, MD: Gryphon House.

Welsh-Smith, S. (1988). *Andy: An Alaskan tale*. New York: Cambridge University Press.

White, E. B. (1952). *Charlotte's web*. New York: Harper & Bros.

Williams, V. B. (1990). *"More, more, more," said the baby*. New York: Greenwillow.

Wilson, S. (1991). *Garage song*. New York: Simon & Schuster.

Wolf, B. (1974). *Don't feel sorry for Paul*. New York: Harper & Row.

Zaffo, G. (1950). *The big book of real trains*. New York: Grosset & Dunlap.

Zaffo, G. (1950). *The big book of real trucks*. New York: Grosset & Dunlap.

Zaffo, G. (1969). *Giant book of things in space*. New York: Doubleday.

Zhensun, Z. (1991). *A young painter: The life and paintings of Wang Yani—China's extraordinary young artist*. New York: Scholastic.

Bibliographical Collections

Bogdanoff, R. F., & Dolch, E. T. (1979). Old games for young children: A link to our heritage. *Young Children, 34,* 37–45.

Buttlar, L., & Wynar, L. (1977). *Building ethnic collections: An annotated guide for school media centers and public libraries.* Littleton, CO: Libraries Unlimited.

Cooper, T. T., & Ratner, M. (1974). *Many lands cooking: An international cookbook for girls and boys.* New York: Thomas Y. Crowell with U. S. Committee for UNICEF.

Council on Interracial Books for Children. (1966–present). *Interracial books for children: Bulletin.* New York: Council on Interracial Books for Children.

Griffin, L. (Compiler). (1970). *Multi-ethnic books for young children.* Washington, DC: National Association for the Education of Young Children.

Maehr, J. (n.d.). *The Middle East: An annotated bibliography of literature for children.* Urbana: ERIC/ECE, University of Illinois.

McWhirter, M. (Ed.). (1970). *Games enjoyed by children around the world.* Philadelphia: American Friends Service Committee.

Mills, J. (Ed.). (1975). *The black world in literature for children: A bibliography of print and nonprint materials.* Atlanta: Atlanta University School of Library Science.

Price, C. (1969). *Happy days, birthdays, names days, and growing days.* New York: UNICEF.

Rollock, B. (Compiler). (1974). *The black experience in children's books.* New York: New York Public Library.

Seattle Public School District No. 1. (n.d.). *Rainbow ABC's.* Huntington Beach, CA: Creative Teaching Press.

Seattle Public School District No. 1. (n.d.). *Rainbow activities book.* Huntington Beach, CA: Creative Teaching Press.

UNICEF (n.d.). *Folk toys around the world: And how to make them.* New York: UNICEF.

Records, Tapes, and Cassettes

Avni, F. *Mostly matzah.* Lemonstone Records.

Big black train. On *The small singer* (Album 1). Bowmar-Noble.

Billowing sails. On *More singing fun* (Album 1). Bowmar-Noble.

A *child's look at . . . what it means to be Jewish.* Kids' Records.

Chug, chug, chug. On *The small singer* (Album 1). Bowmar-Noble.

Fire truck. On *The small singer* (Album 1). Bowmar-Noble.

Hopping around from place to place. Educational Activities.

I can fly. On *The small singer* (Album 1). Bowmar-Noble.

Lakota/Dakota flute music. (Played by K. Locke.) Featherstone.

The laundry and the bakery story. Scholastic Book Services. (R7671)

Let's be friends. Tickle Tune Typhoon.

Little lonely sailboat. On *More singing fun* (Album 1). Bowmar-Noble.

Little old train. On *More singing fun* (Album 1). Bowmar-Noble.

More learning as we play. Folkways Records.

Musical media show. UNICEF.

My community. David C. Cook.

My mommy is a doctor. Educational Activities. (AR580 or AC580)

Sing around the world. Miss Jackie.

Sing, children, sing. UNICEF.

Sing, children, sing I—U.S.A. UNICEF.

Sing, children, sing II—Austria. UNICEF.

Sing, children, sing III—British Isles. UNICEF.

Sing, children, sing IV—France. UNICEF.

Songs and rhythms from near and far. Educational Activities.

Songs to grow on. Folkways Records.

Travellin' with Ella Jenkins (a bilingual journey). Educational Activities.

Trucks. On *More singing fun* (Album 1). Bowmar-Noble.

Pictures

Cherokee alphabet card. Cherokee Publications, Cherokee, NC.

Children around the world. The Child's World.

Children in America. The Child's World.

Children in school. UNICEF.

Communities provide resources. Society for Visual Education.

Communities provide services. Society for Visual Education.

Dairy helpers. Society for Visual Education.

Fire department helpers. Society for Visual Education.

Going places by air. The Child's World.

Going places by land. The Child's World.

Going places by water. The Child's World.

Home and community helpers. David C. Cook.

Hospital helpers. Society for Visual Education.

My community. David C. Cook.

People who come to my home. The Child's World.

Police department helpers. Society for Visual Education.

Postal helpers. Society for Visual Education.

Supermarket helpers. Society for Visual Education.

Transportation. David C. Cook.

What is a community? Society for Visual Education.

Also available: several sets on ethnic groups and children around the world. David C. Cook.

Multimedia Kits

Air transportation. Eye Gate Media.

The development of the Spanish language. Eye Gate Media.

Ethnic holidays. Walt Disney.

Holidays around the world. Walt Disney.

Water transportation. Eye Gate Media.

Films, Filmstrips, and Videos

American Indians. WorldWide Slides. (Viewmaster reel)

Appalachian children. Campus Film.

The autistic child: A behavioral approach. CRM/McGraw-Hill.

Child care in three cultures. Campus Films.

Child day care in China. Campus Films.

Childhood problems worldwide. UNICEF.

Children near and far. Eye Gate Media.

Christmas in many lands. National Geographic.

Early childhood mainstreaming series. Campus Films.

Education for All Handicapped Act (P.L. 94-142). Eye Gate Media.

Eskimos of Alaska. WorldWide Slides. (Viewmaster reel)

Families are different and alike. Coronet Films.

Families: Food and eating. Churchill Films.

Families: A series. Churchill Films.

Going to the doctor, dentist, and hospital. Eye Gate Media.

Growing up with deafness. Campus Films.

Helpers at our school. Coronet Films.

Holidays and celebrations around the world. National Geographic.

International Year of the Child. UNICEF.

Laton: a handicapped child in need. Campus Films.

The life of the American Indian. National Geographic.

The little engine that could. Coronet Films.

Mexican American children. Campus Films.

Minorities and majorities. Eye Gate Media.

Montana Indian children. Campus Films.

Multicultural folktales. Educational Activities.

Multicultural living experiences. Eye Gate Media.

My new friend series (special needs). Eye Gate Media.

Neighborhoods change. Coronet Films.

North America: Land of many peoples. National Geographic.

People serving your community. National Geographic.

Place and transportation. Eye Gate Media.

School children in the U.S.A. Eye Gate Media.

Special children/different needs. Campus Films.

Special children/special needs. Campus Films.

Stories from many lands and cultures. (31 different). Weston Woods Studios.

That the deaf may speak. Campus Films.

Transportation around the world. Coronet Films.

Walk safe! Young America. Pyramid Films.

What is a neighborhood? Coronet Films.

Workers who come to our house. Coronet Films.

five

Myself and My Family

Introduction

To be able to relate to and work effectively with others, one must first be able to relate positively to oneself. Unfortunately, some people care so little about themselves that they are unable to care for others. Children come to the classroom with various backgrounds, values, and points of view regarding themselves and their family. They must be accepted as they are and encouraged to like themselves. Indeed, children need concrete experiences, moments, and ideas directed toward building positive feelings and attitudes about themselves.

The basis of a high-quality program in early childhood is promoting feelings of self-esteem and dignity in each child. As caregivers, we are better able to help children develop positive feelings about themselves if we understand some basic generalizations and suggestions regarding building children's self-esteem.

It is also important that we recognize situations causing stress, how children react to stress, and how they can be helped to cope with stress.

Children's families are very much a part of how they feel about themselves; and even though family structures and makeup might vary, still the family's role in facilitating character education is paramount.

A Healthy Self-Esteem

One's attitude toward oneself is usually referred to as *self-esteem.* Children's self-esteem affects their actions, behavior, learning, playing, and how they relate to others. Self-esteem is a feeling or attitude of personal worth, and it determines the extent to which each child believes himself or herself to be capable, attractive, worthy, responsible, important, and lovable. "It is the core of each happy human being" ("Ideas that work," 1988, p. 57).

A person with healthy self-esteem:

Emotional health and well-being, aspects of a child's self-esteem, are often evidenced in facial expressions, physical actions, and general behavior.

- Accepts the self and limitations while trusting the self to cope with most situations that occur.
- Accepts and assumes responsibility.
- Is proud of successes and accomplishments but does not have to use them in proving the self to others.

- Approaches new challenges, assignments, and experiences with enthusiasm.
- Has a broad range of emotions and feelings, but the general attitude and feelings focus on the positive.
- Recognizes that an innate sense of self-esteem determines how he or she feels and acts.

A person with unhealthy self-esteem:

- Avoids situations or experiences in which he or she may not be successful.
- Feels incompetent, unsuccessful, untalented, unloved, and powerless.
- Blames others for anything that goes wrong.
- Tears down or views negatively any strengths or talents he or she may have.
- Easily gives in to pressure from others.
- May have problems such as drug and alcohol abuse, depression, hostility, or an inability to make and keep friends. ("Ideas that work," 1988). "Low self-esteem poisons a person" ("Ideas that work," 1988, p. 57).

Generalizations Regarding Self-Esteem

- Our behavior matches our self-image. Much of children's behavior, both positive and negative, is influenced by the way they view themselves, that is, their self-image.
- The significant people in children's lives have a great influence on how children see themselves. Children tend to view themselves as they think others see them. Others provide a mirror image, or reflect to children a view of themselves (Kostelnik, Stein, & Whiren, 1988).
- A child cannot grow in confidence and self-esteem without positive feelings, without being praised for appropriate behavior, accomplishments, and successes. Warm and loving approval from others is essential to the development of positive self-esteem.
- Children with healthy self-esteem are poised, confident, and pleasant to be with. Their social skills are generally good. They are less

influenced by peers and tend to make better decisions.

- Whenever an act results in a feeling of satisfaction, that act is likely to be repeated. Within each child, there is an innate need for attention, preferably positive; but if there is no attention for positive behavior, children soon become conditioned to misbehaving in order to receive attention, even if it is negative attention.
- Self-esteem affects the relationships, actions, interactions, and play of children. It influences stability, integrity, and creativity. Creative activities involve risk, and being able to take a risk requires self-confidence. Therefore, to be able to respond creatively, one must be able to trust that those one likes and loves will accept one through both failures and successes. Also, a child who is overly concerned with success, approval, and acceptance will not venture a risk, but will find security in assuming that it is better not to try at all than to try and fail.
- What we are and how we feel about the child has more effect than anything we do. Feelings are modeled—caught, not taught.
- Children with low self-esteem feel isolated, unloved, and defenseless. They often feel powerless to attain goals they desire in life and are often withdrawn and passive about life and experiences.
- Children with low self-esteem are more influenced by the negative experiences in their lives and allow these experiences to control their feelings and perceptions of the environment.
- Because we cannot give away what we do not possess, because we cannot teach what we have neither learned nor understood, because we cannot build with materials we have not purchased, we cannot strengthen children with more positive self-esteem until we first find the courage, insight, wisdom, and determination to strengthen and build our own self-esteem. Thus, the stronger and richer the teacher's own self-esteem, the more successful she or he will be in creating like attitudes and concepts in the children being taught.
- Children and parents need to learn that "I can" is more important than IQ. Self-confidence can often compensate for deficits in other areas.

Positive self-images are developed as children learn more about themselves and have numerous successes resulting in increased confidence and a sense of self-worth. This, in turn, tends to give children the feeling that they are important to others and contributors to society. At the same time, children also develop feelings of the importance of and need for others. Children, in fact, cannot accept others until they accept themselves. Esteem for others begins with esteem for, and acceptance of, oneself.

Suggestions for Building Children's Self-Esteem

- Be honest, sincere, and consistent in expressing feelings.
- Value the children's work and efforts.
- Accept each child for himself or herself. This means not only accepting but searching for individual differences. As you assist children in discovering and accepting their strengths and limitations, help them capitalize on strengths and work with limitations that can be changed.
- Do whatever is possible to help children overcome any physical problems, but also help them accept those things that cannot be changed.
- Praise children for specific efforts and accomplishments. Encourage the development of skills.
- Encourage children to help, build, and support others. This results in positive feelings of joy and internal satisfaction, in addition to healthy social skill development. There seems to be a close relationship between early social

adjustment in the peer group and later adult adjustment.

- Independence breeds self-esteem; allow children to do things for themselves. Children gain confidence in themselves as they accomplish new developmental tasks. Giving children responsibilities, and trusting them to complete these tasks, helps build capabilities and self-confidence. Children learn to make competent decisions by being allowed to make decisions and accept responsibility for them.
- Smile and be cheerful, happy, courteous, and positive with children. These attitudes must be genuine and come from within; remember, your attitude is the key.
- Your actions must convey the worth and value of the children. Little acts of kindness, individual attention, and positive deeds become very important. For example, a short note or phone call expressing a positive feeling or congratulations for a new accomplishment can make a child feel valuable and accepted.
- Your words make a difference. "Children perceive themselves as worthy and competent or the opposite" by what teachers say and the tone in which they say it (Kostelnik et al., 1988, p. 29). Words or phrases such as "Congratulations," "I'm proud of you," "I'm sorry," "Excuse me," and "Thank you," should be included frequently in conversations with children. Phrases either build up or tear down, depending on how they are worded. For instance, put the "problem" on the action, rather than directing it toward the child. Say "That water fountain is too high," rather than "You are too short to reach the water fountain"; "That shoe is too hard to tie," rather than "You are too little to tie your shoe"; "That water is too deep," rather than "You're too young to go in the water."
- Listen to the child in order to understand the child.

- Invite the child to sit by or interact with you (Kostelnik et al., 1988).

Children's emotional well-being largely hinges on how well they like themselves. Psychotherapists have found that the most common denominator of mental health problems is a deficiency of self-esteem. Regardless of the symptoms, most children with such problems suffer feelings of self-doubt, inadequacy, guilt, and helplessness. In their efforts to defend themselves against self-esteem deficiency, they may develop problems in behavior, motivation, and even physical health. Teachers working with young children need to do everything they can to inculcate in each child feelings of importance and self-respect. In addition, teachers should help children understand that this basic psychological need is, to a degree, determined by the children's own attitudes toward themselves and their choice of values and goals. In other words, it is not totally up to parents and teachers to build this feeling; children must add their share of the building blocks—they need to find themselves.

Leslie and Megan were playing hide-and-go-seek and had hidden from Kyle and Curtis. When Kyle and Curtis became frightened because they could not find Leslie and Megan, the four children decided to play hide-and-go-seek all together at the same time. They covered their eyes and counted "One, two . . . nine, ten." Then Megan instructed, "Come on, let's go find ourselves!"

Each Child Is Unique

Most of the foundation concepts presented in this chapter show that children in many ways are alike—and in many ways are not alike. Remember to stress their similarities more than their differences. From the suggested teaching approaches, children will gain insight into their feelings, names, roles, families, friends, abilities, foods, homes, clothes, travels, and many other characteristics. Children must sense that they are unique and special.

I Have Feelings

I have feelings and you do too,
I'd like to share a few with you.
Sometimes I'm happy and sometimes I'm sad,
Sometimes I'm scared, and sometimes mad.
The most important feeling you see, is that
  I'm proud of being me.

I feel just right in the skin I wear,
There's no one like me anywhere.
I feel just right in the skin I wear,
There's no one like me anywhere.

No one sees the things I see,
Behind my eyes is only me.
And no one knows where my feelings begin
For there's only me inside my skin.
No one does what I can do,
I'll be me, and you be you.

I feel just right in the skin I wear,
There's no one like me anywhere.
I feel just right in the skin I wear,
There's no one like me anywhere.

It's a wonderful thing how everyone owns
Just enough skin to cover his bones.
My dad's would be too big to fit,
I'd be all wrinkled inside of it.
Baby sister's would be much too small,
It wouldn't cover me up at all.

I feel just right in the skin I wear,
There's no one like me anywhere.
I feel just right in the skin I wear,
There's no one like me anywhere.

Stress in Children

One precursor of self-esteem deficiency is stress in young children. Honig (1986a) lists several components of stress in young children: "a stressor, how a child perceives that stressor, the coping resources a child has, the support systems available internally and externally for the child, and the child's skill in making coping or adjusting responses when stressed (p. 52). A stressor is "an acute life event or a chronic environmental situation that causes disequilibrium" (Blom, Cheney, & Snoddy, 1986, p. 9). Such stressors may include situations, events, or people and are not necessarily good or bad; they are just particular demands. Variables associated with different kinds of stress in children's lives include age, sex, intellectual capacity, neurological sturdiness, living environment, socioeconomic status, family events or situations, and parenting practices (Honig, 1986a). Stress is produced by the very process of living—many events in our lives over which we have little or no control. One of the great stressors in the lives of young children is hurrying them—from one location to another, to get ready, to do well on work or assignments, to grow up. To counteract this, we can either decrease our demands or increase our support.

Often the cause of the stress response in children is not the actual situation or person, but the child's attitude toward that particular situation or person. For example, stress in young children can be created by fears of unreal things such as monsters or witches. Children misconstrue situations, events, or conversations to mean something they do not mean. This results in worry, anxiety, concern, and stress. Children also experience personal fears and concerns that result in stress. Separation itself is not stressful and harmful to children, but too much separation too soon causes stress (Elkind, 1981). When children become surrounded with fears, anxieties, quarreling, complaining, bickering, and other potentially anxious situations, they can experience emotional overload.

School often creates many stressors for children. There is competition for grades, high expectations, demand for excellence, and social concerns. At every educational level, there is a feeling that we must master certain concepts at this particular level; that is, we must get through this material by a specific time. On the other hand, school can stress some children if they find it dull, boring, and unchallenging. Children in this situation become fatigued, inattentive, un-interested, and stressed. Adults suffering job burnout, especially when their work is meaning-less and repetitious, react with the same symptoms.

Television and movies can create stress by giving children more information than they can understand and information that is too complex. This results in a discrepancy between the amount of information children have and the amount they can process (Elkind, 1988). Children between the ages of 2 and 5 years spend an average of 28 hours a week watching television. These estimates do not include VCR use, which is found in over two-thirds of all households with a television (Nielson Media Research, 1990).

Children's Reactions to Stress

Considering individual differences among children, remember that what may cause stress in one child will not necessarily cause stress in another. Children respond to stress in various ways. They have different coping abilities, as do adults, so what causes one child to fall apart may make another child stronger. The child's reaction relates in part to the notion of accumulation: in one child, stress and anxiety build up faster than the natural adaptation process can handle; another child naturally adapts to the stress. How children respond and react to stress is an individual matter.

We do know some of the signs that suggest that children may be experiencing undue stress. These include:

Crying, fussing

Reverting to less mature behaviors

Nervous habits such as twisting or pulling hair; sighing deeply; nail biting; thumb sucking; or tapping feet, fingers, or pencils

Increased irritability, sometimes to points of tantrums

Lethargy or withdrawal from activities

Subtle reactions, such as a strained look about the eyes, a tightened mouth, or a furrowed brow

Excessive energy, restlessness, or aggression

Inability to stay on the task or concentrate

Nausea, eating disorders

Aches: head, stomach, neck, back, tooth, muscle

Pounding heart

Susceptibility to colds, illness

Difficulty in breathing; asthma

Proneness to injury or accidents

Tiredness

Depression

Nervousness, tenseness

Forgetfulness

Difficulty sleeping and staying awake

Uncommon personality or behavior patterns

Picking at scabs or sores

Frequent physical/verbal/emotional outbursts

There are also some children who keep all the stress and symptoms of stress inside, learning to cover up.

Helping Children Cope with Stress

There is much literature on helping children cope with stress. The atmosphere and feeling tone surrounding the child are vital. Listen to children and encourage them to communicate. Talking about the "worst thing that could happen" or asking them to "Tell me what is worrying you" helps children express such feelings openly. Care for the child: With loving guidance, the child can be emotionally equipped to face whatever life brings. Understand and accept (and sometimes encourage) crying and tears. Tears shed for emotional reasons are chemically different from those shed because of irritations to the eyes. It is possible that emotional tears remove toxins from the body (Solter, 1992). "Crying seems to be a healing mechanism, a natural repair kit that every person

Crying is one way in which a child handles stress, and it actually has healing qualities.

has. It allows people to cope with stress" (Solter, 1992, p. 66). Other suggestions for helping children cope with stress include the following:

Reading

Riding in cars, in wagons, on bicycles or tricycles

Lying down, resting, taking a nap

Listening to music, playing music, singing, whistling, humming

Daydreaming, mental imagery, positive self-talk

Breathing deeper and slower

Laughter and humor

Slowing the pace down

Video games, computer activities, movies, television

Physical contact—hugging, touching, holding

Pets—playing, watching, petting

Constructing or building

Eating, chewing gum or soft candy

Swinging (playground, lawn, hammock)

Warm baths

Art activities and materials

Speaking quietly or softly to the child

Physical activity

Playing with a friend

Consistency, routines, schedules, limits

Honesty, openness from others

Talking, drawing, or writing about concerns

Planting and caring for bush, tree, flower, plant

Training in physical and mental relaxation or self-induced relaxation skills tend to reduce stress and its effects on children (Margolis, 1987). For example, one technique is meditation; the teacher's primary function is to provide a quiet, comfortable environment for relaxation and meditation (Margolis, 1987). Another technique is progressive muscle relaxation, because one cannot be simultaneously relaxed and stressed, and because mental relaxation is a natural consequence of physical relaxation. By tensing and relaxing muscle groups, children can learn to relax muscles when necessary (Margolis, 1987). Another technique, visual imagery, encourages children to imagine a peaceful and happy scene or experience. Or they can imagine a warm ball of liquid gold that starts from the top of their head and slowly flows down their whole body. This visual imagery can be turned into creative brainstorming as children imagine similar kinds of things while both their minds and bodies relax.

Another way of teaching children to deal with stress is to encourage children to use positive, rather than negative, self-talk. Train them to think that "I can" instead of "I can't." Have them brainstorm positive self-talk—positive attitudes and ideas that they think about themselves. Help them clarify their values by asking "Is it worth worrying about right now?" or "Will my worrying about it solve it?"

Help children develop a sense of humor and enjoy laughing. During the early childhood years, they enjoy telling riddles and "knock-knock" jokes; they can learn that it is fun and relaxing to laugh at and enjoy a good joke. One clinical and consulting psychologist calls himself the World's One and Only Joyologist, and explains that his favorite motto is "If it's not fun, I don't want to do it." Steve Wilson tells us "that teachers who encourage laughter in their classes have children who learn quickly, retain more, and have fewer classroom problems." He continues by reminding us that "we demonstrate through our behavior and our own freedom of speech how to minimize tensions with a joke; how to loosen uptight, closed-in thinking systems with good-natured joking ..." (Chenfeld, 1990, pp. 56, 59).

Children should be encouraged to eat a healthy diet with foods from the basic food groups. They should be surrounded with adults who model relaxed living. The curriculum and feeling tone in the classroom should model happy, peaceful living. This atmosphere will not only affect the children's feelings in a positive way but also influence their attitudes toward, and treatment of, others in the classroom. Faith that things will work out can "be sustained, even under adverse circumstances, if children encounter people who give meaning to their lives and a reason for commitment and caring" (Werner, 1984, p. 72).

Character Education

Changes in family structure and makeup are influenced by time, economy, society, culture, education, crisis, and many other situations. One aspect of the family that never changes, however, is the role it plays in assisting children to develop positive character traits. *Character* involves possessing and demonstrating such qualities as honesty, courage, compassion, integrity, industriousness, and patriotism. In a poll addressing family values in the United States, the following were identified as the 10 most important character traits: being responsible, providing emotional support, showing respect for others, having a happy marriage, having faith in God, living up to potential, following a moral code, earning a good living, helping the community, and being free (Massachusetts Mutual Insurance Company, 1991). Since the family is the first unit of society to which the child is introduced, it has paramount responsibility for encouraging character education of young children. Skanchy (n.d.) includes the following basic principles as necessary ingredients of character education: worth and potential, rights and responsibilities, fairness

Character education includes helping children develop feelings of empathy for others and being willing to cooperate with and help others.

and justice, care and consideration, effort and excellence, social responsibility, and personal integrity.

As children develop these character traits and internalize them as worthwhile values, their ability to function and behave as responsible, valuable citizens rapidly expands. *Values* represent standards or principles of worth. When people value something, they deem it worth doing, having, or trying to attain. Many values are explicitly taught or implicitly caught within both the family unit and classroom. Through example and specific curriculum activities, teachers and families attempt to teach responsible behavior and strive to help children acquire a sound set of values with which to make decisions. Children learn fair play, justice, and morality from how they are treated by their families, teachers, and peers. The foundation for strong values rests in empowering children with the following principles:

1. One must develop self-esteem and courage to defend one's convictions, values, and beliefs.
2. One must have the self-motivation to set and accomplish individual goals.
3. One must be tolerant of, and show respect for, *all* other people regardless of their gender, race, social class, or abilities.
4. One must have the ability to judge right from wrong as defined by laws and to make moral judgments.
5. One must be honest with self and others.
6. One must do his or her best and act responsibly.

Approach to Teaching

Concepts and Ideas for Teaching

1. I am a person, and I have a name.
2. I have a body.
   a. Children learn about body parts.
   b. They learn how and why to care for various parts—hair, teeth, nails.

3. I have different physical characteristics.
   a. Freckles.
   b. Glasses, contacts.
   c. Brown eyes.
   d. Red hair.
   e. Braces worn on teeth.
   f. Braces worn on leg(s).
4. I am growing.
   a. I weigh more than I did a year ago.
   b. I am taller than I was a year ago.
   c. I was once a baby.
5. I am sometimes sick.
   a. Colds.
   b. Diseases.
   c. Headaches.
6. I have strengths, talents, and capabilities, but I also have some weaknesses.
   a. What are my talents?
   b. What are my strengths?
   c. What are my weaknesses?
7. I have some goals for myself. I would like to be . . .

8. I have a particular race and nationality.
9. I have feelings, and they are always acceptable, but I must learn to express them in acceptable ways.
10. I have unique thoughts and ideas that are important.
11. I live in a neighborhood.
12. I live in a city (on a farm, in a small town), in a state that is part of a nation that is part of the world.
13. I have favorite
    a. Songs.
    b. Colors.
    c. Seasons.
    d. Friends.
    e. Things I like to do.

f. Television programs.

g. Movies or videos.

h. Holidays.

i. Foods.

j. Things to collect.

k. Subjects in school.

14. When I grow up, I want to be . . .

15. I have a family.

a. My family takes care of me.

b. I learn many things from my family.

16. My family is unique.

a. I may have one or two parents.

b. I may have brothers and sisters.

c. I may have a grandmother and grandfather.

d. I may have cousins, uncles, aunts.

e. My family lives in a house, apartment, shelter.

17. I have fun with my family.

a. We play together.

b. We go places together.

c. We work together.

18. My family sometimes changes.

a. Divorce.

b. Death.

c. Parent remarriage.

d. Illness, disease.

e. Move to a different home, city.

f. Job changes.

g. New baby.

h. Adoption.

19. I depend on many people and need the help of many people.

20. There are many elderly people in my community; I can serve and help them.

Activities and Experiences

1. Take photographs of individual children, especially in action shots. Photograph the entire child, not just the head. These photographs can be used to build the self-concept, and can be displayed on the child's locker or desk.

2. Take or collect photographs of children with their families. These can be used to discuss family characteristics, diversity, similarities, and differences. Remember: Always stress how families and individual children are more alike than different.

3. Provide mirrors for the children to use—on the tables for use during free play and on the walls in various locations. Every classroom should have a full-length mirror.

4. From magazines, children can cut out pictures that they like or that remind them of themselves and/or their families.

5. Draw body images of the children. The children lie on a sheet of butcher paper while a teacher (or another child, if older) draws around the body shape. After being decorated, the images are displayed around the room so that the size and shape variations of the children can easily be observed. As a variation, the children can cut body parts from magazines or newspapers for collaging onto the drawing.

6. Create songs (words and music), with the children initiating ideas. These songs should become an important part of daily singing times.

7. Make hand or foot prints in plaster. They can be compared with those of other children in the classroom, and also with the hands and feet of parents or other family members.

8. Do posters and sheets titled "All About Me" or "This Is Me." Include such topics as My Favorite Things to Do, My Family, A Picture of Me, Physical Characteristics, and so on. These could be put together into a booklet.

9. Set up areas for makeup and cosmetic exploration, as well as for dressing in clothes representing various roles.

10. Put articles of clothing in a sack or box (gloves, boots, sweater, hat, sandals, swimsuit, etc.) As one child reaches in and pulls out an article, the other children say when and where it would be worn appropriately.

11. Provide charts, models, and pictures of the human body; include bones, muscles, and so on.

12. Weigh and measure each child who wishes to be weighed and measured. Repeat this activity often so that comparisons can be made.

13. Make a neighborhood or community map, including the area and house where each child lives, if possible. Lay this map out flat, and provide small "people" and cars for the children to play with.

14. Have children complete open-ended sentences relating to their feelings. For example:

    a. I wish . . .

    b. The best thing I can do . . .

    c. I feel proud when . . .

    d. I feel angry when . . .

    e. I am happy when . . .

    f. When I get big, I'm going to . . .

    g. I get scared when . . .

    h. I like it when my family . . .

    i. I wish my family would . . .

15. Collect cartoons or pictures that depict emotional qualities, and have the children write comments or captions for them.

16. Have each child decorate an envelope, with "Love Notes" written on the outside. The envelope can be left at school or taken home so that other children or family members can write or draw pictures of what they like about the child.

17. Make "I Can Do" cards with pictures or drawings of tasks and skills that the majority of the children in your class can do. As the cards are held up, the children do the skill or pretend to do it.

18. Make a puzzle of each child's name, using both first and last names. Example:

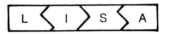

19. Collect many songs, stories, poems, and fingerplays that help to increase each child's self-esteem by focusing on the child's name or other personal characteristics such as physical size or heritage.

20. Make "Guess Who" riddles describing individual children. Suggest clues that reflect the child's positive characteristics.

21. Make job or "To Do" charts. Assist children in individualizing these charts to their own responsibilities and activities. It is satisfying for children to see their accomplishments on paper as they mark off daily tasks. (See Figure 5–1.)

22. Use the following selection for role playing, creative dramatics, memorization, program presentations, ideas for visitors and field trips, development of literacy skills through reading and listening enjoyment, and so on:

When I Grow Up

I can't decide just what to do
When I get big someday.
There are so many different things—
It's really hard to say.

I know I can be more than one,
More than two or three;
But what to be when I grow up?
I'll have to wait and see!

Maybe I will drive a bus,
A taxi, or tow truck;
And when the snow gets very deep,
I'll help you get unstuck.

Maybe I will put out fires,
Or save a frightened cat.
I'll ride upon the fire truck
And wear a fire hat.

I could become a dentist, too,
And care for people's teeth.

(*continued page 142*)

	Sunday	Monday	Tuesday	Wednesday	Thursday	Friday	Saturday
 Get dressed							
 Set the table							
 Brush teeth							
 Pick up toys							
 Fold clothes							
 Take a bath							

FIGURE 5–1

I'd clean the ones in front, behind,
Above, and then beneath.

Maybe I'll a butcher be,
And cut up lots of meat.
Bologna, hot dogs, hamburgers
Are what I like to eat.

Maybe I'll clerk in a bank
And count "four, five, and ten."
When they cash a check, they'll ask,
"May I, please, use your pen?"

I could be a custodian
And make the buildings shine.
They would ask, "Whose careful work?"
I'd proudly answer, "Mine!"

Maybe I'll take care of hives,
And learn about the bees.
When I serve honey sandwiches,
They'll say, "Another, please!"

Maybe I will take a pen
And write a reading book
'Bout how to plant, or how to fix,
Or how to jog or cook.

I'll likely be a parent and will
Mend my children's toys.
When I eat and play with them,
I won't mind the noise.

Maybe I'll a pilot be,
And fly a big jet plane.
I'd be brave through clouds and sun,
Through snows, and fog, and rain.

Maybe I'll take care of cats,
Or horses, dogs, and snakes.
I'll check their health and give them shots,
And put casts on all their breaks.

I could be a farmer and plant
Beets, or corn, or wheat.
Everyone would know that I
Grow healthy food to eat.

Maybe I'll a plumber be,
And hear the people say:
"The pipes won't drain, the faucet drips.
Please help me right away!"

Maybe I will sell new cars
To folks who trade their old.

They'll say, "I think I'll take this one."
And I will answer, "Sold!"

I could engineer a train,
And speed along the track.
As people pass and wave at me,
I will wave right back.

Maybe I will gather trash,
And empty garbage, too.
I'll keep clean the city streets,
The playground, and the zoo.

Maybe I could work with wood—
A carpenter become.
When people need new blocks or chairs,
I'd say, "I'll make you some."

I could be a magician with a
Traveling magic show.
They'd ask me how it works, I'd say:
"That's just for me to know!"

Maybe I could sell new shoes—
Check fit at toe and heel.
I'd say, "Now walk around a bit,
And see how those two feel."

Maybe I will fix up cars,
And keep them good as new.
They'll ask me, "How long will it take?"
"I'll call you when I'm through."

I could be a night watcher, and check
All the doors with keys.
If someone made suspicious sounds,
I'd bravely call out, "Freeze!"

Maybe I'll help students learn—
A teacher then to choose.
I'd work with 4's, or 8's, or 12's,
16's, or 22's.

Maybe I'll make people laugh,
And be a circus clown.
I'll show them that a frown is just
A smile turned upside-down.

I'll likely be a grandparent
With tales about "Back when . . ."
After I am through, they'll say:
"Please tell that one again."

A miner works beneath the ground—
A miner must be bold.

Maybe I would look for silver,
Copper, coal, or gold.

I could become a baker, and make
Cookies every day.
They'd ask me which kind was the best.
"Chocolate chip," I'd say.

You see, there are so many things
That I could grow to be;
But what I'll be when I get big—
I'll have to wait and see.

Reprinted by permission from Loa T. Jenkins.

23. Help children make character decisions about what is right and what is wrong. The following situations readily lend themselves to cooperative learning in smaller groups:

    a. You are in a store and see something you really want to have. In your pocket is enough money to buy milk for your family. What would you do?

    b. You are supposed to take an object starting with the letter "B" to school, and you have forgotten to bring one from home. Your friend sitting next to you has a rubber ball in his coat pocket. What would you do?

    c. You are shopping with a friend and your friend takes a candy bar without paying for it. You are the only one who saw this happen. What would you do?

    d. You are on the school playground, and a child is teasing and hurting another child. What would you do?

    e. You are with a group of friends, and several begin saying negative and mean things about another friend who is not present. What should you do?

24. Seat the group in a circle. As each person's name is said, a positive adjective that begins with the same letter as the person's name is added: Friendly Frank, Happy Heidi, Jolly Justin.

25. In cooperative learning groups, play the game "If you could choose to be a *food*, what would you be?" After each answer, ask "Why?" and allow the child time to respond with the reason. Use such categories as animal, flower, bird, shoe, television show, sound, book, color, bug, car, building, piece of furniture, fruit, and so on ("SEEK," 1991).

26. Do the activity "Give them a hand." All children trace one of their hands on a sheet of blank paper. Their names are written on the bottom part of the traced hands. Then as a child says something good about another child, that compliment is written down on the recipient's hand print. For younger children, teachers will need to do the writing. For older children, the hand prints can be passed around and children can write their own comments on the prints passed to them ("SEEK," 1991).

27. Have the children write their names vertically and then think of a word that describes them for each letter in their name. For example:

    Adorable   Bashful
    Merry   Redheaded
    Young   Energetic
        Tall

28. Have the children write or tell 5 (or 10 for older children) words that describe themselves.

29. Honor the children on their birthdays. You may have a birthday chair cover, a badge, or a crown for the birthday child to wear. Let them do a show-and-tell; lead the group in a game, poem, or fingerplay; or pick their favorite story to be read. Classmates can do a card or a "hand" as described in Activity 26.

30. Have parents help children prepare a time line beginning with the child's birth and including special events of the child's life. Photographs or drawings could be added.

31. Have their families help the children do a family tree with pictures and/or names of ancestors. It could be as simple as the one shown in Figure 5–2.

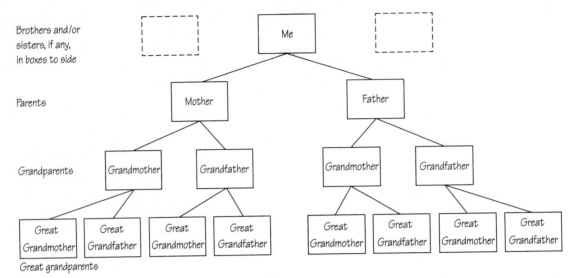

Brothers and/or sisters, if any, in boxes to side

Parents

Grandparents

Great grandparents

FIGURE 5–2

32. In cooperative learning groups, have each group brainstorm what makes children happy. For children focusing on the alphabet, they could think of at least one thing for each letter of the alphabet. For example: A=art classes, awards; B=babies, bubble gum; C=cookies, cousins; D=dancing, ducks. Certain letters of the alphabet could be assigned to each group.

33. In cooperative learning groups, using the Numbered Heads Together strategy, discuss what people the children rely on for help, both in the family and outside the family. Next, discuss how the children can help other people. Following the cooperative learning experience, each child could do a page for a booklet titled "We Help Others."

34. Have children who are able to write (usually first and second graders) keep a journal. Encourage them to share their experiences and feelings.

35. Have each child draw a circle with a picture or photograph of himself or herself in the middle of the paper. Then have the child draw a circle for each family member; these circles will be positioned around the child's circle. Under each circle the child can write or dictate that person's name, and over it write or dictate one word or a sentence to describe the person.

36. Have second grade children write cinquains about themselves or a partner. If done in partners, use the cooperative learning strategy Think-Pair-Share (Curran, 1991: p. 33, among others).

Line 1—Name
Line 2—Two adjectives to describe yourself (or your partner)
Line 3—Three verbs to describe what you (or your partner) like to do
Line 4—Simile for yourself (or your partner) (as _____ as _____)
Line 5—Synonym (another word for you or your partner)

37. Using the cooperative learning group strategy Think-Pair-Share, have the children, in partners, talk to one another and find out first things they have in common and then differences from one another. For

sharing, have them tell one interesting thing they learned about their partner. To get them started in their communicating they can discuss family, number of family members, where they were born, a favorite book they have read, pets, a favorite movie, places they have lived or visited, what they want to be when they grow up, accidents they have had, or trips to the hospital.

38. In cooperative learning groups, students discuss what they like best about their neighborhood, a favorite place in their neighborhood, and how they would change the neighborhood to make it better. Each group has a spokesperson to report.

39. As a class, watch for concerns in your community. When you see a particular concern, take some action as a class. Write a letter to the editor of your local newspaper, or call or write a public official.

40. Read books about elderly people such as *Now One Foot, Now the Other* (DePaola, 1981); *Miss Maggie* (Ryland, 1983); *Emma* (Kesselman, 1985); *Annie and the Old One* (Miles, 1972); *Grandpa* (Burningham, 1985); and *I Know a Lady* (Zolotow, 1984). (See "Suggested Resources" at the end of this chapter for complete references.) Come up with a class project to help an elderly person or persons. The children could help with yard work, visit and perform at a nursing home, visit a shut-in, or do artwork for an elderly person.

41. In concentric circles, have the children pair up as partners. Ask questions and give the children a short time to discuss each question between themselves. Examples of questions include the following: "What are some things that make you afraid?" "What is your favorite . . . (book, color, movie, activity, restaurant, animal)?" "Describe a time when you were embarrassed." "What is your favorite family tradition?" "What is the best thing about your family?" After a question or two, the children could change partners.

UNIT PLAN ON MYSELF

Field Trips

- Dance studio or ballroom where children can see themselves move in front of large mirrors
- Own homes, playgrounds, or yards
- Doctor's office
- Dentist's office
- Beauty shop
- Beauty college (children could have their hair done)
- Eye doctor's office
- Hospital nursery

Visitors

- Dentist
- Doctor
- Nurse
- Barber
- Beautician
- Parent(s)
- Grandparent(s)
- Sibling(s)
- Person to perform and involve the children in mime

Music

- Children make and decorate their own musical instruments, and then accompany familiar songs, as well as songs they have created themselves
- Body sounds to accompany the songs in rhythm (snapping fingers, clicking tongue, clapping hands, etc.)
- Music to skip, jump, hop, run, exercise, relax, and listen to
- Teaching sessions in which children learn to play musical instruments (depending on the ages of the children, these may be rhythm sticks, drums, autoharps, harmonicas, etc.)

- Songs (music and words) created from children's own ideas
- Songs and creative movement about feelings

Art

- Decoration of handmade musical instruments
- Body images—trace around children's bodies while they are lying on paper; the children paint and decorate
- Shapes of eyes, noses, mouths, ears, and so on, cut by the teacher or the children and pasted onto a face-shaped base by the children
- Foot or hand prints set in plaster, dried, and then colored
- Self-portraits
- "Me Posters" (can be collaged or drawn)

Food

- Any food activity that allows and encourages children to develop skills and make something themselves
- Favorite snacks or foods

Science

- Health care activities that help children understand and learn good health habits
- Looking at germs from their hands under a microscope
- Studies relating to growth: bones, hair, healing, fingernails
- Magnifying glass for a closer look at eyes, teeth, freckles, fingers, pores, hair, nose, tongue, scars, and so on.

Literacy Development

- Any stories that the children write themselves about their experiences, feelings, families, and selves. (These can be dictated if the children do not have handwriting skills.)
- Stories or thoughts that are the children's own ideas

(*Note*: For a unit plan or web on families, see Figure 5–3.)

LESSON PLAN ON EMOTIONS (4-DAY)

Overall Goals

- To become aware of individual children and their needs and begin to establish goals for each of them.
- To encourage each child to become independent in putting toys and other materials away, cleaning up, and putting clothes on.
- To help the children gain an understanding of themselves, particularly their emotions.
- To increase each child's awareness of the kinds of things that stimulate emotions and how to work with them.

(*Note:* Many of the whole- and small-group activities in this lesson plan work well as cooperative learning projects, especially those that address happy and unhappy emotions, curiosity, fear, anger, and so on.)

Day 1

Whole-Group Activity

Introduction to Unit on Feelings and/or Emotions

- Place felt cutout faces representing various moods or emotions on the flannel board and discuss them with the children. Afterward, tell the children a story about feelings and discuss it with them.

Objectives

- To establish an understanding of what feelings and emotions are, how they are stimulated, and how they can be worked with.
- To help the children understand their own feelings by relating to the same kinds of feelings in others.
- To ensure that the children know that we often can tell how a person feels by the person's facial expression.

Small-Group Activity

Art—Construction-Paper Collages

FIGURE 5–3

Each child will bring a photograph of his or her family and have an opportunity to talk about it.

Discuss the uniqueness of each child's family.

Make a booklet titled "My Family." For younger children, each child does one page; older children can do their own booklets.

Language & Literacy

Read or tell stories. Examples:
<u>Always, Always</u> (Dragonwagon, 1984);
<u>Bedtime for Francis</u> (Huban, 1960);
<u>Blueberries for Sal</u> (McCloskey, 1948);
<u>I'll Fix Anthony</u> (Viorst, 1969);
<u>Owl Moon</u> (Yolen, 1987);
<u>The Patchwork Quilt</u> (Flournoy, 1985);
<u>When I Was Young in the Mountain</u> (Rylant, 1982);
<u>The Way Mothers Are</u> (Schlein, 1963);
<u>Bye Bye Baby</u> (Ahlberg & Ahlberg, 1989).

Visit extented family members of children in the class.

Visit places of work of family members.

Field Trips

Visit the homes of class members.

Illustrate family booklets.

Do drawings of family members.

Art

Draw favorite characters from stories.

Families (Each family is unique)

Sing songs about families

Music

Food

Make a treat or a snack to be shared with the family.

Make a favorite recipe of a class member's family. Do a class recipe booklet including a favorite family recipe of each class member.

Visitors

Invite a family in to perform musically.

Invite principal or director in to share pictures and thoughts about his/her family.

Invite some of the children's family members in to share hobbies, jobs, and family traditions. Emphasize the value of diversity

• Provide school paste, a sheet of white construction paper, and many cutout shapes of colored construction paper for each child. Divide the children into small groups after the introduction to the unit. The cutout shapes (similar to the felt ones used in the introduction) can be put together to represent faces with different moods. The children may wish to make faces, or they may want to paste the shapes in any collage design.

Objectives

• To discuss various emotions and feelings with the children in their small groups, focusing on what might cause an emotion, how they feel, and what they do when they have that feeling.
• To determine which children make faces out of their cutout shapes, and to encourage them to talk about the mood they may be depicting.

- To find out how children interpret various emotions.

Individual Activities

- Large trough with wheat
- Paint at the double easel

Day 2

Whole-Group Activities

Discussion and Story on Happy Emotions—Love, Joy, and Excitement

- Show the children a picture of a child with a happy expression and ask them such questions as "How do you think this child feels?" "What could have caused the feeling?" "Have you ever felt happy, excited, joyful?" "What told you that this child was happy?" Share a story about love between a parent and children, and then follow it with a discussion on love. Emphasize that loving others or being loved by others makes us happy.

Objectives

- To help the children think about how they feel when they experience love, joy, excitement, or happiness.
- To help the children think about different things that bring joy or happiness to them.
- To help the children want to bring joy and happiness to others.

Visitor—Clown

- Have a visitor come dressed in a clown costume. While the children are gathered as a group, the visitor puts on the greasepaint and makes up a clown face. The clown discusses the concept that dressing up as a clown makes people happy.

Objectives

- To enable each child to know that underneath the costume and painted face is a real person.
- To help children understand that clowns enjoy dressing up to make people, and especially children, happy.

- To give the children the knowledge that if the clown's mouth is painted in a frown, it is painted that way to make people laugh and does not mean that the clown is actually sad.

Discussion and Story on Unhappy Emotions—Sadness, Loneliness

- Tell an open-ended story to the children, and, with a partner or in cooperative groups, encourage them to supply possible endings. Show the children a picture of a crying child, and use the same kinds of questions listed in the preceding discussion. Tell a story to the children that will elicit how it feels to be rejected.

Objectives

- To establish an understanding of feelings opposite to those of happiness, and to help each child understand that everyone experiences these kinds of emotions, too.
- To help each child understand the various reasons for sadness, loneliness, and so on.
- To help the children learn some ways of dealing with these feelings.

Individual Activity

- Large trough with snow or ice

Day 3

Whole-Group Activities

Discussion and Introduction to the Emotion of Curiosity

- Use an unfamiliar book, a pair of magnets, and a picture of children observing and playing with a frog to stimulate interest in the emotion of curiosity. Since the word *curiosity* will probably be new to the children, describe what it is: wondering about, investigating, and exploring something. Use questions to stimulate thought and discussion.

Objectives

- To acquaint the children with the new word *curiosity* and its meaning.

- To enable the children to name and discuss some things that stimulate curiosity.
- To stimulate curiosity in the children.

Discussion and Open-Ended Story About Anger

- Tell an open-ended story about a girl who is angry. The children will discover that the girl is angry; have them describe what made her feel that way. Show several pictures of angry children to the children, and have them discuss what might have made the children angry and what can be done to solve the problem. Also introduce *frustration* to the children as a new word, and have them talk about things that frustrate them and how they may become angry about them. Show the children a picture of a new baby, and discuss jealousy. (These pictures could be distributed among cooperative groups so more children would have an opportunity to participate and share ideas.)

Objectives

- To help each child understand different reasons for anger, including jealousy and frustration.
- To show that anger is not necessarily bad, but that it must be handled correctly. Children can

think about and say what they can do when they are angry.
- To provide an introduction to making up original stories relating to emotions.

Music—Creative Movements with Plastic

- Music of various moods will be played. Give the children a piece of plastic, allow them to move about the area, and encourage them to interpret the music and how it makes them feel. Ask them whether the music makes them feel afraid, curious, happy, excited, or sad. Accept any answer or response.

Objectives

- To help the children feel free in using their bodies to express a mood or feeling.
- To provide opportunity for self-expression through music.

Small-Group Activity

Making Up Stories for Pictures

- After the discussion on anger, divide the children into small groups for cooperative learning. Send the groups to various areas of the room,

With the help of a caring teacher, children are able to work through feelings of frustration that arise in daily interactions with others.

where they will be given several pictures of children depicting specific emotions. In the groups, have the children make up stories for their pictures. If they want the stories written down, make lined paper available.

Objectives

- To provide information about many of the emotions discussed, as well as concepts related to these emotions.
- To provide an experience in problem solving and creative thinking.

Individual Activities

- Trough with sawdust
- Magnets on science table

Day 4

Whole-Group Activity

Science—Discussion on Fear

- Have the children discuss some of the situations that stimulate fear: going to the doctor or dentist, getting shots, taking medicine, going on an elevator, hearing loud noises, being near animals, being in the dark, parents leaving. Discuss how to overcome these fears, mainly by having more experiences with the things feared.

Afterward, discuss and display some things the children should be cautious with: fire, matches, poisons, broken glass, medicines, and so on.

Objectives

- To enable the children to understand that they will outgrow some fears by having more experiences.
- To teach caution about some objects or situations of which children should be aware, and to show examples of some of these things.
- To discover some of the things that bring about fear in the children and to discuss them.

Small-Group Activity

Food—Popcorn with Cheese

- (See recipe in Chapter Seven).

Objective

- To reinforce one of the things we need to be very careful with: hot pans and hot butter

Individual Activities

- String painting
- Trough with manipulative toys

Summary

As infants discover early the existence of their bodies, they also begin to become aware of others around them. Through the development of positive self-images, children are able to accept and value other people. Children must be able to relate positively to themselves before they are able to relate effectively and successfully with others. The family provides the child's first social interactions, and it has a significant role in helping the child establish a positive self-image and healthy, realistic expectations. At the same time, teachers and caregivers need to accept children as they are, and from those acceptances provide a caring,

supportive, high-quality program designed to help the children progress in their continuing quest for self-esteem.

In our effort to understand the influences of stress in the lives of children, it is helpful to recognize situations causing stress, how children react to stress, and how they can cope with stress. We also have a great responsibility to help children learn and develop values and positive character traits; that is, to provide character education. Our values are the traits we deem to be worthwhile; they determine our behaviors and goals throughout our lives.

This chapter includes important basic principles in the development of self-concept, along with suggestions of techniques for building self-esteem in children. A teacher's own self-acceptance and attitude are of utmost importance when seeking to assist young children in developing self-concepts that will destine them for success.

Student Learning Activities

1. Prepare a unit plan on one of the following: "My Family," "My Friends," or some other concept relating to the self. For your unit plan, or web, include a section titled "Literacy," and include stories, poems, and other appropriate activities.

2. Using your unit plan prepared for item 1, prepare a 5-day activity plan using the suggested format on page 67.

3. Observe in a classroom of young children and describe how the teacher enhanced individual children's feelings of self-worth.

4. Prepare a list of teacher-made learning materials you would like to make that focus on teaching children concepts related to the self.

5. Prepare and make at least two of the materials you have listed in item 4.

6. The text discusses stress in children. Using the lists given as possibilities, add ideas that are applicable to your own life: What situations cause you stress? How do you react to stress? How do (or can) you cope with stress?

7. Study children's books relating to "myself and my family." Select one to share with the class. How would you present this story to an early childhood class? Why do you like this book? Is it free of sexism and racism?

Suggested Resources

Children's Books

Alexander, M. (1977). *Nobody asked me if I wanted a baby sister.* New York: Dell.

Anglund, J. W. (1960). *Love is a special way of feeling.* New York: Harcourt Brace Jovanovich.

Anglund, J. W. (1983). *A friend is someone who likes you.* New York: Harcourt Brace Jovanovich.

Anholt, C., & Anholt, L. (1992). *All about you.* New York: Viking.

Berger, T. (1971). *I have feelings.* New York: Human Science Press.

Birdseye, T. (1990). *A song of stars.* New York: Holiday House.

Brown, M. W. (1958). *The dead bird.* New York: William R. Scott.

Brown, R. (1988). *100 words about my house.* San Diego, CA: Gulliver.

Buckley, H. E. (1959). *Grandfather and I.* New York: Lothrop, Lee & Shepard.

Burningham, J. (1985). *Grandpa.* New York: Crown.

Church, K. (1991). *My brother John.* New York: Tambourine.

Clarke, G. (1990). *Eddie and Teddy.* New York: Lothrop, Lee & Shepard.

Cohn, J. (1987). *I had a friend named Peter.* New York: Morrow.

Cooney, B. (1988). *Island boy.* New York: Viking Kestrel.

Couzyn, J. (1990). *Bad day.* New York: Dutton.

Dale, P. (1987). *Bet you can't.* Scranton, PA: Harper Collins.

Demuth, P. B. (1991). *The ornery morning.* New York: Dutton.

DePaola, T. (1981). *Now one foot, now the other.* New York: Putnam.

DeRegneirs, B. (1964). *May I bring a friend?* New York: Atheneum.

Dijis, C. (1990). *Are you my daddy? A Pop-Up Book.* New York: Simon & Schuster.

Dijis, C. (1990 *Are you my mommy? A Pop-Up book.* New York: Simon & Schuster.

Dutton, C. (1990). *Not in here, Dad!* New York: Barrons.

Ets, M. H. (1965). *Just me.* New York: Viking.

Fassler, J. (1983). *My Grandpa died today.* New York: Science Press.

Fox, M. (1989). *Shoes from Grandpa.* New York: Orchard.

Garland, S. (1992). *Billy and Belle.* New York: Viking Penguin.

Green, M. (1961). *Everybody has a house and everybody eats.* Reading, MA: Addison-Wesley.

Green, P. (1991). *Chucky Bellman was so bad.* Morton Grove, IL: Whitman.

Greenfield, E. (1991). *First pink light.* New York: Black Butterfly.

Hamm, D. J. (1991). *Laney's lost mommy.* Morton Grove, IL: Whitman.

Hines, A. G. (1985). *All about myself.* New York: Clarion.

Hoban, L. (1985). *Arthur's loose tooth.* New York: Harper & Row.

Isadora, R. (1990). *Babies.* New York: Greenwillow.

Isadora, R. (1990). *Friends.* New York: Greenwillow.

Keller, H. (1991). *Horace.* New York: Morrow.

Kesselman, W. (1985). *Emma.* New York: Harper Collins.

Kingman, L. (1990). *Catch the baby!* New York: Viking.

Krause, U. (1989). *Nora and the great bear.* New York: Dial.

Krauss, R. (1971). *Leo the late bloomer.* New York: Windmill.

Kurtz, J. (1990). *I'm calling Molly.* Niles, IL: Whitman.

Lasker, J. (1974). *He's my brother.* Niles, IL: Whitman.

Leonard, M. (1988). *What I like series: Going to bed, getting dressed, eating, taking a bath.* New York: Bantam.

Levinson, R. (1988). *Our home is the sea.* New York: Dutton.

Lionni, L. (1986). *It's mine! A fable.* New York: Knopf.

Lyon, G. E. (1991). *Cecil's story.* New York: Orchard.

Mandelbaum, P. (1990). *You be me, I'll be you.* New York: Kane/Miller.

Mayer, M. (1983). *All by myself.* New York: Western.

Mayer, M. (1983). *When I get bigger.* New York: Western.

Miles, M. (1972). *Annie and the old one.* New York: Little, Brown.

Nemiroff, M. A., & Annunziata, J. (1990). *A child's first book about play therapy.* Washington, DC: American Psychological Association.

Patterson, B. (1992). *In my house.* New York: Holt.

Patterson, B. (1992). *In my yard.* New York: Holt.

Patterson, B. (1992). *My clothes.* New York: Holt.

Patterson, B. (1992). *My toys.* New York: Holt.

Rice, M., & Rice, C. (1987). *All about me.* New York: Doubleday.

Ricklen, N. (1988). *Grandma and me.* New York: Simon & Schuster.

Ricklen, N. (1988). *Grandpa and me.* New York: Simon & Schuster.

Ricklen, N. (1988). *Mommy and me.* New York: Simon & Schuster.

Ricklen, N. (1992). *My first day at school.* Hauppauge, NY: Barron's.

Ringgold, F. (1991). *Tar Beach.* New York: Crown.

Rogers, F. (1985). *Going to day care.* New York: Putnam.

Rylant, C. (1983). *Miss Maggie.* New York: Dutton.

San Souci, R. D. (1987). *The enchanted tapestry.* New York: Dial.

Schlein, M. (1963). *The way mothers are.* Chicago: Albert Whitman.

Sendak, M. (1963). *Where the wild things are.* New York: Harper & Row.

Sharmat, M. W. (1977). *I'm terrific.* New York: Holiday House.

Silverman, J. (1988). *Some time to grow.* New York: Addison-Wesley.

Steig, W. (1969). *Sylvester and the magic pebble.* New York: Simon & Schuster.

Steiner, B. (1988). *Whale brother.* New York: Walker.

Torre, B. L. (1990). *The luminous pearl.* New York: Orchard.

Tucker, S. (1991). *At home.* New York: Simon & Schuster.

Tucker, S. (1991). *Going out.* New York: Simon & Schuster.

Tucker, S. (1991). *My toys.* New York: Simon & Schuster.

Tucker, S. (1991). *My clothes.* New York: Simon & Schuster.

Udry, J. M. (1969). *Let's be enemies*. New York: Harper & Brothers.

Viorst, J. (1972). *Alexander and the terrible, horrible, no good, very bad day*. New York: Atheneum.

Viorst, J. (1983). *I'll fix Anthony*. New York: Atheneum.

Wellington, M. (1989). *All my little ducklings*. New York: Dutton.

Williams, B. (1974). *Albert's toothache*. New York: Dutton.

Yashima, T. (1955). *Crow boy*. New York: Viking.

Zolotow, C. (1972). *William's doll*. New York: Harper & Row.

Zolotow, C. (1984). *I know a lady*. New York: Greenwillow.

Records, Tapes, and Cassettes

Be my friend. On *Getting to know myself*. Hap Palmer Record Library. (AR543 or AC543)

Brush away. On *Learning basic skills through music* (Vol. 1). Hap Palmer Record Library. (AR526 or AC526).

Cover your mouth. On *Learning basic skills through music* (Vol. 1). Hap Palmer Record Library.

The downtown story. Scholastic Book Services. (R7670)

Everybody cries sometimes. Educational Activities. (AR561 or AC561)

Everybody is somebody. On *It's a happy feeling*. Cheviot. (T-305)

Everyone has feelings. Scholastic Book Services. (R7567)

Exercise everyday. On *Learning basic skills through music* (Vol. 1). Hap Palmer Record Library. (AR526 or AC526)

Feelings. On *Getting to know myself*. Hap Palmer Record Library. (AR543 or AC543)

The frog's party. A Gentle Wind.

Fun and fitness for primary children. Bowmar-Noble. (B2057)

Helping and sharing. David C. Cook.

Hopping around from place to place (Vols. 1 and 2). Educational Activities.

I've got a reason to sing. Cheviot. (T-307)

Keep the germs away. On *Learning basic skills through music* (Vol. 1). Hap Palmer Record Library. (AR526 or AC526)

Left and right. On *Getting to know myself*. Hap Palmer Record Library. (AR543 or AC543)

Lullabies from 'round the world. Cheviot.

Rainy day dances, rainy day songs. Educational Activities. (AR570 or AC570)

Sing around the world. Miss Jackie.

Take a bath. On *Learning basic skills through music* (Vol. 1). Hap Palmer Record Library. (AR526 or AC526)

You can do it. *Ooo we're having fun*. Cheviot. (T-306)

What are you wearing? On *Learning basic skills through music* (Vol. 1). Hap Palmer Record Library. (AR514 or AC514)

Won't you be my friend? Educational Activities. (AR544 or AC544)

Pictures

Developing my values. The Child's World.

Disney safety study prints (series). Walt Disney.

Guidance. The Child's World.

Health and cleanliness. David C. Cook.

Health and personal care. The Child's World.

Keeping physically fit. The Child's World.

Learning about careers. David C. Cook.

Learning about values. David C. Cook.

The many moods of Mother Goose. The Child's World.

Moods and emotions. The Child's World.

Moods and emotions. David C. Cook.

Safety. David C. Cook.

Social development. David C. Cook.

Understanding my needs. The Child's World.

Multimedia Kits

Careful with strangers. Walt Disney.

Safety at school with Winnie-the-Pooh. Walt Disney.

Safety through the year. Walt Disney.

What should I do? Walt Disney.

Winnie-the-Pooh and the right things to do. Walt Disney.

Winnie-the-Pooh on the way to school. Walt Disney.

Films, Filmstrips, and Videos

All kinds of feelings. Scholastic Filmstrips.

The angry movie. Coronet Films.

Beep, beep. Churchill Films.

Being healthy. Eye Gate Media.

Being safe. Eye Gate Media.

Children, enfants, niños. CRM/McGraw-Hill Films.

The creeps machine. Churchill Films.

The emotional lives of children. Educational Testing Service.

Fables from today's world. Eye Gate Media.

Families: Food and eating. Churchill Films.

Families: A series. Churchill Films.

Feelings (series). Churchill Films.

The five senses. David C. Cook.

Friends. Churchill Films.

Fun of making friends. Coronet Films.

Furthering values. Eye Gate Media.

Getting along with others. Coronet Films.

Hope for children. Health Communications. (Alcoholic parents).

Hush, little baby. Weston Woods Studios.

I am how I feel. Churchill Films.

I am how I look. Churchill Films.

I am what I know. Churchill Films.

I'm feeling alone. Churchill Films.

I'm feeling happy. Churchill Films.

I'm feeling sad. Churchill Films.

I'm feeling scared. Churchill Films.

I'm mad at me. Churchill Films.

I'm mad at you. Churchill Films.

Inside your body. National Geographic.

The joy of being you. Scholastic Filmstrips.

Just me. Weston Woods Studios.

Khan Du (series). National Archives.

Learning to look at hands. McGraw-Hill Films.

Lentil. Weston Woods Studios.

Let's be enemies. Weston Woods Studios.

Let's find some faces. McGraw-Hill Films.

Little things that count. Eye Gate Media.

Madeline. Pyramid Films.

My new friend (series). Eye Gate Media.

The one and only, very special you. Eye Gate Media.

Our family works together. Coronet Films.

Our wonderful body: The heart and its work. Coronet Films.

Our wonderful body: How it grows. Coronet Films.

Our wonderful body: How it moves. Coronet Films.

Our wonderful body: How its parts work together. Coronet Films.

Our wonderful body: How we breathe. Coronet Films.

Our wonderful body: How we keep fit. Coronet Films.

Our wonderful body: Medicines, drugs and poisons. Coronet Films.

People need you. Eye Gate Media.

Safety and school. Eye Gate Media.

Safety signs on street and highway. Eye Gate Media.

The social lives of children. Educational Testing Service.

Soft is the heart of the child. Operation Cork/PGP. (Alcoholic parents.)

Sounds of silence. ACT Productions. (Alcoholic parents.)

They need me. David C. Cook.

Values. Eye Gate Media.

We go to school. Coronet Films.

What is a family? McGraw-Hill Films.

The who we are series. Pyramid Films.

Why we behave as we do. Eye Gate Media.

Your mouth speaking (also in Spanish). Walt Disney.

Computer Software

Facemaker, Golden Edition. (1986). Bridgeport, CT: Queue.

The Human Being Machine (1990). Dana Point, CA. R. J. Cooper & Associates.

Mask Parade. (1984) Bridgeport, CT: Queue.

PART THREE

LANGUAGE AND LITERACY DEVELOPMENT

Language allows the child to translate raw experiences into meaningful symbols that can be used for both communicating and thinking. Literacy involves the speaking, listening, writing, and reading skills. The foundation of literacy is language development. Because the development of language skills begins in infancy and relies heavily on experiences, children exhibit great differences in their language acquisition and growth. These differences are individual, normal, and acceptable. The following chapter covers development of early language, literacy, listening and speaking, reading and writing, and poetry. Included are suggested activities for increasing skills and facilitating development in speaking, listening, reading, and writing. Also included are guidelines and methods for selecting, preparing, presenting, and evaluating stories.

Language and literacy should be active ingredients in all curriculum activities and experiences, rather than separate elements assigned to specific times to be taught.

CHAPTER
six

Language and Literacy Skills

Introduction

One of the most important responsibilities of early childhood teachers is helping children develop skill in language and literacy. Language development separates humans from all other species and is the common link among people. Through language, we are able to exchange and understand communicated thoughts and feelings. Language functions in many ways for the child, and it may well be the most significant feature of the child's early learning. Considering the complexities of learning and language, it is imperative that activities and experiences involving language and literacy be developmentally appropriate.

By the time most children reach 5 years of age, they have a large vocabulary, speak in sentences, and are often able to use proper syntax or grammar (Burns & Broman, 1983). Table 6–1 gives a brief overview of normal language development.

Language is the instrument of thought, personal expression, and social communication. Children's power to grasp, enter into, and reflect on their experiences depends largely on their facility in using verbal symbols. Thus, language is the device through which raw experiences are translated into meaningful symbols that can be dealt with coherently and used for both thinking and communicating. As experience is broadened and deepened, language acquires meaning and further growth and learning become possible. Also, it is through language that they are able to express their own thoughts and emotions and share vicariously in those of others. Therefore, we might say that language is both action and interaction.

Language skill is also important in concept formation, school performance, and problem solving. In order to develop competence in organizing, classifying, categorizing, and understanding concepts, one must have a wide range of

TABLE 6–1
Normal Language Development

By the Age of	Development Activity
1 year	Imitates sounds Between 9 and 18 months, begins to use words intentionally to communicate Responds to many words that are a part of experience
2 years	Puts several words together in a phrase or short sentence (telegraphic language) Can recognize and name many familiar objects and pictures Has a vocabulary of about 30 words
3 years	Uses words to express needs Uses pronouns as well as nouns and verbs in speech Identifies the action in a picture Rapid increase in vocabulary—may average 50 new words a month
4 years	Loves to talk Verbalizes experiences by putting many sentences together Recites songs, poems, and stories Uses words to identify colors, numbers, and letters Sentences grow longer Likes to make up new words Likes rhyming
5 years	Generally has few articulation problems Talks freely and often interrupts others Sentences are long, involving five to six words Describes artwork Learns plurals Enjoys silly language
6 years	Asks the meanings of words Describes the meanings of words Makes few grammatical errors Talks much like an adult Is interested in new words
7 years	Speaks very well May still be mastering some sounds or learning to articulate the following sounds: *s, z, r, th, wh*

appropriate vocabulary. A certain level of attainment in language skills is essential in order for the child to begin formal education successfully. Literacy development is growth in communications skills, including initial speaking and listening, and then writing and reading. "A need to read and write, and for someone to guide you through the intricacies, are basics to literacy" (Schickedanz et al., 1990, p. 10). Language awareness, or metalinguistic skill, focuses on the actual skills children need to master in order to gain literacy. The NAEYC Position Statement (1988) states that "the goals of the language and literacy program are for children to expand their ability to communicate orally and through reading and writing, and to enjoy these activities" (p. 72).

Development of Early Language

Since the foundation of literacy is language development, early childhood teachers must be aware of the development of language, as well as the factors that influence its development.

Children make the language of their family and neighborhood their own language as they imitate the accents, usage, structure, and colloquialisms of the people around them. Verbal imitation begins in the first year of life. Babies imitate rhythms and patterns of pitch and stress, and they begin to be aware of differences in word order and intonation. Children learn to pronounce words primarily through imitation. When children produce sounds, responding adults usually repeat actual words that closely approximate these sounds, which provides auditory reinforcement. As they practice these sounds, correct or incorrect speech forms are reinforced through feedback. Careful observation of language progression determines that children's speech is actually a systematic reduction of adult speech, with function words that carry little information being omitted. For example, an adult might ask: "Do you want some more milk?" The toddler will often respond with "More milk." The fact that children learn the language of their environment reinforces the importance of imitation.

Vocalizations that normally occur in the first year of life are the forerunners of language. These vocalizations must be reinforced or rewarded by certain kinds of responses from others if they are to persist and develop into language. The more reinforcement, the better. Problems with language are often rooted in the early stages of language development, when imitation of a model is relevant. Sometimes the linguistic patterns learned from model imitation are both limited and wrong by the standards of the school the children will attend. In low-income homes, for example, there are reportedly less verbal play, less verbal interaction, and less reinforcing behavior on the part of family members than are generally found in middle-income homes. Adults need to provide exemplary imitation standards and shape children's language behavior through differential reinforcement.

Passive language precedes active or oral language; children hear and understand language before they produce it. The child's language does not proceed from word to concept to experience, but from action or experience to concept to words (Genishi, 1988). Piaget (1955) asserted that infants do think and that thought develops before children are even capable of speech. When babies first begin to speak, they have learned that words are symbols for things or feelings. The Russian cognitive psychologist Vygotsky (1962) believed that it was children's language that made them capable of thought. We concur with Piaget that understanding of language precedes oral speech. We also believe that young children draw language meaning from the context in which it is used. In other words, children may not initially understand the meaning of a word, but they understand what the person using the word means.

Motor and mental readiness are prerequisites for children to begin verbalizing or using oral language. Association of word meanings depends on memory and reasoning. A lag in oral language may be due to the lack of motor or mental readiness; children may not have the memory or reasoning capacity to form oral language.

Children begin using oral language by blending real words in a stream of jargon, but the jargon quickly disappears and is replaced by one-word utterances. Initially, a sentence or phrase is combined and understood as one unit—for example, "awgone" instead of "all gone."

Oral language continues with the combination of words into utterances—two at a time, then three, and so forth. Whether the child is uttering a stream of jargon or a four-word sentence, others extend the child's language by filling in missing prepositions, conjunctions, verbs, and other parts of speech that reflect the way the language is used in the child's environment.

Children progress in language just as they do in other developmental areas—at their own rates and in their own individual ways. Some are very talkative and engage in rather extensive language play. Others appear reticent in using oral language. These differences are normal, and "what differs is oral production, not the underlying cognitive abilities. . . . [The] lack of profuse oral communication does not necessarily indicate intellectual weakness" (Salinger, 1988, p. 11).

Before their second birthday, most children are forming sentences of two or more words. Although the grammar of these sentences is not identical to that of the adult model, one can usually translate the child's sentence by adding function words and inflectional affixes. Although there is no syntax in children's early utterances, nouns, verbs, and interjections are the most common classes of words used. These reflect vocal stress, frequency in adult speech, or semantic importance.

Semantics

Children's development in semantics, or the meanings of words, is directly related to the experiences and interactions they have. Children can program sentences they have never heard before, but they cannot use a word they have not heard. The more experiences children have—whether in the context of language, real experiences, or vicarious experiences such as books and other media—the more they expand their language meanings and vocabulary. A rich variety of well-planned experiences that involve labeling and drawing meaning helps children expand their language and become more literate. However, an experience without attached language does not develop understanding. The following example illustrates the importance of labeling children's experiences. Four-year-old Amy was given one-half of a grapefruit. When asked, "What is this?" Amy confidently replied, "It is vitamin C." Amy's association with grapefruit may have included the instruction "Here, eat your vitamin C." Therefore, the experience with grapefruit lacked real meaning because an incorrect label had been attached to it.

It is imperative that adults constantly share, converse, interact, extend, and exchange language as children have experiences at the zoo, grocery store, park, school, home, or in the car. A word with no meaning is an empty sound, not a word. The meanings of a word for a particular individual depend on previous associations with it; and the more limited the experience, the more limited the resulting language and meanings.

A child's early utterances are often global or generalized, and a sound may represent several different objects or persons. As children continue hearing the verbal contexts of words and have a rich variety of labeled experiences, they increase their knowledge of meanings. For example, *dog* may refer to all animals. As vocabulary and experiences increase, the child is able to narrow the range and to organize, classify, and categorize words and their meanings. The child discovers not only that everything has a name, but also that "this is the name for that." As experiences are made meaningful through word attachments, these words are stored in the brain and used to understand later experiences and communications.

Syntax

Syntax is the set of rules for creating or understanding a sentence. As children first begin to use words, they display no evidence of systematic grammar; yet, by about 4 years of age, most observers agree, the fundamentals have been learned. Training in the use of word sequence to relate and unify cognition is important. Since the sentence is the smallest complete unit of thought, sentence structure is a key to the logic of thinking. Symbols and sounds need to be put together correctly to make words that are understandable; then the words must be placed in a particular order to make a sentence that conveys meaning. Children's ability to form complete sentences is also an index of their growth in thinking and cognitive understanding.

Children learn syntax by first imitating sentences or phrases or by extracting their meaningful parts. Expansion is another process in the acquisition of grammar. Adults often expand what the child has said. If the child states, "Me drink water," the adult will often expand the phrase with a complete sentence such as "You want a drink of water." In effect, the adult is saying, "Is this what you mean?" as well as expanding the child's phrase to a complete sentence. However, these two processes alone teach no more than the sum total of sentences that speakers have either modeled for a child to imitate or built up from a child's reductions. The child's linguistic competence extends beyond this. All children are able to understand and construct sentences they have never heard but that are, nevertheless, well formed. Somehow, then, children process the speech to which they are exposed in order to derive from it latent rule structures or innate abilities to think and form sentences on their own. Thus, children are intuitively able to master the rules of language and make inductive generalizations that go beyond what they hear. As children grow, they gain increased facility with syntactic structures, leading us to believe that maturation is a variable in syntax growth.

Caregivers should expand children's vocabulary and semantic understandings, as well as their syntax or sentence structure. Additional factors in language development include maturation, experiences, the amount and quality of verbal interaction provided the child, relationship to and rapport with the model, motivation for acquiring language, and television habits. When there is restriction in the range, variety, or quality of language input, there is also restriction in the output of expression. Language acquisition and use depend greatly on interaction with another person. Therefore, teachers and caregivers must sense their responsibility in the language development of children and create a rich language environment that includes labeling, classifying, comparing, contrasting, and questioning, in addition to observation of the child's language development.

An additional variable in language acquisition is whether or not the child is a bilingual/bicultural learner. Many teachers recognize the need to support a child's native language and give enrichment in the second language, which is English. This philosophy is referred to as additive because it recognizes the need to *add* new language skills but not to replace the child's existing language skills. We must value children's language diversity (Soto, 1991).

Literacy Development

Children seek to become literate for both survival and pleasure. We must give them opportunities to use language in both the spoken and the written form. Children should frequently see a written copy of what they are hearing. Even when they are not yet able to read, seeing the written images helps them make connections between what is heard and the written symbols (Salinger, 1988). Schickedanz (1986) asserts that we can always find ways to include print, regardless of what activities or materials we are using—and the print must make sense! Children frequently see printed words in their environment; they learn, whether they read or not, that things have spoken and written labels. Children who are successful readers in school have had written language as a dominant part of their daily activities. Children learn very early—because of literacy artifacts such as wallpaper with alphabet letters and print, nursery pictures, picture books with print, stickers with print, cereal boxes, mail and letters, signs, newspapers, and many other things with print—that print corresponds to oral language and represents ideas that can be read.

Children learn that the symbols called *words* convey meaning and tell something. Even though most preschool children cannot actually read, they have a great deal of competency and knowledge related to the functions and nature of print

(VanKleeck & Schuele, 1987). For children who come into early childhood classrooms without this feeling for and background in literacy, teachers must provide a nurturing atmosphere of literacy—exposure to books, print, reading, and writing.

Whole-Language Approach

Literacy development includes listening, speaking, reading, and writing. The interrelationships among these components should be obvious, since they all involve words. In listening, ideas are received through words; in speaking and writing, idea are expressed through words; and in reading, ideas are communicated through printed words. Children learn to

listen by listening;

speak by speaking;

read by reading;

write by writing;

listen by speaking, reading, and writing;

speak by listening, reading, and writing;

read by writing, listening, and speaking;

write by reading, listening, and speaking.

Figure 6–1 shows the interactive relationships among listening, speaking, reading, and writing.

Every part of a rich early childhood curriculum should offer the opportunity for literacy development. Music, science, art, food activities, social studies, math, and any other kind of experience should provide opportunities for literacy skill development. Language learning must be integrated into, not separated from, all aspects of the curriculum. This integration is defined as the *whole-language approach*, or perspective, to literacy development. Some people mistakenly believe that as soon as you advocate the whole-language approach to literacy, you assume that teaching strategies in reading such as the sight- or whole-word approach and the phonics approach are eliminated. With the whole-language approach, we feel that teachers create a literate environment and then use the best tools available

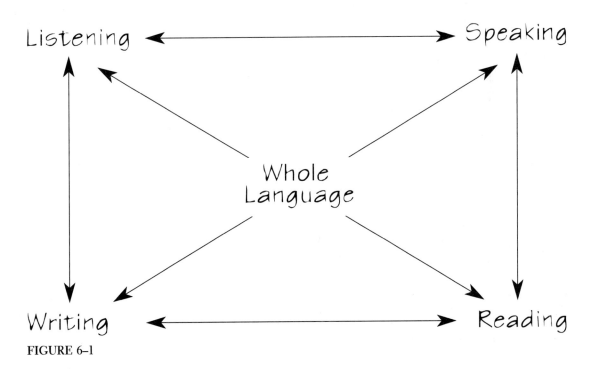

FIGURE 6–1

to teach the components of literacy. These tools include the language experience approach (LEA), in which children dictate to the teacher their thoughts and ideas; the sight- or whole-word approach, in which children see the representation of the whole word and begin to read it; or phonics, in which children learn the letter sound in order to facilitate sounding out the words as they read.

When the whole-language approach is incorporated, there is much to talk about, listen for, write about, and read about. Without meaningful experiences, listening and reading cannot make sense; and one certainly does not talk or write about things that are not understood. An adult with good reading skills could read the words in a textbook on advanced psychology, but actually understanding the meaning of the content would be difficult without previous background experience. So it is with young children: The more experiences they have, the better able they will be to understand what is read to them and later what they read for themselves. We must "build instruction on what the child already knows about oral language, reading, and writing. Focus on meaningful experiences and meaningful language, rather than merely on isolated skill development" (Schickedanz, 1986, p. 13).

High-Quality Children's Literature in the Whole-Language Approach

The language and content of high-quality children's literature are generally more complex than those of basal readers. When reading in early childhood classrooms involves only basal readers, children may feel that reading is not very interesting, because the basal readers are often sterile and lack real-life stories to which the children can relate. When children select stories on their own, they do not choose basal readers. "Simplified in vocabulary and sentence structure, basal stories are often simplistic in content as well. Anticipating that they will read for meaning and fun, children find little in their beginning readers to comprehend" (Salinger, 1988, p. 222).

The whole-language approach encourages teachers to read aloud to children at least once a day from high-quality children's literature. Children who have stories read and told to them are more likely to become good story writers (Hayes, 1990). Reading to children fosters reading development, increases reading comprehension, and expands oral language abilities. For younger children, this is more often done individually or in small groups; whole groups are often used with older children. However, this does not mean that whole groups of very young children do not enjoy having teachers read to them. On the contrary, they do; but the stories need to be shorter and should not be continued from one day to another. Children in first and second grades still enjoy having teachers read from picture books in small groups, but they also begin to enjoy books that are not completed in one sitting but are carried over from day to day, such as *Charlotte's Web* (White, 1952); *Indian in the Cupboard* (Banks, 1981) or the sequels, *The Return of the Indian* (1986), *The Secret of the Indian* (1989); *The Cricket in Times Square* (Selden, 1960); *James and the Giant Peach* (Dahl, 1961); *The Hundred Dresses* (Estes, 1944); *Little House in the Big Woods* (Wilder, 1932) or others in the series; and *Sarah, Plain and Tall* (MacLachlan, 1985). (See "Suggested Resources" at the end of this chapter for complete references.)

One important ingredient, then, of the whole-language approach is to saturate the environment with wonderful books—books about characters with which children can identify; about both familiar and unfamiliar places and events; and about experiences that encourage children to think, laugh, cry, or feel sad. The literature selected must be developmentally appropriate. For example, picture books should be provided for toddlers, with pictures that depict various ages, ethnic groups, and disabilities in positive ways (Bredekamp, 1986). Wordless books should include both the concept type, which works well for children at the labeling stage, and the story type, which can lead children to constructing their own stories (Raines & Isbell, 1988). As children develop good reading skills, they should be guided toward making responsible choices and judgments in selecting reading materials. Certainly not all children's literature is high quality. Providing children with reading lists appropriate to their reading level, including Caldecott and Newbery Award books, is helpful in guiding them to excellent choices.

Language Experience Approach (LEA) as a Part of Whole Language

In the language experience approach, children write and read about their experiences. When they go on a field trip, for example, they return and write about it. Younger children dictate to the teacher; older children write their own stories, poems, ideas, or summaries. Perhaps each child could draw a picture following the field trip and write or dictate to the teacher a description of the picture. These words could be compiled into a class book so that the experience can be enjoyed as well as reinforced in the future. Another approach is to have the class participate together in writing an experience chart. The teacher initially begins with a statement such as "We had an exciting time at Mr. James's farm. Tell me about our trip, and I will write about our experience." The children are invited to participate as they dictate to the teacher where they went, what they did, what they liked, what they did not like, and any other individual perceptions and feelings. The language experience approach can also be used in writing a thank-you letter following a field trip or a meeting with a visitor. The children dictate to the teacher what to say, including their individual reactions. Experiences such as these are termed *whole language* because they incorporate all the components of literacy development.

Prior to the field trip, in addition to the discussion and other preparations (which include speaking and listening), the children could write a note home, or take one written by the teacher, that tells of the forthcoming field trip and activities. Also, directions for getting to the field trip destination could be written down and followed as the trip is made. Children then learn that we communicate with people by speaking, writing, listening, and reading. They also learn that their own thoughts can be both written and read, whether they do the writing and reading themselves or someone else does it for them.

Throughout the planning and carrying out of the field trip, the children listen for the purpose of gaining meaning and understanding. In addition, they are able to use oral language before, during, and after the field trip as they ask questions, participate in discussions, comment, make inferences, answer questions, and use other forms of oral language. Following the trip, they write about the experience by making an experience chart, individual or class book, or thank-you note. Afterwards, they read—sometimes many times—what they have written.

The described environment and experiences focus on the values and meanings of literacy. In whole language, literacy is woven in a natural way throughout the curriculum.

Encouraging Literacy Development

We suggest the following general ways to encourage literacy development:

1. The free play period provides a prime time for teachers to interact with children on a one-to-one basis or in small groups. As children play with manipulative toys, work with blocks, enjoy books, play in the dramatic play area, use sensory materials, or use any of the areas provided during free play, teachers should encourage them to talk and listen to one another. Also, teachers and caregivers should talk with, listen to, and read to children. Often teachers use free play time as a break period for themselves; they do not realize the opportunity for individual and small-group speaking, listening, and reading so beautifully provided in free play. Discussions with children can address the project with which they are involved, or they can be unrelated and ad-

dress their home, hobbies, or other interests.

2. Provide many opportunities for talking, and then be sure to listen. Provide a model for listening. Do not talk too much—the voice that goes on and on is often tuned out. If you do not listen to children, how can you expect children to listen to others? Let the children know that you are listening to them by being attentive and focusing your eyes upon them. Find time to listen to each child.

3. Teachers should not only inquire of children often, they should provide for stimulating inquiry. (*Inquiry* refers here to the use of questions.) Two practices that stifle inquiry are emphasis on exact answers and emphasis on competition. Teachers should ask questions that require thinking responses; they should also encourage and respect the questions children ask. Unusual questions and answers lead to deeper thinking; deeper thinking requires greater communicative ability; and greater communicative ability means language growth. Use thought-provoking questions often.

4. Recognize and accept individual language diversity in children (Soto, 1991). However, teachers must be diagnosticians. Thus they must determine literacy deficiencies and then select the procedures they will use in trying to overcome these deficiencies. They evaluate where the children are in their literacy development and how they can be stimulated and challenged to progress further. Teachers also determine readiness levels for instruction.

5. Teachers should keep in mind the factors influencing the development of language, and therefore strive to be high-quality models, speaking distinctly, calmly, pleasantly, and with well-chosen words. Teachers should also give and encourage language feedback and provide new experiences.

6. Teachers should use the sentence as the basic unit of speech, as well as teach children to speak likewise in complete thoughts or sentences. When we speak in sentences, we express complete and meaningful thoughts. This instruction is also excellent for reading readiness, since books are written in complete sentence form.

7. Establish a comfortable, relaxed atmosphere that stimulates children to talk freely with others.

8. Recognize that grammatical errors, particularly verb and pronoun problems, are typical in the early childhood years. Rather than putting too much emphasis on exactness of speech, repeat the sentence to the child, using correct grammar so that the proper form is heard. Thus the child will not feel a sense of failure but will nevertheless be made aware of correct usage.

9. Use specific words that will help expand the children's vocabularies as well as teach the meanings of words. Too often we speak in general terms such as "Put the book over there," as opposed to "Put the blue book on the middle bookshelf."

10. Verbalize what children are doing. Paint word pictures for them about whatever activity they are involved in—for example, "I see Amy climbing very high on the jungle gym."

11. Help children draw meaning from their listening, speaking, reading, and writing experiences with literacy. For example, when someone speaks it may be necessary to rephrase or ask, "Is this what you mean?" When a visitor comes, or when the class goes on a field trip, it may be helpful to rephrase some of the conversation in order for the children to draw meaning from and understand what is communicated. Rephrasing may also be necessary as selections of children's literature are read and shared. Sometimes it is only necessary

to define the meaning of one word in order for the context and ideas to be understood. Our goal in literacy development is to encourage children not only to speak, listen, read, and write, but to do so with meaning and with understanding of what has been spoken, heard, written, or read.

12. Take advantage of opportunities for using written instructions, even when the children themselves cannot read. For example, the recipe should be available during a cooking experience so that the teacher can read the instructions and the children understand that the recipe communicates what to do. On a field trip, the children can follow a map of instructions that tells them how to get to their destination, as well as what to look for when they get there.

13. Teachers and caregivers should label and read the items seen and used in the classroom. For example, during science or food activities, ingredient labels can be read to the children. When children are away from the classroom, labels on signs, doorways, billboards, and other areas can be read and pointed out.

14. The classroom environment should include print in areas besides the book or story area. Again, even before children read, they should see words and print in their environment—word lists, phrases, charts, signs, labels, calendars, recipes, and so on.

15. The importance, value, and rewards of daily reading aloud to children of *all* ages cannot be overemphasized. These daily readings aloud "will become one of the best parts of your day and the children's day. These moments and hours will be cherished for years to come" (Trelease, 1985, p. xviii). Choose books suited to the experiences and needs of children in your classroom (Wolter, 1992). Recently, Big Books (enlarged textbooks or children's oversized books) have become valuable tools for enhancing children's enjoyment and understanding of literature. They can be obtained commercially or prepared by the teacher or individual children. In addition, interest centers for listening should be encouraged. Earphones can be attached to a tape recorder, and children can listen to commercially prepared stories. Cassettes of teachers reading favorite stories can be enjoyed over and over again by the children, either individually or in a small group.

16. Have children write their own books and stories, which are placed in the story area to be read and enjoyed again and again. Children's self-directed writings demonstrate how much they know and can do (Juliebö & Edwards, 1989). If children are able to write, they can be encouraged to write and illustrate their own stories. If they do not write, they can illustrate their stories (pretend or real experiences) and dictate them to a teacher or caregiver. Children in early childhood classes will enjoy making calendar books. For each day of a particular month, cut a sheet of paper approximately 4 × 5 inches. Put the numeral representing the day at the top of the paper, and then put the papers on a bulletin board in the correct order and placement representing that month. After each day, have a child in the class draw a picture on the paper representing that day and perhaps something that happened at home, at school, or with the weather. Children who are able to write can write about what was drawn. Children who do not write should dictate something about the picture to the teacher. At the end of the month, take the numbered pictures down and put them in order. Add a cover sheet with the name of the month and then staple or bind the pages together. Add this "book" to the book center for the children to enjoy reading again and again. They will especially enjoy "reading" the pages they have created.

A valuable literacy experience is having children of all ages write or draw personal journals in which they make periodic entries.

Listening and Speaking

Listening

Listening is a skill that needs to be taught deliberately in the early childhood years. It is a serious mistake to ignore the need for instruction in listening. "Children do not need to listen *more*, they need to listen *better*" (Winn, 1988, p. 144).

Listening skills include *auditory perception*, the ability to perceive and understand what is heard; *auditory discrimination*, the ability to make fine discriminations among sounds; *auditory memory*, the ability to remember the sequence of sounds within words and sentences; *auditory association*, the ability to associate sounds or words with experiences, objects, ideas, or feelings; and *rhyming skills*, the ability to recognize and reproduce words that rhyme.

Speaking

"Children learn to speak by being immersed in a verbal atmosphere, a rich broth of words, gestures, and expressions" (Freidberg, 1989, p. 13).

Speaking or oral communication influences, and is influenced by, every other aspect of development. Most children in the early childhood years have the ability to speak, but their oral language skills need enhancement and refining. Teachers must respect and accept the language of the child and provide an exemplary role model for good listening. In other words, encourage oral language by being a good listener!

Activities for Listening and Speaking

The following are some suggested activities for listening and speaking with a focus on helping children to acquire literacy. Remember, good listening skills influence reading abilities, and good speaking skills influence writing abilities.

1. In question periods, questions are given and answers are brainstormed and shared. The questions might be thought-provoking realistic questions, or they might be thought-provoking nonsense questions. For example:

What new machine might you invent?
What would you do if you could only walk backward?
What would you make red to make it more beautiful?
What would you do if you woke up one morning to a backyard full of elephants?
What would be your one wish?
What would you purchase if you could purchase anything in the whole world?
If you could make a contribution to the world, what would it be?
What would you like instead of school?
What would you give feathers to make it softer?
What is your greatest hope?
What changes would you like to make in yourself?
What if everyone had a long neck like a giraffe?

Once the children catch on to this type of questioning, they will enjoy making up questions. Perhaps this activity could be done in cooperative learning groups, using Think-Pair-Share as a strategy. Remember that all questions and answers are correct and acceptable.

2. Simple question-answer games can be played, in which the children sit in a circle while questions are asked. Then a ball or bean bag is thrown to a child, who answers the question in a complete sentence. This same child asks another question in complete-sentence form, and the bean bag or ball is tossed to another child for answering.

3. A sack of objects can be used for discussion and language development. The children can learn about and discuss the objects; then directions will be given, in complete sentences, about what will be done with the objects. The teacher or a child might say, "Put the green block on top of Jenny's head," or "Put the gerbil food underneath Stephanie's chair," or "Put the box on the floor and hop over it three times." This game not only teaches new words, or labels, but also develops prepositional understandings.

4. Divide the children into smaller groups and give a picture to each group for discussion. The pictures could be snapshots the children brought from home, which would encourage children to talk as their pictures are shown to the group.

5. Show-and-tell, or sharing time, is enjoyable if it is not presented too often. In one preschool class, the children are assigned a particular day during one week when they can bring something from home and tell about it. Each day during the set-aside time, five chairs are placed in front of the class, and five proud children bring their sacks holding the secret of the item they are anxious to tell the class about. In another class, the teacher uses a large duffle bag and calls it the *mystery* bag. Each day, one child brings something to show or tell about and places it in the mystery bag. The class can guess what is in the bag; if they have trouble guessing correctly, the child who brought the object can give clues. The child who guesses what is in the mystery bag is allowed to take it home that day if he or she has not had a turn for a while.

6. Whenever there is a focus on a basic concept such as numbers, shapes, colors, or textures, there are numerous questions that can be posed to stimulate thinking, speaking, and listening. Many of these questions have been suggested in the chapters on the various concepts; however, additional questions might include: "What is your favorite_____[animal, shape, color, etc.], and why is it your favorite?" "If you could give this_____[animal, texture, shape, etc.] another name, what might it be?" "What things that are not already

_____[name, color, shape, size] would you make_____[same word]?"

7. During a discussion, problem-solving statements, questions, and riddles or other language stimulators can be taped to the bottoms of chairs, picked from a bulletin board, or drawn from a sack. This approach also maintains attention in an unusual way.

8. Listening can be encouraged through games that induce the children to listen to instructions given. "Put Your Finger in the Air" and "Simon Says" are examples of such games.

9. In cooperative pairs, give each child a blank piece of paper and crayons. Give simple directions such as "Draw a ball in any color, but put it in one of the corners of your paper." After the children have had a chance to follow the directions, they tell their partners what they did. Jane might say, "I drew a red ball in the upper corner of my paper." Adults should be nearby to give assistance when it is needed.

10. Pages from workbooks can be torn out and covered with clear plastic or contact paper. Shapes from paper, felt, plastic, heavy poster paper, or other material are cut out so that various colors are available for each worksheet. Instructions might state: "Pick any shape, but it must be a blue one, and put it on a picture of_____[name a picture or a description of a picture]." After the action, the instruction is repeated. There are numerous speaking and listening games that can be developed from old workbooks, such as sequence stories and discrimination and perception exercises, and all can be adapted to literacy activities. Once the children are familiar with a page, cover one section or picture and have them try to remember what is covered. Questions can be asked and clues given as reminders.

11. Show a film or filmstrip, but do not include the sound. Instead, have the children make up the story.

12. Rhyming couplets can be shared with children; the last word of the couplet, which rhymes with the word at the end of the first line, can be left off so that the children can guess what the word is. This activity can also be used with poems that rhyme, with the second word in a rhyming sequence left out for the children to guess. Younger children can listen to the couplet and tell the two words that rhyme. Children could work in cooperative learning groups on these activities.

13. To encourage participation from children who neither listen nor speak well, sometimes a warning is helpful. Instead of calling on the children after the listening is over, tell them *before* they listen that they need to listen especially well because you will have a question for them afterward. For those children who always want to answer and speak, you might call them by name and say, "You might know the answer to the question I am going to ask, but see if you can keep it a secret while I give Jared a turn to answer." Or you might let them whisper the answer in your ear; the joy of having a secret will encourage them to give other children a chance to respond.

14. Give three or four words in sequence, all but one of them beginning with the same consonant sound. Ask the children to listen for the one that is not the same (e.g., *tomato, trunk, egg, tumble*).

15. After experiences involving field trips, stories, food activities, science activities, or visitors, have the children summarize the experiences, and write this summary in the form of a story on a chart or chalkboard to be read back to the children.

16. After a story with a definite sequence of events, have the children recall the events in the order in which they occurred.

17. Make use of sequence stories in workbooks or cartoons. The various parts of the story

can be glued to wooden blocks, plywood, or poster paper to make sequence puzzles. The children must find the correct sequence and then tell the story.

18. Have one child start to tell a story and the next child add to it.

19. Encourage conversation and listening between two children through the use of two telephones.

20. In cooperative learning groups, brainstorm specific items within a given category. For example, after the teacher says the word *animal*, the children can brainstorm all the animals they can remember. Children who read can have their brainstorm topics written down.

21. Make surprise boxes by wrapping them up and having the children guess what might be inside. Then unwrap them and have the children describe the object or objects and how they are used.

22. Wrap boxes with materials used by specific professions. For example, one box might be a mail-carrier box, with envelopes, stamps, rubber stamps, and other items that can be located representing the postal profession. As the children unwrap this box, they can tell each item's use and any other points they wish to make. Other boxes could be wrapped for a plumber, teacher, secretary, police officer, farmer, and so on. Another alternative would be to have each child bring from home a wrapped box representing a parent's profession. The children could exchange these boxes so that each child has one to unwrap; then they could guess whose box they have.

23. Have the children draw pictures representing specific experiences and then discuss the pictures. Instead of drawing the pictures, they can be asked to think of the experience and then relate it to the group. For example, they might be asked to share the most embarrassing experience,

the saddest experience, the funniest experience, the most frightening experience, or the most exciting experience they have ever had.

24. As stories or poems are read or told, words or phrases can be left out, and the children can guess what the missing words might be.

25. A group of rhyming words can be shared (for younger children, three words are enough), including one word that does not rhyme. The children listen and then tell which word does not rhyme.

26. What can it be? The children close their eyes, while the teacher makes familiar sounds behind a screen and asks the children to identify each sound. The following might be used: crushing paper, whistling, pouring water, peeling a carrot.

27. What am I? The children divide into two parallel lines. In one line, each child makes some sound, such as an animal sound, machine sound, or weather sound, and the children in the opposite line try to guess what the sound represents. For younger children, pick a single category such as animal sounds.

28. Give the children in cooperative learning groups various "Tell me . . ." statements and encourage brainstorming. Examples: "Tell me what colors the sky can be." "Tell me how many things you can wear on your head." "Tell me things that fly."

29. Give rhyming riddles for the children to guess. Examples: "I rhyme with damp. I sit on the table. What am I?" "I rhyme with chose, and I am on your face. What am I?"

30. Have each child pick an object out of a sack and describe the object.

31. Give a category, such as fruits, vegetables, or toys, and have the children name and describe items that fit into that category.

32. In cooperative learning groups, brainstorm things you would send on a train. Have a

spokesperson report. Read to the whole group, *The Little Engine That Could* (Piper, 1930). Have the children return to their groups and add to the list of things you would send on a train.

33. Using inside-outside circles (children form two concentric circles), have partners and ask questions. Each partner has a turn to listen and to answer. Ask questions about the theme being explored or open-ended and questions such as "What makes you happy?", "What makes you upset?", "What is your favorite place to visit?", or other questions children could explore comfortably with one another.

34. Children form inside-outside cooperative learning circles and face their partners. The teacher gives a word and the outside circle thinks of a synonym, then the inside circle gives a word that rhymes with it. The activity can progress in this way with the teacher giving new words to explore. Other ideas: Include a word that begins or ends with the same sound and use the word in a sentence; or give a word that is an antonym. The teacher adapts the way the word is approached to the developmental needs of the children.

35. After reading *There's a Nightmare in My Closet* (Mayer, 1968), or *Where the Wild Things Are* (Sendak, 1963), divide the children into cooperative learning groups. Using a large piece of butcher paper, as a group the children will create their own monster using crayons, marking pens, or paints. Each group will have a spokesperson to tell about their project, then all drawings will be displayed in the room.

36. Divide the children into two groups. One group will be the "when" group and the other will be the "where" group. The children will listen as you give two phrases, then decide as a team whether either phrase describes when or where. If the "when" group thinks one of the phrases

describes "when," they raise their hands and repeat the phrase; or if the "where" group thinks one of the phrases describes "where," they raise their hands and repeat the phrase. Examples of phrase pairs include:

on the beach	as fast as can be	(where)
at midnight	green as grass	(when)
calling loudly	in the morning	(when)
happily	yesterday	(when)
too soon	in the closet	(where)
angrily paused	up the hill	(where)

37. Assign each cooperative learning group a topic to brainstorm. What can go *into*: a car truck, a pocket, a wallet, a suitcase, a treasure chest, a tackle box?

Throughout the day, there will be many opportunities to develop listening and speaking skills in young children. Be alert to these opportunities and cognizant of their importance. Also remember that children's attempts to express themselves and share their ideas are more important than perfect language usage. Do not drill on perfect grammar or articulation. Let children learn to enjoy listening and speaking.

Reading and Writing

Reading and writing are the other two main ingredients of literacy in early childhood. Before children learn about letter sounds and names, they must have numerous developmentally appropriate opportunities to observe the values and usefulness of reading and writing (Bredekamp, 1986). If a teacher believes (and teaches accordingly) that children will be successful readers and writers, generally the children *will* be successful readers and writers (Mills & Clyde, 1991).

Reading

Often when parents are selecting preschools for their children, one of the first questions they ask is, "Do you teach reading?" Any knowledgeable preschool teacher, aware of the importance and directions of the early years, should enthusiastically respond with "Yes, reading readiness." Many of the study areas presented in this book are specific reading readiness concepts (i.e., shape, sound, and color). Before children have reading facility, they need to have had numerous experiences to sharpen their visual and aural perception. Kontos (1986) points out that before children can become readers, they "must learn *why* people read and *what* people do when they read. This is called print awareness" (p. 58). Remember, reading involves the ability to differentiate similarities and differences in visual patterns, forms, and sounds.

Children must also have reached a certain cognitive maturity and readiness resulting in their desire to read. There are "two kinds of children: those who love to read and those who think they don't" (Fadiman, 1984, p. xviii). Fadiman refers to Fitzhugh's *Harriet the Spy* (1964), where "Harriet sits down to read. 'How I love to read,' she thought. 'The whole world gets bigger'" (p. xix). Fadiman continues, "As for those who think they don't like to read, well, they're making a mistake, just as all of us do when we try to judge ourselves" (p. xix).

Like any other skill, learning to read takes time, patience, desire, and readiness. One of the most important ingredients in children's readiness for reading is whether or not they have been read to. Children who have enjoyed picture, alphabet, nursery rhyme, and storybooks from early infancy will have a greater desire to read because they know that reading opens new doors, provides information, and is enjoyable. Some ask how young children should be when parents start reading to them. Our answer is, early infancy. From the earliest days, infants learn how books look and feel, how to turn pages, how to be careful with books, how to develop listening skills, and that words and pictures have meaning. "There is nothing magic about the way contact with books in early years produces early readers. One would surely expect it to. A baby is learning

about the way language arises from the page each time his parent opens a book, from earliest days" (Butler and Clay, 1982, pp. 9–10). We advocate reading to very young children and suggest giving children as much as they are ready for as early as they are ready for it.

In addition to reading to children, speaking clearly, distinctly, and with a broad and ever-expanding vocabulary will also foster reading readiness. Reading is a communicative art involving both recognizing and understanding words (Maxim, 1989). We cannot read with understanding and comprehension something that we do not understand the meaning of ourselves. As we speak to and communicate with children, we should endeavor to expand their vocabulary to include both word pronunciation and definition. A child who reads a word but attaches no meaning to it is not reading with comprehension. The meaning of words must evolve through experiences with them. The more experiences children have, and the more these experiences are labeled with words, the more effective their reading experiences become. Therefore, we support the experience approach to reading. During the reading readiness and beginning reading stages, stories about the children's experiences should be written on chart paper and read aloud often. At approximately 6 or 7 years of age, when most children begin writing, they can write and read about their own experiences.

Other related skills prerequisite to fluent reading include large- and small-muscle development, social and emotional maturity, and intellectual and language experiences. Teachers can do much in the early childhood years to prepare children for reading. Ideally, effective early learning activities are combined with the teacher's understanding attitude, resulting in the development of positive attitudes toward reading. The ability to read is important in academic success.

Johnson (1983) suggests that to begin to read fluently, the child must master the following skills:

1. Name the letters of the alphabet, both upper and lowercase;
2. Associate one sound with each letter;
3. Recognize some basic sight words;
4. See a connection between speech and print;
5. See a relationship between letters and words;
6. See a relationship between words and sentences;
7. Know that we read from left to right, top to bottom. (p. 118)

Before recognizing and naming letters of the alphabet, children must be familiar with letter shapes. It is important for children to be familiar with letters and to recognize that these letters are related to reading. We believe it is difficult to teach letter shapes and functions without teaching the names of the letters. Usually, among the first letters children are able to recognize and name are those in their own name. In teaching letter recognition, make children aware that 11 of the letters have basically the same shape in both lower and upper case (i.e., *Cc, Kk, Oo, Pp, Ss, Uu, Vv, Ww, Xx, Yy, Zz*). Five of the letters are similar in upper and lower case (i.e., *Tt, Mm, Nn, Jj, and Hh*). It is most difficult to find similarities between upper and lower case in the other 10 letters because of their differences (i.e., *Aa, Bb, Dd, Ee, Ff, Gg, Ii, Ll, Qq, Rr*).

As children begin to recognize words, they discover that letters also have sounds. In fact, all but two letters in the alphabet have one major characteristic sound. W and Q are the exceptions; they do not indicate a representative sound. Children eventually learn that some of the letters, such as the vowels, have more than one major sound. Children learn alphabet recognition in context or as they interact with materials relating to their written language (books, chalk, chalkboards, paper, pens, markers, and so on).

Children can be encouraged to develop and strengthen reading skills. To become readers in the sense that they seek out and enjoy reading, children must develop skill in drawing meaning from the printed word, which gives purpose to reading. "Comprehension and meaning [should be] emphasized from the beginning, not after a child learns to read" (Throne, 1988, p. 11).

When using phonics, there are many words that are not sounded out. Some words may be best attacked using the sight-word strategy. Children are often faster and smoother readers when they build up a repertoire of sight words; otherwise, they tend to try to sound out each word, sound by sound.

Phonics is a strategy using the sounds letters represent and the resulting sounds made as they

Tyson knows how to spell Megan, his sister's name, but has difficulty solving the problem of making curved letters with straight sticks.

are combined with other letters. Once children are able to sound out words, they also begin to spell words. Spelling, in fact, is practice for phonics strategies. However, the same words that are difficult to sound out using phonics are also difficult to spell. For example, if you ask a young child to spell *wait*, a word unknown as a sight word to this child, the child would probably apply some beginning phonics to the problem and spell it *w-a-t-e*.

Reading is a vital part of literacy development. It is our hope that teachers sense their responsibility in helping children acquire both the ability and the desire to read. We believe that too much emphasis in early childhood classrooms is put on dittos and worksheets. "Children have a right to learn to read from people rather than procedures and programs" (Reutzel & Cooter, 1992, p. 22). We suggest that dittos and worksheets make reading a task and create a feeling of drudgery and boredom for many children. Salinger (1988) explains:

Copying is manually reproducing a graphic image, again with little or no regard for meaning. . . . Because forms of copying and deciphering have been the core of much early childhood reading and language instruction for many years, it is logical to assume that at least some educators have trusted them to promote literacy. Too much emphasis on deciphering or sounding out encourages children to believe that reading involves no more than making the correct oral response for each printed word they see. (p. 72)

There are many ways of preparing teacher-made learning materials that focus on reading skills. Some of these are pictured in Appendix A. These ideas also adapt readily to reading activities. For example, lotto games could be adapted to a word game in which the children classify words as a person, place, or thing. To explain further, a number of words (such as *girl, park, baby, ball, hammer, store, pen,* or *man*) can be written in boxes drawn on a poster paper or card stock paper. A number of cover category cards would individually read *person, place,* and *thing*. The children then match these cover cards on top of each word. This activity not only helps children to classify but also facilitates drawing meaning from words.

An additional suggestion for reading games involves making flowers. On a flower center (or circle), write a word ending such as *er* or *est*. With a paper fastener, attach petals to the flower center. On each petal, write a word such as *fast, slow, bright,* or *light*. As the petals are rotated around the center, new words are formed. A variation could have *ing* or *ed* as center suffixes, with words such as *work, talk, jump,* and *walk* as petal words. This same concept can be used with two wheels made from card stock or tagboard attached together with a paper fastener. The inside wheel could have consonant sounds, blends, root words, or prefixes. The outside wheel could have suffixes or word endings.

Another example is to cut word cards out of index card stock or use precut 3 × 5 inch cards. Fold the right-hand side of the card under about 1 inch from the edge. Now write a word that uses the silent *e* rule on each of the cards. For example words such as *cape, tape,* or *care* can be used. Write each word on the card in such a way that the *e* can be folded under. The children then read the word both without and with the silent *e* on the end.

Writing

Handwriting

Matthew was drawing circle-type shapes on the fogged-up car window. "I'm writing in cursive," he proudly announced. "What does it say?" asked his father. "Oh, I don't know. I can only write in cursive, I can't read in cursive!" answered Matthew.

Another ingredient in the language and literacy program is handwriting, which should be an integral part of the oral and written language program. There is a connection between listening, talking, reading, and writing. Experiences in these areas are best when they overlap one another.

Lamme (1982) lists six skill areas that are prerequisites for handwriting: "small muscle development, eye–hand coordination, holding a writing tool, basic strokes, letter perception, and orientation to printed language" (p. 109). We suggest that children need many experiences with tools such as paper, paints, pens, markers, chalk, brushes, pencils, and crayons to develop abilities not only in handling and using these tools but also in making refined strokes. As children begin to understand symbols and expand their awareness that these symbols have meaning, alphabet letters begin to appear in their artwork (Dyson, 1990). Children should be able to copy simple shapes, differentiating likenesses and differences in both the shapes and sizes of objects and letters. Just as with reading, children must display a keen interest in learning to write and a desire to do so. For example, children who are ready for writing activities often try to write or copy letters, words, and even sentences.

Alphabet letters may be abstract to the child, and should be kept in units or words. Teaching them apart from the words would make them developmentally difficult for young beginners to learn. Because many children develop writing skills at home, parents should be aware of when children might begin writing, specific signs indicating readiness for writing instruction, and how to teach correct skills.

Before children begin to write and use the alphabet letters in writing activities, they should have many experiences using alphabet and sight-word manipulative toys. For example, matching games with upper- and lower-case alphabet letters can be made using any of the lotto game patterns in Appendix A. Alphabet cards, either teacher made or purchased, can be used for various alphabet games and activities.

Learning to form, remember, and read letters is a difficult and slow process (a monumental task!), and each letter offers a unique challenge. Teachers must allow for mistakes, reversals, and incorrectly formed letters. It is challenging for children to maintain uniform size and stay within the lines. "Legibility will come with increased small-muscle control, practice, and motivation" (Salinger, 1988, p. 97). Writing takes much prac-

tice before it becomes natural, attractive, and neat. Teachers must be patient, allow plenty of time, praise positive efforts, and avoid pushing children who are not ready for the experience. Early experiences can be tracing activities; first experiences should be words, followed by short sentences and then short stories.

Creative writing or composing. Children learning to write need patient, supportive, accepting, and appreciative adults who realize that errors are a part of the learning process (Atkins, 1984). In fact, we strongly urge teachers to provide many opportunities for creative writing or composing, beginning with those experiences where children dictate their ideas, stories, or poems to the teacher. When children begin their first composition efforts, there should be no focus on the form of the writing, spelling, or punctuation. These mechanics can come later. Spelling, punctuation, neatness, and accuracy can be worked on once the child has had many experiences writing for the sake of communicating an idea. The initial focus in composing should be on the idea and the effort that the children make. "Unfortunately, the close connection between reading and writing is often ripped apart in the early grades by emphasis on subskills and by fragmented drill-and-practice activities" (Salinger, 1988, p. 257).

When children are routinely involved in the writing process, their reading ability grows rapidly: Readers become better writers and writers become better readers (Reutzel & Cooter, 1992). A delightful writing activity throughout the year for first and second graders is keeping a personal journal. At the end of the year, teachers and parents enjoy the sequence of activities and feelings expressed by the children, while seeing progress in the children's abilities to compose and write. Hatch (1992) presents the following five generalizations for effective writing experiences and activities:

1. every primary classroom should have a writing center;
2. children should write every day;

3. teachers should model effective writing behavior;
4. children's writing should grow out of real experiences; and
5. young writers should be given opportunities to share their work with others. (p. 55)

Activities for Reading and Writing

Hopefully some of the first reading experiences teachers provide for young children will be those which children have composed or "authored" themselves. Very early, children should learn that what they have spoken and has been written down can be read by someone. Therefore, as the children describe an experience, a picture they have drawn, or their feeling about an idea, teacher and assistants can write down their exact words, which can then be read back to the children. Class books can be made by giving the children an idea, having them illustrate it, and then dictating to an adult their description, which the adult writes on the illustration. Pages can then be put together, with each child "authoring" a page. These books will become favorites to read again and again. Examples of class books are "Our Favorite Animals," "Zoo Animals We Like," "Favorite Dinosaurs," "Vacations We Have Taken," and ideas that tie into themes being explored.

Many of the activities listed under "Speaking and Listening Activities" can be adapted for reading and writing. Instead of listening, the children read; instead of speaking, they write. Simply adapt the activities to the developmental abilities and levels of the children in your class.

There are a number of ways, beyond the early experiences just described, to help children who are ready for writing. To encourage children who are ready for more advanced writing experiences, you may wish to use one of the following approaches:

1. Show them how to build a web. For example, perhaps they will write about a summer vacation. The title of the vacation would be the center circle, and circles around that might be things they did each day. One circle might be the beach, one an amusement park, one a visit to the zoo, and another a visit to Aunt Mary's. For each of these, ask children to describe what happened or what they remember about the experience, then write these ideas around each circle, connecting them to the center circle. When they finish their web, each circle can represent a paragraph they can write about.

2. A second approach is to give them steps to writing. For example, you can teach them to think about their ideas and what they might write about, then brainstorm or organize these ideas and even number the order the ideas should be in. Next, they should read what they wrote and make changes if they desire. Children's early writing experiences should not emphasize grammar, spelling, neatness, or other things that will come later. The focus should simply be on sharing their ideas through writing.

Following are some additional writing and reading activities that can be used in early childhood. Remember, just because children do not have handwriting skills does not mean they cannot write. Instead, they can speak or dictate as an adult writes down word for word what they say.

1. Use open-ended proverbs. Each child is given an open-ended proverb to write or dictate and then illustrate. The children fold their paper in half. On the left side, they write the part of the proverb assigned, and on the right side, they finish it. Or, the first part of the proverb can be written at the top of the paper and the children write or dictate the ending at the bottom of the page and then illustrate it in the middle of the paper. Examples of open-ended proverbs include the following:

   "Don't count your chickens . . ."
   "He who is too greedy . . ."
   "Think twice before . . ."
   "Borrowed feather . . ."
   "Kindness works better . . ."
   "You can't tell a book . . ."
   "One good turn deserves . . ."

"The apple doesn't fall . . ."
"Half a loaf is . . ."
"Do unto others as . . ."
"Think before . . ."
"Biggest is . . ."
"Slow and steady . . ."
"A soft answer . . ."
"What goes up . . ."
"An ounce of prevention is worth . . ."
"Spare the rod and . . ."
"Silence is . . ."

Following are some examples of how first grade children completed some proverbs:

"If you can't stand the heat . . . go in the snow."
"A penny saved is . . . money in my bank."
"The grass is always greener . . . on the ground."
"Everything comes to him who . . . reads and makes money."
"Money is the root of all . . . trees."
"Early to bed and early to rise makes . . . me cry."
"If at first you don't succeed . . . wait until you're stronger."
"All that glitters . . . isn't the stars."
"You can't teach an old dog . . . to read."

2. Show the children a picture and have them dictate or write about it. Calendars, magazines, and photographs are sources for pictures.

3. Have the children create an ABC of pretend monsters. Each child selects a letter of the alphabet, imagines a monster, then writes or dictates a description of that monster. For example, "A" might be an "Atarox"—a 17-foot-long garbage-eater that loves "rox" (rocks) for dessert. The children would illustrate their monsters on their pages.

4. Have the children write "bubble gum" poems. In cooperative learning groups, each group writes a poem titled, "To Chew or Not to Chew." The children write a positive comment about gum as the first line, then a negative comment for the second line. The groups can put the pairs of lines together for a class poem. (Adapted from Wayman & Plum, 1977, p. 72.)

5. Have the children bring a favorite possession from home, and place it in a bag. On the outside of the bag, write at least five words that describe it without telling what it is. Class members guess what is in the bag.

6. Divide the children into cooperative learning groups and give each group a different hat. Each group will write five words to describe the hat and then write who would use the hat.

7. Give each cooperative learning group five words and have them write a synonym for each word. Examples include the following:

scream—yell	cent—penny
fast—speedy	little—small
glad—happy	leap—jump
pal—friend	share—divide
large—big	start—begin
hurry—rush	smell—sniff
town—city	smile—grin
skinny—thin	angry—mad
scared—afraid	save—keep
close—shut	stop—quit

(This activity can be done with rhyming words, words that start with the same sound, antonyms, or other language activities.)

8. Give the children open-ended similes to complete in the same way as the proverbs in activity 1. Examples include the following:

As quiet as . . .	As busy as . . .
As sly as . . .	As slow as . . .
As slippery as . . .	As free as . . .
As wise as . . .	As red as . . .
As silly as . . .	As hungry as . . .

9. Give the children story-starters to complete. These can be done individually or in cooperative learning groups. Examples include the following:

> I make the most unusual sundae! First I take . . .
>
> I have an unexpected house guest in the bottom drawer . . .
>
> While working in my lab late one night . . .
>
> I opened the door and . . .
>
> How to make a lizard laugh . . .
>
> My Mom says, "Don't . . ."

10. Have the children write and illustrate their own riddles.

11. Using stickers, illustrations from workbook or other sources, have the children describe each object and develop a picture dictionary.

12. Have the children write recipes or directions for their favorite dishes.

13. After reading a story, have the children describe and write about their favorite character.

14. After reading a story or book, have the children describe a present they would give to the main character or a character of their choosing.

15. Pick an item that will change over time, and once every few days or so have the children use 5 to 10 words to describe it. Items might include a seed that will sprout, a flower, a glass of milk, or a slice of bread in a moist wrapper.

16. Have the children form cooperative learning groups. Assign each group a different topic or word and have them brainstorm and write as many ideas as they can for each spoke on the wheel. Topics might include insects, books, a yo-yo, homes, cages, umbrellas, spaceships, water, red, weekends, or spring, or they might relate to a theme being studied. (See Figure 6–2.)

17. Set up a "mailbox" in the room and have the children write letters to a character such as Barnaby Bear or Lassie. When a child "mails" a letter, he or she should always receive a reply. Perhaps a volunteer parent could be assigned to answer each letter during the year.

Writing activities can be used for children who need an extra challenge as well as for those who enjoy the opportunity of using this creative means of communication. Too often it is left out of the curriculum, and then we wonder why older children lack writing skills.

Other Activities in Language Arts

There are several other areas of literacy that are vital to early childhood education and therefore need specific discussion. Stories, poetry, and fingerplays are all activities that involve listening, speaking, reading, or writing. It is hoped that toward the end of the early childhood years, children will be given many opportunities and much stimulus for writing their own stories and poems.

Children's Literature

There should be ample room for fun, play, and self-expression in the literacy curriculum. Stories capture the attention of children and adults and give enjoyment and relaxation. In addition, stories provide information, teach new words and concepts, are often remembered more easily than general information, and encourage an appreciation for literature. A story, although a vicarious experience, can often teach a concept or give information that otherwise might be impossible to learn.

Stories can be used to teach social skills and values; children learn from the "friends" they identify with in stories. Stories offer opportunities for children to enjoy the world of pretend, encourage appreciation of beauty and various cultures (Harris, 1991), and help children learn to follow a sequence of events. Try telling a story, and then retelling it using the "What happens

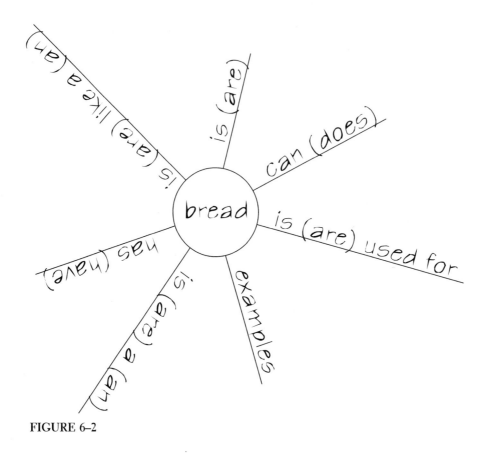

FIGURE 6–2

next?" approach. Begin the story, then allow the children to relate the sequences and events. Well-chosen and well-told stories will also provide appropriate patterns of speech and foster language skills. Reading aloud satisfies emotional needs as the listeners enjoy physical closeness with the reader, and it facilitates development of social skills through pictures, content, and learning appropriate behavior during the reading experiences (Conlon, 1992, p. 15). Children learn early to value stories, and they learn that the printed word is the key that opens the door to the world.

Often when children are restless or when the teacher is in need of an immediate activity, a well-told story is the best solution. For this reason, teachers of young children should know many stories. What a teacher needs most to tell

a story effectively to young children is a love of stories, and enthusiasm for telling them.

Guidelines for selecting stories. The various ages of children in the early childhood category should be remembered when stories are selected. The following guidelines also include additional criteria for selecting books and stories. Just because a story has been published does not mean that it is appropriate for young children.

1. For 3- *and 4-year-olds*, avoid stories with a strong fear element. For this reason, some of the fairy tales should be avoided until children can better separate fact from fantasy. The stories should be short; if a story is told from a book, there should be few printed words in relation to the number of pictures.

Choose stories with a simple, linear plot, as well as stories with repetition; children will enjoy chanting or saying the repetition after they have heard it several times. Stories should be realistic. Children prefer stories about animals, children, and other people.

For 5- *and* 6-*year-olds*, stories can be more complicated, and they can distinguish fact from fantasy. These children like adventure and nonsense stories, and those with surprise endings.

The 7- *and* 8-*year-olds* like legends, folk literature, animal stories, fiction, science stories, stories that relate to their hobbies and other interests, and adventure stories. They enjoy longer stories and can be read to without having to see pictures; however, they still prefer being told a story more than reading a story.

2. Select books and stories geared to the child's age level, interests, levels of understanding, and attention span.

3. For younger children, a book or story that is being read should include illustrations that are colorful, attractive, clear, and appropriate. (However, remember that you can tell a story with no visual aids or pictures and still be effective.)

4. Select a well-balanced diet of books and stories to tell and have available for the children. Have samples of many categories, including those of various cultures, genders, and ethnic origins.

5. The books and stories that children especially enjoy will be repeated and retold often (Wolter, 1992). However, books that are selected for use in individual play should be rotated so that not too many are available at one time. Public libraries loan books to classrooms for this purpose.

6. The theme or main point of selected books should have value and importance. Books and stories used should have memory value; in other words, good stories and books will be remembered by the children.

7. The characters in stories and books should be strong, having worthy character traits. Avoid stories that stereotype people and cultures.

8. Plots should be fresh and well paced.

9. Stories should be short and simple.

Guidelines for preparing stories. Once the story is selected, it must be prepared and presented. Unfortunately, many teachers do not adequately prepare stories before reading or telling them. If stories must be read, we suggest preparing ahead of time so that you are acquainted with the story and its message.

1. Careful preparation is needed to create a vivid experience for children (Wolter, 1992). Allow adequate time before presentation to learn the story thoroughly.

2. Outline in your mind the sequence of the story events; recall the characters, their names, and where they fit into the sequence of events.

3. Practice telling the story, but do not try to memorize the author's exact words.

4. If visual aids will accompany the story, practice using them.

5. Practice appropriate gestures.

6. Make a note of words or references the children might not understand so that you can give explanations before the story begins; then the story can continue without interruptions.

Methods of presenting stories. Remember, a story can be told while using your own body and facial expressions as the visual aids.

1. Flip chart. Illustrations or pictures representing the story are put on heavy paper and attached with large rings. Words for each page are printed on the back of the following page so that they are easily read, and then the page is flipped around. The children can view the illustrations while the

Flip-chart stories made by the children are read and reread many times and soon become favorites.

teacher retains eye-to-eye contact during the presentation.

2. Single object or picture—a doll, animal figure, or puppet for single focus.

3. Flannel board story. Use medium-weight Pellon® colored with marking pens or crayons. Often the figures can be traced from picture books or coloring books. A small piece of masking tape with a number on the back of each figure helps order the sequence of each figure in the story.

4. Record or record book.

5. Tape-recorded story presented with or without pictures.

6. Demonstrations.

7. Dramatizations during or following the presentation.

8. Films, filmstrips, slides.

9. Movie-box story. Put story illustrations on a long piece of butcher paper, then roll the paper on rollers or dowels. Show each illustration as it is unrolled and viewed in a box with a hole cut in it, resembling a television screen.

10. Chalk-talk story. Use simple chalkboard illustrations to accompany a story.

11. Child involvement. Give each child a picture or object to hold during a particular part of the story, or give each child a part in the story.

12. Overhead transparencies.

Guidelines for presenting stories. Stories can be read to children, but they are much more effective and meaningful when told.

1. Make sure that all the children are comfortable and are able to see the storyteller; if visual aids are used, all children should be able to see them.

2. Generally, the smaller the group listening to the stories, the more effective the experience (Miller, 1990). Teachers can effectively group children by their developmental abilities, including their listening ability and their experience level (Wolter, 1992).

3. Use eye-to-eye contact in telling stories.

4. Keep a natural voice that is conversational and clear and that reaches all the children. Change the pitch and tempo of your voice to add interest.

5. Use gestures that are spontaneous and natural; use appropriate facial expressions. "Relax and allow your face to mirror your words and inner feelings" (Sherman, 1979, p. 26).

6. Relax and enjoy the story yourself. Keep it full of life, as well as simple and direct. Live the characters—feel their joys and sorrows, their laughter and struggles.

7. Draw on your own experience to add richness and meaning to the story.

8. Do not hesitate to ask an occasional question or give an explanation, but do not lose the flow and feeling of the story.

9. Younger children especially enjoy having their names in stories, so that they become the characters in the story.

Guidelines for evaluating stories. Once the story has been told, the teacher should evaluate whether the desired goals and objectives were reached.

- Did I tell the story instead of reading it?
- Did the story maintain high interest throughout?
- Did I clearly make the point intended?
- Was eye-to-eye contact maintained?
- Were my facial expressions suitable to the actions of the story?
- Was my voice natural, enthusiastic, and appropriate in tone and pitch?
- Were my gestures natural and spontaneous?
- Were visual aids appropriate and easy to use?
- Did the children listen to and enjoy the story?

Teachers should constantly acquaint themselves with the best in children's literature, both old and new. It is also suggested that each early childhood teacher have an anthology of children's literature available.

See Figure 6–3 for a web constructed around the story "The Jolly Postman."

Poetry

Poetry stirs imagination and creative thinking. Through poetry, children become more keenly aware of sensory impressions. They find enjoyment and satisfaction in these impressions as they are expressed through the imagery of poetry. They also delight in the sound and rhythm of language as it is expressed. Poetry sings, and it is rich, warm, and definite.

Poetry allows children to experience various emotions, feelings, and moods; become familiar with creative language; expand concept and language development; model desirable behaviors; and increase attention spans. Young children enjoy writing their own impressions in the form of poetry, especially when they learn that poetry does not require lines that rhyme.

Many types of poems are appropriate for children in the early childhood years. Children throughout time have loved Mother Goose and other nursery rhymes, perhaps because of the variety of subject matter, the surprise quality found

On an outline of a mailbox, each child can decorate his or her personal box with a pen or collage materials.

Children use felt-tipped pens to make drawings, and then each child mails his or hers to a grandparent or relative.

Mail drop box

Food Activities

Field Trips

Art

Post office

Make and mail a treat to a child who has moved from the area or a class member's grandparent. Or, collect and prepare a box of treats and supplies such as toiletries to send to an area where they have suffered a natural disaster. Take it to the post office and mail it.

Songs about mail carriers. Example: "What Do You Want To Be When You Grow Up?"

Jolly Postman

Music

In cooperative learning groups, children come up with three reasons they would like to be a mail carrier.

Mail carrier

Visitors

Female mail carrier

Discuss with the children the label "postman." What is wrong with it? Discuss other sexist labels and brainstorm better choices. Make a chart titled "Use this instead of this."

Language & Literacy

Children write letters and then mail them. (Could write to a family member so they could see them received.) (If children do not write, letter can be dictated.)

Post office worker

Make a class booklet. On each page it will say: "A mail carrier experiences. . . ." Each child completes the sentence and then illustrates it.

FIGURE 6–3

in many, the rhyme, the musical movement, the repetition, or the short, easy-to-remember actions. Since they are easily memorized, after just a few readings children will be saying them with you—and should be encouraged to do so. Young children also enjoy nonsense verse or poetry, ballad and story poems, poems based on fact, and those that are make-believe or fanciful. There are poems about nearly everything experienced in our world. If a poem cannot be found relating to a subject or concept, one can surely be written!

Poetry should not be read or presented in a singsong pattern, but with directness and sincerity. It should appeal to the emotions and flow with the right meter or rhythm. Most poems should not be explained, but read and enjoyed for the sake of the poem and its appeal to the individual child.

Many of the suggestions presented in this chapter regarding stories are also appropriate for poetry. Poetry can be presented with pictures (or a single picture), puppets, objects, recordings, flannel board illustrations, slides, overhead transparencies, or other visual aids.

In addition, many poems lend themselves to dramatizations; even short nursery rhymes can be dramatized and put into action. For groups of children who are beginning to read, their favorite poems can be put on charts so that they can follow along as the poem is read. Children enjoy illustrating the poems they hear.

Poems lend themselves to choral readings. The older the children, the more sophisticated the choral readings can be. Even young children can repeat their favorite poems and rhymes in choral speaking or reading. To begin choral speaking or reading, you will want to say the poems in unison first. Younger children can be divided into separate or solo parts from the group. For older children, there are other alternatives; for example, the children could be divided by voice pitch into groups of high, medium, and low voices or soft, medium, and heavy voices. When dividing a poem into choral speaking parts by voice pitch, have the high or soft voices take the delicate or lighter lines. Usually these are the lines that ask questions. The low voices should take the lines that suggest mystery, gloom, or solemnity or that answer questions. The medium voices carry the narrative, give explanations, or introduce characters. When teaching choral speaking, be careful not to drill, and remember that it should be enjoyable and therapeutic. Choral speaking also improves speaking ability, helping children to create a crisp, vigorous speech.

Fingerplays

Fingerplays and chants are especially suited for younger children, and very often they are repeated in unison as a type of choral speaking. Fingerplays are short poems accompanied with finger motions; thus they are also a type of dramatization. They are useful attention getters and rest exercises. Whenever you prefer, change dramatizations, finger motions, or words to fit the developmental level, desired objectives, and enjoyment of the children.

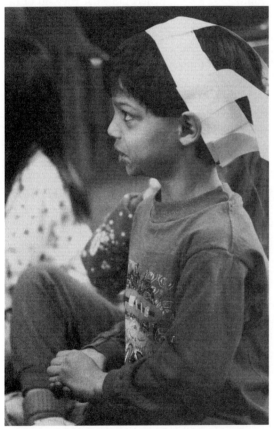

Fingerplays, with or without music, help sustain interest and increase memorization skills and retention.

Summary

Language and literacy development should be an ingredient of every activity and experience in the early childhood classroom. We advocate an environment rich in opportunities for speaking and listening and also rich in print—where children see adults reading and writing, and where they are given opportunities to make sense out of print and to express their thoughts both orally and in print.

Teachers must make certain that practice in writing is purposeful and that children see writing as a way to communicate meaningfully (Salinger, 1988). Make certain that you provide many writing tools: pencils, pens, markers, chalk, and crayons.

The primary factors influencing the development of language appear to be (1) the child's innate ability to learn language, (2) the quality of the model or the early stimulation and variety provided by the model, and (3) the ability of caregivers to expand or extend the child's language. Oral language can be encouraged in early childhood by conversing, discussing, clarifying, reporting, explaining, reacting, dramatizing, storytelling, fingerplays, poems, and rhymes.

Young children should have many opportunities to read for enjoyment from excellent literature. Children's experiences provide a frame of reference for them to draw on in order to make sense of what is read to them or what they read themselves.

The whole-language approach takes children from where they are, accepts what they do or do not bring with them, accommodates differences, and then builds on each child's language competencies and guides the child toward becoming literate and finding joy, meaning, and pleasure in literacy.

Children need to view others around them as being literate; and then, as maturation, readiness, and experiences allow, children need to be given many opportunities to talk, read, and write so that they view themselves as literate. Early childhood teachers can stimulate the child's interest in literacy and facilitate the child's efforts to become literate.

Student Learning Activities

1. Study the language development of a child 2 to 8 years of age and compare it to the chart of "Normal Language Development" (Table 6–1). What similarities do you find? What differences do you find? You may wish to make comparisons with another child of approximately the same age.

2. You have learned that there is much variation in language development in young children. From your own experiences, describe situations in which variation in language has been obvious. Then try to determine some of the factors influencing the language development of a particular child.

3. As a teacher of young children, how can you be influential in helping young children expand, refine, and enhance their language development?

4. Observe in an early childhood classroom with a focus on literacy activities. Describe the activities you observed, and identify the ways each activity contributed to the development of the children. For example, did the activity enhance listening or speaking skills? Did the activity teach new words? Were the activities appropriate, or can you think of ways to achieve the desired objectives and goals in a more appropriate way?

5. Plan, implement, and evaluate at least two activities to encourage listening skills in young children.

6. Plan, implement, and evaluate at least two activities to encourage speaking skills in young children.

7. Based on the criteria given in this chapter for selecting appropriate stories, begin a story file with at least five excellent culturally diverse stories for children 2 to 8 years of age. Make a card for each story. On the card, include the title of the story, author, illustrator, publisher, copyright date, age level the story is appropriate for, and a brief summary of the story.

8. Based on the guidelines for selecting, preparing, and presenting stories, select a story appropriate for preschool, kindergarten, first-, or second-grade children and then prepare and present it. Afterward, use the questions suggested in this chapter as a guide for evaluating your story presentation.

9. Prepare two stories using two different methods of presentation suggested in this chapter. For example, prepare a flannel board story and a flip chart story.

10. Begin a poetry file representing many varied cultures for use with children 2 to 8 years of age. Include on your file card the title, author, citation of the source of the poem, and the poem.

11. Begin a collection of appropriate culturally diverse pictures to accompany poems. Mount the pictures neatly, and make them durable. Attach or write the poem on the back.

12. Memorize at least three fingerplays and teach them to children. Use cooperative learning strategies to teach at least one.

Suggested Resources

Resources for Children's Literature

Cullinan, B. E. (1987). *Children's literature in the reading program*. Newark, DE: International Reading Association.

Lipson, E. G. (1988). *Parent's guide to the best books for children*. New York: Times Books.

Norton, D. (1991). *Through the eyes of a child: An introduction to children's literature*. New York: Merrill.

The list of suggested resources for language and literacy and development could be limitless, because any pictures, books, records, tapes, multimedia kits, films, filmstrips, and videos could be used to stimulate speaking, listening, reading, and writing. Only a few selected examples will be listed here. Use these kinds of resources to stimulate language development in young children.

Children's Books

Abolafia, Y. (1991). *Fox tale*. New York: Greenwillow.

Ahlberg, J., & Ahlberg, A. (1986). *The Jolly Postman*. Boston: Little, Brown & Co.

Ahlberg, J., & Ahlberg, A. (1990). *Peek-a-boo!* New York: Viking.

Aliki, (1986). *How a book is made*. New York: Crowell.

Anglund, J. W. (1977). *In a pumpkin shell*. New York: Harcourt Brace Jovanovich.

Anglund, J. W. (1977). *Nibble nibble mousekin: A tale of Hansel and Gretel*. New York: Harcourt Brace Jovanovich.

Baba Yaga: A Russian folktale. (1991). Retold by E. A. Kimmel. New York: Holiday House.

Banish, R. (1982). *Let me tell you about my baby*. New York: Harper & Row.

Banks, L. R. (1981). *Indian in the cupboard*. New York: Doubleday.

Banks, L. R. (1986). *The return of the Indian*.

Banks, L. R. (1989). *The secret of the Indian*.

Brown, M. W. (1972). *The runaway bunny*. San Diego: Harcourt Brace Jovanovich.

Burton, A. (1991). *Where does the trail lead?* New York: Simon & Schuster.

Butler, D. (1991). *Higgledy piggledy hobbledy hoy*. New York: Greenwillow.

Butler, S. (1991). *Henny, Penny*. New York: Tambourine.

Cameron, A. (1986). *More stories Julian tells*. New York: Knopf.

Carle, E. (1985). *The very busy spider*. New York: Philomel.

Dahl, R. (1961). *James and the giant peach*. New York: Knopf.

dePaola, T. (1986). *Tomie de Paola's famous nursery tales*. New York: Putnam.

Estes, E. (1944). *The hundred dresses*. New York: Harcourt Brace Jovanovich.

Fitzhugh, L. (1964). *Harriet the spy*. New York: Harper & Row.

Gifford, H. (1991). *Red fox*. New York: Dial.

Hughes, S. (1988). *Out and about*. New York: Lothrop, Lee & Shepard.

Hurwitz, J. (1991). *"E" is for Elisa*. New York: Morrow.

Jacobs, D. (1990). *What does it do? Inventions then and now*. Milwaukee: Raintree.

Kalan, R. (1979). *Blue sea*. New York: Greenwillow.

Koss, A. G. (1991). *City critters around the world*. Los Angeles: Price Stern Sloan.

Lear, E. (1991). *The owl and the pussycat*. New York: Lothrop, Lee & Shepard.

Livingston, M.C. (1986). *Sea songs*. New York: Holiday House.

MacLachlan, P. (1985). *Sarah, plain and tall*. New York: Harper & Row.

Martin, B. (1983). *Brown bear, brown bear, what do you see?* New York: Holt.

Martin, B., & Archambault, J. (1989). *Chicka chicka boom boom*. New York: Simon & Schuster.

Martin, J. (1991). *Carrot/parrot*. New York: Simon & Schuster.

Mayer, M. (1968). *There's a nightmare in my closet*. New York: Dial.

Mayer, M. (1987). *There's an alligator under my bed*. New York: Dial.

McDonald, M. (1992). *Whoo-oo is it?* New York: Orchard.

McNaught, H. (1973). *500 words to grow on*. New York: Random House.

Miller, M. (1991). *Whose shoe?* New York: Greenwillow.

Nikola-Lisa, W. (1991). *Night is coming*. New York: Dutton.

O'Neill, M. (1961) *Hailstones and halibut bones*. Garden City, NY: Doubleday.

Piper, W. (1930). *The little engine that could*. New York: Grosset & Dunlap.

Potter, B. (1902). *Peter Rabbit* (series). New York: Frederick Warne.

Prelutsky, J. (1990). *Something big has been here*. New York: Greenwillow.

Scarry, R. (1976) *Early words*. New York: Random House.

Scheer, J., & Bileck, M. (1964). *Rain makes applesauce*. New York: Holiday House.

Selden, G. (1970). *Cricket in Times Square*, New York: Farrar.

Sendak, M. (1963) *Where the wild things are*. New York: Harper & Row.

Shaw, N. (1991). *Sheep in a shop*. Boston: Houghton Mifflin.

Sierra, J., & Kaminski, R. (1991). *Multicultural folktales: Stories to tell young children*. Phoenix, AZ: Oryx.

Sieveking, A. (1990). *What's inside?* New York: Dial.

Stone soup. (1991). Retold by J. W. Stewig. New York: Holiday House.

Tolhurst, M. (1990). *Somebody and the three bears*. New York: Orchard.

Trelease, J. (1989). *The new read-aloud handbook*. New York: Penguin.

White, E. B. (1952). *Charlotte's web*. New York: Harper & Bros.

Wilder, L. I. (1932). *Little house in the big woods*. New York: Harper & Row.

Williams, M. (1985). *The velveteen rabbit*. New York: Knopf.

Wilson, S. (1991). *Garage song*. New York: Simon & Schuster.

Winter, J. (1984). *Hush little baby*. New York: Pantheon.

Children's ABC Books

Anglund, J. W. (1960). *A Mother Goose ABC*. New York: Harcourt, Brace & World.

Anno, M. (1975). *Anno's alphabet: Adventure in imagination*. New York: Crowell.

Auerbach, S. (1986). *The alphabet tree*. Mt. Desert, ME: Windswept House.

Base, G. (1987). *Animalia*. New York: Abrams.

Bayer, J. (1984). *A—My name is Alice*. New York: Dial.

Cleaver, E. (1985). *ABC*. New York: Macmillan.

Crews, D. (1984). *We read: A to Z.* New York: Greenwillow.

Feelings, M. (1974). *Jambo means Hello: Swahili alphabet book.* New York: Dial.

Fujikawa, G. (1974). *Gyo Fujikawa's A to Z picture book.* New York: Grosset & Dunlap.

Gag, W. (1933). *ABC bunny.* New York: Putnam.

Garten, J. (1964). *The alphabet tale.* New York: Random House.

Greenaway, K. (1886). *A apple pie.* New York: Frederick Warne.

Hague, K. (1984). *Alphabears: An ABC book.* New York: Holt, Rinehart & Winston.

Hepworth, C. (1992). *Antics.* New York: Putnam.

Hyman, T. S. (1980). *A little alphabet.* Boston: Little, Brown.

Lionni, L. (1968). *The alphabet tree.* New York: Pantheon.

Lobel, A., & Lobel, A. (1981). *On Market Street.* New York: Greenwillow.

MacDonald S. (1986). *Alphabatics.* New York: Bradbury.

Miller, E. (1972). *Mousekin's ABC.* Englewood Cliffs, NJ: Prentice-Hall.

Musgrove, M. (1976) *Ashanti to Zulu: African traditions.* New York: Dial.

Phillips, T. (1989). *Day care ABC.* Niles, IL: Whitman.

Wildsmith, B. (1970). *ABC.* New York: Pantheon.

Children's Poetry, Rhyme, and Chant Books

Anglund, J. W. (1980). *Almost a rainbow: A book of poems.* New York: Random House.

Baldwin, R. M. (1972). *One hundred nineteenth-century rhyming alphabets in English.* Carbondale: Southern Illinois University.

Colgin, M. L. (Compiler). (1982). *Chants for children.* Manlius, NY: Colgin.

DeAngeli, M. (1979). *Marguerite de Angeli's book of nursery and Mother Goose rhymes.* New York: Doubleday.

DeRegniers, B., Moore, E., & White, M. M. (1969). *Poems children will sit still for.* New York: Scholastic.

DeRegniers, B. (1976). *A bunch of poems and verses.* Boston: Houghton Mifflin.

Dodson, F. (1978). *I wish I had a computer that makes waffles. . . . Teaching your children with modern nursery rhymes.* LaJolla, CA: Oak Tree.

Dunn, S. (1987). *Butterscotch dreams.* Markham, Ontario: Pembroke.

Dunn, S. (1990). *Crackers & crumbs: Chants for whole language.* Portsmouth, NH: Heinemann.

Frank, J. (1968). *Poems to read to the very young.* New York: Random House.

Frank, J. (1982). *More poems to read to the very young.* New York: Random House.

Geismer, B., & Suter, A. (1945). *Very young verses.* Boston: Houghton Mifflin.

Greenaway, K. (1882). (illustrated). *Mother Goose: Or the old nursery rhymes.* New York: Frederick Warne

Hague, M. (1984) *Mother Goose: A collection of classic nursery rhymes.* New York: Holt, Rinehard & Winston.

Hearn, M. P. (1981). *A day in verse: Breakfast, books, and dreams.* New York: Frederick Warne.

Larrick, N. (1983). *When the dark comes dancing: A bedtime poetry book.* New York: Putnam.

Milne, A. A. (1961). *Now we are six.* New York: Dutton.

Milne, A. A. (1961). *When we were very young.* New York: Dutton.

Poems teachers ask for. (1979). New York: Granger.

Prelutsky, J. (1977). *The snopp on the sidewalk and other poems.* New York: Greenwillow.

Prelutsky, J. (1982). *The baby uggs are hatching.* New York: Greenwillow.

Prelutsky, J. (1983). *The Random House book of poetry.* New York: Random House.

Prelutsky, J. (1983). *Zoo doings: Animal poems.* New York: Greenwillow.

Prelutsky, J. (1984). *The new kid on the block.* New York: Greenwillow.

Prelutsky, J. (1991). *For laughing out loud: Poems to tickle your funnybone.* New York: Knopf.

Silverstein, S. (1974). *Where the sidewalk ends: Poems and drawings.* New York: Harper & Row.

Silverstein, S. (1981). *A light in the attic.* New York: Harper & Row.

Sutherland, Z. (1990). *The Orchard book of nursery rhymes.* New York: Orchard.

Tompert, A. (1984). *Nothing sticks like a shadow.* Boston: Houghton Mifflin.

Tudor, T. (1944). *Mother Goose.* New York: Henry Z. Walck.

Weissman, "Miss J." (1991). *Higglety pigglety pop! 233 playful rhymes and chants for your baby.* Overland Park, KS: Miss Jackie Music Co.

Wildsmith, B. (1970). *Mother Goose.* New York: Pantheon.

Withers, C. (1948). *A rocket in my pocket.* New York: Scholastic.

Wright, B. F. (1961). (illustrated). *The real Mother Goose,* Chicago: Rand-McNally.

Records, Tapes, and Cassettes

There are many kinds of recordings that can often be used to stimulate language development. Frequently, records can enhance listening skills. Children can listen to records to learn songs and sing along; they can be encouraged to listen for rhythms or beat patterns of rhythm records; and they will be anxious to listen to many story records. Thus specific suggestions will not be given, but teachers are encouraged to find new approaches to using records, tapes, and cassettes in order to stimulate the language development of young children.

Pictures

The Child's World. A variety of subjects organized into sets. Resource booklets giving additional activities and language experiences accompany the sets. Examples are *The many moods of Mother Goose* (eight pictures), and *Moods and emotions* (eight pictures).

D. C. Cook. Many sets to select from, and suggested activities accompany each picture. Examples are *Nursery rhymes* (30627) and *Storyland* (68510).

Society for Visual Education (SVE). A variety of subjects organized into sets. Information for discussions, activities, questions, and other language activities appear on the backs of pictures. Sets deal with science themes, seasons and holidays, community helpers, and children around the world.

Multimedia Kits

Beginning auditory reading skills with Winnie-the-Pooh. Walt Disney.

Beginning visual reading skills with Winnie-the-Pooh. Walt Disney.

Creative dramatics. The Child's World.

Let's talk with Winnie-the-Pooh. Walt Disney.

Sing consonants with Winnie-the-Pooh. Walt Disney.

Sing short vowels with Winnie-the-Pooh. Walt Disney.

Tales of Jiminy Cricket. Walt Disney.

Walt Disney read-along libraries 1, 2, 3, 4. Walt Disney.

Films, Filmstrips, and Videos

Films, filmstrips, and videos can be used in a variety of ways to enhance language development. Many of the ones presented throughout this text as suggested resources could be used. Have the children tell the story, or once the children hear the story, they could use the film or filmstrip in small groups to tell the story themselves. Often the film, filmstrip, or video could be stopped before the end, and the children asked how they think it might end; or they could be encouraged to make up a possible ending.

BIM. CRM/McGraw-Hill.

Foundations of reading and writing. Campus Films.

The joy of writing: stories! Churchill Films.

The joy of writing: words! Churchill Films.

More alphabet (N–Z). Eye Gate Media.

Our alphabet (A–M). Eye Gate Media.

Snowman's dilemma. CRM/McGraw-Hill.

Computer Software

Choose your own adventure (series). (1985). New York: Bantam.

Cosmic osmo. (1985). Menlo Park, CA: Activision.

Macwrite. (1984). Cupertino, CA: Apple.

Playwriter. (1987). Old Bridge, NJ: Woodbury.

The puzzler. (1987). Pleasantville, NY: Sunburst Communications.

The semantic mapper. (1986). Gainesville, FL: Teacher Support Software.

Super story tree. (1989). Jefferson City, MO: Scholastic.

Talking text writer. (1986). Jefferson City, MO: Scholastic.

The writing adventure. (1985). Allen, TX: Developmental Learning Materials. (DLM).

Action music. (1985). Calabasas, CA: P.E. A.L. Software.

The alphabet academy. (1985). Dimondale, MI: Hartley Courseware.

Alphabet blocks. (1987). Bellevue, WA: Bright Star Technology.

Animal alphabet and other things. (1986). Heightstown, NJ: McGraw-Hill Media.

The bald-headed chicken. (1988). Lexington, MA: D. C. Heath & Co.

A brand new view. (1988). Lexington, MA: D. C. Heath & Co.

Dr. Peet's talk/writer. (1986). Dimondale, MI: Hartley Courseware.

Easy as ABC. (1984). Bridgeport, CT: Queue.

First letter fun. (1985). St. Paul, MN: MECC.

KidTalk. (1988). Santa Ana, CA: First Byte.

Muppet slate. (1988). Pleasantville, NY: Sunburst Communications.

The playroom. (1989). San Rafael, CA: Broderbund Software.

The princess and the pea. (1989). Acton, MA: William K. Bradford Publishing.

Reading 1. (1985). Bridgeport, CT: Queue.

The sleepy brown cow. (1988). Lexington, MA: D. C. Heath & Co.

Stone soup. (1989). Acton, MA: William K. Bradford Publishing.

PART
FOUR

SENSORY EXPERIENCES

Frequently, teachers rely too heavily on the sense of seeing, or the visual process, rather than encouraging expansion and use of the other four senses. As children develop perception and the ability to distinguish differences in seeing, hearing, tasting, smelling, and touching, they learn more quickly because all five senses are "tuned in" instead of only one or two.

Included in this part is a chapter on food and nutrition, because as food is both prepared and eaten, the experience involves especially the senses of taste and smell. Teachers of young children should recognize the value of using food activities as a part of the curriculum. Not only do children enjoy them, but there are also many social, cognitive, small-muscle, math, science, and other values that can be learned and developed through well-planned food activities—many of them as cooperative learning experiences. Early childhood teachers should select nutritionally sound food activities. In a time when we recognize the strong influence of a balanced diet on health and well-being, it behooves all early childhood teachers to teach basic nutrition principles through the careful selection and addition of high-nutrient food experiences.

Also included in this part is a chapter on sensory explorations. Children are naturally curious as they use their senses to explore the world. They try to touch, poke, pinch, taste, lick, chew, smell, watch, listen to, or examine objects, people, and situations in great detail (Beaty, 1992b.) We need to encourage children to maintain their sensory tools and use them to explore their world and answer their questions. "Our world is a huge hands-on museum, a well-stocked laboratory, a fascinating never-ending field trip. . . . Children should be taught to use seeing, hearing, tasting, smelling, and touching, for that is how young children learn everything—they touch, they taste, they smell and listen and look" (Ziemer, 1987, pp. 44–45).

CHAPTER
seven

Nutrition and Food Experiences

Introduction

"Good nutrition is essential to . . . proper growth during childhood. . . . Not only does poor nutrition significantly increase the likelihood of low birthweight, infant death, and lifelong disability, it is financially costly as well" (Children's Defense Fund, 1991, pp. 64–65). To grow up healthy, with vitality and energy, children need adequate nutrition. Their early experiences of preparing, tasting, and eating nutritious foods can have an impact on their long-term eating preferences and habits (Cosgrove, 1991).

For developmentally appropriate practices relating to nutrition of young children, "only healthy foods" should be provided and "eating is considered a sociable, happy time" (Bredekamp, 1986, p. 38). Children generally have a natural curiosity about and interest in food activities. From the time they are born, food is vital to nurturing; it brings security, comfort, and love. To help children make proper food choices, a wide variety of wholesome foods should be available (Goodwin & Pollen, 1980). In accomplish-

ing these goals, food should neither be used for reward nor withheld as punishment (Bredekamp, 1986).

Being involved in food activities is an important way of teaching good nutrition to young children. In selecting a food experience, one of the first questions a teacher should ask is, "Will the food be nutritious?" Traditionally, early childhood classrooms have prepared cookies, candies, ice cream, and other foods that provide little nutritional value or have a low nutrient density. Most preschool programs provide a time for snack and opportunity for occasional food activities, and careful judgment must be used with both. To judge whether or not a food should be served as a snack, one must determine whether the food (1) can be classified as part of a basic food group, and (2) contains enough nutrients to justify its calorie value (Endres & Rockwell, 1990). Acceptable snacks can be chosen from each food group. These are also excellent criteria for any other food prepared or served in the early childhood education classroom.

As this child peels an orange for snack time, she is learning about nutrition while increasing her independence and self-esteem.

Nutrition Education

Nutrition must be of primary concern to early childhood teachers and an integral part of the setting. Nutrition units, as well as food activities, should be planned carefully to teach nutrition concepts specifically and directly to children. Listed at the end of this chapter are many excellent curriculum guides on nutrition for preschool and primary-grade children. As a nation, we are becoming more concerned about this important aspect of health and well-being. Articles, books, programs, school units, extension programs, and White House Conferences all have served to alert and educate us. Now we must put into practice those things we know. Nutrition activities should encourage children to explore the limitless potential for learning by providing open-ended experiences that allow them to extend their understanding beyond any specifically outlined objectives. Although we choose food and nutrition activities with objectives we desire to achieve, there are numerous other learnings that occur as children are (and should be) allowed to

explore in an attempt to answer the questions How?, Why?, What if?, How come?, and I wonder.

Many early childhood programs, such as day care or Head Start, serve complete meals. The subject of nutrition provides many learning opportunities—and it must not be viewed as only preparing, serving, and cleaning-up food activities. The potential for nutrition education in the early childhood programs is limitless (Endres & Rockwell, 1990)!

It is more difficult today to remain aware of nutritional values because of prepackaging, vending machines, and fast-food restaurants. Too often "formulated, fabricated, fake foods . . . are displacing wholesome foods in the diet" (Goodwin & Pollen, 1980, p. 14). We subtly teach children that sweets are the best kinds of food when we make comments such as "Eat your salad and meatloaf, and then you can have your cake and ice cream."

It is imperative that both children and parents be well education in nutrition. It would be beneficial to plan parent meetings and workshops to educate parents on good nutrition. Children are building bodies that are to last them a lifetime, and both children and parents must know that the food they eat has a direct relationship to the quality of their health. They must be informed of the interaction between early eating choices and habits and the development of diet-related diseases later in life. Nutritionally healthy eating habits are acquired early in life. "The goal of nutrition education should be that children eat a well-balanced diet that contains a wide variety of foods, and that children learn to make wise food choices independently" (Herr & Morse, 1982, p. 10). Eating habits that condition children to consume processed foods or foods high in sugar, salt, and fat are physically detrimental and instill in children a taste for foods that are unhealthy, in the long term (Goodwin & Pollen, 1980).

People in the United States each consume about 100 pounds of sugar annually. Sugar-laden foods provide empty calories and dull the appetite, leaving children uninterested in nutritious foods. In addition, overconsumption of sugar causes dental caries. Caregivers must try to reduce children's sugar consumption by avoiding high-sugar foods, selecting alternate sources of sweetness, and finding ways to celebrate special events other than with sugary foods (Rogers & Morris, 1986). Sugar substitutes or artificial sweeteners should not be ingredients in the diets of young children. A decade ago, the Surgeon General of the United States issued a report titled "Healthy People," in which he urged Americans to eat a diet lower in cholesterol, saturated fat, sugar, and salt.

Values of Food Experiences

Families today are eating fewer meals together, and they are eating more fast foods and snack foods. All family members need to be taught to eat a well-balanced diet and select nutritional foods. As teachers, we send many messages about food and nutrition to young children. Herr and Morse (1982, p. 5) make an interesting observation in terms of the materials that decorate the classroom: "Do candles on a cake or oranges on a tree indicate the birthdays of individual children? Is the growth chart an ice cream cone or a carrot? Does the bulletin board show Cookie Monster eating cookies or an elephant eating peanuts? What is the nutrition message of food puzzles, grocery store items, and mobiles?"

The sensory experiences in food activities offer the greatest learning value (Vonde & Beck, 1980). In addition, children enjoy working with and manipulating food—mixing, measuring, pouring, stirring, and eating. Food experiences provide natural means for exploring and developing basic concepts such as size, shape, number, color, measurement, weight, smell, taste, sound, touch, texture, flavor, preservation, and temperature change. Food activities provide opportunities for increasing language skills and labels. Teachers can teach what a particular food is, where it comes from, what it looks like, and how it compares to familiar and unfamiliar foods. Children can describe and label foods, equipment being used, and what is being done with the food (grating, mashing, kneading, stirring, beating, pouring, spreading, grinding, or peeling). Food experiences offer opportunities for teaching safety concepts and proper uses of utensils such as knives, forks, beaters, and peelers. If a stove, hot plate, or frying pan is being used for cooking, children can be taught safety concepts related to fire and heat. Cleanliness must also be stressed: Children should be encouraged to wash their hands before any food activity and to help clean up.

So that children are not required to wait unnecessarily, food should be ready before they are called to meals or snacks (Bredekamp, 1986) unless the preparation of the food involves the children. Especially for toddlers, bowls, spoons, and cups should be easy to handle. Children also benefit from working cooperatively together as a team while interpreting directions in the recipe, following sequences, and keeping time. Social values include learning table manners, sharing, and developing appropriate eating habits. The children's self-images are enhanced as they set the table, prepare the food, eat their own product, and then clean up. Cooking gives a sense of personal achievement by allowing them to do something adults do (Cosgrove, 1991). Working with recipes provides young children with foundational understandings of measuring and fraction concepts: They can best learn the concept of one-half by measuring $1/2$ cup water, $1/2$ teaspoon vanilla, $1/2$ apple, and so on. Also, working with food recipes exposes children to concepts relating to various units of measure. Collecting and sampling recipes from diverse cultures helps children develop an awareness of and respect for people of other cultures.

Seven Basic Nutrition Concepts

The White House Conference on Food, Nutrition and Health (1969) outlined seven basic nutrition concepts with which teachers should become familiar. These form the basis of understanding why nutrition is important. When teachers understand the concepts, they can provide classroom food activities.

1. Nutrition is the process by which food and other substances become you. The food we eat enables us to live, to grow, to keep healthy and well, and to get energy for work and play.

2. Food is made up of certain chemical substances that work together and interact with body chemicals to serve the needs of the body.

   a. Each nutrient has specific uses in the body.

   b. For the healthy individual the nutrients needed by the body are usually available through food.

   c. Many kinds and combinations of food can lead to a well-balanced diet.

   d. No natural food, by itself, has all the nutrients needed for full growth and health.

3. The way food is handled influences the amount of nutrients in the food, its safety, appearance, taste, and cost; handling means everything that happens to food while it is being grown, processed, stored and prepared for eating.

4. All persons, throughout life, have need for about the same nutrients, but in varying amounts.

   a. The amounts needed are influenced by age, sex, size, activity, specific conditions of growth, and state of health, altered somewhat by environmental stress.

   b. Suggestions for kinds and needed amounts of nutrients are made by scientists who continuously revise the suggestions in the light of the findings of new research.

   c. A daily food guide is helpful in translating the technical information into terms of everyday foods suitable for individuals and families.

5. Food use relates to the cultural, social, economic, and psychological aspects of living, as well as to the physiological.

   a. Food is culturally defined.

   b. Food selection is an individual act but it is usually influenced by social and cultural sanctions.

   c. Food can be chosen so as to fulfill physiological needs and at the same time satisfy social, cultural, and psychological wants.

   d. Attitudes toward food are a culmination of many experiences, past and present.

6. The nutrients, singly and in combination with chemical substances simulating natural foods, are available in the market; these may vary widely in usefulness, safety of use, and economy.

7. Foods play an important role in the physical and psychological health of a society or a nation, just as they do for the individual and the family.

   a. The maintenance of good nutrition for the larger units of society involves many matters of public concern.

   b. Nutrition knowledge and social consciousness enable citizens to participate in the adoption of public policy affecting the nutrition of people around the world. (p. 151)

Food and Nutrition Concepts for Young Children

Herr and Morse (1982) developed the following 10 food and nutrition concepts appropriate for young children. Many of these can be incorporated as objectives for food experiences, meals, and even snack time.

1. There is a wide variety of foods.
2. Plants and animals are sources of food.
3. Foods vary in color, flavor, texture, smell, size, shape, and sound.
4. A food may be prepared and eaten in many different ways—raw, cooked, dried, frozen, or canned.
5. Good foods are important to health, growth, and energy.
6. Nutrition is how our bodies use the foods we eat for health, growth, and energy.
7. Food may be classified according to the following categories:

   a. milk
   b. meat
   c. dried peas and beans
   d. eggs
   e. fruits
   f. vegetables
   g. breads
   h. pastas
   i. cereals, grains, and seeds
   j. nuts

8. A good diet includes a wide variety of foods from each of the food categories.
9. There are many factors that influence eating:

   a. attractiveness of food
   b. method of preparation
   c. cleanliness/manners
   d. environment/atmosphere
   e. celebrations

10. We choose the foods we eat for many reasons:

   a. availability and cost
   b. family and individual habits
   c. aesthetics
   d. social and cultural customs
   e. mass media influence (pp. 6–7)

Many children believe that foods originate in the supermarket, vending machine, or restaurant. Children need to know where foods come from and opportunities to help in preparing whole-some foods. Children's diets often include large quantities of soda pop; potato chips; french fries; candy; and other sweets such as cookies, cakes, jams, and jellies. These may be termed *junk foods*; nutritionists label them *foods with low nutrient density*, which means they have few nutrients in relation to their calories. It has been said that "Rich foods with low nutrient density in relation to caloric content are not appropriate in the diets of preschoolers because they may lead to obesity and are likely to crowd out more important foods" (Vonde & Beck, 1980, p. 3). Teachers of young children should be aware of opportunities to help children learn to select and enjoy nutrient-dense foods, or those with high amounts of nutrients for the amount of calories they have. Examples are fruits, vegetables, dairy products, and meats. Children can learn that certain foods aid and support good health, while others do not. The key to adequate nutrition is variety, which means that many different foods are needed in order for the body to develop and grow normally (Vonde & Beck, 1980).

The primary focus of this chapter is on nutritious food activities for use with young children. White flour is often replaced by whole-grain or wheat flour; sugar content in the recipes is reduced or completely eliminated; flavored gelatins are replaced by unflavored gelatin and fruit juices in most cases.

Even young children can learn to follow the "Food Guide Pyramid" in order to ensure a well-balanced diet. This pyramid was developed by the U.S. Department of Agriculture to provide a guide to eating for good health. The five major groups that form the pyramid are described here.

Grain Group (Bread, Cereal, Rice, and Pasta)

- Six to eleven servings daily.
- Select only whole-grain and enriched or fortified products, but include *some* whole-grain bread or cereals for sure!

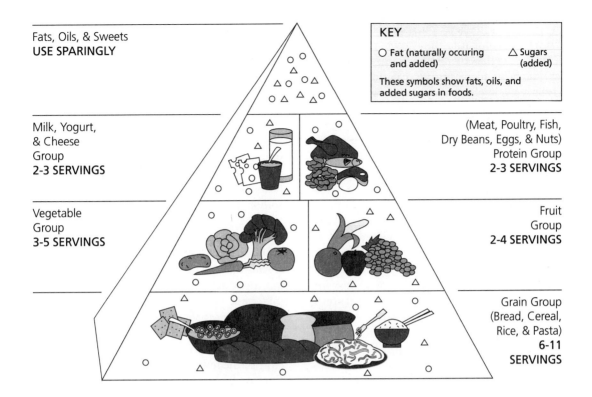

Fats, Oils, & Sweets
USE SPARINGLY

Milk, Yogurt,
& Cheese
Group
2-3 SERVINGS

(Meat, Poultry, Fish,
Dry Beans, Eggs, & Nuts)
Protein Group
2-3 SERVINGS

Vegetable
Group
3-5 SERVINGS

Fruit
Group
2-4 SERVINGS

Grain Group
(Bread, Cereal,
Rice, & Pasta)
**6-11
SERVINGS**

· Includes all products made with whole grains or enriched flour or meal: bread, biscuits, muffins, waffles, pancakes, cooked or ready-to-eat cereal, cornmeal, flour, grits, macaroni and spaghetti, noodles, rice, rolled oats, barley, and bulgur.

Vegetable Group

· Three to five servings daily.
· Frequently include deep yellow or dark green vegetables (for vitamin A).
· Include other vegetables, such as potatoes.

Fruit Group

· Two to four servings daily.
· Include one citrus fruit or other fruit that is a good source of vitamin C.
· Frequently include unpeeled fruits and those with edible seeds such as berries (for fiber).

Milk Group (Including Yogurt and Cheese)

· Two to three servings daily.
· Children aged 2 to 7 should have 2 to 3 cups of milk per day.
· Includes milk in any form: whole, skim, low-fat, evaporated, buttermilk, and nonfat dry milk; also yogurt, ice cream, ice milk; and cheese, including cottage cheese.

Protein Group (Meat, Poultry, Fish, Dry Beans, Eggs, and Nuts)

· Two to three servings daily.
· Includes beef, veal, lamb, poultry, pork, fish, shellfish, dry beans or peas, soybeans, lentils, eggs, seeds, nuts, peanuts, and peanut butter.

Most other foods fit into a sixth category of fats, oils, and sweets. This is not a food group, and foods in this category should be used sparingly. This area includes such foods as butter, margarine, mayonnaise, candy, sugar, jams, jellies, and unenriched, refined bakery products. These kinds of foods provide calories but relatively low levels of vitamins, minerals, and protein compared to the number of calories.

Approach to Teaching

Food experiences planned in the classroom must be well organized and explicitly planned, and adequate time must be allowed for completion. If the food activity takes place in small cooperative groups, care should be taken to explain the procedures and methods to the teachers working with these groups, and each group should have its own copy of the recipe. If the activity takes place in a large group, the recipe could be written on the chalkboard or an experience chart. The teacher should discuss the recipe, ingredients, and procedures with the children before they begin.

Tasting experiences can easily be set up in a classroom as interest centers for use during free play, or they can be group activities. Children can taste several different foods, such as familiar foods, unfamiliar foods, different foods with similar flavors, or different forms of such foods as potatoes or tomatoes.

Children can also be introduced to new and interesting foods. It may be wise to begin with sensory experiences other than tasting. For example, the children may be encouraged to smell, feel, listen to, and look at a new food before tasting it. New foods can also be compared with familiar foods. For example, lima beans or kidney beans can be compared to familiar beans; brussels sprouts to cabbage; an avocado to a pear; a lime to a lemon, a kiwi to a strawberry. It should also be remembered that when first introducing children to a new food or unfamiliar recipe, very small servings should be given. The family style of serving, in which the children serve themselves, is preferred.

Another food activity consists of acquainting children with the origins of foods. Many children assume that milk, for example, comes from the store or the milk delivery person, rather than from the cow. This activity provides an opportunity for teaching categorization games. Children can sort picture cards into categories, such as plant products or animal products. Even more specifically, cards could be sorted into underground plant

Dissolving flavored gelatin in hot water combines science and food activities in an enjoyable nutritional experience.

products, tree products, vine products, cow products, and so on. Also, picture or flash cards can be used simply for naming the food item. Pictures can be found in magazines or discarded workbooks, or stickers can be purchased from stationery stores.

Foods and food activities can be integrated into every aspect of the curriculum in early childhood (Herr & Morse, 1982). Most learning is through the senses; and since food appeals to all senses, it is a powerful learning tool (Goodwin & Pollen, 1980). Food experiences can potentially contribute to every area of the early childhood curriculum. In physical development, there is opportunity for both small-muscle and large-muscle coordination. In mathematics or number work, there are experiences for counting, classifying, and measuring. In science, possibilities abound for using the process skills in food activities —questioning, observing, interpreting, categorizing, and solving problems. There are opportunities for studying and discovering the nature and origin of foods, the changes they make, and their physical properties. In terms of social studies, children can study cultural aspects of foods and become acquainted with other people and the foods common to their culture, ethnic group, or region. Opportunities for language and literacy development are limitless: Learning new words, reading directions and labels, following recipes, questioning, and naming and labeling foods are just some of the language activities inherent in food activities. There are also possibilities for art and creative expression. Many food projects, such as salads or sculptures, are creative processes in themselves. With foods such as a pineapple slice, a lettuce leaf, one-half of a banana, and a maraschino cherry, there is no limit to creative ideas (e.g., a candlestick or a tree). In music, children can do creative movements to interpret the growth and changes in foods. Empty food containers are useful as shakers or music instruments. In addition, every food activity provides practice in socialization as children learn patience, sharing, respect for one another, and cooperation.

Food Activity Guidelines

Following are considerations for incorporating food activities into the curriculum:

1. Plan and organize all cooking activities (Cosgrove, 1991). Generally, the younger the child, the more simple the project—perhaps one or two steps. Use seasonal produce.

2. Make sure that all foods, utensils, and other items necessary for cooking are ready and assembled.

3. Plan adequate time for the food activity, remembering that children take longer to prepare foods than adults. Allow enough time to question, taste, touch, smell, discover, and compare. Utilize each step in the food activity as a learning experience.

4. Show the children a copy of the recipe so that they know that specific directions must be followed. Write the recipe on a large chart or on individual cards for small groups. Draw pictures or use children's recipe books with directions in picture form. Review the recipe before starting the activity.

5. Adhere to rules of cleanliness: Wash hands before beginning, wipe spills up as you go, and involve the children in cleaning the area at the end of the activity.

6. Follow all safety rules appropriate for the particular food activity. Demonstrate proper use of utensils and supervise their use. Caution about the dangers of hot items and electric appliances.

7. Provide for unlimited learning by allowing the children to explore the questions How?, Why?, What if?, How come?, and I wonder.

Foods, whether approached as a general area or as specific food items, make excellent choices for unit themes. The following ideas for activities have been grouped into basic food groups, although this approach to teaching is not the only possibility. For example, a unit may be presented on dairy products, the cow, milk, or the person who delivers milk. These suggestions for activities could fit into a variety of units. A food activity can be included in a unit as an unrelated activity; therefore, many of the suggestions given here could be utilized in any unit to support food activities.

Fruits and Vegetables

Fruits and vegetables can be approached either in general units or in units featuring specific fruit or vegetable concepts. The children should first be made aware of the foods growing in the local surroundings, and units can easily take advantage of particular growing seasons.

In general or specific units on fruits or vegetables, some of the following concepts could be incorporated.

1. Where and how the food grows—on a tree, underground, on a vine, in a pod, on a bush; singly or in bunches.
2. Growing climate and season.
3. Number, size, and location of seeds.
4. How to tell when food is ripe.
5. Various forms and preparations of food— fresh, cooked; mashed, sliced, cubed, shredded, crushed, juiced, chunked.
6. Varieties or kinds of food (apples— Jonathan, Roman Beauty, Delicious; beans—kidney, green, lima, pinto).
7. Sizes.
8. Color (ripe compared to unripe; variations in different kinds).
9. Parts to be eaten (skin, seeds, leaves, pulp).
10. Methods of storage and preservation (freeze, can, dehydrate).

—————————————————

UNIT PLAN ON FRUITS OR VEGETABLES (GENERAL OR SPECIFIC)

(*Note:* Some of the listed activities may be specifically related to fruits or vegetables. Make appropriate selections to suit your plans.)

Field Trips

- Processing plant or cannery
- Orchard, garden, grove, farm—before, during, and after harvest
- Food stand
- Grocery store
- Sorting shed
- Ride on pickup wagon during harvest
- Fruit and vegetable picking
- Truck loading freight for store
- Bakery
- Ice cream store
- Nursery or greenhouse

Visitors

- Orchard, garden, grove, farm owner
- Person demonstrating food storage and preservation
- Grocer
- Fruit or vegetable picker
- Food stand salesperson
- Employee of a cannery or processing plant
- Baker
- Ice cream maker—to demonstrate use of fruits in ice cream
- Employee of a nursery or greenhouse
- Home economist from the county extension service or a home economics teacher

Food

- Making jam, jelly
- Making juice
- Blending fruits or vegetables into drinks or shakes
- Peeling, slicing, grating, mashing foods
- Fruit or vegetable salad
- Fruit or vegetable pies, pastries, or turnovers
- Fruit or vegetable leather
- Sherbet or ice cream
- Gelatin salad
- Cobbler, strudel, or crisp
- Baked vegetables or fruits
- Fruit cocktail
- Stew
- Soup

- Casseroles
- Fruit or vegetable cakes, cookies
- Fruits and vegetables used with dips, cheese fondues, white sauces
- Breads

Science

- Observation of food during the decaying process
- Tasting familiar and unfamiliar foods
- Observation of wormy food
- Where food grows—trees, vines, shrubs; above, under, or on the ground; in gardens, orchards, farms
- Edible parts—peelings, seeds, flesh, stem, root, flower
- Number of seeds—many, few, one
- Sizes of seeds
- Number of sections
- Kinds of food that taste the same
- Kinds of food that taste different
- Sizes of food
- Texture of food
- Noise made during chewing—loud or soft
- Seed or plant in classroom—cared for by children
- Observation of various types of one specific food
- Smells of vegetables and fruits
- Climates and seasons of food
- Preservation of food
- Seeds sprouted for tasting or using with other foods
- Method of teaching how plants obtain water—piece of celery cut in half lengthwise, but not all the way up; each half is put in glasses of different-colored water; within a short time, the leaves at the top of the stalk will be the same color as the water, with the veins of the stalk also filled with colored water.

Art

- Pieces of food traced on paper
- Pieces of food shapes cut from paper
- Pictures of food cut from magazines
- Seed collages

- Collages made from food pictures
- Shakers made from empty food containers
- Paintings or printings on food shapes
- Food sculpture—pieces of vegetables and/or fruits attached to a base with toothpicks (prepared for eating later)
- Food puppets—drawn or outlined; then decorated or given faces; then cut out and mounted on tongue depressors, dowels, or sticks

Music

- Shakers made with seeds on inside and outside—shaken while singing and marching; shaken loudly, softly, quickly, slowly, like an elephant walks, like a kitten creeps
- Musical chairs—pieces of fruits or vegetables placed on chairs for children to identify when they sit down
- Creative movement—children pretending to be various fruits or vegetables being planted, picked, harvested, falling to the ground
- Singing of expandable songs in which fruit or vegetable names can be included

Language and Literacy

- Booklets made by class or individuals, "Fruits (or Vegetables) I (or We) Like"
- Fruits and vegetables cut from magazines and made into a booklet with children's descriptions of them

Additional Activities

- Unusual fruit or vegetable presented for tasting and for exploring with a magnifying glass
- Trough or tubs filled with soil, then foods planted; root vegetables or bush fruits placed in the soil just as they grow
- Trough filled with pea, potato, bean vines—vegetables to be eaten

LESSON PLAN ON FRUIT (2-DAY)
Overall Goals

- To increase the children's facility in labeling a variety of fruits both familiar and unfamiliar.

- To help the children understand that fruit comes in many different sizes, shapes, colors, textures, and tastes.
- To familiarize the children with the concept that fruit has seeds, and to help them match the fruit with its seed.
- To increase the children's understanding about the fruits that can be eaten—how they can be eaten, which parts of the fruit we eat, and which parts we throw away.
- To help the children understand that fruit must be preserved to avoid spoilage.

Day 1

Whole-Group Activities

Introduction and Labeling. Have an apple, orange, and banana at the rug. Talk about each one with the children. Determine whether the children can identify fruit as a category. Discuss each fruit with the children—what it is, what part we eat, what part we throw away, whether it is soft or crunchy to eat, where it is seen on the bulletin board, where it grows, how many seeds it has, and whether it tastes like anything else. (The bulletin board will display several familiar fruits in several different forms: on the tree, in a bottle or can, peeled, cut, sectioned, etc.)

Objectives

- To introduce the concepts and determine what is known already.
- To have the children verbally label the fruit in its normal appearance and in at least one other form.
- To reinforce concepts of color, taste, and texture through a discussion of fruit.

Visitor—Demonstration of Making Fruit Juices. Have the children gather at the rug and watch as the visitor makes a variety of juices. (The visitor's demonstration should precede the children's own juice-making experience.)

Objectives

- To show the children one way to eat fruit, introducing the food activity.

- To give the children the opportunity to meet new people in the class environment.

Small-Group Activities

Food—Making Fruit Juice. Divide the children into four cooperative groups. Have enough grapefruits, juicers, knives, strainers, and cups for one group; enough oranges and equipment for another; enough limes and equipment for another; and enough lemons and equipment for the fourth group. Each group makes its own kind of juice. They then go to the rug to taste the various juices and talk about the experience.

Objectives

- To develop small muscles through cutting and juicing activities.
- To give the children firsthand experience in making juice.
- To provide experimentation and manipulation of different fruits.
- To create a situation for smelling and tasting juice flavors.

Music—Musical Chairs. Divide the children and teachers into two groups to create more room for each group. Place fruit shapes in a circle around each group. The fruit shapes that are being used should be presented first to the children; use only familiar fruits at this stage. Play music, and when the music stops, ask the children what fruits they are sitting on. Be sure that there is a fruit for each child. Do not leave anyone without a fruit. Use oranges, apples, bananas, peaches, strawberries, grapes, cherries, pears, and grapefruits.

Objectives

- To provide an opportunity to identify fruits by shape and color.
- To provide experience with listening, cooperating, following directions, and matching skills.
- To obtain feedback from the children in smaller groups on their understanding of fruits.

- To give the children practice in labeling a greater variety of fruits than the three most familiar ones.

Individual Activities

- Red sand in trough, together with funnels, utensils, and bottles
- Science bench with dried fruit, jar of moldy fruit, jar of good fruit

Matching Fruit Lotto. Set out lotto games and dominoes made with various fruit pictures from seed packets or catalogues.

Objectives

- To reinforce the concept being taught.
- To provide a situation in which the children will discuss fruit with each other.

Day 2

Small-Group Activities

Field Trip to a Fruit Stand or Store. Divide the children into groups, and contact parents to drive cars. First, check with the store or stand, and notify the owner before you go. Tell the children that they may each choose one piece of fruit to buy, and that the fruit they choose will go into a fruit salad that they will help to prepare. At the stand, have one supervisor for every few children to watch them for safety reasons and to supervise what they choose for the salad. Let each group buy its fruit separately so that the children will have a more individual involvement in the buying process. Each supervisor should tell the children something about the fruits they see at the stand.

Objectives

- To give children experience in selecting and buying fruits.
- To extend the learning from the classroom to the community.

Food—Making Fruit Salads. Have the children remain in their field trip groups. Set up tables with peelers and knives, a bowl, cream, a beater,

and individual cups and spoons. Have the children peel, slice, or section their pieces of fruit into the bowl. They can all take turns holding the beater as cream is whipped, adding vanilla, and stirring the salad. The children dish out their own servings and eat them at the table. (You can use plain yogurt instead of cream as the dressing.)

Objectives

- To involve children in the preparation of fruit, providing opportunities for using peelers and knives.
- To reinforce concepts introduced at the store.
- To provide further opportunity for discussions on texture, which part of the fruit we eat, seeds, and labeling by taste and color.

Fruit Stand Center. Open an actual fruit stand with fruit on it for the rest of the unit during free play. Make shopping bags and money available to create a more realistic situation.

(See Figure 7–1 for a web on apples.)

Grain, Rice, and Pasta Products

Cereals, like the other food groups, can be approached in many ways as units. Units might be presented on wheat, breads, macaroni, rice, or oats. When any of these units are taught, some of the following ideas could be incorporated as teaching concepts or goals:

1. Where and how the grain grows.
2. How it looks when it is ready to harvest.
3. How the seeds of some of the grains (e.g., wheat) can be used—eaten raw, sprouted, or used in food preparation.
4. Number of forms in which the cereal or grain can be eaten.

Perhaps one of the most stimulating units features wheat—including experiences with raw wheat, cooked whole-wheat cereal, and wheat ground into whole-wheat flour to be used in many different food activities.

The following are suggested unit plans for some of the familiar cereal or bread products.

UNIT PLAN ON BREAD[*]

Art

- Sculptured bread dough—worked and molded, then baked and eaten
- Sculpture made with different kinds of breads—small cubes or pieces of rye bread, sweet bread, sourdough, and so on; may be combined with chunked fruits and/or vegetables (prepare to be eaten later); Styrofoam base could be used

Food

- Open-faced sandwiches made in different shapes—cookie cutters used to cut shapes of bread; spreads or toppings added
- Toast or cinnamon toast (no sugar)
- French toast
- Rolls—any kind, in any shape
- Bread—pumpkin, zucchini, onion, honey, raisin, or garlic
- Dilly bread—made with cottage cheese and onions
- Muffins
- Biscuits
- Blueberry muffins, rolls, bread
- Scones—made from bread dough or sweet bread dough
- Eggs in a ring—hole cut in center of a slice of bread, both sides buttered, bread put in frying pan, egg broken into center of bread; turned when white begins to look firm
- Canned refrigerator biscuit recipes—listed at the end of this chapter

Field Trips

- Bakery
- Cafeteria or other restaurant where breads are prepared

[*] For a unit plan on wheat and flour, see Chapter 15.

- Child's home where a parent is baking bread
- Zoo or other place where animals are fed bread or bread crumbs
- Grocery store—kinds, shapes of bread; bread products

Visitors

- Baker
- Parent—rolls made in interesting and unusual shapes
- Home economist/community nutritionist
- Bread deliverer—delivery truck brought, if possible; children encouraged to climb in and observe many kinds and forms of bread

Music

- Songs relating to bread

Science

- Discussion of grains used to make breads—wheat emphasized
- Kinds of bread and their different tastes; tasting activities
- Observation of process of grinding wheat into flour
- Comparison of taste, texture, and smell of raw versus cooked bread—dough form compared to baked form
- Comparison of size of bread before and after baking—1/4 cup sugar, two packages dry yeast, and 1/2 cup warm water combined; mixture put into pop bottle with a balloon over the neck of the bottle; mixture causes air to expand in the bottle, just as it does in the bread; balloon inflates.
- Animals that eat breads and/or bread crumbs (birds, insects); ant farm, with a focus on observing the ants as they carry bread crumbs

Language and Literacy

- "Little Red Riding Hood"—story adapted so that the children will not be frightened; used as object story by focusing on the different breads that filled her basket; sampling of such breads.
- Make booklet of different kinds of breads

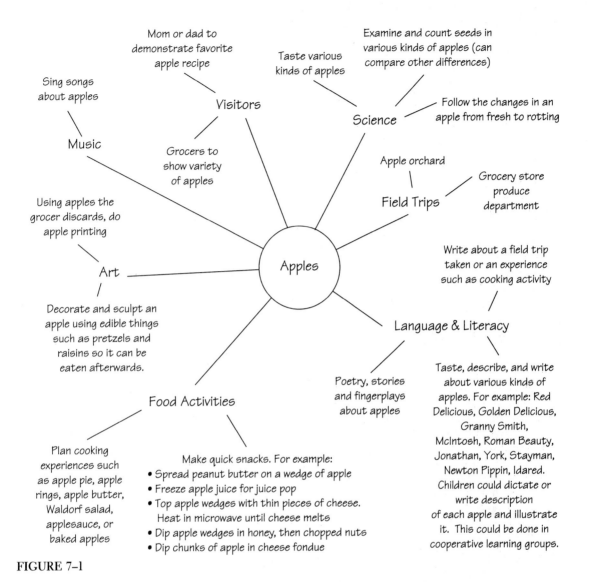

Mom or dad to demonstrate favorite apple recipe

Taste various kinds of apples

Examine and count seeds in various kinds of apples (can compare other differences)

Sing songs about apples

Visitors

Science

Follow the changes in an apple from fresh to rotting

Music

Grocers to show variety of apples

Apple orchard

Field Trips

Grocery store produce department

Using apples the grocer discards, do apple printing

Apples

Art

Write about a field trip taken or an experience such as cooking activity

Decorate and sculpt an apple using edible things such as pretzels and raisins so it can be eaten afterwards.

Language & Literacy

Food Activities

Poetry, stories and fingerplays about apples

Taste, describe, and write about various kinds of apples. For example: Red Delicious, Golden Delicious, Granny Smith, McIntosh, Roman Beauty, Jonathan, York, Stayman, Newton Pippin, Idared. Children could dictate or write description of each apple and illustrate it. This could be done in cooperative learning groups.

Plan cooking experiences such as apple pie, apple rings, apple butter, Waldorf salad, applesauce, or baked apples

Make quick snacks. For example:
• Spread peanut butter on a wedge of apple
• Freeze apple juice for juice pop
• Top apple wedges with thin pieces of cheese. Heat in microwave until cheese melts
• Dip apple wedges in honey, then chopped nuts
• Dip chunks of apple in cheese fondue

FIGURE 7–1

Dairy Products

Milk can be used in such foods as baked custard, yogurt, and soups such as cream of potato.

Cream can be used in food such as ice cream, or whipped cream can be used in desserts, in salads, and as toppings on gingerbread or other cakes.

Butter made by the children and then spread on bread or crackers can be made in several ways. Approximately ½ pint of whipping cream should be left out to warm to room temperature and then put into a container with a tight lid. As the children shake the container, the cream separates and becomes butter. Yellow food coloring and salt may then be added and the buttermilk drained off. To allow each child to make butter, a small amount of room-temperature cream can be put into a baby food jar and shaken until butter forms. How delighted the child will be to take the butter home and share it with the family (if it lasts that long!). From this activity the children will learn that butter comes from cream, which is a product of the cow.

Sour cream and plain yogurt are used in making dips, fruit salads, and stroganoff and as a topping on baked potatoes.

Cottage cheese is used plain, as well as in making salads, dilly bread, chip dips, lasagna, and other dishes. Many recipes for casseroles, desserts, sandwiches, dips, tacos, and so on use other cheese. The children can learn that cheese comes in different forms, such as spreads, cream cheese, bricks, curds, melted, or grated.

UNIT PLAN ON DAIRY PRODUCTS

Art

- Cheese sculpturing—more economical if used in combination with additional foods, such as fruits and vegetables (then eaten)
- Collages made with magazine pictures of dairy products—additional media such as yarn and paper scraps can be added for variety
- Decoration of milk cartons to be used as litter containers, planters, or puppets
- Musical shakers made with milk cartons, cream cartons, cottage cheese containers; decorated with glue and collage items, or by dipping paper scraps, tissue paper, and other materials into liquid starch and then putting on the carton

Science

- Milk separating
- Butter made from cream
- Milk curdling
- Discussion of the need for milk in the diets of both animal and human babies; actual experiences of seeing babies drinking milk

Music

- Creative dramatics—exploring such movements as milking a cow or dramatizing a cow chewing its cud, swatting flies with its tail
- Rhythm shakers—milk cartons (half-pint size easiest to handle) or cottage cheese cartons partially filled with rice, beans, wheat, or other grains

Field Trips

- Dairy farm
- Cheese factory
- Creamery
- Dairy
- Farm with cows
- Grocery store
- Milk depot

Visitors

- Dairy farmer
- Grocer
- Ice-cream shop proprietor—may discuss flavors, colors, ingredients
- Person who delivers milk (and milk truck, if possible)
- Person to make a food product in class using milk

Food

- Any of the activities presented and discussed previously
- Any food activity featuring dairy products
- Tasting different forms of milk (skim milk, buttermilk, evaporated milk, condensed milk, cream)
- Tasting and using different kinds of cheeses
- Making butter
- Making ice cream

Language and Literacy

- Experience charts relating to trips, visitors, movies, and other activities
- Poetry and story writing
- Movie, The Cow[*]—opportunities for sensory experiences with young children; speaking or writing about experiences in the film
- Stories and poems about cows, dairies, and persons who deliver milk
- Booklet titled, "I Like Milk" (include ways we use milk)

[*] Churchill Films, Los Angeles.

Protein Products

Meat units most often tie in with animal units in which meat is the product of the animal. For example, a unit on beef cows could elaborate on different forms of beef—hamburger, steaks, roasts, wieners, liver, stew meat, and others. In a unit such as this one, it is not necessary to have food experiences with each form of beef. The children synthesize the concept of beef and its different forms by observing pictures of these different meat cuts and by visiting a butcher shop or meat market to see various meat cuts. Additional meat units could include pigs (bacon, sausage, wieners, pork chops, pork roast), poultry (turkey, chicken, eggs), and fish (tuna, salmon, halibut, trout, shrimp, cod, turbot). A general area of meat could be approached as a unit, with subcategories such as those just listed (beef, pork, fish, poultry, etc.).

Whatever approach is chosen in developing units of study on meat, teaching should include both the origins and methods of preparation for the various meats. The taste of the meat changes as the method of preparation is varied: for example, the taste of chicken varies according to whether it is fried, put in a salad, baked, and so on.

The following unit plans present each of the basic meat categories. Again, these categories can be combined and activities selected for teaching a general unit on meat. These suggested activities could also be applied to other meats, such as wild game or sheep.

UNIT PLAN ON BEEF COWS AND BEEF PRODUCTS*

Art

- Paper-sack cow puppets
- Pictures of cows painted or drawn
- Print with designs similar to cattle brands

* Foods such as cheese, bacon, eggs, and fried foods are high in cholesterol and should be used in moderation.

Music

- Creative movements or dramatics—dramatizing an auction or a roundup, lassoing a cow or calf, branding
- "Galloping" music—children pretending to lasso or herd cattle

Food

- Hamburger
  - Foil dinners
  - Spaghetti
  - Pizza
  - Casseroles
  - Meatloaf
  - Patties—baked, fried, or broiled
  - Tacos
  - Unusual foreign foods
  - Lasagna

- Wieners
  - Pizza
  - Casseroles
  - Broiled, boiled, or fried
  - Sliced with cheese in the center and broiled or microwaved

- Stew
- Soups made from beef soup bone, hamburger, or stew meat
- Chili
- Beef pie or shepherd's pie made from leftover roast or stew meat

Field Trips

- Livestock auction
- Grocery store
- Farm to observe beef cattle
- Butcher shop to see beef carcass and meat cuts
- Child's home, where parent will show meat cuts in freezer and/or cook a beef cut such as a roast

Visitors

- Leather tanner or tooler
- Parent to cook some beef cut
- Butcher
- Rancher
- Cowboy or Cowgirl

Science

- Comparing size of meat before and after cooking (meat shrinkage)
- Preservation of beef—frozen, canned, dried; discussion of what happens when not properly preserved
- Observing the processing of meats such as hamburger or wieners—grinding, seasoning, and so on
- Observing a carcass
- Uses and preparation of leather
- Tasting different forms of beef—jerky, liver, steaks, roasts, and others
- Diet of beef cow—hay and silage in winter, grass in summer
- Calves—appearance after birth, diet, growth changes

Language and Literacy

- Stories and poems relating to cows
- Creative story and poetry writing
- Films, filmstrips relating to cows
- Class or individual booklet titled "I Like Beef"

UNIT PLAN ON POULTRY AND POULTRY PRODUCTS*

Art

- Paper-sack chicken puppets
- Painting with chicken feathers
- Collages made with chicken feathers
- Eggshell collages—colored with egg coloring or food coloring mixed in alcohol or water; may be combined with media such as chicken feathers, cut straws, or paper scraps
- Chicken wings made to wear on the children's arms—attach with string and decorate with feathers, paper scraps, and other objects; beak made out of paper (could be used for creative movement)

*Foods such as cheese, bacon, eggs, and fried foods are high in cholesterol and should be used in moderation.

Music

- Creative movements or dramatics—dramatizing chickens and their movements; a chick pecking its way out of the shell, learning to stand and walk, drinking water, eating

Food

- Eggs
  Eggnog (commercial or cooked)
  Baked, fried, broiled, scrambled, poached
  French toast
  Custard
  Bakery products using eggs as ingredients
  Desserts using eggs
  Omelets

- Chicken
  Croquettes
  Baked, fried, broiled
  Casseroles
  Salads
  Sandwiches
  Ground chicken used as a chicken spread
  Chicken and dumplings
  Chicken pie
  Chicken soup
  Stir fry

Field Trips

- Poultry farm
- Grocery store—observation of chicken in meat section, eggs in dairy section, and canned chicken
- Hatchery
- Place where egg candling and sorting can be seen
- Child's home—parent to show poultry cuts in freezer, cook poultry cuts such as chicken, make chicken casserole or salad
- Restaurant selling or specializing in chicken

Visitors

- Parent to prepare chicken product—possibly an unusual product such as an omelet, cooked eggnog, or chicken croquettes
- Poultry farmer

- Someone with an egg candler to demonstrate egg candling
- Butcher

Science

- Parts of eggs—shell, yolk, white
- Process of beating eggs or egg whites—become foamy as air is beaten in
- Eggs used as thickening
- Various kinds of eggs—brown, white, chicken, turkey, swan, duck, bird, and so on
- Hatching of chicks from the incubator stage—watching as they peck out of the shell and then grow to be mature hens and roosters
- Candling of eggs
- Preservation of eggs—refrigerated, frozen, dried
- Food eaten by chickens

Language and Literacy

- Stories and poems relating to chickens
- Creative story writing—"Chicken Is Good."

UNIT PLANS ON BEANS

(There are actually foods from two different food groups in this unit—green beans from the vegetable group and dried beans from the protein group. This can be explained to the children.)

Art

- Collages made with different kinds of beans
- Costume for dramatization—large bean leaves made to cover the arms and then decorated with crayons; or painting of a large bean on stiff paper, to be worn on the body
- Hat—large paper plate decorated with different kinds of beans; the bottom of this large paper plate is attached to the bottom of a smaller paper plate; string, yarn, or ribbon is attached to the smaller plate to secure it on the head

Field Trips

- Farm where beans are being grown or harvested
- Grocery store—different kinds and forms of beans

- Child's home—parent demonstrating food activity relating to beans or showing how beans are canned and stored

Visitors

- Parent to demonstrate either a food activity relating to beans or forms or kinds of beans
- Grocer
- Parent to show different kinds of bean seeds and demonstrate how they are planted

Science

- Discussion—beans are seeds and grow in a pod
- Bean sprouts grown and used in salads
- Bean seeds planted; growth observed when proper care is given
- Observation of day-by-day growth of bean. (See Chapter 18, "Size and Seriation")
- Discussion of how beans grow—on a vine, in a pod
- Kinds of beans—pinto, lima, chili, white; tasting of the different kinds
- Bean seeds sprouted for later planting outside; may be harvested and eaten if time is sufficient

Music

- Shakers partially filled with beans; decorated with the same type of bean as is in the container
- Creative movements or dramatizations to music relating to growth of beans, picking, and other activities

Food

- Bean sprouts in green salads
- Bean salads made with several different kinds of beans—yellow wax, kidney, green, garbanzo; oil-and-vinegar dressing
- Pork and beans
- Green beans
- Green-bean casseroles
- Chili
- Bean soup—lima beans with ham or wieners
- Beans—fried, refried, baked

Additional Activities

- Bean vines and/or pods placed in the trough or on a tarpaulin or drop cloth—beans to be picked from vines and/or pods

---

Recipes for Food Experiences

Recipes are grouped under Fruit-Vegetable, Grain, Milk-Cheese, or Meat-Poultry-Fish-Beans to assist in planning a variety of good activities from each group using the Food Guide Pyramid described earlier in the chapter as a reference. Some recipes include foods from more than one group, and some include foods from all the groups. The "Quick and Easy" ideas at the beginning of each section, along with many of the recipes, have been taken from a publication on food and nutrition by the United States Department of Agriculture titled *Food*. This publication is not copyrighted and contains public information. We appreciate it as a source for nutritious food recipes for children!

During snack time, crackers last longer when they are sucked than when they are chewed.

In presenting recipes, the goals have been fourfold: (1) emphasizing ingredients that provide nutrients, (2) being practical in the selection of foods, (3) planning activities that are developmentally appropriate, and (4) allowing children to learn through less restrictive, more open-ended avenues of exploration.

A modest number of recipes that are rich in fat, cholesterol, sugar, or salt have been included; these should be used sparingly. Also, meat and eggs should be adequately cooked, and children should not be allowed to taste dough containing raw eggs.

Fruit-Vegetable Group

Quick and Easy!

- Finger fruits such as grapes, apple sections, pear sections, and so on
- Dried fruits such as apricots, raisins, prunes, bananas, pineapple, or dried fruit leathers
- Minikabobs of bite-sized fruit chunks strung on a toothpick
- Banana chunks dipped in orange juice; shaken in a bag with chopped peanuts; speared with toothpicks
- Juice cubes made by freezing fruit juice in an ice cube tray; other fruit drinks chilled with the cubes
- Grapefruit half, sprinkled with brown sugar and broiled
- Tomato half, sprinkled with bread crumbs, Parmesan or grated cheese, and broiled
- Tomato sections, cucumber slices, and cauliflowerets marinated in French dressing
- Raw vegetable sticks or pieces (radishes, celery, cauliflower, zucchini, green pepper, carrots, cucumbers, parsnips); cutting them in various shapes may be tried
- Minikabobs of bite-sized vegetable chunks strung on a toothpick
- Celery stuffed with cottage cheese, cheese spread, or peanut butter; raisins added for "ants on a log."

- Add sliced zucchini, raw cauliflowerets, raw broccoli, and alfalfa sprouts with greens to greens such as lettuce
- Cooked baby lima beans, sliced mushrooms, and green onions, seasoned with oregano; served with dressing as desired

Banana Smoothie

The children mash pieces of banana on waxed paper. Add this to vanilla ice cream and milk. Stir together.

Orange Frost

1 6-oz can frozen orange juice concentrate	¼ cup sugar
	½ tsp vanilla
1 cup milk	10 ice cubes
1 cup water	

Place all ingredients in a blender. Cover and blend until smooth. Serve immediately.

Fruit Dip

10-oz frozen strawberries
1 8-oz pkg. cream cheese
½ tsp. lemon juice

Thaw and drain strawberries. Combine all ingredients in a blender and blend until smooth. Use as a dip for bite-sized fruit pieces.

Fruit Cup

3 T frozen lemonade concentrate
1 med. apple, cored and diced
1 med. orange, peeled, sectioned, and diced
1 med. peach, peeled, pitted, and diced
1 med. banana, peeled and sliced
½ cup halved seedless grapes
½ cup blueberries
2 T finely chopped walnuts

Place lemonade concentrate in large bowl and mix lightly with fruits as they are prepared. Chill. Garnish each serving with chopped walnuts.

Fruit-Nut Snack

6½-oz can Spanish peanuts, salted
1 cup raisins
4 oz chopped dates

(Other fruits and nuts such as dried banana slices, sunflower seeds, coconut, or other raw nuts can be added for variety or taste. Carob pieces can also be added if desired.)

Mix all ingredients.

Frozen Fruit Pops

1 cup frozen or fresh unsweetened fruit (strawberries, peaches, raspberries, blueberries, kiwis, mixed fruit)
1 cup plain low-fat yogurt
5 T honey

Put fruit in blender. Cover and blend for 45 seconds at medium speed until smooth. Pour into 1-quart measuring cup, add yogurt and honey, and mix well. Pour mixture into 3½-oz. paper or plastic cups (about seven) and put a wooden stick in the center of each cup. Freeze for 1 to 2 hours until firm. Remove cup from frozen pop and serve.

Date Treats

Grind dates and nuts. Form into balls and roll in coconut.

Apple Crisp

3½ cups sliced apples	½ cup quick-cooking oats
1 T lemon juice	
2 T water	⅜ cup brown sugar
½ cup flour (may use whole wheat)	⅜ tsp salt
	¼ cup melted butter
	1 tsp cinnamon

Combine apples, lemon juice, and water. Place in baking dish. Mix together remaining ingredients and sprinkle on other mixture. Bake at 375° for 35 to 40 minutes.

Applesauce

6 apples
4 T honey or brown sugar

Wash, core, and slice apples. Put in saucepan with a little water. Cook slowly until tender. Strain or force through sieve or food mill, or puree in blender.

Squash Bread

1½ cups unsifted flour	½ cup oil
2 tsp cinnamon	2 tsp vanilla
1 tsp baking powder	1⅓ cups summer squash
½ tsp baking soda	(or zucchini) coarsely
¼ tsp salt	shredded, lightly
2 eggs	packed
¾ cup sugar	

Mix dry ingredients except sugar thoroughly. Beat eggs until fluffy. Add sugar, oil, and vanilla. Beat until lemon colored, about 3 minutes. Stir in squash. Add dry ingredients. Mix just until dry ingredients are moistened. Pour into 5- by 3-in. loaf pan and bake for 40 minutes in 350°F oven or until toothpick inserted in center comes out clean. Cool for 10 minutes before removing from pan

Pumpkin Drop Cookies

⅓ cup shortening	4 tsp baking powder
¾ cup sugar	1 tsp cinnamon
1 egg	¼ tsp ginger
1 cup pumpkin	¼ tsp nutmeg
2¼ cups flour	½ tsp salt
(part whole-wheat)	½ tsp vanilla

Cream sugar and shortening; add egg, blend well, and add pumpkin. Add dry ingredients, sifted together, and flavoring. One cupful of raisins and ½ cup chopped nutmeats could be folded in. Drop by spoonfuls on greased cookie sheet. Bake at 350°F for 15 minutes (makes about 3 dozen cookies).

Raggedy Ann Salad

1 peach half	Shredded cheese
1 stalk celery	Nuts and raisins

Use peach for body, celery for legs, and cheese for hair. Make face with raisins and nuts. Place on a lettuce leaf.

Stew

Vegetables
Liquid
Browned stew meat, if desired

Have each child bring a vegetable. Prepare vegetables and add liquid. If desired, add browned stew meat. Simmer for at least an hour and a half.

Vegetable Dip

¼ cup chives or onion tops
¼ cup parsley
⅙ pkg. fresh spinach (not frozen)
½ tsp salt
½ tsp ground pepper
1 cup mayonnaise

Place chives (or onion tops), parsley, and fresh spinach in blender with a small amount of mayonnaise. After blending, add remaining ingredients and run blender again. (Half-and-half cream can be used to make the dip thinner.) Dip zucchini slices, cucumber, carrots, celery, and other vegetables into the dip.

Tempura Vegetables (single portion)

Batter: 1 T water
2 tsp beaten egg
2 T flour

Combine to make batter. Put carrot strips, green pepper, green beans, or other vegetables on a skewer, and dip into batter. Cook in hot oil and serve with soy sauce.

Vegetable Soup

¾ cup dry vegetable soup mix or alphabet soup mix
1 qt boiling water
1 T salt
Beef soup bone or short ribs
1⅓ cups chopped celery
1 cup diced carrots
1 cup chopped onion
1½ cups sliced cabbage
8-oz. can tomato sauce

Add soup mix to water with remaining ingredients, except tomato sauce. Simmer gently for 2 hours. Add tomato sauce and simmer for 1 hour.

Coleslaw

4 cups shredded or finely chopped cabbage
Salt
1 cup plain yogurt or salad dressing

Mix together. (May add diced apples, raisins, pineapple, marshmallows, etc.)

Marinated Vegetable Salad

Cooked green peas	Red kidney beans
French-style green beans	Cauliflowerets
Chopped green pepper	Sliced cucumber
Chopped onion	Sliced carrots
Chopped celery	Garbanzo beans
Julienne carrots	

Marinate in oil-vinegar dressing or ½ cup wine vinegar, ½ cup oil, ¼ cup sugar, salt, and pepper. Mix and refrigerate overnight.

Salads with Vegetable and Fruit Combinations

To grated carrots, add any or all of the following:
   Drained crushed or tidbit canned pineapple
   Raisins
   Diced banana
   Coconut
   Salad dressing or plain yogurt to moisten
To chopped or shredded cabbage, add any or all of the following:
   Diced celery
   Diced apple
   Chopped peanuts
   Raisins

Grain Group

Quick and Easy!

- Raisin bread, toasted and spread with peanut butter
- Sandwiches using a variety of breads—raisin, cracked wheat, pumpernickel, rye, black
- Date-nut roll or brown bread spread with cream cheese
- English muffins, served open-faced for sandwiches such as hot roast beef or turkey, chicken salad
- Individual pizzas: English muffin halves topped with cheese slices, tomato sauce and oregano, then broiled
- Waffles topped with yogurt and fruit
- Wheat or rye crackers topped with seasoned cottage cheese, cheese, meat spread, or peanut butter

Bread or Bread Sticks

1 cup milk	1 cup warm water
3 T shortening	3 T sugar
1 T salt	8 cups flour (or 4
1 cup cold water	cups white and 4
2 yeast cakes	cups whole wheat)

Scald milk, shortening, and salt; dissolve. Then add cold water. Soak yeast cakes in large bowl with warm water and sugar. Next, add 2 cups flour to yeast mixture and mix well. Add the milk, shortening, salt, and water mixture; add 6 cups flour. Mix well, pour out, and knead for 5 minutes on floured board. Place mixture back in bowl and let rise until double in bulk, about 90 minutes. Turn out on floured surface and knead for 5 minutes. Makes two loaves about 1 lb in size; let rise in lightly greased pans until doubled in bulk, about 45–90 minutes, or let children shape into individual rolls or sculptures. Bake for 20 to 30 minutes at 425°F.

Navaho Fry Bread (Pahnelaquiz)

2 cups flour	¾ tsp salt
½ cup dry milk	2 T shortening
1 T baking powder	¾ lukewarm water

Mix flour, milk, baking powder, and salt together and then cut in shortening. Mix in water (more if necessary) and knead until smooth and elastic. Let stand at least 30 minutes or refrigerate overnight. Cut into pieces and deep fry in small amount of hot oil.

Fry Bread (single portion)

2 T flour	pinch of salt
¼ tsp baking powder	2 tsp water

Mix and then shape into thin pancake shapes. Deep fry and drain on paper towel.

Hot Grits

1⅓ cup grits	1½ tsp salt
6⅔ cups boiling water	3 T butter

Pour grits into boiling water, add salt, and stir until it thickens (2–3 minutes). Cover and cook over low heat 25 minutes and stir twice during that time. Dot with butter and serve.

Hoecakes (single portion)

2 T cornmeal
pinch of salt
1 T boiling water

Mix, form into pancake, and cook on greased griddle. Serve with syrup or molasses.

Popcorn with Cheese

⅓ cup popcorn, popped   ½ cup Parmesan
2 T melted butter   cheese
   or margarine   ½ tsp salt, if desired

Placed popped corn in a shallow baking pan. Drizzle with melted fat; mix. Sprinkle with cheese; salt, if desired; mix. Heat for 8 to 10 minutes in oven, stirring frequently.

Scones

2 cups unsifted flour
¼ cup sugar
2 tsp baking powder
½ tsp baking soda
½ tsp salt
¼ cup butter or margarine
2 eggs
⅓ cup sour milk (combine 1 tsp vinegar or lemon juice
   with enough sweet milk to make ⅓ cup)

Grease a baking sheet. Mix dry ingredients thoroughly. Mix in fat only until mixture is crumbly, using a pastry blender, two table knives, or a fork. Beat eggs; add milk. Stir into dry ingredients, mixing just until moistened. Divide dough in half. Place on baking sheet and shape each half of the dough into a 7-in. circle about ½ in. thick. Divide each circle of dough into six wedges. Prick with a fork. Bake at 375°F for 12 minutes or until lightly browned.

Bran Cereal or Whole-Wheat Muffins

1 cup whole bran cereal
½–1 cup milk
1 egg, beaten
¼ cup oil
¼ cup honey, molasses, or brown sugar
1¼ cups unsifted whole-wheat flour
2 tsp baking powder
¼ tsp baking soda
½ tsp salt

Grease muffin tins. Stir bran cereal and milk together in a bowl. Let stand for a minute or two, then add egg, oil, and honey. Beat well. Stir remaining ingredients together until well mixed. Add to liquid mixture and stir only until moistened. Put into muffin tins, filling only about two-thirds full. Bake in 400°F oven for about 20 to 25 minutes or until lightly browned. (*Option*: Eliminate bran cereal and increase whole-wheat flour to 2 cups. If bran is eliminated, mix milk with other liquids.)

Red Beans and Rice

½ cup chopped onion   2 cups cooked rice
½ cup chopped celery   1 T chopped parsley
1 clove garlic   ½ tsp salt
2 T butter or margarine   ⅛ tsp pepper
16-oz. can kidney beans

Cook onion, celery, and garlic in fat until tender; remove garlic. Add remaining ingredients. Simmer together for 5 minutes to blend flavors.

Whole-Wheat Drop Cookies

2 cups brown sugar, packed
1 cup shortening
2 eggs, beaten
2 tsp baking soda dissolved in 2 T water
½ tsp baking powder
¾ tsp salt
2½ cups whole-wheat flour
1 cup chopped dates or raisins
½ cup nuts (optional)

Cream shortening and sugar. Mix remaining ingredients and add to creamed mixture; mix to a soft dough. Drop about 2 in. apart on baking sheet. Bake for 8 to 10 minutes at 375°F.

Individual Carrot Cakes

⅓ cup grated carrot   Pinch nutmeg
3 T yellow cake mix   6 raisins
¼ tsp cinnamon   2 T beaten egg

Mix all ingredients together. Bake in muffin tin at 375°F for 10 to 15 minutes. Frost if desired.

Recipes Using Refrigerator Biscuits

Pigs in a Blanket

Small sausages or hot dogs
Refrigerator biscuits

Fold refrigerator biscuits around sausages. Place in pans and bake at 450°F for 8 to 10 minutes. Cool slightly and serve with mustard or catsup, if desired.

Doughnuts or Scones

Refrigerator biscuits
Cooking oil (approximately ¼ in. deep in skillet)
Sugar, cinnamon-sugar mixture, or glaze

Cut small hole in biscuit with finger or thimble. Fry in heated oil for about 2 minutes or until done, turning once. Drain on paper towels. Roll in sugar or cinnamon-sugar mixture, or glaze. (For scones, eliminate hole in center.)

Bread Sticks

Refrigerator biscuits
Butter
Seeds such as sesame seeds

Roll each biscuit into a long cylinder. Roll in butter and then, if desired, in any kind of seed, such as sesame seeds. Bake according to package directions. Serve in a basket with any kind of desired preserves or honey, or just butter.

Individual Pizzas

Refrigerator biscuits
1 lb ground beef

2 cups tomato sauce
¼ cup finely chopped onion, if desired
Finely chopped small garlic bud, if desired
Grated cheese

On lightly greased cookie sheet, flatten biscuits and press up rim on edge. Fill with mixture of tomato sauce, browned hamburger, onion, and garlic. Top with grated cheese. (Other ingredients that may be used include sliced wieners, pepperoni, Parmesan cheese, oregano, parsley flakes, onion, garlic, basil, pepper.) Bake at 425°F for 10 minutes.

Milk, Yogurt, and Cheese Group

Quick and Easy!

- Milkshakes with mashed fresh berries or bananas
- Parfait of cottage cheese, yogurt, or ice milk combined with fruit, sprinkled with chopped nuts, wheat germ, or crisp cereal
- Fruit-flavored yogurt
- Custard
- Ice-milk sundae topped with fresh, canned, or frozen fruits
- Cheese cubes plain, or speared with pretzel sticks, or alternated with mandarin orange sections on a toothpick

Following food activities from the beginning of preparation through measuring, mixing, serving, and eating not only increases healthy nutritional concepts, but fosters independence and confidence.

- Assorted cheeses with crackers or chilled fresh fruits
- Dips for vegetables sticks. For fewer calories and to make more nutritious, substitute cottage cheese or plain yogurt for sour cream and mayonnaise in preparing dips.

Butter

½ pt whipping cream
Dash of salt
Yellow coloring, if desired

Warm cream to room temperature. Shake in bottle until butter and milk separate. Pour milk off and continue to separate the milk from the butter. Salt to taste. Add yellow food coloring, if desired.

Chili con Queso Dip

16-oz box pasteurized processed cheese spread, cut in cubes
¾ cup canned tomatoes, chopped
1 T finely chopped chili peppers

Place cheese cubes in the top of a double boiler over boiling water. Stir constantly until cheese is melted. Stir in tomatoes and peppers until well blended and creamy. Serve hot with tortilla or corn chips.

Eggnog

3 eggs, slightly beaten	½ tsp vanilla
½ cup sugar	1½ tsp imitation
¼ tsp salt	rum flavoring
3 cups milk	Nutmeg as desired
1 cup half-and-half	

Mix beaten eggs with sugar and salt in the top of a double boiler. Add milk and half-and-half. Cook over boiling water, stirring constantly, just until mixture coats spoon, about 10 to 15 minutes. Cool. Add vanilla and rum flavorings. Chill. Immediately before serving, strain eggnog. Beat with rotary beater until frothy. Pour into chilled cups. Sprinkle each serving with nutmeg, as desired.

Banana Smoothie (single serving)

Mash ½ banana, mix with ½ cup ice milk and ¼ cup milk.

Banana-Orange Shake

4 ripe bananas, sliced	¼ tsp vanilla
⅓ cup orange juice	4 cups reconstituted
6 T honey	nonfat dry milk
Salt	

Put in blender and beat until smooth.

Strawberry-Yogurt Pops

2 10-oz cartons frozen strawberries, thawed	16 oz plain yogurt
1 T unflavored gelatin	3-oz paper cups
	Wooden sticks

Drain strawberries. Place drained liquid in a saucepan and sprinkle with gelatin. Cook over low heat, stirring constantly, until gelatin dissolves. Mix strawberries, yogurt, and gelatin mixture in a blender until smooth. Place cups on a tray or in a baking pan. Fill with blended mixture and cover cups with sheet of aluminum foil. Insert a stick for each pop by making a slit in the foil over the center of each cup. Freeze pops until firm. Run warm water outside of cup to loosen each pop from the cup.

Cheese Fondue

1 slice American cheese
1 slice Swiss cheese
8 oz onion dip

Melt slices of cheese mixed with onion dip slowly in pot until thick. Dip pineapple chunks, French bread cubes, banana slices, celery bites, carrots, cauliflower, wiener slices, apple pieces, zucchini slices, or bread sticks into the fondue.

Protein Group (Meat, Poultry, Eggs, Nuts, Fish, and Beans)

Quick and Easy!

- Nuts, sesame seeds, or toasted sunflower seeds
- Sandwich spread of peanut butter combined with raisins or chopped dates
- Peanut butter and honey spread on an English muffin, sprinkled with chopped walnuts and heated under broiler

- Grilled open-faced peanut butter and mashed banana sandwich
- Tomatoes stuffed with egg salad
- Melon wedges topped with thinly sliced ham

Toasted Sunflower Seeds

1 cup sunflower seeds
1 tsp oil, if desired
1/4 tsp salt, if desired

Mix sunflower seeds with oil only if salt is used. Spread plain or oiled seeds on baking sheet. Bake at 325°F for about 8 minutes or until lightly browned. (Watch carefully, these seeds brown quickly.) Sprinkle oiled seeds with salt while hot.

Quick-Cook Chili

1 lb ground beef
1/2 cup chopped onion
1 16-oz can pinto beans
1 can (10¾ oz) condensed tomato soup
2–3 tsp chili powder

Heat beef and onion in a skillet until beef is browned and onion is tender. Drain off excess fat. Stir in remaining ingredients. Cover. Simmer for 30 minutes, stirring occasionally.

Chao fan

Scramble eggs with a bit of chopped green onion. Add chopped ham and cooked peas. Serve over cooked rice. Add soy sauce, if desired. (Adapted from Kositsky, 1977, p. 30)

Wontons

Wonton skins   bean sprouts
hamburger   green onion
soya sauce

Combine raw hamburger, a little soya sauce, some cut-up bean sprouts, and a little minced green onion. Put a teaspoon into the center of the wonton skin and then fold in half to make a triangle. Dampen the edges so they stick together. Simmer in chicken soup or deep fat fry for 1 to 2 minutes. (Adapted from Kositsky, 1977, p. 30)

Chicken-Fruit Salad

3 cups cooked chicken, cut in chunky pieces
3/4 cup chopped celery
3/4 cup grape halves, seeded
20-oz can pineapple chunks in natural juice, drained
11-oz can mandarin oranges, drained
1/4 cup chopped pecans
1/4 cup salad dressing or plain yogurt
1/8 tsp salt
Lettuce leaves

Toss chicken, celery, grapes, pineapple, oranges, and 3 T of the pecans together lightly. Gently mix salad dressing or yogurt and salt with chicken mixture. Chill. Serve on lettuce leaves. Garnish with remaining pecans.

Mexicale Hot Dog

1 flour tortilla   1 hot dog
1 slice cheese   Salsa (optional)

Lay flour tortilla out. Put slice of cheese on tortilla, spread with salsa, put hot dog on top, and roll up. Microwave for 1 minute.

Open-Faced Submarine Sandwiches

6 English muffin halves, toasted
1 T butter or margarine
6 slices meat
1 cup chopped lettuce
1/2 small onion, thinly sliced and separated into rings
1 medium tomato, thinly sliced
1/2 tsp basil leaves
6 slices pasteurized process American cheese

Spread toasted muffin halves with butter or margarine. Layer meat quarters, lettuce, onion, and tomato slices on toasted muffin halves. Sprinkle with basil. Top each sandwich with cheese slice. Broil until cheese is melted and lightly browned, about 5 minutes.

Refried Beans

1 lb pinto beans   Dash of cumin
1 qt water   1/2 cup lard or bacon fat
Salt to taste

Sort and wash pinto beans. Cover with water generously; let stand overnight. Next day, pour off liquid. Put in large pot and add twice as much water as there are beans. Stir in salt and cumin. Quickly bring to a boil. Lower heat. Simmer for 2 to 3 hours (until tender). Drain; mash beans. Heat lard. Add very hot lard to beans. Stir and simmer until fat is absorbed. Use as is or refry. To refry, fry mashed beans in hot lard until completely dry.

Peanut Butter

1½ T oil
1 cup peanuts
Salt

Put the oil in a blender and gradually add the peanuts and sprinkle with a little salt. Blend well.

Peanut-Butter Balls

15 oz graham crackers	½ cup peanut butter
2 T corn syrup	4 T butter or margarine
2 T milk	2 T vanilla

Crush crackers with a rolling pin or in a blender. Cream butter and add syrup, milk, vanilla, and peanut butter. Add 1 cup of the graham cracker crumbs and set the remainder aside. Mix the ingredients thoroughly, then roll into 1-in. balls. Roll the balls in the remaining cracker crumbs, and serve.

Baked Kidney Beans

3 cups kidney beans	1 T salt
2 large onions, sliced	2 T brown sugar
2 cups canned tomatoes	3 T vegetable oil
3 T chopped green pepper	

Cover beans generously with water and soak overnight. Parboil with onions in morning and then turn into bean pot. Add rest of ingredients and bake for 5 to 6 hours.

Mexican Loaf

1-lb can kidney beans	2 eggs
½ lb cheddar cheese	Seasonings
1 finely chopped onion	Green pepper rings
1 T margarine	Tomato sauce
1 cup bread crumbs	

Drain liquid from beans. Grind beans with cheese. Saute onion in margarine. Combine beans, cheese, bread crumbs, onion, eggs, and seasonings. Put in buttered baking dish, cover with bread crumbs, and bake in 350°F oven for 30 to 40 minutes. Garnish with green pepper rings and serve hot with heated tomato sauce.

Miscellaneous Group

Pudding Squares

5 envelopes unflavored gelatin
1 pkg. (3½ oz) vanilla or butterscotch instant pudding mix
1½ cups boiling water
1½ cups cold milk

In large bowl, combine unflavored gelatin and pudding mix. Add boiling water and beat with wire whisk or rotary beater until well blended; stir in milk. Pour into 8- or 9-in. square pan and chill until firm. Cut into squares to serve. Makes five to six dozen squares.

Gelatin Squares

(Sometimes Called Finger Gelatin)

2 pkgs. (6 oz. each) flavored gelatin
3 cups water
½ cup sugar
3 envelopes unflavored gelatin
2½ cups cold water

Boil the first three ingredients together and add 3 envelopes unflavored gelatin that have been dissolved in 2½ cups cold water. Pour all ingredients into a 9- x 13-in. pan. Set for about 2 hours. Cut into bite-sized pieces and eat with fingers, or cut with cookie cutters into desired shapes.

Additional Food-Related Activities and Experiences

1. Prepare a "Basic #5," snack. Using the Food Guide Pyramid, prepare a snack plate of small, bite-sized pieces of food. As the children use toothpicks to taste each snack, they should identify the corresponding food group. Make sure that at least one food from each food group is included. The following are examples:

   a. Fruits: fruit pieces such as apple, orange, banana

   b. Vegetables: vegetable pieces such as carrots, celery, cauliflower

c. Bread and cereal: small crackers or pieces of bread (preferably whole grain)

d. Milk and cheese: small pieces of cheese

e. Protein group: hard-cooked egg slices, small pieces of meats such as wieners, cooked ham, or beef

2. Name-a-food game. The teacher tosses a ball or bean bag to a child. When the teacher names a food group, such as milk and cheese, the child must name a food within the food group. Or, if the teacher names a food, the child must name the food group to which it belongs.

3. Sort the foods. Pictures of different foods are pasted on heavy paper or cardboard. The children then name the foods and sort them into the five basic food groups. Or foods can be sorted into two groups: foods that are good for us and foods that are not good for us. (Some seed companies will provide teachers with empty seed packets. The fruit and vegetable packets make excellent pictures for this food group.)

4. Teach the following fingerplay:

What do we need to grow on? and
What do we need to go on?
From head to feet,
The food we eat
Is what we go
And grow on.

5. Favorite food song. Sing to the tune of "Skip to My Lou":

We have to eat so we might as well eat
Some food we think is a special treat.
_____'s my choice. It can't be beat,
So serve it every Sunday.
(Second time) So serve it every Monday,
(and so on through the week).

Assign cooperative groups each a day of the week. When the verse of that day is sung, the group names a favorite food to fill in the blank.

6. Discuss the relationship between food and exercise and the value of exercise. Food gives us energy to run, play, and exercise. We must eat right to have the energy we need to play, run, and exercise.

You can't feel fit
If you just sit
Skip and jump and run!
Play some ball,
And stretch up tall.
Exercise is fun.

7. Talk about the different parts of plants that are eaten as vegetables. Let the children taste a sample of each part. For example: leaf—lettuce, spinach; root—carrot, parsnips; flower—cauliflower; stalk or stems—celery; seeds—peas, corn.

8. Obtain a catalog from a nursery or seed distributor, and cut out pictures of fruits. Have the children name each fruit and discuss individual characteristics, such as one large seed, skin that is peeled, skin that is eaten, or color. Have tasting samples of some of the unusual fruits, such as dates, fresh pineapple, cranberries, or other fruits of the season that the children may taste less frequently.

9. Fishing for foods. Make fishing poles out of dowels, string, and magnets. Cut food pictures from magazines and catalogs; then attach paper clips. Let the children fish for the foods, and as each food is "caught," its name and/or food group should be mentioned.

10. Food riddles. Make up riddles about foods. For example: "I am a fruit. I am yellow. I have a skin you peel off. I am long and thin and delicious to eat. What am I?" (Banana.) Break up into cooperative learning groups and have each group make up a riddle.

11. Play "Which One Does Not Belong?" Have a group of three to four pictures. For younger children, three may be foods and

one not a food. They need to find the one that does not belong. For older children, have three in one food group and the fourth in another food group, or have three good foods and one food that is not nutritious.

12. Food sequence. Find or make pictures of the growing or processing stages of a particular food. For example, several pictures could be used in the sequence of wheat to bread. The children put the pictures in the proper sequence.

13. Make a scrapbook of foods grouped into the five food groups. This could be done in five cooperative learning groups with each group assigned a food group.

14. Compare raw and cooked vegetables. For example, compare raw versus cooked broccoli or raw versus cooked cauliflower.

15. Put different foods, one or a few at a time, into a "feely" box, and have the children identify the food by feeling it. If possible, have them tell which food group it belongs to.

16. Have children identify the sources of food—for example, plant, animal, or even more specifically milk, potato.

17. Divide the children into cooperative learning groups, using Numbered Heads Together.* Give each group an unfamiliar fruit such as a pomegranate, kiwi, strawberry, pineapple, raspberry, or whatever you can find in season and available. Each group will sample the fruit and then prepare a description using descriptive words. Call out a number, and that child in each group will be spokesperson to describe the fruit for the rest of the class.

* When using Numbered Heads Together, the children are divided into groups with each child in each group assigned a number. Each group is given a task, or all groups are given the same question or different questions. The group solves the problem together, making sure each group member knows the answer. The teacher says a number and each child with that number is responsible for reporting on the answer or assignment (Curran, 1991).

Summary

Society as a whole is becoming more aware of the importance of nutrition in maintaining physical and psychological health. This is especially important in the early childhood years, when habits and patterns are being learned and internalized. Food activities with young children should largely include fruits, vegetables, and grains, with less fat, cholesterol, refined sugar, and salt. Children, by becoming aware of the Food Guide Pyramid (basic five), are better able to make individual selections that help to ensure a well-balanced diet. Food activities can contribute to learning in every aspect of the curriculum—math, music, social studies, language and literacy, cultural diversity, creative arts, science, and others. When we, as teachers, incorporate sound nutritional concepts into our various teaching experiences, not only will young children benefit now, but the positive influence will be evidenced for years to come. Remember, children *learn* to select good, nutritious foods. The foods children eat affect their growth, behavior, and health. Good food habits must be learned; they are not instinctive.

Student Learning Activities

1. Using the Food Guide Pyramid and suggestions from this chapter, plan one snack time and one meal per day for children for a 5-day period.

2. Using the Food Guide Pyramid, plan two days of meals (three meals each day) for children. These meals should be balanced, nutritious, and inviting.

3. With a group of children, try out at least one of the food experiences from each of the five food groups in the recipe section of this chapter. Evaluate the experiences. Would you use this recipe again? Would you organize the experience in the same way the next time? If not, what changes would you make?

4. Plan an appropriate food experience for children for each of the food groups.

5. Implement at least one of the food experiences you have planned with children. Evaluate the experience. Was it appropriate? Was it organized in the most efficient way? Would you offer the same experience again? If so, would you make any changes?

6. Try out at least two of the food-related activities suggested in this chapter. Where materials are suggested, prepare them. Evaluate each experience.

7. Select a food theme and prepare a unit plan or web on it.

8. Prepare a lesson plan on a food theme. Try to include at least one food experience during the week. Use the unit and lesson plans in this chapter as a guide.

Suggested Resources

Nutrition Curriculum Guides

Association for Childhood Education International. (1974). *Cooking and eating with children.* Washington, DC: Author.

Ball State University. *Teacher training manual in nutrition* (preschool through grade 12). Muncie, IN: Department of Home Economics, Ball State University.

California State Department of Education. (n.d.). *Nutrition education—choose well, be well: A curriculum guide for preschool and kindergarten.* Sacramento: California State Department of Education.

Cobb, V. (1979). *More science experiments you can eat.* New York: Harper & Row.

Cobb, V. (1984). *Science experiments you can eat.* New York: Harper & Row.

Endres, J., & Rockwell, R. (1990). *Food, nutrition, and the young child.* Columbus, OH: Macmillan.

Goodwin, M., & Pollen, G. (1980). *Creative food experiences for children.* Washington, DC: Center for Science in the Public Interest.

Hendrick, J. (1988). *The whole child.* (4th ed.). Columbus, OH: Macmillan.

Humboldt County Office of Education. *Peanut butter and pickles: A nutrition project for pint-sized people: Curriculum guide and instructional activities for grades 1–6.* Eureka, CA: Author.

Josephson, J. P., & Fine, E. (1985). Making mealtimes fun. *American Baby,* 47(2), 53–55.

Marbach, E., Plass, M., & O'Connell, L. (1978) *Nutrition in a changing world: A curriculum for preschool, nursery and kindergarten.* Washington, DC: Nutrition Foundation

McWilliams, M. (1986). *Nutrition for the growing years.* (4th ed.). Columbus, OH: Macmillan.

Minnesota Curriculum Services Center. (1980). *Students, parents, educators, administrators, children for nutrition: A cooperative adventure in preschool nutrition education.* White Bear Lake, MN: Author.

National Dairy Council. (1979). *Food: Early choice.* Rosemont, IL: Author.

Pipes, P. (1988). *Nutrition in infancy and childhood* (4th ed.). St. Louis: Mosby/Year Book.

Randall, J., Olson, K. C., & Morris, L. (1979). *Early childhood nutrition program* (Nutrition curriculum guide for incorporating nutrition activities in the classroom). Ithaca, NY: Cornell University.

Society for Nutrition Education Staff. (1984). *You're in charge: Nutrition for preschool children.* Minneapolis: Author.

U.S. Department of Agriculture Yearbook. *What's to eat? and other questions kids ask about food.* Washington, DC: U.S. Government Printing Office, 1979.

Utah State University, Department of Nutrition and Food Sciences. (1975). *Nutrient density nutrition education: A nutrition education curriculum for grades K–1* (Teachers' Manual, Unit I). Logan: Utah State University Foundation.

Wanamaker, N., Hearn, K., & Richarz, S. (1979). *More than graham crackers: Nutrition education and food preparation with young children.* Washington, DC: National Association for the Education of Young Children.

Cookbooks

Akerman, C. (1981). *Cooking with kids.* Mt. Rainier, MD: Gryphon House.

Avis, J., & Ward, K. (1990). *Just for kids.* West Monroe, LA: Avis and Ward.

Baxter, K. M. (1989). *Come and get it: A natural foods cookbook for children.* Ann Arbor, MI: Children First.

Berman, C., & Fromer, J. (1991). *Meals without squeals: Child care nutrition guide and cookbook.* Menlo Park, CA: Bull.

Betty Crocker's new boys' and girls' cookbook. (1992). New York: Prentice Hall.

Bruno, J., & Dakan, P. (1983). *Cooking in the classroom.* Belmont, CA: Fearon Teacher Aids.

Christenberry, M. A., & Stevens, B. (1985). *Can Piaget cook?* Atlanta: Humanics.

Croft, K. B. (1971). *The good for me cookbook.* San Francisco: Rand E. Research Associates.

Dishes children love. (n.d.). (Order from: Family Weekly Books, 1727 S. Indiana Ave., Chicago, IL, 60616.)

Domke, L. (1991). *Kids cook too!* Rock Hill, SC: Carolina Consultants Network.

Faris, D. (Ed.). (1987). *Favorite foods for pre-school.* Dallas, TX: Stone Canyon.

Ferreira, N. J. (1986). *Learning through cooking: A cooking program for children two to ten.* Saratoga, CA: R & E.

Goodwin, M., & Pollen, J. (1980). *Creative food experiences for children.* (rev. ed.). Washington, DC: Center for Science in the Public Interest.

Greene, K. (1992). *Once upon a recipe: Delicious, healthy food for kids of all ages.* New York: Putnam.

Herick, N. (1990). *Natural, nutritious recipes for children.* Birmingham, AL: EBSCO.

Hughes, P. (1976). *Pueblo Indians cookbook.* Santa Fe: University of New Mexico Press.

Jello desserts kids' stuff recipes. (n.d.). (Order from: General Foods Corp., Kids' Stuff, P.O. Box 4157, Kankakee, IL, 60901.)

Johnson, B. (1990). *Cup cooking: Individual child-portion picture recipes.* Rainier, MD: Gryphon House.

Kendrick, A. S., Kaufmann, R., & Messenger, K. (Eds.). (1991). *Healthy young children: A manual for programs.* Washington, DC: National Association for the Education of Young Children.

Kiddie cookery. (n.d.). (Order from Marie's Educational Materials, Inc., 193–195 S. Murphy Ave., Sunnyvale, CA, 94086.)

Kositsky, V. (1977). What in the world is cooking in class today? (Multiethnic recipes for young children.) *Young Children, 33*(1), 23–31.

Lansky, V. (1988). *The taming of the c.a.n.d.y. monster.* New York: Bantam.

Lansky, V. (1988). *Vicki Lansky's kid's cooking.* New York: Scholastic.

McClenahan, P., & Jaqua, I. (1976). *Cool cooking for kids.* Belmont, CA: Pitman Learning.

Miller, M., & Richardson, T. (1974). *The merry metric cookbook.* Hayward, CA: Activity Resources.

Moore, C. E., Kerr, M., & Shulman, J. (1990). *Young chef's nutrition guide and cookbook.* Hauppauge, NY: Barron.

Niethammer, C. (1974). *American Indian food and lore.* New York: Collier.

Olmsted, C. (1990). *Alphabet cooking cards.* Carthage, IL: Fearon.

Parents Nursery School Staff. (1974). *Kids are natural cooks.* Boston: Houghton Mifflin.

Paul, A. (1985). *Kids' cooking without a stove: A cookbook for young children.* Sante Fe, NM: Sunstone.

Perl, L. (1967). *Rice, spice and bitter oranges: Mediterranean foods and festivals.* Cleveland, OH: World.

Potter, B. M. (1985). *The just for kids cookbook.* Chanhassen, MN: Branches.

Rhoades, J. (1986). *Nutrition mission.* Carthage, IL: Good Apple.

Robson, D. (1991). *Cooking: Hands-on projects.* New York: Watts.

Sledge, S. (1988). *Guess what I made? Recipes for children around the world.* Birmingham, AL: Womens Mission Union.

Stephens, F. (1991). *Baking projects for children: Fun foods to make with children from 4–10.* Nazareth, PA: Murdoch.

Veitch, B., & Harms, T. (1981). *Cook and learn.* (A child's cookbook of pictorial single portion recipes from a variety of cultures.) Reading, MA: Addison-Wesley.

Veitch, B., & Harms, T. (1981). *Cook and learn recipe step cards.* (Fifty favorite recipes from *Cook and learn* and ready-to-use, enlarged steps for classroom use. Also included are 20 parent newsletters about the learning through cooking program that can be duplicated and sent home.) Reading, MA: Addison-Wesley.

Veitch, B., & Harms, T. (1981). *Learning from cooking experiences.* (Teacher's guide to be used with *Cook and learn.*) Reading, MA: Addison-Wesley.

Warner, P. *Healthy snacks for kids.* Benicia, CA: Nitty Gritty. 1983. (Sugar-free, salt-free recipes for snacks, drinks, desserts, and meals.)

Warren, J. (1982). *Super snacks.* Everett, WA: Warren.

Wilms, B. (1984). *Crunchy bananas and other great recipes kids can cook.* Layton, UT: Gibbs Smith.

Wishik, C. S. (1982). *Kids dish it up . . . Sugar-free.* Port Angeles, WA: Peninsula Washington.

Children's Books

Adams, R. (1976). *The Easter Egg artists.* New York: Scribner's.

Aliki. (1963). *The story of Johnny Appleseed.* Englewood Cliffs, NJ: Prentice-Hall.

Aliki. (1976). *Corn is maize: The gift of the Indians.* New York: Corwell/Harper & Row.

Blanchet, F., & Doopernekamp, R. (1974). *What to do with an egg.* New York: Barrons.

Brown, M. (1974). *Stone soup.* New York: Scribner's.

Brown, M. W. (1959). *Nibble, nibble.* Reading, MA: Addison-Wesley.

Carle, E. (1969). *Very hungry caterpillar.* New York: Philomel.

Carle, E. (1970). *Pancakes, pancakes.* New York: Knopf.

Carle, E. (1982). *What's for lunch?* New York: Putnam.

Cauley, L. B. (1977). *Pease porridge hot: A Mother Goose cookbook.* New York: Putnam.

Charlott, M. (n.d.). *Sunnyside up.* (Order from: Island Heritage Ltd., 1819 Kahai St., Honolulu, HI 96819–3136.)

Cooper, J. (1977). *Love at first bite: Snacks and mealtime treats the easy way.* New York: Knopf.

Darling, L. (1955). *Chickens and how to raise them.* New York: Morrow.

Degan, B. (1983). *Jamberry.* New York: Harper & Row.

De Paola, T. (1978). *The popcorn book.* New York: Holiday House.

Ehlert, L. (1987). *Growing vegetable soup.* New York: Harcourt Brace Jovanovich.

Esme, E. (1971). *Eggs.* New York: Wonder Starter.

Fenton, C.L., & Kitchen, H. B. (1971). *Plants that we live on.* New York: Harper & Row.

Fisher, A. (1975). *Once we went on a picnic.* New York: Harper & Row.

Flores, J. (1975). *ABC of poultry raising.* New York: Dove.

Galdone, P. (1973). *The little red hen.* New York: Seabury.

Gibbons, G. (1985). *The milk makers.* New York: Macmillan.

Greenaway, K. (1886). *A-apple pie.* London: F. Warne.

Hoban, R. (1964). *Bread and jam for Frances.* New York: Harper & Row.

Hoban, R. (1972). *Egg thoughts and other Frances songs.* New York: Harper & Row.

Ikeda, A. (1972). *Humpty Dumpty was an egg.* Los Angeles: University of California, Agriculture Department.

Kent, J. (1975). *The egg book.* New York: Macmillan.

Krauss, R. (1967). *The happy egg.* New York: Scholastic.

Krauss, R. (1971). *The carrot seed.* New York: Scholastic.

Lenski, L. (1942). *The little farm.* New York: McKay.

Lenski, L. (1975). *My friend the cow*. Chicago: National Dairy Council.

Lerner, S. (1967). *I like vegetables*. Minneapolis: Lerner.

Lionni, L. (1963). *Swimmy*. New York: Pantheon.

Lynn, S. (1986). *Food*. New York: Macmillan/Aladdin.

McCabe, T. W., & Mitchell, H. W. (1970). *Animals that give people milk*. Chicago: National Dairy Council.

McCloskey, R. (1946). *Blueberries for Sal*. New York: Viking.

Milhous, K. (1950). *The egg tree*. New York: Scribner's.

Milne, A. A. (1961). Rice pudding. In *When we were very young*. New York: Dutton.

Numeroff, L. J. (1985). *If you give a moose a muffin*. New York: HarperCollins.

Pluckrose, H. (1986). *Think about tasting*. New York: Watts.

Pope, B., & Emmons, R. (1967). *Let's visit a dairy*. Dallas, TX: Taylor.

Pope, B., & Emmons R. (1969). *Let's visit a farm*. Dallas, TX: Taylor.

Potter, B. (1903). *The tales of Peter Rabbit*. London: F. Warne.

Rockwell, A., & Rockwell, H. (1982). *How my garden grew*. New York: Macmillan.

Rylant, C. (1984). *This year's garden*. Scarsdale, NY: Bradbury.

Sawyer, R. (1953). *Jouney cake ho!* New York: Viking.

Seixas, J. S. (1984). *Junk food*. New York: Greenwillow.

Seixas, J. S. (1986). *Vitamins: What they are, what they do*. New York: Greenwillow.

Selsam, M. E. (1976). *Popcorn*. New York: William Morrow.

Selsam, M. E. (1981). *The plants we eat*. New York: William Morrow.

Selsam, M. E., & Wexler, J. (1980). *Eat the fruit, plant the seed*. New York: William Morrow.

Sendak, M. (1962). *Chicken soup with rice*. New York: Harper & Row.

Seuss, Dr. (1953). *Scrambled eggs super!* New York: Random House.

Seuss, Dr. (1960). *Green eggs and ham*. New York: Beginner Books.

Seuss, Dr. (1968). *Horton hatches the egg*. New York: Random House.

Sharmat, M. (1980). *Gregory the terrible eater*. New York: Four Winds.

Showers, P. (1985). *What happens to a hamburger*. New York: Harper/Crowell.

Smaridge, N. (1982). *What's on your plate?* Nashville, TN: Abingdon.

Spier, P. (1981). *The food market*. New York: Doubleday.

Tolstoy, A. (1968). *The great big enormous turnip*. New York: Franklin Watts.

Tresselt, A. (1951). *Autumn harvest*. New York: Lothrop, Lee & Shepard.

Tudor, T. (1962). *Pumpkin moonshine*. New York: Henry Z. Walck.

Records, Tapes, and Cassettes

Kinds of food. On *Learning basic skills through music —vocabulary*. Hap Palmer Record Library (AR521 or AC521).

Your body—how to use food and stay healthy (9). Society for Visual Education.

Pictures

Common fruits. Society for Visual Education.
Food and nutrition. David C. Cook.
For your good health. David C. Cook.
Fruits and vegetables. Scholastic Book Services.
The rural environment. Scholastic Book Services.

Multimedia Kits

Nutrition around the clock. Walt Disney.

Films, Filmstrips, and Videos

The cow. Churchill Films.
How apples grow. National Apple Institute.
The little red hen. Teaching Resources Films.
Nutrition for little children. Educational Activities.
The story of bread. Society for Visual Education.
The story of fruits and vegetables. Society for Visual Education.
The story of Johnny Appleseed. Teaching Resources Films.
The story of meat. Society for Visual Education.
The story of milk. Society for Visual Education.
Swimmy. Distribution Sixteen.
Winick, M. *Food and nutrition*. New York: Parents' Magazine (five filmstrips and tapes).

eight

Smell and Taste,
Texture and Touch,
Sound and Pitch

Introduction

Although several senses are discussed in this chapter, each will be considered separately to assist you in curriculum planning. Included are smell and taste, texture and touch, and sound and pitch. Infants respond to sounds, tastes, smells, and touch very early in life. As children learn to use their senses with precision, they become more aware of their environment and use these senses to build and determine concepts.

Smell and Taste

It is through the two important senses of smell and taste that many new ideas are learned. These two concepts may be incorporated into a unit on the senses, taught together, or taught as separate unit themes.

Even though taste and smell are separate senses, they are closely related, and one greatly influences the other. Often a child may dislike a food because of its smell—not because of its actual taste. Chewing a food while the nose is being held diminishes the taste of the food. Likewise, nasal congestion from a cold results in a decrease in the sense of taste.

The teacher's own sense of taste may be enhanced (so that children can be made more aware of their sense of taste) by a review of the location of the taste buds for the four basic tastes. The salt taste buds are located on the tip and sides of the tongue; sweet is on the tip of the tongue; bitter and sour are on the sides of the tongue and on the palate.

Too often in learning activities, children are not encouraged to use their senses of smell and taste. They hear a teacher say, "Look at it. What do you see?" But there are times when it is better to say, "Smell it [or taste it]. Now what do you know about it?" Children should be given the opportunity to taste and smell during food experiences, as well as after the product is finished.

A child relies on previous experiences when learning through smell and taste. For example, when learning textures, the child can use other senses in addition to touch—taste, hearing, and sight. However, smells or tastes cannot be seen, felt, or heard unless the child has had previous experience with the items being smelled or tasted. For example, if a child who had never had experiences with a lemon were asked to describe its smell or taste, the child could not rely on touch or sound for clues; the child would have to taste or smell the lemon. Also, the way a child describes a taste or smell will depend on his or her experience with it. The child must have experience in hearing and using the word *sour* for example, and must know the meaning of this word (the concept) before he or she can describe the smell or taste of a lemon.

Children understand that they learn about some things and identify them by smelling and/or tasting them. A good experience for assisting in this understanding is to paint the outside of a bottle so that the children cannot see the contents (or use a small brown glass bottle) and fill it with root beer, orange juice, or other liquid. The children then taste this liquid, and the teacher asks them whether they would like to learn what they have been tasting. The teacher can follow this experience with ways in which the children could learn what the bottle contains—by smelling or tasting the contents. In this case, it would probably be better to have each child smell the liquid to discover what it is. Teachers need to approach this activity with one specific safety precaution—teach children *never* to taste the contents of bottles or other containers unless they have been told and are certain that the contents are edible and something they should taste. They

must understand that this practice can be very dangerous.

Also, if the children are smelling cleaning agents, gasoline, or other such fluids, mark the containers with the poison sign or a large red X so that the children know that those containers are for smelling only. They are not to be left unattended, and they should be taken from the room when the smelling is completed.

Other health precautions to consider are sanitation and cleanliness when participating in all tasting activities.

Children should be encouraged to rely more often on their senses of smell and taste. Smells and tastes are frequently tuned out of daily experiences. One meaningful activity is to have children write down or discuss all the smells and/or tastes they have experienced during a particular day. They might do a follow-up exercise in which they make it a point to be aware of smell and taste.

In teaching smell and taste, exploratory questions can be asked. For example, you might ask, "What else smells like_____?" or "What else tastes like_____?"

Smell

Approach to Teaching. A broad base for understanding smell can be built by increasing the child's vocabulary. Many opportunities for describing smells and using smell words should be provided, and new smell words should be introduced, along with their meanings. Whenever a smell word is learned, opportunities for smelling items described by the word should be provided. For example, learning the word *bitter* will have no meaning unless something bitter is smelled, and it would be better if several bitter items were smelled. Following is an incomplete list of possible words describing smells; various objects representing these smells are easily accessible for meaning and reinforcement.

Sour	Lemony	Strong
Dusty	Pleasant	Burned
Moldy	Salty	Smoky

Rancid	Rusty	Fishy
Sweet	Bitter	Fresh
Dirty	Offensive	Clean
New	Crisp	Delicious
Piney	Sharp	

After experiences with these words, exciting brainstorming or creative writing sessions may evolve. Children can discuss or write about items, foods, or experiences related to the words. For example, they may think, talk, or write about an experience or memory related to anything that smells smoky. Simple poetry can evolve from smell words.

Smells can be divided into categories and unit themes can be developed on the sense of smell or on one or more of these "smell" categories. Each day the teacher can introduce a different category of smells, providing examples of smells relating to that category through experiences. For example, if the teacher chooses a unit on cleaning smells, a visit to a motel can be planned whereby the children meet the motel cleaning personnel, learn about the job, and smell some of the solvents and materials used for cleaning. Another experience during this unit might be a visit by the school custodian, in which cleaning materials are shared with the children. A salesperson who sells cleaning aids might also visit. The children could participate in a food experience, including the cleanup, with emphasis on smelling the cleaning aids. It is easy to see how exciting it would be to correlate a unit with the theme of cleaning smells. Following is an incomplete list of some of the categories of smells:

Inside	Hospital	Cleaning
Outside	Food	Kitchen
Animal	Holiday	Store
Automobile	Nature	School
Seasonal	Bakery	Cosmetic

Concepts and Ideas for Teaching

1. Some smells give messages or direct behavior
   a. Smoke—leads people to discover what is burning and to take necessary action
   b. Favorite foods—may create hunger for a particular food, especially if a person is already hungry
   c. Medicine—indicates when someone is ill, has a cold, or is sucking a cough drop, which in turn points to sore throats, colds, coughs, and so on
   d. Food smells—often are strong enough and distinct enough to signal what a parent, teacher, or friend is cooking
   e. Fire or matches—may tell us that children are playing with matches
   f. Unfamiliar smells—may make a person curious about the source
   g. Undesirable smells—may remind a person of previous experiences and sometimes even cause nausea
2. The same items do not always smell the same.
   a. People—perfume, soap, foods, culture, and other factors
   b. Automobiles—age, care, places parked, and so on
   c. Flowers—tulips, roses, violets, and others
   d. Perfumes—kind, type of container, age, and other factors
3. Items that look the same do not always smell the same.
   a. Potato flakes and soap flakes
   b. Strawberry gelatin and cherry gelatin
   c. Root beer extract and vanilla extract
4. Different items may have the same smell.
   a. Campfire smoke and cigarette smoke
   b. Vinegar taffy and liquid vinegar
   c. Various items with a lemon smell—lotion, cleaning solvents, shampoo
5. Not all things have a smell.
   a. Dish
   b. Wall
   c. Some types of water

d. Some fabrics

e. Glass

6. Smell may be changed or modified.

   a. Cooking—foods in various stages of the cooking process, such as meat before and after cooking, bakery products before and after baking, any food product before and after burning, or bread before and after being toasted

   b. Aging—a tomato that is fresh and one that is old and spoiled; a freshly cracked nut and one that is becoming rancid because of age; new perfume and older perfume that is partially evaporated

   c. Temperature—frozen items, which lose their smell or develop distinct or stronger odors; melted butter; melted plastics

   d. Drying—fruits, paste, glue, paints, which usually acquire a less distinct smell in the drying process.

   e. Additions—modification of smells in food experiences, science experiences, and art activities by adding or combining ingredients

Activities and Experiences

1. The children could smell items and group them into categories, or the teacher could name a smell and the children could tell which category or categories it fits into.

2. Colored bottles or containers with the outsides painted or taped could be used to identify the ingredients by smell. Care should be taken to select mostly those ingredients with which the children have had previous experience. If the ingredients are not edible, caution the children against tasting them.

3. To help the children differentiate by smell items that look alike, the teacher can select combinations of the following items within each category. Bottles or containers can be coded for older children; they can

write down the number code of the bottle and its ingredients. Children must be cautioned that these items are to smell, not to taste.

1-A Alcohol
1-B Polish remover
1-C Water
1-D White vinegar
1-E Clear carbonated drink
2-A Perfume
2-B Vanilla
2-C Cider vinegar
2-D Root beer extract
2-E Steak sauce
2-F Dark flavorings
3-A White glue
3-B School paste
3-C Lotion
3-D Cold cream
3-E Thick dairy cream
4-A Glycerin
4-B Liquid detergent
4-C Rubber cement
4-D Honey
4-E Baby oil
4-F Some shampoos
5-A Molasses
5-B Maple syrup
5-C Dark corn syrup
6-A Soap flakes
6-B Potato flakes
6-C Onion flakes
6-D Oatmeal
7-A Salt
7-B Sugar
7-C Garlic salt
7-D Onion salt
7-E Celery salt
7-F Sand
8-A Powdered sugar
8-B Cornstarch
8-C Flour
8-D Baby powder
8-E Soda
8-F Baking powder

Identifying aromas is an interesting way to increase the development of the sense of smell. Dark bottles with lids prevent identification by sight and also decrease evaporation of contents.

But if you cannot identify the aroma by smelling, just look inside and see if you can tell what is in the bottle.

9-A Cinnamon
9-B Chili powder
9-C Cloves
10-A Oregano
10-B Parsley flakes

4. Once the children have identified an ingredient by its smell, they can then use descriptive words for it. Similes can also stimulate creativity: "It smells as salty as a soda cracker," or "It smells like a soda cracker."

5. For a "smell" walk or field trip, the children could walk around their own classroom, building, or neighborhood searching for smells.

6. Make up a "smell" story, with the children smelling actual smells at various intervals.

7. Put sensory materials in a trough, large tub, or other similar container for exploring and smelling. Items could include mud, flour, lemonade, barley, and wheat.

8. Discuss with the children how their sense of smell can protect them from danger

9. Brainstorm with the children their favorite or most pleasant smells and their least favorite or most offensive or unpleasant smells. These can be dictated or written into a booklet or chart.

10. Demonstrate the interrelationship of taste and smell. Have the children, while blindfolded, taste a piece of apple and at the same time hold a piece of cut onion near their nose. Some children may believe that they are tasting an onion.

11. Fill various salt shakers with different flavors of red gelatin, sprinkle gelatin on the children's hands, and have them determine the flavor by the smell. Follow this with tasting. (Remember: Have the children wash their hands prior to this activity.)

UNIT PLAN ON SMELL

Field Trips

- Outside walk
- Bakery
- Meat market
- Paint store
- Cosmetic representative's home
- Drugstore or department store where a cosmetic counter could be visited
- Pet store
- Farm
- Hospital
- Flower shop
- Pharmacy

Art

- Collages with scented papers
- Collages made out of foodstuffs that have particular odors (use those discarded because of age).
- Finger painting with soap flakes and/or whipped cream (no longer edible)—comparison of smells of the two; alternatively, finger painting with creams that look like soap flakes but smell different
- Lemon halves dipped into tempera paint for lemon printing—the combination of lemon juice and paint releases an offensive odor (use lemons that are no longer edible)

Music

- Various media put into opaque bottles or other nontransparent containers to be used for rhythm shakers after an experience in smelling. The teacher says, "All those with cinnamon smell in their bottle, shake or play with me on the next song"
- Creative expressions and movements, dramatically portrayed as the teacher or the children give suggestions for how they would respond or move if they were smelling amonia and other suggested smells

Food

- Any food activity, planned with a focus on smell
- Pickles
- Root beer or milk shakes
- Vanilla ice cream, made and then flavored with peppermint or other flavoring
- Gelatin—different groups of children making different flavors and guessing individual flavors through their sense of smell
- Bread or other bakery products—smelled during the mixing process and then during the baking process

Visitors

- Cosmetics representative
- Brush dealer
- Paint dealer or distributor
- Father, to bring in shaving creams and lotions
- Mother, to bring in various cosmetics
- Custodian, to bring in cleaning solvents and other cleaning agents
- Animals
- Parent, to conduct a demonstration on foods

Science

Salt garden (see Chapter Eleven on science experiences for directions)

- Smelling of bread each day as it progresses toward the moldy stage
- Smelling of changes in any item as it is changed or modified
- Smelling and identifying substances in opaque bottles or other containers

Language and Literacy

- The children write or dictate and illustrate booklets such as "Smells I Like" or "Smells I Don't Like"
- Write down a category of smells such as "Strong Smells" or "Summer Smells" and have the children write or brainstorm specific ideas

Taste

Approach to Teaching. To build a broad base for understanding taste, begin with building vocabulary and an understanding of taste words. Many opportunities for describing tastes and using taste words should be provided; new taste words should be introduced and the meaning behind them taught. Whenever a taste word is introduced, the children should have an opportunity to taste an item that the word describes. For example, the word *sour* will have no meaning unless a child tastes something sour. It is best to provide several items that are sour tasting, such as a lemon, a grapefruit, or powdered drink mix. Following is an incomplete list of possible words describing tastes; various objects representing these tastes are easily accessible for meaning and reinforcement. The reader can add additional words to this list.

Salty	Tart	Moldy
Soapy	Sticky	Bitter
Sour	Puckery	Strong
Sweet	Wet	Spicy
Lemony	Juicy	Pleasant
Burned	Cold	Unpleasant
Fishy	Hot	Offensive

After experiences with these words, exciting brainstorming or creative sessions can evolve. The children can discuss or write about items, foods, or experiences related to the words. For example, they might think about, write about, or discuss everything they can remember that tastes fishy and the experiences they have had in tasting items that are fishy.

Tastes can be divided into categories. Unit themes can be developed on taste, or on one or more of these categories. Each day a different category of tastes could be introduced, with examples of tastes fitting into that category being provided through experiences. Following is an incomplete list of categories of tastes:

Inside	Hospital	Fruit
Outside	Bakery	School
Holiday	Fish	Store
Seasonal	Vegetable	Sweet

Concepts and Ideas for Teaching

1. Tastes may affect behavior or reactions.
   a. Lemons or chokecherries—may make mouths pucker
   b. Salty or sweet foods—often create cravings or a desire for more, or create thirst
   c. Bitter foods or other substances—may make one want to spit out what is being tasted

2. The same items do not always taste the same.
   a. Apples—some might be sour, others sweet
   b. Cakes—come in many flavors
   c. Gum—comes in many different flavors

3. Different items may have the same taste or flavor.
   a. Lemon-flavored items—ice cream, cakes, cookies, pie, pudding, gelatin
   b. Cherry-flavored items—lollipops, gelatin, cakes, soda pop

4. Items that look the same do not always taste the same.
   a. Salt and sugar
   b. Cinnamon, cloves, nutmeg
   c. Olive juice, prune juice, root beer

5. Tastes may be changed or modified.
   a. Cooking—foods in various stages of the cooking process, such as vegetables before and after cooking; bakery products before and after baking; overcooked foods, which may have been wet or juicy but after overcooking have a dry taste or even a burned taste
   b. Aging—change in the taste of foods such as fresh bread to stale, moldy, or rancid; change in the taste of a fresh green-yellow banana after it has turned brown and is overripe
   c. Temperature—freezing or melting of foods, which will often change the taste as well as the texture

d. Drying—apricots, cherries, apples, jerky

e. Additions—adding or combining ingredients, such as adding even a drop of flavoring to a bowl of frosting, causing the flavor or taste to change

Activities and Experiences

1. Have a blindfolded child taste various foods and then guess their flavor or identity.

2. Have a blindfolded child sample various items and then group them into taste categories, or name a taste and have the child fit it into a category or categories.

3. Have the children make a taste book. For example at the top of a large piece of poster paper write the word *salty*. The children can then go through magazines and cut out pictures of salty foods or tastes for that page. The word descriptions should be included.

4. Have a child poke a toothpick into an opaque bottle or other container, withdraw the toothpick, and try to guess the contents (a food item) by tasting the flavor on the toothpick.

5. Have the children identify an ingredient by its taste and then think of descriptive words for the taste. Similes and metaphors can be used for creative thinking and brainstorming. These can be written down and used later for a poem.

6. Tell a "taste" story, and at various intervals in the story have the children sample actual flavors.

7. Put sensory materials into a trough, large tub, or similar container, and encourage the children to taste them. Items used might include flour, wheat, gelatin, cornmeal, cooked or uncooked rice, and cooked or uncooked macaroni.

8. Encourage the children to list tastes they like and do not like. Develop an experience chart that includes the children's likes and dislikes.

9. Have the children play tasting games such as identification of the various tastes in a prepared dish of blended ingredients to increase the children's awareness of their sense of taste.

10. Brainstorm with the children the following: sweet tastes, sour tastes, bitter tastes, and salty tastes.

11. Let the children grow plants with characteristic flavorings such as mint, onion, chives, sage, or parsley. Have the children taste these plants.

12. Prepare a food activity, but leave out the spice or seasoning. For example, make two custards—one with nutmeg, and one without. Have the children taste the difference.

13. Prepare puddings that look alike but taste different—lemon, coconut, pineapple, vanilla. Have the children identify and compare the tastes.

UNIT PLAN ON TASTE

Field Trips

- Restaurant
- Picnic
- Cookout
- Canyon or park—roasting marshmallows
- Grocery store
- Child's or teacher's home—tasting or cooking activity
- Factory where food is made or packaged

Art

- Finger painting with whipped cream—tasting it before and after it turns into butter
- Vegetable printing (use vegetables that are no longer edible)

Music

- Creative movements—children pretend to milk a cow; to pull a carrot, peel it, grate it, and eat it; to eat something sweet, salty, bitter, or sour

Food

- Any food activity planned with a focus on taste—children are encouraged to taste the ingredients
- Gelatin—different groups making different flavors of red gelatin, for example, with children guessing the various flavors by taste alone
- Cooking of unusual foods
- Cooking of common foods in unusual ways

Visitors

- Nutritionist
- Baker
- Butcher
- Parent—cooking or food demonstration featuring some aspect of taste, such as talking about the various tastes of nuts; making something using various spices, with the children tasting the spices beforehand
- Grocer

Science

- Pineapple juice colored red or green—will not change the flavor
- Children blindfolded and asked to guess various flavors by the taste or to describe the taste
- Various activities in which the children can learn that tastes can be modified by such processes as aging, adding, or melting

Language and Literacy

- The children write or dictate and then illustrate booklets such as "Tastes I Like" or "Favorite Tastes"
- The children or teacher write down a category of taste, such as "Sweet" or "December," and the children write or brainstorm specific examples. Illustrations can be made and pages collected into a booklet

Texture and Touch

Texture is an identifying quality. It is the way we describe substances or things in our environment when they are touched. Maxim (1989) points out that children are fascinated with different textures. It is important for children not only to identify things by the way they feel, but also to use descriptive words in explaining how things feel when touched.

Assisting children in learning about texture requires that the teacher's own awareness of touch first be increased. Teachers need to acquaint or reacquaint themselves with touch sensations they experience but do not notice.

After the teacher's own awareness of touch has been increased, the children are more likely to be made aware of the various common and uncommon textures in their environment. Becoming more cognizant of familiar textures automatically also makes one more aware of unfamiliar or uncommon textures.

Children need to know that the word *texture* refers to the surface feeling of an item. The words *feel* and *feeling* have various meanings that may need to be clarified so that the children can understand the relationship of feeling to texture. The children's first response to *feel* or *feeling* is likely to be in terms of happy, sad, tired, or other emotion-depicting words.

Texture words are usually adjectives, but often they are used as nouns. For example, when pointing to a brick, the teacher may say, "This is rough." It would be clearer to say, "The brick is rough" or "That is a rough brick." The child, having had no experience with bricks, may refer to the next brick seen as a *rough*. It is important, then, that texture words be used as adjectives.

The child can be encouraged to use many senses when exploring and building concepts related to texture. The sense of touch should be the main sense used in learning texture, even though many teachers point to an object and say, "Look, how does it feel?" Eyes are not always able to tell how objects feel; one must have had experiences in feeling or touching honey, pine needles, sheep's wool, or some kinds of plants in order to be familiar with their textures. Although textures can be described through sight, it is much more valuable to feel and then describe them. Even then, they are difficult to explain. Texture can also be tasted and heard, but again, the most valuable texture experiences will include feeling objects, surfaces, and materials.

The way a child describes a particular texture will be based on previous experiences with that texture. The child who has never had an experience with a wiry, stiff texture would have difficulty in describing the raw wool of the sheep. Again, feeling a texture is one thing, but describing it is another. Knowing how grass feels is much easier, even for adults, than describing it in a way that can be understood by others; how much more difficult the task becomes with children, whose experiences are more limited.

To build a broad base for understanding textures, it is wise to begin by building the child's texture vocabulary. Many opportunities for describing textures and using texture words should be provided, and new texture words should be introduced and taught. Whenever a texture word is introduced, the child should have an opportunity to feel a texture that the word describes. For example, if the word *bumpy* is being learned, it will have no meaning unless the child feels what bumpy is—unless the word takes on a meaning. Following is an incomplete list of words describing texture; various objects representing these feelings are easily accessible for meaning and reinforcement.

Coarse	Crunchy	Prickly
Rough	Sticky	Wiry
Slimy	Spongy	Grainy
Slick	Gritty	Sharp
Smooth	Sandy	Wet
Stringy	Velvety	Furry
Hard	Bumpy	Dry
Soft	Fuzzy	Slippery
Crinkly	Hairy	Waxy

When teaching texture, begin with familiar textures and then progress to more difficult or unfamiliar ones. Children draw from previous learning experiences to build new concepts, and experiences with familiar textures will help them understand and categorize the feelings of unfamiliar textures.

Textures can easily be narrowed down to specific categories, including words already mentioned as texture descriptions: animal textures, human textures, fabric textures, nature textures, textures we taste, and so on.

Approach to Teaching

Concepts and Ideas for Teaching

1. Most things have a texture.
2. Single items may vary in texture.
   a. Trees—leaves, bark, limbs, buds, others
   b. Cars—tires, seats, carpet, fenders, steering wheel, and other parts
   c. Insides and outsides of items—suitcase, sandpaper, fabric, corrugated cardboard, leaf, bark, banana, orange, and so on
3. Different items may have the same texture.
   a. Glass and ice
   b. Mirror and metal
   c. Brick and cement
4. Texture may be modified.
   a. Heat—items that become stiff or even "set up"; items that dissolve or become liquid; items that become hard, smooth, thick, or lumpy; foods, which offer many possibilities for changes in texture; items such as wood, plastic, and paper, which also change texture
   b. Cold or freezing—hardening of most items; making ice cubes and discussing changes in the texture of the water as it freezes and then melts
   c. Drying—change in the texture of wet clothes, fruits, paste, glue, and finger paint
   d. Sanding—change of a rough surface or edge to a smooth surface

e. Additions—in food experiences, science experiences, and art activities, texture changed by adding additional ingredients

f. Pressure—application of pressure to a rough surface, creating a smooth surface (such as wet cement), creating a rougher one

g. Aging—food in various stages showing changes in texture from hard to soft or from soft to hard; skin texture of an elderly person changed from childhood skin texture

h. Chewing—food items changing texture in the chewing process

i. Beating or whipping—whipping cream or egg whites showing changes in texture through the whipping and beating process

j. Natural changes—weather changes such as frost, wind, freezing, and erosion creating changes in texture

Not many objects have textures as rough as coal clinkers. Describing the clinkers itself is an experience in literacy!

Activities and Experiences

1. A texture packet or book can be made by giving each child an envelope containing items with textures that match those found on the pictures that will be shown. As each picture is shown and a particular texture is described, the child selects the item with the matching texture. For example, show a picture of a cat having a tongue made of sandpaper. Tell the child, "Put your hand in your envelope and find something that feels just like this cat's tongue." The child will need to feel the cat's tongue and be encouraged to describe how the tongue feels.

2. A texture book can be made by giving each child a piece of poster paper (all will be given the same size) and a piece of some kind of texture. The texture is pasted on the paper and then described in terms of how it feels or what else feels similar. The exact words, phrases, and sentences are recorded on the page, either by the child or

the teacher, depending on the child's age level and ability. The pages can be put together with rings so that the children can enjoy their own books.

3. Place handprints of various textures around the room at the children's level. When they match their hands on top, encourage them to describe the textures they feel.

4. Pass around materials of various textures (paper, wood, fabric, etc.), and when music or drumbeats stop, have the child describe the texture being held.

5. Pass around sacks or put them on a table or rug. Have each child put a hand inside a sack and then describe the texture and item without using visual clues.

6. Use texture collages to teach textures. Have a manila envelope with the ends stapled or sealed and one side cut open. After items of various textures have been put into the envelope, a child puts a hand into the en-

velope and then describes the texture of one item. The item may then be pasted on the front of the envelope. Many kinds of texture collages may be made by using items of various textures for background surfaces.

7. Put sensory materials into a trough, large tub, or similar container. Examples might be sand, soapy water, rock salt, computer card punches, and mud—substances that can be used to introduce new texture words and concepts.

8. Invite a person who is blind to the classroom and have the person describe the importance of touch in the life of someone who is blind. If possible, have this person demonstrate reading Braille through using the sense of touch.

9. Have the children bring, describe, and write descriptions of items they like to touch. Have them collect or describe items they do not like to touch, and write the descriptions.

10. Encourage the children to brainstorm words that describe textures (suggestions were given earlier in this section). Now encourage them to find objects or items representing these textures. This makes an exciting interest center.

11. Let the children feel cornstarch and describe the texture. Now add some cold water and mix it to about the consistency of white glue. Give the children about ½ teaspoon on the palm of their hand and let them experiment. Can they roll it into a ball? What does it feel like? Tell them to leave it on the palm of their hand without working it. What happens? How does it feel now?

12. Encourage the children to list feelings they can touch, as well as those they feel emotionally. The following examples depict both things children feel and how they feel emotionally.

I feel *things* that are:

scratchy	hot	wet
bumpy	velvety	greasy
crinkly	slivery	silky
ripply	waxy	oily
fuzzy	sticky	mushy
cold	rubbery	glassy
prickly	rough	gooey
slimy	grainy	gritty
slithery	oozy	pliable
slippery	sandy	

but *I* feel:

empathy	lucky	sympathy
anger	rejected	fear
pain	sorrow	sorry
depressed	joy	hurt
delight	defensive	pleasure
imaginative	courageous	carefree
happy	excited	fortunate
lonesome	trusted	loved
eager	cautious	sensitive
strong	faithful	to feelings

13. Put some foods with varying textures in a bag and have the children identify the textures they feel, such as waxy, hard, bumpy, sticky, prickly, seedy, or moist. Also, they can try to identify the foods. Now take these same foods, adding additional ones if desired, and have the children taste them and describe the "eating" textures. Are they the same as or different from the "feeling" textures?

14. Obtain a pumpkin, clean out the insides, and then prepare the seeds for roasting. Describe the various textures in the process. To carry the activity further, keep the pumpkin and observe the changes, particularly in texture, over the next weeks.

15. Fill a lightweight rubber glove (such as a sterile surgical glove) with flour. Tie a knot in the wrist end. Have the children manipulate it for sensory exploration.

16. Fill a sealable plastic sandwich bag with shaving cream. Blindfold the children and

have them guess what might be producing that kind of "feel."

17. For sensory exploration, use the following recipe for "Goo." Use two parts white liquid glue with one part liquid laundry starch. Shake the starch well, then combine it with the glue. Stir until the mixture is completely blended (this takes some time). When it is completely blended, test it as follows: Squeeze some "Goo" in your hand, then open your hand. If the mixture sticks to your hand, add a little more starch. If the mixture breaks when you slowly stretch it, add a little more glue. This mixture becomes stretchier with use. After using it, cover it tightly and refrigerate.

UNIT PLAN ON TEXTURE

Art

- Melted crayon pictures
- Mud pies
- Collage items of different textures—a variety of textures to be pasted, as well as a variety of background textures
- Seed collages—seeds of different textures
- Fabric collages
- Texture smearing
- Collage of items found on a texture walk
- Cotton swabs used for painting on different grains of sandpaper
- Finger painting with sawdust, sand, or other media added

Visitors

- Person who is blind
- Carpenter
- Butcher
- Skin diver
- Sculptor
- Cake decorator
- Person from fabric store
- Grocer
- Dairy farmer or person who delivers milk
- Baker
- Upholsterer
- Two persons with different skin and/or hair textures

Food

- Hamburgers—comparison of textures before and after cooking
- Smooth and chunky peanut butter
- Candied apples
- Gelatin—quick-setting, with ice cubes to see changes as the mixture thickens
- Sponge cake
- Angel food cake
- Soups
- Root beer floats
- Cream puffs or popovers
- Candies
- Macaroni and cheese
- Apples—apple cider, applesauce, chopped in salad, apple strudel
- Cookies
- Popcorn
- Potatoes prepared in various ways

Music

- Creative movements that depict textures—interpreting butter melting; an ice cube freezing and then melting; a person walking on sand or rocks, walking barefoot, walking or skating on slippery, cold ice
- Texture band with sandpaper blocks, different textured sticks; band with various items such as washboards, vegetable graters, pots and pans, corrugated cardboard, and sticks or spoons used for striking
- Shakers or containers partially filled with media of various textures—sand, water, macaroni, sawdust, and so on; "instruments" used to accompany familiar songs or rhythm record

Field Trips

Sawmill	Lumberyard
Furniture store	Park
Dairy	Fabric store

Zoo
Farm
Bakery
"Texture" walk
Gravel pit

Greenhouse
Upholstery shop
Carpet store
Hat store

Science

- Two ice cubes with rock salt rubbed or pressed between them—change in texture of ice cubes
- Chemical garden (see Chapter Eleven for recipe)
- Any experiment or experience in which there is a change in texture beforehand and afterward
- Making Styrofoam—two chemicals, purchased where Styrofoam or boats are made, mixed together to create an immediate reaction that results in Styrofoam
- Freezing of various substances
- Mixing of soda and vinegar together
- Clay or play dough mixed by children
- Melting of butter, ice, and other substances
- Observation of mold growing during the aging and spoiling process of a substance such as bread

Language and Literacy

- Make texture booklets by having the children describe textures and write their own words down
- Encourage the children to dictate and/or write similes for textures such as "as soft as . . ." or "as sticky as . . ."

LESSON PLAN ON TEXTURE (5-DAY)

Overall Goals

- To acquaint the children with textures that are common to their environment, and to assist them in attaching descriptive language labels to textures. By the end of the unit, each child will have had many experiences with textures and will be able to identify and verbally describe

various textures, as well as understand basic concepts related to textures.
- To observe children individually, so that teaching goals for continued development may be created.

Day 1

Whole-Group Activity

Introduction to the Concept of Texture. To lay a foundation for the study of textures, introduce the word *texture* to the children, along with the meaning of the word. Items having various textures will be available for the children to feel, see, and hear. Adjectives such as *rough, hard, soft, smooth, bumpy,* and *velvety* will be applied to the texture feelings.

Objectives

- To introduce the unit by explaining that all things have texture and what texture is.
- To explain that texture can be seen, heard, felt, and tasted.

Small-Group Cooperative Activity

Making Clay. The children prepare clay in three small groups. Each group has 4 cups of flour and 1 cup of salt, as well as water and some coloring. Since all of the clay is approximately the same color, it can be put into one plastic container to ripen.

Objectives

- To encourage later participation with clay, since the children assisted in preparing it.
- To show the children how the texture of clay changes as liquid is added to the powdered mixture.
- To show how the texture of clay changes during the ripening period before it is used.
- To work together in a cooperative group.

Individual Activities

Autoharp

Material and Yarn Sewing. Make various pieces of textured material, along with threaded needles, available for sewing and stitching.

Trough with Water in Various Forms. Put containers of ice, snow (if available), and water in the trough, along with various measuring and pouring utensils.

Art—Crayons at the Easel. Provide crayons to be used for drawing and sketching at the easel. Along with the regular easel paper, provide background papers of various textures. One side of the easel has textured material underneath the easel paper; the other side has textured wallpaper and other materials.

Objectives

· To make the children more aware of textures.
· To provide for the children's artwork to be displayed around the room during the unit on texture.
· To allow for textures to be felt, seen, heard, and possibly even tasted.
· To illustrate that the same item may have various textures.

Day 2

Whole-Group Activity

Music with Texture Sounds. Demonstrate musical "instruments"—such as sand blocks, corrugated cardboard, and washboards—that have various textures and that make sounds of various textures. Then let the children use the instruments to accompany familiar songs. Then the children go to the large table to eat the gelatin that they have made.

Objectives

· To review language labels for texture descriptions.
· To help the children recognize an "instrument" by the sound it makes.

Small-Group Activity

Food—Setting Gelatin. Have four groups of children make gelatin, each group making a different flavor. The gelatin will be set with ice cubes and then put into the refrigerator until firm. Later in the day, allow the children to eat the gelatin in a large group at the table.

Objectives

· To demonstrate one way texture can be changed.
· To promote recall as the children remember, later in the day, the flavor of the gelatin they assisted in making.

Individual Activities

· Small trough containing sawdust and wooden cars
· Double easel with sponges and brushes

Texture Collage on Styrofoam Meat or Pastry Trays. Make materials and items having various textures available for pasting on the meat or pastry trays, which also provide an example of an unusual texture. Put paste into individual containers, and put out a jar of warm water for soaking the used brushes.

Objective

· To reinforce the concepts of texture, texture words, and variations in texture.

Day 3

Whole-Group Activity

Field Trip to a Lumberyard. As the children arrive, attach an identification badge to each child's coat. Explain the visit to the lumberyard in a large group. Then divide the children into smaller groups according to their badges. At the lumberyard the children will feel and see the various textures of wood, glass, and other products. They will also be able to see ways in which texture may be changed.

Objectives

- To reinforce and review various textures of wood, and to allow for observation of materials with other textures.
- To explain further that various items may have the same texture, and that the same items may have various textures.

Small-Group Activity

Stories About Field Trip to the Lumberyard. After the field trip, have the children return to the same groups they had at the lumberyard. While the groups discuss the field trip, have a teacher or aide write down what the children say. Then read the "story" back to the children while they are still in the groups.

Objectives

- To allow the teacher to reinforce important ideas gained from the field trip.
- To provide an opportunity for the children to express their thoughts both verbally and in written form to hear their own expressions being read aloud.

Individual Activities

- Finger painting
- Small trough containing bark, with wooden and rubber cars and trucks

Day 4

Whole-Group Activities

Science—Changing Texture. Demonstrate changes in texture by adding an antacid tablet to water and then combining soda and vinegar. Have the children perform similar experiments of their own as they make root beer floats.

Objectives

- To review texture concepts discussed previously.
- To show that texture can be heard, seen, tasted, felt, and also changed.

Small-Group Activity

Food—Root Beer Floats. After the science experiments, divide the children into smaller groups to have root beer floats. Put ice cream into the containers first, and then add the root beer.

Objectives

- To allow for the textures to be tasted in various stages of the preparation of the food.
- To reinforce the scientific concept of expansion as the texture changes.

Individual Activity

- Small trough with wooden blocks, hammers, and nails

Day 5

Whole-Group Activity

Visitor. Have a person who has various materials and items of similar and different textures visit the classroom. Explain the uses of the items and review appropriate language labels.

Objectives

- To provide a summary and reinforcement of the experiences in the texture unit.
- To listen for any possible misconceptions related to textures that may need to be corrected or explained.

Small-Group Activity

Texture Books. Give each child a sheet of poster paper and a sample cut from fabric. Each child in each group will have a different texture. Have the children discuss the texture and how it feels, then paste it on the paper. Their ideas will be written on their own sheets as they suggest. If children are able to write, they should write their own ideas. These sheets will then be combined to form a book for the children to read.

Objectives

- To allow the children to express their thoughts and to see their thoughts in writing

- To review the previous discussion of the concept of textures.

Individual Activities

- Small trough with dolls and sponges
- Xylophone

———————————————————

Sound and Pitch

Auditory discrimination, according to Maxim (1989), is the "ability to differentiate sounds—usually detecting likenesses and differences in tone, rhythm, volume, or source of sound. Since reading involves hearing the difference between *on* and *and*, or *gain* and *gang*, and telling which of the four words *ball*, *big*, *pin*, and *bone* begin with the same sound, auditory discrimination activities were considered vital in reading readiness programs" (p. 530).

Hearing is one of the five senses, and when we teach children to listen carefully, we are teaching auditory discrimination.

Children learn much about their world from others by listening. Infants, unable to respond to many stimuli, do obviously respond to sounds around them—both familiar and unfamiliar sounds.

Perhaps children can be helped to sharpen their awareness of sound when a teacher's own awareness of sound is refined. Considering individual differences also, it must be remembered that people do not respond to sounds in the same way. Even though some adults have lost their sensitivity to pitch (which describes whether a sound is a low, middle, or high tone), young children are extremely sensitive to it; in fact, a very high sound can actually cause pain. By discovering that sound occurs when something vibrates, children will often overcome fears relating to sounds (Harlan, 1991).

New emphasis on hearing and sound can be made by assisting children to learn by listening.

For example, when children are taken across a street, they are told: "Stop and look. Do you see any cars coming?" They might also hear: "Stop and listen. Do you hear any cars coming?" A brainstorming session could be the children's responses to the question "What have you heard today?" or "What sounds do you hear right now?" In addition to this exercise, sounds could be selected and then described without using the sound word itself. Riddles could be made in which a child describes and gives clues to a sound while the other children guess what sound is being described. Older children should be able to write these clues as riddles. For example: "A loud piercing, sharp, continuous sound. It varies regularly from high to low and back. What sound am I?" (siren).

In teaching the concept of sound, or the skill of auditory perception or discrimination, teachers should give children daily experience in careful listening, in developing awareness to sound, and in describing sounds. Motivating questions should often be asked, such as "What might that sound be?" or "What else has the same sound?" or "How would you describe that sound?" Creative thinking and stimulating brainstorming emerge from explorations with similes and metaphors relating to sounds. For example, the children could describe sounds that are "soft as _____," "loud as _____," or "noisy as _____." Adults have trite phrases such as "quiet as a mouse," but children will come up with new ideas such as "quiet as cutting thread," "quiet as a snowflake hitting my nose," or "quiet as my mother kissing me goodnight."

As teachers begin providing experiences with sounds, it is wise to start with the familiar before going on to the unfamiliar. Many adults find it difficult to identify specific sounds on the basis of hearing alone. They often use their sense of sight, along with listening, even for identifying familiar sounds. Less familiar sounds are much more difficult to recognize, not only for adults but especially for the less experienced child.

Another skill is auditory memory, the ability to remember and recall sounds. Often achievement tests for children as young as 4 or 5 years test for auditory memory. A good way to teach younger children this skill is to clap rhythm patterns and have the children clap the exact rhythms back to you. Older children can repeat concept sequences in the exact order; these can be objects, names, colors, numbers, or any variety of items.

Approach to Teaching

Concepts and Ideas for Teaching

1. There are different categories of sounds. For example:
   a. Cleaning
   b. Holidays or other special days
   c. Seasonal
   d. Home
   e. Country and farm
   f. Musical
   g. Machines or automobiles
   h. Animals
   i. Nature and weather—water, wind, thunder, leaves, fire, rain
   j. Cooking
   k. Human
      (1))External—hopping, eating, chewing, scratching, snapping fingers
      (2) Internal—stomach growling, swallowing, hiccuping, burping

2. Sounds have different qualities and thus can be described in different ways. For example:

a. Light	h. Noisy
b. Heavy	i. Pleasant
c. Soft	j. Fearful
d. Loud	k. Comforting
e. Happy	l. Silly
f. Angry	m. Frightening
g. Sad	n. Exciting

3. We learn from sounds; they give us information and motivate our behavior.
   a. Hungry baby crying

   b. Something boiling over
   c. Time of day—the clock chiming; children outside playing, indicating that school is over and it is late afternoon
   d. School dismissal—school bell
   e. Someone at the door or waiting outside—doorbell, knock, honking horn
   f. People outside—walking sounds, vocal sounds, laughing
   g. Activity of parent—pounding nails, washing windows, preparing dinner, running sewing machine
   h. Feelings of animals or people
   i. Emotional quality of such things as movies, homes, music, television

4. The same sounds can influence or affect people differently.
   a. Alarm clock—pleasant if it rings on the morning of a long-awaited vacation, but unpleasant on a morning when one wants to stay in bed
   b. Telephone—unpleasant in the middle of the night but pleasant when a call is expected from someone special

5. We can hear things we do not see.
   a. Wind
   b. Jet breaking the sound barrier
   c. Stomach growling
   d. Cat purring
   e. Furnace clicking on
   f. Voices in another room

6. Some things are so soft that they cannot be heard

a. Snowflakes falling	d. Worms crawling
b. Feathers falling	e. Butterflies flying
c. Eyes blinking	f. Foods baking

7. Some sounds are alike.
   a. Thunder and fireworks
   b. Dog barking and seal barking
   c. Telephone and alarm clock
   d. Hair dryer and vacuum cleaner

8. The same items sometimes make different sounds.
   a. Child
   b. Musical instrument
   c. Dog
   d. Cars
9. Sound travels both long and short distances.
   a. Via systems of communication such as the telephone, telegraph, radio, television, satellite
   b. By walkie-talkie—on tightly stretched wire or string
   c. Through a tabletop; a child with an ear placed on the table can easily hear sounds made on the underside at the opposite end of the table
   d. Through vibrations—a rather abstract concept for young children, but can be introduced by feeling a tuning fork, striking a tuning fork and then putting it in water, or feeling musical instruments that have definite vibrating qualities.

Activities and Experiences

1. Tape-record sounds and have the children determine what the sounds are. The sounds selected should be familiar ones and should be heard long enough on the tape so that the children can hear them adequately. Some sounds should be made twice—for example, a squeaky door. The following are kinds of sounds that can be used with this activity:
   a. Liquid boiling
   b. Food frying
   c. Batter being stirred
   d. Carrot being peeled
   e. Doorbell ringing
   f. Oven timer buzzing
   g. Water running
   h. Toilet flushing
   i. Bathroom scales—as a person steps on or off
   j. Car starting, windshield wipers working, seat belts being fastened, gears being shifted
   k. Traffic moving
   l. Dog barking, other familiar animal sounds
   m. Telephone ringing

   There are commercial records or tapes of these and other sounds; check your library's audio department.

2. The preceding activity could be modified if the teacher performs the task that would make the sound. The teacher could make the sound behind a screen; if the children cannot guess the sound, it can be made in front of the screen so that the children can watch the task being performed and listen to the accompanying sound.

3. Have the children listen to a particular sound and then suggest several adjectives or descriptive words for the sound.

4. Encourage the children to tell stories containing numerous sounds. This activity is especially effective at Halloween time.

5. Set out pairs of containers, such as empty film containers, with matching sounds so that children can find the pairs having the same sound. The older the children, the more pairs that can be included.

6. Allow the children to feel and/or see things that vibrate, such as a rubber band stretched between two nails and plucked or a radio, timer, music box, or simple machine that vibrates as it runs. Ask the children what they feel and hear.

7. Assign the children to cooperative learning groups, and give each group a small, wrapped, jewelry-size box. Have each group try to discover what the four items are in the box by listening carefully as they shake and tap the box at their ears. Each box could contain a small, rubber ball; a flat object such as a coin, paperclip, or washer; a marble; and a nail, screw, or similar item.

Many sounds echo through the chambers of a large sea shell.

Each box could have the same items, or they could each have different items. After they have guessed and explored, have the children open the box and see what is in it. If just the lids of the boxes are wrapped in wrapping paper, the boxes can be tied and used again without having to be rewrapped each time.

8. Have the children compare loud and soft sounds. Ask, "Can the same sound be either loud or soft? How about a whistle or pounding with a hammer—can they be either loud or soft?" Tap softly on a wooden table and describe the sound. Then have the children put one ear to the table and cover their other ear. Now tap the table again. Ask, "Was the sound loud with the ear close to the table?"

9. Play a pretend sound game. Have a child pretend to be something that makes a particular sound. As the children guess what the child is, instead of saying the name of the object, they should try to make the sound of the object. This same game can be played with a focus on particular categories such as machines, animals, or weather.

10. Obtain a set of six or eight bottles of the same size and shape. Fill them with water to various levels. Have the children strike each bottle with a spoon and compare the sounds; order the bottles from lowest to highest sounds; and blow across the tops of the bottles to compare the sounds.

11. Have the children compare various lengths of conduit pipe or the lengths of each section of a child's xylophone. Now ask them to strike these lengths with a spoon or other striker and compare the sounds.

12. Have some children try to describe particular sounds with words. Then have the other children try to guess what the sound is. For example, they might try to describe a typewriter sound, a toilet flushing, boiling water, or a siren.

13. Have the children brainstorm and/or describe their favorite or happiest sounds and their most frightening or unpleasant sounds. Write their responses on a chart or collect them in an illustrated booklet.

14. Tape-record each child's voice. Let the children listen to the recordings and discuss the differences.

15. Make a simple telephone system using two tin cans or paper cups and string, wire, or thread. Punch two small holes in the bottom of each can (cup) and fasten the ends of the wire (string) to the can. Stretch the system out and have a child at each end of the wire with the can. The system functions best when the wire is tight; it should not be allowed to touch anything between the cans. The wire can be several yards long. As a child talks into the can, the sound waves travel from that can along the

wire to the other can, where the sound is reproduced.

UNIT PLAN ON SOUND AND PITCH

Visitors

- Person to play musical instrument—one instrument making many sounds; many instruments making the same sound
- Ensemble from portion of band or orchestra
- Custodian to bring in materials, equipment, and supplies that make various sounds
- Vocalist
- Baby—comparison of baby's sounds with the sounds the children in the classroom make; listening to sounds made by the baby's equipment and toys
- Parent to bring in materials or equipment relating to job, hobby, or home activities—electric shaver, power tools, hammer and nails, and so on; pitch of parent's voice compared to that of children's own voices also noted
- Tap dancer
- Garbage collector with truck
- Pet store owner—or anyone with animals that make sounds
- Plumber
- Mechanic
- Native American dancer
- Piano tuner

Field Trips

- Farm
- School where music room, band, or orchestra could be visited
- Pet shop
- Zoo
- Service station or automobile repair garage
- Outside walk to listen to sounds of nature in the everyday environment
- Bird refuge
- Factory—machine sounds
- Office
- Music store

- Sawmill
- Fire station
- Construction or building site
- Barbershop
- Cafeteria—cooking sounds

Science

- String and cans to make walkie-talkie
- Dry-cell circuit—hooked up to make a buzzing sound or ring a bell
- Lengths and widths of strings on musical instruments (and bottles of water at various levels)—variation of the pitch of the sound made when they are struck
- Experiments with the tuning fork
- Experiences with sounds traveling or vibrating
- Activities with elastics

Food

- Popcorn
- Marshmallow squares
- Grilled or broiled hamburgers or other foods
- Boiled vegetables or other foods
- Grated foods such as cheese or apples—then used in food activities
- Chopped foods
- Shredded foods such as cabbage for making coleslaw
- Homemade root beer

Art

- Decorated sound shakers
- Other instruments made and decorated—tambourines, hummers, drums

Music

- Making any kind of musical instrument for musical band or orchestra
- Shakers made by groups of children, with each group using a different medium; for a music activity using the shakers, the first verse of a song accompanied by one group whose shakers have a particular sound, and the chorus accompanied by another group whose shakers have another sound; alternatively, various parts of a record accompanied by individual groups

Literacy

- At Halloween, write or dictate and illustrate a booklet titled "Spooky Sounds"
- Develop a chart or booklet, with or without illustrations, titled "Sounds We Like—Sounds We Don't Like." Have each child do a page for "Sounds We Like," and a page for "Sounds We Don't Like." The pages can be illustrated, then described with a written or dictated sentence.

LESSON PLAN ON SOUND (5-DAY)

Overall Goals

To help the children discriminate among sounds, categorize them, and catch their meaning, so that on completion of the unit they will be able to accomplish the following goals:

1. Recognize the loudness/quietness and highness/lowness that can be characteristic of most sounds.
2. Move from this understanding of sound to the emotional qualities of sound (happy, sad, fearful, light, comforting sounds).
3. Then be able to identify and classify sound further by the object or objects that created it, such as human, animal, farm, and city sounds.
4. Finally, be able to understand the ideas that sounds can communicate (e.g., the sound of a siren can mean an accident or a fire, or a car pulling into the driveway at the end of the day can mean that Mom or Dad is home).

Day 1

Whole-Group Activity

Discussion of Loudness, Quietness, Highness, and Lowness of Sounds. At the rug, sing songs (with fingerplays) loudly then quietly, and then in normal voices. Then play several sounds that have been tape-recorded. These sounds will be high or low, and in some cases the same object will create both sounds. Then imitate the sounds and discuss which ones are liked or not liked, and how they make one feel when they are heard.

Objectives

- To pull the group together at the rug at the end of individual activities and to see whether this procedure will prepare them better for discussion at the rug.
- To conclude the first concept of the unit and lead into the next one.

Small-Group Activities

Sound Hunt for Treasure. This activity takes place outdoors if the weather permits, and each group has a different route to follow. This game is comparable to a treasure hunt. Each new clue is found only when the children answer questions on whether or not certain objects make high, low, loud, or quiet sounds. Show the children that some objects can produce all these sound qualities. The treasure should be hidden inside a large chest or buried in the sandpile, depending on what the treasure is.

Objectives

- To serve as an introduction to the unit and provide the children with some experience with sound before it is discussed again later in the day.
- To discover how much is already understood about sounds.

Art—Starch-and-Tissue Sculptured Drums. Give the children an opportunity to create a collage on the sides of drums made from large empty cans obtained from cafeterias, with a piece of inner tube stretched over the open end and secured with wire. The drums will be used the following day during a story. Explain this plan to the children while they are making their collages. Tissue paper dipped in starch is the collage medium.

Objectives

- To have the children participate in making an object with which they can make loud, quiet, and kinesthetic qualities of sound.

- To make drums that will be used in a story and music experience the following day.

Individual Activities

Feathers, Hammers, and Water-Filled Pop Bottles. Place the feathers in the trough, place the hammers on stumps with nails, and line up the pop bottles on a table. Vary the water level in the bottles so that a person blowing on the openings will be able to produce both high and low sounds. The hammers, when used to pound nails, provide a loud sound, and the feathers provide an almost noiseless quality, bordering on a soft sound, which is discussed along with the emotional qualities of sounds.

Objective

- To reinforce the concept that activities are centered on sounds even during free play.

Day 2

Whole-Group Activity

Flannel Board Story. Tell the story outside. Pass out the drums made the previous day before telling the story. Have the children help tell the story by playing the drums when given certain signals.

Objectives

- To involve the children in helping to tell the story, and to observe how well they are able to follow their entrance cues.
- To reinforce the concepts of loudness and softness and the type of sound a drum makes.
- To reinforce the idea that sounds create various feelings by having the children make various sounds to dramatize the story.

Small-Group Activity

"Sound" Walk on the Playground and in the Classroom. Have two groups of children begin outside and two inside. With eyes closed and ears close to objects so that sounds can be heard, the children strike or listen to various objects, such as a drum, an autoharp, a seashell, or a music box.

Objectives

- To provide a sound activity in which the discussion will be carried on by the children after they hear the sounds. Loudness, softness, or happiness will not be stressed.
- To observe the interest in and comments of the children about the sounds around them.

Day 3

Whole-Group Activity

Human Sounds. Ask a small group of high school drama students to perform a segment of the children's theater version of "Hansel and Gretel."

Objectives

- To bring out ideas regarding the emotions that sound produces, and to lead into the concept that these actors are making human sounds.
- To observe the children's reactions to the visitors and the acting out of a familiar story.

Small-Group Activity

Animal Sounds. Bring four animals to the class and place them around the room. For this activity, each group of children has an animal (or a figure of an animal) at its table. The children discuss the sounds the animal makes, then use clay to sculpt either an animal or an object representing an animal sound.

Objective

- To provide a meaningful experience with real animals, introducing another category of sounds.

Individual Activity

Recording the Children's Own Voices. Provide two or more tape recorders in various areas of the room, such as in the block or manipulative area. Have teachers in these areas record the voices of the children there and then play the tape back to them. Emphasis is placed on the idea that children make human sounds and that these sounds are meaningful.

Objectives

- To develop self-worth by allowing the children to recognize their speech as being meaningful.
- To categorize the sounds the children make as being human, as opposed to machinery, automobile, or animal sounds, and so on.

Day 4

Whole-Group Activity

Music—Rhythm Band. Provide each child with an instrument, and use several different instruments. Have the children accompany a musical selection on a record or their own singing.

Objective

- To provide an experience with several different sounds, observing the children's involvement in an activity of this type.

Small-Group Activities

Science—Guessing Objects by the Sound They Make. Assign the children to cooperative learning groups. Give each group a wrapped, jewelry-size box containing three or four objects such as a coin, marble, bell, and screw or nail. Have them listen carefully, then brainstorm possibilities for what is inside. After they have guessed, have them open the container and see what is inside.

Objectives

- To use the sense of hearing to discriminate sounds.
- To work cooperatively as a group, brainstorming and hypothesizing.

Art—String Painting. Have small groups of children gather at the tables. The children dip strings into liquid paint and then put them between two pieces of paper. With one hand, they press the two pieces of paper together; with the other hand, pull the string out. Make sure they leave an end

of the string protruding from the sheets of paper so that it can be grasped for pulling out.

Objective

- To make sounds with the strings before they are used for painting, and then to identify those sounds.

Individual Activity

Matching Sounds. Use small boxes or film cans and put duplicates of different objects inside pairs of containers. For example in each of two cans, put six paper clips; in two others, put five buttons; in two others, put one tablespoon of rice. Ask the children to shake the cans or boxes and listen to identify which pairs match.

Objectives

- To use auditory discrimination to try to match the pairs of containers that have the same sound when shaken.
- To have the children be able to correct the matches by removing the lids to make sure the pairs match.

Day 5

Whole-Group Activities

Sirens. As the children brown meat for sloppy Joes, turn on a recording of a siren. From the sound heard, have the children try to determine what it could have been. Have some pictures to show possibilities. A review of the week may be given at this time.

Objectives

- To have the children try to guess what something is by hearing it and not seeing it.
- To observe the children's interest in the siren.
- To get the children outside while the meat cooks.

Food—Making Sloppy Joes. Have the children gather at the rug as you combine the indgredients. Use a hot plate or electric fry pan. (The hamburger will have been browned by the children in their small groups.) Call attention to the cooking sounds.

Objectives

- To help the children notice the cooking sounds.
- To provide further opportunity for discussion on the characteristics of sounds and what sounds tell us.

Small-Group Activities

Food—Setting the Table and Browning the Hamburger. Have the children set up the tables while listening to the sounds of setting the table. After establishing the idea that the sounds made while setting the table are dish sounds, introduce the final concept for the week by asking, "What do we think of when we hear the sounds of dishes being set on the table?" Since these sounds usually mean food, begin browning the hamburger to be made into sloppy joes later in the day.

Objective

- To introduce the final concept of the meanings that sounds can convey.

Food—Eating Lunch. Go inside and dish up the sloppy joes. Have the children eat them with carrots and juice, observing the sounds the different foods make as they chew.

Objective

- To help the children notice and discriminate among the sounds they make as they chew.

Summary

Although smell (olfactory) and taste (gustatory) perceptions involve separate senses, they are closely related and influence each other. Texture is the way the touch of an object can be described. It is important that children be able not only to identify items by feel, but also to use appropriate descriptive words. As children have experiences in listening, they also develop the skill of auditory discrimination. The ability to distinguish sound and pitch is an important aspect of reading readiness. Even very young infants respond to smells, tastes, touch, and sounds. As we increase our own sensory awareness, we become better able to make children more cognizant of using their senses for learning. Experiences with familiar smells, tastes, textures, sights, and sounds should be presented before unfamiliar ones, allowing children opportunities to solidify concepts and continue building new understandings on already established foundations. These sensory skills readily adapt to combined units, separate units, or incorporation into other areas of study.

Student Learning Activities

1. Write down your most favorite and least favorite tastes and smells. Have a group of children aged 2 to 8 brainstorm and share their most favorite and least favorite tastes and smells.

2. Make yourself aware of the smells and sounds around you on a particular day. List the many smells or sounds you become aware of. Which of these alerted you to danger? Made you aware of something important? Taught you something? Created certain feelings or emotions?

3. Plan, create, and write down an activity for teaching any one of the sensory concepts.

4. Go on a "texture" walk, and follow your experience with some creative writing about what you felt on your walk. You may wish to use similes or metaphors, but be sure to describe what you felt and how things felt.

5. Prepare a demonstration or experience for young children to show that texture changes.

6. Prepare and implement at least two of the different activities and experiences suggested in this chapter. Select a group of children from a classroom or a small group of relatives or neighborhood children to work with in implementing your activity. Evaluate your experience.

7. Using qualities of sounds such as loud, soft, frightening, and so on, make up creative similes and metaphors. Interview children aged 2 to 8, and have them help you brainstorm sound similes.

8. Brainstorm additional ideas for any sensory unit plan in this chapter, or do a sensory web, and then prepare a 5-day activity plan on one of the senses.

9. Prepare at least one teacher-made material or piece of equipment relating to sensory concepts for children 2 to 8 years of age. (Refer to the ideas in this chapter and Appendix A for suggestions.)

Suggested Resources

Children's Books

(*Note:* Also refer to the list of children's books in Chapter Seven, "Nutrition and Food Experiences.")

Brandt, K. (1985). *Sound.* Mahwah, NJ: Troll Associates.

Carle, E. (1986). *My first book of touch.* New York: HarperCollins.

Carle, E. (1986). *The secret birthday message.* New York: Harper & Row.

Engvick, W. (Ed.). (1985). *Lullabies and night songs.* New York: Harper & Row.

Fisher, A. (1964). *Listen, rabbit.* New York: Harper & Row.

Fowler, R. (1986). *Mr. Little's noisy car.* New York: Putnam.

Howard, K. (1971). *Little bunny follows his nose.* New York: Western.

Hughes, S. (1985). *Noisy.* New York: Lothrop, Lee & Shepard.

Iveson-Iveson, J. (1986). *Your nose and ears.* New York: Bookwright.

Keats, E. (1964). *Whistle for Willie.* New York: Viking.

Kunhardt, D. (1988). *Pat the bunny.* New York: Western.

Lemieux, M. (1985). *What's that noise?* New York: Morrow.

Martin, B. (1991). *Polar bear, polar bear, what do you hear?* New York: Holt.

McGovern, A. (1967). *Too much noise.* Boston: Houghton Mifflin.

Pluckrose, H. (1986). *Think about hearing.* New York: Franklin Watts.

Rice, M., & Rice, C. (1988). *All about me.* Garden City, NY: Doubleday.

Sathre, V. (1992). *Carnival time.* New York: Simon & Schuster.

Showers, P. (1961). *Find out by touching.* New York: Harper & Row.

Showers, P. (1961). *The listening walk.* New York: Crowell.

Showers, P. (1968). *Hear your heart.* New York: HarperCollins.

Wells, R. (1973). *Noisy Nora.* New York: Dial.

Multimedia Kits

Bambi discovers the five senses. Walt Disney.
The senses. National Geographic.

Films, Filmstrips, and Videos

About sounds. Eye Gate Media.
Fall, winter, spring, summer, Educational Activities.
Five senses series. Campus Films.
Learning with your ears. Coronet Films.
Listening. Churchill Films.

Moving machines. BoPeep Productions.
Sound for beginners. Coronet Films.
Sounds, sounds, sounds. Educational Activities.
What you can see and hear. National Geographic.
Your senses and how they help you. National Geographic.

PART FIVE

AESTHETIC DEVELOPMENT

The two chapters in this part address the aesthetic development of young children, especially in the areas of creativity in music and art. Perhaps it would be wise to define what is meant by *creativity* and *aesthetics*. "Most definitions of aesthetics involve the capacity to perceive, respond, and be sensitive to the natural environment and to human creation" (Feeney & Moravcik, 1987, p. 7). Aesthetic development encompasses the young child's individual taste, love of beauty, and criteria for judging beauty (Feeney & Moravcik, 1987). There are numerous definitions and approaches to defining creativity, but whether it is being defined in terms of art, thinking, writing, or any other activity, certain words and ideas come to mind. Creativity appears to involve intuition, elaboration, fluency, flexibility, originality, evaluation, and divergent thinking. Most researchers believe that creativity is a capacity or potential possessed, at least in some degree, by all human beings (Mearns, 1958; Taylor, 1968). Mearns (1958) states that "all God's chillun got wings [but] all God's chillun are not permitted to use them" (p. 229). He goes on to point out that adults, as they work with children, must believe that everyone possesses creativity. When children express thoughts, feelings, or actions in original, self-initiated, or inventive ways, they are being creative (Maxim, 1989).

Remember, all children are creative, but in different areas and to different degrees (Maxim, 1989; Mearns, 1958). Children who are the most creative will often manifest a determination to express their creativity. Creative children, it has been suggested, often manifest characteristics such as the following:

• Have the ability to perceive unusual and broad relationships
• Have different time/space perspective

- Have a sense of humor
- Enjoy inquiring and asking questions, as well as problem solving
- Show great ingenuity and imagination
- Offer many ideas and a variety of valid alternatives in problem solving
- Enjoy taking risks and participating in adventure
- Are often persistent in reaching a goal
- Enjoy firsthand investigative activities that provide the opportunity to probe, explore, discover, and create
- Use elaborate language and often express themselves in unique ways

Creativity is a continual process, and the best preparation is creativity itself (Lowenfeld & Brittain, 1987). The joy of discovery is its own reward and provides the incentive for continuing exploration and discovery.

Too often our schools are not designed to promote or encourage creative thinking or creative art. Frequently, children's thinking and art work must be exact and must fit into a mold or pattern. Many times there is no room for individuality, but only the opportunity to give back to the teacher the "right" or expected answer. Convergent thinking, arriving at the same "right" answer, is often the type of conformity encouraged and rewarded. This type of thinking is uncreative, less time-consuming, easy to evaluate, and, in some areas, essential to education. A balanced view makes room for divergent thinking, too. We must continue to struggle to understand and find use for that powerful catalytic agent children have at their command—imagination! Our schools need to be designed to encourage children to think (Torrance, 1976). Society and schools seem to be against divergence, and pressures on children often cause them to surrender their natural creativity. Teachers often cover too much material and do not ask enough questions or give children adequate time to think and respond verbally, in writing, or in art expression. Our schools often expose children to the constant fear of evaluation.

Researchers suggest there is only a small relationship or correlation between intelligence and creativity (Torrance, 1976). Children can be taught in such a way that their creative thinking abilities become useful in attaining educational competencies. These creative skills and abilities are very different from those measured by intelligence and scholastic aptitude tests, but they are important to both mental health and vocational success. It is imperative that teachers strive to foster creativity during the early childhood years, because it is the child's creativity that allows dreaming, that sparks or kindles a new idea, that motivates the child to accept a challenging task or assignment. Creativity offers the child the chance to change things that are or have been to things that might be or things that may yet be discovered. Ideas for better ways of doing things do not exist in machines, but rather in the minds of humans. It is only when children are given the opportunity and even the responsibility to release their creative potential that these changes and new ideas are born.

Children grow, work, and learn better when there are periodic times set aside for self-expression. Experiences and activities in the creative arts reduce stress, enhance development, facilitate learning, and balance the often hurried lives of children (Elkind, 1988).

"The ability to solve problems is one of the most important skills for children to develop" (Hitz, 1987, p. 12). Yet, only a small percentage of the time in schools is spent encouraging students to think at the higher levels necessary for problem solving (Goodlad, 1984). "There is clearly a need for all teachers to provide more opportunities for children to solve problems" (Hitz, 1987, p. 12). Music and creative art provide numerous opportunities for solving problems with creative thinking. Conditions that facilitate the development of creativity in the classroom include the following:

- Giving responsibility and independence
- Valuing the expression of feelings and individual divergence
- Emphasizing self-initiated exploring, observing, and questioning
- Creating a feeling of freedom and openness, and encouraging spontaneous expression
- Developing an accepting atmosphere
- Providing a wealth of stimulation from a rich and varied environment
- Asking provocative, thoughtful questions
- Valuing originality
- Providing many opportunities for achievement
- Providing differentiated, meaningful interaction

The arts provide children opportunities for creative thinking as well as creative production. Children love to experiment with words, paints and other materials, and music; they find it enjoyable to dream and to create something of their own, something unique and original. Music and creative arts can give children the opportunities for a creative outlet—to use divergent, as opposed to convergent, thinking. However, teachers must be careful not to teach these art areas in rigid, structured ways, thereby stifling children's creative potential. Teachers' techniques, approaches, and activities need to be open-ended, giving children the opportunity to use their creative imagination.

Chapter Nine provides many different approaches and techniques for using songs in the classroom. In addition, a variety of suggestions for rhythm instruments and creative movements are given. Children in the early childhood years enjoy creative art activities. These activities take extra effort to prepare and clean up, but the effort is worthwhile. Care must be taken not to provide structured art activities, but rather the kinds that give children the experience of creating, planning, imagining, and exploring; many suggestions for these kinds of activities are given in the chapter.

Children need experiences that allow them to use creativity and originality in expression or thought. Some children exhibit more potential for creativity than others, but the challenge comes in encouraging *all* children to use the creative potential they have. Music and creative arts are areas that can encourage imagination, self-expression, and creativity; they should have an important place in every early childhood teacher's curriculum.

Teachers model and teach those things they value and feel are worthwhile (Feeney & Moravcik, 1987). When teachers respond emotionally and verbally to the aesthetic qualities in the environment, children learn to enjoy and appreciate things of an aesthetic nature.

CHAPTER
nine

Music and Movement

Introduction

Children want to express themselves through music, and "music and movement are a natural part of most childhood activity" (Maxim, 1989, p. 288). There are many reasons for including music in early childhood programs. Through music children experience pleasure, joy, and creative expression. Music is one of the acceptable avenues for release and expression of feelings, moods, and emotions. Music allows for the development of desirable feelings and moods, and for dissolving undesirable feelings and moods. It can quiet or calm children, create listening moods, or soothe hurt and troubled feelings. Music has therapeutic value and, as a result, can also enhance the child's feelings of self-worth. Songs can be sung that include the child's name, or children can write words, phrases, or verses of songs. Children should be permitted to "put themselves into" music—to interpret music in their own style and to make up new words, new melodies, and new movements. Music can also

foster "appreciation of one's cultural heritage" (Maxim, 1989, p. 289). In addition, children enjoy learning songs and dances from other cultures and nations.

Many songs can also call attention to clothing worn by the child or physical attributes possessed. Children can sing about their activities. They can name a locomotor skill or other activity and dramatize it while singing about it. Children's "focused listening" (Wolf, 1992), attention span, auditory discrimination, and memory develop through music. Listening especially to songs that tell a story (ballads) or give directions to follow provides an excellent opportunity for careful concentration and attention. Language and concepts can be developed through music as children sing correct language form: New songs often introduce new words and cognitive skills (Dumtschin, 1987; McDonald & Ramsey, 1982). Children are able to build language fluency through singing. Reading and singing are closely connected, because as songs are sung, language is whole and correct. When children show an interest in print, the songs can be printed in their entirety; children sense the meaning of the print as the songs are sung (Barclay & Walwer, 1992). Concepts can be better committed to memory when they are attached to melodies.

Music skills such as rhythm, meter, pitch, and tone are introduced to young children. Opportunities for participation should always be available for individuals; however, the sense of belonging to and functioning with a group is always enhanced through music participation. Most of all, children enjoy music. They enjoy the intricate tunes and melodies; the words, which often tell a story or capture their sense of humor; and the rhythms, which often create spontaneous body movements such as toe tapping or hand clapping. Music in early childhood classes is a must; it is a teaching tool and has aesthetic qualities. "Sounds and music are everywhere; with just a little teacher preparation, the joy that is music can pervade the preschool classroom" (Warner, 1982, p. 134). Through fingerplays, action songs, music games, writing words for songs, composing melodies (Hitz, 1987), and other music-related activities, children are able to utilize creative thinking in problem solving.

Music Goals

Since music should be an integral part of the early childhood curriculum, its main objective for this age group is the child's enjoyment of music. Therefore, emphasis should be on the child, not the teacher; the enjoyment, not the skill; the process, not the product. Musical experiences defy time limits, exacting goals, and expectations. The time for music is any time! Through the music program in early childhood, the child should acquire the following benefits:

1. Success, joy, and pleasure through participation
2. Opportunities to experience music through a variety of activities, materials, instruments, and movements
3. Acquaintance with a variety of types of music
4. Provision for listening activities to foster music understanding
5. Awareness of contrasts in music such as fast and slow, high and low, loud and soft
6. Responsiveness to simple rhythms through locomotor movements, body movements such as clapping, or the use of rhythm instruments
7. Opportunity to sing a variety of songs
8. Ability to express the mood or feelings of a musical selection through body movements, and opportunity to express emotion through music

The teacher should individualize these goals for the particular group, and also for the individual children within the group. Too often teachers plan from an activity approach—they think of a "fun" activity instead of a music activity that is developmentally appropriate for the children (Andress, 1991). The teacher must know each child's functioning level with regard to musical skills and interests. "Music should be included daily for infants as well as older children. The presence of music, whether through recording or the teacher's singing or playing, can awaken early responses to musical sound and can encourage infants to *learn to listen*" (McDonald & Ramsey, 1982, p. 187). A good music program should incorporate the goals of music in singing, rhythm experiences, movement, and listening (Mooman, 1984). These music activities must be developmentally appropriate (Bredekamp, 1986) if they are to be effectively incorporated into all curriculum areas.

The teacher's role is to show an interest in the spontaneous beginnings of music that the child creates. There should be time available for music. Not only should music be planned for every day, but it should also be used spontaneously to support other parts of the curriculum, to create variety, and to provide transitions to activities. Care should be taken to provide adequate space for musical activities, particularly during creative movements and expressions. Allow for freedom of expression, as well as some freedom regarding participation. Young children should be free to become involved in music and to express their own feelings, moods, and interpretations. Criticism and demands for perfection in performance skills have no place in these early music experiences. The teacher's role includes planning activities that will encourage music participation and expression, as well as providing materials and experiences that will stimulate creative thinking and action.

Since young children are highly motivated by praise, the teacher should further motivate musical competencies by praising individuals. Comments such as "Jimmy has found a different way to use the rhythm sticks" or "Lori has learned that you can even jump sideways" provide individual motivation.

As mentioned, an important part of the teacher's role is planning musical activities and experiences. These teacher-initiated activities include teaching songs and musical games, planning music activities that support and relate to

Music and singing should be frequent activities in an early childhood education curriculum. These activities are especially effective when they are spontaneous.

curriculum areas, planning and musical dramatizations, using rhythm activities and rhythm instruments, and encouraging creative body movements. However, the teacher should also take advantage of child-initiated activities. The children may begin singing or chanting during play. They may sing familiar songs, make up their own tunes, or use new words to familiar melodies. A child may begin spontaneously to hum or move rhythmically; the teacher should take advantage of the opportunity to praise the effort and encourage the child to continue.

Teachers should create opportunities for increasing their own musical competencies. They should develop enthusiasm for the music program, since their own feelings will be *caught* by the children, rather than *taught* to them. "The teacher's positive attitude and approach to musical experiences are crucial factors in the young child's success in music" (Haines & Gerber, 1988, p. 25). Although teachers may not see themselves as musicians, music can still be a valuable part of the program. The teacher need not have an operatic voice or voice training to teach songs to children. Teachers who enjoy music and sing with enthusiasm, regardless of ability or training, are the ones who receive the greatest response and involvement from children. Your voice is your most important musical instrument ... [and] when you view yourself as a participant rather than a performer, you can relax and concentrate on the activity, not on yourself" (Jalongo & Collins, 1985, p. 20). Music is a universal language; one does not have to understand the terminology or musical mechanics to enjoy it. It is most effectively approached as an experience to be lived, rather than a subject to be taught.

Songs and Singing

Learning songs and singing are probably the most common musical experiences in the early childhood years. The key to the child's total musical growth is "happy and successful singing" (Haines & Gerber, 1988, p. 17). Again, the attitudes of enthusiasm for and enjoyment of singing are of the utmost importance. Teachers should build a repertoire of singable songs, and it is imperative that they use caution and wisdom when selecting songs to teach to young children. "Singing should be included in the daily activities of preschool children, but expectations of achievement should be based upon knowledge of the developmental nature of their ability. Songs for classroom use should be chosen with careful consideration of tonality, range, melodic configurations, and vocal developmental stages of the children" (McDonald & Ramsey, 1982, p. 188). Toddlers imitate singing and often tag on to the end of a phrase or song. They move to the music and enjoy very simple songs (Wolf, 1992). During preschool and early school years, singing becomes more ritualized and group oriented (Wolf, 1992).

The following are guidelines for teaching songs in early childhood:

1. Competition has no place in teaching children to sing; often it distorts their voices and makes the melodies unpleasant. Comparisons between children should not be made.
2. Know the song well yourself, and then sing it to the children several times while they listen. Listening to good singing is a significant factor in children's vocal development (Haines & Gerber, 1988). Do not teach a song by repeating the words separately from the music. You might play a recording of the song for the children to hear; then they can join in and sing with the recording and the teacher. When selecting records or tapes, make sure the voices are in tune and the instrumentation is uncomplicated (Wolf, 1992).
3. Some songs should be taught in sections— phrases, sentences, or short verses at one time. This is particularly true of longer songs that are more difficult to learn. Then these sections can all be put together. However, when the children are first intro-

duced to the song, they should hear it in its entirety so that they experience it as a whole unit.

4. Use a variety of approaches and teaching techniques (discussed throughout this chapter) in teaching songs and singing familiar songs. Do not always teach songs in the same way. Use pictures, hand and finger actions, and simple props that will involve the children to assist them in remembering the words.

Songs with accompanying actions add variety and increase participation in music activities.

5. Do not force children to sing. Often a child does not sing at school but sings all the songs at home. For some children, it takes time to feel comfortable singing with the group, and pressure to sing does not make them more willing to participate. However, involve the reluctant singer whenever possible. The more involved the children become in a song, the more the words become a part of the activity (Bayless & Ramsey, 1987).

6. Eye-to-eye singing, like eye-to-eye teaching, is most effective. The mood and feeling of the song, along with the teacher's enjoyment of singing, will be caught through expressions you convey to the children.

7. Sing songs to the children in a lower range (i.e., A or B below middle C to G or A above) (Wolf, 1992).

8. Make sure that children understand the meanings of new words in the song, as well as the meaning of the song. However, make certain that the content of the song is on the level of the children's understanding and interest.

9. You may want to discuss the feeling, mood, repetition of melodies or words, tempo, or rhythm of the song.

10. As you teach songs, enunciate clearly and distinctly.

11. If there is a part of a song that is particularly difficult for the children to learn, isolate that part and sing it to the children while they listen. Also, sing that part of the song much more slowly until the children have learned it. Other suggestions include having them clap the rhythm or use their hands to show how the melody moves.

12. Use instruments often to accompany the children's singing, but *teach* the songs without accompaniment (Wolf, 1992). Even if you are not skilled in music reading, there are still many instruments that can be learned or played easily (e.g., autoharp, baritone or tenor ukelele, guitar, rhythm sticks, other rhythm instruments).

13. Children enjoy songs with simple and clear melodies, although they are also eager to learn longer and more intricate tunes. When selecting songs for young children, remember that those with repetition of melody and words are generally both easy and enjoyable to learn.

14. When teaching new songs, hum and sing the song spontaneously to the children as they work and play; they may also hum along.

15. Songs with half-steps in the melody line, unusually large intervals between tones, or a broad range should be avoided because they are often too difficult for very young children to learn.

16. Whenever simple actions, motions, or dramatizations are appropriate, incorporate them into the singing time.

17. Sing confidently, and do not apologize for your singing.

18. When involved in a singing time, you may invite the children to sing along; usually you need only begin to sing and they will join in. Beware of asking, "Do you want to sing this song?" unless you are prepared to accept a negative answer.

19. Sing songs about familiar things or feelings.

20. Make a tape recording of favorite classroom songs, and add new favorites to it. Encourage parents or children to take it home for listening and singing along.

Variety in Singing*

Routine approaches or techniques in any curriculum area tend to become boring to children. Thus we need to become aware of possible ways to add variety and spice to singing songs.

1. Use visual aids (such as overhead transparencies, movie boxes, charts, posters, chalk talk) to help teach a song. The children will also enjoy assisting with the visual aids. Puppets (finger, sack, stick, commercial, cone) add friendly interest. Stories that tell the content of the song can be used. As you tell stories about animals, places, or things, sing songs about them also. Objects representing familiar songs can be put into a sack or box; children reach in and select the songs to be sung. Use pictures representing songs that the children know. Also, many songs that utilize action words such as skipping, painting, and so on can be depicted in pictures.

2. Make up guessing games to utilize variety in songs. Say, "I'm thinking of a song that tells me to put my finger in different places" ("Put Your Finger in the Air"). Or start the singing time with a question that will arouse interest and gain attention (see item 12 in this section).

3. Put the names of songs on the backs of objects or pictures pinned to a chart or bulletin board, or put the names of songs in a sack or box. The children select the object from the chart or the paper from the box to determine the songs to be sung.

4. Have children sing songs, or parts of songs, as a solo, duet, or trio.

5. Where accompanying chants are appropriate, have some of the children chant, and others sing the song. For example, in the song "I've Been Working on the Railroad" (familiar folk song), some of the children chant "choo, choo, choo." In the song "Little White Duck," (familiar folk song), have some of the children accompany with "quack, quack, quack." In the song "Hush, Little Baby" (familiar folk song), have the accompaniment of "hush, hush, hush."

6. Use sounds or instruments as accompaniment. Some of the children accompany while others sing.

7. Sing a song and pause while the children sing the end of the line, the next phrase, or the end of the sentence; the children fill in the words.

* Consult a variety of song books for melodies and lyrics of traditional and old familiar songs. Specific song books will be noted where available.

8. Write the word of a song on the chalkboard or a chart. Erase or cover words or phrases as the children are learning the song.

9. Have children pantomime a song for the rest of the group. Follow up with singing the song.

10. Have the children add new words to a familiar song in order to make or weave nonsense into them. For example, when singing "London Bridge," change "Build it up with iron bars" to "Build it up with bacon and eggs" or "Build it up with cats and dogs." In the song "Mary Had a Little Lamb," ask what silly thing Mary might have instead of a lamb—a centipede, for example.

11. Use pitch-level conducting in teaching a song. In other words, use your arm and hand to show the changes in pitch level.

12. Before you sing or play a new song, create a listening experience by asking the children the following kinds of questions:

    a. Who? ("Listen to this song and tell me *who* it is about.")

    b. Where? ("Listen to this song and tell me *where* the animal is going.")

    c. What? ("Listen to this song I am going to sing for you and tell me *what* new word you hear" or "*What* words rhyme? or "*What* parts of the melody or tunes are alike?" or "*What* words are repeated?")

    d. How? ("Listen to this song I am going to sing for you and tell me *how* Michael Finnegan's whiskers got in again" ["Michael Finnegan," familiar folk song].)

    e. Why? ("Listen to this song and tell me *why* Cindy should go home" ["Cindy"].)

13. Incorporate a variety of other teaching methods, such as role playing or dramatizing a song.

14. Hum the song or parts of it.

15. Sing a song from a record or a tape by children's recording artists such as Ella Jenkins, Joe Wayman, Raffi, Miss Jackie, Hap Palmer, Steve Millang, and Greg Scelsa. Discover your favorites at educational toy stores or at your library, where they can be checked out. Include them in your classroom for easy sing-alongs!

16. Teachers can use song picture books such as *The Lady with the Alligator Purse* (Westcott, 1990) or *I Know an Old Lady Who Swallowed a Fly* (Rounds, 1990) to link songs to literacy. The song can be sung, the picture song book read, and then a variety of activities in other curriculum areas planned to extend the learning (Barclay & Walwer, 1992). To expand the activity, the children can participate in art activities, dramatic activities, field trips, and any other experiences that relate in a meaningful and age-appropriate way.

17. See Figure 9–1 for a web for the song picture book *The Wheels on the Bus* (a variety of authors and illustrators have done this song in picture book form).

Specific Kinds of Songs

There are literally thousands of excellent songs that can be selected in teaching young children. Some of the categories of songs from which teachers should surely make some selections are discussed here. There are songs to teach almost every one of the concepts discussed in this book. A teacher who desires a song about a specific concept for which a song cannot be found should write new words about the concept to a familiar tune, or make up both the words and melody for a new song. We believe that the following categories of songs are valuable in teaching young children.

Expandable songs. Expandable songs offer opportunities for children to help create the songs, thus creating a sense of pride and enhancing self-worth. Expandable songs enable children to make

FIGURE 9-1

up their own words or phrases for particular parts of the songs. For example, the familiar folk song "If You're Happy and You Know It" becomes an expandable song as children add their own phrases: "If you're happy and you know it (blink your eyes)." Another way of changing this song is to change the word *happy* to different moods or emotions, such as "If you're mad and you know it, take a walk." Following are a few suggestions of songs that contain expandable phrases and words:

"I Went to Visit a Friend"

(to the tune of "Oats, Peas, Beans, and Barley Grow.") Underlined words and phrases are those that can be changed by the children.

I went to visit a friend one day,
She only lived across the way.

She said she couldn't come out to play,
Because it was *her cleaning* day.
This is the way *she cleans* away,
This is the way *she cleans* away,
This is the way *she cleans* away,
Because it was her *cleaning* day.

"Mary Wore a Red Dress"

"Look Around the Room"

"I See a Boy"

"Sing with Me"

"My Little Soul's Gonna Shine"

"Over in the Meadow"

"Bumble Bee"

"The Wheels on the Bus"

"Come on and Join Into the Game"

"Put Your Finger in the Air"

"Rig-a-Jig Jig"

"Johnny Works"

"Blue, Blue"

To the tune "Mary Had a Little Lamb," sing the following:

Pass a napkin to your friend, to your friend, to your friend.
Pass a napkin to your friend. Now take one yourself.
or
It's time for us to go outside, go outside, go outside.
It's time for us to go outside, for soon we're going home.
or
Jimmy has some jingle bells, jingle bells, jingle bells.
Jimmy has some jingle bells, that he plays for us.
or
Martha brought a part of skates, pair of skates, pair of skates.
Martha brought a pair of skates to our sharing time.
or
Eric has a shape that's blue, shape that's blue, shape that's blue.
Eric has a shape that's blue. What shape and color can you find?
or

Now it is cleanup time, cleanup time, cleanup time.
Now it is cleanup time, I will need your help.

To the tune "Lazy Mary" (also "Here We Go 'Round the Mulberry Bush"), sing the following:

What is the color of the shoes, of the shoes, of the shoes?
What is the color of the shoes you're wearing on your feet?
or
Stand up if you are wearing red, wearing red, wearing red.
Stand up if you are wearing red; and show us what to do.
or
This is the way I nod my head, nod my head, nod my head,
This is the way I nod my head, you can join me too.
or
We are getting ready, ready, ready,
We are getting ready, To go outside and play.
or
Jimmy and Susie, you can go out, you can go out, you can go out.
Jimmy and Susie you can go out; Bobby, you can go too.
or
We are working stirring the batter, stirring the batter, stirring the batter.
We are working stirring the batter, soon our cake will be done.

To the tune "Skip to My Lou," sing the following:

Johnny's birthday is today, Johnny's birthday is today,
Johnny's birthday is today, and he is 5 years old.
or
Put your finger on your eye, put your finger on your eye,
Put your finger on your eye, and tell us what you see.
or
Little red wagon painted blue, little red wagon painted blue,
Little red wagon painted blue, skip to my Lou, my darling.

(The children then decide what color to paint the blue wagon, and another verse is added.)

or

I have a buddy who is wearing pink, I have a buddy who is wearing pink.

I have a buddy who is wearing pink, and his name is Jamie.

or

The bus on the street goes beep, beep, beep,

The bus on the street goes beep, beep, beep,

The bus on the street goes beep, beep, beep.

Skip to my Lou, my darling.

or

The cow on the farm goes moo, moo, moo,

The cow on the farm goes moo, moo, moo,

The cow on the farm goes moo, moo, moo,

Listen to the sound it makes.

To the tune "The Farmer in the Dell," "A-Hunting We Will Go," "I Put My Right Foot In," or "Looby, Loo," sing the following:

It's time to go inside, it's time to go inside.

Hang up your coat, sit on the rug; for now it's story time.

or

Stand up and touch your nose, stand up and touch your nose.

Touch first with left, and then with right.

Spin and then sit down.

or

I see a friend in stripes, I see a friend in stripes.

I see a friend in stripes. Can you guess who it is?

or

We're going to the zoo, we're going to the zoo.

We're going to the zoo. What animals will we see?

or

We'll see a tall giraffe, we'll see a tall giraffe.

We'll see a tall giraffe. His neck is longer than mine!

To the tune "London Bridges," sing the following:

Time to put your crayons away, crayons away, crayons away.

Time to put your crayons away, until another day.

or

Find a person wearing green, wearing green, wearing green.

Find a person wearing green. What's that person's name?

or

Ann's the first one on the rug—Roger, Marilyn, Kathy, Todd,

Mary, Eric, Marsha, Gary—Now here's Michael.

or

What would you do if I gave you some paints, gave you some paints, gave you some paints?

What would you do if I gave you some paints?

I would paint with them!

or

Will you answer "here today," "here today," "here today?"

Will you answer "here today," when I call your name?

Many of the songs you already know and sing are expandable, and they provide a valuable exercise in creative thinking and problem solving as children create their own words and phrases. Many other songs in addition to those listed here can also become expandable songs.

Nursery rhymes. Preschool and kindergarten children always delight in singing nursery rhyme songs. The simple melodies and short verses (most of them four-line songs) make them so appropriate for these young children. The familiar, simple, and catchy tunes also make them easily adapted to new words. Jalongo and Collins (1985) suggest learning a few traditional tunes that can "lead to many different songs because folk music has many parodies" (p. 20).

These suggestions should only serve to stimulate your own imagination. Think of additional possibilities for other nursery rhymes. Some of the favorite nursery rhymes follow:

"Twinkle, Twinkle Little Star"

"Old MacDonald"

"Sing a Song of Sixpence"

"Hickory, Dickory, Dock"

"Baa, Baa, Black Sheep"

"Jack and Jill"

"Peter, Peter Pumpkin Eater"

"The Muffin Man"

"Three Blind Mice"

Old traditional and folk songs. Children's musical heritage surely must include many of the songs that have been sung by children for centuries. One need only consult favorite songbooks and observe the citations in the upper-right-hand corner of the music to realize that a majority of children's songs are traditional or folk songs from around the world. Some of the favorites include the following:

"This Old Man"

"Pop Goes the Weasel"

"Eensey-Weensey Spider"

"Where Is Thumbkin?"

"Rig-a-Jig Jig"

"If You're Happy"

"Little Peter Rabbit"

"My Pigeon House"

"I'm a Little Teapot"

"Yankee Doodle"

"Bingo"

"Six Little Ducks"

"Michael Finnegan"

"The Noble Duke of York"

"The Bear Went Over the Mountain"

Lullabies. Lullabies often have a quieting and calming effect on children. Have preschool and kindergarten children pretend that they have a baby they are trying to get to sleep. They may rock it in their arms or pretend to rock it in a cradle. How quiet they will be to make sure the baby is not awakened! The following lullabies are suggested:

"Hush, Little Baby"

"Brahm's Lullaby"

"Rock-a-Bye Baby"

"All Through the Night"

"Kum Ba Yah" (familiar African folk song)

Ballads or story songs. These traditional songs have been handed down from generation to generation and enjoyed by many. Children love them because of the stories they tell. After a ballad was sung to a group of children, Rachel immediately said, "Oh, sing me that story again!" Some of the following will be enjoyed by the children time and time again:

"Hush, Little Baby"

"I've Been Working on the Railroad"

"Mister Frog Went a-Courting"

"I Know an Old Lady Who Swallowed a Fly"

Haines and Gerber (1988) suggest an approach they call *add-a-song:* Children role play or dramatize favorite fairy tales or nursery rhymes, then add "a song or two, with simple words and a familiar tune" (p. 143), and repeat them when certain actions occur or recur in the story line. This approach combines music and storytelling and adds a new dimension to storytelling.

Rounds. Even preschool children enjoy singing simple rounds, and they like to hear different words sung at the same time. However, when using rounds in early childhood, it is important that you have a leader for each group. For younger children, usually two groups are adequate, even though some songs have more parts to them. One of the simplest ways to sing a round with the very young is to combine two songs: Have one group sing one song while the other group sings another song. Examples of such combinations include "Three Blind Mice" with "Row, Row, Row Your Boat" and "Are You Sleeping" or "The Farmer in the Dell" with "Skip to My Lou." These combinations have different tunes or melodies. You can also have the children sing rounds by combining two or more songs that have the same melodies:

"Twinkle, Twinkle Little Star" with "Baa, Baa, Black Sheep" or "The ABC Song"

"Farmer in the Dell" with "A-Hunting We Will Go" or "I Put My Right Foot In"

"Frère Jacques" with "Are You Sleeping?" or "Where Is Thumbkin?"

"The Mulberry Bush" with "Lazy Mary" or
  "The Wheels on the Bus"

"The Bear Went Over the Mountain" with
  "My Thumbs Are Starting to Wiggle"

When teaching rounds sung in the traditional way, make sure that the children know the song well first before trying it as a round, remembering to have a leader for each group. Some rounds that can be sung in parts and are simple enough for children in the early childhood years include the following:

"Frère Jacques" or "Are You Sleeping?"

"Row, Row, Row Your Boat"

"Sweetly Sings the Donkey"

"Kookaburra"

Writing and creating songs. It has already been mentioned that new words can be written to familiar old tunes or melodies. Children will also enjoy learning new words to familiar melodies of television commercials. They hear these melodies so often, and they are so catchy, that children will not have any difficulty with them! Children and teachers can also enjoy writing new words to new tunes. It is amazing how easy it is to create original words and a simple, original melody to go with them. Just be sure to record or write the words and melody, because they are so often difficult to remember until they become familiar. Choose a topic, and then begin brainstorming short phrases about that topic. A small group of children could work cooperatively on an appropriate melody for these short phrases. The entire group could work on the words and then in small groups—each group being responsible for one or two lines—the melody could be developed and finally recorded.

A simple way of creating songs is to work with *scale* songs. The melody is the scale, beginning at middle C (do), or lower, and then climbing to upper C (or to the note on which you began). Then go back down the scale. For example, the following words could be sung up and down the scale:

Mr. Jones, the carpenter, came.
He showed us how to build a cage.

For each scale song, you will need a sentence or phrase with eight syllables to go up the scale, and then a sentence or phrase with eight syllables to go down the scale.

Musical Games

Young children enjoy the involvement that comes with musical games, which spark enthusiasm and excitement. Musical games can be taught and carried out in a number of ways. Some are simple enough that the children need only follow along and do as the words tell them. However, others need careful instruction, and it may be wise to role play or go through these games before combining music and game. Also, the musical backgrounds can be provided in a number of ways. For familiar songs, the children can sing as the game is played. Sometimes a piano or other musical instrument is available for accompaniment. Many of these musical games are also on records. Following are some of the most popular musical games for young children.

"Hokey-Pokey"

"Looby-Loo"

"Bluebird"

"Skip to My Lou"

"Oh Where, Oh Where Has My Little Dog
  Gone?"

"Farmer in the Dell"

"The Mulberry Bush"

"Sing a Song of Sixpence"

"Pop Goes the Weasel"

"The Muffin Man"

"A-Tisket, A-Tasket"

"Put Your Finger in the Air"

"Did You Ever See a Lassie?"

"Come on and Join into the Game"

Musical rhythm instruments add variety and interest to music activities, and help children identify and duplicate the rhythms.

Rhythm Activities

In many ways, each musical experience a child has will be a rhythm experience, because children begin to feel the rhythm pattern of music very early. Even infants begin to sense the beat, or rhythm, of musical selections. However, it is not at all unusual to find a young child who has difficulty in sensing the rhythm pattern of music. Care should be taken not to make such a child feel uncomfortable or pressured, which will take away the enjoyment of the music. Children's first experiences in finding or experimenting with rhythm patterns will probably be with clapping or playing them on a rhythm instrument. Initially, some children may simply enjoy the experience of hand clapping or playing the instrument, and may not be aware of the rhythm. The teacher should not be concerned. The teacher's role in these early rhythmic experiences should be to encourage sound and rhythm exploration and participation, not duplication (McDonald & Ramsey, 1982). During rhythm experiences, the teacher can pat the beat on the child's knees (Weikart, 1985). Being able to keep time to music develops gradually, and there is much individual variation among children.

Early exposures to rhythm should have simple and definite sounds, with even or steady rhythm patterns. A good beginning to rhythm activities is the exploration of sounds in the environment, not necessarily actual musical sounds. For example, encourage the children to listen for sounds that have definite beat patterns, such as a clock ticking, a water faucet dripping, or a jackhammer drilling. Then encourage them to listen to the sounds twice and try to reproduce them by clapping hands or tapping feet. Another possibility is to listen to the sound of different rhythmic vocal sounds. One could select a particular vowel or consonant sound and sing it to a familiar melody. Other vocal sounds that can be set to rhythm patterns include buzzing, laughing (ha-ha-ha or ho-ho-ho), hissing, and chanting. Games can be made out of this kind of rhythm experience. In one game, the children sit in a circle, and as a ball or bean bag is thrown to a child, that child repeats a vocal rhythm pattern and then tosses the bean bag or ball to another child. That child must repeat the same rhythm pattern; then the bean bag or ball is tossed to others, and they must come up with new patterns.

Chants can also be used for early rhythm exploration. Four- or five-word sentences can be made into chants and different rhythm patterns clapped or beaten out as the children repeat the sentences. For example, the sentence "You can't catch me!" can have a variety of patterns. Emphasis may be put on the first, second, third, or fourth words (*You* can't catch me; You *can't* catch me; You can't *catch* me; You can't catch *me*.) Chants can be altered in other ways: They can be soft or loud, fast or slow, steady or wavering. Chants adapted from rhymes, stories, or fingerplays can be developed for children's actions, including jump-the-rope chants. If young children are not familiar with the chants, invite a person into the classroom to teach some of them to the children. After they listen, they can play the rhythm patterns of these chants on rhythm instruments or use "body instruments" such as hand clapping.

Children can pretend to do some of the following activities and develop a rhythm pattern by clapping or beating the rhythm pattern of each sound: chair rocking, clock ticking, knocking on a door, washing machine agitator turning, water dripping, hammering a nail, sawing a log or piece of wood, sweeping the floor, shining a window.

Many excellent records can give children experience in rhythm exploration. Some can be used for basic introductions to rhythm, and others are used for more advanced explorations. (See the resources at the end of this chapter.)

Body Instruments

Clapping is probably the most commonly used body rhythm instrument, and we have cited it often. However, other instruments can be used in rhythm activities:

Whistling	Singing
Humming	Speaking
Hissing	Thigh slapping (patting)
Snapping fingers	Head tapping, head nodding
Stamping feet	Gasping
Clicking tongue	Sh-h-h-h (gentle, or explosive
Blinking eyes	and loud)

In addition, the children could take just one part of the body, such as the hands, elbows, or feet, and discover ways of using that body part to beat rhythm. For example, the hands could be used to clap, tap on the floor, or tap some part of the body such as the chest or back. The tapping could also alternate from head to floor or from shoulder to knees.

Rhythm Instruments

Give children frequent experiences using rhythm instruments. Many early childhood teachers do not like to use them because the children become difficult to control when the instruments are brought out for use. If these instruments are seldom used, the children may become too excited about them. Lack of variation in presentation and direction also encourages lack of control. When introducing an instrument, make sure to use its proper name, and give the children ample opportunity to become familiar with it. Freedom to explore instruments should be provided in various ways—not always in a rhythm band marching around in a circle and following a leader. The teacher might even allow exploration during free play.

Instruments can be purchased, collected, or made by the teacher or children (see Appendix A for pictorial suggestions of teacher- and/or child-made instruments). Usually school budgets determine the kinds and amounts of rhythm instruments purchased. With handmade instruments, it is usually possible to have greater numbers of the same kinds. Following is a discussion of many rhythm instruments that can be obtained in one, two, or all three of the previously mentioned ways.

Bells. Bells and jingles can be made simply by lacing bells on a string and tying the ends of the string together. Another method is to sew bells onto a mitten or glue them across the top of a wide elastic band. You can also drill holes in bottle caps, string them on a string, and then tie the ends of the string together.

Clappers. The effect of castanets can be obtained by selecting a stiff piece of cardboard approximately the size of a matchbook (an empty matchbook could be used). If a matchbook is not used, fold the cardboard piece in the middle, just as a matchbook is folded. Tape and glue a bottle cap on each inside end, but do not put the tape over the outside of the caps. The clapper is held between the thumb and the index and middle fingers, and then is secured in this position with an elastic band. As the fingers and thumb are moved together and apart, the bottle caps should strike each other, making the sound of castanets. (See Figure 9–2.)

Corrugated cardboard washboard.   Pieces of heavy corrugated cardboard (or lighter pieces pasted on heavy cardboard or wood) are strummed with a spoon, dowel, or nail for a washboard sound effect.

Cymbals.   Kettle lids, or other lids with knobs attached, will serve as cymbals. (Small pieces of wood screwed onto the lid will also serve as knobs.)

Drums.   Use coffee cans, or obtain from cafeterias their largest metal cans. On the open end, stretch inner-tube rubber or similar material as tightly as possible, and then secure it with wire or cord. A drumstick can be made out of a dowel or stick, to one end of which a piece of fabric-covered foam rubber is secured. The drum can be decorated by dipping magazine scraps and pieces of tissue paper in liquid starch and then placing them on the sides of the can. When making a drum, the tighter the ends, the sharper the sound. The covering can be made from chamois, inner-tube rubber, or Naugahyde. Wiring is recommended over lacing, since lacing does not seem to be tight enough, and the lacing holes may tear easily. Drums can also be made out of oatmeal or hat boxes, nail kegs, or large barrels; or two different-sized cans may be tied together to make bongo drums. Drumsticks that can be improvised include a dowel, spoon, eraser end of a new pencil, wire brush, rubber spatula, drawer-pull nailed to a dowel, or dowel inserted in a Styrofoam ball.

Gongs.   The sound of a gong can be obtained by setting a steel or brass hubcap on a block of wood to strike it, or by drilling a hole in the hubcap and attaching a wire or string as a handle. The sound will differ according to where the gong is struck and what is used to strike it. Possible strikers include a dowel, stick, spoon, or nail.

Hummers.   Obtain cardboard tubes from the inside of paper rolls (waxed paper, paper towels, toilet paper, etc.). On one end of the tube, punch a hole, using a paper punch and punching down as far as possible. Cover that same end of the tube with either waxed paper or aluminum foil (about a 3-inch square is adequate for each hummer). Secure this covering with an elastic band, but make sure that the punched hole is not covered. The tube can be decorated in any desired way. The children put their mouths up to the open ends of the tubes to blow and hum at the same time.

Jingle clogs.   These instruments can be made by flattening bottle tops and then making a hole in the middle of each bottle top with a nail. (This hole should be larger than the nail used to attach the tops to the dowel, so that the tops can jingle.) Loosely nail the bottle tops to the ends of a 4- to 6-inch dowel. Bells may be used in place of bottle caps. Decorate them. Small wooden wheels, buttons, or metal washers could be used in place of bottle tops. Also, a hole could be drilled in one end of a dowel. Bells are then joined loosely on a string, and the string is tied to the end of the dowel (See Figure 9–3).

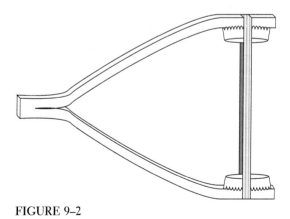

FIGURE 9–2
Clapper

or

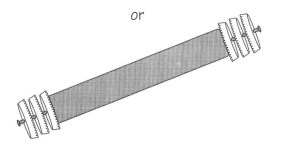

FIGURE 9–3
Jingle Clogs

length, and make enough to provide the children with two each. These sticks can be struck together or tapped on an aluminum pie plate, a steel bowl, or the floor. One stick could be serrated so that a different sound would be made by rubbing the smooth stick over the serrated one. (See Figure 9–4.)

Shakers. Dried seed pods or gourds often make the sound of maracas or shakers. Empty containers such as gourds, metal cans, or film containers; small boxes or cartons such as gelatin boxes, cottage cheese cartons, or half-pint milk cartons; paper plates stapled together; baby food jars; plastic bottles; or empty bandage boxes can be partially filled with sand, rice, dry beans, macaroni, pebbles, shells, paper clips, or similar items. Small amounts of these items are used. The shakers can be decorated (See Figure 9–5.)

Tambourines. Tambourines can be made using either two lightweight paper plates held to-

Paper cups, coconut shells. Two same-sized paper cups are provided for each child. They may be decorated. They are played by bringing together either of the two ends or alternating them—the larger ends together, then the smaller ends together. When using a coconut, cut it in half, hollow out the meat, and then strike the cut ends of the halves together.

Plucking instruments. Drill a hole through the bottom of an old washtub. Fasten a screw eye or a large bolt through the hole. Secure a heavy wire to the bolt; to the other end of the wire, fasten a broomstick or dowel. Secure the free end of the stick or dowel in the bottom of the washtub by drilling a hole in the tub. Play it by plucking the wire; obtain pitch variations by tightening the wire. A rubber-band banjo can be made by obtaining a sturdy open box and stretching a few rubber bands of different sizes, spaced widely, around it. The box may be placed on a wooden table for more resonant tones.

Rhythm sticks. Cut dowels of any width into lengths of 8 to 12 inches. Cut them all the same

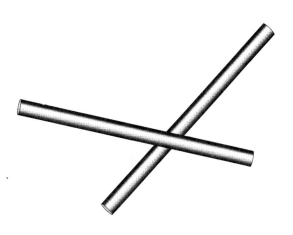

FIGURE 9–4
Rhythm Sticks

FIGURE 9–5
Shakers

Tuned glasses or bottles. Fill glasses, soda bottles, or other glass bottles with water to different levels. If the water levels are properly varied, the tones achieved will represent a scale. Tap the bottles lightly to produce the sound. (If these bottles are covered, the measured water will not evaporate as readily.)

Tuning fork. A tuning fork, which can be obtained commercially, will vibrate and produce a certain tone, depending on the size of the fork.

Wooden blocks. Wooden blocks are made of hardwood and provided in pairs. They can be cut into any shape, including geometric shapes, and sanded. Handles of spools, knobs, and wooden pieces can be bolted or screwed on. For variations, different sizes and kinds of materials could be thumbtacked or attached to create different sounds. Such materials as corrugated cardboard, sandpaper, or foam rubber may be attached. (See Figure 9–7.)

gether or one heavy paper plate. Bells or bottle caps are attached to the edges. Aluminum pie plates also work well.

Triangles, nails. A triangle can be made by obtaining a 3- to 5-inch length of metal pipe and a piece of heavy string 10 to 15 inches long. Run the string through the pipe and tie the ends of the string together. The children hold the string and strike the suspended pipe with a nail or other metal implement. Nails make good instruments, producing the sounds of chime bands or triangles. Purchase one nail 5 inches in length or longer for each child in the class (a variety of lengths or the same length may be used). In addition, purchase a striker nail approximately 4 inches in length for each child. To the head of the longer nail, tie a string to be used as a handle for the nail. The shorter nail is held by the other hand and strikes the longer nail. A horseshoe sus-pended by a string, with a nail for a striker, can also be used. (See Figure 9–6.)

FIGURE 9–6
Triangles and Nails

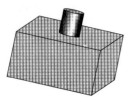
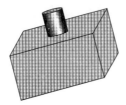

FIGURE 9–7
Wooden Blocks

Xylophone. Obtain electrical conduit pipe from a hardware store. It should be cut into the following lengths, but the cutting must be exact. Therefore, it is best to use a power saw. (If the hardware store has a power saw, have the pipes cut there.)

Middle C	12½ in.	G	10 in.
D	11¾ in.	A	9½ in.
E	11 in.	B♭	9⅜ in.
F	10¾ in.	B	9 in.
F#	10½ in.	C	8¾ in.

Make a wooden xylophone using balsa wood 1½ inches wide and the following lengths:

Middle C	9 in.	G	7 in.
D	8½ in.	A	6½ in.
E	8 in.	B	5½ in.
F	7⅝in.	C	5 in.
F#	7⅜ in.		

Other kinds of rhythm instruments

1. Hair-comb harmonicas or kazoos (waxed paper over the side of a comb)
2. Pots and pans
3. Pages of a book ("strummed")
4. Wooden rungs of chair
5. Vegetable grater

Specific Activities with Rhythm

There are many delightful ways of using rhythm activities in the classroom, and the teacher should incorporate rhythm activities into the music curriculum, as well as other parts of the curriculum.

Have the children use body instruments or rhythm instruments to beat the rhythm of nursery rhymes, poems, names, colors, places, or songs. Alternatively, rhythm patterns can be suggested by using marks on the chalkboard or felt pieces on the flannel board. The following patterns could be put on the chalkboard and the children asked to clap them:

.. .. *or* ... .. *or* ... .

More difficult patterns can be given as children's experience increases. Tell the children that you are clapping the names of some children, and have them stand if they think their name is being clapped. For example, the pattern for Allison McKean would be ... .. You can combine names such as Brandon and Marilyn (.. . ...). As the children grow in experience, substitute note patterns for the marks or felt pieces. For example, Mary Lou Smith might be ♫♩ ♩; Phillip White might be ♩ ♩ ♩ (White, 1981). The children will learn that the pause indicates the separation between words. Also, make guessing games out of colors, locations, nursery rhymes, foods, animals, and other categories.

Give each child one rhythm stick or dowel. On the verse of the song, use locomotor movements to move around or over the dowel. On the chorus, the dowel is picked up and the rhythm tapped out on the floor. For example, on the first verse of the song "Rig-a-Jig Jig," the children find some way of walking around or over the dowel (backward, sideways, forward, etc.), and on the chorus the children pick up the dowel and tap the rhythm. On the second verse, the children might hop as they sing, instead of walking; thus they must find a way of hopping around or over the dowel. Then, once again, on the chorus they use the stick to tap out the rhythm. Songs can either be sung by the children or played on records. Directions can be given to find a way to go *around* the dowel on the first verse and *over* the dowel on the second verse. On the third verse, encourage the children to find a different way of moving to visit their neighbors—but always on the chorus to pick up the dowel and tap out the rhythm.

Have the children pretend to be conductors, inventing their own arm and hand movements. They could use a dowel for a baton.

As the children are given an instrument, they can be encouraged to find two different ways of playing it or holding it.

As an accompaniment to the children's singing or to a recording of "Horsey, Horsey,"* provide each child with a pair of paper cups. As they play or beat the rhythm of the song, first striking the tops and then the bottoms of the paper cups together, the sound will resemble the "clip-clop" of horses' hooves.

Accompaniments for stories, songs, poems, and nursery rhymes can be devised. For example, drums of three different sizes could be used to tell the story of "The Three Bears." The larger, deeper-sounding drum would be the papa bear; the middle-sized drum, the mama bear; and the smallest drum, the baby bear. As an alternative, on a four-line song, one instrument (such as a triangle) could play the first line, wooden tone blocks could play the second line, the maracas could play the third line, and all could join in for the last line. For a nursery rhyme such as "Hickory, Dickory, Dock," some of the children could pretend to be the pendulums on grandfather clocks and ticktock back and forth to the rhythm of the rhyme or song. On the first line, instruments (such as wood blocks or the triangles) could accompany; on the second line, when the mouse runs up the clock, the xylophone could be played; on the third line, when the clock strikes one, the cymbal or gong could play; and on the last line, when the mouse runs down, the xylophone could play.

Fundamental Locomotor Movements

Another aspect of music and rhythm consists of developing and exploring locomotor movements. Some of the basic locomotor movements include

* *Learning as We Play.* Folkway Records and Service Corp. (Distributed by Scholastic Book Services) (FC7659).

walking, climbing, marching, running, hopping, jumping, skipping, galloping, rolling, crawling, leaping, sliding, and trotting. The most basic of these movements, and the one to begin with, is walking. Rhythmically, this movement has a basic, steady, beat pattern that can be slower or faster. Background stimulus for locomotor movements can be provided by a drumbeat or other instrument beat, a musical recording, a song, or an accompaniment on a tuned instrument such as a piano. As children develop skill in each of the locomotor movements, they should be given the opportunity and encouragement to use them in a variety of ways and to find different ways of exploring the movement. For example, the following are some ways to explore walking; many of these same suggestions could be applied to other basic locomotor movements.

Fast	Like . . . (a tin soldier,
Slow	etc.)
Heavily	Happily, sadly, etc.
Lightly	In the rain
Low	In the wind
In the middle	In the cold
High	In the snow
With toes in	When it is hot
With toes out	Barefoot
On heels	in the sand
Backward	on the grass
Sideways	on pebbles
In big steps	on a hot pavement
Stamping	in cold water
In short steps	In the dark
On tiptoe	When going some-
Skating	place special
Diagonally	When going some-
On the outside of the	place you do not
foot	care to go
With knees out	Following your hand
Lazily	as you walk
Long	Leading with your
With knees high	ear
In slow motion	eye
With eyes closed	elbow
On hands and feet	shoulder

Some further examples of exploring different locomotor movements might be variations of running. Children could run lightly or heavily, stop suddenly, or change directions. Bells and triangles could be used to evoke lighter running, and drums and tambourines for more vigorous action. Marching is an often used locomotor movement in early childhood classrooms. Unfortunately, however, the goal is usually to keep time to music, to keep in step, or to stay in the circle. We propose that the goals should not always be to keep time or to keep in step. Children should not always have to be in a line or circle; they can learn to march in different directions without interfering with others. Explore variations with marching.

Axial Movements

There are other types of movements, often referred to as *nonlocomotor*, or *axial*, movements. They include the following (suggestions for stimulating these kinds of movements are given):

1. Swinging and swaying
   a. Swing arms like the pendulum on a clock, from side to side.
   b. Swing arms over and around, as though winding yourself up.
   c. Swing arms and body back and forth, as though getting ready to take off in flight or rocking in a chair.
   d. Swing and sway any part of your body like a monkey.
   e. Make some part of your body move like a railroad signal.
   f. Make some part or parts of your body move like trees and leaves moving in the wind.
   g. Make some part or parts of your body move like windshield wipers.
2. Bending and stretching
   a. How many different parts of your body can you bend? How many parts can you

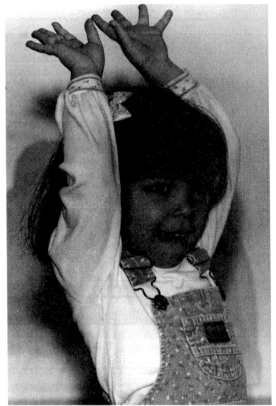

"I can stretch as tall as a tree!"

   stretch? In how many different directions?
   b. Bend yourself small and then stretch yourself tall.
   c. How many ways can you stretch your face?
   d. Can you stretch some part of you like a rubber band, and what happens when you pop?
   e. Pretend you are walking on stilts.
   f. Stretch, move, and bend your body through the stages of a sneeze.
   g. Move your body as though you were reaching for something on the highest shelf in your home.
   h. Pretend to be an inchworm.

3. Pushing and pulling
   a. Pretend that you are pushing a wagon.
   b. How many ways can you pretend to be pushing and pulling a piano?
   c. Pretend you are digging and hoeing weeds in the garden.
   d. Show me how you would move to work the oars of a boat.
   e. Pretend that you are swimming. How about pretending that you are rescuing someone who is drowning?
4. Rising and falling
   a. Pretend to be a jack-in-the-box.
   b. Show me how you would move if you were the sun rising and then setting.
   c. Pretend to be an airplane taking off in flight and then landing.
   d. Pretend to be a seed growing into a flower, and then a petal on that flower falling and blowing away.
   e. Pretend to be a ball bouncing up and down. Do you always bounce to the same height?
5. Twisting and turning
   a. How would you move if you were a top?
   b. Pretend that you are using a Hula-Hoop.
   c. Show me how you would move if you were an ice skater making a turn.
   d. Pretend that you are a lid being screwed onto a jar.
6. Shaking
   a. Shake like Santa Claus.
   b. Pretend to be some jelly.
   c. Show me how you would move if you were being washed in a washing machine.
   d. Shake as though you were a milk shake being mixed.

Using Locomotor and Axial Movements

There are many ways to teach and use both locomotor and nonlocomotor movements. By ex-
ploring and getting children involved in these kinds of movements, you will enhance their co-ordination, give them experience with both rhythm and movement, provide opportunities for creative problem solving, and encourage physical activity and development. Following are some further suggestions for accomplishing these goals:

1. Many songs offer opportunities for locomotor and nonlocomotor movements. For example, use "I Went to Visit a Friend One Day," "Rig-a-Jig Jig," or an adaptation of such songs as "If You're Happy and You Know It" or "Mary Had a Little Lamb" (the lamb could walk, run, or skip to school with Mary).
2. Use a follow-the-leader approach.
3. Suggest movements that resemble those of animals.
4. Suggest ways to "cross the river" or go across the room.
5. Use nursery rhymes to stimulate movements.
6. Suggest ways to go around a dowel or other stick.
7. Use records to stimulate ideas for movement.
8. Lay foot patterns out on the floor for fundamental locomotor movements.
9. Draw shapes using different parts of the body (include shapes, letters, and numbers, making them different sizes).
10. Jump into the middle of a space and find various ways to move to get out.

Once children have explored locomotor and nonlocomotor movements, they are ready for what we often refer to as *creative movements*. Having had the basics of movement, they are ready to create more on their own and use more freedom. Much of what we have suggested with both locomotor and nonlocomotor movements leads to creative movements, and the two categories become difficult to separate.

Creative or Expressive Movements

To the young child, music and movement are often one and the same. Movement to music gives children another way to explore music (Ludowise, 1985). When children hear music, they move spontaneously. Movement and dance are children's play (Hsu, 1981). Even adults often nod heads, tap feet, and move bodies to the rhythm and sounds of music. Teachers need not try to "teach" children creative movements, but rather help them discover and release those creative movements that already exist (Stinson, 1977). Creative movements require limitations and rules that must be explained carefully to the children. When and if they break a rule, they need to be reminded that if they choose to participate, they must abide by the rules; if they cannot abide by the rules, they must be watchers. One basic rule of any movement experience is that children must move in their own space and not touch others. This rule helps children to become responsible for their own behavior. Another basic rule is to stop when the signal is given (music stops, hands clap, whistle blows). You may need additional rules, depending on your space, materials, and the children you are working with.

A few guidelines for effective creative movements are as follows:

1. Children need as much space as possible; therefore, if a game room, gymnasium, or similar space is available, use it. If you must stay in the classroom, move furniture aside to give adequate space. If you are planning the experience for outside, provide some limitations as to space.
2. Inhibitions can be avoided more easily if the teacher is not inhibited and is an active participant. Teachers can describe, suggest, and model for children (Andress, 1991). Do not press a child to join the group; sometimes shy children need to observe several times before joining. This is one of the values of having movement activities during free play. Inhibitions may begin with too much adult interference or with negative comments from either children or adults. Build confidence and give individual praise, especially to children who show some signs of hesitation.
3. Do not set yourself or any child up as a model to be copied by others. Rather, the modeling is a suggestion; and to be successful, the teacher must be aware of the children's motor capabilities (Andress, 1991). Do not make comparisons among children. In creative movements, the idea is to develop individuality of expression.
4. Do not use music as the only stimulus for creative movements. Sometimes no music at all is appropriate. Perhaps a story or poem will give a suggestion for creative movements, and sound effects made by the children could serve as the background for these movements.
5. As children become involved in movement explorations, try to redirect, challenge, and stimulate their discoveries by suggestions such as "Do what you are doing now in a slower way," or "Try moving in a different direction or at a different level," or "Try the same thing you were doing, but make it smoother or lighter." Verbalize or describe to the child what she or he is doing.
6. Avoid trite phrases such as "light as a feather." Instead, use phrases such as "Move as if you were a feather," "as if snow were hitting your nose," or "as if you were a butterfly landing on a flower." Children will make their own suggestions.

Movement Interpretations

Movement explorations and creative movement experiences can be used to interpret nearly every experience, thing, or phenomenon. (See the sections on music in the unit plans in the various chapters.)

The following are some suggested movement interpretations. This list can be expanded.

1. Life cycle of the butterfly
    a. Caterpillar crawling
    b. Caterpillar eating milkweed
    c. Caterpillar hanging very still from a branch or twig
    d. Chrysalis hanging very still
    e. Butterfly emerging from the chrysalis
    f. Butterfly drying its wings
    g. Butterfly flying
2. Piece of cellophane or lightweight plastic
    a. Item put in the teacher's hands without children seeing; children encouraged to guess what is too large, interpreting their guesses through movement; children encouraged to guess what the item might be, again interpreting their guesses through movement
    b. Teacher's hands opened, with children watching plastic move, and then interpreting what they see through movement
    c. Piece of plastic used for movement exploration
3. Shaving cream
    a. Spurting from aerosol can
    b. Foaming up
    c. Spreading on face
    d. Being used for shaving
4. Airplane sequence
    a. Starting motor
    b. Taking off
    c. Flying
    d. Coming in
    e. Landing safely
5. Popcorn
    a. Butter melting
    b. Popping
    c. Everyone ending in a ball shape on the floor, all "popped"

6. Water
    a. Dripping
    b. Flooding
    c. Flowing in a fountain
    d. Freezing
    e. Melting
    f. Spilling
    g. Sprinkler
7. Laundry
    a. Inside washing machine
    b. Inside dryer
    c. Being scrubbed on a washboard
    d. Being pinned to clothesline
    e. Drying in a breeze
8. Fishing
    a. Casting out
    b. Reeling in
    c. Pretending to be a fish
    d. Fly fishing
    e. Pretending to have a hooked line
    f. Frying and eating fish

These suggestions offer opportunities for sequences and a number of interpretations relating to a single idea. Also, there are many items, activities, and experiences that allow for a single possible interpretation, such as "Move like a pair of scissors," "Show me how you would move if you were a needle on a sewing machine," or "Show me how your dog moves when you have just come home after being gone for a while and the dog is glad to see you." As teachers train themselves to become aware of movement opportunities, they will be amazed at the daily experiences that lend themselves to these kinds of activities.

Although materials are not necessary for movement interpretations, they can add variety, and for some children may stimulate more movement exploration (Andress, 1991). Following are a few suggestions:

1. Plastic or cellophane (with a rule that the plastic cannot be put up to the face)
2. Scarves, drapery materials, or pieces of lightweight fabric
3. Ribbons, pieces of string or yarn, strips of crepe or tissue paper
4. Hoops
   a. Placed on floor to determine space—children do movements inside the hoop or around the outside
   b. Used with a partner
   c. Children moving in and out of a hoop in different ways
5. Balloons
   a. Children throwing and catching them with music
   b. Children following movements
   c. Balloon let go and deflated—and then movements followed
6. Balls
   a. Many different kinds
   b. Different parts of body moved to represent a bouncing ball
   c. Comparison of movements of different kinds of balls (e.g., table tennis, foam)
7. Ropes
8. Batons
9. Boxes
10. Rubber or elastic bands
11. Feathers
12. Crumpled paper
13. Tubes (inside waxed paper or paper towel rolls, decorated as desired)
    a. Story told, with children allowed to imitate and move with tubes
    b. Many different kinds of objects created for interpretations—oar, ski pole, gun, bow and arrow, spear, telescope, fishing pole
14. Parachute
    a. Children encouraged to move around the parachute, using locomotor movements or any kind of movement patterns.
    b. Parachute moved up and then down, with children and adults gathered around; then movements interpreted without the parachute
    c. Ball placed on top of the parachute, with each person trying to prevent it from going out or off the parachute at a particular spot.
    d. Each child encouraged to do sit-ups to music or in rhythm while sitting on the floor with legs extended

Musical Dramatizations

Musical dramatizations also tie in closely with creative movements; children again move and interpret something. Many stories have possibilities for excellent dramatization, or parts of stories can be dramatized as the children interpret some situation, action, or incident. Songs also have possibilities for musical dramatization, since they allow opportunities for children to interpret through body movements. Many music books for early childhood provide musical dramatizations and tell stories interspersed with music (Haines & Gerber, 1988).

Children also enjoy dramatizing poetry and nursery rhymes, often wishing to repeat the same activity over and over again.

Musical Instruments

Whenever possible, children should be exposed to musical instruments. We have mentioned the use of rhythm instruments because children will enjoy playing them. However, if other musical instruments can be played by the children, their use is encouraged. A tuba was placed in one preschool classroom to be explored and tried out during free play. Although many of the children had difficulty getting enough wind into the tuba to produce sound, they enjoyed having an adult blow into it while they pushed the buttons to alter the sounds. Other kinds of instruments can be explored by the children, and including visitors in this objective broadens the many possibilities.

We also hope that if teachers play instruments, they use them often as accompaniments or as listening experiences. There are many instruments that a teacher can learn to play with relative ease—the ukelele, guitar, autoharp, resonator bells, song bells, recorder, or Orff instruments. Children should be exposed to a variety of instruments, and many visitors are delighted to perform for the children. In one preschool classroom, a grandfather who played the fiddle entertained the children with his music for 45 minutes. Another group of children was entertained when a visitor played a saw. Take the children on field trips to places having instruments and musicians—music stores, junior high school band period, high school orchestra period, a concert or concert rehearsal. A group of Head Start children visited a nearby high school during the orchestra period and listened to the orchestra practice for a performance. Then they were invited to wander among the musicians, who encouraged the children to touch and explore. The children could begin to classify or sort instruments into groups such as stringed, percussion, wood, and metal instruments, or even to organize them by size.

Pictures of musical instruments have been produced by Bowmar Publications, Inc. (Glendale, CA). Each instrument is photographed individually, with educational material printed on the back of the photo. Also, young children can become familiar with musical symbols and notes through matching or lotto games. It is not intended to teach music theory in early childhood, but rather to encourage children to become acquainted with such symbols as bass and treble clefs, rests, whole notes, quarter notes, half notes,

and so on (Dumtschin, 1987). Music and stationery stores often carry stickers, posters, and other items with pictures of musical symbols or instruments.

Development of Appreciation for Music

Hopefully, if music is made an important part of the curriculum, children will develop an appreciation for music and its many assets. In addition to the planned musical activities, it is hoped that teachers will see the value of music used spontaneously throughout the day and in different areas of the curriculum. Often, all that is needed is to provide a setting and materials and an encouraging comment (Haines & Gerber, 1988). It is also hoped that throughout the day music will provide a background for play and activities. However, music should often be really listened to—without other distractions. Children should listen to others, to themselves, to live music, and to recorded music (including marches, polkas, and waltzes). They should eventually learn to listen to various elements of the music. "Creativity exists both in the performance and enjoyment of listening to the music of others" (Matter, 1982, p. 305). Children can be exposed to the masterpieces in music directly through listening experiences. (If you do not have them in your classroom or library, they can often be borrowed from the public library in your area.) These masterpieces can provide a musical background for free play, art activities, science activities, or other desired projects. Children can listen to and learn to appreciate the music of different cultures, which provides a link among people (Wolf, 1992). All these associations with good music assist the children in developing appreciation for music.

Summary

"A good musical environment is necessary if the child is to realize his or her maximum potential" (Matter, 1982, p. 306). Early experiences with music should be varied and should consist of both listening and participation (Matter, 1982). Music, a universal language, is a most important element of the early classroom curriculum. It allows and encourages enjoyment, attentive listening, moving to the beat, pleasure, creative expression, emotional balance, positive self-concept, music appreciation, and development of musical-related skills (i.e., rhythm, meter, pitch, tone). The most important emphasis on music, however, should be enjoyment. As teachers' own musical competencies and abilities increase, they become much more capable of providing the kinds of activities that result in the development of children's own musical competencies and abilities. Although songs and singing are the most common experiences, there are many others: musical games, rhythm activities, fundamental locomotor movements, musical instruments, and development of musical appreciation. Music ought to be an integral part of the early childhood experiences for each child.

Student Learning Activities

1. Why is music an important part of the early childhood curriculum? How do you plan to implement it as a part of your curriculum? How could you improve your music skills? Are there particular areas you could work on?

2. Begin a music file of songs you plan to use in your curriculum. Use the references suggested in this chapter for both records and books.

3. Using at least one of the suggestions for providing variety in singing given in this chapter, teach a song to a group of children between 2 and 8 years of age.

4. Visit a preschool, kindergarten, or first-grade classroom and observe how music is included in the curriculum. Are music tools and instruments a part of the learning environment? Are appropriate tapes and/or records available and used? Does the teacher sing to and with the children? Did you see any musical games, rhythm activities, or creative movements being used with the children? Were rhythm instruments available? Were they teacher made and/or commercial?

5. Make a list of music equipment and supplies you would want in your classroom.

6. Listen to and evaluate at least three recordings suggested either in this chapter or by your instructor. How would you use these recordings?

7. Evaluate at least three of the music books suggested as references and resources for this chapter. What do you like and what do you not like about each book?

8. Make at least two teacher-made rhythm instruments. (Refer to Appendix A for suggestions, in addition to those included in this chapter.)

9. Add to the list of suggested movement interpretations or creative movements given in this chapter. With a group of children, use one of the suggestions and evaluate your experience.

10. Plan a musical dramatization.

11. Do a web or unit plan for an early childhood song or song picture book, or evaluate and add to the one illustrated in this chapter.

Suggested Resources

Children's Books and Early Childhood Music and Songbooks

Many excellent early childhood songbooks are no longer in print. However, they are often available and have good selections of songs. Consult libraries, book stores, schools, and other sources for out-of-print books and for those currently on the market.

Amery, H. (1989). *Children's songbook.* Tulsa, OK: EDC.

Baby's book of lullabies and cradle songs. (1990). New York: Dial.

Beal, K. (1990). *Big book package* (4 vols.). (Multicultural sing-along big book program series.) Reading, MA: Addison-Wesley.

The big book of children's songs. (1990). Milwaukee: H. Leonard.

Cassidy, N. (1990). *Kids songs jubilee.* Palo Alto, CA: Klutz.

Cassidy, N. (1991). *Kids' songs: Sleepyheads.* Palo Alto, CA: Klutz.

Clark, K. B. (Ed.). (1993). *Traditional black music.* New York: Chelsea House.

Cooper, D. (1992). *Recycled songs.* New York: Random House.

Davol, M. (1992). *The heart of the wood.* New York: Simon & Schuster.

Fox, D., & Marks, C. (1987). *Go in and out the window: An illustrated songbook for young people.* New York: Metropolitan Museum of Art and Henry Holt.

Glazer, T. (1983). *Music for ones and twos: Songs and games for the very young.* New York: Doubleday.

Glazer, T. (Ed.). (1988). *Tom Glazer's treasury of songs for children.* New York: Doubleday.

Glazer, T. (1990). *Mother Goose songbook.* New York: Doubleday.

Goode, D. (1992). *Diane Goode's book of silly stories and songs.* New York: Dutton.

Gutmann, D. P. (1990). *Nursery songs and lullabies.* New York: Putnam.

Hoermann, D., & Bridges, D. (1988). *Catch a song.* Nashville: Incentive Publications.

Marzollo, J. *Pretend you're a cat.* (1990). New York: Dial.

McGee, S. (1992). *I'm a little teapot.* New York: Doubleday.

Mettler, B. (1976). *Creative dance in kindergarten.* Tucson, AZ: Mettler Studios.

Mettler, B. (Ed.). (1979). *Materials of dance as a creative art activity.* Tucson, AZ: Mettler Studios.

Mettler, B. (1980). *The nature of dance as a creative art activity.* Tucson, AZ: Mettler Studios.

Nelson, E. L. (Ed.). (1986). *The fun-to-sing songbook.* New York: Sterling.

Nelson, E. L. (1992). *Musical games for children of all ages.* Woodstock, NY: Beekman.

Raffi. (undated). *The Raffi singable songbook.* Toronto: Chappell.

Raffi. (1986). *The second Raffi songbook.* Toronto: Chappell.

Raffi. (1989). *The Raffi everything grows songbook.* New York: Crown.

Raffi. (1992). *Baby beluga.* New York: Crown.

Ramsey, M. E. (Ed.). (1984). *It's music.* Wheaton, MD: Association for Childhood Education International.

Richards, M. H. (1985). *Let's do it again!* Portola Valley, CA: Richards Institute of Music Education and Research.

Rinehart, C. (1980). Music: A basic for the 1980s. *Childhood Education, 56,* 140–145.

Roth, K. (1992). *Lullabies for little dreamers.* New York: Random House.

Rounds, G. (1990). *I know an old lady who swallowed a fly.* New York: Holiday House.

Sale, L. (1992). *Growing up with music: A guide to the best recorded music for children.* New York: Avon.

Scelsa, G., & Millang, S. (1992). *Dancin' machine.* New York: Random House.

Scelsa, G., & Millang, S. (1992). *The world is a rainbow.* New York: Random House.

Seeger, R. C. (1992). *American folk songs for children.* Hamden, CT: Shoe String Press.

Sharon, L., & Sharon, B. (1985). *Mother Goose.* Boston: Atlantic Monthly.

Smith, R. B., & Flohr, J. W. (1984). *Music dramas: For children with special needs.* Denton, TX: Troostwyk.

Warren, J. (1987). *Mini-mini musicals.* Seattle: Warren.

Weikart, P. (1988). *Movement plus rhymes, songs, and singing games*. Ypsilanti, MI: High/Scope.

Weissman, J. (1984). *Sniggles, squirrels, and chicken pox*. Overland Park, KS: Miss Jackie.

Westcott, N. B. (1990). *The lady with the alligator purse*. New York: Little Brown.

Wickstrom, S. K. (Illus.). (1988). *Wheels on the bus* (Raffi songs). New York: Crown.

Williams, V. B. (1988). *Music, music for everyone*. New York: William Morrow.

Winn, M. (Ed.). (1974). *The fireside book of fun and game songs*. New York: Simon & Schuster.

Wirth, M., & Stassevich, V. (1983). *Musical games, fingerplays, and rhythmic activities for early childhood*. Englewood Cliffs, NJ: Prentice-Hall.

Wiseman, A. (1979). *Making musical things*. New York: Macmillan.

Zeese, D. (1988). *Sing a song of concepts*. Washington, DC: Looking Glass.

Zeitlin, P. (1982). *A song is a rainbow: Music movement and rhythm instruments in the nursery school and kindergarten*. Glenview, IL: Scott, Foresman & Co.

Records, Tapes, and Cassettes

We suggest the following because we are familiar with them and have achieved musical successes in using them. You may have others you enjoy using just as much as these; perhaps the choice will depend on what you have available. Many of these recordings serve various purposes: teaching a song, playing a game, experiencing rhythms, or moving creatively.

A.B. LeCrone Co.
  Activities for rainy days
  The Hokey Pokey and other favorites
A&M Records
  Raffi with K. Whiteley
Alcazar (Kids' Records)
  A child's look at what it means to be Jewish
Alcazar (Lemonstone)
  Mostly matzoh
Alfred Publishing Co.
  It's Time for Music
B/B Records
  Rabbits dance: Marcie Berman sings Malvina Reynolds

Bowmar-Noble
  Bowmar orchestral library
  Children's rhythms in symphony
  Dance-a-folk song
  Folk songs for little singers
  Fun with music
  Kindergarten songs
  Know the orchestra
  Little favorites
  More singing fun, No. 1
  Nursery and Mother Goose songs
  The rainy day record
  Rhythm is fun (rhythm and locomotor activities)
  Rhythm time. No 1 (basic locomotor skills and rhythms)
  Rhythm time, No. 2 (creative interpretations)
  Rhythms to reading
  Singing fun
  Singing games
  Singing games and dances
  The small dancer
  The small listener
  The small player
  The small singer
  World of marches
Camden—RCA Records
  Lullabies for sleepy-heads
Campus Film Distribution Corp.
  Dance, sing, and listen (5101)
  Dance, sing, and listen again (5111)
  Dance, sing and listen again and again (5121)
  Dance to the music (5161)
  The electronic record for children (5141)
  The way out record for children (5131)
Cheviot Corporation
  Action songs for everyday (T-316)
  Action songs for indoor days (T-311)
  Singing games (T-321)
The Child's World
  Birds, baboons, and barefoot bears
CMS Records, Inc.
  Music for 1's and 2's
Columbia Records
  Little white duck and other children's favorites
  The sounds of India
Discovery Music
  Lullaby Magic
Educational Activities/Adventures in Rhythm
  Adventures in rhythm
  And one and two

Call-and-response rhythmic group singing
Counting games & rhythms for the little ones
Growing up with Ella Jenkins
I know the colors in the rainbow
Jambo and other call-and-response songs and chants
Little Johnny Brown
Looking back and looking forward
My street begins at my house
Play your instrument and make a pretty sound
Rhythm and game songs for the little ones
Rhythms of childhood
Seasons for singing
Songs, rhythms and chants for the dance
This-a-way-that-a-way
This is rhythm
You'll sing a song and I'll sing a song

Educational Activities
Altogether songs and marches
Basic concepts through dance
Circle games, activity songs, and lullabies
Clap snap and tap
Creative movement and rhythmic exploration (AR533)
Dancing numerals
Dancing words
Easy does it
Everybody cries sometime
Feelin' free
Finger games
Fingerplays and footplays
Folk song carnival (AR524)
Getting to know myself
Holiday songs and rhythms
Homemade band (AR545)
Honor your partner
Ideas, thoughts, and feelings
Learning basic skills through music, Vols. I, II, and III
Marches
Modern tunes for rhythms and instruments (AR523)
Mod marches (AR527)
Movement exploration
Movin' (AR546)
Patriotic and morning time songs (AR519)
Perceptual motor activities using rhythm instruments
Perceptual motor rhythm games
Pretend

Rainy day dances, rainy day songs
Rhythms for today
Rhythm stick activities
Sea gulls
Sensorimotor training in the class
Simplified folk songs (AR518)
Spin, spider, spin
Witches' brew
Won't you be my friend

Elephant Records
Mainly Mother Goose

Featherstone
Lakota/Dakota flute music

Folkway Records and Service Corp. (Distributed by Scholastic Book Services)
American game and activity songs for children (FC7674)
American Indian dances
And one and two
Children's activities to music for kindergarten
Counting games and rhymes for the little ones
Early childhood songs
Edgar Kendricks sings for the very young
Learning as we play (FC7659)
More learning as we play (FC7658)
More songs to grow on (FC7676)
Nursery rhymes—Rhyming and remembering
Plan your instruments and make a pretty sound
Rhythms of childhood
Song and play time with Pete Seeger (FC7526)
Songs to grow on (FC7675, FC7501)
This-a-way, That-a-way
You'll sing a song and I'll sing a song

G. K. Mayer Distributors
Favorite animal songs
Nursery songs and lullabies

Ginn & Co.
Dance-a-story

Golden Glow Recordings
Good morning, sunshine! Songs for a day full of wonder

Hart Stone Press
Imagination and me
I like me
Dandy-lions never roar

High Windy Audio
Stories and Songs for Little Children

Kimbo Educational
Bean bag activities
Dances for little people

Fun activities for fine motor skills
Get a good start
I like myself
It's toddler time
Nursery rhymes for little people
Preschool playtime band
Simplified lummi stick activities
Sing-a-song of action
Songs and activities for children with special needs
Toddlers on parade

Look At Me Productions
Amazing musical movements
Look at my world

Lyons Band
Chicken fat
Childhood rhythms
Lullaby time for little people
Nursery rhymes for little people

Miss Jackie
All about me
Hello rhythm
Let's be friends
Lollipops and spaghetti
Peanut butter, Tarzan, and roosters
Sniggles, squirrels and chicken pox

Moose School Records
Take me with you!

Pearce-Evetts Productions
Animals, Vol. 1
Family and friends, Vol. 2

Red Rover Records
Did you feed my cow?

Scholastic Book Services
Adventures in rhythm (SC7682)
American folk songs for children
American Negro folk and work songs
Call-and-response rhythmic group singing
   (SC7638)
Rhythm and game songs (SC7680)
Song and play-time

Ta-Dum Productions
Dance in your pants

Tickle Tune Typhoon
Hug the earth

Troubadour Records
Raffi: Baby beluga
Raffi: Corner grocery store

Raffi: More singable songs
Raffi: One light, one sun
Raffi: Raffi's Christmas album
Raffi: Rise and shine
Raffi: Singable songs for the very young

Young People's Records/Children's Record Guild
All aboard—train to the zoo; train to the farm;
   train to the ranch
The carrot seed (1003)
Grandfather's farm (5004)
Me, myself, and I; My playful scarf; Nothing to do
My playful scarf (1019)
Ride 'em, cowboy (5001)
Sunday in the park (1010)
Train to the farm (1011)
A visit to my little friend (1017)

Youngheart Records
Holidays and special days
On the move with Greg and Steve
Quiet moments with Greg and Steve
We all live together (Vols. 1, 2, 3, 4)

Multimedia Kits

Disney's greatest musical moments. Walt Disney.

Films, Filmstrips, and Videos

All about music. Pyramid Films.
Dance with joy. Documentary Films.
Developing rhythm in young children. Miss Jackie.
Developing skills with music. Miss Jackie.
Fast and slow. Coronet Films.
Feeling good with music. Miss Jackie.
Hello rhythm, Miss Jackie.
I've got music in me. Miss Jackie.
Learning through the arts. Churchill Films.
Lollipop opera. Pyramid Films.
Music makes me feel good. Miss Jackie.
Peter and the wolf. Pyramid Films.
Sing, you'll feel better inside. Miss Jackie.
Singing with young children. Miss Jackie.

Computer Software

Magic melody box. Human Touch. (Atari).
Music. Lawrence Hall of Science. (Apple).

CHAPTER
ten

Creativity and Art

Introduction

Matthew, a preschool child, ran to the teacher anxiously one morning and announced: "Come over to the easel. I just painted a red bird with yellow eyes, and it looks like it is *really* flying!" As the teacher went to the easel, she beheld a red bird with yellow eyes that did indeed look as if it were *really* flying. The freeness of Matthew's painting created an impression of movement—a red bird with yellow eyes, in flight!

Art, if presented properly, offers great potential for developing the child's creativity. Creative art is *not* imitation; rather, it is self-expression (Clemens, 1991). One's own work is never like anyone else's work (Mearns, 1958). Remember—not all children respond to art experiences and materials in the same way!

Art materials should be readily accessible to young children. Markers, paste, clay, crayons, and paints should be in a place where children have access to them whenever they desire (Clemens, 1991). As children draw, they learn about such art qualities and properties as color, line, shape or form, space, design, mass or volume, pattern, and texture (Dyson, 1988; Feeney & Moravcik, 1987; Schirrmacher, 1986). "When children draw, they are not simply communicating about their experiences; they are solving visual problems as well" (Dyson, 1988; p. 26). As children paint and draw their ideas on paper, they "think and talk their way through a picture" (Throne, 1988, p. 13).

Even though we often are unable to recognize and identify a child's particular drawing or painting, the progressive steps and understandings are valuable. "Much of young children's art is private, egocentric, and not intended to look like something" (Schirrmacher, 1986, p. 4). As the young artists smear, brush, dab, and swirl paint or glue, we must remember that the efforts and process are more important than the product (Schirrmacher, 1986). Appropriate comments, sincerely and carefully expressed, provide encouragement and support to young children in their art endeavors and explorations. "Just as too much seasoning can ruin a gourmet meal, excessive

Coloring with markers provides a change from using crayons and tends to stimulate extended interest and creativity in self-expression.

comments from an adult can turn off the child artist" (Schirrmacher, 1986, p. 6). Remember, too, the importance of making sure that the creative art curriculum and environment are developmentally appropriate for young children (Bredekamp, 1986).

Values of Children's Artwork

The child's artwork has many values, and art should be included as an important area of the curriculum. It does require careful preparation on the part of the teacher, as well as close supervision, and it may be messy; nevertheless, it has great worth in programs for young children. Often it is avoided because of lack of conviction regarding its value, or because of messiness and the cleanup requirement. Early childhood teachers should recognize the great values of children's artwork and provide many varied art experiences. Following are some of the benefits of art experiences for young children:

1. Art offers opportunities for self-expression and individualism. For some children, art media experiences may be one of the few means of self-expression (Clemens, 1991). Young children's art expresses their thinking *and* feelings (Francks, 1979). There are children who do not communicate feelings well through verbal language, music, physical activities, writing, or other areas; however, they are able to express themselves through art media. For every child, art materials should offer the opportunity for self-expression, for celebrating individual uniqueness. "Before our eyes, young child make their own personal, visual, written statement as a map of the mental and emotional strides they have already taken and as proof of their uniquely creative personality" (Francks, 1979, p. 21).

2. Art experiences are satisfying to most children. They enjoy creating, working with the raw materials, the processes involved in the art activity, and the product achieved through creative art endeavors.

3. Art activities are therapeutic. Whatever the kind of art project, it offers a catharsis for the child's feelings and emotions that may not be expressed in any other kind of activity. Art activities provide a time to relax from the structure, and sometimes the rigidity, of the school day. They can be the means by which many children free themselves of pent-up tension and frustration, and create feelings of pleasure and joy (Maxim, 1989).

4. Art activities offer training, skill, and development in eye–hand coordination. Children learn to use scissors, manipulate and handle glue and paste, and work with a paintbrush and other tools, all of which promote eye–hand coordination. Most art activities re-

quire small-muscle skill, and as the child practices, this skill is improved.

5. As children mature and advance through the stages of art, they devote more thinking, planning, and organizing to their projects. Thus the way they interpret ideas, solve problems, and think through concepts can be reflected in their artwork. Much can be learned about a child's feelings and knowledge through artwork.

In addition, art activities provide opportunities for language and communication skills as children listen to directions, talk to one another as they work, and describe their efforts and products as they finish. Science skills and concepts are often demonstrated before their eyes as they work with and combine various media. For example, finger painting provides hands-on experience in combining colors or making shades of colors. Children find great satisfaction in sensory exploration with the various media provided in art activities. Their satisfaction in the process and their pride in the product can make valuable contributions to boosting self-esteem in young children. There must be some wonderful, inherent, positive reasons why young children approach creative art activities with the drive, interest, and eagerness that is so often seen. Creative art is a vital and important part of the early childhood curriculum.

Fostering Creativity Through the Arts

There are a number of guidelines for teachers in using art as a method of fostering creativity in the young child.

1. Avoid patterns, ditto outlines, and coloring books; they do not promote creativity (Clemens, 1991). Children enjoy experiences with art materials and media. The young child who has not been exposed to the rigid structures of dittos and coloring books or the structured expectations of adults or older children enjoys the freedom of expression that unstructured art activities offer. Only when art activities are unstructured and utilize raw materials does the child have an opportunity for creative expression. If approached in the right way, every art project offers possibilities for encouraging creativity. Unfortunately, when activities are structured (coloring, painting, or collaging dittoed or precut patterns), art is a powerful force that works against the child's creativity. How does this happen? When children become dependent on the lines or patterns of others, they begin to think that they cannot perform on their own. For example, when a pattern of a horse is given to them to color, they will notice the sophistication of the drawing and how much it really does look like a horse. When they next try to make a horse, the pattern comes to mind, and since they might not be able to duplicate it, they say, "I can't draw a horse." Perhaps not long before they had colored the horse, they had happily and confidently sketched a picture of a horse. To many adults it may not have looked exactly like a horse, but they had enjoyed the freedom of using their self-expression in creating their horse. That freedom, that creative expression, becomes lost for many children when they become dependent on the outlines of adult artists. According to Lowenfeld and Brittain (1987), children may enjoy coloring books because they are not required to think for themselves. They become dependent on someone else's art, impression, or outline, and in so doing become less confident in their own expression. The outlines of others so closely resemble the actual objects that children no longer consider their own efforts correct or worthwhile. Art is an activity that is a personal expression of one's own ideas or reactions. It is never like anyone else's work. Note the individualism expressed in the following poem:

*Patterns**

by Jean Warren

Too soon
The patterns
Tell us how

To move

Too soon

Leave your dreams
Outside the door.

All sit!
All stand!
Listen now!
The sky is blue.
Cut the line.
Make a star.
Stop!
Story time.

Too soon

And soon
The patterns
Tell us how
To think
To feel

Too soon
The originals are gone
And in their place
The pattern of a single face.

2. Through art, help the children develop positive views of themselves. Let them know that you have faith in their efforts. Tell them often, "You can." Discourage the use of models and patterns, and particularly praise their own unique efforts. Help the children to know that what they create is their own, and that they should strive to please themselves—not you, not other children, and not other adults. Combs (1962) says: "With a positive view of self one can risk taking chances; one does not have to be afraid of what is new and different. . . . A positive view

* Reprinted by permission from *Young Children*, Vol. 33, No. 2 (Jan. 1978), p. 53. Copyright © 1978, National Association for the Education of Young Children, 1834 Connecticut Avenue N.W., Washington, DC 20009.

of self permits the individual to be creative, original, and spontaneous" (p. 141).

3. Give affirmation and praise of the children's work. Let them know that you value uniqueness, diversity, and difference. As you praise and talk to the children about their work, do not force or pressure them into telling you what it is; it may not be anything at all but rather an exploration of the materials (Clemens, 1991). This is particularly true with younger children. In visiting with them and discussing their work, you can comment on design, shape, and color, and invite them to tell you about their picture or how it makes you feel. However, Francks (1979) feels that teachers should take the role of quiet observers during children's art experiences. She states: "Whether or not young children wish to talk about their drawing is of far less significance than the fact that they have chosen to set down their thoughts in a manner they selected, unaided and unhampered" (p. 21). She goes on to point out that teachers should let children either talk or be silent about their artwork, whichever they choose. If they describe it, you may wish to write their descriptive words (exactly as they were said) on the picture—but you must have their permission to do so.

   You will also show interest, appreciation, and affirmation for their work by putting their names on their pictures (if they are unable to write their names themselves) and by displaying their pictures. However, it is unwise to display any of the pictures unless they can all be displayed, particularly if only the "best" ones are selected. It is also best to display artwork at the children's eye level—not yours.

4. Do not do the children's artwork for them, do not edit their work, and do not provide models for them to follow. You may want to show them how to use the materials provided, but then allow them to explore, experience, try out, and manipulate the media themselves. As you observe children working,

there may be times for needed assistance, especially if the materials are being presented and used for the first time.

5. Do not evaluate the children's artwork. Teachers are conditioned to evaluate, but children should be free in the art area to express themselves without fear of being evaluated. The teacher's role is to "provide time, space, place, materials for children, and then allow them the dignity of 'doing their own thing'" (Francks, 1979, p. 21). Do not grade art.

6. Help parents value their children's creative efforts. The children not only enjoy the process but are very proud of the product. Shane had painted his first finger painting, but he was unable to take it home because it had not dried adequately. It was difficult for him to leave the painting at school, and he made sure that he knew where it would be waiting for him the next day. His first words after arriving at school the following day were, "Do I get to take my picture home today?" Young children are proud of their work; teachers should also be proud of the work, and parents can be helped to gain an appreciation for it as well. Many parents do not understand that children go through stages of development in art just as they do in every other aspect of growth. Children universally progress through the same series of stages in their early art development. Scribbling begins at age 2 or earlier, extending up to the age of 4 or 5, at which time the child begins to draw symbolically (Kellogg, 1967). Kellogg (1970) has described at least 20 basic scribbles used by children, such as vertical, horizontal, diagonal lines, and other lines and patterns.

Parents may not understand that scribbling is a valuable stage of art (Francks, 1979). Many times they do not value children's artwork as an artistic and creative effort. Sharing with parents guidelines for fostering creativity in art is therefore a worthwhile educational endeavor. Most of-

ten they will appreciate the insight and enlightenment given to them. It is difficult to measure the long-term effects this new appreciation may have on promoting the child's creativity.

7. Expose the children to works of art. Visit art galleries, and borrow from your public library reproductions of paintings by famous artists and display them in your room. Comment on the art or illustrations in picture books. Using postcard-sized reproductions of artwork available from museum gift shops, have the children match or pair those that are identical. They can also be grouped into such categories as subject, color, artist, size, or others. If the children know how to read, they can learn the names of artists and the titles of paintings. Why not, as Wolf (1986) suggests, let children "begin to cultivate good taste during their impressionable years" (p. 19)?

Preparing and Organizing Art Activities

Art activities require careful planning and preparation on the part of the teacher. Very often, the success of a project rests on its preparation not on the project itself. The following guidelines are useful:

1. Establish rules with the children concerning the care and use of art materials. They need to know that supplies and materials cannot be wasted. They cannot damage school property or other children's property with art supplies. Young children must be taught that art supplies are not for eating; many children cannot resist eating the tempting school paste.

2. Have all the materials and supplies needed for the project set up and organized. Since you have also carefully thought about what will be needed, all the supplies and materials are available.

3. Try out art activities ahead of time so that you know how to use the materials and can assist the children in learning how to use them. A student teacher was planning an art activity using plaster of Paris. She did not work with it beforehand to become familiar with its properties. In making preparations for the day's activity, she carefully mixed the plaster of Paris before class began. Two hours later the children were prepared for their art activities, but the plaster of Paris had already set when it was brought to them. The teacher should know, for each activity planned, what kinds of materials are needed, what thickness of paint is desired for that particular activity, how long the string should be for string painting, or whether glue or paste works better with a button collage. All these questions, and others, need to be answered before the children begin; they are best answered when the teacher tries out the project ahead of time.

4. A sponge, soapy water, and other necessary cleanup materials should be available for the children to use; they can be encouraged to clean up when they are finished.

5. Cleanup should be made as easy as possible. For many art activities, tabletops can be covered with butcher paper or old newspapers for rapid change and cleanup. Containers of soapy water can be provided for glue brushes or paintbrushes as soon as children are finished with them. Aprons or old short-sleeved shirts should be worn by the children to protect their clothing.

6. The children should have adequate working space during the activity. If there is no large space available, perhaps the activity can be done in smaller groups during free play. Or the children could be divided into groups; while one group is participating in the activity, the other children are involved in other projects.

7. Art activities need plenty of time—time for setting up, time for exploring and creating with the raw materials provided, and time

for proper cleanup. Too often art experiences become rushed, taking the enjoyment and even some of the creativity out of the projects.

8. If paintings need to dry, plan ahead of time for a drying place. A place for finished products should be provided. If one child's picture is displayed, all the other children should have their pictures displayed.

Materials for Art Activities

Materials for art activities should be handled carefully and should not be wasted. Children need ample supplies. Thus, if costly supplies are desired, use them less frequently, but when they are used, supply an adequate amount! Many of the items used in projects were previously discarded and should be collected for storage in clean containers in an art-supply storage area. Empty plastic containers, aluminum containers and plates, aerosol lids, and so on are useful for many art projects. Some of the supplies may belong to an individual child, whereas other materials are shared by several children.

Many of the materials discussed in the following sections can be combined with other media. For example, instead of using finger paint alone, add sand, confetti, or glitter. Combine crayon drawings with finger painting. First make crayon drawings and then finger paint over them. Or use cut-up tissue paper with the paint at the easel. Let the child first paint a picture or explore with the paints and brush; then place pieces of tissue paper on the paint. The paint will act as a glue, and the tissue paper will adhere to the picture when it is dry.

Surfaces

Include butcher paper (cut into small pieces or left longer for murals), construction paper, paper bags, paper towels, newspaper, sandpaper, newsprint, cardboard, scraps of wood. Styrofoam meat or pastry trays, paper plates, wallpaper, wrapping paper, print-shop end rolls (often available from newspaper printers), boxes (any kind or size), cans, and ice-cream cartons. Art activities such as finger painting could be done directly on a table-top, or on a tabletop covered with butcher paper or other materials.

Variety so often increases interest! Vary the surface of the child's artwork; the novelty makes the activity and the product exciting for the child. Vary the size and shape of the paper. Art activities can be done on various sizes of paper, from very small bits to large pieces. Murals may be displayed either outside or inside the building. The individual child's portion may be cut for taking home, or the mural may be done as a class project, with none of it taken home. Use simple geometric shapes and unusual shapes and designs of paper, as well as shapes and designs cut into the paper.

Finger Painting

Using fingers and hands in a paint medium is called *finger painting*. Some children are hesitant to become involved in this kind of activity and are concerned about being messy. Provide encouragement for these children, but do not force them to become involved. Heather was not willing to finger paint the first three times the class finger painted. However, the fourth time the activity was provided, she painted with one finger; the next time, she became completely involved with all her fingers. Finger painting must be well organized and supervised, and children should wear aprons. The painting can be done on many of the previously mentioned surfaces. Some kinds of paper should be either taped down or dampened on the underside so that they will adhere to the table. Children will enjoy finger painting directly on the table top, and then will not worry about sliding, slipping, or tearing paper. If the child wants a picture, you can print a reverse simply by blotting the design onto paper. Children may sit or stand while painting, depending on the freedom

Finger paint is not only a creative art activity, but also can provide a most unusual texture experience.

of movement desired. The following are possibilities for finger-paint mixtures:

1. Soap flakes—water added to soap flakes and the mixture beaten to the desired consistency
2. Cream—shaving creams or other cosmetic creams; food coloring or dry, powdered paint added to change the color
3. Liquid starch—dry, powdered paint added for color

Foot Painting

Using any of the previously mentioned media, have the children paint with their feet instead of with their fingers and hands. After the children remove their shoes and socks, the desired kind of paper can be put on the floor, which has previously been covered with newspapers. The paper should be taped down at least on the corners.

One successful method is to put two rows of children's chairs parallel and facing one another. Then put one long strip of large-sized butcher paper between the two rows of chairs. Put a spoonful of finger paint in front of each chair. While painting, the children should stay seated in their chairs so that they do not slip. When they are finished, a small plastic tub of water and a bar of soap can be brought to their chairs so that their feet can be washed. This activity can also be done outside in warm weather, with a hose handy to wash the feet.

Painting and Printing

Although liquid paints may be purchased from commercial supply houses, mixing paint from powder is more economical and provides many opportunities for child involvement. Vary the color and the consistency of the paints. Sometimes provide only one color; at other times, provide two or more colors. Combine some of the colors to obtain more unusual colors. Try adding small amounts of dark colors to darken the colors, or add white paint to make pastel colors. The consistency of the paint will often be determined by the project. Straw painting requires fairly thin paint, whereas other paintings require thicker consistencies. Various media can be added to change the consistency of the paint. A frequently added medium is soap or detergent, which makes the paint go further, makes cleanup easier, and makes the paint adhere to waxy surfaces (such as those on milk cartons). Other added media include sand, sawdust, and confetti, which vary both in consistency and in texture. One teacher added strong spices to the paint during a unit on smells. Paints are used differently for painting and printing projects. In painting, the tool (brush) is used to rub or brush the paint on the surface. In printing, the tool is dipped into the paint and then applied to the paper. In this case, a sponge or paper towel saturated with paint may work better than a container of paint. Often printing turns out to be painting, but the wise

teacher is not concerned, since interest and involvement are of much more value than the end product.

Brush painting. Probably the most frequently used type of painting is brush painting. Although it is often done at the easel, it can be done in different areas and on a variety of surfaces. Vary the size of the brushes and the consistency of the paint.

Sponge painting. Cut sponges into small pieces; clip each piece inside a clothespin for a handle, or tie it to a tongue depressor or stick. Sponges can be used for both painting and printing.

Feather painting. Use several feathers clipped inside a clothespin, a feather duster, or a single feather of any size or kind dipped into paint and used similarly to brushes. If single feathers are used, they may be attached to the picture, resulting in both a painting and a collage of feathers.

Cotton-swab painting. The cotton swabs are dipped into the paint and used as brushes, pens, or sponges.

Vegetable and fruit printing. Pour the paint over a sponge or absorbent paper placed in a small dish or container. The fruit or vegetable is pressed onto the sponge and then onto a surface. Oranges, lemons, apples, grapefruits, onions, potatoes, green peppers, celery, pieces of corn on the cob, corncobs, and others work well. When potatoes are used, designs may be cut into the potatoes, or the potatoes may be cut around the design. (Use vegetables and fruits that are no longer edible.)

Button printing. Using epoxy glue, glue buttons onto small wooden dowels, and then use the buttons for printing. Vary the sizes, shapes, and designs of the buttons.

Spool painting. Empty wooden thread spools are attached to a handle made from an old coat hanger or other wire. Small nicks can be made on the ends of the spools to create variation in the design.

Yarn-on-a-metal-can painting. Yarn or string is glued with a strong glue to a small metal can. Paint is brushed over the yarn or string, and then the can is rolled over a surface.

Burlap, nylon netting, or other fabric printing. Small pieces of burlap, nylon netting, or other textured fabrics (2½ to 3 inches square) are wrapped over a sponge that has been attached to a clothespin or secured to a dowel with a piece of string or elastic. The fabric is then dipped into paint and printed or painted onto a surface.

Pinecone printing. Whole pinecones can be rolled in paint or cut into small pieces. The large ones with flat bottoms can be dipped into paint to make impressions on surfaces.

String-block printing. String, yarn, rickrack, lace, or similar materials are glued to small wooden blocks or scraps of wood. The blocks are dipped into the paint (or the paint is brushed onto one side), and the design is printed onto a surface.

Blot painting. The paper or other material is folded in half; small amounts of paint are dropped with either a spoon or an eyedropper on one inside half. The paper is then folded over, and the halves are blotted together.

String painting. One end of a piece of string or yarn, 8 to 10 inches in length, is attached to a clothespin. The string or yarn is then dipped into a container of paint. A piece of paper or other material has been folded in half and the string placed in a design on one inside half. The paper is folded over the string. One hand presses on the paper and string, and the other hand pulls the string out in different directions to make a design. If desired, the string can be dipped into paint of a different color and the same procedure repeated.

Straw painting. Paint is dropped onto a surface with an eyedropper or spoon. Then the paint is blown in different directions with a short straw.

Gadget printing. Gadgets found around the home are dipped into paint and then onto a surface to make the design. Gadgets such as forks, potato mashers, jar ring tops, and rubber door stoppers make interesting choices.

Collages

Many different kinds of materials and scrap items can be used for pasting collages. When collages are made, some materials or combinations of materials are glued onto a surface. Children can tear or cut their collage materials.

Glues. A variety of substances can be used for glue or paste. For gluing paper of any kind, an inexpensive paste may be used, such as *library* or *school paste.* It can be thinned, if desired, by whipping or beating with a rotary beater. Do not add water. It can also be used directly out of the jar. For heavier items, such as scraps of fabric or macaroni, *white glue* is suggested. Homemade *flour paste* can be used as a glue, along with homemade *cornstarch paste. Wheat paste* can be purchased inexpensively. *Plaster of Paris* can be purchased economically in bulk and mixed to a thick consistency. A small amount can be put on a base, and then various collage items can be pressed into it. Tissue paper, cut-up scraps of magazines, or similar light media can be glued to any kind of surface with *liquid starch.* The papers or tissue scraps are dipped into the starch and then pressed onto such surfaces as plastic aerosol caps (two of the same size could be glued together, with some objects placed inside, to make a musical shaker), glass baby food jars (to make banks, vases, pencil holders, etc.), or half-pint milk cartons (to make musical shakers). Although a little more difficult to use, *rubber cement* is another possibility. The kinds of glues and pastes mentioned can be put as a blob on waxed paper, aluminum foil, a metal lid, or a paper towel (easily cleaned up) and applied with the finger or a brush; or the collage items can be dipped into the paste or glue and then onto the surface.

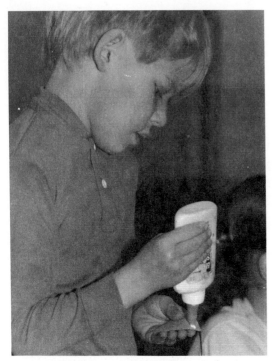
Successfully regulating the bead flow of glue from the bottle top is a great achievement.

Elastics
Keys
Sequins
Any kind of tape
Gummed stars,
    reinforcements, or
    labels
Confetti
Feathers
Bottle caps
Fabric
Sand
Beans
Colored salt
Seeds
Sawdust
Styrofoam
Wood chips
Toothpicks
Rocks and/or gravel
Leaves
Lace
Yarn scraps

Linoleum scraps
All kings of paper
    Wallpaper
    Tissue paper
    Crepe paper
    Newspaper
    Magazine scraps
Straws
Old jewelry
Spices
String
Washers
Brads
Canceled stamps
Eggshells
Cotton balls
Wrappers from candy
    bars
Labels from cans
Dried flowers and
    weeds
Hardware items
Carpet scraps

Suggested media. When children make a collage, they arrange, on a surface, a medium or combination of media in desired ways. Often their designs become intricate and unusual. Collage media can be found anywhere, including the garbage can, and practically everywhere indoors and outdoors. Paper can be torn or cut for collage work; three-dimensional objects also offer good possibilities. Collages can become part of class murals in various sizes and shapes. Be sure that the glue is strong enough to hold the medium or media chosen. The following list of suggested media is only a beginning; use your own imagination, along with the materials and discarded items on hand in your environment. You may use combinations of items; one item; a variety of one item such as buttons; or even a category of items such as beans, seeds, sewing items, or wood.

Sculpturing

When children sculpt, they pile on, build high, pat, roll, flatten, poke, and squeeze, depending on the materials provided.

Clay. The most frequently used sculpture medium is clay. It should always be available in every early childhood classroom. Clay must be neither too sticky nor too dry. It should be pliable, workable, and mobile. Children should be exposed to different kinds.

1. Play dough
    2 cups boiling water
    Food coloring (about 4–6 drops)
    3 T oil
    2½ cups flour
    ½ cup salt
    1 T alum
    Mix the food coloring with the water, and then add the oil. Add the liquid ingredients to the dry ingredients and knead them to-

gether. Form the material into balls and re-frigerate it in an airtight container. This play dough must be kept refrigerated when not in use, and it will not dry out like other salt-flour doughs. The texture and consistency are excellent!

2. Salt-flour clay or dough
   3 cups flour
   ³/₄ cup salt
   ½ tsp oil
   Water to achieve the right consistency

Mix the dry ingredients together with dry powdered paint for coloring, or add food coloring to the water. Gradually add water, and continue kneading and mixing until the clay is the desired consistency. This clay can be mixed and stored in an airtight container for a long period of time.

This clay can be used for making beads by rolling it into small balls and poking holes through each bead with a nail. The clay can also be used for making handprints, or it can be molded around a can, with collage items pressed into it for decoration. The clay can be left out to air-dry or can be baked until hard.

3. Oil-base modeling clay is very pliable and workable. It can be purchased from school stores or art-supply stores. It can be used over and over, and should be stored in plastic bags so that it retains moisture.

4. Pottery clay is a moist clay used by potters. It can be purchased from art-supply stores or from a college art department. It should be stored in plastic bags so that it remains moist and workable.

5. Bread dough can be molded like clay, and baked in the oven like ordinary bread, then eaten.

Wood sculpture. Small scraps of wood (obtained from a mill or construction site) are combined with other items and glued or nailed to a wood base. Paint the dried sculpture.

Box sculpturing. An assortment of boxes of different sizes and shapes is glued together. A cereal box makes an excellent base, and then smaller boxes are used to complete the sculpture. The sculpture can be painted; if powdered detergent is added to the paint, it will adhere to a wax-coated box.

Styrofoam sculpture. A structure can be built with a styrofoam base, scraps and pieces of Styrofoam, and toothpicks.

Miscellaneous Art Activities

Necklaces. Children enjoy making things they can wear. Both boys and girls delight in constructing necklaces. Make sure that a piece of tape is put on one end or a small object tied to it to hold the objects on. The end being used for stringing should be stiff; yarn or string can be dipped in wax, glue, or nail polish, or tape can be put around the end. Following are suggestions for stringing media.

1. *Colored macaroni.* Use smaller-sized macaroni, because it will go further and the child can spend more time stringing it. If large macaroni is used, the necklace will hold only 6 to 10 pieces. To color macaroni or similar media, put rubbing alcohol and food coloring in a jar. The darker and more intense the desired color, the more food coloring should be added. Put the macaroni in the jar and shake it for a few minutes. Then spoon it out onto paper towels to dry. (Use macaroni that is too old to eat.)

2. *Paper.* Use small pieces of paper cut into shapes or designs with holes punched in the middle. Flower shapes are easily made this way.

3. *Horse chestnuts or small blocks of wood.* Drill holes through each for stringing.

4. *Plastic straws.* Cut into varying lengths for stringing.

Hats. Various kinds of hats can be made for use in parades, games, musical activities, and so on.

1. *Paper plate hats.* Paper plate hats work best if a smaller paper plate is stapled to the back of a larger plate so that they are back to back. The smaller paper plate may have a hole punched on each side, with ribbons or strings attached to make the ties. The smaller plate then fits around the child's head and is not decorated. The larger paper plate will appear to sit on top of the head and can be decorated with collage paper flowers, cotton balls, flowers, or other objects.

2. *Crowns.* Cut a crown pattern for each child out of heavy paper such as poster paper. The paper can be decorated by painting, collaging, or printing. Add such items as gummed stars, glitter, aluminum foil, or old jewelry stones. Attach ties to the crown, staple bands of the heavy paper to the crown, and then staple these two ends together to fit the child's head.

3. *Newspaper hats.* Fold newspapers into various hat shapes and then decorate them.

4. *Spring hats or bands.* Make a band of paper about 1½ inches wide and long enough to extend about three-quarters of the way around the child's head; attach string or ties to the ends. Paper flowers can be cut out and glued on. Flowers can also be made by extending 1-inch squares of crepe paper over the end of a pencil to make a flower formation, which is then glued to the headband. Bows can be made by twisting rectangular-shaped crepe paper in the middle and then gluing the bows to the band. Another spring band can be made by cutting out the inside portion of a paper plate, decorating the rim, and attaching ties.

5. *Wig.* A brown paper bag is used to make a wig. Cut a face hole in one side of the bag, and then cut the rest of the bag into strips. Roll each strip on a pencil, crayon, or pen to curl it.

6. *Davy Crockett hat.* Cut a face hole in a brown paper bag, and then cut the rest about the length of the child's hairline.

However, in the back center, cut a long portion representing the tail. Decorate with crayons or other desired media.

Cotton-ball painting. Dip cotton swabs or balls into dry, powdered paint and smear them on paper. Pastel colors or shades work best. When the picture is finished, spray it with lacquer hair spray so that the paint does not rub off.

Melted crayon pictures. Using a vegetable grater or a small plastic pencil sharpener, make crayon shavings using old crayons. Do not use many of the darker colors. Mix the shavings together and put them in small containers. Sprinkle a few shavings onto half of the inside of a folded paper. Waxed paper works especially well because the finished picture is transparent and the two sides of the paper are sealed together. After the crayon shavings have been sprinkled onto one side of the paper, the other side is folded on top of the shavings. The picture is then placed between several layers of newspaper and ironed with a hot iron. The heat will melt the crayon shavings together. If waxed paper is used, the two portions will melt together. Small collage items may also be added with the shavings. For example, at Christmastime, cut holiday objects and shapes from tissue paper and add them, with glitter, to the shavings. Things from nature and the outdoors could be collected and added with the shavings. For example, one group of children made place mats in the fall by adding small seeds, dry weeds, and other outdoor fall treasures to the crayon shavings.

Salt or sand painting. Although termed *painting*, this process is actually a collage activity. Glue is spread onto a surface, and then sand or salt that has been put in saltshakers or other containers is sprinkled onto the wet glue. The excess salt or sand is then shaken off. (Color the salt or sand by adding a few drops of food coloring or powdered paint.)

Paper plates. Some suggestions for using paper plates have already been presented. Paper plates can also be stapled together and then decorated to make snow figures. They can also be decorated to make turtles or masks. Eye holes can be cut out, with big, floppy bunny ears and a bunny nose and mouth added, to make a bunny mask.

Egg cartons. Egg cartons can be used to make insects, ants, caterpillars, or other animals. They can be painted and then items glued on to make faces. Pipe cleaners can be used for legs and feelers.

Coffee filter butterflies. Dip the filters in water colored with food coloring. After they dry, they are pulled together across the diameter of the circle and attached with a clothespin. Glue a head on and attach pipe cleaner feelers for a completed butterfly.

Milk cartons. Milk cartons can be decorated and used to make the sections of a train or to make other vehicles such as boats or wagons. They can also be decorated as planting boxes or as baskets.

Ice-cream cartons. These cartons can be made into wastebaskets, flowerpots, drums, curler boxes, helmets, hats, or storage containers by collaging, painting, or finger painting them.

Paper cups or cans. Paper cups or cans can be decorated with desired media and used for pencil holders, planting containers, flowerpots, clay gardens, or musical instruments.

Rocks. Rocks can be painted and decorated as animals, pets, or other objects. They can also be glued together for sculpturing.

Cameras. Provide each child with a box that has holes punched in the longest sides so as to create a lens hole through which the child can see. Put a picture of the child inside the box, along with cutout magazine pictures of other people. Decorate the cameras. When dry, put an elastic band around the two sides of the box without holes. As the children peer through the punched holes, they pretend to take the picture by flipping the elastic. Then pretend that the picture is inside and already developed.

Soap bubbles. Make blowers out of old coat hangers bent to the desired size, or use plastic holders that link six-packs of sodas. Mix one of the following two recipes and give each child a small portion in an aerosol lid or similar small container. Let them blow bubbles outside; it prevents a sticky film from collecting on the floor.

Recipe 1

½ cup liquid dishwashing detergent
¼ cup sugar
A little water to dilute solution, if necessary

Recipe 2

8 oz liquid detergent (quality brand)
1 oz glycerin

Crayons and felt-tip pens. These art tools are easy to obtain and offer great creative opportunities for children when used on a variety of surfaces. Use water-based markers, rather than permanent markers, because the permanent markers may contain toxic solvents.

Chalk. Chalk can be used dry and then sprayed with lacquer hair spray to prevent it from rubbing off. Wet a paper with water, buttermilk, or liquid starch, and then use the chalk. Using these dampening methods makes the paintings much more brilliant, and the chalk sticks to the paper. Chalk can also be dipped into sugar water (a few tablespoons of sugar mixed with half a cup of water), buttermilk, or water for the same results.

Large boxes. Large boxes can be painted, sculpted, collaged, or decorated for play. A train could be made from a number of boxes, with ice-cream cartons being used on the front box to make the engine.

Summary

So many values emerge from children's creative art activities. A great deal of freedom lies within the bounds of limits, rules, and responsibilities. Individualism flourishes, self-expression flows, and there is satisfaction in both the process and the product. Art activities also have sensory qualities, often involving several of the senses at one time.

As teachers foster creativity in art during the early childhood years, children's abilities to dream and kindle new ideas, accept challenging tasks, and discover horizons not yet imagined are expanded. Ideas for better ways of doing things exist in the human mind, not in computers or other machines. The sooner the mind is encouraged and invited to create, the more able it will be to expand its capabilities and the more time it will have to reach its potential. It should be easy for teachers to defend the value of art experience in the curriculum.

Student Learning Activities

1. Visit an early childhood classroom when children are participating in an art activity. Evaluate how effectively creativity was fostered. Notice the various stages of art of the children participating. Was the activity well planned and set up, implemented, and cleaned up?

2. Collect art samples from children and study the various stages of art. One way to do this is to have a group of children draw a self-portrait, or simply give the children each a circle or paper plate and have them draw face portraits of themselves. What did you learn from this activity?

3. Make a list of the art supplies and equipment you would want to have in your classroom.

4. Begin an art portfolio of children's art activities by completing a sample of at least two art activities suggested for each section in this chapter. For example, do two finger paintings, at least two paintings and two printings, at least two collages, and so on. Label them, and describe the materials needed on the back. Add to the collection each time a new art activity is done.

5. Prepare and try out at least one of the playdough or clay recipes. Evaluate your results. Do you like the texture and consistency?

6. Visit several early childhood classrooms and evaluate the kinds of art experiences the children are having based on the children's artwork you see displayed in the rooms.

Suggested Resources

Early Childhood Education Creative Art References

Bos, B. J. (1982). *Don't move the muffin tins: A hands off guide to art for the young child.* Roseville, CA: Turn the Page Press

Chenfield, M. B. (1983). *Creative activities for young children.* New York: Harcourt Brace Jovanovich.

Cherry, C. (1990). *Creative play for the developing child: A teacher's handbook for early childhood education.* Carthage, IL: Fearon Teacher Aids.

Cherry, C. (1976). *Creative play for the developing child.* Carthage, IL: Fearon Teacher Aids.

Copple, C., Siegel, I., & Saunders, R. (1984). *Educating the young thinker: Classroom strategies for cognitive growth.* Hillsdale, NJ: Erlbaum.

Herberholz, B. (1985). *Early childhood art* (3rd ed.). Dubuque, IA: William C. Brown.

Jenkins, P. D. (1980). *Art for the fun of it: A guide for teaching young children.* Englewood Cliffs, NJ: Prentice-Hall.

Johnson, M. (1992). *Understanding and appreciating your child's art: How to enhance confidence in drawing, ages 2–12.* Los Angeles: Lowell House.

Lasky, L., & Mukerji, R. (1980). *Art: Basic for young children.* Washington, DC: National Association for the Education of Young Children.

Lowenfeld, V. (1988). *The nature of creative activity.* Irvine, CA: American Biography Service.

Taylor, C. W. (1986). Be talent developers. *Today's Education, 57,* 67–79.

Torrance, E. P. (1987). *Save tomorrow for the children.* Buffalo, NY: Bearly.

Wankelman, W., Wigg, P., & Wigg, M. (1989). *A handbook of arts and crafts* (7th ed.). Madison, WI: Brown & Benchmark.

Davis Mass, 50 Portland Street, Worcester, MA 01608, specializes in creative art activities and has many materials available. By writing to this company, you may obtain a complete list of its available art publications as well as information on its periodical, *School Arts.*

Films, Filmstrips, and Videos

Art for beginners: Fun with lines. Coronet Films.
Brush painting. Campus Films.
Building puppets with Pierrot. Coronet Films.
Clay. Campus Films.
Creating collages with Pierrot. Coronet Films.
Dough. Campus Films.
Early expressionists. Modern Talking Pictures.
Easy crafts. Eye Gate Media.
Fingerpainting. Campus Films.
Modeling clay with Pierrot. Coronet Films.
My art is me. University of California Extension Media Center.
Paste and collage. Campus Films.

Computer Software

Color 'n' canvas. Wings for Learning. (Apple IIGS).
Color me. Mindscape. (Apple, IBM, Commodore 64).
Magic Crayon. C & C Software. (Apple).
Picture perfect. MindPlay. (Apple, IBM).
Rainbow painter. Queue. (Apple, Commodore 64).

PART SIX

DEVELOPING SCIENCE AND CRITICAL THINKING SKILLS

Science and critical thinking skills encompass virtually every aspect of the early childhood curriculum. This part includes chapters on weight and balance; color; animals; plants; and temperature, weather, and seasons. However, math, sensory, social studies, and various art activities are also valuable in the development of science and critical thinking skills, when science becomes a way of thinking, communicating, and doing. It is not just a curriculum area, but also a learning style that entices a child to wonder, question, and discover, and to know and understand (Holt, 1989).

In every part of the curriculum, it is important for teachers to provide opportunities for children to refine and sharpen their thinking skills. Teachers should seek for ways to encourage questioning, experimenting, and discovery throughout the curriculum (Klein, 1991). "Thinking skills are mental abilities that help one to think, reason, and evaluate" (Brown, 1987, p. 102). Through sharing experiments, reading stories, and engaging in discussions and spontaneous conversations, children should be taught to think and use such questions as Who?, What?, Where?, When?, Why?, and How? "Redirecting, probing, and prompting techniques during discussion facilitate student thinking at higher levels" (Brown, 1987, p. 103). Teachers should value inquiry and thoughtfulness or reasoning above all other skills (Brown, 1987). Science especially provides opportunities for exercising these critical thinking skills. The following unfinished phrases will serve as springboards to deeper thinking for children:

What if . . . ?

I wonder why . . . ?

Were you surprised that . . . ?

Did you notice . . . ?

Did you think about . . . ?

Did it remind you of . . . ?

What do you think happened . . . ?

Can you think of another way to approach . . . ?

Is there another alternative . . . ?

How would you feel if . . . ?

These kinds of questions and inquiries encourage students "to question, to analyze and to look beyond the superficial for all possible answers" (Carr, 1988, p. 69). Children should learn to explain, add to, and validate their responses and answers. "Every teacher should create an atmosphere where [all] students are encouraged to read deeply, to question, to engage in divergent thinking, to look for relationships among ideas, and to grapple with real-life issues" (Carr, 1988, p. 73).

One approach for encouraging children to think is to have them become the teacher (Foley, 1988). When children explain an idea to someone else, they synthesize that idea into their own thinking more thoroughly. They should be encouraged to observe, question, find out, and then share what they have learned with others.

We must reach the point where we integrate thinking with the content of our curriculum (Carr, 1988). In other words, critical thinking should not be just tacked on as part of the curriculum where critical thinking exercises are scheduled; rather, it should be part of an integrated approach to the entire curriculum. Teachers should create an environment that stimulates critical thinking and inquiry (McMillen, 1986).

Young children think neither logically nor abstractly, but rather in concrete terms. Their reasoning is not systematic and does not lead to generalizations or the formation of logical concepts, but often to gross misinterpretations. These children are egocentric and view the world from their own perspective. Their thinking is bound by their perception; things are seen as they appear to be, or in terms of their external or surface features. Young children generally focus on only one attribute at a time. Science in the early childhood years must be taught in very concrete terms, using exploring, manipulating, questioning, comparing, and other process skills.

Science explorations happen in almost every unit and occur spontaneously nearly every day. Taking advantage of questions and incidental learning opportunities allows for limitless science and critical thinking skill development. Teachers of the young must seek to help children think in scientific ways, to foster thought processes that encourage children to utilize scientific ways and methods. The questions teachers ask, the comments they make, and their approaches to problem solving can do much to help children incorporate scientific thinking. "Adults facilitate children's engagement with materials and activities and extend the child's learning by asking questions or making suggestions that stimulate children's thinking" (Bredekamp, 1986, p. 10). The teacher must "guide scientific thinking through skillful questions and comments . . .

[and] . . . through such questions and comments, the teacher helps the children to evaluate and extend their experiences" (Maxim, 1989, pp. 468–469). However, explanations should not be too involved, intricate, or mystical. Teachers must communicate simple and honest facts that are appropriate for the child's level of understanding and interest.

Selected science activities must take into consideration the experiences and interests, ages, and special needs of the children (Modigliani, Reiff, & Jones, 1987). To be developmentally appropriate, these materials and experiences should be concrete, real, and relevant to the lives of young children, while allowing learning to take place through active exploration and interaction with adults, other children, and materials (Bredekamp, 1986). As children develop understanding and skills, then, teachers should increase the difficulty, complexity, and challenge of the activities (Bredekamp, 1986).

We should encourage children in their science education to learn the value of keeping records. Teachers can do the writing for young children who have not yet acquired writing skills; when children are able to write, they should write their own observations and keep their own records. Just as scientists are recordkeepers and record information such as how much, where, when does it happen, and what makes it happen, so must we teach young scientists the importance of recording the information they have observed (Beaty, 1992b).

Science is "asking questions, searching for answers, exploring, experimenting and perceiving. Science can teach patience and persistence, inquiry, open-mindedness, respect for honest evidence, resourcefulness, self-reliance, and respect for other people's opinions" (Holt, Ives, Levedi, & von Hippel, 1983, p. 6).

Some basic guidelines have been suggested to help children develop their science and critical thinking skills:

Encourage them to pay attention

Share science observations you make

Suggest activities that give them opportunity to explore scientific notions

Encourage them to notice causes and effects

Give them opportunity to talk about their experiences

Urge them to try new experiments and make new discoveries

Provide materials that will encourage scientific discoveries

Be curious and open minded yourself and have a positive attitude toward science discoveries (Holt et al., 1983, pp. 14–16)

Science is discovering and learning about the world through hands-on experiences with things in the environment (Smith, 1981). "When science is a firsthand experience, children not only learn science but also improve their other learning skills" (Kotar, 1988, p. 40).

An early childhood program should be child centered and activity oriented; it should provide children with a varied environment to explore at their own pace and according to their individual cognitive abilities. Both girls and boys should be encouraged in science activities and inquiry (Rivkin, 1992). In their active explorations, children should be encouraged to observe carefully, note similarities and differences, make predictions, test their predictions, ask questions, and interact with one another and with the teacher. They should be constantly encouraged to think and talk about what they are doing and seeing (Smith, 1981, p. 9). Science should be fun and provide joy for teachers and children as they explore and discover.

Be aware of the children's abilities and levels of cognitive growth, remembering to focus on the concrete. "Abstract concepts outside the realm of immediate experience should not be included in an early childhood science curriculum" (Smith, 1981, pp. 5–6). An overall goal of science in the early childhood classroom is to interest the children in the world in which they live. They can learn about and appreciate animals, plants, and all parts of the world, as well as learn to protect and preserve their environment. In any study of nature, children should learn the concept that all forms of life are interdependent, that there is a delicate balance and harmony in nature, and that as humans we must preserve this balance (Rivkin, 1992). They can develop meaningful, clear, and substantial concepts through their involvement in "child-centered and activity-oriented" experiences (Maxim, 1989, p. 494).

CHAPTER
eleven

Science Experiences*

Introduction

Science for young children is not so much a body of facts and information as it is a process of doing and thinking. Children have a natural curiosity about the environment in which they live. Their questions reflect their interest in everything about them—nature, people, animals, plants, and so on. "What does an earthworm eat?" "Do trees have birthdays?" "Why do magnets pick up pins?" These endless questions often open up avenues into the realm of science. As we answer questions through exploring, providing experiments and materials, and problem solving, we are supplying answers and encouraging the child's continued curiosity. This great emotion of curiosity and its importance in learning has been discussed by Carson (1956).

If I had influence with the good fairy who is supposed to preside over the christening of all children, I should

---

* The areas of physical science are presented in this chapter. For other discussions of the general sciences, refer to specific chapters.

ask that her gift to each child in the world be a sense of wonder so indestructible that it would last throughout life, as an unfailing antidote against the boredom and disenchantments of later years, the sterile preoccupation with things that are artificial, the alienation from the sources of our strength. (pp. 42–43)

The Teacher Sets the Stage for Science

The teacher's interest and curiosity will often kindle the child's interest in exploring and finding out. "Children's curiosity leads them to experiment and the more they experiment the more they learn science" (Holt et al., 1983, p. 6). When the teacher's behavior demonstrates a sense of wonder and curiosity, the children are able to model this (Harlan, 1991). Answered questions add to children's reserves of knowledge and increase their interest in, awareness of, and understanding of the world in which they are living. However, it is best to allow them to discover the answers themselves through exploring, reading, listening, observing, and other process skills.

To teach science effectively, it is suggested that teachers:

1. Give time, because children take time when they are engaged in exploring and discovering.
2. Know something, because the teacher's knowledge is what sparks and directs the children's learning.
3. Be open to their own lack of knowledge, but demonstrate their excitement in learning.
4. Value their own opportunity to interpret a question from their own perspective and interests.
5. Demonstrate for children how to record observations, because writing down what is observed and remembered enhances learning.
6. Provide materials and supplies for science explorations (Perry & Rivkin, 1992).

Daily Experiences with Discovery Science Add Depth and Interest for Young Children

Science is, and should be, a part of a child's daily experiences—"it is everywhere!" (Ziemer, 1987, p. 45). It is not a separate subject to be reserved for specific experiences in the curriculum; it is present in the world around the children, and they are anxious to explore it, discover answers, and build new understandings. Take advantage of the unplanned experiences, and select planned activities from the children's daily experiences, because these will be the most comprehensible and concrete (Rivkin, 1992).

Values of Science Activities

Science should not emphasize teaching children facts but should involve them in the process of understanding their world through observing,

manipulating, and becoming involved with science activities and materials (Neuman, 1992). The benefits of science for young children include the promotion of intellectual growth, greater potential for success in school, and opportunities for the development of positive self-images.

Process skills provide the framework for science education in early childhood and children should be encouraged to develop them as they participate in science experiences (Maxim, 1989; Neuman, 1992; Roche, 1977). Examples of process skills are observing, investigating, comparing, classifying, explaining, inferring, verifying, creating, communicating, analyzing, predicting, computing, recording, measuring, organizing, and hypothesizing. These skills are important in the cognitive, reasoning, and thinking processes. Process skills are, in fact, thinking skills; these skills will affect every area of learning, and can be particularly encouraged and developed in science activities. "Learning science process skills is the important thing, along with learning that science is fun" (Kotar, 1988, p. 40).

Teachers should pay careful attention to the skills just listed and should write direct objectives for science activities and other appropriate experiences that will assist in the development of these skills. Skillful, careful, and wise teaching is essential for children to be taught to observe, compare, create, communicate, analyze, and hypothesize. The kinds of comments, questions, and approaches to planned activities, as well as the activities themselves, make a difference in whether these process or thinking skills are developed. Teachers should constantly be aware of children's individual development in science and try to stretch their abilities by expanding process skills and teaching higher-level process skills as children are ready for them.

To elaborate further on the process skills that will be particularly utilized in early childhood: In *observing*, children are taught to use all their senses to learn about things and experiences. In *comparing*, children compare likenesses and differences among objects and ideas. For *classifying*, children are asked to group or sort by categories, to find something that does not belong, and to be able to name the group or say how the members of a group are alike. *Communicating* is using words orally, and for children in the later early childhood years, writing to explain or describe an event or happening. In *measuring*, children are involved in using standard or nonstandard units of measure; in either case, the children give a quantitative description. It may involve time, distance, volume, temperature, weight, or numbers. When children *infer* something, they observe and add meaning to their observation. When they are *predicting*, they guess what they expect will happen. When they *record* information, they either dictate or write down what they observe.

However, science is more than these processes alone. Science experiences in early childhood should help children form scientific concepts. "[Science] is knowledge and a way of knowing, knowledge of the universe, of the earth, of living organisms. It is the belief that the world is knowable and worth knowing, and that we can, by our actions, attain some knowledge of it!" (Howe, 1975, p. 58).

Science, then, enables children to better understand their world. By understanding their environment, some of their fears are alleviated, they are more comfortable with nature, and they have an increasing awareness of the events, people, and materials surrounding them. Science is of value because it creates high interest, is fun and exciting, and is enjoyable for the child (Rivkin, 1992). Through science studies, particularly open-ended or discovery activities, children develop methods of thinking that include problem solving, inquiry, reasoning, and rationalizing.

Science activities encourage children to observe, explore, inquire, and make generalizations, and they provide opportunities to use and develop sensory capacities—to see, hear, taste, smell, and touch. The children will learn to use skills that scientists use—inferring, observing, interpreting, classifying, and drawing conclusions. In addition, they will gain scientific knowledge.

Approach to Teaching

To be most effective in stimulating learning, the teacher should (a) encourage the child's curiosity, and (b) provide learning experiences that extend children's daily activities (Harlan, 1991).

Blowing bubbles is fun and engaging, and teaches about air.

Since concepts are built slowly from numerous activities and facts, teachers should plan many related science experiences to reinforce a single theme or topic (Harlan, 1991). Science activities become less meaningful to children if they are offered as isolated events. Random experiences are not sufficient to allow children to link important ideas together and fit them into other situations that have meaning in their lives (Harlan, 1991). Science notions and concepts should also be built on what the child already knows. Therefore, teachers need to inventory what the children know, understand, and are familiar with—and then add concepts that are new and unfamiliar.

As science activities are approached, it is hoped that teachers will see the value of some experiences that are structured—that is, the answers or conclusions are predetermined, and only one conclusion is correct. (For example, if a plant has neither water nor light, it will die.) However, it is hoped that many of the activities will have an open-ended or discovery approach—that is, there is no single correct answer, but rather many possibilities or hypotheses. (For example, while exploring with water, ask the children, "How many different ways can you think of that we use water?") Both types of activities are valuable and encourage the kind of thinking we are endeavoring to develop in young children.

Carson (1956, p. 45) presents a guide for persons who desire to assist children in the process of learning:

I sincerely believe that for the child, and for the parent seeking to guide him, it is not half so important to *know* as to *feel*. If facts are the seeds that later produce knowledge and wisdom, then the emotions and the impressions of the senses are the fertile soil in which the seeds must grow. The years of early childhood are the time to prepare the soil. Once the emotions have been aroused—a sense of the beautiful, the excitement of the new and the unknown, a feeling of sympathy, pity, admiration or love—then we wish for knowledge about the object of our emotional response. Once found, it has lasting meaning. It is more important to pave the way for the child to want to know than to put him on a diet of facts he is not ready to assimilate.

Some of the science activities suggested in this book are of the more structured type in which a conclusion can be made as a result of the experience. Examples include the salt–chemical garden, as well as experiences involving changes in properties such as texture, size, and shape. However, even with these kinds of experiences, it is hoped that the teacher will still take advantage of the discovery approach and not be too hasty in giving the answers or conclusions. Allow the children to discover them. Caution: Do not smother a child's interest and curiosity with too many facts and instructions (Harlan, 1991).

There are also experiences that lead children to question and explore, but the conclusions must remain open-ended. For example, one may ask, "How many hairs do I have on my head?" This problem may lead to a study of hair and the average number of hairs a person may have, but it is doubtful that the child will be able to obtain a specific conclusion or answer, nor can the teacher supply that answer! Children should not be discouraged by unanswerable questions and problems. They should be reminded that thousands of scientists are working today to discover the answers to many unanswered questions—what kinds of life exist in outer space, what are the causes and cures for cancer, and many others.

As has already been mentioned, one of the most exciting ways to teach science is by taking advantage of spontaneous learning experiences. Teachers need to be "aware of daily experiences that involve science," such as those with animals, plants, numbers, nutrition, creative art, music, social studies, and numerous others (Smith, 1987, p. 36). The child may ask a question that could lead to an entire unit of study. A child may ask where a butterfly sleeps. This could result in a unit on butterflies, insects, or sleeping habits of animals. Take advantage of the daily happenings and of the materials often brought into class. The child bringing in an icicle could be the one to stimulate a unit of study on the forms of water, especially focusing on ice and how it is formed and used. Illustrations from the authors' own experiences include the day a cement mixer poured a cement platform in the children's playground. A science experience emerged relating to the ingredients of cement and the mixing, pouring, and setting of cement. Another activity occurred when people entered the classroom to fix a broken radiator. The children were invited to gather around and watch as the radiator was repaired. The experience included a discussion of heat and its source. As steam escaped, it was discussed as a form of water, and the tools needed to repair it were named while the children observed them in use.

Another approach to teaching science is the use of a science center or science interest table. This area, like other areas of the room, can be used continually or just occasionally. Materials can be put out for the children to explore, or science activities can take place on an individual basis in these areas. The materials used and activities selected need to be simple. For example, some modeling clay and toothpicks can be placed beside a tub of water. The children are challenged to work with and model the clay in such a way as to make cargo ships, with the toothpicks becoming cargo. In this subtle way, concepts of sinking, floating, and displacement can be learned. The materials and experiences are simple and easy to obtain and set up. If a science theme has been selected as a unit of study, the science center or table can serve as reinforcement and review.

Science should be integrated throughout various aspects of the curriculum. As food activities are being carried out, there are many opportunities for exploring and including scientific concepts. What will happen to the butter when the electric pan is turned on? What will happen to the dry ingredients when the milk is added? What is happening to the cream as it is being whipped—is something being added? Is it getting larger or smaller? Will it weigh the same before and after it is whipped? Music activities also offer opportunities for exploration of science. Experiment with sound, and the changes in sounds as the sizes of the strings of instruments change. Explore the parts of instruments and how they work. Additional science opportunities can be found in the realm of art. What happens to media such as glue and papier-mâché as they dry? The secondary colors are often successfully taught through exploring and combining different colors of paints. Individual activities during free play such as the sensory table or trough, blocks, easel painting, books, and manipulative materials all offer opportunities for critical thinking and science exploration. Outdoor play offers limitless experiences in science concepts.

Field trips and visitors, providing the first-hand experiences so valuable for scientific learning, offer natural ways for teaching science. Field trips frequently require no resource persons other than the teacher; however, if field trip resource persons or classroom visitors are involved, they should be well informed about the concepts you are teaching and should be given specific instructions regarding age-appropriate discussions or experiences.

Many activities in science lend themselves to recordkeeping, thereby enhancing measuring, observing, and recording skills. For example, when sprouting a bean seed in a glass jar between a wet towel and the jar, the children can record how many days it takes for their seed to sprout (see Figure 11–1). On a daily basis, the children can record the weather with symbols on a calendar, and then at the end of the month they can compute how many days of sunshine, rain, clouds, or snow there were that particular month. Still another example is observing the incubation period of eggs and recording how many days it takes for the eggs to hatch (see Figure 11–1)

The safety of the children should be of primary concern in planning science activities. As well as eliminating fears, science offers the opportunity to teach the use of some cautions. The teacher must model intelligent caution and still encourage exploration and investigation (Holt, 1989). The teacher must always know and understand what is going on and help children understand where and why precautions are necessary. Never assign children a task or let them participate in activities for which they are not developmentally ready. However, as they become ready

Susan

How many days for the seed to sprout?

N = No
Y = Yes

1	2	3	4	5
N	N	N	N	Y

How many days before the chicks hatch?

N = No
Y = Yes

1	2	3	4	5	6	7	8	9	10	11
N	N	N	N	N	N	N	N	N	N	N
12	13	14	15	16	17	18	19	20	21	22
N	N	N	N	N	N	N	N	N	Y	

FIGURE 11–1

Sample Charts for Recording Observations

for new tasks and adventures that involve safety factors, supervise them closely and carefully as they are learning. Give them rules that are necessary for their own health and safety, as well as that of their classmates.

Science activities can be planned on an individual, small-group, or whole-group basis. In small groups, cooperative learning works well as the children use experimentation and discovery to reach possible solutions. Often when a science experience is explained and demonstrated to a whole group, it readily adapts to follow-up either individually or in small groups. This enables the children to try out the materials while the experience is clarified, explained, and reinforced.

As with other concepts, once a science concept has been taught, the teacher needs to receive feedback from the child to determine whether the ideas and information have been properly synthesized and understood.

Science is important. It brings children into closer touch with themselves and the world they live in. Children enjoy science; they love to discover, explore, and find out! The values of science can be summarized in the following way:

Science is a way of doing things and solving problems. It is a style which leads a person to wonder, to seek, to discover, to know, and then to wonder anew. It is a style in which good feelings of joy, excitement, and beauty accompany these active interactions with one's world. Not only children but adults can experience science. It is a way of life. (Holt, 1989, p. 118)

A wise, commonsense guideline for determining appropriate activities in early childhood education is: "Q. How do we know what age children would enjoy these activities? A. If they enjoy them, they aren't 'too bad' " (Ziemer, 1987, p. 51).

Some Dos and Don'ts

DO have actual materials for children to explore.

DO use the water trough or similar container for science materials and equipment. For example, fill the trough with soil, often including some earthworms and/or other insects. Put the balance scales in the trough with boxes, blocks, or other toys—or even with sensory media such as sand or wheat. Put egg cartons, eyedroppers, and colored water in the water trough for color-mixing experiences.

DO frequently provide science tools such as magnifying glasses, thermometers, magnets, and scales. Include them with the sensory media, at the science table or corner, or outdoors.

DO develop an interested, curious, and enthusiastic attitude toward science yourself. The children will have some inherent interest in and enthusiasm for science, but they will also catch much of the teacher's spirit. "Your eyes should be open to [the wonders of the physical world], because your enthusiasm about environmental phenomena will support and enhance the child's" (Maxim, 1989, p. 494).

DO relate science activities and units to the children's environment to their daily experiences. For example, it may not be wise to do a whole unit on the walrus unless the children are familiar with it. However, such a unit would provide an excellent study in some locations. There are so many possibilities for units and activities for children in these early childhood years that relate to *their* world—*their* weather, the plants in *their* locality, the animals in *their* environment—and there will be adequate time later for learning about the world beyond their surroundings (Rivkin, 1992).

DO perform experiments and activities ahead of time to have confidence in what is being done. The success of many experiments depends on the specific ways they are carried out. Previous try-outs provide knowledge and assurance in the performance of the experiment.

DO scale ideas and concepts down to the child's level of understanding. During activities, ask questions frequently to determine whether the information being taught is also being understood. So often with science explorations, it is erroneously assumed that the child already knows some of the basic concepts.

After a science unit on chickens, the children were watching some baby chicks hatch in the incubator. Nearby was a picture of a hen and her baby chicks. A puzzled child asked when the mother hen was going to hatch. The teacher had taken for granted that the children knew that baby chicks grow into hens and roosters.

DON'T make science activities magic; make them a part of the real world, and help children see the cause-and-effect relationship. Magnets are not magic; they are tools of science. Thunder and lightning are not magical or unidentified happenings; they are acts of nature that have a cause and an effect.

DON'T be afraid to say, "I don't know." But do attempt to help children find the answers to their questions. Seek answers through books, materials, encyclopedias, and knowledgeable persons in the sciences (Perry & Rivkin, 1992). Remember, too, that there are some questions that cannot be answered, even with study. When questions are asked that cannot be answered, tell the child that no one knows the answer to that question. However, if the situation can be explored, encourage the child's curiosity and self-discovery.

DON'T let children use equipment, materials, or substances that are dangerous. For example, when doing experiments involving fire, the teacher should perform the activity. However, this does not mean that children should not be taught how these materials are used and the caution necessary in handling them.

DON'T just teach scientific facts; assist children in learning to think, discover, and solve problems.

Ecology

Children can begin early to learn that they need to protect our environment—that they can make a difference. They can learn that there are many natural beauties on our planet to be enjoyed, appreciated, and protected by all people. They can learn that the quality of the soil, air, and water is determined by human treatment and care. Some of earth's problems are:

- *Air pollution.* This is caused by combustion and burning fuel. Factories, woodburning stoves, and cars all emit harmful pollutants into our air.
- *Water pollution.* People allow waste into our water supplies or spill chemicals or oil into our rivers and lakes.
- *Solid waste.* We throw away tons of garbage each year, and the earth is running out of space to put this huge amount of garbage.
- *Soil erosion.* We farm soil so much it becomes poor, and we cut down trees and clear away land for cities and buildings.

Teach the children what they and others can do to save the earth and protect our environment:

- Recycle glass, aluminum, newspapers, some plastics, and clothing.
- Stop wasting water. Turn off the water while brushing teeth, and do not let the water run to waste outside in yards and on playgrounds. Keep cold water in the refrigerator for drinking so it does not have to run from the faucet each time to get cold. Take a shower instead of a bath.
- Encourage families to buy products that are biodegradable—that rot or decompose when discarded.
- Never litter. Always put trash in a trash can.
- Pick only what they plant themselves, and leave other things in nature for all to enjoy.
- Care for toys and other possessions so they do not need to be replaced and can be passed on to others.
- Learn to conserve such things as paper. For example, school lunches can be brought in lunch boxes instead of paper bags, and bags, sacks, and other consumables can be reused.

- Turn the lights off when leaving a room, turn appliances off when not in use, and turn the thermostat down in winter and up in the summer to conserve fuel.
- Learn to reduce, reuse, and recycle and, by so doing, save our beautiful earth. One child can make a difference by cleaning his or her street, by planting a tree, by helping her or his family start a family recycling program.

Schools can develop partnerships with parks or nature centers and become responsible for some of the cleanup and other duties of maintaining a park or environmental center for the enjoyment of all (Jacobson & Padua, 1992).

The study of ecology for young children must provide for interactions with nature (Cole, 1992). Experiences with trees, parks, flowers, and their community all help children to acquire an appreciation for and commitment to our world and its environment. Teachers should build an awareness in young children, and there is a need to change behaviors and attitudes (Cohen, 1992). The best approach to support ecological and nature themes and concepts is to provide hands-on activities (James, 1992). For example, children can adopt a tree by naming it; studying and learning everything they can about that kind of tree; watering it; having a picnic under it; enjoying its shade; observing it during different seasons; seeing how animals use it; and making sure it is free of insect or other problems that could be treated. Teachers do have an important role in helping young children cultivate an attitude and sense of caring, understanding, and appreciation for their natural environment.

Science Experiments Unrelated to Specific Units

Scientific explanations are presented simply in many of the experiences suggested in this chapter. Older children can understand and be introduced to scientific explanations in more detail. Younger children will find the demonstrations themselves adequate. Many experiments help children understand about ecology and being sensitive to preserving the earth and its environment.

Vinegar and baking soda. To a small amount of vinegar (¼ cup), add 1 teaspoon baking soda. Watch, hear, and feel what happens. (Carbon dioxide gas [bubbles] is formed when vinegar and baking soda are mixed together.)

Buoyancy of raisins or alfalfa seeds in carbonated soda or in soda and vinegar solution. Add 3 tablespoons of vinegar and 2 teaspoons of baking soda to 1 cup of water. Add 1 teaspoon of alfalfa seeds or other tiny seeds; observe as the seeds rise to the surface of the water and then sink to the bottom of the container. Carbon dioxide bubbles pick the seeds up and carry them to the surface. When the bubbles pop, the seeds return to the bottom, where they are surrounded again by bubbles and are carried to the surface. As an alternative, drop raisins, whole or part, into a cup half filled with carbonated soda. Count how many times a raisin surfaces and sinks in a given time period, such as 3 minutes.

Blowing up a balloon. Pour an inch of vinegar into a pop bottle. Put 1 or 2 teaspoons of baking soda inside a balloon and affix the balloon opening to the open top of the bottle. Then allow the soda and vinegar to mix together. The balloon will slowly inflate.

Crystals. Unique crystals can be grown with ordinary table salt or alum. Heat some water, and then dissolve as much salt as possible in the water. The solution will then be saturated. Pour the solution into an old open pie pan (the disposable aluminum kind works well, since the solution may be corrosive to some metals). Then place it in a corner of the room where it will not be disturbed. As the water starts to evaporate, small crystals will be observed forming. If these crystals are viewed through a microscope, they will show a crystal shape unique to that particular salt. Also note that the slower the water evaporates, the larger the crystals will grow.

Chemical garden. Combine the following ingredients: 2 tablespoons ammonia, ¼ cup bluing, ¼ cup salt, ¼ cup water. (Caution the children against smelling the ammonia, except at a safe distance.) Pour the ingredients over coal, bricks, charcoal, or other materials. Drops of food coloring may be added on top. In a few hours, salt-crystal formations will begin to appear. Use glass containers for this experiment, since the chemical may corrode aluminum. The chemical growth that occurs is made up of salt formations created when the liquid evaporates. The growth can be continued if more of the chemical ingredients are added or if a teaspoon or two of ammonia is added.

Floating an egg and pencil. Partly fill two containers, one with fresh water and one with salt water (4 tablespoons salt to 1 cup water). Let the children try floating the egg in each container. Try a hard-boiled egg. Now place a pencil in the water with the lead end up and the eraser end down. What happens to the pencil in the fresh water? What happens in the salt water? Do the items float in the salt water or the fresh water?

Rainbow. On a sunny day, stand a mirror in a bowl filled with water. Set the bowl near a wall. Now turn the mirror to reflect (and refract) the sun's rays onto the wall. This exhibits the colors of the spectrum. What colors are seen?

Mirror images. Hinge two mirrors together with tape. Stand the hinged mirror on its edge. Place bits of colored paper in the mirror angle. Observe the different patterns in the double reflection. Try using a penny instead of the colored paper bits. Place the penny in the mirror angle. How many pennies can you see? Open and close the mirror and observe as the number of pennies reflected in the mirror changes.

A–Z science fair. Hold an A–Z Science Fair during school, after school, or in the evening, with parents and other classroom students being invited to attend. The teacher and children collaborate and think of a science experiment, activity, demonstration, or concept to represent each letter in the alphabet. Each child selects a letter of the alphabet or a science idea to be presented during the Science Fair. Flags or labels identify each letter, enabling participants to progress from activity A through activity Z—observing, trying out, manipulating, and inferring with each one. Following is a list of possible general concepts or ideas to represent each letter in the alphabet. These are only suggestions; there are numerous other possibilities.

A—Air

B—Bubbles

C—Crystal garden

D—Degrees (Celsius and Fahrenheit)

E—Electric current

F—Floating and sinking

G—Gravity

H—Hive

I—Ice

J—Jack (observe and try out a jack)

K—Keys (which key fits the padlock)

L—Light and shadows

M—Magnets

N—Nests

O—Owl facts

P—Plants

Q—Quarts (measuring liquids)

R—Rainbows

S—Sounds

T—Tasting

U—Unhatched eggs

V—Violin strings

W—Water

X—Xylophone sounds

Y—Yards (measuring)

Z—Zucchini (observe differences between zucchini and cucumber)

Following the Science Fair, write a book about the experience. Each page represents a letter, with a picture drawn by the child and then a sentence or two in the child's words about that experiment or activity.

Teaching About Air

Young children soon learn that air is all around us, is real, and takes up space. Air can also be touched and felt, as we feel the blowing wind, the cold and hot temperatures of the seasons, our breath, or the air from a compressor or pump. An exploratory science activity taking place in the preschool classroom is described in the following example:

The teacher had given the children small boxes, of various sizes, wrapped as gifts. They were told to explore the boxes in any way they wished (except opening them) and try to discover what might be inside them. One young boy said, "I know for sure one thing that is inside." The teacher, wondering how he could "know for sure," asked, "What do you think might be inside?" He confidently answered, "I don't just think, I know for sure air is inside!"

Once children learn the concept that air is all around us, they can "know for sure" that air is in a wrapped package, even though it is not known what else is actually contained in the mystery box.

Air concepts could be taught as a separate unit or as individual activities supporting other themes. There are numerous supportive curriculum activities relating to air.

Concepts and Ideas for Teaching

1. Air is part of the earth and is all around us.
2. Air takes up space.
3. Animals, people, and plants need air for survival.
4. Fire needs air to burn.
5. Air has weight.
6. Air has force.
7. Air moves.

8. There is air in dirt.
9. There is air in water.
10. Bubbles are formed with air. If you are blowing bubbles, the air comes from inside your body.
11. Air expands when heated, and warm air rises.
12. Air helps many items to float on water.
13. Air has many uses.
14. Air can be hot or cold.
15. Air can make noise.
16. The quality of air is affected by humans.

Activities and Experiences

1. Have the children hold their hands close to their mouths and noses to feel the air as it is exhaled. Also, have them put their hands on their chests to feel their chests (lungs) expand and contract as air is inhaled and exhaled.

2. Obtain a flexible cardboard box no smaller than a gelatin box and no larger than a cereal box. Cut a hole in one end and wrap the box with paper, making sure to wrap around the hole but not cover it. Above the hole, glue tiny tissue-paper streamers so that they hang across the hole. Pass the box around so that all the children can shake it or feel it. Then ask them, "What is inside the box?" Unless the children have had a previous discussion on air, they will probably reply that the box is empty. When the box comes back to you, squeeze the box in the center and ask the children, "If nothing is in the box, what is making the tissue paper move?" The conclusion should be drawn that there is air in the box; when the box is squeezed, some of the air is forced out through the hole, making the tissue paper move.

3. Place a tissue in the bottom of a glass. Invert the glass in a large glass bowl that has been filled with water. Ask the children why the tissue does not get wet. If they do not know, explain that the glass is full of air and that air takes up space. When the tissue stays dry, it is because the glass is full of air and there is no room for water to enter. If the glass is tipped to the side, air bubbles will escape and water will take the place of the air, allowing the tissue to get wet.

4. Fill a glass or jar half full of dry soil or dirt. With the children gathered very close around the jar, pour water onto the soil. Ask the children what they see and hear. They should be able to both see and hear air bubbles come up out of the soil. Explain that there is air in dirt, and water that is poured onto the soil and seeps down into it takes the place of the air and forces the air to the surface.

5. Fill a clear glass container with water. Allow it to stand for a brief period of time. Soon air bubbles will begin to form against the edge of the container. The air from the water has formed the air bubbles.

6. Fill a trough, tub, or sink with water. Obtain a small plastic container with a lid, such as an empty detergent bottle or small plastic bottle. Put the lid on and place the container on the water. Ask the children whether it will float or sink. It will float because of the upward force (buoyancy) of the water and because the container is light, being full of air. Take the lid off and fill the plastic container with water. Will it still float? A similar activity can be carried out in a larger body or pool of water. Show the children a deflated inner tube. Will it float or sink? Now inflate it with air and see what happens. Air helps things to float.

7. To demonstrate that fire needs air, obtain three pie plates or saucers and put identical small candles on each one (you may need to melt a little wax to hold the candle in place). Select three glass jars of varying sizes (pint, quart, and gallon jars work well). Light one of the candles, and then put a jar over the candle. Ask the children to observe what happens. When the candle

Peter is discovering that fire needs air to burn.

goes out, ask the children if they know why the candle went out. Now perform the same demonstration while using the other two jars. If possible, put the jars on the candles at exactly the same time. Why does the candle under the smallest jar go out first? Why does the candle under the largest jar go out last? Explain that fire needs air to burn or that air has oxygen in it, and once the air (oxygen) in the jar is used up, the fire goes out; it cannot burn without the air (oxygen). This same experiment can be demonstrated at Halloween time with two carved jack-o'-lanterns. Put

candles in both, and set the eyes and other carved features back in one. Light both candles and replace the lids. Ask why one candle stays lighted and one goes out. Explain that the jack-o'-lantern with the carved face allows air inside, but the other one is sealed and does not allow air inside. Thus, when the fire has used up all the air on the inside, the flame goes out because it needs air (oxygen) to burn.

8. Discuss what would happen if people, animals, and plants did not have air. Put a glass jar over a plant and observe what happens in a few days. Make sure that the

plant still has water and sunlight. The plant will die without adequate air. Do all plants need air? (No, mold will grow in an airtight jar.)

9. Put a balloon on the edge of a table or desk. Put a book on top of the balloon and then blow the balloon up. The air in the balloon will force the book up.

10. Even on a day that is not windy, go outside and observe the trees and other plant life. They will be moving slightly because of moving air. Blow some soap bubbles and watch them float on the air. Turn on a fan or vacuum and observe as the air moves items.

11. Give the children a container of water and a straw. While blowing, they will see and hear the bubbles created when the air inside them blows through the straw and makes the bubbles in the water. Once the children have mastered blowing (and not sucking), add a small amount of detergent to water in a bowl, cup, or other container. Give them a straw and let them blow bubbles. Keep sponges close by to absorb water.

12. Make kites and pinwheels. Explain that it is both the construction of the objects and the moving air that make them fly or move.

13. Blow soap bubbles outside and explain that air from inside the child fills the bubbles, whereas the air outside makes the bubbles move; the more wind (moving air) there is, the faster and farther the bubbles will move. A good solution for bubble blowing can be made from either 8 ounces liquid detergent and 1 ounce glycerin, or 8 ounces liquid detergent and ½ cup sugar. Blower wands can be made by bending and twisting wire coat hangers or other heavy wire such as pipe cleaners.

14. For activities to teach that air has weight, see Chapter Twelve.

15. Hold a long piece of paper (longer than it is wide, such as 4 inches by 10 inches) be-

tween your thumb and forefinger. As you blow across the top of the paper, it will rise (actually, will be lifted). This is because as air speeds up, the air pressure decreases. Another example: A shower curtain will be pulled toward a running shower.

16. Challenge the children to invent new bubble machines. Each child could bring something from home to use to blow bubbles. In addition, if the children are blowing bubbles outside, food coloring can be added to the bubble solution and a large piece of butcher paper put on the fence or building so the blown bubbles make a bubble mural. The children's names can be put on their own spots, and the mural can be cut up so the children can take their own parts home. The children can measure and see which bubble is the largest. In addition, the children can autograph their bubbles on the mural.

17. Assign the children to cooperative learning groups, and give each group different materials to make miniature parachutes. Materials might include a cupcake liner, a handkerchief, and a small square of plastic. The groups will make parachutes by tieing each corner with string or yarn and then taking the other end of the yarn or string and threading it through a bead or tying it to a washer. Have the children in each group experiment by dropping their parachutes from the same height and finding out which one reaches the ground first. Then make comparisons among groups, with each group dropping their fastest parachute.

18. If you have access to compressed air, suspend round objects in the jet of air, using a hose with a nozzle. Objects that work are Ping-Pong balls, beach balls, or Styrofoam balls. Point the nozzle up, then start the air flowing. Balance a ball in the jet of air. As the nozzle is moved or tilted downward, the ball will still remain suspended for a short period of time.

19. Obtain a large, empty thread spool; a small nail (shorter than the spool), about 1–1½ inches long with a flat head; and a small square of cardboard (about 1½–2 inches on each side) about the weight of an ordinary 3- by 5-inch card. Push the nail all the way through the center of the cardboard square, so that the head is against the cardboard. Hold the spool in one hand with your mouth against one end so that you can blow through it. Then poke the nail into the other end of the spool until the cardboard rests gently against it. Tell the children that you are going to blow the cardboard off. As you start to blow hard, let go of the cardboard and nail. To the amazement of the children, it will not be blown away, but will be drawn toward the spool. You can even blow downward and it will not fall off until you stop blowing. This works because as the air flows rapidly between the end of the spool and the cardboard square, air pressure is less than on the other side; thus the cardboard is drawn toward the spool.

20. Make a simple weather vane to detect wind direction. Use a wooden dowel (perhaps ½–1 inch in diameter) about 1½ feet long. A triangular-shaped fin can be made of plastic, metal, Formica, or other nonabsorbent material (rain will cause cardboard to deteriorate). Nail or screw the fin to the back end of the dowel, and then sharpen the front end of the dowel somewhat. Find the center or mass of the vane by balancing it on your finger, and then drill a hole through the dowel large enough to insert the head of a 1½- to 2-inch finishing nail. Drive the nail into a board, post, or other convenient location; then place the vane on it with the nail through the hole. The vane will point into the wind. Care should be taken so that the vane will not be obstructed as it turns completely around. Try to eliminate any obstacles around the vane that would disturb the wind.

21. Blow up a balloon, and then release it. The air being forced out of the open end results in a backward force, producing a reaction force forward. The balloon is propelled forward because of the reaction force, *not* because the air pushes against anything.

UNIT PLAN ON AIR

Art

- Hummers decorated to be used as rhythm instruments
- Straw painting
- Inflated balloons decorated with paper scraps, felt scraps, rickrack, gummed stars, or other objects; perhaps they could be decorated as human heads
- Pinwheels
- Paper airplanes (to make and fly)
- Fans (to make)
- Miniature parachutes made from different materials

Visitors

- Someone to play a wind instrument
- Someone to demonstrate household machines and how they utilize air
- Fire fighter to show how a fire can be smothered—with the air taken away

Field Trips

- Dentist's office—use of air in the equipment (air hose)
- Service station
- High school, junior high, or college music department
- Pet store—observation of fish and how they breathe air through the gills
- Place where there are machines that use air—vacuum, hair dryer, clothes dryer, appliances, fans

Food

- Food activity featuring whipped cream—air beaten into cream

- Food activity featuring meringue—air beaten into egg whites

Science

- Any of the activities mentioned in this chapter
- Pictures or slides of animals and plants—discussion of how they need air
- Pictures or slides of machines that use air
- Observe what happens on a windy day when you open a milkweed pod
- Explore bubbles

Literacy

- Use the language experience approach to write about the uses of air
- Write or tell about things that fly
- Study and write about keeping the air clean

Physical Motor

- Play with a large parachute. Develop simple games to use with it

Music

- Creative movements interpreting bubbles, kite flying—faster music as air moves more rapidly or the weather becomes more windy
- Use of hummers, with discussion of how the air vibrating on the waxed paper makes the sound (see Chapter Nine for directions on making hummers)

Teaching About Fire

Fire is an interesting part of the child's world, since it stimulates curiosity, but it is often not approached with necessary caution. Therefore, along with teaching young children about fire, its dangers must be emphasized—and, if not already acquired, a certain caution toward it must be taught.

A unit on fire may be planned in conjunction with the fire fighter. Often a unit of study focuses on the fire fighter as a community helper but never brings in concepts related to fire. We suggest that many concepts relating to fire be taught to young children so that they know that fire has many uses, but that it is dangerous and is not to be played with.

On one occasion when Smokey Bear visited the classroom of 3- to 5-year-olds, his role had been previously discussed—that he is a symbol of fire safety and is not actually a live bear. It was also explained that there was a real bear named Smokey Bear living in Washington, DC. However, excitement ran high when Smokey walked in with the forest ranger—heartbeats stepped up, eyes widened, breathing increased, and one child exclaimed: "It's the real Smokey Bear. I thought I would never get to meet you." Even when Smokey Bear removed his head and an actual person's head emerged, the reality of Smokey Bear still remained in the minds of those 3- to 5-year-olds.

Concepts and Ideas for Teaching

1. Fire has many uses: heating, lighting, cooking, and burning of waste material.
2. Fire needs air (oxygen) and fuel (wood, paper, or other flammable material) to burn.
3. Fire can be ignited in many ways: striking rocks together, using matches or heat, or focusing light on one spot for some time, combustion.
4. There are several ways to extinguish a fire: Douse with water or salt; smother with dirt or a blanket; eliminate the air supply by smothering; use a fire extinguisher.
5. People have different feelings toward fires. We may be frightened if our lives or homes are in danger because of a fire; we may experience pain if our bodies are burned with fire; we may feel warm and safe if we are gathered around the fireplace when it is cold and stormy outside; we may feel excitement and warmth as we are gathered around a campfire cooking our dinner and singing campfire songs; or we may feel relief and security when the power goes off and the candles are found and lighted.

Activities and Experiences

1. Demonstrate that fire needs air (see Activity 7 in the section on air).
2. Demonstrate ways to put out a fire; role play.
3. Demonstrate first aid in treating a burn. If it is not severe, put it under cold water and then treat it with ointment.
4. Demonstrate how to build a fire outdoors and then how to put it out.

UNIT PLAN ON FIRE AND THE FIRE FIGHTER

Art

- Collages of flammable and nonflammable materials
- Melted crayon pictures—take care with the iron so that no fire will start and no one is burned.

Food

- Hot dogs roasted over a fire
- Marshmallows roasted over a fire
- Any food cooked over a fire
- Foil dinners baked on coals
- Fondue

Field Trips

- Fire station
- Home or school on fire-safety inspection
- Picnic at a park, canyon, or picnic site—fire built in designated safe place; hot dogs cooked, marshmallows roasted; fire put out carefully

Visitors

- Fire fighter
- Smokey Bear
- Scout to show how to start a fire and how to put it out properly

Science

- Necessity of air in building a fire or keeping it going

- Ways to start or build a fire
- Ways to put out a fire

Literacy

- Stories and poems about fires and fire fighters
- Story of Smokey Bear
- Open-ended story: "I like fire because . . ."

Music and Dramatic Play

- Dramatization of putting out a fire
- Dramatization of sitting around a campfire cooking food, and singing songs

---

Teaching About Light

The question posed to a group of preschoolers, "What would you do if you had no light?" resulted in some interesting comments and answers. One child said, "I would get a blind man's dog," and another said, "God would help me." Another replied, "I would light a candle." "But a candle is one source of light," the teacher replied. "Then I would get a flashlight," the child responded quickly. "And that is another source of light," the teacher told him. "Then I guess I would just have to sit," concluded the child. It is difficult for children to imagine a world without light, and it is interesting for them to begin to understand the several sources of light. In every situation in which people are without natural light and there is a power failure preventing the use of electricity, there are still sources of light, such as flashlights and fire.

Shadows, an aspect of light, are so fascinating that even babies find them interesting. Very young children may find shadows frightening, but as preschool children learn the cause of shadows, their fears are alleviated, and they delight not only in watching them but in making them. What child, at the conclusion of a movie when the projector is still casting light on the screen, does not love to make hand and finger shadows on the screen? Another activity is to hang a sheet in front of a group of children. After putting a light behind the sheet, have some of the children perform shadow dances, shadow dramatics, or shadow games behind the sheet (but in front of the light), so that the other children can watch the shadows on the sheet. After a story, one teacher decided to have the children dramatize it by means of shadow dramatics. There was awe, fascination, and excitement as the children in the audience watched the shadows of the performing children as the story was dramatized. Children also enjoy guessing who other children are by their shadows. One young boy said, "I know that is Stacy, because the shadow has pigtails!"

Concepts and Ideas for Teaching

1. Light is either natural (e.g., sunlight) or artificial (e.g., flashlights, lanterns).
2. Plants need light and will grow toward the light
3. Light has many uses.
   a. Used by people
      (1) Lamps—used by people to see in the dark
      (2) Lighthouses—used to warn ships and boats of nearness to land
      (3) Freeway and street lights, lighted airport runways, traffic lights, headlights, lighted signs—used with forms of transportation to light the way and let people know where they are going
      (4) Light or fire at a campsite—used for warmth, cooking, and to discourage wild animals
      (5) Natural sunlight—used for warmth and also as a source of telling time
   b. Used by animals
      (1) To see in the dark
      (2) For warmth
      (3) To determine the approximate time
   c. Used by plants—warmth and sunlight needed by most plants to grow
4. Shadows are produced when an object passes in front of light; shadows result from interruption of light. If the object making the shadow is removed, the shadow also disappears.
   a. Relation of object's shape to its shadow
   b. Relation of the size and shape of a shadow to a change in the location of the object and the position of the light source

Activities and Experiences

1. Collect as many sources of light as possible—flashlights, lanterns, candles, matches, lighters, and so on.
2. Try growing a plant in a closet or room where there is no light.
3. Watch a plant "follow" the sun or light.
4. Show pictures or slides of the uses of light.
5. Show, discuss, and demonstrate the effect of sunlight on photographic paper, ice, cold water, colored construction paper, material.
6. Explore shadows.

   a. On a sunny day, divide the children into pairs to trace each other's shadows.

   b. Play shadow tag, with the one who is "it" trying to step on another person's shadow.

   c. Make a sundial—string tied around the end of a dowel; the other end of the dowel put in some sand or soil next to cement; and string on the end of dowel extended across the cement and secured with tape. During the day, draw a line on the cement with a piece of chalk where the shadow is being cast

   d. Use an overhead projector for making shadows of objects, letters, numbers—encourage the children to make hand and finger shadows

7. Give an ordinary flashlight battery, a piece of wire, and a flashlight lamp to a pair of children and have them figure out how to make the lamp glow.

LESSON PLAN ON LIGHT (SHADOWS) (4-DAY)

Overall Goals

- To introduce the children to the concept of shadows and their origin.
- To acquaint the children with the types of shadows, and the knowledge that a shadow's size and darkness are changeable, according to the light source and the distance from the object.
- To identify the shapes of objects by their shadows.
- To stimulate interest in and appreciation for poetry.
- To increase body awareness through creative movement, body shadow pictures, and rhythm activities.

Because of the nature of this lesson plan, one corner of the room will be darkened to be the "shadow corner," where many of the individual activities throughout the unit will be performed. The plans may have to be altered or changed if the weather is not sunny.

Day 1

Whole-Group Activity

Introduction to Unit. As an introduction to this unit, give a slide presentation. The slides will consist of many delightful pictures of shadows dealing with children's lives and what causes shadows. A cassette tape will accompany the presentation. Questions that may concern the young child will be answered during this presentation. Such topics as the causes of shadows, the shapes of shadows, the light source, and the size of shadows will be illustrated during this short presentation. Read a poem about a shadow.

Objectives

- To introduce the unit on shadows.
- To acquaint the children with types of shadows.

- To provide new experiences in seeing a slide–tape presentation and hearing poetry.

Small-Group Activities

Science—Shadows. After dividing the children into cooperative learning groups, tell them to go outside. Each group will have a dowel or stick to place in the ground; then they will measure its shadow. Later in the morning, each group will go back to its own stick and again measure the shadow. A marker will be placed at the locations of both shadows to allow the children to see how shadows change as the day progresses.

Objectives

- To show that shadows change at different times of day.
- To provide for group cooperation and interaction to achieve a common goal.

Art—Paper Hats. After the groups have measured the shadows, have them go as groups into the classroom and make pointed paper hats, which will be used for the "shadow parade" on day 2. They can decorate the hats with paint, crepe paper streamers, scraps of paper, and other materials.

Objectives

- To provide an experience for creative expression.
- To increase manipulation skills by pasting and cutting.

Individual Activities

Tracing Shadows Outside. Provide butcher paper and trace each child's complete body shadow while the child stands still and watches. Encourage the child to find a unique position or stance. Emphasize the body parts and help increase the child's body awareness during this experience. Cut out the bodies so that the children can paint them on day 2. Each picture must be carefully labeled.

Object Printing. Have the children print with various types of objects using a variety of colors of paint.

Lotto Shape Games. Develop a set of black "shadow" shapes as a lotto game for matching and discrimination purposes. This game can be used at any time, but it will be especially effective during this unit or a shape unit.

Trough Full of Bubbles. Place the trough in the shadow corner. Mix 1 cup of granulated soap in 1 quart of warm water. Small cans and straws should be available for each child. It is interesting for the children to observe the bubbles they blow and to see whether the shadows are cast on the wall when the light in the shadow corner is switched on.

Objectives

• To increase body awareness by tracing each child's body shadows.
• To experiment in science areas with shadows.

Day 2

Whole-Group Activity

Music—Shadow Parade. Have the children participate in a "shadow parade" with musical instruments. They wear the hats they made on day 1 and carry a flag, baton, or rhythm instrument. Beat a rhythm on a drum, and encourage the children to beat out the rhythm as they march around the playground and especially to watch their shadows during the parade.

Objectives

• To allow for rhythmic body movement and self-expression.
• To observe the shadows of children dressed with hats and instruments.

Small-Group Activity

Food—Fruit Salad (Cooperative Learning). Ask the children to guess the shapes of certain fruits from their shadows. Place the fruits behind a sheet, with a light shining on them. Each fruit will be guessed separately. Show the following fruits (easily identified): grapes, pineapple, watermelon, cantaloupe, bananas, and apples. They will be combined to make a fruit salad in each group. Each child will have a chance to cut some fruit into pieces and then each group's salad will be shared among the group. Since sharp knives will be used, this activity must be carefully supervised, and the children must be thoroughly cautioned about the dangers of sharp instruments.

Objectives

• To strengthen manipulation skills through cutting, reinforcing safety.
• To identify the shape of an object by its shadow.

Individual Activities

Painting the Shadows Outside. Hang the traced shadows on the fence on the playground to be painted. Offer several colors of paint. Leave the pictures on the fence to dry.

Shadow Puzzles. Cut the silhouettes of certain objects into puzzles, which the children will have the opportunity to play with and use, along with the other manipulative toys.

Puppets and Overhead Projector. Set up an overhead projector in the shadow corner. Here the children can have creative play with the puppets and their shadows on the wall. Music may be played to stimulate creative movement.

Science Table. On the science table, place several shoe boxes with balls of clay, a small flashlight, and a pencil. Help the children observe the various angles of shadows that can be produced, making the pencil shadows both long and short. The pencil is supported in the shoe box by the clay. The flashlight is then used at various angles and distances from the box to produce different types of shadows.

Day 3

Whole-Group Activities

Visitor—Person to Demonstrate Shadow Plays. Ask a visitor to show a variety of finger shadow plays on a screen or wall in the classroom. In these plays, use simple shapes that children can quickly learn, such as those of a rabbit, duck, elephant, or dog. A light shining on the wall helps produce the dark shadows. Encourage group involvement and have the children practice some of these shadow plays while the visitor is there to assist.

Objectives

- To introduce a new person to the children.
- To show that not all shadows are what they appear to be.
- To facilitate small-muscle coordination in learning the shadow plays.

Discussions—Shadow at Night. Encourage discussion of the kinds of shadows that the children see at night in their bedrooms. Talk about how quiet, dark, and dim the shadows are. Help the children talk about their fears, but minimize this aspect of the darkness. Discuss how shadows are not always what they seem to be. Emphasize the positive.

Objectives

- To encourage an honest approach to emotions such as fear.
- To reinforce the concept of shadows and their appearances at night.

Small-Group Activity

Shadow Tag. Divide the children into small groups and have them go outside. There each group will play "Shadow Tag." In this game, one person is "it" and tries to step on another child's shadow. When a child does step on another child's shadow, that child then gets to become "it." Several children can be "it" at once. Be sensitive to each child and careful not to let anyone feel that he or she is not a part of the game. Another variation to this game is "Shadow Touch Shadow," in which the children try to let their shadows touch hands, feet, and so on.

Objectives

- To increase the social interaction and cooperation of children.
- To encourage awareness of space, coordination, and shadows.

Individual Activities

Trace Silhouettes. Trace the children's profiles on black paper as silhouettes (with a sheet and light). Later, cut the silhouettes out and mount them on pieces of white paper. Provide a learning experience on day 4 with the silhouettes, and then let the children take their own silhouettes home.

Shape Collage. Cut all kinds of shapes out of black paper, and have the children paste collages on white paper. Provide scissors if the children want to cut.

Shadow Plays. Place the screen in the shadow corner so that the children can experiment with the shadow plays they have been taught. Other media and shapes may also be provided to increase experimentation with the light and shadows.

Objectives

- To provide an identity experience for children with silhouettes.
- To let the child explore with various shapes and sizes in collages.
- To provide good finger skills in shadow plays.

Day 4

Whole-Group Activities

Field Trip to See a Shadow Play. Take the class on a field trip to a school to see a shadow play performed by students from that school. The shadow play will be performed completely behind a sheet, so that the children will see only shadows of what is happening. The shadows are very misleading, as the doctor keeps taking huge things out of a boy's stomach. When the play is over, talk about what happened and remove the sheet so the children can see what really took place.

Objectives

- To observe the misleading ideas shadows can give.
- To give the children a chance to express their feelings after the play is over and to share their reactions.

Music—Creative Dramatics. Try creative dramatics with the children in the classroom. Give each child a piece of plastic to move creatively with the music. Place a light behind the children to cast shadows on the wall. Encourage discussion about the shadows and why the plastic shadows are so much lighter than the children's shadows.

Objectives

- To allow children to express themselves freely.
- To increase body awareness through shadows.

Small-Group Activity

Silhouette Game. Divide the silhouettes into small groups, and have each child try to guess his or her own silhouette.

Objectives

- To identify shapes and objects.
- To increase self-awareness.

Individual Activities

Shape Game. Cut shapes of familiar objects out of black Pellon®, and have the children match pictures of them to the actual objects.

Trough. Set a trough full of sand in the shadow corner. Put figures of animals and people in it to promote play. The children can observe the shadows cast from the animals and other objects.

Shadow Toy. This simple toy, when put in direct light, makes a variety of shapes: square, circle, triangle. It can be used either inside or outdoors.

Objectives

- To encourage recognition of shapes and objects.
- To allow for expression of ideas and sensory experiences.

Teaching About Magnets

"I've never seen a pin jump before," exclaimed one excited child as magnets were introduced. Another child said, "I didn't know pins were alive," as she observed the magnets attracting the pins. Magnets are fascinating for children to explore. Simply showing the children magnets and telling them what they can do takes away the excitement; children need opportunities to experiment and discover for themselves what magnets are and can do. Ideally, each child should have a magnet; however, magnets can be put on a science table for use in individual exploring.

The children need many objects for experimenting with the magnets so that they can determine what kinds of materials the magnets attract. A container of common objects such as a cork, scrap of material, pencil, eraser, paper clip, scissors, tack, coin, soap, washer, pin, needle, fastener, and tape provides continued motivation for exploration. The objects in the box could be sorted into two groups—those attracted by the magnet and those not attracted by the magnet. (A dog's two-sided food dish works very well for this sorting or classifying activity.) After adequate experimentation, the children will be able to see some similarities in the objects the magnet attracts.

During a sorting activity, one child replied, "All the things that the magnet picked up are silver. Magnets

Exploring with a magnet enables a child to discover what a magnet will and will not pick up.

must pick up silver things." True, many iron and steel objects are silver in color, but this concept was not accurate. Then the teacher said, "Let's test your idea to see whether it is correct." The teacher selected some silver paper, aluminum foil, a piece of aluminum, a nickel coin, a silver button, and silver fabric. After trying to pick up each of these objects with the magnet, the child concluded that magnets do not necessarily pick up items that are silver in color. The teacher took the opportunity to explain that the objects attracted by the magnet were made of iron and steel. Also, even though an object of iron or steel may be too large for the magnet to pick up, the pull or attraction can still be felt.

It is sometimes difficult to present an entire unit on magnets; therefore, they are presented here as a science concept, with several supporting ideas and activities. Perhaps an experience with magnets could be presented each day for a week or two, or incorporated as a science activity within another unit of study.

Concepts and Ideas for Teaching

1. Magnets attract objects made of iron and/or nickel and/or steel. (Although it is not nec-essary to teach the components of magnets to young children, they are actually made from rock called *magnetite*, which does attract iron and steel. Magnetite is also called *lodestone*.)

2. Magnets come in many shapes, sizes, and strengths; some have stronger magnetism than others.

3. Stronger magnets will attract through paper, glass, cardboard, wood, and water.

4. Magnetism can be transferred. It is possible to magnetize such objects as iron nails, paper clips, needles, and knitting needles by stroking them 30 to 50 times in one direction with a magnet. However, as the children will discover, these homemade magnets do not retain their magnetism for very long.

5. Opposite or unlike poles attract (the north pole attracts the south pole), whereas like poles repel each other.

6. A compass needle is a magnet, always pulling to the north. When a magnetized needle is floated in water, it acts as a compass and points north.

7. All magnets have a north pole and a south pole, and magnets are strongest at their poles.

Activities and Experiences

1. Collect magnets of different sizes, shapes, and strengths. Also collect objects that use magnets, such as clips for holding notes to bulletin boards or refrigerators, toys using magnets, and potholders with magnets attached.

2. Compare the strengths of magnets by counting or comparing the number of pins or paper clips each magnet can pick up by "hooking" them one to another until the magnet can no longer hold another pin or paper clip. Order the magnets from strongest to weakest. In this experience, the children can discover that the strength of a magnet is not necessarily determined by its size.

3. Have the children put a piece of paper between their magnet and paper clip to see whether the objects still attract. During this activity, children will discover that magnetism works through glass, cardboard, wood, fabric, and other materials. Fill a glass bowl with water and drop the paper clip into it. The children will learn that the magnet will attract the paper clip through the glass and the water.

4. Suspend a bar magnet from a thread or string tied to its center; in a few minutes, the magnet will align itself with the earth's magnetic field and point north and south. It becomes a simple compass. Notice that as some types of metal are brought close to the magnet, there will be an attraction and the compass will not work.

5. Put iron filings on glass, a paper plate, or cardboard. Put a magnet underneath and let the children discover what happens as the magnet is moved around. Sprinkle the iron filings over a glass slab and touch a magnet underneath the glass. Now put this slap on an overhead projector so that the iron-filings designs can be enlarged on the wall or screen.

6. Make small fishing poles from ¼- by 12-inch dowels and attach small magnets to them with fishing line. The children fish from a box containing assorted items—iron and steel, as well as objects that will not be attracted by the magnet. "Fish" are cut from paper, and paper clips are attached to them so that they can be "caught." If desired, basic concepts such as color, number, and shape can be put on the fish to enable the children to tell about their "catch." Larger poles can also be made from dowels or sticks, and a dramatic-play fishing area can be built in one area of the room. Use large-unit blocks for the "rocks" surrounding the "fishing pond" or "lake"; the children sit on these rocks and proceed to "fish."

7. Place a horseshoe or bar magnet on a table and cover it with a white piece of paper. As iron filings are sprinkled onto the paper, they will align themselves with the magnetic field. If you put two bar magnets with like and then unlike poles next to each other, the iron filings will show the interaction of the magnetic fields.

Note: After a period of time, magnets may lose their force. They can be remagnetized in high school or university physics or electronics departments. Also, you can rejuvenate a weak magnet by pulling it lengthwise across the pole of a powerful magnet (Hardy & Tolman, 1993). To preserve their magnetism when the magnets are not in use, attach the iron keeper over the poles of a horseshoe or bar magnet, do not store the magnets with the north and south poles together, and do not store magnets in metal boxes. Remember, magnets can be damaging to electronic products (Hardy & Tolman, 1993).

Teaching About Rocks

"Teacher, I have something really, really valuable for you in my sack. I was going to give it to my mom, but I have given her one before, so I decided to give it to you." As the first-grade teacher opened the brown paper bag, she found a rock with fool's gold on it! The child proceeded to tell her of the value of gold, and, therefore, of this rock's value. Rocks are of interest to young children and are readily available. Early in life, children become aware of the many variations; rocks come in different sizes, shapes, colors, textures, and weights. Children enjoy classifying rocks in many of these ways. Probably one of the first ways of classifying is by kind, even though specific names may not be known.

The children learn that rocks are made up of minerals and are unique because of the variations and characteristics of these minerals.

Concepts and Ideas for Teaching

1. There are many kinds of rocks.
2. Most rocks are made up of minerals or smaller particles, and they are formed in different ways.
3. Rocks have different hardness values. Some rocks can be broken more easily than others. (Mineralogists and geologists use Mohs' scale of hardness to classify rocks according to relative hardness from 1 to 10; 10 is the hardest, and the diamond has a hardness value of 10.)
4. Rocks have different uses, depending on their hardness (hard and long-lasting rocks may be used for buildings), beauty (many are used for jewelry), or other qualities.
5. Some rocks may be used for writing and drawing on other rocks.
6. The inside of a rock often differs from the outside.
7. Rock fossils are specific kinds of rock. During the rock's formation many years ago, a plant or animal became embedded in the rock and left its imprint.
8. A person who collects, cuts, and polishes rocks as a hobby or profession is called a *lapidary*.
9. Rocks cannot burn.
10. Very small or fine rocks are called *gravel* and are used in making cement or concrete. Sand consists of extremely fine rocks.
11. Water changes rocks, making most rocks smooth.

Activities and Experiences

1. Collect rocks to sort and classify by general groups such as igneous (formed from cooling lava; examples: pumice and obsidian); sedimentary (formed from rocks, sand, and stones that are compacted by pressure; examples: sandstone, limestone, and shale); and metamorphic rock (formed when igneous or sedimentary rocks are completely changed through pressure and heat; examples: limestone becomes marble, shale becomes slate, sandstone becomes quartzite).
2. Collect rocks to sort and classify by specific kind of physical characteristics such as color, shape, or size.
3. Collect rocks from bodies of water, streams, creeks, and other locations, and note their smoothness.
4. Make "fossils" from clay, and then let the clay harden.
5. Visit a lapidary shop, or invite a lapidary or jeweler to visit the classroom to explain the hobby.
6. Visit a gravel pit and notice the different sizes of gravel.
7. Visit a construction site and watch concrete being poured.
8. Visit a geological museum.
9. Obtain Mohs' scale of hardness and classify rocks (minerals) by hardness. Determine whether they can be scratched with a fingernail, penny, nail, or by other means.
10. Crack rocks open to examine them on the inside. Make sure safety precautions are taken for protecting the eyes.

11. Invite a geologist to visit your classroom.
12. Collect geodes for children to observe.
13. Investigate how weathering changes rocks.
14. Have each child bring a rock from home or the playground. The children will write or dictate descriptions of the rocks. They can weigh them, measure them, and describe their physical characteristics. They can draw illustrations of their rocks, then put the pages into a class booklet.
15. Order rocks by weight from lightest to heaviest.
16. Make plant or insect "fossils" by coating a plant or insect with petroleum jelly and then putting it between lumps of clay or pressing it into a mixture of plaster of Paris. When the clay or plaster of Paris dries, remove the plant or insect and observe the imprint.
17. In small groups, blindfold one child at a time and have that child feel a rock. While the child is investigating blindfolded, he or she should be encouraged to describe the rock orally: "It feels like . . . ; It reminds me of . . . ; It is about the same size as . . . ; I like it because . . ." (Charron & Jones, 1992). The rock is then put in a group of rocks and the child's blindfold is removed. Then the child feels the rocks to identify the rock he or she initially felt.
18. Have the children investigate to see whether any rocks float. If they do, they are pumice. Air bubbles in pumice make it the lightest rock there is.
19. Rub an iron file against various rocks to make rock dust. Keep each rock's dust separate. Examine a little of each rock's dust under a magnifying glass or microscope and observe the differences. The differences will be obvious because rocks are made of crystals and some can be recognized by their patterns.
20. Put a drop of vinegar on a variety of rocks. A rock will "fizz" if it contains limestone.
21. Visit or invite into the classroom a jeweler to talk about the rocks he or she sells.
22. Have the children look for and bring to class objects in their homes that are made from rocks.

Teaching About Water

Water! Even though it is one of the substances most familiar to children, they never tire of exploring it. We have found that even unusual media such as rock salt and Styrofoam packing material placed in a trough do not capture as much attention as water—ordinary water! Water play not only seems to interest all children, it holds and maintains their attention for longer periods of time than do many other media. Ordinary water is exciting, but adding new dimensions to water or changing its form adds further interest. New concepts can be learned as various changes are made in the water. In addition to using ordinary water as a sensory medium, the following ideas are suggested: adding food coloring, adding detergent to make bubbles (perhaps adding some straws to go with the bubbles), and adding ice to the water. On the other hand, it would be possible to begin with another medium, such as sand, and then let the children add water to it in the trough. These suggestions are only a few of the ways to utilize water in exploring and discovering.

Matthew wiped across his mouth with the back of his hand and announced: "I just had a drink of water so I wouldn't waste all that thirst!"

Although water is a substance with which the children have daily contact, many concepts can be taught relating to it. The children can, of course, learn that it is a liquid, and therefore can be poured. It can be compared to other liquids, or it can be pointed out that water is often the base of many liquids, such as punch or reconstituted orange juice.

Like other science areas, water can be used as an independent experience or it can be developed and expanded into a unit. Following is a discussion of some of the possible units relating to water: characteristics of water, forms of water, ice, uses of water by people, the water cycle, and general uses of water.

Concepts and Ideas for Teaching

1. Characteristics of water. (Teachers should not attempt to investigate the components of water with young children.)
   a. Has weight
   b. Is a liquid
   c. Is colorless, but can be colored by adding substances (food coloring, gelatin, ink, bluing)
   d. Takes the shape of the container into which it is poured
   e. Natural taste is changed with addition of chemicals used in purifying
   f. Temperature is changed by heating and cooling
   g. Evaporates (goes into the air)
2. There are different forms of water.
   a. Liquid (as previously explained)
   b. Ice—water in frozen form
   c. Steam—water that has changed to a gas or vapor
3. Water has many uses.
   a. People—drinking for survival; washing and cleansing of self, clothes, home, food; watering crops, gardens, and all plants in the surroundings; cooking; ice for preserving and cooling foods; steam for cleaning, ironing or pressing, removing wallpaper, stamps, or other items glued to surfaces, in generators, and in steam turbines
   b. Animals—survival; habitat
   c. Plants—survival; habitat
4. There is a water cycle. Water in the air condenses into clouds and comes to the ground in various forms—rain, snow, and so on. It then collects in lakes, seas, and ponds. From there, rivers and streams carry it to reservoirs and storage tanks. After purification, it is carried through underground pipes into homes, schools, buildings, and other places. Children may also be interested to learn that water collects underground, so that a well can be dug to pump the water from the ground. Children could observe the water pipes in a home under construction or in a home where the water pipes are easily viewed.
5. Many forms of recreation utilize water.
   a. Fishing
   b. Boating
   c. Swimming
   d. Water Skiing
6. Water is involved in many professions.
   a. Fire fighting—extinguishing fires
   b. Fishing
   c. Sailing—protecting the seas
   d. Plumbing—repairing water pipes and water systems
   e. Water quality engineer
7. Some objects sink in water, and some objects float.
8. Some materials dissolve in water, and some do not.
9. Some items absorb water, and some do not.
10. The quality of water is affected by humans.
11. The surface of the earth is mostly water (400 billion billion gallons), and most of the earth's water is in the oceans (97%), and so is salt water. About half of our fresh water is in ice caps and glaciers, so we must conserve and protect our fresh water.
12. People use more and more water all the time. The average person uses 125 gallons of water each day. That is too much; we need to conserve.

Activities and Experiences

1. Observe the forms and cycles of water by first discussing ice cubes and how they are formed. Then put them in an electric frying pan with the temperature on low. Observe as the ice cubes change first to water and then to steam as the water boils. Hold an aluminum pie plate above the steam to collect some of the moisture, and then observe the drops of water on the pie plate.

2. Bring into the classroom animals that live in water—fish, tadpoles, and other aquatic life.

3. Allow the children to discover what kinds of objects float and what kinds of objects sink in water. Provide a container of water and a box of materials (paper clips, marbles, cork, sticks, beads, rocks, sponges) for experimenting with sinking and floating. The children will discover that heavier items sink and lighter items float. However, through experimentation, they can also discover that items that sink are not always heavier than those that float. Begin with two equal-sized balls of oil-base clay. Ask the children if they think the clay balls will sink or float; then let them see that the balls will sink. Shape one of the balls of clay into a boat so that it will float. As an alternative, provide each child with a container of water, or have the children gather around a trough of water. Give each of the children a ball of the oil-base clay and ask whether they can do something to it so that it will float and not sink. If oil-base clay is not available, aluminum foil can be used. Ships do not sink for the same reason that this small clay boat does not sink. The boat is larger than the ball and pushes aside, or displaces, more water than the ball. The amount of water displaced by the boat weighs more than the boat itself. The water pushes the boat up until the weight of the boat and its cargo equals the weight of the displaced water.

4. Children will also enjoy decorating boats that have been cut from foam core, attaching and winding up a propeller with an elastic, and then racing the boats in wallpaper trays partially filled with water.

5. Put an empty, capped detergent bottle in a bowl or tub of water. It should float. Put a small amount of water in it, and it should still float. As more water is added, it sinks lower and lower, because an object will float if it is lighter in weight than the amount of water that would take up an equal amount of space. This same experiment can be performed with smaller plastic bottles.

   For younger children, a simple explanation might be that some objects are too heavy to float, or some objects are not porous enough (do not have enough air in them), or some objects need to be shaped like a boat in order to float.

6. Allow children to experiment with substances that dissolve in water and substances that do not. Compare sand, salt, marbles, an antacid tablet, flour, tapioca, soda, sugar, gelatin, and a powdered drink.

7. Give children two ice cubes each. Have them sprinkle rock salt on one ice cube, and then press the ice cubes together. The children should be able to see that the salt melts the ice. Try the same experiment with small rocks and note the difference.

8. Build a terrarium and observe the rain cycle. (See no. 21 of plant activities in Chapter Fifteen for directions for making a terrarium.)

9. Fill a large glass or plastic container partly full of water and mark the water level. Put the container in the freezer, or outside if the temperature is below freezing. After the water freezes, determine whether the ice line is above or below the water line. The children should discover that when water freezes, it expands. Allow the container of ice to melt back into a liquid. Compare ice and water lines again.

10. Fill two clear glass containers with water and mark the water levels. Leave the lid on one of the containers; leave the other container uncovered. Each day, observe and mark the water level in the uncovered bottle. Frequently compare the current water levels in both containers. Include the word *evaporation* often in the discussion.

11. Have the children take turns lifting different containers of water. They can lift a glass of water, but what about a pitcher or large bucket of water? Can they lift the pitcher or bucket without the water in it? Water has weight.

12. Compare the weight of a dry sponge with the weight of a wet sponge. Compare the weight of clothes that are dry with the weight of clothes that are damp and those that are wet.

13. With water tables, basins, or tubs, provide opportunities for pouring and measuring. Provide a variety of containers of various sizes for the children to play with, along with funnels and measuring cups. Encourage exploration of the concepts of more or less, substance, volume, and weight. Also provide small plastic bags to demonstrate that water has no definite shape but takes the shape of the container it is in.

14. Water play in a water table or basin can interest children for long periods of time. Other materials that can be included with the water on various occasions are sponges, straws, strainers, eggbeaters, medicine droppers, syringes (without needles, of course), a rubber bulb with a perforated nozzle, a hollow rubber ball with a hole in it, and rubber or plastic tubing.

15. Place an ordinary drinking glass in a dish and fill it carefully with water. As it is filled, carefully pour more water into the glass; the water will bulge above the edge of the glass and form a convex shape. This is because of surface tension. To show the effect of detergents on water, a drop of liquid detergent placed in the water will cause it to flow over the edge of the glass.

16. A needle, which is more dense than water, will float on top of water. This can be accomplished in two ways. One way is to hold the needle between the thumb and forefinger, lower the needle down toward the surface of water in a glass as close as possible without getting the needle wet, and then drop it. If the needle is dropped parallel to the surface from such a short distance, it should float. Use hard water, if possible. The second method is to place a small, single layer of toilet paper or tissue on top of the water and then place the needle on top of the paper. Then, with a small pointed object such as a toothpick, gently push the paper downward away from the needle.

17. Punch four or five small holes in a gallon can or a quart juice can, starting at the bottom and having the holes about an inch apart. Plug the holes with small pieces of wood, and then fill the can with water. As the plugs are pulled out rapidly (beginning with the bottom one), the water will shoot out the farthest from the bottom hole and least from the top hole. This shows that the deeper the water is, the greater the pressure.

18. Fill a large, small-mouth bottle with water. Fill a small test tube or small, cylindrically shaped bottle about half full of water. Invert it, placing it upside down into the large bottle. The amount of water in the test tube is critical; it should be just enough so the test tube will not sink. Make sure that the water comes to the top of the large bottle. Place your hand on top of the bottle, and as you push down the test tube will sink to the bottom. As you lift your hand and push down again, you will find that the small test tube will go up and down. This is because air will compress and water will not; so when you push down with your hand, water is forced

into the test tube, making it heavier so that it sinks.

19. Wipe the chalkboard with a damp cloth. Watch the dampness disappear as the water evaporates. Also, water can be observed to evaporate as a pan of water is boiled away on the stove.

20. Construct a simple, accurate rain gauge using an 8-inch funnel mounted in a box with a 2½-inch-diameter can underneath the funnel. The funnel should be mounted so that no rainwater seeps past the outside down into the catch can. The ratio of the area of the funnel to the catch can (an ordinary soft-drink can works well) is 10:1. So, when measuring the accumulated water in the can with a ruler, you must divide the water level by 10. For example, if, after a rainfall, 1½ (1.5) inches of water were measured in the can, this would indicate 0.15 (or fifteen hundredths) inch of rain.

21. Have the children compare the prices of a gallon of water, a gallon of punch, and a gallon of milk. The average price of water in the United States is one penny a gallon.

UNIT PLAN ON WATER

Field Trips

- Water laboratory
- Creeks, rivers, streams
- Fire station
- Fire hydrant
- Ice pond
- Place selling bricks of ice and dry ice
- Car wash
- Frozen-food locker plant
- Gymnasium—water fountain, swimming pool, shower room, steam room
- Pet store or place where children can observe an aquarium

Art

- Painting with water (this works best outside on a fence or sidewalk)
- Watercolor painting
- Easel painting
- Paper-sack fish
- Mixing paint
- Papier-mâché
- Plaster of Paris molds
- Soap-flake finger painting
- Salt-flour clay

Music

- Moving like water—locations, stages, sounds
- Sounds of water used for rhythms
- Rhythm sticks—tapping out rhythm of falling rain, thunder, and so on
- Containers with varying amounts of water—containers tapped with metal rod

Visitors

- Someone who will bathe a baby in the classroom
- Animals that need water (fish)
- Person to cook with water
- Custodian—water vacuum
- Forest ranger
- Fire fighter
- Parent to wash car

Food

- Boiled vegetables
- Cooked rice, macaroni—absorbing water
- Liquid for leavening
- Drinks
- Ice used for cooling
- Snow cones
- Homemade vegetable soup
- Gelatins
- Drink made from powdered mix

Science

- Floating objects
- Terrarium—rain cycle
- Stages and forms of water
- Items that absorb water and those that do not
- Items that dissolve in water and those that do not
- Uses of steam

- Uses of water in cleaning
- Animals that live and survive in water
- Overhead projector—colors mixed together

Literacy

- Write or tell "I like water because . . ."
- Write or tell "Water is . . ."
- Read and recite poems about water
- Read stories relating to water, such as *Fish Is Fish* (Lionni, 1970)

Additional Activities

- Water, ice, snow in trough
- Blowing bubbles
- Painting with water and brushes—outside
- Role playing with fire fighter's clothes, hats, fire trucks

LESSON PLAN ON WATER (1-DAY)

Overall Goals

- To help each child realize that humans have many uses for water—to dissolve some things, to drink, to cleanse some of the foods we eat, to swim, to wash our own bodies, to wash automobiles, to cool our bodies on a hot day, to put out fires, to cook, as an ingredient in many substances.
- To enable each child to name five of the preceding uses of water by humans.
- To increase awareness that water has three forms.

Whole-Group Activity

Introduction to Unit. Tell a story about a child who went swimming. The story leads into a discussion about some other uses humans have for water. Put pictures illustrating some of these uses on a flannel board as they are discussed.

Objectives

- To introduce the unit's theme and activities.
- To find out what the children already know about the uses of water by humans.

- To provide a visual aid to help in learning some of the uses of water.

Music—Rhythm Sticks. Give each child a pair of rhythm sticks and have the children tap the rhythm as an appropriate record is playing that imitates the falling of rain and then the sound of thunder.

Objective

- To increase the children's awareness of the sound and rhythms of rain and thunder.

Small-Group Activities

Field Trip to a Gymnasium. When the children first arrive, give them the opportunity to take a drink from the water fountain. At the gymnasium, lead the children on a tour and give them an explanation of the swimming pool, shower room, and steam room. Take special precautions to ensure the safety of the children. Soon after returning, hold a discussion on the field trip.

Objectives

- To demonstrate that often on a hot day and/or after physical exercise such as walking, our bodies are thirsty; water will quench this thirst.
- To observe three uses of water: enjoyment and exercise, to cleanse our bodies, and to relax our bodies (steam).
- To see two forms of water: liquid and steam.

Food—Vegetable Soup. Form cooperative learning groups for making homemade vegetable soup. Provide each group with a large bowl, scrub brush, paper towels, peeler, cutting board, and small knife. The children in each group will take turns doing the various steps. First, they will wash and scrub the vegetables in a large dishpan. Then, under close supervision, they will peel and slice the vegetables. One child will take the group's sliced vegetables to a large pan placed on a hot plate in the classroom. When all the groups are finished, add several quarts of hot water to the vegetables. Caution the children that the pan will soon be hot. Allow the soup to simmer for several hours to be eaten the next day.

Objectives

- To become aware that some foods we eat first need to be washed in water.
- To become aware that water is one of the ingredients in soup.
- To have the experience of using a peeler and a knife.
- To observe the water escaping from the soup as steam.
- To reinforce the idea that cooking foods have a smell.

Individual Activities

- Water and ice cubes in the trough

- Watercolor painting with primary colors at the double easel

Objectives

- To give the children further opportunity to explore the feel, smell, taste, and color of water.
- To give children the opportunity to beat, pour, and mix water.
- To demonstrate two forms of water as children observe ice melting in the water.

Summary

Because children are naturally curious about their environment, science is frequently a part of their exploration, play, questioning, and experimentation. Many science activities are preplanned into the curriculum, but most often, science-related experiences result from natural, spontaneous environmental stimulation. As children gain more knowledge in the areas of science, they become more able to understand their world. As they become more familiar with the earth, they also should learn that they can make a difference in protecting our environment—that the quality of air, soil, and water is determined by human treatment and care. They become more aware of, and comfortable with, nature, people, events, and materials surrounding them.

Valuable science activities for children include hearing, tasting, smelling, touching, inferring, observing, interpreting, classifying, drawing conclusions, solving problems, inquiring, reasoning, rationalizing, exploring, generalizing, comparing, creating, verifying, analyzing, predicting, and hypothesizing. Possibly no other single area of the curriculum involves as many process skills that are so important to the development of understanding and thinking in young children.

Student Learning Activities

1. From your reading and study of this chapter, develop some criteria for science activities and units for children. For example, science activities and units should provide opportunities for firsthand or real experiences.

2. From your study of this chapter, write down at least five of the process skills science helps to develop in young children. Now, for each skill you listed, suggest one science activity that would specifically give children practice in developing that skill. For example, to develop the skill of inferring, a good activity would be to pass around a gift-wrapped box containing several objects, such as paper clips and pennies. Have the children guess or infer what might be inside the box.

3. Make a list of science equipment and materials you would begin collecting for science

kits. Examples might be rocks, seed collections, thermometer, magnifying glass, tape measure, and others. Pick an area, such as magnets, and develop a science kit. Time will be provided in class to share your kits.

4. Plan and make at least one science material or piece of equipment.

5. Study some of the references listed for this chapter. From your study, write down three additional science activities.

6. Obtain, study, and evaluate at least three of the children's books suggested as references for this chapter. What science concepts does the book teach? How would you use the book with children? How effective would the book be in teaching a science concept to children?

7. Plan and carry out with children at least three science activities.

8. Select a science theme and prepare a unit plan or web for it.

9. From the unit plan or web prepared for item 8, complete an activity plan on the science theme you have selected.

10. From your work in items 8 and 9, prepare a lesson plan on a science theme.

Suggested Resources

Additional Science Resources

Althouse, R. (1988). *Investigating science experiences with young children.* New York: Teacher's College Press.

Butzow, G. M., & Butzow, J. W. (1989). *Science through children's literature.* Englewood, CO: Teacher Ideas Press.

Charlesworth, R., & Lind, K. K. (1990). *Math and science for young children.* New York: Delmar.

Caduto, M. J., & Bruchac, J. (1988). *Keepers of the earth: Native American stories with environmental activities for children.* Golden, CO: Fulcrum.

Edom, H. (1992). *Science activities.* Tulsa, OK: Educational Development.

Herman, M. L., Passineau, J. F., Schimpf, A. L., & Treurer, P. (1991). *Teaching kids to love the earth.* Duluth, MN: Pfeifer-Hamilton.

Katz, A. (1986). *Naturewatch: Exploring nature with your children.* Reading, MA: Addison-Wesley.

Lingelbach, J. (1986). *Hands-on nature.* Woodstock, VT: Vermont Institute of Natural Science.

Neuman, D. B. (1992). *Experiences in science for young children.* Prospect Heights, IL: Waveland.

Neuman, D. B (1993). *Experiencing elementary science.* Belmont, CA: Wadsworth.

Rockwell, R. E., Sherwood, E. A., & Williams, R. W. (1983). *Hug-a-tree: And other things to do outdoors with young children.* Mt. Rainier, MD: Gryphon House.

Sherwood, E. A., Williams, R. W., & Rockwell, R. E. (1990). *More mudpies to magnets.* Mt. Ranier, MD: Gryphon House.

Williams, R. A., Rockwell, R.E., & Sherwood, E. A. (1987). *Mudpies to magnets.* Mt. Ranier, MD: Gryphon House.

Periodicals

Chickadee: The Canadian Magazine for Children. Young Naturalist Foundation, 56 the Esplanade, Suite 304, Toronto, Ontario, Canada, M5E 1A7.

Child Life. P. O. Box 10681, Des Moines, IA 50381.

Children's Playmate Magazine. Children's Better Health Institute, 1100 Waterway Boulevard, P.O. Box 567, Indianapolis, IN 46206.

Koala Club News. Zoological Society of San Diego, Inc., P.O. Box 551, San Diego, CA 92212.

National Geographic News. P.O. Box 2330, Washington, DC 20009.

Ranger Rick's Nature Magazine. The National Wildlife Federation, 1412 16th Street, N.W., Washington, DC 20036.

Scholastic Let's Find Out. Scholastic Magazines, 1290 Wall Street, W., Lyndhurst, NJ 07071.

Scienceland, Inc. 501 5th Avenue, Suite 2102, New York, NY 10017.

Science Weekly. P.O. Box 70154, Washington, DC 10088.

Sesame Street. Children's Television Workshop, P.O. Box 2896, Boulder, CO 80322.

3 2 1 Contact. P.O. Box 2933, Boulder, CO 80322.

World. National Geographic Society, P.O. Box 2895, Washington, DC 20077-9960.

Your Big Back Yard. National Wildlife Federation, 1412 16th Street, N. W., Washington, DC 20036.

Zoo Books. P.O. Box 85382, San Diego, CA 92186-5384.

Children's Books

(See also lists of children's books in other text chapters.)

Baron, B. (1989). *Dinosaurs, dinosaurs.* New York: HarperCollins.

Barton, B. (1987). *Machines at work.* New York: Crowell.

Barton, B. (1990) *Bones, bones, dinosaur bones.* New York: HarperCollins.

Brandt, K. (1985). *Air.* Mahwah, NJ: Troll Associates.

Brandt, K. (1985). *Sound.* Mahwah, NJ: Troll Associates.

Branley, F. M. (1986). *Air is all around us.* New York: Scribner's.

Carle, E. (1991). *The tiny seed.* Saxonville, MA: Picture Book Studio.

Edom, H. (1992). *Science with light and mirrors.* Tulsa, OK: Educational Development.

Edom. H. (1992). *Science with magnets.* Tulsa, OK: Educational Development.

Edom, H. (1992). *Science with water.* Tulsa, OK: Educational Development.

George, W. T. (1991). *Fishing at Long Pond.* New York: Greenwillow.

Gibbons, G. (1982). *Tool book.* New York: Holiday House.

Hiscock, B. (1991). *The big tree.* New York: Antheneum.

Hoban, R. (1960). *Bedtime for Frances.* New York: Harper & Row.

Hoban, T. (1990). *Shadows and reflections.* New York: Greenwillow.

Jeffers, S. (1991). *Brother Eagle, Sister Sky: A message from Chief Seattle.* New York: Dial.

Keats, E. J. (1964). *Whistle for Willie.* New York: Viking.

Knowlton, J. (1985). *Maps and globes.* New York: Harper & Row.

Lionni, L. (1970). *Fish is fish.* New York: Pantheon.

Livingston, M. C., & Fisher, L. E. (1986). *Earth songs.* New York: Holiday House.

Locker, T. (1991). *The land of Gray Wolf.* New York: Dial.

MacGill-Calihan, S. (1991). *And still the turtle watched.* New York: Dial.

McGovern, A. (1971). *Stone soup.* New York: Scholastic.

Mitgutsch, A. (1986). *From wood to paper.* Minneapolis: Carolrhoda Books.

Most, B. (1991). *A dinosaur named after me.* San Diego: Harcourt Brace Jovanovich.

Patent, D. H. (1990). *Yellowstone fires: Flames and rebirth.* New York: Holiday House.

Pluckrose, H. (1986). *Thinking about hearing.* New York: Franklin Watts.

Rockwell, A., & Rockwell, H. (1971). *Machines.* New York: Harper & Row.

Rockwell, A., & Rockwell, H. (1971). *The toolbox.* New York: Harper & Row.

Scarry, R. (1971). *The great big air book.* New York: Random House.

Steig, W. (1969). *Sylvester and the magic pebble.* New York: Windmill Books.

Testa, F. (1983). *If you look around you.* New York: Dial.

Wade, H. (1977). *Sand.* Milwaukee: Raintree.

West, D. (1992). *Why is the sky blue: And answers to all of the questions you always wanted to ask.* New York: Barron's.

Wilkes, A. (1991). *My first green book.* New York: Knopf.

Wyler, P. (1986). *Science fun with toy boats and planes.* New York: Julian Messner.

Pictures

Astronomy. The Child's World.

Common rock and rock-forming minerals. Society for Visual Education.

The desert. The Child's World.

Earth movements. The Child's World.

Ecology: The pollution problem. David C. Cook.

Ecosystems. David C. Cook.

Erosion. The Child's World.

Glaciers. The Child's World.

Important minerals. Society for Visual Education.

Land forms of running water. Society for Visual Education.

Learning about energy. David C. Cook.
Learning about nature. David C. Cook.
Polar regions. The Child's World.
Safety. David C. Cook.
Science themes no. 1. David C. Cook.
Science themes no. 2. David C. Cook.
The sea. The Child's World.
Volcanoes. The Child's World.

Multimedia Kits

Disney's beginning map skills series. Walt Disney.
Our planet earth. National Geographic.
Simple machines for primaries. Eye Gate Media.
What air can do. National Geographic.

Films, Filmstrips, and Videos

About air. Eye Gate Media.
About motion. Eye Gate Media.
About water. Eye Gate Media.
All things change. Eye Gate Media.
The big sun and our earth. Coronet Films.
Conservation for beginners. Coronet Films.
Day and night. Eye Gate Media.
Earth, moon, sun, and space. National Geographic.
Fire: Friend and foe. National Geographic.
Five billion years. McGraw-Hill/CRM.
Foundation of science. Campus Films.
Gravity and what it does. Coronet Films.

How levers help us. Coronet Films.
How light helps us. Coronet Films.
How ramps help us. Coronet Films.
How simple machines make work easier. Coronet Films.
How wedges help us. Coronet Films.
How wheels help us. Coronet Films.
Land and waters of our earth. Coronet Films.
Learning with your eyes. Coronet Films.
Learning with your senses. Coronet Films.
Light and shadows. Eye Gate Media.
Living and non-living things. Coronet Films.
Magnets for beginners. Coronet Films.
Making shadows with Pierrot. Coronet Films.
My world . . . earth. Churchill Films.
My world . . . water. Churchill Films.
S.P.L.A.S.H. McGraw-Hill/CRM.
Saving our planet. National Geographic.
Shadows, shadows everywhere. Coronet Films.
Soil: What it is and what it does. Coronet Films.
Solids, liquids, and gases. National Geographic.
A space flight around the earth. Churchill Films.
Turn a handle, flick a switch. Churchill Films.
Wonders in a country stream. Churchill Films.
Wonders in your own backyard. Churchill Films.

Computer Software

Computergarten. Scholastic, Inc.
Micros for micros: Estimation. Lawrence Hall of Science.

twelve

Weight and Balance

Introduction

Weight and balance are difficult but exciting concepts to explore with young children. Like many of the other concepts that have been discussed, this one must be explored through concrete experiences. Children usually judge the weight of an object by its size. As a result, children often misjudge the weight of an object and how much strength they need to pick it up (Hurlock, 1977).

An understanding of weight is necessary before one can comprehend the meaning of balance. A discussion of the relationship between gravity and weight will depend on the age and understanding of the children. Weight is the result of gravity, and gravity is stronger closer to the center of the earth. Therefore the farther away an object is from the earth's center, the lighter in weight it is. An object at sea level will weigh slightly more than the same object on a high mountain.

The same principle accounts for the pressure felt on the ears when one rapidly changes altitude. The air is heavier near the surface of the earth, and changing altitude alters the pressure (or weight) of air on the ears.

Older children will be able to understand the effect gravity has on an object, as well as the air pressure on ears. Younger children will understand weight in terms of heaviness.

Weight is the heaviness or lightness of an object as it is weighed on a scale by use of a standard of measure. The terms *heavy* and *light*, commonly used in defining weight, are relative, or comparative. One must have two objects to compare before being able to determine that one object is heavier or lighter than the other. It is impossible, technically, to state that a single object is heavy unless it has been determined that an amount greater than so many pounds is heavy. One must also consider to whom an object would seem heavy. What is heavy to a child is much different from what is heavy to a teenager or an adult. What is heavy to a dockworker, a farmer, a furniture mover, or someone with great strength is much different from what is heavy to someone with little physical strength.

An object is *balanced* when stability has been achieved by an even distribution of weight on each side of a fulcrum, or point of support. A *fulcrum* is a point of balance between two objects. It is not necessarily located at a central point between these objects, however. When objects are balanced, their weight or number is equalized on both sides. Thus two objects of unequal weight can be balanced by either (1) moving the fulcrum or (2) moving the two objects in such a way that the lighter of the two is farther from the fulcrum on one side, and the heavier of the two is closer to the fulcrum on the other side. If objects are of equal weight, such as blocks or chips, two or more can be put closer to the fulcrum and one farther from the fulcrum, thus equalizing the weight on both sides. This discovery is exciting to children; it can be achieved in another way by having children of different weights balance on a teeter-totter.

Children acquire the concept of balance by balancing themselves. They may try to balance on one foot with their eyes open and then with their eyes closed. They may then change feet and try the same activity again. Soon they begin to recognize the state of stability of the object or objects in balance.

Daily Experiences with Weight and Balance

It is important to remember that daily experiences are valuable in developing an awareness of weight and balance. Riddles and guessing games are easily used in teaching weight and balance. For example, say: "I weigh the same as a pound of hot dogs, and you use me on toast in the morning. What am I?" The answer is a pound of butter or margarine. Or one may say: "You use me in cakes and cookies and on your cereal, and I weigh the same as 5 pounds of flour. What am I?" The answer is 5 pounds of sugar. Guessing games are especially adaptable with weight and balance. Display objects of different weights and ask which ones weigh the same, which one weighs the most, and which one weighs the least. Which toy is heaviest? Which of these two books weighs more? Can you find at least three objects in our room that weigh more than 5 pounds each? Can you balance the balance board or the balance scales with sand on one side and blocks on the other side? A balance scale is an excellent piece of equipment to include in the water table or trough with small, dry media; it gives children an opportunity for practical exploration of both weight and balance. Similes and metaphors also can be used with weight. For example, the phrases "as heavy as _____" and "as light as _____" could be completed with the children's own ideas of heavy and light objects. Exploratory questions asking what makes an object heavier or lighter could also be used frequently.

Walking on a balance beam is easier when assisted by an encouraging, supportive helper.

As young children begin to have experiences with weight, they need many opportunities to compare weights by using their own muscles. They should have practice in determining *equivalents*—weights that are the same. Scales or balance scales can be used for these activities. Experiment with directive questions, such as "How many pennies are the same weight as 20 buttons?" or "How many little rocks weigh the same as two pencils?" Children also need activities requiring balance—using their bodies as the means of balance or using equipment such as the teeter-totter or the balance scales to achieve a balanced state.

Many opportunities to become familiar with weight vocabulary should be provided. As children have many exposures to words and their meanings, the words soon become possessions and are active parts of the children's vocabularies. The following are examples of weight words:

heavy/light   heaviest/lightest   ponderous
heavier/lighter   weighty

Children must also relate weight to the standard units of weight measurement. They must therefore understand that weight is measured in ounces, pounds, and tons. Eventually they will need to know what these terms mean and how they relate to one another—for example, 16 ounces in a pound or 2,000 pounds in a ton. Children should also be exposed to the standard units of weight measurement in the metric system: grams, milligrams, kilograms, and so on. Broman (1982) simplifies the metric units of meter, liter, and gram as follows: 1,000 = kilo-; 100 = hecto-; 10 = deka-; 1/10 = deci-; 1/100 = centi-; and 1/1,000 = milli- (pp. 289–290). In addition, inches can be compared with centimeters, feet with decimeters, yards with meters, rods with dekameters, miles with kilometers, ounces with grams, pounds with kilograms, and Fahrenheit with Celsius. All dry and liquid quantities are measured in liters.

Children often relate weight to themselves and their own body weight. They may know that they weight 42 pounds, though they may not know exactly what that means. It would be interesting, then, for them to find other things that weigh 42 pounds: How many large-unit blocks would it take to weigh 42 pounds? How many books could weigh 42 pounds? What could you pack in a suitcase to make it weigh 42 pounds? Probably anything the child can lift is "light," and anything that cannot be lifted is "heavy."

Approach to Teaching

Concepts and Ideas for Teaching

1. Gravity determines weight and depends on an object's distance from the center of the earth. The farther from the earth's center, the less the weight. Weight is the force with which a body is attracted toward the earth by gravitation.

   a. A parent weighing 180 pounds on the seacoast would weigh less on a mountaintop and only 30 pounds on the moon.

   b. The higher in the sky an airplane flies, the less it weighs.

2. Anything that takes up space has weight; even items having apparently no weight still have weight that can be measured on a fine scale.

   a. Feather

   b. Scrap of paper

   c. Penny

   d. Small piece of candy

3. Weight is measured through the use of instruments called *scales*.

4. Weight can change.

   a. Additions

      (1) People gaining weight by adding pounds

      (2) Air added to an inner tube

(3) Water added to a dry sponge

(4) Balloon inflated

b. Subtractions

(1) Release of air from a balloon

(2) Drying out of a wet sponge

(3) Removal of a baby's clothes (making the total weight less)

c. Physical growth and aging

(1) Children generally gaining weight as they grow

(2) Older people often losing weight as they become very old

(3) Old, shriveled apples weighing less than young, firm apples

5. A change in weight may result in an alteration of appearance.

   a. Either adding or subtracting many pounds from a person

   b. An inflated balloon compared to a deflated balloon

6. Changing the form or rearranging the structure of an item will not change its weight.

   a. A pound of butter weighs the same when melted

   b. A tower of 10 blocks weighs the same as those 10 blocks in a pile

   c. An amount of water weighs the same when it is frozen into a solid as when it is a liquid

7. Weight is not determined by size, shape, age, or equal amounts. Some items may look heavy but are light; and some items may look light but are heavy.

   a. A pound of nails is not equal in amount to a pound of feathers

   b. A large Styrofoam container, such as that used to hold a tape recorder, weighs less than a smaller cardboard container, such as a jewelry box

   c. Older people do not necessarily weigh more than younger people

d. Gifts of various shapes do not vary in weight merely because of a variation in shape

8. Different items may have the same weight.

   a. An 11-year-old child may weigh about the same as a bale of hay

   b. A 10-pound bag of sugar may weigh the same as a child's dog

   c. A pound of butter weighs the same as a pound of bacon

9. Many items are sold and packaged in 1-pound units of measure.

   a. Bacon   f. Candy
   b. Butter   g. Nuts
   c. Rice   h. Nails
   d. Cereal   i. Plaster
   e. Meat   j. Salt

10. The same items may vary in weight.

    a. Apples   d. Rocks
    b. People   e. Marbles
    c. Boxes   f. Automobiles

11. Air has weight.

12. Weight experiences may involve making comparisons between the weights of two or more objects, in addition to ordering items from lightest to heaviest.

13. Balance is not necessarily achieved by supporting an object or a group of objects in the middle, but by obtaining stability through an even distribution of weight on either side of a fulcrum, or vertical axis.

14. Materials do not have to be of the same kind, substance, or amount to be balanced.

    a. A roll of cellophane tape balanced on one side of the balance board, with a wooden block on the other side (heavier object moved closer to the fulcrum to achieve balance)

    b. Wheat on one side of the balance scale, rice on the other.

    c. Two wooden blocks, balanced with one wooden block

Activities and Experiences

Experiments with weight comparisons

1. Place wrapped packages of different sizes and shapes in order, from lightest to heaviest.

2. Visit a pumpkin patch, or collect as many pumpkins as you can find. Weigh and measure them, and order them from lightest to heaviest. (Use other seasonal items such as icicles or apples or other objects such as shoes, blocks, and so on.)

3. Have the children match duplicate weights of items—even when the items are not the same or the items are not the same size, shape, or equal in amount.

   a. Boxes of different sizes filled with various items and then wrapped
      (1) Ordered according to weight by children
      (2) Scales kept nearby to weigh those that are difficult to determine by lifting
      (3) Paper sacks containing various items used as an alternative
   b. Balance scales used to match items of same weight
      (1) Scales or pans in the same position on either side of the fulcrum
      (2) Children try to choose items of similar weight and verify the weights by using a scale
      (3) If possible, a scale measuring both pounds and ounces showing actual weights
   c. Different amounts of various items—feathers, candies, nails, bolts, wheat, balloons, dry cereal—weighed by children to determine how much of an item is required to equal a pound

4. Have the children close their eyes and determine, by lifting various objects, which ones are heavier.

5. Ask the children to examine groups or pairs of objects and decide by observation which ones are heavier. Have them follow up by lifting objects or weighing them to determine whether the selections are correct.

6. Have the children keep a record of their own weight and record the changes. The children can then find things that weigh less than they do, things that weigh more than they do, and things that weigh the same as they do.

   a. Number of large-unit blocks equaling their own weight
   b. Comparison of weights
      (1) Children weighed on scales
      (2) Children weighed holding an item such as a book, a pound of butter, or some blocks

7. Introduce the children to units of measure by introducing them to scales. Focus first on scales that weigh in pounds, and give them many experiences with pounds. Then introduce the concept of ounces (a unit for measuring less than a pound), and let the children measure items on an ounce scale (e.g., a diet scale). After this exposure, intro-

Melissa is intrigued with the vacillating dial as she climbs off and on, off and on the scales.

duce older children to a unit of measure less than ounces—grams—and try to locate a scale sensitive enough to weigh grams. In addition, older children may be exposed to the unit of measure representing 2,000 pounds (a ton). Many heavy items are weighed in tons. A weigh station or trucking corporation are possible places to see items being weighed in tons.

8. Use the balance scales with sensory media such as wheat, rice, or buttons to enable the children to explore the concepts of balance and weight. Various kinds of items can be used with the balance scales for making weight comparisons, as well as for balancing items of equal weight and for distributing weight in order to make the balance scales stable.

9. Perform experiments to show that air has weight.[1] For example, select two balloons that are exactly the same (put them on the balance scales). Measure two lengths of string that are exactly the same kind and length (about 10 inches). Tie the string to the deflated balloons. Suspend a yardstick with a string in the middle, or balance it on the spine of a book, using the book as a fulcrum. Tie a string with a balloon attached to each end of the yardstick in the same location. Whether the yardstick or the balance scales is used, the balloons should balance evenly. Now remove one of the balloons and blow air into it. Tie the string back on it and return it to the same place on the yardstick. It will be obvious that the balloon containing air has more weight because the yardstick or balance scales will tip lower on the side with the inflated balloon.

Experiments with sinking and floating

1. Put a number of different objects—feathers, corks, small wooden sticks, hairpins, pebbles,

[1] See Chapter Eleven for additional experiments with air.

coins—near a bowl, basin, or trough of water. Let the children predict which objects will sink and which will float. Have a box for the objects that sink, as well as a box for those that float.

2. Give each child an equal amount of oil-base clay (a ball about an inch in diameter). Challenge the children to see whether the clay will float in a trough of water or large bowl of water. Ask them to see whether they can change its shape in such a way that it will float. If the children are not successful, show them how to press the clay flat and then mold the edges up to make a little boat.

3. The previous experiment can also be done with pieces of aluminum foil.

Experiments with balance

1. From a school physics laboratory, obtain an analytical balance scale, which is sensitive to weights of less than an ounce. Then have the children experiment with balancing such objects as feathers, scraps of paper, toothpicks, hairpins, needles, and thumbtacks. They can also determine which is the heaviest of the objects they are using for the experiment. Working with this balance scale is the same as working with the larger balance scale, except that objects of lighter weight can be balanced.

2. Put two children of different weights on the teeter-totter and challenge them to find a way to make it balance. The heavier child will be closer to the fulcrum, and the lighter one will be farther away.

3. Provide a balance board made from plywood about 1/2 by 2 1/2 by 24 inches. The fulcrum can be made with a block of wood measuring 1/2 by 1/2 by 3 inches. With a marking pencil or pen, rule off the board in equal inch divisions and draw a line across the board at each division. Be sure to start at the middle and work toward both ends. Begin labeling the marks on each side from the

Alexis is discovering the challenge of balancing a ruler on the spine of the book.

center to the ends, beginning 1, 2, 3, . . ., but do not label the middle mark. Now give the child six or eight 1-inch blocks (made by the teacher or commercially). Many experiences with balancing can be performed with these simple materials. One of the best ways to begin is to let the children experiment with the materials without giving any directions. After the children have balanced the board on the fulcrum, some of the following activities will provide reinforcement (see Figure 12–1):

a. Two blocks placed on either side of fulcrum after balancing the board on the fulcrum—children to determine whether each block must be placed at the same distance from the fulcrum to make the board balance

b. Four blocks (two on each side) placed on either side of the fulcrum—children to discover ways to position the blocks and still have the board balance

c. Two sets of three blocks each, four blocks each, and so on used to balance the board on the fulcrum by placing each equal set on either side of the fulcrum

d. Two sets of unequal numbers of blocks used to balance the board on the fulcrum
   (1) One block placed on one side and two blocks on the other side of the fulcrum; three blocks on one side; and one on the other; many more variations
   (2) Older children are encouraged to discover an additional principle: that one or two blocks placed farther from the fulcrum can balance several blocks closer to the fulcrum; for example, blocks placed on positions 1, 3, and 5 on one side balance one block placed on position 9 on the other side, since $1 + 3 + 5 = 9$

e. Fulcrum moved by the children so that it is not at the midpoint (perhaps under position 1 or 2 on either side). The children determine whether balance can be achieved

UNIT PLAN ON WEIGHT AND BALANCE

Art

- Wrapped packages decorated with paint or collage materials (packages of various weights, then used for balancing or weighing)
- Decorated music shakers—empty juice cans, milk cartons, or boxes filled with items of varying weight such as rice, feathers, rocks, sand
- Papier-mâché molded around an inflated balloon; let dry, then pop the balloon, and paint or decorate ball as desired

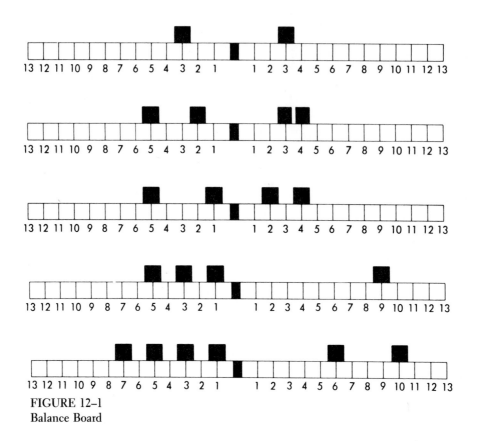

FIGURE 12–1
Balance Board

Food

- Any food experience dealing with items sold in 1-pound quantities (bacon, rice, meat, butter, bread, etc.)
- Baking of cake and weighing it in various stages—cake mix first, then total weight changed by adding water and eggs, and then again by putting it in baking pan
- Spaghetti or macaroni, which has changed weight from lighter when dry to heavier after being cooked in water

Visitors

- Persons from school physics department—various scales brought to the classroom
- Doctor or nurse—use of scales
- Grocery clerk with items in 1-pound packages

- Employee from state department of weights and measures
- Parent with bathroom scales

Music

- Decorated music shakers to use with selected records
- Musical boxes (instead of musical chairs) of different sizes, shapes, and weights. (As music stops, children lift box they are sitting on; then when game is finished, see if they have been able to determine which box was lightest and which box was heaviest.)
- Creative movements—pretending to carry a heavy rock; pretending to toss a light rock into the air; pretending to be a balloon being filled with air and suddenly bursting

Science

- Deflated inner tube weighed, then inflated one weighed
- Deflated balloon weighed, then inflated one weighed
- Dry sponge weighed, soaked with water, weighed, allowed to dry, weighed again
- Teeter-tooter set up for comparison of children's and teachers' weights; also for comparative weighing of various objects in the room
- Wrapped packages matched by weight
- Pound of butter weighed in cube, then after melting
- Rice, wheat, or spaghetti weighed, soaked in water, then weighed again

Field Trips

- Physics department in a school—observation of scales and their uses
- Doctor's office—use of scales with people
- Medical supply store—observation of various scales and their uses
- Weigh station—use of scales with vehicles
- Trucking corporation—use of scales with vehicles
- Grain elevator—use of scales with crops and produce
- Grocery store—scales at checkout stand, meat scales, and scales near fresh produce
- Livestock auction yards—use of scales with animals
- Beach or sandy hills—different-sized containers for filling and weighing amounts of sand
- Post office—observation of weighing of packages

Literacy

- Write and illustrate a story. "_____ Is One Pound."
- Write and illustrate a story using the comparisons "_____ Is Heavier Than _____" and "_____ Is Lighter Than _____."

Summary

Children usually judge an object's weight by its size, and many experiences with weight are necessary before a correct understanding of weight is achieved. Numerous concrete activities with gravity, air pressure, balancing, and comparing assist children in determining the meanings of weights and balance. As children become more familiar with weight- and balance-related vocabulary words, their knowledge broadens to include the various standard and metric units of measurement.

Student Learning Activities

1. Interview and visit with children ages 2 to 8 about concepts relating to weight. Ask them how much they weigh. Ask the children to make weight comparisons of objects in the environment. How do concept understandings of weight vary between the older and younger children you interview?

2. Prepare at least one teacher-made material for teaching weight or balance to young children.

3. With a group of children, implement at least one of the activities and experiences related to weight or balance suggested in this

chapter. The group of children may be a classroom group or a gathering of relatives or neighborhood children. Evaluate your experience.

4. Think of additional ideas for the unit plan on weight and balance.

5. Prepare an activity plan on weight and balance.

6. Visit a children's library or media center and see whether you can discover books, pictures, recordings, or filmstrips relating to weight and/or balance.

Suggested Resources

Computer Software

How to Weigh an Elephant. (Panda/Learning Technologies). Apple, C64/128.

CHAPTER
thirteen

Color

Introduction

Children delight in learning colors, and the world opens new doors for them as color concepts are mastered. The environment is full of colors; color is a concept that children live with daily. They see, feel, use, and respond to colors (Hubbard, 1990). Infants are quick to notice brightly colored objects and patterns in their surroundings. This is a concept that very young children are interested in and quick to understand.

Using color names is one way a child can describe his or her world. "Colors also serve as one basis for classification. . . . The child also experiences seriation as he orders colors from lightest to darkest. . . . The child who discovers color concepts becomes more aware of his environment and can relate his knowledge to new situations" (Althouse & Main, 1975, p. 1). Being aware of various properties of color enables us to understand better how color concepts can be approached in the early childhood curriculum. These properties include name (or hue), intensity or saturation (brightness or dullness), pure (primary) or mixed (secondary), temperature (coolness and warmth), and value (lightness or darkness) (Feeney & Moravcik, 1987).

Color Concepts and Labels

Color often is used as a clue in identifying and describing objects before other concepts such as size, shape, and number are used. When becoming interested in color, the child first recognizes what color is and will describe items in terms of color. However, frequently the color label is wrong; it takes time to learn correct color labels. When beginning to learn colors, the child is unable to label or name the colors, and yet is able to recognize that a particular item is the same color as another item. In effect, the child is able to match colors. Comments such as the following may be heard: "My shoes are licorice color" or "I want to wear the lemon shirt" or "I'll use the book that's fire-engine color."

One day as Creighton entered the classroom, the teacher asked him if he remembered the color of his eyes. When his expression indicated that he had forgotten, and since there was no mirror close by, the teacher gave him a clue by saying, "They're the same color as my eyes." As he looked at the teacher's eyes, he responded excitedly, saying, "Them there eyes are root beer!" The teacher recognized that although he did not yet know the label brown, *Creighton knew that his eyes and hers were the same color as root beer—surely the beginning of understanding the color brown.*

Thus the child should not be assumed to be wrong if, in the process of naming colors of familiar items, nontraditional names such as *chocolate brown, fire-engine red, lemon yellow,* and *lime green* are used. When a child uses such a label, the teacher might suggest that that is one name for the color and then also say the traditional name.

Brady announced to his teacher, "Today I wore my coat with flag colors!" as he hung up his red, white, and blue jacket.

A teacher asked a child to examine his plaid-colored shirt and tell her any of the colors in the shirt. He responded with a quick "My shirt is rainbow-colored," and he was indeed correct.

Before young children are taught the labels of colors, they can be given many experiences in matching and sorting colors. A deck of cards can be sorted by color, or construction paper can be cut into squares, circles, or other shapes and then sorted into piles of similar colors. Even before children label colors, they have the ability to point to a particular color when asked to find it. For example, on a particular page of a story being read, if there are several animals of different colors, the teacher might say, "Point to the animal that is yellow." Or, while eating, say, "Find something that is red." As long as this game is not overused, children will continue to enjoy playing it.

While learning a specific color (e.g., yellow), the child may readily identify objects that are yellow while not yet being sure which ones are not yellow. The child who knows that apples, to-matoes, and stop signs are red may then ask whether the banana is also red. Or the child may know what green *is* but not yet know what green *is not*.

Once children begin to identify colors by their names or labels, there should be many opportunities for using colors. One way is to give children color choices. For example, when crayons or papers are distributed, the children can be asked what color they chose. Since they often have favorite colors, when it is feasible allow them to select items on the basis of their color preferences. Most children prefer lighter and brighter colors to darker and duller colors. Kane (1982) states that "stimulated by response to colors, glandular activities can alter moods, speed up heart rates, and increase brain activity" (p. 36). According to Kane, red is the "exciter"; pink is restful and even has a tranquilizing effect; blue evokes a mood of tranquility and serenity and is a cool color; yellow is the "energizer" because it lifts spirits and is said to make people feel peppy and optimistic; and green is the "masquerader" because people think it is calming (but studies actually show it to be irritating).

Teaching Color Concepts

Since the world is saturated with colors, there are numerous opportunities for encouraging children's awareness of the world of color. Color should be used often in everyday conversations with children. The teacher can comment on the color of the sky, trees, flowers, clothing the child is wearing, eyes, hair, or the book being carried. Questions such as "What else is this color?" or "This is the same color as what?" should be used often for problem solving relating to color.

To avoid confusion when teaching color, it is important to remember that color is an *attribute*, not an object. Grammatically speaking, color names are both nouns and adjectives, but when they are taught as adjectives, children understand them more easily. In other words, use the name of both the color and the object being described. For example, of a seashell, say, "That is an orange seashell" or "That seashell is orange in color" rather than "That is orange."

As a lesson plan on color is being prepared, the teacher should be well aware of the needs and abilities of the particular group of children before deciding on an approach. Several alternatives are available, depending on the developmental level of the children in terms of their color understandings. For children who have little understanding of color, begin the experiences with color by focusing on what color is. Then spend perhaps 1 or 2 days or even a week on each of the primary and secondary colors. This approach will provide a sure understanding and knowledge of these six basic colors. Along with each of the colors, the various shades could also be taught. For example, as blue is being studied, also teach dark blue, navy blue, light blue, turquoise blue,

and so on. Another approach is to begin with the primary colors and then advance to the secondary colors. While learning secondary colors, the children discover that they are made by combining the primary colors. After the study of the primary and secondary colors, the children then go back to shades of colors. Since they have learned that the secondary colors are made by combining colors, it is exciting to learn how shades of a particular color are made—by adding white paint to make it lighter, by adding black paint to make it darker, or by adding another color to change the shade. Color mixing provides other opportunities for young children to explore.

Psychological Influences of Color

The psychological influences of color should be included in discussions about color. Colors are symbolic and often influence feelings. People react differently to colors for cultural reasons, and different cultures attach various meanings to color. For example, to the Irish, green is lucky; to the Chinese, red means good luck or happiness. A person's color preferences tell something about personality, and in some studies color tests have been developed that reveal personality characteristics that are a result of color preferences. In an article in *Time* magazine ("The Bluing of America," 1983), Marielle Bancou, Executive Director of the Color Association of the United States (CAUS), is said to have studied the psychology of color; "his studies also indicate that different colors appeal to specific types of people: red to the active, yellow to the high-minded, orange to the friendly, blue-green to the fastidious" (p. 62).

Colors can affect some people's moods and create particular memories. Colors in the environment can influence behavior, reactions, and morale; but usually colors are *associated with* particular behaviors; they are not the *reason for* the behaviors. However, adults who are working with children should select the colors that are to be part of the children's surroundings carefully. It

Sherrie is mixing primary colors in Styrofoam® egg cups and discovering secondary colors.

would be well to paint classrooms for children in "beautiful" colors and avoid too many kinds of distracting and overstimulating patterns (Feeney & Moravcik, 1987).

Another interesting article in *Time* magazine, "Blue Is Beautiful" (1973), states that the child's intelligence and imagination are influenced by a favorite color. Researchers found that popular, or "beautiful," colors such as light blue, yellow, yellow-green, or orange stimulated alertness and creativity, whereas "ugly" colors such as white, black, and brown had negative effects on the children studied. Color is symbolic, since children associate certain things with particular colors. For children, color is a way of describing and communicating the details of something, symbolizing a mood, and creating metaphors (Hubbard, 1990).

Approach to Teaching

Concepts and Ideas for Teaching

1. Colors have names and these names are used to describe objects.
2. Most objects have a color.
3. Some objects do not have a color.
   a. Water
   b. Clear plastic
   c. Clear glass
4. Many items are similar in color.
   a. Red: apply, cherry, tomato, berries, items of red clothing, hair, material
   b. Green: plants, vegetables, books, sweaters
   c. Yellow: lemon, sun, yellow butterfly, corn on the cob
5. The same items may vary in color.
   a. Cars: red, black, green, and so on. The same model and kind will come in various colors
   b. People: red, white, black, brown
   c. Eyes: blue, black, green, brown, hazel
   d. Apples: yellow, green, red, brown

6. Single items may vary in shades of the same color.
   a. Trees: shades of green
   b. Fabric: shades of any color
   c. Paint: shades of any color
7. Single items may have various colors.
   a. Fabrics: plaids, stripes, others
   b. Trees: in the fall, a tree may have leaves of many colors
   c. Pictures or paintings
8. Color may be modified or changed.
   a. Combining: When two or more colors are combined, the color will be changed and a new one made, or the shade of the original color will be different. Working with colored water or paints offers many possibilities for exploring new colors by combining colors. The child should learn that the secondary colors (green, orange, and purple) are made by combining the primary colors (red, yellow, and blue). Red and yellow will make orange, red and blue will make purple, and yellow and blue will make green. When combining these colors, start with the lighter of the two colors and then add the darker color. (It is easier to make colors darker than lighter.) The child who has learned these combinations can easily understand that every other color is made by combining the primary colors in various ways.
   b. Adding: In food, art, and science activities, colors can be changed by adding additional ingredients. For example, when making gingerbread, the original ingredients of sugar, eggs, and shortening will change color when the molasses is added.
   c. Heat, cooking, or the sun: Exposure to the sun or the process of heating or cooking will often change the color of an item. Meats will change, when cooked, from red color to brown; bakery items such as gingerbread or chocolate cake will

often become lighter in color. Toast, waffles, or pancakes will become darker, as will anything that burns. Roasted marshmallows or hot dogs become darker. Exposure to the sun will often fade or lighten items, but people become tanned or sunburned.

d. Freezing or cooling: Most items become lighter when frozen. When comparing the changes in color before and after freezing, make sure to have examples of the item both before and after the freezing process.

e. Drying: The colors of fruits or other foods will change as they are dried. The colors of some art media may change as drying occurs.

f. Aging: Food in various stages shows changes in color. Physical characteristics of people may change color during the aging process, and the skin, hair, and eye colors of babies often change in a short period of time.

g. Natural changes: Weather changes such as frost, freezing, rain, and sun can result in changes in color. It is exciting to teach the changes of the autumn leaves resulting from cooler temperatures.

h. Camouflage: Some animals will change color to camouflage, disguise, or hide themselves. Examples are the snowshoe rabbit and the chameleon.

9. Colors may be symbolic:

a. Seasons: green for spring and summer; yellow, orange, and brown for fall

b. Holidays: red and green for Christmas; orange and black for Halloween

c. People: red, black, white, yellow

d. Clothing: particular shades and colors are worn more typically during certain seasons; black clothing signifies mourning

e. Feelings: moods described in terms of color—blue for depressed, black for angry, or red for angry

f. Safety: red meaning stop, green meaning go, yellow meaning caution

g. Danger: red

h. Sickness: yellow, red (flushed), white (pale), green

i. Injury: black-and-blue or red

j. School colors: football teams

k. Patriotism: red, white, and blue for the United States, or patriotic colors representing other native countries of students

l. Foods: possible alteration of taste when food is not the expected color. (It is assumed that the taste *is* altered.)

Activities and Experiences

1. Let the children observe and have opportunities for mixing colors, especially the primary colors into the secondary colors. The following media and methods are possibilities:

a. Food coloring: Use either a quart jar or gallon jar filled with water, and put enough drops of yellow in it to make it a dark yellow color; mix well. Then add a few drops of red and watch as the yellow water changes to orange; mix well. Repeat this experience with other colors. Use baby food jars, clear glasses, or plastic containers with the primary colors in them. In additional containers, mix the secondary colors. (Always begin with the lighter of the two colors when mixing.) Use white Styrofoam egg cartons and cut the tops off. In each carton, in one of the holes put some red-, in another some blue-, and in another some yellow-colored water. Let the children use eyedroppers or spoons to mix new colors in the empty holes. This activity can be used with the cartons in a trough or at a table for an individual activity, or as a whole-group activity, with each child having a carton.

b. Mix some instant powdered milk with enough water to fill a pie tin or similar shallow container one-third to one-half full. Using small plastic containers of food coloring, the children drop a row of four or five drops of red and a row of four or five drops of yellow, and continue with two or three more rows of different colors with four or five drops of color on each row. Next, they drop one or two drops of liquid dish detergent in the middle and watch the colors blend into a rainbow.

c. Finger paint: Begin with white paint and sprinkle dry powdered paint on it. After that color is mixed in, sprinkle a second color on it for another change. Or start with a particular color of finger paint and add a second color of finger paint to it.

d. Paint: Provide opportunities for mixing colors at the easel or in other areas. Also provide for mixing shades of colors and for mixing more than two colors.

e. Collect three Styrofoam meat or pastry trays, and cut the centers out so that they resemble frames. Staple sheets of

Cellophane windows are covered with cellophane sheets of primary colors red, yellow, and blue. Holding two windows together shows how secondary colors result from combining primary colors.

cellophane, in the primary colors, to each of these frames, producing a red frame, a yellow frame, and a blue frame. When these frames are put on top of one another and held against white paper or up to the light, the secondary colors are seen. For a similar activity in color mixing, drop small amounts of colored water (the three primary colors) between two pieces of acetate and then put the acetate on an overhead projector. Press on the acetate in different areas to make the colors mix together. Also using an overhead projector, once again show color mixing by using pieces of colored cellophane.

2. Once the children have discussed how colors often reflect particular moods, ask them to describe their day in terms of a color. Older children could be encouraged to "write" stories, describing everything in the story in terms of colors.

3. For older children, read the book *Hailstones and Halibut Bones* (O'Neill, 1961); then discuss or write additional similes and metaphors for each of the colors.

4. As each of the colors is studied, ask the children to wear clothing of that color.

5. Use the plastic rings from six-pack can holders and cut them apart into separate rings. Thread a piece of yarn through the top of each one; then let the children glue pieces of colored cellophane on each one. They will enjoy hanging them as mobiles, hanging them at the window, or putting them on top of one another to form different colors.

6. Tell the story *The Color Kittens* (Brown, 1959). As the kittens mix particular colors, mix the same colors; then paint with them on an easel or other paper.

7. Cut, from paper, patterns that have the same shape but different colors. To make them more durable, laminate or cover them

with clear adhesive paper. Spread them on the floor and tape them down. Cut smaller corresponding shapes and colors, and give one to each child. Put on music and have the child march, slide, skip, and so on to the music; when it stops, the child must find and stand on a shape the same color as the one being held. As an alternative, instead of giving each child a color, give verbal directions. For example, say "Donna, please stand on an orange circle." Another approach would be to use a drum or another instrument to create a particular rhythm, rather than using a record or tape. With a little innovative thinking, this activity could be approached in many different ways. The game "Twister" could also be used.

8. Have the children sort colored items—buttons, paper shapes, marbles, colored macaroni, pieces of fabric. You can make a color-sorting tray from a white Styrofoam egg carton. Using felt-tip pens or acrylic paints, make each of the 12 holes a different color. Now provide small shapes of colored paper, colored beads, or colored buttons for the children to sort according to the various colors.

9. Have the children play color lotto. Use paint chips from a paint store or colored construction or poster paper. Cut two squares (or other shapes) the same size of each color. On a base of poster paper or cardboard, paste the desired number of colors; for older children, 8 to 12 colors, or shades of the same color; for younger children, 4 to 8 colors. Cover with clear adhesive paper or laminate; then cover duplicates individually to be matched to the corresponding color on the larger base.

10. Make a color wheel of wood or heavy cardboard. The colors can be felt pieces or paper (colored with felt-tip pens) glued to the base. Now put corresponding colors on clothespins, using felt or colored pens, one color per clothespin. The clothespins are clipped to the corresponding colors of the color wheel. Older children may use shades of a single color, but younger children should use distinct colors.

11. Fill a glass or container partly full of water. Drop a single drop of food coloring into the water and stir. Add another drop and stir, continuing this procedure so that the children can see how the same color can be changed from light to dark. Let the children follow up with the same experiment. For a similar experience, instead of using the same container of water, use different or separate containers, such as clear medicine bottles. Each time, add one or two more drops of coloring to the water. Then order the containers from the lightest to darkest.

12. Sing songs that create awareness of the colors children are wearing and the colors in their environment.

13. Show outlines of objects such as fruits, vegetables, flowers, trees, and the sun. Do not show them colored. Have the children name the color or colors of the object.

14. Name a color and have the children respond with names of objects of that color.

15. Make up color riddles and have the children guess the color being described. For example: "I am the color of strawberries, cherries, and fire engines. What color am I?" Have older children make up the riddles and share them with one another. The riddles could be written and illustrated for a book. One page could have the riddle and the next page could have the answer, either written or drawn.

16. Obtain paint chip samples from paint or hardware stores. Cover them with clear adhesive-backed paper or laminate them. Cut them up into separate chips and put each series of a single shade into a container or envelope. Children can then order them from lightest to darkest.

17. Cut up old white sheets into squares or rectangles for "scarves." Let the children pull up small sections of the scarves and then tie a string around those sections. The sections can be dipped into bowls of dye or food coloring and then hung to dry. These tie-dyed scarves may be used for scarf dancing.

18. Have a color day when the majority of activities focus on one color. If the children are alerted to this event, they can even be encouraged to wear clothing of that color.

19. Dye hard-boiled eggs. Use Easter egg dye or food coloring. You may wish to give the children the opportunity to mix colors or have them dip the egg into one color and then into another to discover the effect.

20. Make fishing poles of sticks or dowels (15 to 18 inches long). Space and attach screw eyes, with one on the end, for threading string. On the end of the string, attach a small magnet. Now let the children fish for fish of various colors that have been cut from colored paper and have paper clips attached. Encourage the children to name the color of each fish they catch.

21. For older children who are ready to expand their color vocabulary, make word cards of the following color words and help the children sort them into color piles. Find examples of each, if possible; paint chips would be a good source.

    a. Red: scarlet, coral, terra-cotta, crimson, vermilion. Castilian red, ruby, cherry, fire red, calypso red, poppy

    b. Green: shamrock, sea green, hunter green, olive green, chartreuse, avocado, army green, celery green, apple green, kelly green, emerald green, jade green, turquoise green, verdant green, viridian green, grass green, cactus green, khaki green, pea green

    c. Brown: chocolate, caramel brown, hazel, mahogany, maple brown, dirt brown, sepia, olive brown, tan

    d. Yellow: mustard, lemon, saffron, chamois, blonde, canary yellow, sunshine yellow, citron yellow, buff, amber, sallow, primrose, tawny, gold

    e. Purple: violet, lavender, orchid, amethyst, grape, lilac, burgundy, damson

    f. Orange: carrot, peach, pumpkin, coral, mandarin orange, tangerine orange, copper, rust

    g. Blue: indigo, royal, navy, cobalt, turquoise, sea blue, robin's-egg blue, baby blue, teal blue, azure, sapphire blue, midnight blue, peacock blue

---

UNIT PLAN ON COLOR

Field Trips

- Color walk
- Art gallery
- Art department of college or other school
- Paint store
- Fabric store
- Flower shop
- Grocery store
- Bakery
- Nursery or greenhouse in the spring

Art

- Mosaic of dyed rice, macaroni, or other media
- Finger painting
- Painting with dry powdered paint or watercolors
- Collages with colored cellophane
- Mixing primary colors of clay to make secondary colors
- String painting
- Melted crayon pictures
- Blot painting
- Clay sculptures or modeling (use primary colors)
- Colored macaroni strung for necklaces or bracelets
- Collages using items that come in various colors—toothpicks, marshmallows, cereal, etc.

Music

- "Color Song" (Hap Palmer)
- Songs that incorporate colors—colors of the children's clothing, colors in their environment, favorite colors.
- "Musical Chairs," with colors on the backs of each chair. (When using a game with younger children, do not exclude children from any game.) After the children have found their chairs, give instructions for each of the colors. For example, say, "All who have red on their chair stand up and hop in a circle."
- In small groups, make shakers that are of different colors, or give groups of children baby food jars with objects of different colors or colored water in them. The teacher might say, "All those with purple shakers play on the next song, or on the chorus of the next song."
- Creative movements with colors. Play some classical music; have the children decide what color the music represents and then move like that color or something representing that color.

Food

- Almost any food activity can be planned with a focus on color or color mixing.
- Make gelatin—ordinary flavored gelatin, or begin with one of the three primary colors, lemon, for example. After the hot water is added and the gelatin dissolved, use ice cubes that have been colored either red or blue. For example, if blue ice cubes are added to lemon gelatin, green gelatin will result.
- Make a white cake, and before it is baked, marble it with drops of food coloring.
- Make cakes, cookies, or breads and add food coloring to change the color.
- Make fruit salad in small groups and have each group whip the cream and add food coloring, or use plain yogurt with color added to it, so that each group has salad of a different color.
- Make an apple salad, using green, yellow, and red apples.
- Make any meat dish in which the children cook the meat first, so that the change in color can be observed.
- Make colored popcorn.

Visitors

- Paint dealer or distributor
- Artist to mix paints and paint picture
- Animals of various colors—perhaps with their babies to see whether they are the same colors (example: baby and adult mouse)
- A mother with her baby, and a suitcase filled with clothing of different colors for the baby to wear
- A parent or other visitor to make snow cones, with children selecting the desired color and flavor
- A clown to put on different colors of face makeup

Science

- Chemical garden, made with food coloring of different colors on top (see Chapter Eleven for directions)
- Coloring or dying carnations or celery by putting in glasses with food coloring or ink in water
- Any experience showing how particular animals use color camouflage
- Any experience in color mixing and color changing
- Color changes of autumn leaves
- Color changes resulting from aging, ripening, or molding

Literacy

- Write or dictate stories on favorite colors. Story springboards might be "My Favorite Color Is . . ." or "I Like _____ [color] Because . . ."
- Make a book for each color studied; the title of the book could be that color. Children could cut pictures from magazines or draw their own pictures of things that are that color
- Encourage children to write or tell color similes and metaphors.

Summary

Because children become aware of color at a very early age, it often is their first clue in describing or identifying objects. Even before they are able to attach correct labels, they can identify items as having the same colors and may describe color in terms of familiar objects. Therefore, it is important that children have many experiences with matching and sorting colors. In teaching colors, concepts should progress through the primary colors, then secondary colors, and finally shades of colors. Since color is a symbolic attribute, not an object, it has various psychological effects and connotations with respect to cultures, personal preferences, and personality characteristics. Because it occurs everywhere in our environment, color is a natural concept to teach children and easily adapts to many areas of the curriculum.

Student Learning Activities

1. Visit a classroom and observe an activity teaching color. Evaluate the activity. Was it appropriate for the age of the children? Would you have made any changes in the activity? Did the activity teach effectively?

2. With a group of children, implement at least one of the activities and experiences related to color suggested in this chapter. The group of children may be in a classroom setting or simply a small group of relatives or neighborhood children. Did the children enjoy the experience? What did they learn about color? Evaluate your experience.

3. Plan, create, and write down an activity for teaching color to children.

4. Prepare at least one teacher-made material or piece of equipment to teach some aspect of color to children. (Refer to ideas in this chapter and in Appendix A for suggestions.)

5. Add your own teaching ideas to the unit plan on color.

6. Obtain, review, and evaluate at least two of the children's books suggested as references for this chapter. What color concepts are taught? How would you use the book with children? How effective would the book be in teaching a color concept to children?

7. Visit a children's library and add at least three additional excellent children's books to the reference list for teaching color to children 2 to 8 years old.

Suggested Resources

Children's Books

Adams, R. (1976). *The Easter egg artists*. New York: Scribner's.

Bang, M. (1991). *Yellow ball*. New York: Morrow.

Bragg, R. G. (1992). *Colors of the day*. Saxonville, MA: Picture Book Studio.

Brown, M. W. (1959). *The color kittens*. New York: Simon & Schuster.

Carle, E. (1985). *My very first book of colors*. New York: HarperCollins.

Carle, E. (1984). *The mixed-up chameleon* (2nd ed.). New York: HarperCollins.

Ehlert, L. (1989). *Color zoo*. New York: HarperCollins.

Ehlert, L. (1990). *Color farm.* New York: Harper-Collins.

Goennel, H. (1990). *Colors.* New York: Little, Brown.

Groening, M., & Groening, M. (1991). *Maggie Simpson's book of colors and shapes.* New York: HarperCollins.

Hoban, T. (1987). *Is it red? Is it yellow? Is it blue?* New York: Morrow.

Hoban, T. (1989). *Of colors and things.* New York: Greenwillow.

Hoban, T. (1993). *White on black.* New York: Greenwillow.

Jenkins, J. (1992). *Thinking about colors.* New York: Dutton.

Johnson, C. (1958). *Harold and the purple crayons.* New York: HarperCollins.

Lionni, L. (1959). *Little blue and little yellow.* New York: Astor-Honor.

Lionni, L. (1976). *A color of his own.* New York: Pantheon.

Martin, B. (1967). *Brown bear, brown bear, what do you see?* New York: Holt, Rinehart & Winston.

McCarney-Muldoon, E., & O'Brien, M. B. (1992). *Fun with colors.* New York: Macmillan.

McKinnon, E. S. (Ed.). (1988). *One-two-three colors: Activities for introducing color to young children.* Everett, WA: Warren.

O'Neill, M. (1961). *Hailstones and halibut bones.* New York: Doubleday.

Scarry, R. (1976). *Richard Scarry's color book.* New York: Random House.

Seuss, Dr. (1960). *One fish two fish red fish blue fish.* New York: Random House.

Slobodkina, E. (1947). *Caps for sale.* Reading, MA: Addison-Wesley.

Taylor, B. (1992). *Over the rainbow! The science of color and light.* New York: Random House.

Turner, B. (1990). *Colors.* New York: Viking.

Williams, J. (1992). *Simple science projects with color and light.* Milwaukee: Gareth Stevens.

Woolfitt, G. (1992). *Blue.* Minneapolis: Carolrhoda.

Woolfitt, G. (1992). *Green.* Minneapolis: Carolrhoda.

Woolfitt, G. (1992). *Red.* Minneapolis: Carolrhoda.

Woolfitt, G. (1992). *Yellow.* Minneapolis: Carolrhoda.

Yenawine, P. (1991). *Colors.* New York: Delacorte.

Records, Tapes, and Cassettes

Colors. On *Learning basic skills through music.* (Vol. 1). Hap Palmer Record Library (AR514 or AC514).

Magic monster mix: Magic monsters look at colors. The Child's World.

Parade of colors. On *Learning basic skills through music* (Vol. 2). Hap Palmer Record Library (AR522 or AC522).

Pictures

Colors and Shapes. The Child's World (Panorama).

Films, Filmstrips, and Videos

Beginning concepts. Scholastic Early Childhood Center.

Caps for sale. Weston Wood Studios.

Color. Eye Gate Media.

Color, color everywhere—Red, yellow, blue. Coronet Films.

Color for beginners. Coronet Films.

Colors and shapes. Eye Gate Media.

Creating with color. Coronet Films.

Green . . . green . . . green . . . blue . . . blue . . . blue . . . Educational Activities.

The gruesome gray monster (finding colors). Coronet Films.

Hailstones and halibut bones. In Part I (1964). Part II (1967), NBC-TV. Sterling Educational Films.

The happy world of color. Educational Activities.

Harold and the purple crayon. Weston Wood Studios.

Little blue and little yellow. CRM/McGraw-Hill Films.

Yellow . . . yellow . . . yellow . . . red . . . red . . . red. . . . Educational Activities.

Computer Software

Color find. E.C.S. (Apple).

Color me. Mindscape. (Apple, IBM, Commodore 64).

Colors and shapes. Hartley Courseware. (Apple).

Fun with colors. Access Unliminted. (Apple).

CHAPTER
fourteen

Animals

Introduction

What possibilities for teaching lie within the realm of animals in the child's environment! It is impossible to imagine going through a year of study at any level of early childhood without some units and experiences with animals. Young children have a sensitivity to, and seek an understanding of, animals. Many concepts can be gleaned from studies of animals—size, shape, number, color, texture, weight, smell, sound, nutrition, and so on. Specific concepts relating to individual animals, or to categories and classes of animals, emerge as a result of animal studies. For example, children will become aware of physical characteristics of the animals, where they live, what they eat, uses of the animals, and how they reproduce and care for their young. Children will also enjoy making comparisons among animals as they become acquainted with the characteristics of the animal categories.

There are additional values and by-products of animal experiences and studies. Children learn how to care for animals properly—how to hold them (if they can be held), how and what to feed them, and how to care for and clean their surroundings. "Young children acquire strong feelings of importance as they feed the classroom animals and provide for their care. Rarely do young children have opportunities to practice themselves the care and treatment they receive at home from their parents" (Maxim, 1989, p. 474). Many children are afraid of animals, but through experiences with these animals, the fears can often be lessened or overcome. Children can become aware of our tremendous reliance on animals as sources of food and clothing, while at the same time becoming aware of animals that are either a potential danger or a nuisance.

Approach to Teaching

Animals make excellent visitors to the classroom, where children observe, investigate, learn about, and care for them. Categories of animals appropriate for indoor interest centers include pets, some farm animals, fish, birds, and insects. Some traditional favorites are tadpoles and frogs, turtles, gerbils, hamsters, guinea pigs, goldfish, caterpillars and butterflies, chicks that hatch, rabbits, and hermit crabs. Children also enjoy ant farms, bug cages, and bird feeders. Individually made bird feeders can be taken home, where they further extend children's interest and understanding through continued observation and feeding of the birds.

The world of animals is a big world indeed, and many units of study can develop from this single category. There are numerous forms of animal life, ranging in size from animals so small they cannot be seen without the aid of a microscope to those that are much larger than humans.

Many of the concepts and units developed may result from the children's inquiries about particular animals or categories of animals, or because the children have brought pets or other animals into the classroom.

A well-planned animal unit should include, if possible, a field trip to visit the animals being studied, a visitor who will bring animals into the classroom, or animals that can stay in the classroom for study and observation. Remember the importance of the firsthand sensory experience. It is difficult to imagine a unit on eggs and chickens without including a visit to the poultry farm; having eggs incubated and hatched right in the classroom; or having chicks, hens, or roosters in the classroom for study and firsthand observation. Even when there are actual animals for classroom observation, misconceptions may occur.

Lyn had been watching the incubator as the chickens hatched from eggs. When only one more egg remained to hatch, Lyn inquired, "But when is the mother going to come out?" After the experience of having a live angora sheep on the playground, the children discussed it and compared it to pictures of sheep with which they were more familiar. However, one child told his mother as she was picking him up from school that day, "We had a real live buffalo come to our class today." On another occa-sion, after several days' experiences with guinea pigs, one child commented, "Baby pigs are guinea pigs." Another child stated that "baby pigs are skinny pigs."

As animal units and experiences are planned, do not be afraid to develop units around the most common animals. For example, many new concepts can be taught and many ideas reinforced and clarified through units on dogs, fish, or cows. Many children are familiar with these animals and may even have some for pets; however, new concepts can be built on those already understood, and broader meanings can be obtained. Children can also be introduced to generally less familiar animals, such as tadpoles, guinea pigs, and lizards.

Categorization games will help children distinguish animals from other groups such as toys, foods, furniture, people, and plants. Even more specifically, animal picture cards can be sorted into categories such as insect, farm animals, circus animals, pets, animals that live in water, birds, and animals that live underground; many additional categories could be developed as well. A set of animal pictures or flash cards can also be used for naming the animals. Pictures can be found in such places as magazines, stickers purchased from stationery stores, or discarded workbooks.

Whether approached in general areas or in specific units, animals make excellent choices for study. Following is a list of suggested animal unit themes. It is not meant to be inclusive, since the ideas and themes are almost endless, limited only by the teacher's own creative thinking and planning. Also, a unit need not necessarily emerge from each theme; it is possible to use one of the suggested themes for a science experience. For example, a teacher might not wish to do a whole unit on the life cycle of tadpole to frog, but it would provide an excellent experience for the science center or a single science activity.

Note: The general theme is italicized, and the subthemes listed may be included in the general unit of study or may stand alone as a unit of study.

• *Farm animals*

Cows	Chicks, hens,
Pigs	and roosters
Rabbits	Sheep
Horses	Goats
Ducks	Turkeys

• *Zoo animals*

Elephants	Tigers	Penguins
Monkeys	Seals	Bears
Lions		

• *Jungle animals*
• *Circus animals*
• *Desert animals*
• *Ocean animals*

Fish	Mammals (whales
Shellfish	and dolphins)

• *Pets (domestic animals)*

Birds	Hamsters	Fish
Dogs	Guinea pigs	Turtles
Cats	Gerbils	

• *Insects*

Bees	Ants
Spiders	Butterflies*

• *Worms*
• *Birds* (perhaps specific birds common to the locale)
• *Tadpoles and frogs* (life cycle)
• *Animal babies*
• *Animal homes*
• *Hibernation*
• *Animals that live in trees*
• *Animals that live underground*
• *Animals that lived long ago*

---

* An excellent unit or science activity is the study of the life cycle of the monarch butterfly, which begins as a caterpillar.

• *Animals suggested for classroom observation*

Hamsters	Worms
Guinea pigs	Insects of various kinds
Gerbils	Turtles
Fish	Mice
Snails	Lizards
Rabbits	Chickens
Ant farm	Birds

Concepts and Ideas for Teaching

1. Animals have various kinds of physical characteristics.

   a. Various body parts that often serve important purposes
      (1) Wings—how many?
      (2) Legs—how many?
      (3) Claws
      (4) Shell
      (5) Eyes
      (6) Tail
      (7) Mouth
      (8) Feet (study footprints)
      (9) Nose
      (10) Arms
      (11) Beak
      (12) Antennae
      (13) Lungs
      (14) Gills
      (15) Backbone (or no backbone)
      (16) Other?

   b. Various body coverings that have characteristic textures and serve different purposes.
      (1) Fur
      (2) Skin
      (3) Feathers
      (4) Shell
      (5) Hair
      (6) Scales

2. Animals move in various ways—some in only one way and others in several ways.

   a. Walk
   b. Swim

c. Fly

d. Crawl

e. Have wings and do/do not use them for flying

f. Use a fin or tail for moving

3. Animals live in various places or environments and in various kinds of homes.

a. Trees

b. Desert

c. Jungle

d. Farm

e. Zoo

f. On the land

g. Underneath the ground

h. Near garbage

i. In cold climates

j. In water but not on land

k. In water but also on land

l. Change in habitat in particular seasons

4. Animals eat various kinds of things.

a. Plants

b. Insects

c. Nuts

d. Other animals

e. Garbage

f. Wood

5. Animals reproduce and care for their young in various ways.

a. Give birth to live young

b. Lay eggs—with hard shells or without shells

c. Abandon young after giving birth

d. Feed milk to young (mammals)

e. Keep young nearby to nurture and care for

f. Usually have multiple offspring

g. Usually have single offspring

h. Provide the food for the offspring

6. Animal babies have different characteristics in relation to their parents. Animals go through life cycles while changing and growing.

a. May or may not look like the parent

b. Sometimes have identifying names

c. May eat different things or the same things as the parent

d. May or may not move in the same way as the parent

e. May or may not sound the same as the parent

f. Change as they grow

7. Animals may make different sounds; the sounds may have a particular purpose.

8. Some animals are extinct, and we learn about them from fossils.

a. Dinosaurs—the largest land animals that ever lived on the earth

b. Mammoths

c. Saber-toothed tigers

9. Some animals are make-believe, such as dragons.

10. Many animals are useful to humans.

a. Animals that provide food for humans—cows, chickens, pigs, turkeys, deer, fish

b. Animals that provide clothing or apparel for humans—sheep; animals that provide furs; silkworms; animals that provide leather for making shoes, purses, wallets

c. Animals that are friends or pets to humans

d. Animals that eat other animals that are harmful or a nuisance to humans—snakes eat mice; cats eat mice; birds eat insects such as grasshoppers

e. Animals that eat plants that are harmful or a nuisance to humans—livestock eat mustard weed, which is harmful to humans

f. Animals that provide humans with entertainment and recreation
    (1) Animals used for sporting purposes, as well as meat—deer, elk, fish, rabbits, pheasants, ducks, geese
    (2) Zoo and circus animals, which are always enjoyable to observe
g. Animals that work for humans
    (1) In some parts of the world, animals that provide transportation—horses, donkeys, camels, and dogs
    (2) Dogs that help herd sheep and cattle
    (3) Dogs that are trained as seeing-eye dogs for people who are blind
    (4) Dogs that are used in detective work or serve as guards
    (5) Cattle, mules, and horses, which do farm work

11. Many animals are harmful to humans.

    a. Animals that are dangerous if they are threatened by humans

    b. Animals whose bites are poisonous—snakes, black widow spiders

    c. Animals whose bites may cause disease—rabies

12. Many animals are a nuisance to humans. Some animals eat plants or animals that are important to humans—insects such as weevils eat wheat and other grains; coyotes eat sheep and chickens; bears eat sheep.

13. Some animals may be useful, while also being either harmful or a nuisance to humans. Many animals are useful, but because of tramping and overgrazing, the possibility of erosion increases.

14. Animals adapt in various ways to seasonal changes.

    a. Animals that hibernate—fish, frogs, bears, snakes

    b. Animals that migrate—birds, geese

    c. Animals that acquire a heavier fur or covering—cows, horses, sheep, dogs

15. Animals respond to temperature in various ways.

    a. Dogs and other animals that pant to cool themselves

    b. Pigs, which shunt their blood away from the skin surface in cold weather but are more susceptible to death in hot weather

    c. Bees, which cluster together in masses to keep warm in cold weather

16. Animals respond to light and dark in various ways.

    a. Animals that move about when it is dark—bats, raccoons

    b. Snakes, which see things in the dark that humans cannot see

    c. Animals that move about when it is light

17. Animals protect themselves in various ways.

    a. Animals that have physical characteristics that they use in protecting themselves—claws, quills, stingers, horns, poisonous bites

    b. Animals that have natural camouflage for protection and thus are difficult for their predators to see—chameleon, many insects, fish, snowshoe rabbit

    c. Animals such as skunks that use a powerful odor for protection

    d. Animals that use sounds for protection

18. A veterinarian is an animal doctor and usually works at an animal hospital, where sick or injured animals are cared for.

19. Animals have needs—food, water, shelter, air, space, and a unique temperature.

20. There are many kinds of pets. Pets are animals that are cared for by people.

Activities and Experiences

1. The most beneficial kinds of activities and experiences with animals are firsthand.

Take field trips to places where animals are found, or bring animals to the classroom. When animals are in the classroom, children need to be told exactly what they can and cannot do with them and, if the animals can be handled, how to do that kindly, gently, and properly. The safety of both the children and the animals should be considered. Teachers should check their program or school policies to see whether there are any restrictions or regulations that need to be observed. When the animals are in the classroom, the children should have the opportunity to feed them and care for their needs. In this way, the children learn that all animals need food, but they do not all eat the same kinds of foods. The children also learn that all animals need water and air.

A favorite observation activity with animals is observing the life cycles of particular animals such as the frog (tadpole to frog), monarch butterfly (caterpillar to chrysalis to butterfly), or chicken (egg to chick).

Sequence pictures provide opportunities for children to arrange pictures in such a way that they tell a story visually (in this case, the life cycle from tadpole to frog).

2. Make a bug cage. Obtain two large lids (at least 3 inches in diameter) of exactly the same size or use two small cake pans. Obtain a piece of heavy, stiff screen about 8 to 10 inches in length and wide enough to fit inside the circumference of the lids or pans plus several inches for overlap. Roll the screen to fit inside the lids or pans exactly, and then, with string or yarn, "sew" around the overlap to hold the screen securely in the roll that will fit inside the lids or pans. Now mix a small amount of plaster of Paris and pour it into one of the lids or pans. Then immediately put one end of the roll or circle of screen into that lid or pan. Hold it until the plaster of Paris dries. A twig or stick may be stuck into the plaster of Paris before it sets so that there will be something for the bugs to crawl on. When bugs are caught in the cage, simply put the other lid or pan on the top of the roll.

3. Collect pictures of many kinds of animals and glue them to cards. They can be sorted into such categories as farm or zoo animals; animals that fly or that do not fly; animals that provide food for humans; and so on. Pass these cards out to the children. Give a characteristic of animals and have the children raise their card (or cards) of animals that have that characteristic. For example, say: "Hold up your animal (or animals) if it eats other animals" or "Hold up your animal (or animals) it if lives in the jungle."

4. Concentrate on a specific animal or group of animals, and provide as many firsthand experiences as possible with that animal or group and the characteristics involved.

5. Make animal scrapbooks. Collect as much information or as many pictures as possible for each animal in the scrapbook. The scrapbook could relate to a particular group of animals, such as pets, or it could be for

Anne studies the characteristics and behaviors of a friendly butterfly.

animals in general. Encourage literacy by writing something about each animal.

6. Present animal riddles. Either the teacher or the children can give the clues for a particular animal. The children guess what animal answers the riddle. These can be written in an animal riddle book, with additional ones added during the year.

7. Use animal stick puppets for dramatizations, for demonstrating animal sounds and other characteristics, or for categorizing by characteristics.

8. Make plaster molds of animal footprints by mixing plaster of Paris (it sets up quickly, so mix it just as you are preparing to make the mold), and putting a cardboard rim around the footprint. (The cardboard rim could be the rim of a small box such as a jewelry box. Cut several sizes out beforehand.) Place the rim around the footprint and pour plaster into the impression. When dry, remove the plaster and return it to the classroom to classify and label it. Put a picture and name of the animal next to the footprint cast.

9. Make written or dictated observations of animals the children see or visit. For example, after visiting a zoo or farm, each child could dictate or write about one animal he or she has carefully observed. The children could illustrate their observations and these could be put together into a class booklet. First- and second-grade children could add research to their observation report. If the

animal is in the classroom, a language experience chart could be recorded on observations made of the animal each day.

10. Following an experience with an animal, have the children help make a web to review what has been learned. For an example, see Figure 14–1.

11. Compare one animal to another, or one group of animals to another group or category of animals.

    a. Similarities

    b. Differences

12. Have the children compare an animal or group of animals to themselves.

    a. Similarities

    b. Differences

Unit and Lesson Plans on Animals

There are many different units and lesson plans that could be done on animals or concepts relating to animals; the following ones serve only as examples. Hopefully, they will spark your imagination and creative planning for other units and lesson plans relating to animals, such as those on hibernation, baby animals, or animal homes.

Following are unit and lesson plans on some animal themes. (See Chapter Seven, Nutrition and Food Experiences, for ideas on other animals and their products.) Whenever possible, select units and lesson plans that will provide experiences with actual animals. Again, be aware that they can be either general (such as zoo or farm

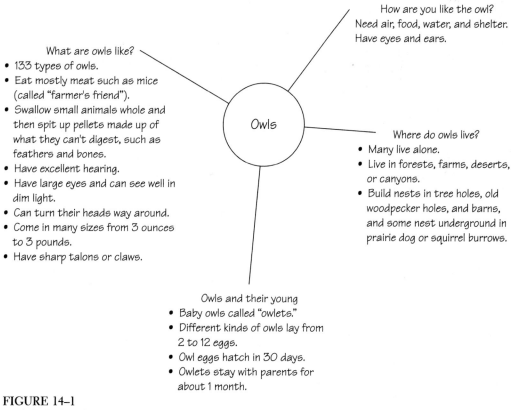

FIGURE 14–1
Sample Web: What Has Been Learned About Owls

animals) or specific (such as cows, bees, frogs, or animal babies).

UNIT PLAN ON FARM ANIMALS

Art

- Farm mobiles
- Farm animal collages
- Salt or oil base clay farm animals
- Finger paint, with media such as oats or wheat—food for farm animals
- Farm animal sack puppets

Field Trips

- Farm
- Grocery store, to look for products from farm animals
- Butcher shop

Visitors

- Farmer
- Someone to bring in a pet that is a farm animal
- Storyteller to tell a farm animal story
- Grocer to bring in farm animal products
- Parent to cook a farm animal product

Food

- Milk shakes
- Eggs prepared any way
- Ice cream
- Bacon-and-tomato sandwiches
- Hamburgers or hamburger used in any way
- Chicken prepared in any way
- Turkey prepared in any way
- Jerky or salami pizza
- Various preparations of pork, lamb, or fish

Science

- Animal corner with live farm animals, eggs incubating, baby farm animals
- What farm animals eat
- Physical characteristics of some farm animals
- Farm animal babies—what they look like, what their names are, how they are cared for, what they eat

- What happens to farm animals in summer and in winter
- Small samples of food products provided by farm animals

Music

- Creative movements dealing with farm animals
- Paper cups decorated and used as rhythm accompaniment to songs about animals walking or running
- Familiar fairy tales sung and dramatized

Language and Literacy

- Poetry and stories relating to farm animals
- Tape of farm animal sounds; identification of the animals by the children
- Puppets or felt figures of farm animals made by the children; stories dramatized about farm animals; stories made up using animal figures
- Dramatized nursery rhymes, poems, and fairy tales relating to farm animals
- Open-ended stories, with children telling the endings
- Display of pictures of farm animals. (Say "I went to the farm and saw a_____"; let the child select a picture and talk about that animal.)
- Slides of farm animals, with discussion about them
- Writing or telling and illustrating stories about favorite farm animals

UNIT PLAN ON BEES

Art

- Bee mobiles—bees and beehive painted or colored; holes punched in hive, and bees hung all around it with string
- Bees made with Styrofoam base and materials such as pipe cleaners
- Bees made and decorated, using toilet-paper roll as base

Field Trips

- Bee farm
- Honey distributor

- Flower garden where bees are collecting nectar to make honey
- Library

Visitors

- Parent or grandparent to make something using honey—honey candy, honey butter
- Beekeeper—description of job, telling how the hive is smoked in order to obtain honey; demonstration of a beekeeping outfit or uniform, including veil, gloves, and clips around trousers to prevent bees from getting inside pants; equipment used, including smoker machine, bee brush, knife for opening hives, and beehive frames
- Someone to show honeycomb

Food

- Honey butter
- Honey candy or cookies
- Muffins with honey butter (see recipe)
- Honey bread (see recipe)

Recipe for Muffins and Honey Butter

2 cups baking mix	1 cup milk
¼ cup sugar	¼ cup oil
1 egg	

Mix baking mix and sugar. Add beaten egg to milk and oil; then add this liquid to the dry ingredients. Stir until moistened; the batter will be lumpy. Fill greased muffin tins two-thirds full. Bake at 400° F for about 20 minutes. Serve with a mixture of butter and honey.

Recipe for Honey Bread

1½ cups honey	1½ tsp salt
1½ cups milk	⅓ cup oil
¾ cup sugar	2 eggs
5¾ cups flour	2 tsp vanilla
1½ tsp soda	

Bring honey, milk, and sugar to a boil and cool the mixture. Mix dry ingredients together; add oil, eggs, and vanilla. Add cooled liquid mixture and beat for 2 minutes. Put in greased loaf pans. Bake at 325° F for about 1 hour.

Science

- Science corner or table with pictures of bees, beehives, and beekeepers doing their jobs; display of objects such as honeycomb, equipment beekeeper uses, bee eggs, bees, and bee products
- Science discussions, experiments, and observations focusing on the following topics: members of the bee family (queen, workers, and drones and their various functions within the hive); making of honey; characteristics of bees; honeycomb (six-sided wall cells in the hive that bees use for storing food and as a place for hatching young bees); collecting nectar from flowers to make honey; bees' role in pollinating flowers and trees (Use pictures and any visual material available.)
- Discussion of first-aid treatment for bee stings; discussion of why bees sting people and animals

Music

- Creative movements and dramatics relating to bees—hatching from eggs, flying, moving about in the hive, searching for nectar in flowers
- Songs and records relating to bees

Language and Literacy

- Stories and poems relating to bees
- Making bee puppets or flannel board figures, with the children telling stories or dramatizing them
- Slides of bees, with discussion and storytelling
- Films and filmstrips relating to bees
- Tape of bee sounds; discussion
- Story writing about bees

LESSON PLAN ON HONEYBEES (1-DAY)

Overall Goals

- To introduce the honeybee and its characteristics—habitat, body parts, food, reproduction, locomotion.
- To help the children understand how the honeybee helps humans. To introduce the children to some uses of honey.

- To help the children calm their fears of bees, explain through the visitor that if we do not harm bees, they generally will not harm us.
- To explain to the children that bees and flowers are necessary to each other for survival.
- To provide the children with firsthand experiences with bees.

Day 1

Whole-Group Activity

Discussion and Introduction of the Honeybee Unit. Tell the children that bees are the only insects that provide any important part of our food. Include questions such as: "What is the food they provide for us?" "What body parts do bees have—do they have a head and legs?" "Where do honeybees live?" Have flannelboard cutouts showing body parts of bees—head, chest, abdomen, legs, wings, antennae. *Note:* Point out fuzz, pollen, baskets, and talk about the nectar or honey sack. Show pictures of honeybee farms and wild-bee hives; compare the differences.

Objectives

- To introduce the children to the new unit on honeybees and the food they provide.
- To arouse interest in honeybees and their identifying features.
- To obtain a general indication of what the children know about bees.

Small-Group Activities

Art—Making Beehives. Provide the children with yellow and brown flour clay, as well as a piece of Styrofoam in the shape of a beehive. Encourage the children to roll their clay into a "worm" and then mold it around the Styrofoam, layering the yellow and brown clay. When the children are finished, each child will be given a purchased bee (purchased by the teacher from a hobby store) to place anywhere on the beehive. Compare the texture of the clay to that of the Styrofoam.

Objectives

- To reinforce the concept of a beehive.
- To introduce ideas of bee "houses" to the children.

Field Trip to a Library. Divide the children into groups by pinning different-colored bees on them. Parents will drive the children to the library. The children will listen to stories about honeybees read by the librarian.

Objectives

- To provide listening experiences concerning bees.
- To become more familiar with community resources.

Individual Activities

- Dome covered to resemble beehive
- Easel with brown and yellow paint
- Bees in cage

UNIT PLAN ON BIRDS

Art

- Finger painting, with birdseed added
- Feather painting
- Feather collages
- Decoration of eggs (made from toilet-paper rolls or plastic colored eggs)
- Bird collages or bird stickers from stationery store
- Birdseed collages
- Decorate birdseed shakers with birdseed and/or other materials
- Use of the outline or form of birds on large sheets of butcher paper; children paint and/or make collages with them
- Bird puppets

Food

- Any food activities using poultry products—chicken, turkey, or eggs

Field Trips

- Pet store
- Bird refuge
- Walk to observe birds and look for birds' nests
- Museum or university ornithology department to observe stuffed birds
- Poultry farm
- Aviary
- Home where pet birds may be observed

Visitors

- Pet store owner
- Ornithologist
- Bird watcher
- Child or other member of family who can bring a pet bird
- Storyteller to tell stories about birds
- Parent to cook a poultry product
- Person who knows birdcalls; demonstration
- Someone who owns a talking bird such as a parrot

Science

- Science discussions, experiments, and observations focusing on the following topics; kinds of birds, sizes of birds, characteristics of birds (such as having feathers and having been hatched from eggs), colors of birds, birds that migrate, birds common to the locale, bird food
- Study of bird eggs—sizes, colors, and so on
- Study of bird's nests—sizes, materials used in construction, matching of specific birds with their characteristic nests
- Bird feeders; a simple one is a pinecone (flour and water mixed into a thick paste and stuffed into the pinecone, which is then rolled in birdseed and hung in tree with a piece of string)

Music

- Musical games about birds
- Sing songs about birds
- Creative dramatics relating to birds—hatching from the egg, drying feathers, swimming, flying, hunting for worms
- Records lending themselves to dramatization of bird characteristics and actions

Language and Literacy

- Slides of birds; discussion
- Tape recording of bird sounds made by teacher
- Picture of birds; discussion and storytelling
- Stories and poetry about birds
- Puppets or flannel board figures, with children dramatizing or telling stories
- Display of pictures of birds with a discussion beginning "I saw a bird that . . . ," with individual children selecting a picture and telling about that bird by finishing the statement. These accounts could be written and collected into a book.
- Dramatization of stories, poems, songs relating to birds

UNIT PLAN ON FISH

Art

- Fish made from a small brown-paper sack stuffed with newspaper, tied with string on the open end so that it resembles a fishtail, then painted or decorated
- Fish drawn by each child and put on an overhead or opaque projector for enlarging (older children can trace their own), then painted or decorated (makes a creative bulletin board)
- Fish made and decorated, then put behind blue cellophane paper to create the illusion of a fishpond or aquarium
- Seafood collage made by cutting types of fish we eat and fish products from newspaper grocery advertisements.

Visitors

- Parent to cook fish by any method
- Parent to bring in fishing gear and demonstrate its use, perhaps cooking fish as well
- Fish and game officer
- Person from a hatchery, cannery, or restaurant
- Grocer to bring in several varieties of fish, perhaps allowing the children to taste some
- Someone to bring in slides of fishing trips
- Some to bring in pet fish

Music

- Creative dramatics or movements representing fishing or moving like fish
- Shakers made from tuna fish or shrimp cans; can be decorated with seashells

Field Trips

- Fish hatchery
- Fish cannery
- Sporting goods store or department store to see fishing gear and supplies such as salmon eggs, flies
- Pet store with several varieties of fish
- Fish market, to see various cuts of fish and to notice fish odors
- Restaurant that serves fish
- Grocery store

Food

- Fish burgers
- Baked, fried, broiled fish
- Casseroles
- Fish patties—salmon, tuna
- Fish salads—tuna, shrimp
- Sandwiches
- Fish and chips
- Chowder

Science

- Kinds of fish and where they live
- Parts of fish—scales, fins, gills, and so on
- What fish eat
- How fish breathe
- Hibernation of some fish
- Spawning habits of some fish
- Aquarium placed in classroom
- Tasting and comparing of various kinds of fish
- Fish placed in a trough or large container for observation and touching
- Characteristics of a specific kind of fish, such as salmon

Language and Literacy

- Slides, pictures, stories, poetry, songs, films relating to fish

- Teacher-made puppets or flannelboard fish characters for children to dramatize or tell stories about
- Stories about fish—tell or illustrate

LESSON PLAN ON FISH (4-DAY)

Overall Goals

- To introduce the children to fish and to provide experiences with fish: kinds, body parts, uses.
- To make the children aware of the general characteristics of fish so that they will be able to name and locate the parts of a common fish (fins, tail, scales, gills).
- To increase awareness that there is more than one kind of fish and to enable the children to describe at least two kinds of fish (goldfish, trout, shark, eel, etc.).
- To help the children learn to identify several uses for fish (food, pets, recreation).
- To acquaint the children with the concept that although there are certain elements that all fish have in common (backbone, mouth, gills, swimming), there are many kinds of fish. Fish differ in size, color, shape, habit, taste, and use.

Day 1

Whole-Group Activity

Discussion—Introduction to Unit and Field Trip. Introduce the topic of the unit, as well as some of the basic concepts, such as what a fish looks like, where a fish lives, and how fish are cared for and used. Ask questions concerning what to observe at the hatchery, such as: "Do all fish look alike?" "Are all fish the same size and color?" "What odor does a fish have?"

Objectives

- To establish objectives for the field trip.
- To introduce the unit of fish and basic concepts to be learned.

Small-Group Activities

Field Trip to a Fish Hatchery. Divide the children into groups by badges shaped like fish that are the same except for the fins. The fins will distinguish the groups. Teachers help the children to label this part of the fish and discuss the number of fins to enable the children to find their own groups. Drive to the hatchery and tour the grounds. A guide will be available to show the children the fish equipment and to answer questions. Point out the various things to be observed—smell, size, and variations of fish.

Objectives

- To enable the children to see various kinds, sizes, parts, characteristics, and colors of fish.
- To show how and what the fish are fed.
- To observe the growth cycle of fish as they move from one tank to another.
- To demonstrate the uses of fish (research, recreation, food).

Experience Chart. Gather the children into groups to make experience charts. Title the piece. Let the children contribute the observations they would like to remember about the trip. Write these observations on a piece of butcher paper as the children watch.

Objectives

- To follow up and reinforce the field trip.
- To show verbal language being put into written form.

Individual Activities

- Aquarium with goldfish
- Paper and crayons at easel

Day 2

Whole-Group Activity

Story About a Fish. Read the story *Fish Is Fish* (Lionni, 1970) at the rug, with special emphasis given to the fish characteristics that are common to the pictures. Point out and label these characteristics.

Objectives

- To introduce basic characteristics of fish and to observe how much the children already know about the parts of fish.
- To lead into small-group discussions about how fish breathe, as well as why they live in water.

Small-Group Activities

Science Discussion—Air in Water. Divide the children into small groups to discuss why the fish in the story just read to them had to live in the water. Let the children express their knowledge of fish. Bring in the concept of gills, and reinforce any correct concepts the children discuss. Then perform the following science experiment: Before the children arrive, transparent glasses will have been filled with water, one for each group. As the children finish discussion gills, underwater breathing, and living on land and in water, fill other glasses with fresh water, one for each group. Show the group the glass that has been previously filled with water. The air in the water will have formed bubbles on the side of the glass. Explain that just as people can breathe air, fish have special equipment, gills, to get the air out of the water.

Objectives

- To allow the children to express their knowledge of fish, and to provide the teacher with feedback on how much each child does know about fish.
- To inform the children about the breathing mechanism of fish and to clarify the concept that fish do not breathe the water but can extract the oxygen (air) from the water by means of gills.

Art—Paper-Bag Fish. Provide the children with a paper bag taped into a fish shape, string for a tail, newspapers with which to stuff the fish, and paint to decorate it. Show the children how to stuff the fish with paper, and tie each bag, with the child assisting. The children can then paint their fish. The fish will be put on the lockers to dry until day 3, when collage items (eyes, gills, fins) will be added. Names will be taped to the fish.

Objectives

- To reinforce knowledge of the basic shape of fish.
- To begin an activity that will be continued the next day, allowing the children to add a second art method to their painted item.

Individual Activity

- Fish in the trough

Day 3

Whole-Group Activities

Art—Collage. As the children enter at the beginning of the day, direct them to the art activity of gluing collage items to their fish (made yesterday). At the large table, set up the fish with collage items. The children can decorate their fish as they wish. Use this opportunity to reinforce knowledge of the parts of the fish.

Objectives

- To stimulate creative imagination by pasting cutouts on the bag to make it appear more like a fish.
- To provide opportunities for feedback on how much the children are assimilating about fish, and to reinforce the concepts of basic shapes and characteristics of fish.

Music—Rhythm. Gather the children at the rug for a rhythm activity. Pass out instruments so that the children can accompany songs, fingerplays, and records. Explore various beats.

Objectives

- To provide opportunities for children to follow directions in a music activity.
- To observe the ability of the children to respond to music through the rhythm.

Individual Activities

- Watercolors and salt at easel
- Water and objects in a container

Day 4

Whole-Group Activity

Discussion and Review—Film About a Fish.* At the rug, involve the children in a discussion of what they have learned about fish: physical characteristics of fish, where fish live, how they breathe, the uses of fish. Then present that all fish are not alike. The class will discuss how the fish they have seen have various characteristics (color, size, location, uses). Then show a film that presents many unusual as well as common fish. Allow for discussion and comments.

Objectives

- To review the unit and observe what the children have gained.
- To provide an opportunity to clear up any misconceptions the children may have.
- To enable the children to see fish in their natural habitat through the film. They will be able to see close-up views of underwater life that would be impossible to bring into the classroom in any other way.

Visitor, with Tasting Experiences. Ask the visitor to demonstrate how fish is cooked, including the preparation required before cooking and the method of cooking. While the fish is being cooked, have the visitor show the children fishing equipment and tell them about fishing as a sport. Then divide the children into groups for a tasting experience. Set up prepared samples of fish at the tables. Use two or three different kinds of fish, including one prepared in class. Encourage the children to try each of the samples and compare the tastes.

Objectives

- To enable the children to see the actual preparation of fish being used as food.
- To provide each child with the opportunity to taste fish, compare tastes, and identify likes and dislikes.

* *Swimmy.* Westport, CT: Connecticut Films.

- To acquaint the children with fishing as a recreational sport and with fishing equipment.

Small-Group Activities

Dramatization of Poems, Songs, or Rhymes. Gather one-half of the children inside, and send the other half outside. Give the inside group a nursery rhyme, poem, or song to act out or perform as they wish. When they have practiced, have the other group come in and practice. Then both groups will get together to dramatize their selections for the uninvolved children, who will try to guess what is being dramatized.

Objectives

- To permit creative thinking and actions to be combined with spoken or sung words.
- To allow for a different approach to small-group activities.

Individual Activities

- Trough with balance scales and corn
- Pictures of various kinds of fish on display
- Fish specimens and aquatic insects

UNIT PLAN ON PETS

For this unit it is suggested that one particular pet be chosen for each day's focus, with concepts relating to that pet brought into the discussion. Hopefully, the children can handle the pets, feed them, and care for them. Baby pets will also add interest for the children.

Art

- Decoration of rocks to resemble a desired pet—felt scraps, hobby-store eyes, beans, materials scraps, and others
- Sock pets—child's sock decorated with felt scraps, yarn, and other fabrics
- Sack-puppet pets
- Pet collages—pictures of pets cut from magazines or animal pet stickers purchased from stationery stores
- Salt dough or salt clay pets
- Collages using dry foods for pets, such as birdseed

Field Trips

- Pet store
- Home where pets can be observed
- Zoo
- Animal hospital

Visitors

- Pet store owner
- Family member of student to share family pet
- Storyteller to tell pet stories

Jason cautiously observes the dog as the dog cautiously observes Jason before the two venture to be friends.

- Veterinarian
- Zookeeper

Food

- Sandwiches cut with pet-animal cookie cutters
- Green salad, with discussion of pets that enjoy vegetables—sesame seeds sprinkled on salad, followed by discussion of which pets enjoy eating seeds
- Bread dough shaped into a favorite pet

Science

- Science discussion, experiments, and observations focusing on the following topics: kinds of pets; sizes of pets; characteristics such as footprints, colors, sounds, diet, sleeping habits
- Care and needs of particular pets
- Pet babies—appearance, care required, diet

Music

- Songs about pets
- Creative dramatics relating to pets—how they move, what they do during the day, how they respond to friends, how they respond to enemies, and so on.

Language and Literacy

- Slides of pets; discussion
- Pets or pictures of current or former pets brought by the children; sharing and discussion
- Puppet or flannel board figures; dramatization or storytelling by the children; or discussion of particular pets by the children
- Tape recording of pet sounds, with the children naming the pet and discussing the sounds it makes and why
- Stories and poetry about pets
- Game in which individual children select a particular pet and then describe it so that other children can guess which pet has been described
- Game in which a child leaves the room, class members select a particular pet, and then the child returns and tries to discover which pet was selected by asking yes/no questions
- Children illustrate a favorite pet, and then dictate or write something about this pet. Children's stories are made into a class booklet

Summary

Teaching units about animals provide numerous possibilities for explorations and experiences regarding various animal-related concepts. Young children generally have a natural curiosity about animals and their characteristics. An environmental curriculum that includes animals abounds with opportunities for studying size, shape, number, color, texture, categorization, weight, smell, sound, and food, along with the physical characteristics, habitats, uses, and habits of animals. By studying animals, children are able to lessen or overcome fears while gaining insight and understanding of the proper care of animals. Most of all, children can appreciate animals and sense the dependence of humans on them.

Student Learning Activities

1. Visit with a preschool, kindergarten, first-grade or second-grade teacher. Find out whether units or activities relating to animals are included in the teacher's programs. (Note the units or experiences included in the curriculum.) Ask the teacher to relate to you the children's (and the teacher's) feelings about animal units and experiences in the classroom.

Does the teacher ever have live animals in the classroom? Discuss with the teacher any other ideas and questions relating to animals as a part of the curriculum. Following your interview, describe what you learn and your reactions.

2. Try to visit a classroom where there is a live animal. What are the children's reactions? Ask the children questions about the animal. Do you see any reinforcement relating to the animal, such as pictures, books, or other materials?

3. Begin a collection of children's poetry relating to animals. Include fingerplays, if you desire.

4. Begin to collect and mount a set or sets of animal picture cards.

5. Visit a children's library and evaluate at least two of the books on the reference list included in this chapter. Then include at least two more books. Evaluate and describe each of the four

books. How would you use them with children? What concepts relating to an animal or animals are taught in the books?

6. Study the unit plans on animals included in this chapter. Then prepare a unit plan or web on an animal, category of animals, or topic relating to animals. From this unit plan or web, prepare a 5-day activity plan. Balance your days with a variety of activities that are not theme related.

7. Think of additional ideas for each of the unit plans included in this chapter.

8. There are many records and tapes that include songs about animals. Visit a library or early childhood classroom and listen to at least three recordings relating to animals. Evaluate each recording. Would the recording teach accurate facts about the animal, or is it a "pretend" song? How would you use the recording with children?

Suggested Resources

There are so many songs, pictures, films, filmstrips, videos, and books about animals that teachers should check available resources for additional suggestions. Whenever a unit is done on a category of animals or a specific kind of animal, check the card catalog at the nearest library under the desired subject heading. Space limits the list provided here to only few of the possible suggestions in this category. However, four excellent resources include (1) *Science and Children*, a journal of the Natural Science Teachers Association that provides in each issue a column on the care of a specific living organism; (2) National Geographic Society, 17th and M Streets, N.W., Washington, DC 20036; (3) National Audubon Society, Route 4, Box 171, Sharon, CT 06069; and (4) National Wildlife Federation, 1400 16th Street, N.W., Washington, DC 20036.

Children's Books and Magazines

Baker, A. (1991). *Two tiny mice*. New York: Dial.

Booth, D. (Ed.). (1990) *Voices on the wind: Poems for all seasons*. New York: Morrow.

Breslow, S., & Blakemore, S. (1990). *I really want a dog*. New York: Dutton.

Brett, J. (1988). *The first dog*. New York: Harcourt Brace Jovanovich.

Brown, M. W. (1979). *The dead bird*. New York: Dell.

Brown, M. W. (1982). *Home for a bunny*. New York: Western.

Brown, M. W. (1977). *The runaway bunny*. New York: HarperCollins.

Carle, E. (1986). *The very hungry caterpillar*. New York: Putnam.

Cole, S. (1985). *When the tide is low*. New York: Lothrop, Lee & Shepard.

Eastman, P. D. (1960). *Are you my mother?* New York: Random House.

Ehlert, L. (1990) *Feathers for lunch*. New York: Harcourt Brace Jovanovich.

Fisher, R. M. (1982). Animals in winter. In *Books for young explorers* (Set 9). Washington, DC: National Geographic.

Flack, M. (1986) *Ask Mr. Bear*. New York: Macmillan.

Gag, W. (1952). *Millions of cats*. New York: Putnam.

Galdone, P. (1973) *The little red hen*. New York: Seabury.

Ganeri, A. (1992). *Animal food*. New York: Barron's.

Gibbons, G. (1985). *The milk makers*. New York: Macmillan.

Gibbons, G. (1991) *Whales*. New York: Holiday.

Gifford, H. (1991). *Red fox*. New York: Dial.

Ginsburg, M. (1980). *Good morning, chick*. New York: Greenwillow.

Greenfield, K. (1992). *Sister Yessa's story*. New York: Harper.

Kitchen B. (1991). *Animal numbers*. New York: Dial.

Kleven, E. (1992). *The lion and the little red bird*. New York: Dutton.

Koss, A. G. (1991). *City critters around the world*. Los Angeles: Price Stern Sloan.

Krauss, R. (1970). *Whose mouse are you?* New York: Scholastic.

Leaf, M. (1936). *The story of Ferdinand*. New York: Viking.

Leigh, O. (1985) *The merry-go-round*. New York: Holiday House.

Lemieux, M. (1985). *What's that noise?* New York: Morrow.

Lewison, W. C. (1992). *Going to sleep on the farm*. New York: Dial.

Lionni, L. (1968). *Swimmy*. New York: Pantheon.

Lionni, L. (1970). *Fish is fish*. New York: Pantheon.

Martin, B., Jr. (1983). *Brown bear, brown bear, what do you see?* New York: Henry Holt.

Marzollo, J. (1990). *Pretend you're a cat*. New York: Dial.

McCloskey, R. (1941). *Make way for ducklings*. New York: Viking.

McDonald, M. (1992). *Whoo-oo is it?* New York: Orchard.

Munsinger, L. (1986). *A porcupine named Fluffy*. Boston: Houghton Mifflin.

National Geographic Society. (1974). *Books for young explorers* (series). Washington, DC: Author.

National Geographic Society. (1980) Life in the woods. In *Wonders of learning* kits. Washington, DC: Author.

National Wildlife Federation. *Ranger Rick's Wildlife Magazine*. Washington, DC: Author.

National Wildlife Federation. *Your Big Backyard Magazine*. Washington, DC: Author.

Parker, N. W., & Wright, J. R. (1990). *Frogs, toads, lizards, and salamanders*. New York: Greenwillow.

Patterson, F. (1985). *Koko's kitten*. New York: Scholastic.

Pope, B., & Emmons, R. (1967). *Let's visit a dairy*. Dallas: Taylor.

Pope, B., & Emmons, R. (1969). *Let's visit a farm*. Dallas: Taylor

Romanova, N. (1985). *Once there was a tree*. New York: Dial.

Ryder, J. (1990). *Chipmunk song*. New York: Lodestar.

Seuss, Dr. (1960) *Are you my mother?* New York: Random House.

Sheldon, D. (1991). *The whale's song*. New York: Dial.

Spier, P. (1971). *Gobble growl grunt*. New York: Doubleday.

Szilagyi, M. (1985) *Thunderstorm*. New York: Bradbury.

Tafuri, N. (1985) *Rabbit's morning*. New York: Greenwillow.

Taylor, K. (1991). *See how they grow* (series). New York: Dutton.

Urquhart, J. C. (1982). Animals that travel. In *Books for young explorers*. Washington, DC: National Geographic Society.

Venino, S. (1981). Amazing animal groups. In *Books for young explorers*, Washington, DC: National Geographic Society.

Viorst, J. (1975) *The tenth good thing about Barney*. New York: Antheneum.

Waldrop, V. H. (Ed.). (1983) *Ranger Rick's storybook*. Washington, DC: National Wildlife Society.

Wildlife Education, Ltd. *Zoo books* (series). San Diego, CA: Author.

Wildsmith, B. (1967). *Wild animals*. Oxford: Oxford University Press.

Wildsmith, B. (1980). *Animal homes*. New York: Oxford University Press.

Wildsmith, B. (1982). *Pelican*. New York: Pantheon.

Wildsmith, B. (1983). *Fishes*. New York: Oxford University Press.

Wolf, A. (1985). *Only the cat saw*. New York: Dodd Mead.

Wood, A. (1984) *The napping house*. San Diego, CA: Harcourt Brace Jovanovich.

Woodruff, E. (1991). *The wing song.* New York: Holiday House.

Yolen, J. (1987). *Owl moon.* New York: Philomel.

Zion, G. (1956). *Harry the dirty dog.* New York: HarperCollins.

Records, Tapes, and Cassettes

Animals are wonderful. Cheviot.

Animal folk songs for children. Scholastic Book Services.

Animal song parade. Columbia Harmony. (Record)

The circus. David C. Cook.

Creepy the crawly caterpillar. Children's Record Guild. (Record)

Dandy-lions never roar! Good Apple.

The farm. David C. Cook.

Folk song carnival. Hap Palmer Record Library, AR524 or AC524.

Folk songs for young folk—Animals (Vol. 1). Scholastic Book Services. (Record)

Folk songs for young folk—Animals (Vol. 2). Scholastic Book Services. (Record)

If a dinosaur came to dinner. The Child's World.

More learning as we play. Folkways Records. (Record)

More singing fun (Vol. 1). Bowmar-Noble. (Record)

The rainy day record. Bowmar-Noble. (Record)

Singing fun. Bowmar-Noble.

The small singer (Vol. 1). Bowmar-Noble.

The small singer (Vol. 2). Bowmar-Noble.

Snoopycat. Scholastic Book Services.

Multimedia Kits

Amphibians and how they grow. National Geographic.

Animal families. In *Wonder of learning* kits (includes cassette and teacher's guide). Washington, DC: National Geographic, 1980.

Animal homes. In *Wonder of learning* kits (includes cassette and teacher's guide). Washington, DC: National Geographic, 1981.

Birds and how they grow. National Geographic.

Butterflies. National Geographic.

Farm animals. National Geographic.

Mammals and how they grow. National Geographic.

Spiders. National Geographic.

Whales. National Geographic.

Pictures

Animal homes. The Child's World. (Foldout)

Animals and how they live. National Audubon Society.

Animals of North America. National Audubon Society.

Animals that help us. The Child's World (Foldout)

Animals without backbones. Society for Visual Education (SVE).

Baby animals of the wild. The Child's World.

Birds. The Child's World.

Birds and other animals. National Audubon Society.

Birds and our land. David C. Cook.

Common birds. Society for Visual Education (SVE).

Common insects. Society for Visual Education (SVE).

Familiar fresh-water fish. Society for Visual Education (SVE).

Farm animals. Eye Gate Media.

Farm and ranch animals. Society for Visual Education (SVE).

Fishes. The Child's World.

Insects. The Child's World.

Insects and spiders. National Audubon Society.

Insects and spiders. The Child's World.

Kinds of animals. The Child's World. (Foldout)

Life cycle of frog. The Child's World. (Sequence chart)

Life cycle of monarch butterfly. The Child's World. (Sequence chart)

Life cycle of robin. The Child's World. (Sequence chart)

Life in the sea (I). The Child's World.

Life in the sea (II). The Child's World.

Mammals. The Child's World.

Moths and butterflies. Society for Visual Education (SVE).

Pets. David C. Cook.

Pets. Society for Visual Education (SVE).

Pets. The Child's World. (Foldout)

Reptiles and amphibians. Society for Visual Education (SVE).

Science themes (1). David C. Cook.

Science themes (2). David C. Cook.

Trip to the farm. David C. Cook.

Trip to the zoo. David C. Cook.

Western birds. National Audubon Society.

Wild animals. Society for Visual Education (SVE).

Zoo animals. Society for Visual Education (SVE).

Films, Filmstrips, and Videos

Animal babies grow up. Coronet Films.
Animal games. National Geographic.
Animal hide and seek: Camouflage for beginners. Coronet Films.
Animal homes. Churchill.
Animal senses. National Geographic.
Animals and how they grow. National Geographic.
Animals and their foods. Coronet Films.
Animals and their homes. Coronet Films
Animals and their ways. Eye Gate Media.
Animals are different and alike. Coronet Films.
Animals around you. National Geographic.
Animals can bite. Pyramid.
Animals hatched from eggs. Coronet Films.
Animals in winter. National Geographic.
Animals that work for people. National Geographic.
Baby rabbit. Churchill.
Bear country. WorldWide Slides. (Slides)
Beaver valley. WorldWide Slides. (Slides)
The biggest bear. Weston Woods Studios.
Birds and their homes. Coronet Films.
Birds of the world. WorldWide Slides. (Viewmaster reel)
Butterflies. WorldWide Slides. (Viewmaster reel)
Caterpillars grow and change. Coronet Films.
Chick, chick, chick. Churchill.
Children's zoo. WorldWide Slides. (Viewmaster reel)
The cow. Churchill.
Curious George rides a bike. Weston Woods Studios.
Dogs. Churchill.
Farmyard babies. Coronet Films.
Fish life. WorldWide Slides. (Viewmaster reel)
Frederick. Distribution Sixteen.
Horses. WorldWide Slides. (Viewmaster reel)
How animals live. Eye Gate Media.
How animals live in winter. Coronet Films.
Insects and their homes. Coronet Films.

Let's learn about animals. Educational Activities.
The life of animals. National Geographic.
Lions, tigers, and other big cats. National Geographic.
Make way for ducklings. Weston Woods Studios.
Millions of cats. Weston Woods Studios.
Monkeys. WorldWide Slides. (Viewmaster reel)
Our animal neighbors. Coronet Films.
The perils of Priscilla. Churchill.
Perry. WorldWide Slides. (Slides)
Pets are fun. Campus Films.
Pets we love: Animals and pets. Eye Gate Media.
Pigs! Churchill.
Places where plants and animals live. National Geographic.
Places and animals depend on each other. Coronet Films.
Rocky Mountain wildlife. WorldWide Slides. (Slides)
Saving our wild animals. National Geographic.
Sheep, sheep, sheep. Churchill.
Snakes. WorldWide Slides. (Viewmaster reel)
Squeak the squirrel. Churchill.
Swimmy. Distribution Sixteen.
The tale of Peter Rabbit. Weston Woods Studios.
Ways animals communicate. National Geographic.
Whales. National Geographic.
What animals are. Eye Gate Media.
Why animals live where they do. Coronet Films.
Why animals live where they live. Eye Gate Media.
Zoo animals behind the scenes. Coronet Films.
Zoo babies. Coronet films.

Computer Software

Animal photo fun. DLM. (Apple).
Cotton's first files. MindPlay. (Apple).
Katie's farm. Lawrence Productions. (Apple IIGS, Mac, IBM, Mac II).
Learn about: Animals. Wings for Learning. (Apple).

CHAPTER
fifteen

Plants

Introduction

"In countless ways, science is at work everywhere and at all times in this beautifully ordered, yet full of surprises, world" (Ziemer, 1987, p. 44). Plants are living parts of the science world. Children enjoy caring for and nurturing plants through their growing stages. There is particular excitement for young children the day they discover that their little seed, carefully planted, watered, sunned, and cared for, is pushing its way through the soil and taking its first peek at the world! In addition to the satisfaction of planting seeds and caring for plants, there are many opportunities for learning about plant life and teaching concepts through the studies of seeds and plants. Concepts such as size, number, color, texture, and shape can be developed easily through discussions relating to plants. Concepts specific to individual plants, or categories or classes of plants, will emerge as a result of plant studies. For example, children will become aware of the characteristics of plants, what plants need

in order to grow, and uses of plants. Children will also learn by making comparisons among plants—comparing sizes, colors, rates of growth, seasons of growth, and other factors. As you and your class observe a tall tree, for example, "Ask wondering questions: 'I wonder what makes the leaves so green.' 'I wonder how long it took this tree to grow so tall'" (Ziemer, 1987, p. 44). We do not need to know all the answers, because we are teaching curiosity rather than just facts. Our questions should "encourage [children] to observe . . . [and] to start thinking" (Ziemer, 1987, p. 46).

Children should have opportunities for exploring plants in the classroom environment. With so many varieties of plants, teachers need to select those appropriate for the climate and season. Rubber plants and geraniums are especially hardy, and children enjoy watching geraniums bloom and observing the beautiful color of the blossoms. When there are plants in the classroom, the children should be allowed to care for them—water them, put them in sunlight, give

There is no better team than a thirsty plant and an eager waterer!

them plant food, and assume many other responsibilities in nurturing or caring for plants. There are a number of plants that are poisonous and should be avoided. Examples include English ivy, philodendron, laurel, and dieffenbachia (Maxim, 1989). Before purchasing plants for your classroom or center, check with your local nursery to make sure that the plants are nontoxic. The specific varieties of plants that are in your environment, both inside and outside, should be named often. Ideally, children should have a garden space outdoors where they can plant and care for vegetables and/or flowers. "The digging, weeding, and watering responsibilities add to the children's awareness of life within their environment and to the concept of what plants need to grow" (Maxim, 1989, p. 482).

Through studies of plants, children become aware of our reliance on plants as a source of food, clothing, and shelter, as well as aesthetic beauty in both indoor and outdoor surroundings. However, children can also learn that many plants, such as noxious weeds and poisonous plants, may be a nuisance or harmful to humans.

Approach to Teaching

As units of study relating to plants are selected, the teacher should utilize the appropriate seasons and climates, and select for study the plants that are most common to the children's surroundings and locality. Where possible, give the children actual experiences with plants.

Plants could be approached as a general theme or unit. However, specific areas such as seeds, vegetables, fruits, trees, wheat, or flowers also provide appropriate units of study. Categorization games help children distinguish plants from other groups such as animals, people, or toys. Even more specifically, plant picture cards could be sorted into categories such as vegetables, fruits, flowers, and trees. The cards could also be used as flash cards for naming the specific plants. Pictures of plants can be found in magazines, stickers purchased from stationery stores, discarded workbooks, or seed packets.

Following is a list of suggested plant unit themes. It is not meant to be inclusive, since ideas and themes are limited only by the teacher's own creative thinking and planning. Furthermore, a unit need not necessarily result from each idea or theme; for example, a suggested theme could be used for a science experience supporting any unrelated unit of study.

Plants	Fruits (also specific)
Seeds	Trees
Nuts	Wood
Wheat	Plants that grow in water
Vegetables (also specific)	Flowers
Plants as food for humans	Berries

After a plant unit such as pumpkins is presented, the children can help complete a web such as the one illustrated in Figure 15–1.

Concepts and Ideas for Teaching

1. Most plants need air, light, water, and food in order to grow.
2. We eat different parts of plants.
   a. Roots (turnips, carrots, radishes, parsnips, onions)
   b. Leaves (cabbage, lettuce, spinach, chard, beet greens)
   c. Stems or stalks (asparagus, celery, broccoli)
   d. Skins (tomatoes, apples, carrots)
   e. Seeds (nuts, peas, beans, potatoes)
3. Plants vary in color, size, texture, shape, and weight.
4. Plants may change in appearance as they progress through various stages of growth and as they are affected by temperature, weather, and season.
5. Some plants can grow only in particular seasons and climates.

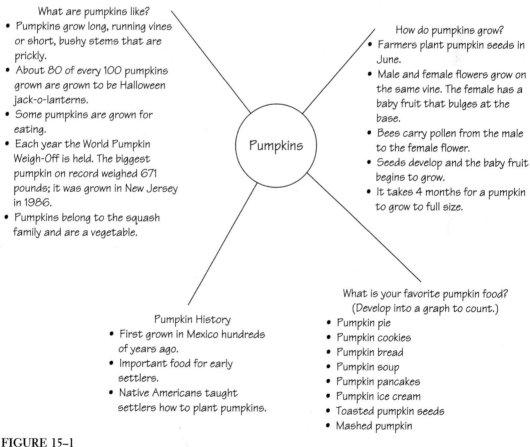

What are pumpkins like?
- Pumpkins grow long, running vines or short, bushy stems that are prickly.
- About 80 of every 100 pumpkins grown are grown to be Halloween jack-o-lanterns.
- Some pumpkins are grown for eating.
- Each year the World Pumpkin Weigh-Off is held. The biggest pumpkin on record weighed 671 pounds; it was grown in New Jersey in 1986.
- Pumpkins belong to the squash family and are a vegetable.

How do pumpkins grow?
- Farmers plant pumpkin seeds in June.
- Male and female flowers grow on the same vine. The female has a baby fruit that bulges at the base.
- Bees carry pollen from the male to the female flower.
- Seeds develop and the baby fruit begins to grow.
- It takes 4 months for a pumpkin to grow to full size.

Pumpkins

Pumpkin History
- First grown in Mexico hundreds of years ago.
- Important food for early settlers.
- Native Americans taught settlers how to plant pumpkins.

What is your favorite pumpkin food?
(Develop into a graph to count.)
- Pumpkin pie
- Pumpkin cookies
- Pumpkin bread
- Pumpkin soup
- Pumpkin pancakes
- Pumpkin ice cream
- Toasted pumpkin seeds
- Mashed pumpkin

FIGURE 15–1
Sample Web: What We Learned About Pumpkins

6. Plants have various characteristics.
   a. Roots   d. Leaves
   b. Stems or stalks e. Seeds
   c. Flowers   f. Skins

7. There are many kinds of plants.
   a. Trees   f. Vines
   b. Flowers   g. Mosses
   c. Foliage   h. Molds
   d. Vegetables   i. Other fungi
   e. Grains

8. Plants have many uses.

   a. Some plants provide food for humans (vegetables, fruits, grains).

   b. Trees provide products such as wood, paper, poles, gum, drugs, paint, waxes, and dyes.

   c. Some plants provide clothing (cotton, linen).

   d. Many plants provide beauty (trees, houseplants, flowers).

   e. Some plants provide shade, shelter, and protection for humans and animals (trees and large plants such as shrubs and bushes).

   f. Some plants provide homes for animals (trees, shrubs, foliage).

   g. Many plants are food for animals.

9. Some plants are harmful to humans (poisonous, such as poison ivy).

10. Some plants are a nuisance to humans (e.g., weeds).

11. Some plants grow on land and some grow in water; some grow in light and some in shade.

12. Most plants grow from seed, although there are variations. Some plants grow from bulbs, some grow in particular circumstances without seeds (moss and mold), some grow from cuttings (geraniums), and some grow from suckers or runners.

13. Most plants "follow," or grow toward, the sun.

14. Plants have different rates of growth.

15. Seeds differ in color, shape, size, and texture.

16. We eat some types of seeds.

17. Seeds travel by rolling; by blowing with the wind; or by being carried by animals, water, or humans.

18. Some plants have one seed, and some have many.

19. Some seeds look like the parent plant, some do not.

20. Plants we eat grow in different ways: Some foods grow on trees, some on bushes, some on vines; some foods grow above the ground and some below it.

Activities and Experiences

1. Observe and discuss characteristic parts of different plants.
   a. Apple tree   c. Broccoli
   b. Geranium   d. Wheat

2. Have a tasting experience in which the children taste different parts of plants. Ask the children to name and give examples of edible parts of plants. (Refer to concept 2 for ideas.)

3. Observe the growing cycle of several different plants from their beginning to maturity.

   a. Observe the day-by-day stages of a growing seed such as a lima bean seed. Line the inside of a straight-sided jar with a paper towel or blotting paper. Keep water or a soaked sponge in the bottom so that the towel remains wet. Each day put soaked lima bean seeds between the jar and the wet paper. Do this each day for about 5 days so that the changes on each of the 5 days can be observed. Record observations in writing, and in drawings or photographs, and put them together in a book to read and reread about the experience. When the seeds are well sprouted, plant them in soil and continue to watch their growth until they bear beans.

    b. Observe the growth of an orange tree from its beginning as a seedling. Record observations in pictures and writing.

    c. Observe the growth of a flower. Record observations in pictures and writing.

    d. Observe the growth of bread mold. Record observations in pictures and writing.

    e. Observe the growth of grass seed by having each child plant some in an egg shell filled with potting soil.

4. Plant some bean seeds. When the bean plant begins to grow, each day cut a strip of paper the length of the plant. Over a period of time, compare the lengths of the strips of paper in order to study the growth of the plant. Maintain the bean plants until the plants flower and reproduce seeds. Count the leaves on the plant as it is growing. When a pod appears, cut it and count the seeds.

5. Observe and record the day-by-day growth of various seeds; compare the ways they are different and the ways they are alike.

6. Have the class adopt a tree in the neighborhood or school yard and observe the tree's changes throughout the year. The class could measure the tree's diameter, examine its bark, observe the leaves during the different seasons, and keep a year-long book or record describing its growth and changes. Photographs of the tree could be taken at different times during the year and then individually mounted for use as a sequencing material or in a book.

7. Observe how plants absorb water and food. Put a fresh stalk of celery under water; trim the end off and cut it up the center while the stock is still under water. Cut it almost the entire length of the stem but not quite all the way. Fill two glasses with water and put food coloring of different colors in each one (red and blue work well). Put half of the celery in one glass of colored water and the other half in the other glass. Within hours, the veins going up the stem of the celery and the leaves on the top of the stalk will assume the color of the water in the glasses. One can also put a white carnation in the colored water, and the petals will change color.

8. To enable the children to see what happens when a plant does not receive one of the necessary ingredients for growth, perform the following experiment: Obtain five similar plants, such as bean plants or flowers. Give one plant all the necessary ingredients except air; another, everything except light (put it in a dark room or closet); another, everything except water; another, everything except soil (food). Provide all the necessary ingredients to the fifth plant. Observe how long each plant grows and lives. Record observations.

9. Put different plants or parts of plants in a paper bag. Have a child describe one of the items, and ask the other children to guess the name or part of the plant from the description given.

10. Compare the sizes of plants, such as a radish plant and a tree, or one kind of bean plant and another.

11. Put plant pictures on cards and have the children sort the plants into categories. Categories might include the following:

    a. Plants that we eat/plants that we do not eat

    b. Fruits/vegetables/trees/foliage/flowers

    c. Plants that grow above the ground/plants that grow below the ground/plants that grow in water

12. Collect leaves and make comparisons. Classify and label those of the same variety.

13. Study and observe plants that do not grow from seeds—plants that grow from bulbs

and plants that grow in particular media such as moss and mold. Allow the children to look at the plants through a magnifying glass. Do forced-bulb planting indoors.

14. To teach the children that stems grow upward and roots grow downward, obtain a clear glass or plastic jar and secure a piece of fine gauze over the top with an elastic band or a string. On top of the gauze, sprinkle seeds such as wheat kernels, and then fill the container with water. Make sure that the first few days the container is watered to the top and that the seeds remain wet enough to sprout. Be sure to put the container in a dish or pie plate, since the gauze absorbs the water. Within a few days the seeds will sprout—the roots growing downward, (because of gravity—this is called *geotropism*) and the stems growing upward.

15. Obtain a tree stump that is fairly old and demonstrate to the children how to count the rings to learn the age of the tree.

16. Hollow out a tree stump and put products of trees on the inside. The children will be fascinated to learn that many products— paper, boards, gum, drugs, paint, dyes, waxes—are obtained from trees.

17. Put a plant near the sun and leave it in the same position for several days. Observe how it follows the sun.

18. Have a variety of plants in the classroom for the children to care for. They should learn how often to water, how much water to give, how often to fertilize, and how much fertilizer to give.

19. In the classroom, observe animals that eat plants. Compare these animals and the plants they eat to other animals and the plants they eat.

20. Plant and care for a garden (indoor or outdoor). Record growth and other observations through writing and pictures. Discuss the importance of fertilizing the garden,

and show the children how to use decayed leaves, grass, and other biodegradable matter.

21. Plant and care for a terrarium (class or individual). Use an empty aquarium, large jar, bowl, or individual baby food jars. Put fine gravel on the bottom, and then add good soil, a layer of vermiculite, some sand, and a little charcoal. Add plants and then sprinkle with water. Cover the jar. The children can observe the plants absorbing moisture, the moisture evaporating from the ground, and the moisture condensing on the lid of the jar.

22. Plant seeds and watch their growth. Sprout between glass slabs, in plastic cups lined with paper towels, or in petri dishes; sprin-

During study of a unit on plants, a container of seeds provides a stimulating texture experience for the children. Later on, the children will plant the seeds and care for the growing plants.

kle on wet sponges; or plant in soil in paper cups, plastic cups, or half-pint milk cartons. Measure and record the growth.

23. Invite each child to bring from home an old sock, preferably one of wool or wool blend. Visit a nature center or a field with a lot of weeds and grasses, and have the children put their sock on over their shoe. When you return to your center or classroom, discuss the variety of seeds stuck to the sock and give each child an empty plastic milk carton or bleach jug that has the top portion cut off. Let each child put his or her sock into the plastic container and surround the sock with potting soil. Water the sock periodically, and a variety of plants will begin to grow in a few days.

24. Have the children collect pictures of foods that come from plants.

25. Make a plant scrapbook and have the children look for pictures of plants. The scrapbook may be divided into categories such as trees, vegetables, flowers, and so on. Nursery and greenhouse catalogs are excellent sources for pictures. Label the pictures for literacy.

26. Collect and categorize a variety of seeds according to the way they travel or are scattered. Collect seeds that are winged, like maple tree seeds or milkweed seeds. Collect seeds that stick or attach themselves to animals or people. Collect other kinds of seeds, and discuss the many ways seeds are carried from place to place. Collect and label or identify seeds.

27. Have a tasting experience with seeds we eat—peanuts, coconut, beans, wheat, peas, and others.

28. Provide a variety of seeds and have the children sort them in a container such as an egg carton. Provide the seed packets and see if the children can then match the seeds to the appropriate packet.

Unit Plans on Plants

Following are examples of unit plans on various aspects of plants, from general to more specific categories. (For unit plans on fruits and vegetables, see Chapter Seven, Nutrition and Food Experiences.)

UNIT PLAN ON PLANTS (GENERAL)

Art

- Plant collages—seeds, dried flowers, leaves, sticks, etc.—in plaster of Paris, play dough, or other media
- Screen painting with parts of plants
- Painting with flowers, leaves, or grains instead of brushes
- Seeds added to finger paint
- Melted crayon and parts of plants (seeds, leaves, flowers) between waxed-paper sheets
- Flowers made out of nut cups, egg cartons, or cupcake holders; attached to a pipe cleaner, put in clay base, and arranged in paper cup vase
- Flowers and leaves cut from wallpaper or fabric to glue on a paper or cardboard base
- Shakers decorated with plant parts

Field Trips

- Home garden
- Nature walk, with emphasis on looking for plants
- Greenhouse
- Plant nursery
- Flower shop
- Houseplants in home
- Plant science department at a college; botany department at a high school

Visitors

- Florist
- Person owning houseplants
- Member of one child's family to show seeds they will plant in a home garden and discuss the care of plants at home

- Person to build a terrarium
- Person to bring in a pet or animal that eats plants

Food

- Any food experience using plants such as fruits, vegetables, seeds, or nuts

Science

- Growth cycle of plants
- Needs of plants—air, sun, water
- Uses of plants
- Harmful plants
- Nuisance plants
- Types of plants
- Places where plants grow
- Parts of plants
- Observe the growth of mold, and study it under a microscope. What objects grow mold?
- Sweet potato supported with toothpicks in a jar of water; observation of growth
- Pineapple planted by twisting the top off the fresh pineapple and then planting it in wet sand
- Carrot tops grown by cutting them 1/4 to 1/2 inch down and then putting them in water

Music

- Songs about plants and seeds
- Seed shakers made and used as rhythm instruments; seedpods and gourds used as rhythm instruments
- Creative movements and dramatics relating to growth of plant from seed to mature plant; plants wilting because of lack of water and then being revived; plants following the sun, moving in the wind; seeds traveling and sprouting
- Dramatization of care of plants
- Dramatization of musical story: growth of plant

Language and Literacy

- Stories about plants
- Poetry
- Slides of plants; discussion
- Different kinds of plants brought by children from their homes; discussion
- Game in which individual children select a particular plant and describe it to the other chil-

dren; guessing which plant is being described
- Children's own stories based on experiences in planting, growing, and caring for plants or gardens
- Take pictures of various garden plants, such as carrots or peas, and then have the children dictate or write a story about each one; assemble the stories into a booklet

UNIT PLAN ON TREES

The children should understand that trees are a kind of plant and that they start from small seeds. The products of trees, as well as other uses, should be among the concepts studied during this unit. The children should also be exposed to the wide variety of trees. The activities selected will be determined by the goals and objectives desired for the particular unit. A unit on trees would be appropriate around Arbor Day.

Art

- Tree product collages using paper and wood products
- Pinecone mice
- Wood collages using wood shavings, sawdust, and wood scraps
- Sawdust painting
- Paper collages
- Tree trunk drawn or pasted on paper, with children using sponge painting or hand prints from finger paint to paint the leaves
- Nutshell animals
- Four-season paintings or drawings of trees
- Shakers
- Texture smears with leaves, wood products, or other parts of trees such as twigs
- Leaf collages
- Pinecone printing

Field Trips

- Nature walk to observe trees
- National or state forest
- Lumberyard
- Carpenter shop
- Home under construction

- Sawmill
- Hobby shop or woodworking shop
- Store where wooden things (furniture, etc.) are sold
- Christmas tree farm
- Grocery store to observe edible tree products such as nuts and fruits
- Tree nurseries
- Visit to tree(s) in which the children could see animal homes, such as birds' nests
- Visit to a site where trees are being planted
- High school or university industrial arts shop
- Museum to see wood sculptures
- Divide the children into pairs. One child in the pair is blindfolded and taken to a tree. The child can hug the tree, feel it, and explore it. The child returns to the starting position, removes the blindfold, then finds the tree that was explored.

Food*

- Fruit salads, desserts, or juices made from fruits of trees
- Foods that have nuts as an ingredient, such as cakes, cookies, candy
- Dried fruits

Visitors

- Forest ranger or urban forester
- Forest-fire fighter
- City fire fighter
- Carpenter
- Wood carver
- Logger
- Owner of a tree nursery
- Grocery store employee

Science

- Examination of circles in tree trunks to determine age of tree
- Discussion of tree products
- Tree planted and cared for
- Discussion and study of tree parts
- Observation of how wood burns

* See also Chapter Seven.

- Tasting of foods that are products of trees—fruits, nuts, pine gum
- Changing characteristics of tree products
- Observation of selected tree over a period of time, preferably a year. Keep a record in writing and with pictures.

Music

- Creative movements relating to trees growing, moving in the wind, heavily laden with snow, leaves falling
- Use wooden rhythm sticks or wooden blocks as rhythm instruments
- "Musical Chairs" in which pictures of different kinds of trees or tree products are placed on the front of the chairs. (Play music and have the children do locomotor rhythms. When the music stops, give directions such as "All pine trees stand and hop to this music" or "All weeping willow trees stand and skate to this music." A variation of this is to tape the pictures of the trees or the tree products securely to the floor. Have each child stand on one when the music stops, and then proceed with the game as suggested.)
- Wooden drums
- Shakers with seeds from trees
- Instruments made from wood
- Drumsticks

Language and Literacy

- Stories about trees—written by the children or other authors
- Poetry
- Pictures of trees, and children brainstorming words that come to their minds as they see each tree
- Slides of trees; discussion of characteristics, season, feelings relating to each tree
- Cinquain poetry for trees
- Prepare a book, with each child doing one page. On this page, the child is to draw a picture of a favorite tree and dictate to the teacher or write why he or she likes that tree.
- Have children finish the sentence "The best thing about a tree is . . ." or "I like trees because. . . ." The children could write or dictate

their answers and then illustrate them. These pages could be put together into a book to be enjoyed over and over again.

Related Activities

- Rope swing in a tree
- Hammering
- Sawing
- Container with wood chips, sawdust, toothpicks, wooden spoons, bark, leaves

LESSON PLAN ON TREES (5-DAY)

Overall Goals

- To help the children become acquainted with the different parts of a tree (roots, trunk, branches, leaves).
- To help the children become more aware of nature around them.
- To help the children realize the many types, uses, values, and products of trees (shade, ornamentation, fruit, nuts, lumber, homes).
- To increase the children's vocabulary of terms relating to trees.

Day 1

Whole-Group Activities

Introduction to Unit. Gather the children together at the rug. Sing a few songs about trees. Then tell the children about the different parts of the tree and show them pictures of many different kinds of trees. Read the book *A Tree Is Nice* (Udry, 1956).

Objectives

- To stimulate interest in the new unit on trees.
- To familiarize children with the names and parts of common trees.

Discussion of Nature Walk. Gather the children at the rug to discuss the nature walk. Then guide them in a discussion on the uses of trees (shade, ornament, building homes, fuel for fires, etc.).

Objectives

- To help the children learn that trees have many uses.

- To give the children a chance to discuss observations on the field trip.

Small-Group Activities

Art—Leaf Collages. Assign the children to small groups at separate tables. Give each group a piece of construction paper and some glue. Make many different shapes and kinds of leaves available for the children to use. The children will glue them on the paper in any desired way.

Objectives

- To help the children see that leaves come in many different shapes and sizes.
- To give the children an opportunity to discuss the parts of trees.

Nature Walk. Divide the children into groups of three or four, with a leader for each group. The groups will walk through the area, looking at the many different trees. The leaders will obtain feedback from the children and help clear up any misconceptions they might have. This is also a good time to reinforce knowledge of the parts of the tree.

Objective

- To let children see many of the trees that were discussed in class and to reinforce their knowledge of trees—the differences, sizes, and parts.

Day 2

Whole-Group Activities

Visitor—Forest Ranger. Invite a ranger to talk to the children about the forests and the trees in them. The discussion should include some of the problems involving trees, such as fires, diseases, winterkill, and insects that destroy the wood, as well as some of the uses of our national forests.

Objectives

- To help the children learn that there are many people who work constantly to keep the forests in good shape for our enjoyment and recreation.
- To teach the children that trees may become sick and sometimes need special help.

- To instill the respect for nature and to let the children know that although they are young, they can help in certain ways to keep the forests safe.

Music and Creative Movements. Gather the children at the rug; after a brief introduction, put on a record. Have the children use their shakers to keep time with the music, and encourage them to move like a tree on a hot summer day, in the wind, in the rain, when thirsty, and so on.

Objectives

- To give a more complete understanding of the many different ways trees move.
- To provide a musical experience with the shakers the children made.

Small-Group Activity

Art–Shakers. At the tables, give each child two paper plates with holes punched all around the outside, as well as snips of colored paper, and liquid starch to use as paste. The children put seeds from a honey locust tree inside the two plates and then lace them up with yarn. They will use these shakers later in the day.

Objectives

- To develop small-muscle control.
- To make a musical instrument from a part of a tree.

Individual Activity

Trough with Wooden Items. Necessary items include wood chips, sawdust, toothpicks, wooden spoons, bark, and wooden boxes.

Objectives

- To acquaint the children with the different textures and products of wood.
- To develop language concerning wood products.

Day 3

Whole-Group Activities

Movie Explaining Logging. Show a movie as soon as all the children have arrived. It lasts for only 10 minutes, so that the children will not become too tired.

Objectives

- To show the children another use for trees.
- To show the children that many people make their living working with trees.
- To introduce the field trip to the sawmill.

Field Trip to Sawmill. In groups of three or four, the children and teachers ride with parents to the sawmill. Here they see how the trees are cut into usable sizes and observe treatments used to cure the wood. The children see how many wood products are made (rough-cut lumber, planed lumber, sawdust, plywood [pressed]).

Objectives

- To provide the experience of seeing an industry that may be new to the children.
- To acquaint the children with different items made from wood.
- To provide an opportunity to observe how large trees are handled after they are cut down and then cut into workable size.

Small-Group Activity

Art—Sawdust Pictures. Give each child a piece of paper and some glue. Make sawdust available at each table in several different colors, to be used as desired.

Objectives

- To carry over the ideas from the field trip.
- To permit handling of a tree product.

Day 4

Whole-Group Activity

Discussion of Things That Grow on Trees. Discuss with the children the many types of trees and the different things that grow on them. Use pictures of the trees and items or the actual items if available. Read the book *Apple Tree! Apple Tree!* (Blocksma, 1983).

Objectives

- To teach the children about other products of trees, including foods.
- To teach the children that different kinds of trees have different purposes.

Small-Group Activities

Food—Nuts. Divide the children into groups by name tags shaped like different kinds of nuts. Give them the opportunity to crack many different kinds of nuts and see how they taste. Save the shells.

Objectives

- To observe nuts both inside and outside the shell.
- To learn the names of several kinds of nuts and to taste different kinds.

Art—Nutshell Animals. Have the children take the nutshells and sort out some they would like to use. Make paint, pieces of paper, and small pieces of yarn available. These materials will be used for making animals out of the shells.

Objectives

- To help develop small-muscle coordination.
- To show that objects can be made out of nutshells.

Art—Mobile. Give the children small pieces of wire to shape as they wish. They will then dip their wires into a liquid plastic substance. It dries very fast and in the shape of the wire, as well as being transparent and colorful. The pieces of wire are then tied to a hanger by means of a piece of string. The hanger is bent into a circle, and the resulting mobile is then hung in a convenient place.

Objective

- To give the children an opportunity to help make something attractive that can be taken home and hung up. To allow them to work with an unfamiliar, creative material.

Day 5

Whole-Group Activities

Music. Set out such things as wood blocks and log drums for the children to make music. They can also use these items with a record for variety.

Objectives

- To encourage the use of musical instruments made out of wood.
- To allow the children to hear different sounds made from wood.
- To increase the ability to feel and move in rhythm.

Science. Set out many different preparations of apples so that the children will be able to see some of the processes that can alter the form of food. Some of the items used can include raw apples, canned applesauce, dried apples, and apple juice. The children will be able to see how the dried apple soaks up water and swells to a larger size.

Objectives

- To show that the same item can have many different forms and tastes.
- To observe how water changes the sizes of items.
- To acquaint the children with another form of food grown on trees.

Visitor. Invite a person with an apple press to come in and show the children how apple juice is made. The children will then drink the juice.

Objectives

- To show how a food product (juice) is made from a tree product (apple).
- To demonstrate how pressure alters items.

Small-Group Activity

Art—Toothpick Sculpture. Give each of the children toothpicks, some fast-drying glue, a cardboard base on which to put his or her sculpture. The children put toothpicks into the glue and stick them together.

Objectives

- To provide another activity in working with wood.
- To reinforce the unit on trees.

UNIT ON WHEAT AND FLOUR

Art

- Finger painting with flour paste
- Finger painting with wheat kernels added
- Shakers—cans filled with wheat kernels, then decorated with tissue paper, kernels of wheat, or parts of the wheat shaft, and glued with wheat paste
- Collages—wheat, parts of the shaft; wheat cereals
- Clay made from flour
- Papier-mâché
- Painting with wheat shaft
- Vase or pencil container made by molding clay around a 6-ounce can and sticking small bits of wheat shaft, kernels of wheat, or other collage items into the soft clay.

Field Trips

- Bakery
- Flour mill
- Wheat field
- Granary, wheat silo, or grain bin
- Home to see how wheat is stored
- Home to see wheat grinder and observe how it grinds wheat into flour
- Cereal company

Food*

- Cooked wheat cereal—whole or cracked
- Sprouted wheat salad

* See bread unit plan in Chapter Seven.

- Chewing of wheat into gum
- Any food activity utilizing flour—cakes, cookies, breads, muffins, biscuits, pancakes, and others
- Dry wheat cereals eaten as cereals or used in recipes

Science

- Sprouting of wheat
- Grinding of wheat (blender may be used)
- Observation of wheat sprouting and growing. Put a piece of gauze over a jar, fill the jar with water, place kernels of wheat on top, and place the jar in the sun. Keep the kernels wet, and within a few days the stems will grow up and the roots will grow down through the gauze and into the water.
- Stages of wheat in the growing process
- Equipment farmer uses to plant, harvest, and store wheat
- Kinds of wheat
- Separating of wheat from chaff (shaft rubbed between hands; chaff blown off)

Music

- Shakers used in shaker band or rhythm activity
- Musical dramatization of the story of the "Little Red Hen"
- Story of "Little Red Riding Hood," with music illustrating the many different ways she moved to grandmother's house—skipping, hopping, sliding, jumping, walking, and so on
- Wheat shafts used to play drums

Visitors

- Farmer showing kinds of wheat
- Baker
- Parent making bread
- Person grinding wheat with stone
- Botanist showing how wheat grows
- Nutritionist

Language and Literacy

- Stories such as "Little Red Hen," "Little Red Riding Hood"
- Poems

- Create own stories—for example, "How We Use Wheat"

LESSON PLAN ON WHEAT AND FLOUR (1-DAY)

Overall Goals

- To introduce to the children the following basic concepts of wheat:

1. What wheat is.
2. What it looks like. Wheat has three basic forms—seed, greens (sprouts), mature shaft.
3. How it tastes. Feels. Smells.
4. How it grows. Where it grows.
5. Flour is ground wheat.
6. Wheat can be used as food: whole wheat, cracked wheat, sprouted wheat, as well as flour. It is a basic element in many products.

- To strive to help children understand what *growing* is by watching wheat sprout.

Whole-Group Activities

Demonstration of Forms of Wheat. Gather the children at the rug. Have containers (glass) of whole-kernel wheat, sprouted wheat (greens), and mature-shaft wheat. Explain to the children the relationship among the three forms. To reinforce this concept, separate the wheat from the chaff of the mature wheat so that they can see that it is a whole kernel of wheat and begin to grasp the cycle. Spread a large tarpaulin so that each child will have the opportunity to explore a shaft of wheat and extract the kernels onto the tarp.

Objectives

- To foster an understanding of the growing cycle of wheat through the use of the five senses.
- To introduce three forms of wheat.
- To provide an actual experience of separating wheat from chaff.

Rhythm and Creative Movement Activity. Gather the children at the rug and have them participate in several well-known fingerplays and songs. Have

them play the game "The Farmer in the Dell," and then introduce them to the following new song by singing it several times to the melody of "I'm a Little Teapot":

I'm a little wheat stock, short and stout.
Here is my kernel, and here is my sprout.
When I get all grown up, then I'll shout—
Just pick me, farmer, and shake me out (Farina, Furth, & Smith, 1959, p. 71).

Objectives

- To reinforce the concept of wheat separating.
- To teach new words to a familiar old song.

Small-Group Activities

Art—Painting with Wheat Shaft. Divide the children into groups by color squares, and ask each child to go to the table that has the appropriate color of paint. Provide the children with white paper on which their name has been printed and a bundle of three wheat shafts tied together to serve as a form of paintbrush. The paint is put on the paper in drops with a spoon (it will have a rather thick consistency), and the children paint with wheat. They may create whatever design they wish.

Objectives

- To reinforce the concept of the mature form of wheat.
- To foster creativity by using wheat in uncommon ways.

Food—Cooked Whole-Wheat Cereal. Cook the cereal beforehand, and divide the children into small groups by means of their names on small disposable bowls. Give each group containers of milk and brown sugar. Serve the cereal from the pan in which it was cooked. Give each child a very small amount, along with a spoon and encourage the children to try it. Serve juice also.

Objectives

- To demonstrate one way in which wheat is eaten—as a breakfast cereal.

- To show the children how wheat is cooked, and to teach them size comparison by having uncooked whole wheat on the table also.
- To provide an opportunity to try a new food.

- Trough filled with whole kernels of wheat
- Role playing of various occupations

Summary

Plants are a natural, living part of the children's science environment both inside and outside the classroom. Regardless of the locality, climate, and season, there are numerous possibilities for plant studies and experiences. At most times of the year, in most areas of the world, there is some kind of vegetation in some stage of development. Young children are generally curious and eager to broaden their understanding of their surroundings, particularly of growing plants. This is especially evidenced by their excitement over the discovery that a newly planted and cared-for seed has begun to grow. Related concepts such as size, number, color, texture, categorization, shape, characteristics, needs, and uses of various plants can be explored.

Student Learning Activities

1. After studying this chapter, add to the list of plant unit themes at the beginning of the chapter.

2. Think of additional plant-related activities and experiences for the list in this chapter.

3. Plan and implement with a group of children at least one of the activities on plants suggested in this chapter or added by you to item 2. Evaluate your experience. The group of children may be a classroom group or a small group of relatives or neighborhood children between the ages of 2 and 8 years.

4. Begin a picture collection of plants or a category of plants such as trees.

5. Think of additional suggestions for each of the unit plans included in this chapter.

6. From a unit plan you have prepared or from one suggested in this chapter, prepare an activity plan (see Chapter Three) on a theme related to plants.

7. Visit a children's library or media center and add to the lists of resources in this chapter. Find additional excellent recordings, pictures, books, or filmstrips relating to plants and add to the lists in this chapter.

Suggested Resources

Children's Books

Ahlberg, J., & Ahlberg, A. (1979). *Each peach pear plum.* New York: Viking.

Blocksma, M. (1983). *Apple tree! Apple tree!* Chicago: Children's Press.

Booth, D. (Ed.) (1990). *Voices on the wind: Poems for all seasons.* New York: Morrow.

Carle, E. (1987). *The tiny seed.* Natick, MA: Picture Book Studio.

Ehlert, L. (1988). *Planting a rainbow.* San Diego: Harcourt Brace Jovanovich.

Gibbons, G. (1991). *From seed to plant*. New York: Holiday House.

Kellog, S. (1988). *Johnny Appleseed: A tall tale*. New York: Morrow.

Krauss, R. (1945). *The carrot seed*. New York: Harper-Collins.

Lavies, B. (1989). *Tree trunk traffic*. New York: Dutton.

Lyon, G., & Lyon, E. A. (1989). *Alphabet of trees*. New York: Orchard Books Watts.

Patent, D. H. (1990) *Yellowstone fires: Flames and rebirth*. New York: Holiday House.

Robbins, K. (1990). *A flower grows*. New York: Dial.

Romanova, N. (1985). *Once there was a tree*. New York: Dial.

Russell, N. (1989). *The tree*. New York: Dutton.

Ryder, J. (1990). *Chipmunk song*. New York: Lodestar.

Silverstein, S. (1964). *The giving tree*. New York: Harper & Row.

Thomas, E. (1992). *Green beans*. Minneapolis: Carolrhoda.

Titherington, J. (1986). *Pumpkin pumpkin*. New York: Greenwillow.

Udry, J. (1956). *A tree is nice*. New York: Harper & Row.

Wilner, I. (1991). *A garden alphabet*. New York: Dutton.

Wood, A. J. (1990). *Look! The ultimate spot-the-difference book*. New York: Dial.

Records, Tapes, and Cassettes

Little Seeds. On *Singing fun*. Bowmar-Noble.
Tick, tock, the popcorn clock. The Child's World.

Pictures

Broadleaf trees. Society for Visual Education (SVE)
Forest. The Child's World.
Life in the sea (I). The Child's World.
Life in the sea (II). The Child's World.
Plant identification. National Audubon Society.
Plant study program. National Audubon Society.
Plants and seeds. The Child's World (Picture foldout).

Plants and seeds. David C. Cook.
Plants that provide food. The Child's World (Picture foldout).
The story of corn. The Child's World (Sequence chart).
Trees. National Audubon Society.
Trees and plants. National Audubon Society.
Tree study program. National Audubon Society.
Wildflowers. National Audubon Society.

Multimedia Kits

Kinds of plants and where they grow. National Geographic.
A look at plants. National Geographic.
What is a seed? National Geographic.

Film, Filmstrips, and Videos

Growing, growing. Churchill Films.
How plants help us. Coronet Films.
How trees help us. Coronet Films.
Learning about leaves. Coronet Films.
Let's watch plants grow. Coronet Films.
Place where plants and animals live. National Geographic.
Plants and animals depend on each other. Coronet Films.
Plants and animals in the city. National Geographic.
Plants are different and alike. Coronet Films.
Plants: What happens in winter. National Geographic.
Rainshower. Churchill Films.
Seeds grow into plants. Coronet Films.
Seeds and how they travel. National Geographic.
Seeds scatter. Churchill Films.
A tree is nice. Weston Woods Studios.
The tree. Churchill Films.
What do seeds need to sprout? Coronet Films.
What plants are. Eye Gate Media.
Wonders of growing plants. Churchill Films.
The world of plants. National Geographic.

Computer Software

Learn about: plants. Wings for Learning. (Apple).

CHAPTER
sixteen

Temperature, Weather, and Seasons

Introduction

The concepts of temperature, weather, and seasons are related to one another because each one influences the others. For example, the season often determines the weather for a particular locale. The temperature influences every aspect of weather and often determines the exact type of weather that is experienced. At the same time, the temperature is usually influenced by the time or season of the year. Thus, none of these concepts can be discussed without involving at least one of the others.

Children and adults are greatly influenced by temperature, weather, and seasons. Activities; feelings; moods; and choices of games, recreation, foods, and clothes are often determined by the temperature, weather, or season. Everyone is interested in the weather report, for it often determines what one can and cannot do and where one can and cannot go. People listen to the weather report to decide whether windows should be washed, cars polished, or picnics planned. The weather report helps to determine whether it will be a good day for skiing, the fruit trees in blossom will be damaged by frost, precautions should be taken to protect gardens and orchards, or a planned trip can still be made. It is amazing to realize the extent to which our lives are controlled by the weather, the temperature, and the season.

Individual Reactions to Temperature, Weather, and Seasons

It is especially interesting to note individual emotional reactions to temperature, weather, and seasons. In her discussion of the child's sensory reactions, Liepmann (1973) presents temperature as a touch reaction and indicates that responses to temperature are individual and unique. We would also suggest that because reactions of individual children and adults vary, they have their own unique preferences regarding weather, seasons, and temperature. For example, some people prefer a particular type of weather and season because they enjoy the activities offered at that time. Thus there are individuals who prefer winter and snow because they enjoy skiing, ice skating, snowmobiling, sleigh riding, watching or participating in basketball, or just playing in the snow.

On the other hand, a person's preference for a particular season or type of weather is often determined by his or her characteristic body temperature. Cold-sensitive individuals will probably prefer the warmer seasons of spring, summer, and fall and the kinds of weather typical of those seasons. Perhaps they will even prefer, if given a choice, to live in a climate that is warmer and does not have a cold winter season. A heat-sensitive person will most likely prefer the cooler seasons—fall, winter, and spring—and the typical kinds of weather that accompany those seasons.

Often it is assumed that everyone reacts to temperature the same way, but this assumption is not correct. Liepmann (1973) says:

It is natural to assume that your child feels hot or cold when you do, but this may not be so. Of course, he can adapt himself, but the next time you're cold and turn up the heat, or feel stifled and throw open the window, or turn on the air conditioner, take a minute to notice your child's reaction. For instance, does your daughter really wilt in summer heat and complain a lot? You can tell her you can't change the weather, but a little sympathy is in order even if you're not affected yourself. By the same token you can ask her to be considerate of you if you're under the weather and she isn't. Perhaps your child is a polar bear. He wants windows open, uses only a light blanket at night in winter, and seldom catches cold. Don't tell him he's wrong, even if it makes you shiver to go into his room. What feels wrong to you feels right to his body. (p. 85)

Even though these thoughts are written for the parent, they can surely be applied to the teacher-student-classroom relationship. Individual reactions to temperature, weather, and seasons often determine feelings, moods, and emotional reactions to these three conditions. Therefore, when anyone is too warm or too cold, discomfort and irritability may occur. When children become too warm they may become sleepy, or their aggressive activity may heighten and they may be more difficult to control. This phenomenon also occurs with changes in the season and weather. For example, the day the first snow flies is usually a more difficult teaching day. On windy days, or on days when the weather is inclement and the children are unable to play outside, they may also be more difficult to control. When spring is "in the air" and the temperature is warmer, it is necessary to plan more time for outside play because children will need and even demand it.

Another emotional reaction that often results in behavioral changes occurs if a season is particularly long or if the children have experienced an unusual amount of one type of weather. For example, winter may be unusually long, with snowstorms still coming in April, May, and June. Adults may experience depression and irritability, and although children are often more adaptable and flexible than adults, they too may become anxious with the long cold season.

In one particular locality, there was an unusually long winter one year. This episode took place in the preschool laboratory on a May morning following another snowfall:

Bessie came into the classroom looking rather disgruntled; when one of the student teachers asked her whether she was not feeling well, she said, "My body feels okay, but I am mad because in my heart and mind I just keep waiting for spring, and it just keeps on wintering!"

Also, temperatures that are too warm or too cold make concentrating difficult. When it is too warm or too cool, people's minds focus on trying to become comfortable, rather than concentrating on projects or work.

Approach to Teaching

In teaching units relating to temperature, weather, and seasons, remember that young children should be exposed first to the seasons and kinds of weather that they actually experience. For example, it may not be practical to have units on snow and/or winter for children in Florida. Also, it is best to teach kinds of weather and specific seasons at the time when the children are most apt to experience those particular conditions.

As with other concepts, the child may not be able to attach a label to a particular picture or object that gives a clue to some aspect of a season or kind of weather. The child may be able to group pictures and objects relating to winter together but may not be able to label that season *winter*. One approach to introducing and teaching a particular season or aspect of weather is to give the children the experience of classifying or grouping objects and/or pictures of that season or aspect of weather together. For example, the teacher may introduce winter by telling the children that they are going to talk about a time of year when the weather is very cold, when snowstorms are typical, and when the trees are usually bare. The label of the season, *winter*, is introduced. Then the teacher shows season pictures and objects, such as snow shovel, a snowshoe, a swimming suit, a hoe, a rake, tire chains, a window scraper, and a flyswatter, and asks the children to select those that are appropriate for the season being studied.

Another teaching approach involves helping the children learn that the seasons always follow the same sequence. Thus winter always follows fall, spring follows winter, summer follows spring, and fall follows summer, or whatever sequence is appropriate for your own region. In addition, children could draw pictures of scenes or objects, such as trees, in each season; then these pictures (or pictures provided by the teacher) could be arranged in sequence. It is interesting to teach the seasonal changes of animals—the snowshoe rabbit, monarch butterfly, and frog.

Since nature always foretells a coming season with signs, daily experiences outside offer the opportunity for spontaneous learning experiences. A sensitive teacher points to the buds on the tree and asks the children what season the buds signal. Or, as the children discover and explore the icicle hanging from the roof outside, the wise teacher relates it to temperature and season. The teacher may also ask such thoughtful questions as "What will happen to the icicle or to your snowman if the sun comes out and gets very warm?"

Through a series of short essays, Humphrey (1950) describes some of her memories with schoolchildren. In one incident, a child who came late into the classroom, bringing a present to the teacher, was directed to put it on the teacher's desk. Later, when a huge wet spot appeared on the blotting paper, the child cried because the icicle she had brought as a present had melted. But the wise teacher said that she still had the icicle, since the shape and form of the icicle were still on the blotting paper—in giant size! When a teacher does not cast this kind of experience aside, concepts concerning icicles' shape, size, and relationship to temperature are taught naturally.

Lesson plans relating to the concepts of temperature, weather, and season can be approached in a variety of ways. For example, it is possible to plan a unit on a particular season, with discussion of the most typical weather and temperatures accompanying that season. Thus emerge units on fall, wind, and cooler temperatures; spring, wind, rain, sunshine, and warmer temperatures; and summer, sun, and hot temperatures. On the other hand, each subject could be treated alone and approached as a separate unit. For example, during the fall season a unit could be done on fall, with perhaps a follow-up unit on wind. Temperature could be included in one or both of the units as it relates to the main subject. A separate unit on temperature could also be linked to the current season and a visit by the weather forecaster with weather instruments, such as the thermometer.

Weather, seasons, and temperatures are a part of the world in which children live; children are curious and interested, and have a desire to learn more about them. Gear your units to the uniqueness of your own area and to the individual situations of the children in your classroom. Thus, depending on the seasons that the children in your locality experience, at least two and as many as eight or nine units could be developed from just these three concepts.

Concepts and Ideas for Teaching

1. Each day we experience a particular season, a particular kind (or kinds) of weather, and temperatures ranging from the high to the low for the day.

2. We live in a particular area where we experience certain seasons, certain kinds of weather, and a temperature variation.

3. The area where we live determines the characteristic temperature range we experience, and this determines the climate in which we live. Thus we live in a warm, cool, cold, humid, dry, seasonal, constant, or changing climate. (The children should describe the characteristics of their climate.)

4. Some animals are particular to certain areas because of the characteristic climate, temperature, weather conditions, or seasons of that area. (Describe your own area.)

5. Some plants are particular to certain areas because of the characteristic climate, temperature, weather conditions, or seasons of that area. (Describe characteristic plants in your own area.)

6. A thermometer is an instrument used for measuring the temperature. The measured temperature goes up when the weather is warmer and down when it is cooler.

7. There are different kinds of thermometers.
   a. Thermometers for measuring the air inside and outside
   b. Thermometers for measuring body temperatures, especially during illness
   c. Thermometers for use in cooking, such as meat and candy thermometers.

8. When the temperature of some items changes, the items either expand (get larger) or contract (get smaller).
   a. Water expands during freezing.
   b. Metal expands during heating.
   c. Breads, cakes, cookies, and other foods that are baked expand in a hot oven because of the effect high temperature has on their ingredients.
   d. Many meats get smaller when they are heated or cooked.

9. People, animals, and plants make changes in varying seasons, kinds of weather, and temperatures.
   a. Observation of a tree during each season
   b. Observation of what particular animals (bears, frogs, insects, birds, monarch butterflies) do during specific seasons or kinds of weather, or when the temperature changes.

10. We are influenced in many ways by the weather, season, or temperature.
    a. How we feel
    b. What we do
    c. What games and sports we participate in
    d. How we dress
    e. What foods we eat
    f. How our bodies react to temperature changes—perspiring in excessive heat or getting "goose bumps" and shivering in cold weather

11. The length of the days varies with the season; in the Northern Hemisphere, the days are shorter in winter and longer in summer.

12. There are many different kinds of clouds. One can often determine the approaching weather by the clouds.

13. Clouds have many different shapes and sizes, often resemble different objects, and may change shape rapidly.

Concepts and Ideas for Teaching Seasons

1. Each season has its own particular characteristics.
2. Each season has sensory characteristics.
   a. Sounds
   b. Sights
   c. Smells
   d. Feels (or feelings)
   e. Tastes
3. For each season, people make particular preparations involving their cars, homes, clothing, and outside grounds.
4. For each season, animals often make particular preparations or changes.

5. For each season, many plants make changes.
6. Each season has jobs, in the home and outside of the home, directly related to it.
7. Each season has characteristic kinds of recreation and activities.
8. Each season has characteristic foods.
9. Each season has holidays that always fall within its boundaries.

In the following material, each season will be treated separately in terms of the preceding teaching ideas. The suggestions presented here are not meant to be inclusive; you may wish to contribute ideas more appropriate to your own locality. Encourage the children to brainstorm their own ideas as a season is being studied.

Winter

1. Winter has its own particular characteristics—cold, wet, quiet, white and gray, sleepy, snowy. It is an indoor season for some and an outdoor season for others.
2. Winter has characteristic sensory qualities.
   a. Sounds—quiet, furnaces turning on, hail hitting the windowpane, wind, cars stuck on icy roads, snowballs hitting the windowpane, snowplows, children playing in

Experiences with various stages of plants help children understand that particular tasks are usually done during specific seasons of the year.

the snow or sleigh riding, snowmobiles, and road graders

b. Sights—snow figures, snow, snowplows, warm and heavy clothing, boots, hats, frost on windows, snow tires, chains for tires, icicles, frost, bare trees, footprints in the snow

c. Smells—crisp air, woolly clothing, wet clothing, soups, stews, Christmas smells, fire, homemade bread, furnace smells, pine

d. Feels—cold, toasty warm, the feel of hands and toes that have almost frozen and are starting to thaw, wool, fur, blankets, fire, snow, ice, wet clothing.

e. Tastes—soup, snow, icicles, hot bread, chili, turkey, hot chocolate; Hanukkah, Christmas, New Year's Day, and Valentine's Day tastes and foods

3. People prepare their cars, homes, clothing, and yards for winter.

a. Cars—antifreeze, chains, snow tires, ice scrapers

b. Clothing—purchased or taken out of storage (out of mothballs in the case of wool clothing); items such as boots, coats, hats, gloves, and scarves located and checked for fit and condition

c. Homes—furnaces checked (if not previously done in the fall), windows sealed or shut tightly, air conditioners covered or stored away, chimneys cleaned

d. Yards and grounds—lawn furniture and gardening equipment stored, snow shovels purchased or taken out of storage, feed for animals obtained, shrubs tied up, coarse salt purchased for icy walks

4. Animals prepare for winter in a variety of ways. Some animals hibernate; some grow thick, warm coats of fur; farm animals are usually provided with shelter; some animals, such as birds, migrate during the fall in preparation for winter; some animals store

nuts, seeds, or other food; some animals change color to blend with the environment.

5. Plants prepare for winter in a variety of ways. Some trees are bare and dormant during the winter; flowers sometimes are nonexistent in the winter, unless they are grown in greenhouses; bulbs of such flowers as tulips and daffodils are dormant underneath the ground; shrubs survive if the temperatures do not fall too low.

6. Jobs related to winter include shoveling the snow from the walks and driveways, feeding farm animals that in other seasons are on the range or graze in the pasture, operating snowplows or sanders, cleaning off snowcovered or icy car windows, and keeping the furnace in good working order. In addition, professional jobs include furnace repair, ski patrol, operation of ski resorts, and the sales of snowmobiles or other winter recreation equipment.

7. Recreational activities characteristic of winter include playing in the snow, building snow figures, snowball fights, hockey games, basketball games, skiing, snowshoeing, sleigh riding, and ice skating.

8. Foods characteristic of winter include soups, chili, hot breads, Christmas foods, Valentine cookies, traditional New Year's foods, oranges, and grapefruit.

9. Holidays of winter include Hanukkah, Christmas, New Year's Day, Martin Luther King Jr. Day, Valentine's Day, Groundhog Day, President's Day, and St. Patrick's Day.

Spring

1. Spring has its own particular characteristics—warmer; sometimes wet and sometimes windy, and with more storms (tornadoes and thunderstorms), but mostly sunny and dry; active; alive; colorful; busy; home and grounds cleanup; gardening and planting; green; new growth; birds; snow melting; flowers blooming; people wearing pastel colors.

2. There are many sensory characteristics of spring.

  a. Sounds—voices of children playing outside, roller skates, roller blades, skateboards, song birds, wind, rain, bees, lawn mowers, motorcycles, cleanup crews using machinery to pick up and clean up trash.

  b. Sights—kites, mud puddles, grass growing, newborn animals, new growth, flowers, people doing home and yard cleanup, children playing outdoors, snow melting

  c. Smells—rain, earth and soil, newly cut grass, fresh paint, washed and cleaned homes (spring cleaning), flowers, dew, fertilizer, fresh-air smells

  d. Feels—chilly temperatures in morning and evening, warmer days; energetic; grass, earth, and soil; pulling weeds and cleaning flower gardens; trimming shrubs, trees, and rose bushes

  e. Tastes—flavored ice pops, salads, wiener roasts, ice cream, fresh vegetable salads, fresh strawberry pie and shortcake

3. People prepare their cars, homes, clothing, and yards for spring in numerous ways.

  a. Cars—snow tires and chains removed, air conditioning checked

  b. Clothing—winter clothing (heavy coats and other outer clothing) put away, and spring and summer clothing brought out of storage; boots and raincoats kept close by; spring and summer clothing purchased

  c. Home—inside spring cleaning, such as washing walls, cupboards, windows, floors, drawers, and closets, as well as sorting household items and throwing some of them away; outside spring cleaning, such as cleaning out flower beds, planting flowers, trimming shrubs and trees, raking and fertilizing grass, painting or fixing up the outside of the home, storing snow shovels and equipment, and bringing gar-dening equipment, lawn furniture, and patio furniture out of storage

4. What animals do in the spring: Many animals come out of hibernation, birds return, baby animals are born, animals may begin to lose fur coats, many livestock and farm animals are taken to the range for the late spring and summer months, sheep are shorn, and birds build nests.

5. What plants do in the spring: Plants that have been dormant during the winter come alive with buds, flowers, and leaves. Pussywillows are in season. Bulbs that have been dormant now poke up through the ground in the form of daffodils, tulips, and other early flowers. Some indoor plants are taken outdoors once the possibility of frost is over. Buds are seen on trees. Fruit trees blossom. Flowers, shrubs, and vegetable gardens are planted. Farmers plant vegetables, grains, and feed for their animals.

6. Jobs related to spring include those of city cleanup crews, gardeners, construction workers, farmers, professional carpet and rug cleaners, and nursery and seed people.

7. Recreational activities characteristic of spring include sandpile play, tricycle and bicycle riding, roller skating, roller blading, skateboarding, baseball, golf, fishing, tennis, outdoor neighborhood games, and picnics.

8. Foods characteristic of spring include strawberries and fresh strawberry desserts, asparagus, avocados, fresh vegetable salads, Easter candy and hard-boiled Easter eggs, and picnic foods.

9. Holiday of spring include April Fool's Day, Passover, Good Friday, Easter, Arbor Day, Mother's Day, sometimes Father's Day, Memorial Day, and May Day.

Summer

1. Summer has its own particular characteristics—hot, humid, lazy, sunny, dry, green, active, busy, vacations, flowers, gardens be-

ginning to produce, lightweight and little clothing, sweating, visits from vacationing friends and relatives, usually no school.

2. Summer has many sensory characteristics.

   a. Sounds—lawn mowers, motorcycles, water splashing, hiking, parades, fire engines, birds, plowing, crickets, children playing outside, sounds that often seem louder because windows are open, bees, water sprinklers

   b. Sights—campers, boats, trailers; people wearing less clothing and people on vacation; fishing, camping, and hiking gear; gardens, flowers, and leaves on trees; parades, sunburned skin; green; people and animals sweating; sprinklers, fans, and air conditioners; sunglasses; swimming suits

   c. Smells—chlorine, beaches, flowers, sunburn ointment, earth, perspiration of people and animals, cold drinks and ice pops, fresh fish, campfires, fresh fruit and vegetables, freshly cut hay, outdoor barbeques, hot asphalt, watermelons and other fruits, overheated cars, bug sprays

   d. Feels—going barefoot on grass, sand, or hot pavement; mosquito and other insect bites; bee stings; being sweaty, hot, and sticky; cool drinks and ice

   e. Tastes—lemonade and other cold drinks, fresh fruits, melons, fresh vegetables, picnic foods, roasted hot dogs and marshmallows, potato salad, barbecued foods or charcoal-cooked meats, ice-cream cones, fresh fish

3. People work in their yards and on their homes and wear cooler clothing in summer. They also take vacations.

   a. Clothing—swimsuits, shorts, and lightweight clothing a must for hot summer weather; sweaters or light jackets necessary for an evening in the canyon or park; shoes often not worn, especially by children

   b. Homes—yards and gardens watered often; flowers in bloom; harvest season in late summer; lawns cut often; bugs and weeds sprayed or treated; home repair; screens put on windows

   c. Recreational activities and vacations—canyons, parks, beaches, and other places outdoors; a day spent away from home relaxing and having fun, or a vacation lasting for several days or weeks

4. Animals are seen in abundance in the summer, including those that are not seen in other seasons. Fish jump from the lakes and ponds, insects buzz or move about everywhere (mosquitoes can be a nuisance), bats and fireflies may be seen at night, and crickets may be heard. Livestock are seen grazing in the mountains and on the ranges, other farm animals are seen away from their winter shelters, and pets often rove freely about the neighborhood.

5. Plants are usually at the peak of their growth in the summer. Farmers are busy keeping their crops of vegetables and grains irrigated and weeded. Yards and gardens are beautiful with flowers, green trees, and green lawns. Fruit trees bear fruit, and the vegetable gardens are productive. In late summer the farmers harvest crops—grains, vegetables, and other plantings.

6. Jobs related to summer include city cleanup operations, gardening, construction work, farming, baseball umpiring, lifeguarding, ice cream sales, home-and-garden sales, and harvesting of crops as a temporary job.

7. Recreational activities characteristic of summer include especially the outdoor activities. Vacations are often taken by families and individuals, and many activities are planned on vacations. The following summer activities are enjoyed by many: picnics, hiking, fishing, baseball, water skiing, sailing, swimming, tennis, golf, camping, boating, volleyball, tricycle and bicycle riding, roller

skating, running through sprinklers, outdoor neighborhood games, and sandpile play.

8. Foods characteristic of summer include fresh fruits; melons, especially watermelon; hot dogs; hamburgers; lemonade and other cold drinks; ice cream; milk shakes and sodas; fresh vegetables; tomatoes; tossed green salads; picnic foods, barbecued foods such as steaks, hamburgers, and shish kebabs; and corn on the cob.

9. Holidays of summer include Father's Day (sometimes), Independence Day, and Labor Day.

Fall

1. Fall has its own particular characteristics—cooler days as compared to summer, quietness, colors (especially red, yellow, orange, rust, brown), harvest, school, new clothing, sometimes windy, the first snowfall, raking leaves, yard and garden cleanup in preparation for winter, warm days and cool nights, first frost, shorter days, and dry leaves.

2. Fall has numerous sensory characteristics.
   a. Sounds—slower chirp of crickets, back-to-school sounds of children, farm machinery sounds as harvesting is done, rain and wind sounds, blowing and crunching of dry leaves as children play in them, football activities.
   b. Sights—colorful leaves, harvest, wheat, children playing in leaves and adults raking, falling leaves, apples, pumpkins, school buses, trees becoming bare, home canning, countertops and storage areas filled with freshly canned fruits and vegetables, children in jackets and sweaters
   c. Smells—leaves, wet leaves, smoke, home canning, harvest smells, carameled apples, cinnamon, chili, brisk cool nights, cut hay
   d. Feels—chilly nights, sometimes warm days and sometimes cool days, dry leaves as they are played in and raked up, fresh fruits and vegetables ready for canning

   e. Tastes—cider, pumpkin pie, cranberries, squash, apples, turkey, chili, doughnuts, stew, hot soup, carameled apples

3. People prepare their cars, homes, clothing, and yards for fall.
   a. Cars—snow tires, chains, antifreeze
   b. Clothing—new purchases for school or last year's garments brought out of storage and checked for fit and good repair; warmer clothing substituted for summer's lightweight clothing; sweaters, jackets, and other outerwear.
   c. Home—screens taken off and windows shut tightly; air conditioners covered or put into storage; furnaces checked and/or cleaned, and new filters installed
   d. Yards and gardens—leaves raked; bulbs such as tulips planted; shrubs trimmed and tied; flower beds cleaned up; yard tools put into storage and hoses put away; outside water shut off so that pipes do not freeze; fall harvesting of farm crops and foods

4. Some animals, such as bears and snakes, go into hibernation in late fall. Other animals grow thick, warm coats of fur; livestock are brought down from summer ranges; birds migrate; other animals store nuts and other foods; and some animals change color as a camouflage for winter. The caterpillar forms a pupa case (chrysalis) from which it emerges as a butterfly in spring.

5. Leaves turn color and fall from the trees. Many trees, plants, and weeds bear seeds, and plants may dry or die. Some plants, like chrysanthemums, bloom in the fall. The first frost often kills many plants.

6. Jobs related to fall include raking leaves and yard and garden cleanup. Many jobs are associated with the harvest season. Farmers and farmhands are especially busy; in homes there is fruit and vegetable canning, and the busy season arrives for turkey farmers.

7. Recreational activities characteristic of fall

include football, volleyball, playing in the leaves, and hunting.

8. Foods characteristic of fall include turkey, apples, carameled apples, apple cider, pumpkin pie, squash, Halloween candy, doughnuts, and cranberries.

9. Holidays of fall include Rosh Hashanah, Yom Kippur, Columbus Day, Halloween, Veterans Day, and Thanksgiving.

Concepts and Ideas for Teaching Weather

1. The particular kind of weather, how it is caused, and where it comes from.

2. What this type of weather does, what its uses are and what its positive and negative aspects are.

3. There are various ways in which this kind of weather is manifested.

4. Each kind of weather has sensory characteristics.

   a. Sounds

   b. Sights

   c. Smells

   d. Feels

   e. Tastes

5. Each kind of weather makes one feel different inside, depending on one's feelings toward that kind of weather.

6. Each kind of weather makes us dress differently.

7. Each kind of weather makes us do different things.

8. We participate in different games and activities in different places, depending on the kind of weather.

9. We go to different places in different kinds of weather.

10. The different kinds of weather are often related to other aspects or kinds of weather.

In the following material, each of the main aspects of weather is treated separately in terms of the foregoing ideas. The suggestions are not meant to be inclusive. You may have to contribute ideas that are more appropriate to your own locality. Encourage the children to brainstorm and to share the resulting ideas as the various kinds of weather are being studied and explored. Other types of weather can also be approached with these same questions.

Snow

1. (Note: Select parts of this explanation that are suitable to your children's understandings.) Snow begins as frozen water vapor that forms around microscopic particles afloat in the air. When this water vapor freezes, transparent ice crystals are formed. As more water vapor condenses around these ice crystals, they become heavy enough to fall out of their clouds. Air currents then toss them about in the atmosphere, causing them to collide and to break into tiny chips of ice that form more ice crystals. The crystals clump together on their trip down to earth, forming snowflakes. The crystals in a snowflake are always in the form of a six-pointed star (hexagon).

2. Snow falls in the colder climates and often blankets the earth during the winter months, especially in the mountains. Snow has many uses. Most of our water comes from snow, because when it melts it builds up the watersheds or melts into the lakes and reservoirs from which the streams and rivers flow to bring water to people. Snow is also used in many winter sports activities. Children play in snow and use it to build things such as snow figures. Snow is also used as an insulation for plants and animals.

3. Snow falls in different ways. It falls as a blizzard, sleet, hail, large flakes, or small flakes. It can be wet or "dry" (powder).

4. Snow has many sensory characteristics.
    a. Sounds—quiet, light; when snow falls against the windowpane, it makes a soft, tapping sound; sleet and hail are louder when they fall.
    b. Sights—white, sparkling; each snowflake is small and fragile and quickly melts when touching a surface warmer than itself.
    c. Smells—damp, wet; there is no other characteristic smell for snow.
    d. Feels—cold, wet, icy; snow can cause stinging or numbness, especially in the fingers and toes, when one has become wet with it in cold weather.
    e. Tastes—wet, tasteless, like ice or ice water; children will find clean, white snow inviting to taste because it looks good to eat, but they will discover its taste to be very bland.

5. Snow creates different feelings in different people. Usually the first snow of the season is welcomed by most people, especially children. However, usually the last snow of the season is not welcomed and creates negative feelings because most people are ready and waiting for spring. We must remember that feelings toward snow depend on whether snow is a favorite kind of weather or not. Children should be allowed to explore and share their feelings toward snow.

6. Snow makes us dress in warm clothing—wools, furs, boots, mittens, heavy coats, hats, sweaters, long socks.

7. Snow makes us do different things. When it snows, we play inside more often than we do in other seasons. We often do not travel very far or take vacations, although some people vacation in warmer climates to get away from the snow and cold. We also build snowmen, play in the snow, go sled riding, and participate in other winter sports.

8. We participate in different games and activities in different places in the snow. We play many inside games, but we also play games and participate in snow activities—"Fox and Geese," ice skating, sled riding, skiing, building snow figures, having snowball fights, building snow structures, snowmobiling, and snowshoeing. Many of these activities take place in our neighborhoods and backyards, but others occur in winter resorts in the canyons or mountains.

9. We go different places when it snows. Usually we stay home, but we may go to resorts or mountain areas to participate in winter sports or travel to warmer climates.

10. Other kinds of weather influence snow. Sun melts snow; wind creates blizzards and snowdrifts; rain melts the snow, but if the temperature goes down after a rainstorm in the wintertime, it can create icy conditions.

Rain

1. Rain is moisture or water that has evaporated from the ground and from bodies of water. This water vapor collects (condenses) into rain clouds and then falls to the earth in the form of rain. Once again moisture from the ground and plants evaporates and forms vapor in the air, and the rain cycle begins anew. (*Note:* Use only those parts of the explanation that are appropriate for your children's understanding and levels of comprehension.)

2. Rain is useful in many ways. Heavy rainstorms, like snow, help build up the watersheds. Rain waters gardens and grass, helps farmers irrigate crops if it comes at the right time, clears dust and smog from the air, and helps plants grow. The water from rain is also used by people for washing, bathing, and drinking, as well as by plants and animals. Rainstorms may also bring rainbows, and their beauty is enjoyed by all, especially children. Rainstorms may cause damage and may occasionally have negative

influences. They can cause thunder and lightning, and the lightning can cause fires, especially forest fires, which are damaging and dangerous. Heavy rainstorms can also cause flooding.

3. Rain has different forms. It comes in torrents, a drizzle, mist, light rainfall, heavy rainfall, thunderstorms, large drops, and small drops.

4. Rain has various sensory characteristics.

   a. Sounds—cars on highway, rain on roof or windowpane, thunder and lightning, windshield wipers.

   b. Sights—rainbows, lightning, gray and dark, blurry, fresh and green after a rainstorm.

   c. Smells—fresh, wet, musty, moist

   d. Feels—wet, clean, fresh, humid, cool

   e. Tastes—drops of water on the tongue have no taste

5. Rain creates different feelings in different people. On a rainy day, the following conversation between two children was once overheard:

Dennis: *I surely like rainy days—they are my favorite kind!*

Sam: *They aren't your favorite kind—they are ugly, and they are the worst.*

Dennis: *They aren't ugly, and they are my favorite day. I love them because they are wet!*

Rain does indeed create different feelings in both children and adults. Some people enjoy it, and some do not like it at all. For some, it creates feelings of enthusiasm, exhilaration, and delight; for others, it stirs feelings of depression, sadness, and laziness. One's reactions and feelings toward rain may depend on the plans for the day or how long it has been since the last rainfall. For example, if a picnic is planned with one's family or friends, rain could bring disappointment or disgust. On the other hand, after many long days of hot, dry weather, a rainfall is often refreshing and welcome. Farmers also have different reactions to rainfall. It may be desperately needed and hoped

for; on the other hand, if farmers are just ready to plant or if the hay has just been cut or baled, rain is not a welcome sight. If rain has been falling for several days, it can often bring disgust or depression, especially to adults. A major city in the Northwest that experiences much rainfall year round is known to have one of the highest suicide rates of any city in the United States. Many psychologists attribute this phenomenon to the fact that so many days are gray, cloudy, and rainy. Thus, there are several factors that determine one's reactions to rain. As children discuss their feelings, it might be well to give them actual situations to explore. For example, ask, "How would rain make you feel if it came on the day we were planning our field trip to the zoo?"

6. Rain makes us dress in special clothing. We wear boots, umbrellas, and raincoats.

7. Rain makes us do different things. When it rains, we probably play inside more often. However, after a spring or summer rainstorm, we may especially enjoy playing in the sandpile or in puddles, or even sailing boats down small streams caused by the rain.

8. We engage in different games and activities in different places when it rains. We play more inside games and activities and are often in a hurry to come out of a rainstorm. Immediately after a rainstorm, children like to play in the sandpile because the water helps them make such good mud pies and molds so readily. They also like to sail boats and other objects in the streams created by rainstorms. Teachers often like to plan musical games and other inside activities for rainy days.

9. We go to different places when it rains. Usually we stay home, and rainstorms often cause us to seek cover if we are enjoying outdoor recreational activities such as a picnic, hiking, or boating.

10. Other kinds of weather influence rain. The sunshine at the end of a rainstorm creates a rainbow. A rainstorm on a hot day may

create steam from the pavement or roof-tops. Wind combined with rain often creates torrents or other miserable conditions. Wind can often blow away a potential rainstorm. Warm temperatures turn spring snowstorms into rain showers.

Wind

1. Wind is the result of moving air currents, caused when hot air rises and cold air takes its place.

2. Wind is good for flying kites, drying clothes or other items, moving storms or other kinds of air masses, making windmills work, and moving sailboats. It is not good for neat hairstyles; keeping dust in place; or freshly painted houses, garages, fences, or other outside structures. Most animals do not like wind. People who wear contact lenses do not like wind because it causes irritation to the eyes. Wind can also cause damage to the environment by contributing to soil erosion or causing other environmental problems. A farmer who has just planted a field does not like wind because of the soil erosion.

3. Wind has different forms, such as light breezes, gusts, windstorms, hurricanes, dust storms, gentle winds or breezes, strong winds, high winds, and tornadoes.

4. Wind has numerous sensory characteristics.

   a. Sounds—whistle, flutter, gusting, rapping, whining, blowing, wailing; may be frightening or pleasant

   b. Sights—hair blowing, trees and other shrubs and flowers moving, branches blown down, people holding their hats on and moving in a hurry, women holding their skirts and dresses down, children flying kites

   c. Smells—dusty; may blow in unusual odors from nearby swamps, farms, industrial plants, lakes, or other areas; may bring the smell of a potential rainstorm

   d. Feels—gritty, sandy, and dusty, cool, stifling, gentle, strong, pleasant, irritating, welcome, unwelcome

   e. Tastes—sand that has blown in to the mouth

5. Wind creates different feelings in different people. Again, the feelings generated by the wind depend on what has been planned for the day and whether or not the wind interrupts the plans and is unwelcome or welcome in terms of the day's activities. Children may enjoy spring winds because they can fly their kites. A soft, gentle wind on a hot summer day or evening may be just the thing needed to cool off. Strong winds are most often unpleasant and unwelcome, at least to adults. During the winter, wind combined with already cold temperatures will create a chill factor that will make the temperature seem even lower and make the weather more unpleasant. Gentle, light winds in summer are often welcome, but heavy, strong winds stir up too much dust in the air. On days when it is extremely windy, children often come into the classroom just like gusts of wind, and the emotional climate in the classroom on those days is often high.

6. Wind makes us dress in heavier clothing. In the spring or fall, we may need only a jacket or sweater. In the winter, if it is windy, we may need to put on extra-heavy clothing and coats.

7. Wind makes us do different things. We have to hold on to things we are carrying and hold down other things. If it is windy, we are often in a hurry to arrive at our destination or to go inside.

8. We engage in different games and activities in different places in the wind. We sail boats, enjoy windmills, and fly kites when it is windy. Children also seem to enjoy running outdoors when it is windy—almost as if they were chasing the wind or the wind were chasing them!

9. We go to different places when it is windy. Usually we stay inside and enjoy inside activities such as puzzles, games, music activities, and reading. However, windy weather is also the time for flying kites and sailing boats, as well as enjoying windmills and pinwheels.

10. Other kinds of weather influence wind, and wind influences other kinds of weather. Wind may blow a storm in or blow one away. If wind occurs with a snowstorm or rainstorm, we have a blizzard or a gusting rainstorm. During dry weather or in dry places, wind creates dust storms.

Sun

1. The sun is a star in our galaxy. It is a source of light, heat, and energy. It does not turn off at the end of the day or on cloudy days. At the end of our day, it is making light and day for people on another part of the earth. On cloudy days the sun is still shining, but the clouds are in front of it so that we do not benefit as much from the rays of sunshine or from the sun's heat. Every day has a sunrise and sunset for most people; however, there are places on the earth (such as the North Pole and South Pole) where, during particular times of the year, because of the position of the sun, children do not see the sun for many days, and there is no sunrise or sunset.

2. The position of the sun, or the position of the earth in relation to the sun, makes or changes the seasons. The sun produces light, heat, and energy, which are necessary for plant growth. The warmth of the sun creates good outdoor play conditions, so that children and adults enjoy being outdoors. In the middle of the summer, the sun can create so much heat and the temperature can get so high that in some places it can be uncomfortable to be in direct sunlight for long periods of time. In some places it is necessary to have homes,

schools, and other buildings air conditioned because of the high temperatures. When the sun is very warm, it can melt such objects as crayons and objects made of wax. It can also fade colors, particularly in draperies, cars, or furniture, that are constantly exposed to the rays of the sun. It can make crops dry up, particularly on unirrigated farms, if rainfall is not adequate; it can wilt flowers and burn grass if they are not watered. It can cause painful and dangerous sunburns.

3. The sun has different effects, usually depending on the particular locality and the season of the year. It can feel slightly warm or extremely hot. In the winter when the sun shines, its rays are welcome and may create some warmth through a windowpane, but outside the temperature may be too cold for the sunshine to feel warm at all. Two of the beauties of nature are sunrise and sunset; they seem to have particular beauty and great variety of color in the summer.

4. The sun has various sensory characteristics.

   a. Sounds and tastes—no characteristic ones

   b. Sights—bright, yellow, orange, beautiful and colorful sunrises and sunsets, shadows, reflections of sunlight

   c. Smells—hot asphalt or tar, dry soil, melted wax or plastic, hot car seats, hot rubber (created by the warmth of the sun's rays)

   d. Feels—warm, hot, sunburn, perspiration, lazy, dry, sticky

5. The sun creates different feelings in different people. Most often the sun is a welcome aspect of weather. Children enjoy the sunshine because it means that they can play outside more often. During the winter, sunshine usually means that there will be no rain or snow; thus, even though temperatures may be cold, children can often play

outside. In the springtime everyone is anxious to see warm, sunny days because outside work and play are possible. The sun also brings growth to trees, shrubs, flowers, and other kinds of plants. To farmers, the springtime sun means that the soil and land will begin to thaw and dry enough for the ground to be worked and planted. The summer sun means that many outdoor activities and games can be enjoyed. We plan many outdoor experiences in the summer, and the sun is welcome because it creates warmth and dryness. The fall sun casts more light on the bright colors of nature and makes them even more beautiful. For most people, the sunshine brings happy feelings. However, during the middle of summer, when the sun brings high temperatures, one feels lazy, sweaty, and lacking in energy.

6. The warmer the sunshine, the lighter we dress. We wear less clothing and lighter weight clothing when the sunshine is very warm. We wear sunsuits, shorts, sleeveless shirts and blouses, and sundresses. We also wear sandals, and we do not need to wear sweaters and coats.

7. The sun allows us to do different things. We go on vacation. We play outside; take sunbaths; run through sprinklers; and go swimming, wading, and on picnics. We play in the summer more than at any other time of the year. We enjoy projects such as lemonade stands, neighborhood plays, and hobbies of every kind. We go bicycle riding and play with outdoor equipment.

8. We participate in different games and activities in different places in the sunshine. We play outside—games and activities of every kind. We play in the sandpile, ride bicycles and tricycles, and play with other wheel toys outside. We play many neighborhood games, such as hopscotch, marbles, and jacks. We ride skateboards and roller skates. We enjoy games and activities in the parks and other recreation areas and use equipment such as slides and swings.

9. We visit different places when the days are sunny, including recreation areas, parks, amusement parks, the zoo, the canyons and mountains. Activities enjoyed at such places include picnics, wiener roasts, campouts, hikes, and boating. Visits to relatives and friends are more frequent, and families often plan outings and family reunions on sunny, warm days. Swimming is a favorite sport on sunny days.

10. Other kinds of weather influence the sun, and the sun influences other kinds of weather. Clouds may prevent the rays of the sun from reaching the earth, creating an overcast day. Rainstorms or snowstorms may hide the sun for hours or days at a time. The wind may decrease the sun's warmth, lowering the temperature. The sun influences almost every other aspect of weather. It may melt the snow, shorten a rainstorm, and dry up puddles and mud.

Shadows are an interesting additional aspect of sunshine. They are created when objects pass in front of light; thus objects that pass in front of the sun create shadows. Clouds are actually objects that pass in front of the sun and cast shade on the earth. In addition, the movement of the sun during the day will create different shadows. For example, a tree, building, home, fence, or other object will cast shadows in different positions as the sun moves during the day. When the day is very hot, people move to the shade—places where shadows are cast—to escape the heat. When the day is cold, people like to move into the light of the sunshine to warm up.

One additional concept is that day and night are caused by the movement of the sun. One child, in a discussion of day and night, said that it was the moon that made it dark. The teacher explained that it was not the moon, but the sun setting, that brought nighttime. It is also the sunrise that brings the beginning of day. Children can also understand that the length of daylight and nighttime will vary with the season.

Activities and Experiences

Very few specific activities and experiences are included here, since many of them are listed in unit plans (particularly the science sections) and other places in this chapter.

1. Plant a garden indoors or outdoors.
2. Plant bulbs in the fall and observe their growth in the spring.
3. Discuss the thermometer and frequently check the temperature. Help the children understand that the temperature goes up when it gets warmer and goes down when it gets colder. Chart the temperature on a graph at the same time each day for a month and observe any changes. The high and low temperatures each day could be graphed the same way.
4. Observe carefully the effects of temperature on a growing plant.
5. Have the children cut pictures that represent hot or cold items from old magazines. These are then collaged onto a poster that has been divided in half: hot items on one half, and cold items on the other.
6. Visit a greenhouse and measure temperature variations in different areas of the greenhouse.
7. Visit a grocery store and measure/compare temperature variations in different food

Each morning in this classroom, the children select an appropriate picture symbol that represents the weather for the day. The picture also helps children determine whether boots, coats, umbrellas, or mittens are needed for outside play.

areas: shelves, frozen food case, refrigerated case, storage areas, and so on.

8. Fill a few containers with different temperatures of water and arrange them in order from hottest to coldest. Record the various temperatures in both Fahrenheit and Celsius (centigrade).

9. Make sets of sequence pictures to be ordered by season. One set might be a tree pictured in fall, winter, spring, and summer. Another set might be a child dressed for the four seasons.

10. Collect picture cards of things representative of various seasons—clothing, weather, trees in various seasons, tools, jobs, and others. Let the children categorize them by season. A similar set of sorting cards could be made to represent various kinds of weather.

11. Brainstorm with the children what they like best and least about each season. Write their ideas down, and have them illustrated and put into a booklet.

12. Make a season scrapbook with a section for each season, and include pictures of jobs, recreation, weather, and many other aspects of that season. Write ideas for each page in a sentence or two.

13. Play a "Guess What?" game for any aspect of weather or a particular season. Example: "Guess what I like to do in the summer?"

14. Interview each child to determine favorite seasons and kinds of weather. Chart or graph the results.

15. Hold a watercolor watch. Assign each child a quiet place and a suggested weather word, such as *rain*, *sun*, *wind*, or *snow* (depending on the current weather conditions). Supply the child with watercolors, crayons, markers, colored pencils, pens, chalk, or pencil. During a period of about 15 minutes, the child draws or tells what is observed (adapted from Charron & Jones, 1992).

From the foregoing material, many ideas for approaching lesson plans should emerge. However, we also include the following unit plans to give additional ideas for organizing activities for lesson plans. We have combined a season with the kinds of weather associated with that season. The units need not be combined, but they often fit together.

UNIT PLAN ON SUMMER AND SUN

Field Trips

- Beach or swimming pool for wading or swimming
- Picnic
- Backyard garden
- Canyon or park
- Zoo
- Outdoor walk to observe summer and sun characteristics
- Planetarium
- Aviary
- Farm
- Early-morning sunrise breakfast or outing

Art

- Blot painting with white paint to portray clouds on gray or blue paper that represents the sky
- Flower pictures made with cupcake holders
- Flowers made out of nut cups, using pipe cleaners for stems; stems placed in clay base in paper cup
- Sponge painting of sunrise or sunset
- Fans made and decorated
- Collage of summer objects—sand, shells, rocks, pebbles, grass
- Rock paint
- Paper-plate hats decorated for a summer parade
- Paint with water outside

Science

- Study and observation of shadows
- Study, observation, and growing of seeds and plants

- Study of the life cycle of the frog
- Fire prevention
- Flowers
- Clouds
- Sunlight and its effect on growing plants

Music

- Shadow dancing behind screen or sheet
- Creative movements relating to summer activities—fishing, swimming, throwing a Frisbee, and others
- Creative movements interpreting a sprinkler, fountain, waterfall
- Creative movements representing the sun rising or setting
- Creative movements interpreting the growth of a seed into a plant, and the wilting of a plant in the summer's heat or sunshine and how it perks up when it is watered
- Creative movements interpreting animals seen in summer—birds, butterflies, insects, life cycle of a frog, fish, and others
- Marching parade with or without rhythm instruments

Food

- Homemade ice cream or frozen yogurt
- Marshmallows and hot dogs cooked over a grill on the playground or at a park
- Fresh fruits in salads and other forms
- "S'mores"—two graham crackers, piece of chocolate bar, marshmallow toasted by the child; "sandwich" put together while marshmallow is warm
- Sandwiches and other picnic snacks, even if the picnic is outside the classroom on the grass or at a nearby home or park
- Potato salad
- Jams and jellies
- Fruits dried in the sunshine and eaten a day or two later
- Flavored ice pops, slush, or other frozen treats
- Gelatin squares

Visitors

- Person from a nursery
- Lifeguard
- Farmer
- Gardener
- Florist or flower arranger
- Person who enjoys fishing
- Golfer
- Ornithologist
- Entomologist
- People to share vacation experiences
- Carhop
- Ice-cream vendor

Language and Literacy

- Slides and/or pictures of summer scenes, with children discussing them—perhaps individually and in small groups
- Objects or pictures of food, recreational equipment, clothing, and so on relating to all seasons—items passed out to all the children, with each child who has something relating to summer telling about it
- Sharing of vacation experiences
- Sharing of a favorite summer activity, food, place to visit, and so on
- Stories, written or told, of most memorable summer vacation or experience
- Writing and illustrating booklets on "Why I Like Summer," "What I Like to Do in the Summer," "Summer Is . . . ," or "What I Did This Past Summer"

UNIT PLAN ON WIND

This unit could easily be related to the concept of air.

Field Trips

- Outdoor walk on windy day to observe characteristics of wind
- Kite flying or watching others fly kites
- Airport
- Dam on nearby lake to watch a sailboat
- Weather station or television station to watch the weather forecast
- University or high school band class where children can see and hear wind instruments
- Music store that sells wind instruments

Art

- Kites made by children
- Straw painting or blow painting
- Hummers made to use in musical activity
- Balloons decorated with papier-mâché or powdered paints

Science

- Study and observation of effects of wind—erosion, wearing away of rocks, sand drifts
- Observation of a weather vane to determine wind direction
- Study of the effects of strong windstorms such as hurricanes and tornadoes
- Study and discussion of positive and negative aspects of wind

Music

- Hummer band (see discussion on hummers in Chapter Nine)
- Creative movements interpreting leaves blowing in the wind, people moving in the wind, kites blowing in the wind, trees moving in the wind, feathers moving in the wind, clothes drying in a breeze
- Visitors with wind instruments—children allowed to try to play instruments; visitors asked to play their instruments while children play their hummers

Food

- Hot soup—children allowed to blow on it to cool it
- Hot chocolate
- Food activities related to air—egg white or whipped cream beaten as a part of a food activity, with emphasis on how air is beaten into it and the concept that wind is also moving air

Visitors

- Musician to play wind instrument or harmonica
- Parent to fly kites on playground
- Weather forecaster
- Pilot to tell about watching the wind direction and speed when flying

- Forest ranger to discuss the effects and influences of wind in the forest and mountains

Language and Literacy

- Pictures or slides of different kinds of weather, with children identifying those that depict wind
- Stories about wind, written or told
- Poems about wind, written or told
- Variety of articles of clothing, with children determining which articles should be worn on windy days
- Booklet written and illustrated on wind, including why the children do and do not like it

UNIT PLAN ON RAIN

Field Trips

- Lake, pond, stream, or river
- Reservoir
- Fish hatchery
- Water laboratory
- Home where the family has a terrarium or rain garden
- Water tower

Art

- Painting or collage of rainy scenes
- Children mixing their own paint so that they see the water base; painting with watercolors
- Paintings of rainbows
- Screen spatter painting—screen mounted on a board (or use an old window screen), which is then placed several inches above and parallel to the tabletop; paintbrush dipped into paint and passed over the screen to give a spatter effect on the paper below; alternatively, "shadow" pictures made by placing an object or shape cutout (or cookie cutter) on the paper and spattering paint around it

Science

- Study and observation of the rain cycle—evaporation and condensation

- Building and observation of a rain garden or terrarium
- Study of rainbows
- Study and observation of what rain does to plants
- Study and observation of a prism
- Foods with a water base, such as root beer or lemonade
- Foods dissolved in water, such as gelatins or powdered drinks
- Foods cooked in water, such as vegetables, macaroni, or rice

Visitors

- Weather forecaster
- A visitor to explain and build a rain garden or terrarium

- Farmer
- Forest ranger

Language and Literacy

- Stories about rain, written or told
- Poems about rain, written or told
- Shared rainy-day experiences
- Pictures or slides of different kinds of weather, with the children identifying those that depict rain
- Variety of articles of clothing, with the children determining which articles of clothing should be worn on rainy days
- Writing and illustrating booklets titled "I Like Rain Because . . ." or "Rain"

Summary

Because the concepts of temperature, weather, and seasons are so closely related to each other, a discussion of one of them usually involves at least one of the others. All people are greatly influenced by temperature, seasons, and weather: they affect clothing, food, activities, games, recreation, feelings, and moods. Many people prefer one season to another because of the kinds of activities that are characteristic of that season. Not all people, however, react the same way to weather variations: for example, a particular temperature could make one person feel cold, another feel hot, and another feel just right. Weather, seasons, and temperature are natural parts of the world in which we live. The spontaneous curiosity and interest of children in their environment makes related learning both enjoyable and rewarding.

Student Learning Activities

1. Write a paragraph or two on your attitudes about temperature, weather, and seasons. How might your own attitudes about the season, temperature, or weather influence the children in your classroom?

2. Interview a preschool, kindergarten, first-grade or second-grade teacher. Find out this teacher's attitudes toward temperatures, weather, and the seasons. Ask the teacher whether and how those attitudes affect the children. In addition, interview and find out how the teacher includes temperature, weather, and seasons in the curriculum. Are units planned relating to any of these topics? How do the children respond?

3. Using one of the unit plans from this chapter complete a 1-week activity plan (see Chapter Three).

4. Using the activity plan you completed in item 3, complete a lesson plan following the format given in Chapter Three.

5. Visit a children's library or media center and add to the lists of references in this chapter. Find additional excellent recordings, pictures, books, and filmstrips relating to temperature, weather, and seasons.

6. Begin a picture collection for weather and seasons. Mount the pictures appropriately.

7. Begin a collection of children's poems relating to weather and seasons.

Suggested Resources

Children's Books

Andrews, J. (1986), *Very last first time*. New York: Atheneum.

Blades, A. (1989). *Winter, spring, summer, fall*. New York: Lothrop, Lee & Shepard.

Booth, D. (1990). *Voices in the wind: Poems for all seasons*. New York: Morrow

Brown, M. W. (1947). *Goodnight, moon*. New York: HarperCollins.

Brown, M. W. (1976). *The winter noise book*. New York: HarperCollins.

Cole, S. (1985). *When the tide is low*. New York: Lothrop, Lee & Shepard.

Garelick, M. (1961). *Where does the butterfly go when it rains?* New York: Scholastic.

Gibbons, G. (1990). *Weather words and what they mean*. New York: Holiday House.

Hader, B. & Hader, E. (1972). *The big snow*. New York: Macmillan

Horton, B. S. (1992). *What comes in spring?* New York: Knopf.

Hughes, S. (1985). *Bathwater's hot*. New York: Lothrop, Lee & Shepard.

Hughes, S. (1988). *Out and about*. New York: Lothrop, Lee & Shepard.

Keats, E. J. (1962). *The snowy day*. New York: Viking.

Larrick, N. (1971). *Rain, hail, sleet and snow*. Eastern, MD: Garrard.

Lenski, L. (1948). *Now it's fall*. New York: Oxford University Press.

Lenski, L. (1953). *On a summer day*. New York: Walck.

Lenski, L. (1954). *I like winter*. New York: Oxford University Press.

Lenski, L. (1959). *Spring is here*. New York: Oxford University Press.

Leslie, C. W. (1991). *Nature all year long*. New York: Greenwillow.

Levinson, R. (1986). *I go with my family to Grandma's*. New York: Dutton.

Nikola-Lisa, W. (1991). *Night is coming*. New York: Dutton.

Oliver, S. (1990). *My first look at seasons*. New York: Random House.

Omerod, J. (1981). *Sunshine*. New York: Lothrop, Lee & Shepard.

Omerod, J. (1982). *Moonlight*. New York: Viking.

Patent, D. H. (1990). *Yellowstone fires: Flames and rebirth*. New York: Holiday House.

Ryder, J. (1990). *Chipmunk song*. New York: Lodestar.

Simon, N. (1991). *Mama cat's year*. Morton Grove, IL: Whitman.

Spier, P. (1982). *Rain*. New York: Doubleday.

Szilagyi, M. (1985). *Thunderstorm*. New York: Bradbury.

Tafuri, N. (1985). *Rabbit's morning*. New York: Greenwillow.

Tresselt, A. (1969). *White snow, bright snow*. New York: Lothrop, Lee & Shepard.

Tudor, T. (1977). *A time to keep: The Tasha Tudor book of holidays*. New York: Random House.

Whitby, J. (1984a). *Emma and grandpa (1) (January, February, March)*. Essex, England: Longman.

Whitby, J. (1984b). *Emma and grandpa (2) (April, May, June)*. Essex, England: Longman.

Whitby, J. (1984c). *Emma and grandpa (3) (July, August, September)*. Essex, England: Longman.

Whitby, J. (1984b). *Emma and grandpa (4) (October, November, December)*. Essex, England: Longman.

Wildsmith, B. (1984). *The north wind and the sun*. New York: Oxford University Press.

Wildsmith, B. (1980). *Seasons*. New York: Oxford University Press.

Wilner, I. (1991). *A garden alphabet*. New York: Dutton.

Zolotow, C. (1983). *Summer is. . . .* New York: HarperCollins.

Records, Tapes, and Cassettes

A child's garden of verses and other songs for children. Walt Disney Productions (DQ1241).

Fall is here. The Child's World.

Holidays. David C. Cook.

Holiday songs and rhymes. Hap Palmer Record Library (AR538 or AC538).

Magic monsters around the year. On *The magic monster mix.* The Child's World.

More singing fun (1). Bowman-Noble.

Rain is falling. on *The rainy day record.* Bowman-Noble.

Seasons and weather. David C. Cook (DC-24190).

Singing fun. Bowman-Noble.

The small singer (2). Bowman-Noble.

Spring is here. The Child's World.

Summer is here. The Child's World.

Time and time again. Educational Activities (AR87 or AC87).

The weather. On *Ooo we're having fun.* Cheviot (T-306).

Winter is here. The Child's World.

Pictures

Fall and winter holidays. Society for Visual Education (SVE).

Familiar cloud forms. Society for Visual Education (SVE).

Holidays. David C. Cook.

In the fall. Society for Visual Education (SVE).

In the spring. Society for Visual Education (SVE).

In the summer. Society for Visual Education (SVE).

In the winter. Society for Visual Education (SVE).

Learning about weather. David C. Cook.

Seasons. David C. Cook.

Seasons and holidays: Fall. Society for Visual Education (SVE).

Seasons and holidays: Spring. Society for Visual Education (SVE).

Seasons and holidays: Summer. Society for Visual Education (SVE).

Spring and summer holidays. Society for Visual Education (SVE).

Take a walk in fall. The Child's World. (Sequence chart)

Take a walk in spring. The Child's World. (Sequence chart)

Take a walk in summer. The Child's World. (Sequence chart)

Take a walk in winter. The Child's World. (Sequence chart)

Weather phenomena. The Child's World.

Multimedia Kits

Four seasons. The Child's World.

A tree through the seasons. National Geographic.

Why does it rain? National Geographic.

Winnie the Pooh discovers the seasons. Walt Disney.

Films, Filmstrips, and Videos

About seasons. Eye Gate Media.

About weather. Eye Gate Media.

Animals in winter. National Geographic.

Attic of the wind. Weston Woods Studios.

Autumn comes to the city. Coronet Films.

Autumn is an adventure. Coronet Films.

The big snow. Weston Woods Studios.

The cat and the collector. Weston Woods Studios.

Climates and seasons. Coronet Films.

Ernest and Celestine. Weston Woods Studios.

Exploring the ocean. Churchill Films.

Fall brings changes. Churchill Films.

Fall, winter, spring, summer. Educational Activities.

First experiences about weather. David C. Cook.

Frederick. Distribution Sixteen.

The happy day. Weston Woods Studios.

Heat for beginners. Coronet Films.

Henry the explorer. Weston Woods Studios.

Hot and cold. Coronet Films.

How weather helps us. Coronet Films.

In a spring garden. Weston Woods Studios.

Josie and the snow. Weston Woods Studios.

The little island. Weston Woods Studios.

Mary of mile 18. Weston Woods Studios.

Millions and millions of bubbles. Churchill Films.

Our sun and its planets. Coronet Films.

Rainshower. Churchill Films.

The seasons. National Geographic.

Secrets of the rain. Campus Films.

The snowman. Weston Woods Studios.
The snowy day. Weston Woods Studios.
Spring brings changes. Churchill Films.
Spring is an adventure. Coronet Films.
Summer is an adventure. Coronet Films.
Time of wonder. Weston Woods Studios.
The tontem and the fox. Weston Woods Studios.

The twelve months. Harcourt, Brace, Jovanovich.
The water says. Churchill Films.
Weather for beginners. Coronet Films.
Where does the butterfly go when it rains? Weston Woods Studios.
White snow, bright snow. Weston Woods Studios.
Winter is an adventure. Coronet Films.

PART
SEVEN

DEVELOPING MATH AND PROBLEM-SOLVING SKILLS

When a child is confronted by a problem is when that child really begins to think. Teachers must provide the kinds of mathematics experiences that teach children to be problem solvers and thinkers, and at the same time make it inviting. When math is intriguing, children will seek it out. We must make math fun, not just a drudgery of learning facts and figures. Children need to learn the joy that comes with problem solving. In early childhood, they should be offered interesting and engaging opportunities for applying the concepts and skills they have learned.

During early childhood, the focus of teaching should be on the thinking, analyzing, and reasoning behind math, rather than on producing the correct written answer (Carr, 1988; Kamii, 1982). "If the process of numerical reasoning is correct and if children are confident of their own ability to figure things out, they are bound to find correct answers and to seek even more challenging tasks" (Kamii, 1982, p. 251). Therefore, our goal should be to teach children to classify, infer, observe, compute, measure, predict, solve problems, think through possibilities, and understand the process (Hitz, 1987). Problem solving is related to all areas of learning, not just to math and science.

For cognitive growth to flourish, children must have problems to solve and opportunities to work at solving those problems by themselves. Then they need to experience the results and consequences of their decisions (Hitz, 1987). In addition to the sensory or real experiences children need to acquire knowledge, they also need to be engaged in those experiences both physically and mentally (Williams & Kamii, 1986). In other words, children need manipulative math experiences during early childhood in order to synthesize the desired math concepts mentally.

Guidelines for Incorporating Math and Problem-Solving Skills in the Early Childhood Curriculum

Teachers must avoid gender bias regarding math and must nurture confidence in and enthusiasm for math, problem solving, and reasoning activities in *all* children. If the concepts are geared to their particular level of interest and ability, and if the emotional inhibitions that promote a feeling of inferiority are removed, all children are capable of mathematical reasoning and problem solving (Piaget, 1974).

Teachers should recognize that opportunities for teaching math abound in children's daily experiences as they encounter concepts relating to time, distance, measuring, weight, number recognition, and other math notions. During the early childhood years, many understandings of math concepts grow out of experiences with objects, food, play materials, nature, the outdoors, time, and space—in effect, their everyday experiences. Teachers should use children's unique experiences as springboards for learning math. Math concepts are often acquired in a spontaneous, natural way because children are normally curious about and interested in them.

However, many math concepts require substantial experience and development time before they are incorporated into the child's thinking. For example, time concepts such as *today*, *tomorrow*, and *yesterday* are often misunderstood by young children, and comments such as "I don't want my bath today, I want to have it yesterday" or "I already did that, I did it tomorrow" are very common among young children.

Math in early childhood must be concrete and manipulative. "Manipulative and concrete objects are the means through which young children develop abstract concepts" (Jelks, 1981, p. ix). Teachers should be cautioned against the use of workbook pages and dittos when teaching math in early childhood. "Where children are required to sit down, quiet down, and write it down, excitement about math may never have a chance to emerge (Stone, 1987, p. 16). Objects and manipulative toys and materials must be an integral part of early childhood math programs. It is difficult, for example, for young children to understand money concepts without opportunities to actually use money. Strategically asked questions will turn children's thinking toward math ideas and concepts. Likewise, by listening and responding to children's questions, teachers can teach math ideas spontaneously. Children often are asked "How many?" or "How much?" questions, and to answer, they have to use math concepts (Katz, 1983).

Math should be taught in all curriculum areas, although math learning centers can be set up and specific times allotted in the curriculum for math activities. Problem-solving skills are related to all areas of learning, not just to math and science. For example, while on field trips, children spontaneously learn concepts relating to money, time, numbers, and other aspects of math; in food experiences, children are exposed to measuring, number concepts, fractions, and other math and problem-solving skills. These skills or concepts include matching (quantities, numbers, shapes, forms, sizes, and so forth); making patterns; classifying, ordering, or seriating in order on the basis of size, number, ordinal position, or weight; and making comparisons. Recognizing and using patterns is a valuable problem-solving tool, as is classifying, which helps develop analytical and logical thinking and abstract concepts (Carr, 1988; Day, 1988). Classification relies on the recognition of likenesses and differences.

It is important to begin with simple concepts and then move to the more abstract.

Once a child has had experiences with beginning number concepts (i.e., recognizing numbers, counting, understanding the meaning of numbers, and even some simple addition concepts), we begin to teach more abstract math concepts, such as time, money, and space. Preschool children have difficulty with math concepts of these kinds because they are of the stage (preoperational) in which their understanding depends on how something appears to them (Katz, 1983). Consider Piaget's example of conservation: Five buttons, pennies, crackers, or other objects of uniform size are placed close together in one row; in a second row, five like items are spread apart. When children are asked whether both rows contain the same number of items, most preschool children will indicate that the row that is spread apart or is longer has more because it *appears* to have more. After 5 or 6 years of age, most children are able to focus on actual numbers and can separate length from number.

Children learn best when allowed appropriate freedom to explore through their senses of touch, sight, sound, taste, and smell. Therefore, a good early childhood education environment for developing math and other problem-solving concepts should include literature and storytelling; blocks and construction; art; science, water, and sand; music; language; food and nutrition; interactions with peers and adults; and other activities suitable for young children.

Use of Computers

Computers become valuable as they enhance, not replace, discovery and exploration through sensory experiences. Children need many concrete experiences with basic math concepts before they can find meaning in the more abstract computer activities. "Only after a sound, basic program has been developed should preschool and kindergarten teachers consider buying a computer" (Anselmo & Zinck, 1987, p. 27). Then, the drill and practice of computer activities can further enhance the development of math and problem-solving potentials.

Computer effectiveness in the early years of learning can be achieved only when teachers develop competence in computer literacy, understanding how a computer functions and the basic principles of programming. Computer literacy programs should teach teachers to assess the appropriate use of computers in the classroom, locate suitable computer hardware and computer-related materials, and evaluate software for young children (Hyson & Eyman, 1986). Use of the computer, like the use of other learning centers, must be carefully planned to meet the level of understanding of the children in the classroom. Care must also be taken to teach the children how to use the computer. How exciting it is to see the effects of computer exploration with young children when it is carefully integrated into a well-planned early childhood curriculum!

Like all teaching tools, computer software must provide a developmentally appropriate approach to early childhood education (Bredekamp, 1986; Haugland & Shade, 1988). Young children can increase such skills as counting, number recognition, and associating a quantity with a symbol through the use of computer exploration (Hungate, 1982). There are many counting and math computer games available for young children, and the thinking processes involved in using the computer often utilize mathematical reasoning.

The computer must act as a supplemental aid in the classroom, not as a basic ingredient or substitute teacher. Computer learning of math concepts and other problem-solving skills should not replace the teacher in early childhood education. Our contention has been, and always will be, that a teacher is the most valuable resource available in the education of children. We must remember that the computer cannot take the place of effective teachers who have programmed themselves to teach.

Early childhood teachers must develop a positive attitude toward math. Since early impressions are often lasting impressions, children need to sense the importance of developing math and number skills. Many activities throughout life rely on the use of math concepts and the ability to use numbers. Early childhood is the time to inculcate enthusiasm for and a positive attitude toward mathematics!

CHAPTER
seventeen

Math Concepts

Introduction

Children become aware of numbers early in life, because daily experiences involve various uses of numbers. Soon after children begin to speak, they use words relating to numbers. But understanding the meanings of these number words comes later, as the child matures, experiences, and develops. The development of number concepts appears to be a function of both age and educational development. Young children are very interested in number or numberlike properties (Wellman, 1982). They like to count and rehearse the sequence of number names. Many experiences with self-correcting manipulatives should be provided for children throughout the early childhood years. Those working with young children should "take advantage of the counting potential in a child's play. If she is playing with pegboards, nesting cups, counting cubes, bead counters, or large beads, or if she is working with clay making cookies, balls, or snakes, count each item as it is finished" (Caplan & Caplan, 1983, p. 88). After

children learn to associate a quantity with a number (idea), then begin to write down number symbols, or numerals, so the children can associate the quantity with the numeral.

The classroom and activities of young children abound with opportunities for using numbers that include counting and simple number reasoning concepts; but many of the understandings children have of number are incomplete or even misunderstood or confused. For example, "the idea that the concept of number relates to the final count of single objects, each counted once, is difficult for young children to understand" (Honig, 1980, p. 3). In other words, children may enjoy counting, but the cognitive understanding of one-to-one correspondence comes some time later, developmentally, than rote counting ability. Children's understanding of numbers develops as they match, compare, sort or group, and order (Katz, 1983, p. 5).

Learning about math should be integrated into all curriculum areas. For example, various number concepts can be explored through children's books and literature. Such concepts include classification, comparison, ordering, ordinal number, one-to-one correspondence, rational counting, number recognition, conservation of number, and cardinal number (Harsh, 1987). However, for the early childhood teacher to be successful in teaching math concepts, the teacher must know the level of understanding of individual children and teach to their needs.

Mathematical and number concepts can be taught in a unit theme, in individual or group activities, and as an integrated part of the entire curriculum or preschool day.

Children can be given engaging problems to solve in cooperative learning groups. For example, in preschool each group could be given a set of beads or buttons and a set of numeral cards. Each group counts its objects and finds the numeral representing that quantity. For first or second grades, once a day in a cooperative group the children could have a story problem to solve relating to the math concept they are learning. For example, if they are working on beginning addition, give a problem such as "There are three goldfish in the aquarium, and a class member brings in two more fish. How many fish are there in the tank all together?" Cooperative learning helps children share, refine, and include all children in elaborating on information.

It is important that adults use math terms correctly in their vocabulary, while listening for any misconceptions children may have in their striving for understanding.

Birthdays and ages are constantly items of importance to children. They become measures of time, abilities, and achievements. Often in children's speech one hears references to ages and birthdays. "I already did this—when I was only three." "Yesterday I was three, today I am four—and tomorrow I will be five!" "I am three now—Clint can have two." "My sister is 14 and I am 4, so we are the same age."

A 3-year-old was involved in a discussion with her 4-year-old brother. He had told her that she could not go to preschool because she was not yet 4. She said, "Someday I'll be 5," to which he replied, "Then I'll be 6." She said,

"Someday I'll be 10,"; he said, "And I'll be 11." "They continued on and finally she said, "Well, someday I'll be 100," and he confidently said, "And then I'll be 101!"

Frequently, the importance of the child's age is apparent in responses to seemingly unrelated stimuli. A 3-year-old may not be satisfied with one cookie or with four cookies—just three. Since that age of 3 years is so important, the child can usually count to 3 and desires things in that amount.

A soldier was visiting the classroom and explaining to the children about independence and being free. Richard, intently listening, suddenly retorted, "I am not free, I am 4!"

The children were being divided into groups for an art activity, the groups being named "ones," "twos," "threes," and so on. "Destry, you are in the 'twos.' " To which he indignantly responded, "I am not 2, I am 5."

Age and size are directly associated, since the child assumes that the larger and bigger a person is, the older that person is. Children also directly associate age and authority: the more authority a person has, the older that person is. Only after gaining more experience and understanding does the child realize that a large 5-year-old child is younger than a small 8-year-old child or that a 40-year-old parent is older than a 30-year-old fire fighter.

References to height and weight are often heard as children continue to experiment with their new vocabulary. "I ate 2 pounds of bacon for breakfast; now I weigh 37 pounds." "I weigh 65 feet."

The children were being measured and weighed, and these amounts were being recorded on a chart. Melissa observed the other children for a short time and then declared, "Pound me next."

Numbers are also familiar to children because they appear in telephone numbers, addresses, speedometers, speed limit signs, mileage distance signs, page numbers, clocks, calendars, and thermometers. Food experiences offer opportunities for measuring, timing the length of cooking, and dividing into portions; elements of fractions are also familiar in recipe measurements.

Following is a partial list of words and pre-fixes dealing with numbers with which children can become familiar:

dozen	tri-	triple
few, fewer	bi-	less than
many	uni-	more than
more	mono-	none
decade	single	same as
century	double	pair

Classification

Classification is a beginning math concept that can be taught in many ways, in different areas of the room, and in various curriculum areas. To classify means to sort or group by some common characteristic such as size, shape, number, color, or other category. Examples of classifying are: workers by things that go with their jobs; fruits, vegetables, or flowers by kind or other characteristics; kinds of transportation; buttons by shape, size, color, or kind; and animals by kind, category, size, color. Children can use marbles to sort by color or size (Lehman & Kandl, 1992).

Space

The concept of *space* at the early childhood level primarily involves using and understanding prepositional words. Space concepts answer *where* questions, *which way* questions, and *distance* questions. In other words, position, direction, and distance ideas are taught through vocabulary and actual experiences.

Money

Because of the importance of money in people's lives, children are made aware of its value long before they understand the value meanings. Most young children's concepts of money relate to the understanding that we earn it by working, then use it to pay for what we buy (Hamilton, 1990). Since it is easy for misconception to occur, many experiences should be provided that allow children to work with various amounts of money. When a child has the opportunity to use money, it becomes meaningful. Many games and types of play involve play money, and certainly play money has value as the child learns about payments, cash exchanges, and other concepts. But it is even more important that the child experience the use of real money, so that the various sizes, amounts, and markings become familiar. Because the child associates size with value, both the nickel and the penny seem to be worth more than the dime. Children are often able to identify different coins, even though the value of the coins is not known. The vocabulary attests to the child's understandings. "I need two-seventy pennies." "It costs sixty-eleven monies."

George asked his mother for a tricycle. She answered that they did not have any money to buy a tricycle. Being accustomed to seeing the store clerk return change, George answered, "Well, let's go to the grocery store for some money."

It is important for children to experience shopping for food, toys, and clothing. Children will learn that not all items cost the same amount of money, that different items may have the same cost, and that the same item may have various costs. They often see change being returned to the buyer, but they need to learn that the buyer paid for the item before change was made. Perhaps an item costing 79 cents was paid for with a dollar. The change of 21 cents would be returned to the buyer as two dimes and one penny. It is difficult for children to understand that one piece of money ($1.00) is of more worth than three pieces of money (21 cents), since three is greater than one.

The use of checks and credit cards further hinders a child's understanding of the value of money. Often if a parent responds to a child's request for money with the comment "We don't have enough money," the child will reply, "Then write a check."

Number Concepts

In the process of learning to understand numbers, there are some basic concepts to be learned. As children work on these understandings, they need the example and encouragement provided by a teacher so that misconceptions can be corrected. These concepts are not self-contained, and they may overlap. There are many number concepts that the child will develop during the early childhood years. Some of the first concepts—becoming aware of the sound and sequence of numbers or counting and one-to-one correspondence—provide a basis for the acquisition of other number skills. The child then moves from counting to understanding what those numbers mean, and that *two* means two objects or things.

Becoming Aware of the Sound and Sequence of Numbers (Counting) and Developing One-to-One Correspondence

Children frequently hear counting—as steps are climbed, objects are stacked, foods are distributed, finger and toe games are played, familiar nursery rhymes and songs are enjoyed, and during many other activities. This repetition reinforces the child's ability to begin memorization of the sequence and sounds of numbers even before the meanings of these numbers are understood. The recitation of numbers in the counting sequence has little meaning to very young children, in fact, they probably perceive it as just sound in a particular sequence. Songs, fingerplays, nursery rhymes, and stories utilizing the fingers as counting objects should be heard often. Because the correct number sequence is 1, 2, 3, 4, 5 . . ., these songs and finger plays should utilize this particular ordering, rather than . . . 5, 4, 3, 2, 1. Learning correct counting is difficult enough for children to grasp; as their understanding increases, they are able to reason about the reverse counting sequences. It is not uncommon in this stage to hear children count 1, 2, 3, 4, 5, 6, 13, 11, 14, 5, 6. . . .

To rote count, verbalizing the number sequence, is one thing; but to count items correctly—one number per item—is more difficult. This requires skill in one-to-one correspondence. Often when a young child is given a series of items to count, the child counts two numbers for one item or two items while verbalizing only one number. Thus children need to be given much time to learn to count; once this concept is mastered, the skill of one-to-one correspondence can be acquired. One way to foster the development of this skill is to have children record what they are counting, using symbols such as rocks, coins, or beads. Another way of helping children to keep record or count something is to give them cards and paper punches and let them punch a hole for everything they are counting (Beaty, 1992b). They could count cars in a parking lot, children in the group, birds that fly overhead, or many other objects in their environment. Other daily opportunities for fostering one-to-one correspondence include table setting or passing papers or other supplies to class members. There are many children's counting books that can be read and objects counted to give further practice.

Understanding the Meaning Behind Numbers

As this memorization takes on meaning, the one-to-one correspondence necessary for actual counting is understood; the child learns that *three* means three objects or items. Even though a child may not yet be able to recognize the numeral, as objects are counted the child can correctly ascribe a number to it and understands what that number means. To understand the meaning of numbers, the child must be able to associate quantities with symbols. Puzzle matches, in which the numeral is on one side of the block or card and items representing that quantity are on the other side, provide good practice and can be geared to the developmental needs of the child. For example, a child just learning this concept may be given only matches 1 through 4, where as another child may be ready for 1 through 10.

Zero, or the empty set, is also a rather difficult concept for children to grasp. Zero is less than 1; but when the numeral one precedes zero (10), then the numeral is 10 times as valuable as the one (1).

Eric had a 6-month-old brother and was asked "How old is your new baby brother?" After thoughtful consideration, he answered, "Zero."

Recognizing Numeral Symbols

Children memorize the sequence of numbers, and this sequence broadens into one-to-one correspondence between object and number. Now the task of recognizing the symbol representing the number (the *numeral*) must be mastered. Suppose you were told to learn the symbols shown in Figure 17-1, which represent the numbers 1 to 5. This makes the child's position easier to understand. Now, if these numerals are written into mathematical problems, the task becomes even more difficult (see Figure 17-2). Through repeated experiences and opportunities, children learn to recognize the numeral symbol and say the name. The old adage that a single experience is not enough to build a reliable concept certainly applies in learning to recognize numerals. It is an exciting accomplishment for children, and demonstrates much work and study on their part.

The teacher had been showing the children how the number 8 could be represented by their fingers. They were told that four fingers plus four fingers equals eight, as does five fingers plus three fingers. At the close of the

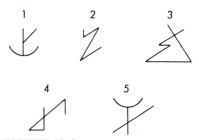

FIGURE 17–1
Example of Symbol-Learning Task

FIGURE 17–2
Sample Symbols in Problem Form

presentation, the teacher asked Lisa to show the number 8 with her fingers, Lisa triumphantly touched her index fingers to the thumbs, forming two circles. Then she put these two circles together so that one circle was above the other, forming the numeral 8.

There are many manipulative toys and materials that can be used effectively in teaching numeral recognition. For example, separate cards for each numeral, with the numeral cut from sandpaper, are effective because they encourage tactile learning; the child feels the shape of each numeral as it is being learned. Numerals can be cut from felt to be used at a flannel board, made from wood to give three-dimensional shape, or cut from index cards or other heavy paper. To make a self-correcting number lotto, numerals can be cut and put on oak tag or poster board; then matching numerals that are exactly the same can be cut and put between clear plastic sheets so that each numeral for matching is separate. As the children match the numerals in plastic to the ones on the board, the plastic allows them to see through and correct themselves if the numerals have been matched backwards or upside down. There are also many excellent commercial toys focusing on numerals that can be used in the early childhood classroom.

Once children understand the meaning of numbers and recognize numerals, they can associate the numeral with the number in the set. For example, the child can now match a set of objects (four peanuts, for example) to the numeral or symbol (4, for example).

Ordering of Numerals and Sets

Once the numeral is recognized, the skill that often follows is the ability to order the numerals in sequence. As the children observe a collection of numerals, they are able to select first the 1, then the 2, the 3, 4, 5, 6, and so on in correct order.

In addition, they develop the skill of putting sets of objects in order, from those with the fewest number of objects to those with the greatest number of objects. The children should also be able to make comparisons such as *more than, less than,* and *as many as.*

Directional Positioning of Numerals

Not only are the numerals correctly ordered and sequenced, but the child is able to place them so that they are positioned correctly. The numerals are not backward, sideways, or upside down; and the numerals 6 and 9 are distinguished.

When teaching numerals, it is helpful if other concepts (such as size and color) are kept constant. For instance, it is easier for the child to concentrate on learning the numeral itself if all the numerals are the same size and color. If the numerals are of various colors, the child might think that the red numeral is a 4 and the blue numeral is a 5—rather than learning that the 4 is a 4 and the 5 is a 5 regardless of color. Varying the color, however, adds an element of difficulty to be introduced later in order to increase the challenge and motivation to the children.

Once children master these basic mathematical concepts, they are ready for more advanced number skills and usually show signs of wanting to write the numerals.

Comparing and Conserving Numbers

In mathematical comparisons, children learn to make comparisons such as those that relate to size and measurement and to quantity, such as more than/less than. Before children begin adding and subtracting, they should have many experiences comparing sets in terms of more than and less than.

Conservation means that if two sets are compared and found to be equal, when they are rearranged to look unequal the child can still determine that the two sets are equal. For example, if two rows of buttons, five in each row, are arranged in such a way that a button on one row corresponds with a button on the other row, it may be obvious to the child that they are the same or equal. If they are arranged so the second row looks like more or less than the first row, this concept will not be as obvious. However, the child who can conserve numbers will still recognize that the sets are equal. Number conservation experiences can also be planned with rows of unequal items, making them look either the same or different.

Conservation relates to judging the amount; as with number, the child recognizes that the arrangement of items does not change the number. Conservation of volume is more challenging, since the child must recognize and understand that the shape of something does not change the volume. To understand conservation of weight, the child must recognize that the shape or size of something does not change the weight.

Ordinal Numbers

As the child develops concepts of ordinal numbers (1st, 2nd, 3rd, etc.), he or she is also able to order items using ordinal numbers and to match ordinal numbers to cardinal numbers (1, 2, 3, etc.).

Adding Sets

As children develop skill in this aspect of mathematics, they are able to determine the number of items in a set when two or more sets are combined. Begin by having the child identify numerals that are one more than a particular number. Again, use real objects for early experiences. The child can then visualize that two buttons and three buttons in one box are the same as five buttons in another box.

As children grasp more advanced math concepts of addition and subtraction, a game using dice to determine specific plays encourages continued interest and concept development through cooperation and socialization.

Subtracting Sets

As children develop skill in this aspect of mathematics, they are able to determine the number of items in a set when one set is taken away from another set. Again, you should begin by having the child identify numerals that are one less than a particular number.

Units of Measure

We use measurements whenever we want to know "How far?" or "How much?" We measure length, quantity, temperature, weight, and time. Young children easily confuse different standards or units of measurement. For example, a mother was trying to get her 4-year-old child to sleep when Kyle said, "Do you know how much I love you, mother?" When she responded with "How much?" he hopped out of bed, pointed to a numeral on a nearby clock and said, "This much, 87 pounds!" Another 4-year-old child was weighing herself on the bath scales; reading the numeral 40, she said, "I weigh 40 inches!" It takes time and experience for young children to

use units and standards of measurement correctly.

We must also point out that early childhood teachers should be familiar with metric units of measurement and vocabulary, understanding how to convert standard units to metric units.

Fractions are also a part of measurement. Children during the early childhood years can begin to understand fractional terms such as *one-half* and *one-fourth*, and to recognize that these terms indicate a part of a whole. An effective and natural way to introduce fractions to children is through many experiences with recipes. Fractions can also be taught by making a whole circle in one color; making a circle the same size in another color and cutting it in half; making the same size circle in a third color, and cutting it in thirds; and making a circle the same size in still another color, and cutting it in fourths. Depending on the developmental level of the children, you could also do a circle for sixths and one for eights. Another idea is to put the children in cooperative groups and give each group the same amount of clay. One group is to divide their clay in half, another group in thirds, and another in fourths, extending as far as developmentally appropriate. Still another possibility is to divide the class into halves, thirds, fourths, and various other parts of the whole.

Time, another unit of measure, is discussed in more detail following the lesson plan on "Numbers" later in this chapter. For more specific information on measurement of temperature and weight, consult Chapter Eleven or the index.

Linear Measure

Learning linear measurement means understanding that lengths are measured in terms of inches, feet, and yards; and understanding and using tools for linear measurement (e.g., ruler, tape measure, yardstick). Teachers should supply tools for linear measurement in the woodworking area, and it is helpful to add a ruler when using pencils and paper. A tape measure can be included in the dramatic play area for measuring height.

Liquid Measure

The concept of liquid measurement includes understanding that quantities of liquids are measured in terms of cup, pint, quart, teaspoon, and gallon and having experiences using containers that equal these amounts. Even more challenging is to determine the number of cups in a pint, quart, and so on; the number of pints in a quart; and the number of quarts in a gallon. In addition to sensory media in the trough, add cups and jars for measuring, comparing, and problem solving.

Approach to Teaching Numbers

Concepts and Ideas for Teaching

1. The words *number* and *numeral* have different meanings. *Number* is the idea, or what is being thought. *Numeral* is the name or symbol of that idea, or what is being written. The numeral, then, represents the number.

2. The correct numeral sequence is 1, 2, 3, 4, 5, 6, 7, 8, 9, 10. . . . Therefore it is important that songs, fingerplays, nursery rhymes, poems, and games utilize that sequence.

3. A group of objects such as buttons, beans, or chips is called a *set*. An *empty set* is 0 (zero).

4. Numbers are used in many ways.

5. Money is used to purchase things. Coins and dollars are U.S. money, and coins have different names and different values.

6. We use different items for measuring: clocks, rulers, measuring tapes, scales, measuring cups and spoons, calendars, and thermometers.

Activities and Experiences

1. Select two pages from a calendar. Leave the numerals on one intact, and separate the numerals of the other. The single numerals are then matched to those on the whole page.

2. Cut face cards in half (make the cutting lines different on the separate cards, so that only the two correct halves will fit together). Then the cards are matched together as puzzles. A variety of number puzzles can be made matching the numeral or symbol to objects and the written name of the numeral to either objects or the numeral symbol. These can be constructed and geared to the developmental levels of the children.

3. On a piece of plastic or canvas, paste or draw numerals. This material should be large enough for a child to carry out the following instructions: "Place your foot on the numeral 4" or "Put your hand on the numeral 6." If the children are older, add instructions involving the right foot, left foot, right hand, left hand, elbow, knee, and so on.

4. Draw a line with numerals in the proper sequence on the floor. Tell the child to stand on a numeral and "move ahead four numerals—now move back two. What nu-

meral are you standing on?" (This exercise also develops basic math understandings of addition and subtraction.)

5. Set up a store area in the classroom, including a cash register and money. Each day change the kind of store, still making sure that number concepts are included (post office, bakery, grocery store, clothing store, variety store, bank, etc.).

6. Cut a pig from heavy paper, and make a square hole near the top of it. Cut a circle about the size of the pig's body, and glue various quantities of money on the circle. Fasten this circle underneath the pig with a paper fastener. Turn the wheel so that the different quantities show through the square hole. Write each of the represented quantities on a small card so that the children can match the two. Include a small box or bag of change so that the same amount of money can be shown in ways other than that represented on the wheel or through the hole. For example, if a dime is shown through the hole, the child should find the 10-cent card and also combinations equaling 10 cents (10 pennies, 2 nickels, or 1 nickel and 5 pennies).

7. Newspapers can be used to cut out advertisements on different items for making comparisons. For example, the children could cut out items and their prices and order them from least to most expensive. The children may need assistance in separating items by price per pound and price per individual item.

8. This activity is for any age level, to give practice in various money concepts, change from purchases, and subtraction concepts. From newspaper grocery ads, workbooks, catalogs, or stickers, gather pictures of items that could be purchased. For younger children, put a picture and an approximate price on a card. For example, for a quart of milk, write $.89. Have a can of change so the children can practice counting out the price of the items. For older children, in addition to the item and price on the card, add "You give $1.00" (or whatever amount of money is given), "Change?" (The children figure how much change should be given.) The answer can be on the back of the card for use in correcting.

9. Make a set of cards from pictures on seed packets. These cards can be grouped by flowers and vegetables; classified by kinds of flowers, by vegetables, or by colors; or used to present even more advanced concepts, such as vegetables that grow above the ground as opposed to those that grow beneath the ground.

10. Use a calendar. Children enjoy either marking off each day or adding the days to the calendar.

11. Use a calculator. Children enjoy seeing the numeral appear in response to the button they have pushed. Older children can do simple addition and subtraction.

12. Make a classroom directory with each child's name, address, and telephone number. Put this list by the toy telephone so that the children can practice dialing numbers.

13. Use the flannel board with felt numerals and felt shapes such as stars, trees, flowers, apples, and others. Challenge the children to organize these shapes into sets representing each numeral. For example, for the numeral 1, one star; for the numeral 2, two apples; and so on.

14. Make a series of cards (at least 5 × 8 inches) with a tree cut from felt glued on the cards. Cut apples from red felt. Children can put apples on the trees and then order them in sequence or make comparisons between trees, such as *more than*, *less than*, or *same as*. They can also match the number of apples on a given tree to the numeral.

15. Allow individual children to pass items for snack time, such as plates, cups, or napkins. This gives practice in one-to-one cor-

respondence and understanding of such phrases as *too many* or *not enough*.

16. Do a variety of fingerplays, songs, poems, and stories that focus on rote counting.

17. Collect 6, 8, or 10 half-gallon cardboard milk cartons and cut them all down, equal in size, to about 3 inches. Staple them together. On the same inside vertical side of each one, glue a number or number card. (On the other sides, you may wish to put colors, shapes, or concepts.) Now give the child a small bean bag, Styrofoam ball, or Ping-Pong ball. The child tosses the bag or ball into one of the boxes and then responds with the number glued inside of that particular box.

18. Adapt pages from worksheets and workbooks to make learning games for number concepts. For example, make a matching game from a sheet on money or time on which the children are expected to write in the time or the amount of money, Write the times or money amounts on cards for the children to match to the clock faces or sets of money on the worksheet.

19. Obtain a shoebag with individual compartments. Ask the children to fill each compartment with one, and only one, shoe or other item. Compartments in egg cartons can also be used (Stone, 1987).

20. Place pairs of items (shoes, socks, earrings, dice, mittens, cymbals) in a bag and then have the children remove them and match them. Trace right and left hands on various wallpaper patterns (matching patterns for left and right), then cut them out, mix them up and have the children match them. (Stone, 1987).

21. Mark a numeral (2, 3, 4, 5, . . . 10) on a card. Have the children use paper clips, staples, hole punches, paper reinforcements, clothespins, or other objects to create sets: five staples on a "5" card, 8 holes punched on an "8" card, and so on (Stone, 1987).

22. Prior to an outdoor walk, give paper sacks to pairs of children and assign specific sets of collect: two pinecones, six leaves, eight rocks, and so on (Stone, 1987).

23. Ask your class, "How many class members have brothers? How many brothers? How many class members have sisters? How many sisters? How many have no brothers or sisters?" Now make a graph of the results. Make other simple graphs for color of hair or eyes, ages, number in family, favorite colors, favorite foods, kinds of pets, favorite books, number of books read, weather for a month, number of letters in name, number of buttons on clothing, and a comparison of the number of seeds found in a variety of fruits.

    Do a graph of the class members' birthday months. Across the top of the graph, write the months of the year; then, to make the graph, have the children draw pictures of their faces and sign their names. Determine how many birthdays fall in each month and then which month has the most and which the fewest (adapted from Charlesworth & Lind, 1990, p. 244).

24. Have the children play a game using a board such as the one shown in Figure 17-3. Each of two to four players has a marker such as a button. The object is to move from square 1 to square 12 and back to 1 again. There are three dice, and each player gets a chance to roll. The child must roll a numeral 1 before being able to move to square 1. Each player can add numbers together to try and get the needed numeral. For example, if the child rolls a 1, a 4, and a 2 and is on square 3, the child can move to squares 4, 5 (4 + 1) and 6 (4 + 2).

25. Play a game called "What's My Rule?" in which the children give you a number and you give it back to them, applying your rule. They try to guess the rule, but they do not shout it out. If they think they know the rule, another child gives them a number and they apply the rule. For exam-

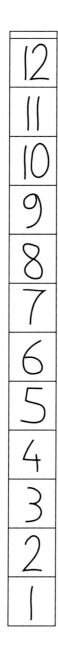

FIGURE 17–3
Board Game

levels. Once the children understand the game, they can divide into cooperative learning groups and take turns thinking up a rule and applying it to numbers given to them by members of their group.

26. Divide the children into cooperative learning groups, and give each group a handout of developmentally appropriate math problems for which they will need to identify the pattern and determine the rule in order to select the number that comes next. For example:

    a. 1, 3, 5, 7, <u>?</u> What is my rule?
                    What comes next?

    b. 15, 12, 9, <u>?</u> What is my rule?
                    What comes next?

    c. 10, 20, 30, <u>?</u> What is my rule?
                    What comes next?

27. Have two sets of cards. On one set, write a numeral on each card; on the other, represent a number set of each card. Have the children put objects such as square blocks on the number set cards to represent the meaning of the matching numeral.

28. Cover 10 soup cans with solid-color contact paper. Using small adhesive circles from an office supply store, put one on the "1" can, two on the "2" can, and so on. Children can put the same number of popsicle sticks or straws in each can as there are circles on the can.

29. "Number Rainbow" is a good game for children to play in cooperative pairs while they develop skill in adding and subtracting. Each child has a card with a rainbow with numerals 2 through 12. The pairs take turns throwing two dice. If player throws a 4 and a 3, a 7 (4 + 3) or a 1 (4 − 3) on the rainbow can be covered by coloring over it. As the children take turns, if they throw the dice on a pair of numerals for which they have already colored in the answers to the addition and subtraction problems, then they lose that turn. The player who

ple, the rule could be to add or subtract a particular amount, or it could be to always add 10 to the number. You will need to make up rules according to developmental first covers all the numerals on the rainbow wins.

30. This activity is for children in first or second grade as they begin to study place value (numbers above 10). To make this concept concrete, they need to see it and work with it manipulatively. Use the soup cans created for activity 28. Show the children that the 10 can, or 10 sticks, is equal to one number ten. Write the numeral on a number card as shown in Figure 17-4. Now do this with a higher number such as 14. Put 10 sticks in the "ten" can and 4 in the "four" can so the children can learn that 10 + 4 = 1 ten and 4 ones = 14. You can do this same activity with blocks and numeral cards (see Figure 17-5). As children become developmentally ready, you can increase your tens place value to 2, 3, and so on.

31. Give each child a number line to learn the number sequence from 1 to 10. Then, for addition and subtraction, have the children use buttons or poker chips on the number line as manipulables to compute problems such as "Find 4 more than 1" or "Find 3 less than 5."

32. Place circles with numerals on the floor. The children can throw a bean bag and name the numeral, or add one more or one less to that numeral. Children who are working on addition and subtraction facts can throw two bean bags and add or subtract the two numerals.

33. Make the points of a triangle with empty circles, and place another circle on each of the sides. Ask the children to figure out how to make each row of three circles total 9 (or any number) (Charlesworth & Lind, 1990). This is called a "magic triangle" (see Figure 17-6).

34. Take advantage of math experiences arising from the background, experiences, and knowledge of the individual children. In one class, the children illustrated and wrote math equations because of one child's response to his experience of losing some of his teeth. The child drew a picture of his smile and left spaces where he had lost teeth. He counted and drew all the rest of his teeth. Then he made a math problem on his paper to show how many teeth he had left. The whole class then wanted to illustrate their smiles and figure out how many teeth they had (Mills, 1993).

35. Play "Target Addition" with the class. You choose a target number such as 10, 20, 25, or whatever seems appropriate. There are two to four players with a board similar to the one shown in Figure 17-7. Players can

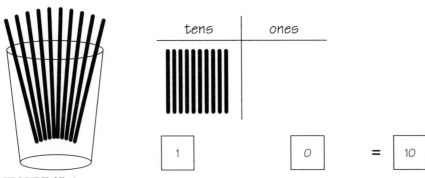

FIGURE 17–4
Sample Number Card Showing the Place Value of 10

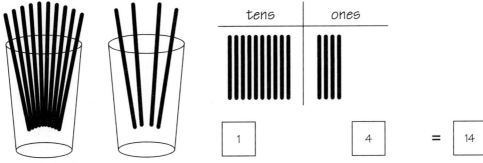

FIGURE 17–5
Sample Number Card Showing the Place Value of 14

work with one board (which would necessitate picking a smaller target number), or each player can have an individual game board. The object of the game is to pick two numbers, add them together, and cover those two numbers with beans or buttons. The next player must start with what the last player's numbers added up to so that each player adds numbers on to the last player's. For example, the first player might select 1 + 1 = 2; the second player, 2 + 1 = 3; the third player, 3 + 2 = 5; the fourth player, 5 + 5 = 10, the fifth player, 10 + 5 = 15, and so on. Once you pass 5, players are only able to cover one of the board numerals since they only go to 5. The first player to reach the exact target number wins (Stenmark, Thompson, & Cossex, 1986).

36. For cooperative learning, have the children stand in two concentric circles facing one another. One partner gives a number, and the other partner has to apply a rule such as "Give a number that is 2 more" or "Give the number that is 3 less."

37. Divide the children into cooperative learning groups, and give each group an age-appropriate addition or subtraction problem such as 3 + 1, 10 − 3, 16 + 4, 26 − 3. Then have them make up a story for their problem.

38. Divide the children into cooperative learning groups, and give each group developmentally appropriate story problems. First have them determine which operation symbol to use (+ or −). Then have them write the number sentence with the answer. For example:

   a. Marti had 4 buttons and then lost 2. How many buttons did he have then?
   (1) __−__ (symbol) (2) __4 − 2__ (number sentence)

   b. José had 4 baseball cards. Tom had 3, and Steve had 2. How many baseball cards did they have in all?
   (1) _____ (2) _____

   c. Maria had 4 stickers and Anthony gave her 2 more. How many stickers did she have then?
   (1) _____ (2) _____

UNIT PLAN ON NUMBERS

Field Trips

• Store—weight of items, cost of items, number of objects in each item (12 eggs in one dozen), money exchanges

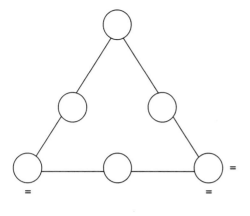
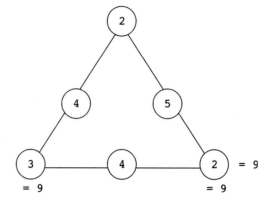

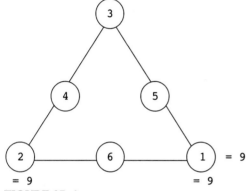

FIGURE 17–6
Magic Triangle

- Bank
- Telephone company and telephone numbers
- Ride that includes seeing the speedometer, mileage signs, speed-limit signs, house numbers
- Weather station, thermometer
- Bakery—numbers of ingredients and baking time
- Carpenter shop
- A place where the children ride an elevator

Art

- Numeral collage—children supplied with cut numerals, glue, and paper; numerals pasted randomly or matched to predrawn numerals on background paper

- Block printing, with the numerals glued on block—numerals glued backward to be correct when printed; block dipped into liquid paint, then pressed onto paper or other background material

Visitors

- Store clerk, with items showing weight and cost
- Bank teller
- Telephone operator
- Police officer—importance of speed limit and mileage signs
- Weather forecaster with thermometer
- Chef, baker, or parent to prepare a food item requiring numbers in amounts and measurements

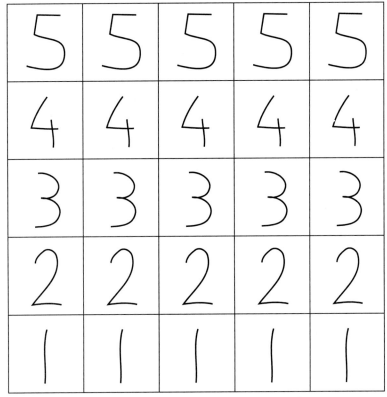

FIGURE 17–7
"Target Addition" Game Board

- Carpenter with measuring tape, yardstick, and ruler

Food

- Food experiences requiring recipes with specified amounts and numbers of ingredients
- Food experiences requiring baking and cooking time
- Numeral cookies—cut numeral shapes from rolled cookie dough

Music

- Musical footsteps—footsteps with numerals put in a circle on the floor; children skip, hop, and jump around the circle until the music stops; children tell the numerals they are standing on
- Clapping rhythms—record with definite beat, clapping varieties of rhythms ("This time we will clap three times, then pause one time, then clap three times again.")
- Clapping rhythms of nursery thymes and familiar songs; clapping the numbers of dots placed on a chalkboard

Science

- Experiences with scales and balances using numbers for measurements
- Activities with yardsticks, rulers, measuring tapes
- Activities with liquid measurements
- Experiences with a thermometer

Language and Literacy

- Make number booklets with pictures from magazines or workbooks, photos, or the children's own drawings. Have the children write or dictate a sentence or two for each page.

LESSON PLAN ON NUMBERS (5-DAY)

Overall Goals

- To help each child participate in whole-group, small-group, and individual activities.
- To assist teachers in becoming acquainted with individual children—their needs, behaviors, and personalities—and to be aware of the goals for each child.
- To ensure that each child will develop the concept of numbers related to his or her development level. By the end of the week, the children will have had experiences in seeing how numbers are used in their environment as well as experiences in counting, ordering, determining the correct position of numerals, and learning the meaning behind the abstract symbol.

Objectives

- To allow the teacher in each group to gain feedback from the children on their understanding of numerals and concepts related to numbers.
- To allow each teacher to lead a discussion on number concepts, including counting, recognition of numerals, ordering, correct orientation, and perhaps the meaning of numerals.

DAY 1

Whole-Group Activities

Introduction to the Unit on Numbers. While the children are gathered on the rug, place a sack in front of them containing various items that use numbers, and ask the children to guess what is in it. It will contain some of the following items:

clock, recipe, book, newspaper advertisement, measuring cup, toy, and other items.

Objectives

- To introduce the unit on numbers, arousing curiosity and interest in the unit's activities.
- To ensure that each child will become aware of how numbers are used in the environment.
- To provide feedback to teachers regarding the developmental level of each child in the area of understanding number concepts.

Flannel Board Story. Have the children gather on the rug to hear a flannel board story.

Objectives

- To provide an enjoyable experience with literature.
- To allow the teachers to observe the differences in the attention spans of the children and, from this observation, to establish goals and needs.

Small-Group Activity

Numeral Collages. Divide the children into small groups, and give each child a 3-gallon ice cream carton, dish of liquid starch, and various numerals cut from lightweight paper, such as gift wrap. The children will paste the numerals, using the starch as glue, on their cartons.

Objectives

- To allow the teacher in each group to gain feedback from the children on their understanding of numerals and concepts related to numbers.
- To allow each teacher to lead a discussion on number concepts, including counting, recognition of numerals, ordering, correct orientation, and perhaps the meaning of numerals.

Individual Activities

- Paint at the single easel
- Soapy water in the trough

Day 2

Whole-Group Activities

Discussion on Counting and Position and Ordering of the Numerals 1 to 10.   Have the children gather on the rug, and count the number of boys, girls, and teachers separately and then all together to give practice in rote counting. After some counting songs have been sung, place poster paper with the numbers 1 to 10 outlined at the top where all the children can see it. Hold up individual numerals in correct order and match them to the corresponding outlined numerals on the poster paper. Emphasize the correct order and orientation of the numerals as they are pasted on the paper. Point out that numerals have to go a certain way, or else they will be upside down or backward.

Objectives

- To give the children practice in rote counting: each child will be able to count to 10.
- To show, through the use of visual aids, correct order and orientation of the numerals 1 to 10.

Art—Gadget Painting.   Place gadgets that make a circular imprint on a large table, along with black and yellow paint and white paper.

Objectives

- To see what the children do in this creative activity with the unusual tool.
- To give the children an opportunity to socialize in a whole group during a creative activity.

Small-Group Activities

Matching Numerals.   Using calendars, give each child one month with the numerals intact and in sequential order. Also give each child a set of numerals that are cut up. Direct the children to match the cut-up numerals to the sheet of numerals. If they have difficulty, select the numerals 1 to 3 and then point to these same numerals on the calendar, asking the child to match them. It is the responsibility of the teacher in each group to simplify the task as needed for individual children. Direct the children to the small groups as they come in first thing in the morning; they will stay in these small groups until all the children arrive and have an opportunity to par-

Number cubes, with graduated sizes corresponding to appropriate numerals, provide a manipulative experience for understanding numbers and beginning addition/subtraction concepts through the use of sight and touch.

ticipate in the matching activity. Give books to each teacher in case the children arriving first tire of the matching activity.

Objectives

- To see which children are able to match and order the numerals, and to see how simple the task needs to be in order for them to do so.
- To again allow the teachers an opportunity to discuss ordering and recognizing numerals.

Field Trip to the Grocery Store. Have the children gather at the rug after their matching activity, and explain the field trip to them. Explain and discuss the use of numbers in the grocery store. Encourage the children to look at prices on food items, weights on food items, and the use of numbers at the checkout stand in determining the total grocery bill. Also encourage them to weigh some produce items. Give them some money with which to purchase one large package of pudding, which will be used in a food activity later in the unit.

Objectives

- To give each child an opportunity to make more/less comparisons with numerals. For example, show two cans of beans, one marked 19 cents and one marked 35 cents, and then ask which is more. Teachers will again be able to teach concepts related to numbers, as well as gain feedback from individual children on concept understandings.
- To help each child see how numbers are used in weight. Some children may be able to understand that weight determines the price of many items.
- To enable the children, as they purchase their package of pudding, to see the numerals on the box appear on the cash register.
- To give children who are ready an opportunity to learn number concepts related to money. For example, 5 cents is the same as a nickel, we pay the grocer for our groceries, we get back less money than we give to the grocer, and so on.

Day 3

Small-Group Activities

Food—Making Pudding. After the visitor's presentation, while the children are still in a whole group, introduce and explain the food experiences. Tell the children that the numerals on the package indicate the price and the weight. Then tell them how they will make the pudding that will be eaten the next day. Place particular emphasis on the use of numerals in measuring and timing the cooking of the pudding. Then divide the children into smaller groups. Two of the groups will go outside while the other two groups stay in and make their pudding. One of the two groups that stays inside will use the hot plate in the room for cooking, while the other uses the stove in the kitchen. Then the four groups will change places, and the ones that were outside will make their pudding. As each group finishes, give each child a small bowl of pudding marked with his or her name.

Objectives

- To allow each child to exercise independence by participating in the pudding preparation.
- To allow teachers the opportunity to teach and reinforce concepts relating to numbers—particularly in measuring, reading the recipe, and timing the pudding as it cooks.

Discussion and Structured Collages—Matching Numerals and Determining the Meaning of 1 to 10. Using the poster paper with the numerals 1 to 10 printed across the top (previously used the day before), have the children review the orientation, counting, and sequence of numerals 1 to 10. Then explain the meaning of these numerals. Under each numeral, paste the number of squares representing that numeral. Then divide the children into smaller groups and give one piece of construction paper to each child. On one side, the numerals 1 to 5 will be outlined; on the other side, 6 to 10. Give each child numerals to match and paste (care must be taken to help in matching, as well as in putting the paste on the backs of the numerals or on the construction paper). Then give the children squares to paste below each numeral to represent the meaning of that numeral. Dots will be placed on the construction paper to aid the children in this task; they can match the square to the dot. For example, one dot will be placed below the numeral 1 for its matching square. This activity must be individualized to meet the developmental needs of each child. It is not expected that all children will complete the activity as described.

Objectives

- To allow each teacher to learn where each child in the small group is in numerical understanding. Some children may be able to match and determine the meaning of numerals 1 to 3, others 1 to 5, and still others 1 to 10.
- To give the children the opportunity to work with paste and to develop coordination in using the paste and paste brush.

Individual Activities

- Bubble blowing
- Trough containing number toys

Day 4

Small-Group Activities

Eating Pudding. In the groups, allow the children to eat their bowls of pudding. During the interaction, review and reinforce concepts relating to numbers.

Objectives

- To see whether the children notice the change in the texture of the pudding after it has set in the refrigerator overnight.
- To provide reinforcement and review of number concepts.

Reading Stories; Manipulative Play with Number Toys. Read various stories to the children. Then give each group several number toys for play and exploration.

Objectives

- To enable each child to use and discuss number concepts related to the various pieces of equipment.
- To enable each child to listen to and participate in story reading; this is often not an activity chosen by some children during free play.

Individual Activities

- Various sizes of paper, such as confetti, hole punches, computer punches, and others in the trough. The trough is filled with the computer punches, along with funnels, cups, spoons, and other measuring and pouring devices.

Locomotor Rhythms Using Numerals. Designate one area of the room for this activity, and tell the children that those wishing to participate may do so. Tape pieces of paper, each with one numeral on it, to the floor (use only numerals 1 to 10). Give each participating child a small card with a numeral, or with dots representing one of the numerals, on it. Put on a record, and have all the children do locomotor movements appropriate to the rhythm of the music (examples are hopping, skipping, jumping, leaping, etc.). When the music stops, the children are to stand on the numeral that either matches the numeral on their small card or represents the number of dots on their card. Cards can be exchanged and the activity repeated many times.

Objectives

- To provide further experience in reinforcing number concepts.
- To give opportunities to recognizing, naming, and matching.

Day 5

Whole-Group Activities

Clapping Rhythms. Have the children first clap the rhythm of some of the familiar nursery rhymes. Then clap some simple rhythm patterns such as - - -, - - - -, or - - - -. The children will listen to the patterns and then clap them. Then place some black dots on the flannel board in different rhythmic patterns, one pattern at a time, and have the children clap them.

Objectives

- To give the children some simple experiences with beat and rhythmic patterns.
- To teach the children that nursery rhymes have rhythm.

Science—Addition and Balance Related to Number Concepts. Have the children gather on the rug, and by means of an addition stick, explain the concept of balance as equal weight on two sides. First, focus on placing a disk on, for example, the numeral 5 on the one side, and then make it balance the numeral 5 on the other side. Then show another way to make it balance by putting a disk on 3 and a disk on 2. Use real objects to illustrate that 3 and 2 are the same as 5. Then with five beans, show ways of grouping to make 5—combinations of 4 and 1, and 3 and 2. Divide the children into four smaller groups, and give each child 10 beans. The teacher in that group asks such questions as "Show me six beans." "Now show me another way of showing six, such as three and three."

Objectives

- To begin to teach elementary addition concepts to children who may be ready. If children are not ready for addition, the teacher can focus on the concept of *same as*: "Here are some beans; now show me the same number of beans."
- To reinforce and review concepts related to numbers, and particularly to emphasize the meaning of numerals.

Daily Activity. During the unit, put out a number-concept table so that children can go there during free play and participate in games and activities or play with pieces of equipment related to numerical concepts.

Individual Activities

- Painting with brushes and water outside
- Dramatization of nursery rhymes

Approach to Teaching Time

Because time cannot be seen, felt, heard, or touched, it is an abstract concept and requires understanding, maturation, and experience to master and measure (Caplan & Caplan, 1983). The notions of *past*, *present*, and *future* are complicated for young children. Children begin to sense the importance and value of time early in

Matching puzzles of clock faces with corresponding digital times helps children understand time-related concepts. Puzzle matches of this type are self-correcting because only the proper matches will fit together.

their lives. Every day they hear references to time, and understanding the meanings of these references is a relatively long and difficult process. To understand quantitative time, children must realize that time flows at a uniform speed that can be divided into equal intervals (VanScoy & Fairchild, 1993).

Time is an abstract concept. Many of the phrases that children hear do not refer to given lengths of time, and it may be an awesome task to grasp the actual meanings. Some of these phrases are *time to go to bed, time for a bath, time to eat lunch, hurry up, we don't have time to, not now, maybe later, just a minute, just a second,* and *in the olden days.*

Time to have a bath may be at 6:30 one evening and at 8:00 another evening. *Just a minute* could be 50 seconds, 3 hours, or possibly never. To a 5-year-old, *in the olden days* might be only 4 years ago, or it could be a long time ago. This phrase has different meanings to a 30-year-old and to an 80-year-old. Thus it is easy to see why the concept of time is challenging both to teach and to learn.

How long is a minute? Specifically, it is 60 seconds, or one-sixtieth of an hour. Generally, however, the length of time varies in relation to experience. The way a person feels may make this minute feel either long or short. If one is anticipating an important long-distance telephone call, the minute seems much longer than if one is engrossed in an exciting novel—then the minute becomes much shorter. Usually in pleasant activities the minute is relatively short, whereas in unpleasant activities it is relatively long. This phenomenon also presents difficulty as children try to grasp time understandings.

Young children are just beginning to understand time concepts, and they are often confused.

They may know "today" but are still confused that "tomorrow," when it comes, is also "today." Such words as "later" or "after awhile" may mean very little to them. While taking every opportunity to introduce the words and ideas of time, the teacher must also keep in mind that "in a little while" may seem like an

eternity to a frightened child waiting for his mother to return. (Murphy & Leeper, 1970, p. 14)

As children get older, their concept of time also undergoes changes. To a young child 18 is old; to an 18-year-old, it is young. To a first-grade child anticipating a summer out of school, the summer is a long time. But to a 20-year-old college student who is weary of studying, the summer may be much too short. Generally, however, the older a person becomes, the faster the time passes. Because of these varying concepts of time, a preschool child might ask, "Were you alive with the cowboys and Indians?" or "Did you know Abraham Lincoln?"

Children invent vocabulary words that are appropriate for their reckoning of time—for example, *yesternight* or *tomorning.* It is difficult to put words in their proper context when *tomorrow* does not refer to the same day as *today* or *tonight.* If today is Wednesday, does *next Saturday* refer to the approaching Saturday or the Saturday following? A child's favorite day might be in January, because that is when his or her birthday occurs. A visit to the circus may be 3 sleeps, rather than 3 nights, away.

Teachers can direct children's attention to time and recognize that time words may need to be defined, such as "*Yesterday* is the day before this day." "Since children understand time concepts based on a sequence of events before they understand those based on intervals, the use of such words as *before, after, fast, next, last, soon,* and *later* will enable them to further their ideas or temporal order" (Caplan & Caplan, 1983, p. 90).

Other vocabulary words relating to time include *yesterday, today, tomorrow, last night, next week, next time, morning, afternoon, evening, midnight, night, day, second, minute, hour, week, month, year, decade, century,* A.M., P.M., *early, late, later, soon, sooner, autumn, winter, spring, summer,* B.C., A.D., *short time, long time, never, forever, past, present, future, now, early, late, new, old, year, then, before, never,* and *next.*

As children work with the calendar in the

classroom, they begin to understand the names of the days of the week, the months, and the concepts that there are 7 days in a week, 28 to 31 days in a month, and 12 months in a year. Calendars promote various number concepts: There are 365 days in a year; these 365 days are divided into 12 months; many months have the same number of days, but some do not; months are divided into weeks, and each week has 7 days; the days of the week have names; calendars tell of special days coming; January 1 begins the new year, and December 31 ends the old year (Maxim, 1989). Through conversations and experiences, children also develop concepts relating to reading the time on the clock and understanding hours, minutes, and seconds. However, teachers must remember that counting is the basis of time concepts (Caplan & Caplan, 1983).

Various cultures and groups structure time differently. Some cultures live life slowly and deliberately, whereas others maintain a rapid pace. Some families have time to relax and participate in recreation, whereas others are much too busy to allow for these luxuries.

Understanding time is much more than being able to "tell time." Often elements other than the clock readings tell of the general time: darkness, overhead sun, snow, jack-o'-lanterns, children playing during recess at the school yard, a rooster crowing, and other events and circumstances indicate the possible seasons, hours, and holidays. Children learn that a specific ordering system exists among units of time, and "learning to attach specific numbers to the gross ordering of the passage of time will also extend their mathematical thinking" (Caplan & Caplan, 1983, p. 250).

Concepts and Ideas for Teaching

1. Time is measured progressively in seconds, minutes, hours, days, weeks, months, years, decades, and centuries.

    a. 60 seconds in a minute

    b. 60 minutes in an hour

    c. 24 hours in a day

    d. 7 days in a week

    e. 4 weeks in a month

    f. 52 weeks in a year

    g. 12 months in a year

    h. 10 years in a decade

    i. 100 years in a century

    j. 1,000 years in a millennium

2. The clock has an hour hand and a minute hand (short hand—hour, long hand—minute), and they move clockwise on the clock.

3. Both the clock and the calendar are measurements of time.

    a. Clock—seconds, minutes, hours

    b. Calendar—days, weeks, months, years

4. Even though time is specific, it is flexible; there are 24 hours in 1 day, but a person can structure what will be done within that 24 hours.

5. Time regulates what children do.

    a. School at 9:00 A.M. on weekdays

    b. Church on Sunday for some children

    c. Bedtime at 8:00 P.M.

6. Time influences the food we eat.

    a. Breakfast food generally differs from dinner food

    b. Snacks during favorite television programs

    c. Plentiful and inexpensive vegetables in season

    d. Shortage of fruit supply during spring frosts

7. Time influences recreation.

    a. Basketball in winter, baseball in spring, football in fall

    b. No skiing if the season is sunny and warm

    c. No picnics when the weather is cold or rainy

d. Outdoor movie theaters often closed during winter

8. Time influences the clothing we wear.
    a. Different clothing styles 20 years ago
    b. Warmer clothing in cold seasons
    c. Cooler clothing in warm seasons
    d. Bedtime clothes different from daytime clothes
    e. Different clothing at home and at work
    f. Warmer clothing in late evenings and early mornings; cooler clothing in afternoons

9. Time is an element of measurement in holidays, birthdays, and other events.
    a. Operation on child 3 weeks ago
    b. Child's lost tooth on the night of a favorite movie
    c. Christmas always on December 25
    d. Child's birthday on same date each year
    e. New baby expected the first part of October
    f. Visit from a child's grandmother on April 4

10. Time is an element of measurement in seasons, weather, lightness and darkness, and speed.
    a. Four seasons—spring, summer, fall, winter—which always begin on the same dates and follow the same sequence
    b. Car traveling 45 miles per hour—45 miles traveled in an hour
    c. Distance of lightning indicated by lapse of time between observing lightning and hearing thunder
    d. Warnings of approaching storms usually given in lengths of time
    e. Inches of precipitation said to accumulate in a specific period of time.
    f. Rotation of earth in 24-hour period, resulting in lightness and darkness—contrary to the usual childhood ideas that the sun makes the day light and the moon makes the earth dark, and that the sun and moon come up and go down

Activities and Experiences

1. Make a year's calendar and include dates of importance to the children—their birthdays, closing date of school, holidays, and special events. Refer often to the past, present, and future and how these time perspectives change from day to day.
2. Make a clock with movable hour and minute hands. Have it show appropriate times at the beginning and end of the school day, lunch, snack, outside play, and so on. Match digital times to a traditional clock's time, or vice versa.
3. Measure a 60-second length of time at two different times—one while the children are sitting with nothing to do and one while they are listening to a good story. Discuss the differences they felt and why.
4. Make a sundial. On a large cardboard circle, attach a perpendicular straw or narrow stick. Leave it in the sun so that the straw will cast a shadow on the circle for 12 hours. Every hour on the hour, mark the position of the shadow of the straw. At the end of 12 hours there will be 12 appropriate marks, but these markings will not be equal distances apart. Then, at the mark indicating when school begins, place a picture or a drawing representing that time. Lunch, school ending, and other events of the day may be designated by drawings or pictures at the appropriate marks. As the day progresses, the children observe the nearness of an event by the shadow of the straw cast on the dial. (This sundial will be accurate for only a few days; then another one must be constructed.)
5. From a calendar, take two month pages. Leave one page as is and cut the day nu-

merals apart on the other page. Then have the children use the cut numerals to match the numerals on the page that has been left intact.

6. Measure the time of different egg timers.

7. Do language experience stories titled "Times I Like" and "Times I Do Not Like."

8. A favorite calendar activity is to use 31 sheets of paper, about 5½ × 4 inches, representing each day of the month. Number them from 1 to 31 and put them up in correct order, representing a calendar. As each day arrives, a different child can write and draw a picture for that day. For example, on May 2, when Daniel announces that his dog had puppies in the middle of the night, he is invited to draw a picture on the paper with the 2. A related sentence is then written on the paper by either the child or the teacher, depending on the child's level of writing skill. When the month is finished, the ordered pages are attached to a name-of-the-month cover sheet. The resulting book will be read over and over again. If saved for an entire year, the sheets can be put together into a school yearbook.

9. Read a story that has a definite time sequence such as *Caps for Sale* (Slobodkina, E. 1947), then go back through the story and label the sequences in terms of the time of day.

10. Using a kitchen timer, have the children first guess how many things can be done in a certain length of time, such as "In 1 minute, how many times can you bounce a ball?" "How many times can you hope on one foot?" Then set the timer to 1 minute and actually count these out.

11. Take a picture of the children under the same tree at various times during the year to see the changes that result in both the tree and the children. The passage of time changes things.

12. After the children are able to read hour and half-hour times, teach them how to count by 5 and tell time to the nearest multiple of 5. Teach them to read both traditional-hand and digital time.

UNIT PLAN ON TIME

Science

- Chemical garden—observation of changes
- Seeds planted—observation of growth over a specific length of time; comparison with original seed size
- Potato left on a table for a period of time—observation of changes
- Sundial

Music

- Musical chairs—music played for varying lengths of time
- Creative movements—being in a hurry, going slowly, pretending to be the hour, minute, or second hand of a clock; dramatizing a day from awakening through going to bed
- Rhythm sticks played along with a metronome, with variation of the beats per minute

Field Trips

- Clock sales and repair shop
- Science center with fossils
- Historical museum
- Bakery
- Weather station
- Any business that uses a time clock for employees to punch in and out of work

Art

- Individual sundials made and decorated
- Clock face made by each child—paper plate and all numerals needed; numerals pasted on the plate, either at random or matched to a numeral previously drawn by the teacher

Food

- Any food activity requiring a specific cooking time—cookies, cakes, candies, casseroles, puddings, breads, pies
- Medium-, hard-cooked eggs, depending on the cooking time

Visitors

- Grandparent, teenager, baby

- Person from museum of history—objects from the past
- Person with a fossil
- Baker—explanation of the time element in baking
- Person who sells or repairs clocks
- Weather forecaster

Summary

Even though children become aware of numbers early in life through daily experiences, the actual understanding of number words depend on experiences, maturation, and intellectual development.

Generally, number concepts are best acquired through incidental learning, rather than from formalized structured lessons. However, developmentally appropriate lesson plans, carefully planned and prepared, assist children in assimilating concepts relating to numbers. For children in the early primary grades, math worksheets are most effective when used following lessons, activities, and play experiences with concrete objects relating to the math concept being taught. Math activities should be enjoyable and challenging, worked on gradually, and repeated often.

As children gain experience and knowledge in measuring, counting, ordering, telling time, matching, comparing, and estimating, their ability to recognize and ascribe appropriate ideas with number concepts increases.

Student Learning Activities

1. Observe and talk with a preschool child, listening for comments and understandings related to numbers. Ask such questions as "How old are you?" "What is your favorite number?" "How far can you count?" and "Where do you see numbers?" Now make a comparison. Observe and talk with a child between ages 5 and 6 and ask some of the same questions. You will want to ask additional questions, such as "Show me how you can add some items. Here are three pencils, and what will you have if you add three more pencils?" You may wish to relate problems to money, time, weight, measurement, and other concepts. Challenge the child with number questions and problems. Now compare the differences in the two children you observed, keeping in mind the differences in their ages.

2. In this chapter are listed words and prefixes dealing with numbers with which children 2 to 8 years old could become familiar. Brainstorm and add to this list.

3. Develop an activity or material for teaching in each of the following areas: sound and sequence of numbers, understanding the meaning behind numbers, recognizing numeral symbols, ordering of numerals, and directional positioning of numerals.

4. Implement at least one of the activities you planned in item 3 with a group of children. Evaluate your experience.

5. To help you understand the challenge in recognizing numeral symbols, develop a set of numeral symbols for 1 to 10, such as those suggested in Figure 17-1 for numerals 1 to 5. Learn these symbols or teach them to a friend. Several days later, see if you remember what each symbol represents, and try some addition and subtraction problems with them.

6. With a group of children, implement at least one of the activities and experiences related to number concepts suggested in this chapter. The group of children may be in a classroom setting or simply a small group of relatives or neighborhood children. Evaluate your experience.

7. Think of additional ideas for the unit plan on numbers, or make a number web.

8. Think of additional ideas for the unit plan or web on time.

9. Review and evaluate at least two of the children's books suggested as resources for this chapter. What number concepts are taught by the books? How would you use the books with children? How effective would the books be in teaching number concepts to children?

10. Visit a children's library or bookstore and add at least three additional excellent children's books to the resource list for teaching number concepts to children 2 to 8 years of age.

11. Visit a classroom and observe an activity for teaching numbers. Evaluate the activity. Was it appropriate for the age of the children? Would you have made any changes in it? Was it effective? Did the teacher use materials? Was a ditto or workbook sheet used and, if so, was it effective?

12. Make at least two number games that can be used in a cooperative group setting in early childhood. Math board games to teach number concepts would be a good choice.

Suggested Resources

Math Pamphlet

McCracken, J. B., *More than 1, 2, 3: The real basics of mathematics*. Washington, DC: National Association for the Education of Young Children.

Children's Books on Counting and Numbers

Anno, M. (1977). *Anno's counting book*. New York: Crowell.

Anno, M. (1982). *Anno's counting house*. New York: Putnam.

Astley, J. (1990). *When one cat woke up: A cat counting book*. New York: Dial.

Bang, M. G. (1983). *Ten, nine, eight*. New York: Greenwillow.

Barton, B. (1981). *Building a house*. New York: Greenwillow.

Carle, E. (1974). *My very first book of numbers*. New York: HarperCollins.

Crews, D. (1986). *Ten black dots*. New York: Greenwillow.

Duke, K. (1985). *Seven froggies went to school*. New York: Dutton.

Ehlert, L. (1992). *Fish eyes: A book you can count on*. San Diego: Harcourt Brace Jovanovich.

Feelings, M. (1971). *Moja means one*. New York: Dial.

Fujikawa, G. (1981). *One, two, three: A counting book*. New York: Putnam.

Gag, W. (1928). *Millions of cats*. New York: Putnam.

Giganti, P. (1992). *Each orange had 8 slices*. New York: Greenwillow.

Gordon, M. (1986). *Counting*. Morristown, NJ: Silver-Burdett.

Hague, K. (1986). *Numbers*. New York: Holt.

Hoban, T. (1972). *Count and see*. New York: Macmillan.

Hoban, T. (1990). *Exactly the opposite.* New York: Greenwillow.

Keats, E. J. (1972). *Over in the meadow.* New York: Scholastic.

Kitamura, S. (1986). *When sheep can not sleep? The counting book.* New York: Farrar, Straus & Giroux.

Kitchen, B. (1991). *Animal numbers.* New York: Dial.

Kopper, L. (illus.) (1990). *Ten little babies.* New York: Dutton.

Langstaff, J., & Rojankousky, F. (1967). *Over in the meadow.* New York: Harcourt, Brace, & World.

Leedy, L. (1985). *A number of dragons.* New York: Holiday House.

Leonni, L. (1962). *Inch by inch.* New York: Astor-Honor.

McMillan, C. (1986). *Counting wild flowers.* New York: Lothrop, Lee & Shepard.

Nozaki, A. (1984). *Anno's hat tricks.* New York: Philomel.

Russo, M. (1986). *The line up book.* New York: Greenwillow.

Sendak, M. (1962). *One was Johnny: A counting book.* New York: HarperCollins.

Seuss, Dr. (1960). *One fish, two fish, red fish, blue fish.* New York: Random House.

Sloat, T. (1991). *From one to one hundred.* New York: Dutton.

Slobodkina, E. (1947). *Caps for sale.* New York: HarperCollins.

Sullivan, C. (1992). *Numbers at play.* New York: Rizzoli.

Tafuri, N. (1986). *Who's counting?* New York: Greenwillow.

Tudor, T. (1956). *I is one.* New York: Rand.

Wahl, J., & Wahl, S. (n.d.). *I can count the petals of a flower.* Reston, VA: National Council of Teachers of Mathematics.

Wildsmith, B. (1984). *One two three.* Topsfield, MA: Merrimick.

Children's Books on Time

Barrett, J. (1976). *Benjamin's 365 birthdays.* New York: Atheneum.

Brown, M. W. (1947). *Goodnight moon.* New York: HarperCollins.

Flournoy, V. (1978). *The best time of day.* New York: Random House.

Flournoy, V. (1985). *Patchwork quilt.* New York: Dial.

Rutland, J. (1976). *Time.* New York: Grosset & Dunlap.

Schlein, M. (1955). *It's about time.* New York: Young Scott.

Schwerin, D. (1984). *The tomorrow book.* New York: Pantheon.

Children's Books on Money

Belov, R. (1971). *Money, money, money.* New York: Scholastic.

Brenner, B. (1963). *The five pennies.* New York: Random House.

Hoban, L. (1981). *Arthur's funny money.* New York: HarperCollins.

Martin, B. (1963). *Ten pennies for candy.* New York: Holt, Rinehart, & Winston.

Rockwell, A. (1984). *Our garage sale.* New York: Greenwillow.

Schwartz, D. M. (1989). *If you made a million.* New York: Scholastic.

Viorst, J. (1978). *Alexander, who used to be rich last Sunday.* New York: Macmillan.

Records, Tapes, and Cassettes

Addition and subtraction. Hap Palmer Record Library. AR541 and AC541.

Counting games and rhythms for the little ones. Scholastic Records.

Learning about numbers. David C. Cook. DC-44685.

Learning math with rods. Educational Activities. AC28.

Magic monster mix: Magic monsters count to ten. The Child's World.

Money, money, money. On T-306, *Ooo we're having fun.* Cheviot.

The number march. On *Learning basic skills through music* (Vol. 1). Hap Palmer Record Library. AR514 or AC514.

Sing a sum . . ., Grade 1. Educational Activities. AR711 or AC711.

Sing a sum . . ., Grade 2. Educational Activities. AR711 or AC711.

Pictures

Counting and ABC's. The Child's World (Panorama).

Earning and suing money. David C. Cook. Set of 20 pictures (74476).

Learning about money. David C. Cook. Set of 12 pictures (51904).
Learning to measure in metric units. David C. Cook. Set of 16 pictures (83287).

Multimedia Kits

Disney's basic math program. Walt Disney.
Disney's telling time program. Walt Disney.
Disneyland magical metrics tour. Walt Disney.
Musical math: I: Beginning concepts. Cheviot.
Telling time with Donald. (Computer Software). Walt Disney.

Films, Filmstrips, and Videos

Addition for beginners. Coronet Films.
Beginning concepts. A filmstrip series in basic concepts. Scholastic Early Childhood Center.
The calendar: Days, weeks, months. Coronet Films.
Computers in your life. National Geographic.
Foundations of mathematics. Campus Films.
Learning about time. National Geographic.
Let's count. Coronet Films.
Let's measure: Using centimeters, meters, and kilometers. Coronet Films.
Let's measure: Using grams and kilograms. Coronet Films.
Let's measure: Using milliliters and liters. Coronet Films.
Let's measure: Using standard units. Coronet Films.
Making change for a dollar. Coronet Films.
Math for every seasons. National Geographic.
Math readiness: This one with that one. Coronet Films.
Math readiness: Up, down, all around. Coronet Films.
Math readiness: Which go together? Coronet Films.
Money. Eye Gate Media.
Numbers. Eye Gate Media.
Numbers and numerals all in a row. Eye Gate Media.
Old woman in a show. Coronet Films.
Order: First always comes before last. Eye Gate Media.
Our gang learns arithmetic. Eye Gate Media.
Over in the meadow. Weston Woods Studios.
Place value: Ones, tens, hundreds. Coronet Films.
Quantity: Something is different. Eye Gate Media.
Science and numbers. Eye Gate Media.
Solving world problems in mathematics. Eye Gate Media.
Subtraction for beginners. Coronet Films.

Telling time is easy. Eye Gate Media.
Ten little Indians. Coronet Films.
Time to tell time. Eye Gate Media.
We use the number line. Coronet Films.
Zero, the troublemaker. Coronet Films.

Computer Software

Alligator Alley. DLM Teaching Resources. (Apple).
Arithmetic critters. MECC. (Apple).
Bears tell time, the. McGraw-Hill Media. (Apple).
Beginning math concepts. Orange Cherry Media Software.
Coin works. Nordic Software. (Macintosh).
Counting critters. MECC. (Apple).
Early games match maker. Counterpoint Software, Inc.
Easy street. MindPlay. (Apple, IBM, Macintosh, Apple IIGS).
Exploring measurement, time, and money. IBM Educational Systems. (IBM).
Finger abacus. Edutek Corporation. (Apple II with Applsoft ROM, 32K).
Fish scales. DLM. (Apple).
Hop to it! Sunburst Communications. (Apple).
KidsMath. Great Wave Software. (Macintosh).
Kidstime. Great Wave Software. (Macintosh, Apple IIGS, IBM).
Kinder concepts. Midwest Software. (Commodore 64/128; Apple II+).
Match-on-a-Mac. Teach Yourself by Computer. (Macintosh).
Match up! Hayden Software Company. (Atari 400, 800; Atari tape 16K; Atari disk 24K; Commodore 64).
Math rabbit. American Guidance Service. (64K. Apple II; IBM PC).
Math and me. Davidson and Associates. (Apple, IBM, Apple IIGS).
Measure works. MECC. (Apple).
Money works. MECC. (Apple).
Number farm. Developmental Learning Materials (DLM). (Commodore 64K, Apple II; IBM PC).
Playroom, the. Broderbund Software. (IBM, Macintosh, Apple).
Preschool pack. Nordic Software. (Macintosh).
Talking alpha chimp. Orange Cherry Software. (Apple IIGS, IBM).
Winker's world of numbers. Wings for Learning. (Apple).
Winker's world of patterns. Wings for Learning. (Apple).

CHAPTER
eighteen

Size and Seriation

Introduction

Although color and form are more functional than size in children's perceptions, size distinctions are still an integral part of early learning. Children realize how much they have grown as they compare their size with that of young infants. They see themselves as big. Activities with size can help them learn to make comparisons and understand size. These activities must be developmentally appropriate for children, and both age and individual differences must be considered (Bredekamp, 1986).

Teaching size involves making comparisons between the sizes of two or more objects. Seriation is arranging items in a specific order according to a specific rule, such as size. When children seriate with regard to size, they arrange items from smallest to largest.

It is important to remember that size is relative or comparative; in other words, the size of a particular object may be larger or smaller, depending on the size of the object to which it is compared or seen in relationship. An exciting brainstorming session can emerge as children are asked, "What is the largest object in the room?" Then they could be asked what would make that object smaller, then what would make even that object smaller by comparison. The questions could continue until the final answer might be the universe. Since size is relative, it is better to use relative size words—*larger* rather than *large*, *smaller* rather than *small*, *bigger* rather than *big*, and so on. With the addition of the suffix *er*, these words become comparative.

In teaching size and seriation, teachers should give children daily experiences in making size comparisons and in seriating objects. "It is not the manipulation of objects in itself that is important . . . [but] the mental action that is encouraged when children act on objects themselves" (Williams & Kamii, 1986, p. 26). Motivating questions and statements should often be used, such as "Which is the smallest fish in our aquarium?" or "Put the cars in order from smallest to largest as you put them away today."

Many opportunities for becoming familiar with size vocabulary should be provided. As a child has repeated exposure to words and their meanings, they soon become possessions and are an active part of the vocabulary. The following are examples of words relating to size aspects:

larger/smaller	deeper/shallower
bigger/littler	older/newer
taller/shorter	older/younger
wider/narrower	gigantic/tiny
longer/shorter	fatter/thinner
higher/lower	thicker/thinner

Children often relate size to themselves or their own bodies. The distance an object is from a child affects how the child judges the object's size; and children have difficulty making comparisons and judgments as the distance between them and an object increases (Caplan & Caplan, 1983). Objects larger than themselves are "big," and objects smaller than themselves are "little." Concepts of age are tied to physical characteristics of size. To a child, the larger people are, the older they are (VanScoy & Fairchild, 1993). Children become aware of size early, since they are constantly reminded that they are "too big to . . ." and "too little to . . . ," as well as being told that "when you are bigger you will be able to. . . ." Thus children begin to feel that with size and age, everything becomes possible, but in the meantime, they have to wait because they are too young—and too small.

Many children, especially those who are shorter or smaller than their peers, equate their size with their character, which strongly influences their self-concept. These children not only feel shorter or smaller physically but also emotionally small, inadequate and unimportant. Teachers have a responsibility and obligation to all children to focus size remarks on objects rather than children. For example, instead of saying, "You are too small to reach the light switch," it might be better to say, "That light switch is too high—let me help you." Children should be frequently reminded they *can* do many things because of their size. All too often, they are constantly reminded of things they *cannot* do because they are neither old enough nor big enough. It is no wonder that some children are discontented with their size, age, and particular stage of life. Over 40 years ago, Davis and Havighurst (1947) explained the child's desire to grow up, and their description is still realistic today:

Age is the ladder by which the young child hopes to climb to his Arcadia. . . . Very early he discovers that other children, whether in his family or his nursery school, measure his prestige by his age. On the ladder of age each step will lead him to higher privileges at home and at school, to sweeter triumphs over more and more "small fry," and to more dazzling signs of prestige. . . . Everything good, he is told by his parents, comes with age. More than anything else, therefore, the child yearns to become bigger and older. . . . To the young child . . . age seems to be the key which unlocks all the forbidden doors of life. It is the magic gift of adults, which brings power and social acceptance. It lifts the barriers to the most inviting and mysterious roads, opening toward freedom and adventure. . . . As long as he is young he must be the underdog, he must yield, he must obey. It is not easy for a child to be always inferior, simply because he is inferior in size. (p. 28)

As children initially make comparisons of size, it is important to focus on only one aspect. For example, if sizes of coins (i.e., larger versus smaller) are being compared, do not add the comparison of thicker versus thinner (Beaty, 1992b). It is also wise to keep other concepts constant, such as color and shape, since changes in these attributes may confuse the child. A piece of equipment such as the familiar stacking cone often fails to focus on size because the child memorizes the color sequence and knows that the top ring goes on the top because it is orange—not because it is the smallest. Care should be taken to avoid this confusion when selecting pieces of either commercial or handmade equipment. However, there are some pieces of equipment relating to size in which variation in color is appropriate. Color can serve as an aid in these kinds of toys, rather than as a distraction. An example is a set of different-sized dowels in which each dowel is a different color.

Cylinder shapes of varying diameters can be fitted into holes of corresponding diameters cut into a board.

Approach to Teaching

Concepts and Ideas for Teaching

1. The child is bigger than some things and smaller than others. This fact often determines what the child can and cannot do.

2. Size may stay the same, even though it appears to change.

   a. Child growing out of a coat thinks that the coat has changed in size

   b. Size changes in terms of perspective; the farther away one goes from an object, the smaller it looks

   c. Airplane in the sky appears smaller and then disappears

   d. Magnifying glass

   e. Microscope

3. We feel different sizes even though our physical size does not change.

   a. When do we feel big?

   b. When do we feel small?

4. Things do not always look the same when size changes.

   a. Distortion mirrors

   b. Items viewed under a magnifying glass

   c. An inflated balloon compared to a deflated one

5. The same items come in various sizes.

   a. People

   b. Trees

   c. Flowers

   d. Automobiles

   e. Buttons

   f. Macaroni

   g. Cans

   h. Houses

6. Size can change.

   a. Physical growth and aging—size of a seed in the growing process (fruits, vegetables, plants, etc); a baby compared to an adult

   b. Cooking—some foods, such as rice, macaroni, and bakery products, become larger during cooking; others, such as meats, become smaller, or shrink

   c. Subtracting—as air is taken out of a balloon, it becomes smaller; as wood is sawed, the pieces become smaller

d. Adding—air in an inner tube; water to a dry sponge

e. Chemical changes—combining ingredients such as vinegar and soda changes their size; combining the ingredients to make Styrofoam causes a chemical reaction in which the material foams up and becomes much larger in size. (These ingredients can be purchased from a place where boats are built)

f. Cutting—changes the sizes of materials and items

g. Temperature—freezing water expands

h. Bending or folding

i. Instruments—microscopes, magnifying glasses, and binoculars all change the sizes of items

Activities and Experiences

1. Have the children seriate Styrofoam balls from smallest to largest, or match duplicate sizes.

2. Put rods or dowels in matched pairs into containers; the child relies on the sense of touch to match two that are the same size.

3. Use materials such as buttons, gummed stars, lids, beads, feathers, and nails as sensory media, as collage material, or to seriate in order of size. Also, have the children make size comparisons between two or more of the objects.

4. Have the children seriate cans or boxes from smallest to largest by placing them inside one another.

5. Have the children seriate or match washers in graduated sizes.

6. Cut geometric shapes in seriated sizes out of wood, felt, or cardboard. Cut two of each size for matching pairs; use one of each size for ordering size.

7. Have the children seriate metal or plastic rings from smallest to largest, or match duplicate sizes.

8. Put lima bean seeds or similar seeds on a glass slab, on a piece of cotton, each day. After several days, the changes in size are evident. The seeds can also be put in a

A magnifying glass increases both the size of an object and the children's curiosity!

glass between a paper towel and the outside of the glass; moisture is maintained by means of a continually dampened sponge in the center of the glass.

9. Use felt geometric or object shapes such as animals. Although they are of different shapes, colors, or sizes, challenge the children to group them by size. For example, if the children are working with shapes, have them find all the different geometric shapes that are the same size.

10. Give the children clay or playdough and have them roll balls of various sizes; then seriate these balls according to size.

11. Encourage the children to make size comparisons of things in their environment.

12. Measure each child periodically, and compare the changes in size.

13. Compare the hand and foot sizes of the children. For older children you may wish to make actual measurements, and they will enjoy making the size comparisons.

14. Using the same geometric shape, cut pairs of matching sizes and then put several matching pairs together into a "feely box" or sack. The children identify matching pairs through the sense of touch.

15. Observe pieces of fine art (in books, calendars, postcards, galleries, etc.) and have the children compare them in terms of sizes and seriations in their lines, shapes, and spaces (Feeney & Moravcik, 1987).

16. "Fill a shopping bag with pairs of objects, with pair members similar to one another except for size" (Stone, 1987, p. 18). The bag is emptied, and the children match and sort pairs of one big and one little object.

17. Supply greeting cards and envelopes that are all mixed together; then have the children match the cards to the correctly sized envelopes (Stone, 1987). A similar activity uses boxes and lids.

18. Cut and compare various paper tubes (from toilet paper, paper towels, gift wrapping paper) for matching like sizes or seriating (Stone, 1987).

19. Divide children into cooperative groups and give each group an orange. Using a string, measure the circumference of the orange. Each group determines how long its string is in inches and centimeters. On the chalkboard or chart paper, each group graphs its results. Comparisons are made. Each group then takes its string and finds at least three objects in the room that are the same measurement as the string or the same size as the circumference of the orange (Adapted from Misifi, 1993).

UNIT PLAN ON SIZE AND SERIATION

Field Trips

- Sports store—observe balls of various sizes
- Clothing store—clothing too large and too small for children; clothing to fit parent(s)
- Grocery store—different items of the same size; the same items in various sizes
- Cycle shop—cycles of different sizes
- Carpenter shop—drill bits, pieces of wood, nails, and screws in various sizes
- Tire store—tires and inner tubes of various sizes
- Bakery—observe process of bread baking
- Greenhouse—many kinds of plants in different stages (sizes) of growth
- Shoe store
- Art gallery

Visitors

- Mother and baby
- Grocer with canned goods of various sizes
- Baker to make doughnuts
- Service station attendant to fix an inner tube
- Teenager to inflate tires on bicycle
- Sports store clerk—seriation of balls (golf, baseball, softball, volleyball, basketball)
- Scientist with microscope or magnifying glass
- Carpenter with saw and boards
- Two grandfathers of different sizes

- Clothing store clerk with some clothes too small, some just right, and some too large for the children

Science

- Planting seeds—compare growing seeds and plants with the size of the original seeds
- Mixing vinegar and soda together
- Two similar sponges—allow one to become saturated with water and then compare the sizes of the two sponges
- Drawing a line on a clear bottle—fill to the line with colored water; let freeze; observe level of ice, and then let thaw and observe as the liquid returns to the original mark
- Planting young tree—caring for it and watching its growth over an extended period of time
- Lighting a candle—observing the change in size (have two candles originally, so that the lighted candle can be compared to the unlighted one)

Food

- Bread—mix and bake, cool, eat
- Raised doughnuts
- Hamburgers
- Marshmallow squares (butter and marshmallows change size as they melt)
- Popcorn
- Cookies
- Ice cream (size changes in ice, salt, and amount of ice-cream mixture)
- Whipped cream or egg whites
- Egg soufflé
- Rice, spaghetti, or macaroni dish
- Snapping spaghetti into various lengths prior to cooking
- Vienna sausages and wieners
- Cake
- Hotcakes cooked in various sizes

Art

- Collage with paper circles of various sizes, either of the same color or of different colors
- Button collage—buttons of many sizes pasted on Styrofoam trays
- Various lengths of straws, cut and strung

- Papier-mâché applied to an inflated balloon and allowed to dry; the balloon is then popped and the resulting ball is decorated
- Box sculpture—boxes of various sizes pasted together, allowed to dry, and then decorated
- Clay modeling of balls or ropes
- Smallest to largest pictures—draw pictures of objects, ordering them from smallest to largest; or pictures of animals, comparing small animals to larger or largest animals

Music

- Creative movements—of a child or seed growing, bread or cake baking, ice cube or icicle melting, balloon being inflated and popped, sponge absorbing water, vinegar and soda being mixed
- Music shakers—of varying sizes or of the same size, containing unlike sizes of materials (sand, berries, rocks, wheat, rice)
- Small musical instrument (such as a harmonica) compared to larger musical instrument (such as an accordion)
- Similar musical instruments of varying sizes (violin, cello, bass violin)

Literacy

- Write stories titled "As Big as . . . ," "As Small as . . . ," "As Tall as . . . ," or use other size words as similes

LESSON PLAN ON SIZE (5-DAY)

Overall Goals

- To study the behaviors and needs of the children so that goals can be established for them.
- To teach and expand concepts of size so that by the end of the unit each child will be able to:

1. Say which objects are larger and which objects are smaller when making comparisons.
2. Say and understand how size changes (perspective, cooking, melting, chemical changes, stretching, growing, and putting media into different-sized containers).
3. Name single items that come in different

sizes, such as macaroni, buttons, children, trees, buildings, and cars.

Note: During the unit, make toys and equipment available that reinforce the concept of size. Place dolls of different sizes in the housekeeping area, as well as many manipulative toys, to reinforce concepts of size. Give children experience in seriating objects according to their size.

Day 1

Whole-Group Activity

Introduction to Size. Use pictures and objects to encourage the children to make comparisons of size. Provide ladders of various heights, as well as single items that come in different sizes (such as milk cartons.)

Objectives

- To introduce the phrases *larger than* and *smaller than*, enabling each child to name things that are both smaller than and larger than the child.
- To have the children become aware that size is relative; we compare one object in relation to another, and what is small in one comparison may be larger in another comparison.
- To enable each child to see that the same item can come in different sizes.

Small-Group Activity

Art—Button Collages. Have the children paste buttons of different sizes on meat trays.

Objectives

- To have the children make size comparisons using buttons.
- To reinforce the discussion of the concept that the same item may come in different sizes.
- To give and receive feedback on the concepts brought out in our introduction on size.

Individual Activity

- Painting at the single easel, one color on each side

Day 2

Whole-Group Activity

Science—Things Change in Size. Lead the children in several experiments to demonstrate change in size: (1) Use two cups with equal amounts of sand. Pour one first into a large, shallow container and then back into the cup. Then pour it from the cup into a taller, thinner container and then back into the cup. (2) Blow up a balloon. (3) Stretch an elastic band. (4) Watch an ice cube melt.

Objectives

- To teach some ways that things can change in size—changing the size of the container, filling it with air, stretching, melting.
- To allow opportunities for thinking and problem solving.
- To give the children the opportunity to perform some of the experiments on their own after the whole-group experience.

Small-Group Activity

Field Trip to a Tall Building. Take the children on a walk to a tall building. On the way, notice such things as the size of a specific tree and a specific car, and then make comparisons of the change in size as these same objects are viewed from the ninth floor of the tall building.

Objectives

- To teach the concept that size stays the same even though it appears to change with distance.
- To give the children the experience of riding on an elevator.
- To have the children, in their groups, make comparisons of size along the way. For example, they might compare the sizes of cars, buildings, trees, and people.

Individual Activities

- Ice cubes in the trough

Pasting Different Sizes on a Square Mural. Provide squares that are the same color and the same shape, but of different sizes. (This activity will be continued on day 4.)

Objectives

- To encourage verbal comparisons of the sizes of squares.
- To give the children more opportunities to develop skill in handling the brush and paste.

Day 3

Whole-Group Activity

Visitor—Musician. Ask the visitor to bring in instruments that are in the same family but of different sizes (flute, saxophone, clarinet).

Objective

- To acquaint the children with two or three different musical instruments within the same family, and then to compare the differences in the sizes and sounds of the instruments.

Small-Group Activity

Make and Decorate Shakers. In the whole group, lead a discussion on the concept that the same items may come in different sizes. After dividing the class into smaller groups, have each group make a shaker of a different size. The group making the largest shaker will use the largest media (beans or macaroni), the group making the next-largest shaker will use the next-largest media, and so on. After small amounts of the media are put into the shaker, the outside of the shaker can be decorated with the media (using media of the same size on the outside and the inside).

Objectives

- To provide opportunities for making size comparisons, teaching and reinforcing the concept that the same items (shakers, as well as beans or macaroni) come in different sizes.
- To make a shaker that will be used in a music experience the next day.

Individual Activities

- Stringing beads of different sizes

Mirrors at Different Heights. Place mirrors at three different levels so that the children will have to position themselves at different levels to see themselves. Hang one mirror very low, one at about the children's level, and one high so that they will have to climb the stairs to reach it.

Objectives

- To enable each child to discriminate tallest and shortest.
- To have the children tell what they did to become taller and what they did to become shorter.
- To provide an opportunity for the children to see themselves and to develop positive self-images.

Day 4

Whole-Group Activity

Music—Rhythm Experience with Different-Sized Shakers. Record some of the songs that are familiar to the children, recording the same song in a slower tempo and a faster tempo so that there will be a variation in rhythm and tempo when the shakers are used.

Objectives

- To reinforce the concept that the same item comes in different sizes.
- To have the children match their shakers to shakers of the same size and sound.
- To give them an experience with basic rhythm and to notice which children are able to shake particular rhythms and tempos.

Small-Group Activity

Food—Whole-Wheat Muffins. In two groups, have the children mix the batter for the muffins and then divide it into cupcake papers. After baking the muffins, divide the children into four small groups to butter and eat them.

Objectives

- To have each child compare the size of the batter before and after baking and to tell what has caused change in size (heat).
- To help each child develop skill in measuring, beating, stirring, and spreading, using utensils such as spoons, knives, and beaters.

Individual Activities

- Stacking cones in the trough
- Pasting squares of different sizes on a square mural (continued from day 2)

Day 5

Whole-Group Activities

Science—Things Change in Size. Review the concept taught on day 2, but use new experiments.

Objectives

- To teach the concept that living things (such as themselves) change size by growing.

Determining the correct ordering of wooden dowels from shortest to tallest is not always an easy task—neither is balancing a dowel on its end.

- To encourage the children to compare their size with that of a baby and with that of the teacher.
- To teach that things change size when two ingredients are mixed together.
- To have the children see and understand that even though many of them are about the same age, they are still of different sizes. (Have them respond to the question "Are you all the same size?")

Pouring Juice into Different-Sized Glasses. Use the same amount of juice, but pour it into glasses of four different sizes.

Objective

- To reinforce the science experience on day 2, showing that we change the size of some things (but not the amount) by pouring the same amount into different-sized containers.

Small-Group Activity

Art—Collages. On the rug, demonstrate how to make collages to the whole group. After dividing the children into small groups, have them use two or three different items (such as pieces of straws, circles, or feathers) and then various sizes of these items, pasting them on pieces of cardboard.

Objectives

- To reinforce the concepts studied and to obtain feedback regarding these concepts.
- To give children who are ready the experience of seriating by size a number of objects that are the same item but of different sizes.

Individual Activities

- Use of paper, brushes, and containers of different sizes at an easel
- Measurement of each child for size comparisons

Summary

Size and seriation involve both making comparisons between two or more objects of different sizes and ordering items from the smallest to the largest. Size is relative; the size of an object depends on the size of another object with which it is being compared. In teaching size and seriation, provide children with many opportunities for practicing size comparisons, seriating objects, and hearing related vocabulary words.

Student Learning Activities

1. Visit a preschool, kindergarten, first-grade or second-grade classroom. Just from the equipment and materials in the environment, list the opportunities you see for teaching size and seriation. For example, you may see unit blocks of various sizes that could be compared on the basis of size or even seriated according to size.

2. Near the beginning of this chapter are listed words dealing with size comparisons with which children 2 to 8 years of age could become familiar. Brainstorm and add to this list.

3. Visit a store or a school supply house, or study an equipment catalog selling toys and learning materials that focus on size. Describe and evaluate them for their effectiveness in teaching size concepts. If they are multicolored, would they be more effective if the color were kept constant?

4. With a group of children, implement at least one of the activities and experiences related to size and seriation suggested in this chapter. The children may be a classroom group or simply a small group of relatives or neighborhood children. Did the children enjoy the experience? What did they learn about size and/or seriation? Evaluate your experience.

5. Now plan, create, and write down an activity for teaching size or seriation to children.

6. Prepare at least one teacher-made material or piece of equipment to teach size and/or seriation to children 2 to 8 years of age. (Refer to ideas in this chapter and Appendix A for suggestions.)

7. Think of additional ideas for the unit plan on size.

8. Visit a children's library and add at least two additional excellent children's books to the resource list for teaching size to children 2 to 8 years of age.

9. Complete a 5-day activity plan for teaching size to young children. Model your format after the lesson plan format given in the chapter.

Suggested Resources

Children's Books

Anderson, L. C. (1983). *The wonderful shrinking shirt.* Niles, IL: Whitman.

Barton, B. (1981). *Building a house.* New York: Greenwillow.

Berkley, E. (1950). *Big and little, up and down.* Reading, MA: Addison-Wesley.

Brenner, B. (1966). *Mr. Tall and Mr. Small.* Menlo Park, CA: Addison-Wesley.

Hoban, T. (1985). *Is it large, is it small?* New York: Greenwillow.

Holl, A., & Reit, S. (1970). *Learning about size.* Indianapolis: Bobbs-Merrill.

Kohn, B. (1971). *Everything has a shape and everything has a size.* Englewood Cliffs, NJ: Prentice-Hall.

Krasilvsky, P. (1952). *The very little girl.* New York: Doubleday.

Krasilvsky, P. (1962). *The very little boy.* New York: Doubleday.

Krauss, R. (1947). *The growing story.* New York: Harper & Brothers.

Lenski, L. (1959). *Cowboy Small.* New York: Henry Z. Walck.

Lenski, L. (1979). *Big book of Mr. Small.* New York: McKay.

Lenski, L. (1979). *More Mr. Small.* New York: McKay.

Lionni, L. (1968). *Biggest house in the world.* New York: Pantheon.

McMillan, B. (1986). *Becca backward, Becca frontward: A book of concept pairs.* New York: Lothrop, Lee & Shepard.

Russo, M. (1986). *The line up book.* New York: Greenwillow.

Spier, P. (1972). *Fast-slow, high-low.* Garden City, NY: Doubleday.

Ward, L. (1952). *The biggest bear.* Boston: Houghton Mifflin.

Films, Filmstrips, and Videos

Big and small. Coronet Films.

Size. Eye Gate Media.

Size: Smaller than large and larger than small. Eye Gate Media.

Computer Software (size)

Observation and classification. Hartley Courseware. (Apple).

CHAPTER
nineteen

Shape and Form

Introduction

As early as 3 weeks of age, children begin to distinguish patterns of shape and form. Color is an important aid for identifying shape, but it is also possible that the form or shape of almost any object—for instance, a chair or a table—is more significant than its color.

By the age of 5 or 6 years, children can differentiate geometric shapes—squares, triangles, and circles. Concepts and understandings are formed from observation and manipulation, rather than by mere definition.

Shape and form are important concepts to teach for a number of reasons. Children are interested in the shapes of things—objects in their environments, the shape of their bodies, the shapes they can make with their bodies, and geometric shapes. They also learn early that most things have a shape, and that the shape of something helps to determine what it is or how it is different from other objects in the same category. One of the most important reasons for teaching

the perceptual awareness of shapes and noticing fine differences in shapes is that a child's reading readiness will depend in part on visual perception of shape and form. Wide exposure to shapes and forms in the environment can also be enhanced through fine art, which involves more than geometric shapes and combines both regular and irregular shapes (Feeney & Moravcik, 1987).

If a child has been taught to notice differences and to look for differences in the shapes and forms of things, he or she will be more able to read and master other academic skills. For example, in math a child must recognize the differences between the numerals 9 and 6 and learn the correct forms of other numerals in order to recognize them and comprehend their meanings. Work and study on shape and form transfer to other areas and assist the child in progressing in academic studies.

Objects are identified by shape or form, and the recognition of various forms depends on previous visual experiences with the objects. The shapes illustrated in Figure 19-1 symbolize a con-

468

Shape sorting boxes take only half as long to fill when two friends cooperate to complete the task.

cept or organized thought, even though verbal labels have not been ascribed to them. When the shape is observed, it is recognized and identified as having a particular meaning.

Most things have a shape, but it must be remembered that liquids and gases assume the shapes of their boundaries or containers. In teaching shape and form, it is also important to include shapes in addition to the common geometric shapes of a circle, triangle, rectangle, and square. Since shapes aid in or are sources of identification, limiting instruction to the basic shapes excludes from the learning environment the important aspects of recognition of shapes in general.

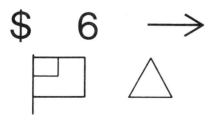

FIGURE 19–1
Examples of Shapes That Symbolize Concepts

Before uncommon shapes are taught, more familiar ones must be assimilated and understood. Recognition of unfamiliar shapes depends on previous shape identification and recognition. Based on an understanding of simple shapes, the child is able to build more complex structures.

The children were on a field trip observing shapes, and the teacher inquired about the shape of the window in the back of the bus. (The window was rectangular, with rounded corners.) After thinking for a moment, Eric replied, "It isn't a rectangle, because it doesn't have any sharps!"

As with the teaching of any ideas, shapes must be found in numerous ways in the child's environment, with many opportunities for manipulation and problem solving involving objects of various shapes (Maxim, 1989). Williams and Kamii (1986) remind us, however, that the mental action that is encouraged when children act on objects is more important to learning than the actual manipulation of objects.

Words defining shapes should be used often, and words that are usually relied on, such as *that*, *there*, and *it*, must be accompanied by more detail. Everyday language should include such statements as "That is a square box" rather than

"That is square"; "The clock is round" rather than "This is round"; and "Put the book on the red, square table" rather than "Put it over there." From such sentences, both the object and its characteristic shape become separate and unique ideas. Later on, more dimensions such as color, size, texture, and number may be added.

When unfamiliar shapes are introduced, a review of already familiar shapes should precede the introduction. Then the children's thinking can be stimulated with such statements as "How is this new shape the same as . . . ?" or "How is this new shape not the same as (or different from) . . . ?" Comparisons provide reinforcement and review of shapes already learned. Leeper, Dales, Skipper, and Witherspoon (1984) indicate that children need many experiences with shapes and with making comparisons between shapes before focusing on naming shapes. Too often we begin with naming shapes. This is also true of letters: Children need experiences and opportunities to observe and compare before learning the names of the letters.

To learn about shapes, children need to play with them—through games, toys, art activities, songs, poems, and stories (Beaty, 1992a). Developmentally appropriate (Bredekamp, 1986) literature, materials, experiences, games, and toys—selected carefully and deliberately—stimulate and increase a child's ability to perceive shapes and forms in the environment. Sutherland and Arbuthnot (1986) stress the importance of children's literature in enhancing the learning of prenumber concepts in the early years. The more difficult abstract concepts to grasp, such as "time, distance, size, mass, color, [and] shape . . . need to be clarified and amplified in books as well as in conversation" (Sutherland & Arbuthnot, 1986, p. 99) and activities.

Approach to Teaching

Concepts and Ideas for Teaching

1. Most things have a shape, and we tell what they are by their shape.

2. Some objects are geometric shapes—circle, square, triangle, and rectangle. (Add the pentagon, octagon, hexagon, rhombus, ellipse, and other names of specific geometric shapes for older children.) Three-dimensional geometric shapes include the sphere, cone, and cylinder.

3. The same items or objects may be found in different shapes.

a. Flowers	h. Tents
b. Hats	i. Houses
c. People	j. Statues
d. Dogs	k. Chairs
e. Boxes	l. Pasta
f. Automobiles	m. Telephones
g. Shoes	n. Clocks

4. The same shapes may be found in different objects.

   a. Circle found in a clock, marble, orange, basketball, coin, plate

   b. Square found in books, fabric patterns, checkerboard, blocks

   c. Triangle found in tents, houses, bridges, musical instruments, highway signs

5. The same shapes may be found in different sizes.

a. Circles	g. Books
b. Suitcases	h. Cans
c. Crayons	i. Balls
d. Shoes	j. Greeting cards
e. Apples	k. Pizza
f. Picture frames	l. Fish

6. Shape can be modified.

   a. Growth and aging—shape of a seed compared to that of a plant; a baby compared to an adult.

   b. Movement—various shapes are achieved by moving various parts of the body or by changing elastic or rope boundaries

   c. Pressure—applied to a tomato, egg, drying mud, wet cement, rough wood, or inflated balloon alters the original shape

d. Temperature changes (heating and freezing)—shapes are changed by turning solids into liquids, as well as some liquids into solids

e. Cutting, crumbling, crushing, bending, folding—not only change the original shape but also may create identifiable new shapes

f. Natural changes in nature—wind, water, and so on

g. Pouring—liquids take the shape of the containers into which they are poured

7. One shape, by adding different dimensions, becomes another shape; for example, combining a triangle and a circle results in a face with a hat or an ice-cream cone.

Activities and Experiences

1. *Shape identification.* Circulate containers of objects to be identified by shape; the child feels the shape within the container and then reports the item felt.

2. *Silhouette identification.* Display outlines of various shapes (simple shapes such as an umbrella, shoe, chair, fish; more complex shapes such as different shapes of shoes, animals, flowers—depending on the age level) for the children to identify.

3. *Shape collage.* Paste variously shaped pieces of paper on a background. Then distribute matching shapes that have been cut smaller than the background shape to the children. As the shape is matched, it is pasted on the background.

4. *Shape bulletin board.* Attach shapes to the bulletin board, with a small container affixed below each shape. The children match loose identical shapes with those on the board and then drop them into the containers.

5. *Sensory exploration.* Put objects of various shapes (of the same category or a different category) in a trough or similar container so the children can feel and see the various

shapes. For instance, objects with circle shapes could include a ball, marble, coin, magnifying glass, and others.

6. *Shape twister.* Attach shape silhouettes to the floor. Instruct the children to place their right hand on the triangle, their left foot on the square, and so on.

7. *Pegboard shapes.* Supply the children with pegboards, pegs, or geoboards and elastics. By stretching the elastic around various patterns of pegs, the children can form shapes. To make a geoboard, sand and finish a board 8 inches × 8 inches × 1 inch. Pound nails at equal intervals using five rows of five nails each and leaving about one-half-inch space between the board and the head of the nail. (Since older children can draw shapes on paper, provide them with pencils and paper on which dots have been placed or drawn. Then they may draw shapes by connecting the dots.)

8. *Shape dominoes.* Make a set of 28, which involves seven different shapes, each domino having two shapes. When the game is played, matching shapes are placed in adjacent positions.

9. *Shape classification.* Cut various shapes (geometric and/or objects) in different colors and sizes from felt. The children classify or sort the items according to shape (i.e., all the squares together, all the rabbits together).

10. *Copying shapes.* The 2-year-olds, 3-year-olds, and young 4-year-olds may have difficulty in copying even shapes such as circles and squares. Most 5-year-olds can begin to copy some shapes. Making a perfect copy will be difficult and challenging, yet enjoyable, for many. By the time children are 6 to 8 years of age, they can copy many-sided geometric shapes and unusual shapes. One way to encourage copying shapes is to draw a particular shape on a series of evenly spaced dots and then, next to this, provide a similar series of dots on which the children can copy the shape.

Small-diameter sticks of various lengths can be placed on top of corresponding lines on basic geometric shapes.

11. Provide graph paper, and encourage the children to draw a variety of shapes in a variety of sizes.

12. *Shape folding.* Give each child either a square or rectangular piece of paper (not construction or heavy paper), and challenge the child to fold it into various shapes. Even very young children can do this activity with a square paper napkin, folding it in half to form a rectangle or folding the opposite corners together to form a triangle.

13. *Tearing shapes.* Have the children tear each shape as it is named and use the shapes on a shape collage.

14. Supply magazines for the children to go through and find objects with obvious geometric shapes. The children can cut these pictures out and make a shape book with a page or pages for each shape.

15. Make an unfinished row of patterns of shapes (e.g., one circle, two triangles, one rectangle; one circle, two triangles, one rectangle). Leave space for the children to complete the pattern at least one more time.

16. On 3 × 5-inch cards, draw two to five shapes, either all alike or with one or two different. The children sort these cards into two piles; the shapes on the card are either the same or different.

17. *Tracing shapes.* Provide shape-sorting toys, three-dimensional shapes of animals or other things, or cookie cutters for the children to use for tracing shapes.

18. "The shape of a particular fruit can be used to explore the movement of round objects" (Smith, 1987, p. 38). For example, as a round fruit (e.g., an apple) is rolled across various surfaces, it can be compared with the way other fruits (e.g., a banana or pear) roll. Encourage the children to find other objects that roll like the apple (Smith, 1987).

19. Make individual puzzles by cutting out shapes (triangle, square, circle, etc.) from the front panels of cereal boxes, leaving the four side borders intact. Store these puzzle pieces in sealable plastic bags (Stone, 1987).

20. Prior to cooking pasta for a food activity, mix uncooked pasta of various shapes

(shell, elbow, twist) in a bowl. Then have the children sort these into separate bowls. The pasta is later cooked, and the shapes of the cooked pasta are identified and compared. Various shapes of Styrofoam packing pieces can also be used for shape and form sorting and identification (Stone, 1987).

21. Assign the children to cooperative learning groups, and give each group a one-page sheet with various geometric shapes drawn on it. The children in each group are to cut out their shapes and glue them on one picture that they work on as a group.

UNIT PLAN ON SHAPE

Field Trips

- Bakery
- Farm
- Shape walk
- Furniture store
- Meat market
- Clothing store
- Shoe store
- Hat store
- Music department
- Bus ride
- Construction site
- Art gallery

Art

- Sponge printing (geometric or other shapes)
- Shape collage
- Easel paper cut in various shapes
- Box sculpturing
- Tracing around objects similar in shape
- Candles from sand molds
- Clay molding
- Different-shaped buttons in a collage
- Shakers of various shapes
- Marshmallow sculpture
- Circle or other shape drawings: Draw several circles on a sheet of paper, and have the children make something different with each one
- Various cut-out shapes can be put into patterns or be used to make figures

Music

- Twister with shapes, using music
- Playing instruments of varied shapes
- Comparison of sounds from instruments of various shapes
- Musical shapes (pass shapes around; identify or describe them when the music stops)
- Different ways we can shape our own bodies
- Ways of moving around shapes or a particular shape

Food

- Variously shaped crackers with juice
- Shaped sandwiches
- Napkins folded in shapes
- Honey candy or taffy pull
- Cakes baked or decorated in different shapes
- Rolled, shaped cookies
- Boiled, fried, or scrambled eggs
- Gelatin in molds
- Popcorn
- Bread, molded and then baked
- Hotcakes cooked in various shapes
- Various shapes of pasta—uncooked and cooked

Visitors

- Carpenter
- Glassblower
- Person from hat store
- Person from shoe store
- Highway flag signaler or police officer
- Artist
- Flower arranger
- Family (comparison of body shapes)
- Parent to make cookie or bread shapes
- Pizza expert
- Wood carver
- Leather tooler

Science

- Shape changed by cutting, crumbling, etc.
- Shape changed by adding yeast
- Demonstration of erosion
- Water, air—take shape of containers
- Balloon experiments
- Making of Styrofoam
- Observation of snake after feeding time
- Crushing, then releasing of plastic
- Identification of objects from cut silhouettes

- Matching of shapes by feeling
- Bubble blowing (½ cup liquid dishwashing detergent and ¼ cup sugar or 8 oz liquid detergent and 1 oz glycerin. Either recipe can be diluted with a small amount of water, if necessary)

Literacy

- Make a booklet composed of pictures of various shapes. Add sentences created by the children (written by the children or teacher, depending on the children's writing ability). Even the booklet pages can be cut into shapes; either each page is different, or all pages within the booklet match.

LESSON PLAN ON SHAPE (5-DAY)

Overall Goals

- To develop a better understanding and a clearer perception of the shapes in the surrounding environment, especially the circle, square, and triangle.

- To show that the circle, square, and triangle are basic shapes and that many other objects have the same basic shape.
- To provide creative experiences for the children with these three shapes.
- To teach the concept that the same object may have different shapes, and that the same shape may be found in different objects.

Day 1

Whole-Group Activities

Introduction of the Circle, Square, and Triangle. Place a circle, square, and triangle on a flannel board. Then discuss what the shapes are and how they are the same and different. Give each child the opportunity to name the shapes and tell what else has the same shape. For example: "What else has the same shape as this circle?" Show familiar objects and pass them around so that each child has one. Underneath the shapes on the flannel board place boxes, each with a shape on it. Ask the children to bring up their object

As the teacher shows a shape, the children match it to the corresponding shape on their individual lotto boards.

and place it in the box that has the same shape as their object.

Objectives

- To introduce the children to the shapes of the circle, square, and triangle.
- To develop the concept that objects can be found in these three basic shapes; different objects can have the same shape.
- To develop language experience through talking about shape.

Music—Pass Around Shapes to Music. Have the children stand in a circle, and pass around a circle, square, and triangle to music. When the music stops, the three children with the shapes call out the name of the shape they have. Then every child is given one of the three shapes, which are passed around the circle to music. When the music stops, those with the circles hold up their shape. Next, the children with the squares, and then the children with the triangles, hold up their shape.

Objectives

- To reinforce the discrimination of the three shapes.
- To provide the children with a musical experience with these three shapes.
- To develop the children's auditory acuity.

Small-Group Activities

Cutting, Painting, and Hanging the Shapes of a Circle, Square, and Triangle. Give each child scissors and a piece of construction paper on which a circle, square, and triangle have already been drawn. Then have the children cut out the shapes and paint on them with finger paints that have already been mixed. Afterward they will place their three shapes on the walls around the room.

Objectives

- To provide the children with the experience of making their own circle, square, and triangle.
- To provide a continuous opportunity to see the shapes on the wall during the unit.

- To show how the three different shapes may have different colors, and that something may be red, for example, and still be a circle.

Food—Crackers with Soup. Serve noodle soup to the children. While they are waiting for the soup to be served, ask the children to fold their napkins into one of the three shapes that were discussed. Place baskets on the tables with round, square, and triangle crackers. Encourage the children to try each of the crackers and to talk about the shape of each while eating their soup. Ask them such questions as "What cracker has the same shape as the noodles in the soup?" and "How are the crackers the same and how are they different?"

Objectives

- To provide an opportunity for the children to talk about shape and to compare the same and different shapes.
- To show the children that the same object has three different shapes and that different items have the same shape.
- To provide the children with a creative experience with napkins and show them how they can fold paper to make different shapes.

Individual Activity

- Square blocks of various sizes for individual play

Day 2

Whole-Group Activity

Visitor—Carpenter. Ask a carpenter to visit and bring tools and the materials needed to build a birdhouse. While building the birdhouse for the children, the visitor discusses the circle, square, and triangle and shows how these three shapes can be used in making a birdhouse. Give the children the opportunity to ask questions, feel the wood and materials, and even help pound in the nails. Ask the children how the birdhouse is the same as or different from their own house. Tell them that the birdhouse will provide a place for the birds to obtain food and shelter. After the carpenter is finished, put birdseed into the house, and hang it outside.

Objective

- To teach the concept that the three basic shapes can be combined to make a birdhouse.

Small-Group Activity

Art—Making Houses with Construction Paper. Divide the children, into small groups, and give them a large piece of construction paper. Put paste and different-sized circles, squares, and triangles on the table. Instruct the children to paste the three shapes on the paper so that they construct a house. Tell them that they can use the square for the main part of the house, the triangle for the roof of the house, and the circles for the smoke coming out of the chimney—or they can make the house any way they want.

Objectives

- To reinforce the idea that certain objects have certain shapes.
- To provide the children with the opportunity to recognize and work with the circle, square, and triangle.
- To give the children the opportunity to compare the work they do with the work of the carpenter.

Individual Activity

Shape Box. A shape box is a box with two holes in each end so that the children can put their hands into it and yet not be able to see what is inside. Place two circle shapes, two square shapes, and two triangle shapes in the box. The children will find two shapes that are alike by reaching into the box and feeling the shapes. When they think that they have the two shapes, they bring them out and see whether they are right.

Objective

- To learn to discriminate shape through the sense of touch.

Day 3
Small-Group Activities

Shape Walk. Place all the children in small groups, with a teacher leading each group. During a 20-minute walk around the area, they will search for the shapes they have learned about thus far in the unit. Ask questions such as "What do you see that is the same shape as the circle?" and "Can you find something else that is the same shape as the square?" Have the children gather small objects to take back to the classroom—leaves, rocks, pop-bottle caps, paper, candy wrappers, and others—objects that are circles, squares, or triangles. Collect the objects for use later on in the unit in making a three-dimensional collage.

Objectives

- To provide the opportunity for shape searching.
- To reinforce the concept that different objects have the same shape.
- To allow the children to become familiar with the idea that shapes are continually around them.
- To reinforce the concept that many objects can be made by combining shapes.

Science—Balloons and Shapes. Place balloons of different sizes and shapes in small groups on the tables. Talk about the balloons and their shapes with the children. Talk about air and tell the children that air will change the shape of the balloon. Have the children blow up the balloons if they can and notice the difference in the shape. If they cannot, blow up the balloon for them and compare the two shapes before and afterward.

Objective

- To teach the concept that air changes the shapes of items.

Food—Cut-Cheese Sandwiches. Place the children in small groups, and give them a knife, two slices of bread, and a piece of individually wrapped cheese. Have them cut the bread into either triangles or squares and then cut the cheese to match the bread. Serve juice with round ice cubes in it, and tell the children to observe the changes in shape as the ice cubes melt.

Objectives

- To reinforce the concept that cutting can change the shape of objects.
- To develop the concept that ice changes shape as it melts.
- To show how common objects are made into different shapes.

Individual Activity

- Domino cards with three shapes

Day 4

Whole-Group Activities

Music—Musical Mix-Up with Shape. Tape large plastic circles, squares, and triangles to the floor. Make these shapes out of plastic that is the same color and that can be bought in rolls. Have three children stand on three different shapes and move around to other shapes while the music is playing. As the music stops, a spinner with the three shapes on it is spun. The child who is standing on that shape when the spinner stops must leave the game. This continues until there is a winner. (This game could also be played without the elimination procedure.)

Objectives

- To provide a game experience with shapes.
- To reinforce shape discrimination.

Visitor—Baker. Have a baker visit the class and show how an elephant can be made out of square and round cakes. The cakes will already be made and ready for cutting. The baker will bring the necessary materials for cutting the cakes and will show the children how an elephant can be made just by cutting the square and round cakes in the right places and putting the pieces together the right way. The baker will also bring in other pastries that are in the shape of a circle, square, or triangle. The children will be given the opportunity to taste these items.

Objectives

- To reinforce the concept that shape changes by cutting.
- To reinforce the concept that objects may consist of combinations of many shapes.

Small-Group Activity

Food—Icing the Elephant Cake. While the children are tasting the pastries that the baker brought, let part of the group ice the cake that has already been made. Give each group an opportunity to ice part of the cake. Provide icing of different colors, and let the children put the icing on in any way they want. Serve the cake on round, square, and triangular plates (shapes cut from the middle of the standard round paper plates, previously prepared by the teachers).

Objectives

- To reinforce the concept that shape changes by cutting.
- To show how the same object (paper plates) can have three different shapes.

Day 5

Whole-Group Activities

Visitor—Parent of One of the Children. Ask one of the parents to bring in a homemade quilt and show the children the pieces of the quilt. They will see that each piece is separate and that the pieces are sewn together to make the quilt. Give the children the opportunity to find the matching pieces on the quilt. Follow this with a discussion about shapes and which shapes are used for the various parts of the quilt.

Objectives

- To reinforce the concept that small shapes can make up one large object.
- To provide an opportunity for matching like shapes and patterns.

Music—Shape Band. Give each child either a triangle, a bell, a pair of blocks, or a tambourine. Lead a discussion about these instruments, and let the children hear how each sounds. Put a tape on, and have the children play their instruments to the music. Each instrument is played individually, and then the whole band plays. The children then march around the room, playing their instruments.

Objectives

- To provide the opportunity for the children to see how instruments are made of these three shapes.
- To provide a musical experience with shape.

Art—Three-Dimensional Collage. Give each child a medium-sized piece of cardboard. On the table provide three-dimensional pieces of Styrofoam cubes, fabric, and all the things that were collected on the shape walk. Ask each child to make a shape collage, pasting the objects on the cardboard. After the paste has dried, the collage can be taken home. During this time, the children discuss the shapes and what things are the same shape.

Objectives

- To provide review and reinforcement of the shapes studied.
- To give the children an opportunity to use the shapes gathered on the shape walk.

Note: The following poem on shape will be used in various ways throughout the lesson plan.

The shape of it*
by Ruth Lundgren

Everything we see has a shape.
  A cat has a shape,
  And so has a dog,
  A rat and a bird,
  A cow and a hog.
Everything we see has a shape.
  A house and a garage,
  An apple and a grape,
  A bed and a chair,
  A bear and an ape.
Even if an ape came in different colors, he would still
  have the shape of an ape.
Shapes tell us what things are.
When we see this shape, we know it is an elephant.
When we see this shape, we know it is a car.
When we see this shape, we know it is a hammer.
And when we see this shape, we know it is a kite.
Shapes change shape.
  A balloon can change.
  An umbrella can change.
Even a boy can change shape.
Some things come in many shapes.
  Dogs come in many shapes.
  Flowers come in many shapes.
  Clouds come in many shapes.
  Cookies come in many shapes.
But everything we see has a shape.
  An ape has a shape,
  And so has a bee,
  A beetle, an ant,
  And even a tree.
Please look all around you.
What shape do you see?

* Used by permission of the editors of *The Friend,* published by The Church of Jesus Christ of Latter-Day Saints.

Summary

Even in their first few months of life, children are able to distinguish shapes. While they are relatively young, they also demonstrate interest in the various shapes in their environment. Familiar and common shapes should be discussed and taught before more unfamiliar and uncommon shapes are introduced. Not only are objects identified by shape, but the recognition and perception of shapes are basic ingredients in reading readiness. Children should have numerous experiences with the shapes in their environment. They can be encouraged to notice the differences and similarities among various shapes.

Student Learning Activities

1. Visit a preschool, kindergarten, first-grade, or second-grade classroom. From the equipment and materials in the environment, list the opportunities you see for teaching shape and form.

2. With a group of children, implement at least one of the activities and experiences related to shape suggested in this chapter. The children may be a classroom group or simply a small group of relatives or neighborhood children. Evaluate your experience.

3. Think of additional ideas for the section on "Activities and Experiences" and for the unit plan on shape.

4. Do a web on shape.

5. Prepare a 5-day activity plan on shape. (See the lesson plan given in this chapter for the format of your activity plan.)

6. Prepare at least one teacher-made material or piece of equipment to teach shape to children 2 to 8 years of age. (Refer to ideas in this chapter and in Appendix A for additional suggestions.)

7. Visit a children's library and add at least two additional excellent children's books to the resource list for teaching shape to children 2 to 8 years of age.

8. List and draw the geometric shapes children 2 to 8 years of age can learn.

Suggested Resources

Children's Books

Bruna, D. (1984). *Know about shapes*. Los Angeles: Price Stern.

Budney, B. (1954). *A kiss is round*. New York: Lothrop, Lee & Shepard.

Carle, E. (1974). *My very first book of shapes*. New York: Crowell.

Gardner, B. (1980). *The turn about, think about, look about book*. New York: William Morrow.

Gordon, M. (1986). *Shapes*. Morristown, NJ: Silver-Burdett.

Groening, M., & Groening, M. (1991). *Maggie Simpson's book of colors and shapes*. New York: HarperCollins.

Hoban, T. (1974). *Circles, triangles, and squares*. New York: Macmillan.

Hoban, T. (1983). *Round and round and round*. New York: Greenwillow.

Hoban, T. (1986). *Shapes, shapes, shapes*. New York: Greenwillow.

Kohn, B. (1971). *Everything has a shape and everything has a size*. Englewood Cliffs, NJ: Prentice-Hall.

Lerner, S. (1970). *Square is a shape: A book about shapes.* Minneapolis: Lerner.

Mackinnon, D. (1992). *What shape?* New York: Dial.

Russo, M. (1986). *The line up book.* New York: Greenwillow.

Sullivan, J. (1963). *Round is a pancake.* New York: Holt, Rinehart, & Winston.

Wildsmith, B. (1981). *Animal shapes.* London: Oxford University Press.

Records, Tapes, and Cassettes

Learning with circles and sticks. On *Learning basic skills through music* (Vol. 2). Hap Palmer Record Library. AR585 or AC585.

Magic monster mix: Magic monsters look for shapes. The Child's World.

One shape, three shapes. On *Learning basic skills through music.* (Vol. 2). Hap Palmer Record Library. AR522 or AC522.

Triangle, circle, or square. On *Learning basic skills through music* (Vol. 2). Hap Palmer Record Library. AR522 or AC522.

Walk around the circle. On *Learning basic skills through music—vocabulary.* Hap Palmer Record Library. AR521 or AC521.

Pictures

Colors and shapes. The Child's World (Panorama).

Films, Filmstrips, and Videos

Beginning concepts, a program in basic concepts and perceptions. Scholastic Early Childhood Center.

Colors and shapes. Eye Gate Media.

Matter, matter everywhere: How materials change. Coronet Films.

Shape: A circle is never square. Eye Gate Media.

Shapes. Eye Gate Media.

Computer Software

Colors and shapes. Hartley Courseware. (Apple).

First shapes. First Byte. (Apple IIGS, Macintosh, Atari ST).

Inside outside shapes. McGraw-Hill Media. (Apple).

Match-on-a-Mac. Teach Yourself by Computer. (Macintosh).

Math and me. Davidson and Associates. (Apple, IBM, Apple IIGS).

Muppetville. Sunburst Communications. (Apple).

Patterns. MECC. (Apple).

Preschool pack. Nordic Software. (Macintosh).

Teddy's playground. Sunburst Communications. (Apple).

PART
EIGHT

PARENT INVOLVEMENT

"Parents are a school's best friends" (Henderson, 1988).

The final chapter of this book focuses on an additional skill that teachers need: working with parents and extending the curriculum into the home. Effective work and communication with parents are necessary in any good early childhood program. Parents need to know about their child from the school's point of view, and teachers benefit as they gain understanding of a child's behavior from parental input (Bjorklund & Burger, 1987). "If schools do not make the effort to include parents in the learning process, children can find it difficult to integrate the separate experiences of home and school" (Henderson, 1988, p. 152). We must plan for optimum involvement and look to parents as friends and helpers (Becher, 1986). The child is in school for only a limited time each day. It is vital that a positive link between the home and the school be made and that parents and teachers see each other as playing an important role in the education of the child. Guidelines for working with parents are given, as well as specific ways to extend the curriculum into the home.

CHAPTER
twenty

Working with Parents

Introduction

Many parents are not aware of how important they are in their child's education (Rich, 1991). The family is the young child's earliest educator, and parents have a lasting influence on children's attitudes, values, learning, concepts, emotions, and ideas. They have the right and the responsibility to influence their children's education (Becher, 1986). There is extensive and convincing evidence regarding the benefit of parent involvement in the development and education of their children (Becher, 1986; Coleman, 1991a; Galen, 1990; Greenberg, 1989; Henderson, 1988). Educators believe parents make the difference between a mediocre school and a great school. Everyone benefits when parents are involved in children's education (Henderson, 1988), and all parents have competencies that, when fully supported, help their children succeed in school (Swick, 1991). In order for the teaching of young children to be effective, a positive link must be made between the school

and the home; they must be partners, since the two are vital parts of the child's life and education. Involving parents in children's education improves the children's achievements and the overall level of achievement in our schools (Henderson, 1988; Walberg, 1984). Involving the parents when children are young has long-term benefits (Swick, 1991).

Both parents and teachers can contribute to the growth and development of children. In addition, parents have much to offer teachers and the school, and teachers have much to offer parents. It is vital that both parents and teachers understand that they have valuable contributions to make. Parents can become better acquainted with the school's programs, and teachers can become more aware of children's home situations. As they learn each others' values and goals, they are able to be more supportive of each other in working together with their children. Teachers must focus on strengthening their relationship with parents (Swick, 1988).

Active Parent Involvement Is Necessary and Takes Many Forms

Programs vary in the kind and amount of parent involvement, but we do know that schools cannot work in isolation. If programs in early childhood education are to succeed, they must have parental support and participation, and children must continue to receive stimulation from parents (Swick, 1991; Hymes, 1980; Greenberg, 1989; Umansky, 1983). Teachers need to appeal to parents' interest in order to have them become involved. In other words, parents must be involved for a reason, not just "be involved" (Coleman, 1991a).

Traditionally, teachers have met with parents twice yearly for parent–teacher conferences and report sessions. Today, however, teachers realize that more interactions between parents and teachers are necessary, with much more dialogue, sharing, and support between the two (Derman-Sparks, 1989). Some believe that "parent involvement is best when it requires actual participation with the children" (Nunnelley, 1990, p. 26). Parents must feel welcome not only at school and program activities, but also in the classroom. In

addition, home–school relationships should be founded on families' strengths.

Parent involvement takes many forms, and it ought to encompass a broad range of activities, including involving parents on governing boards to influence policy and decision-making that affects children, observing in the classroom, helping in learning centers, assisting at the computer center, listening to children read or reading to children, or working on specific concepts such as math with individual children. Parents can provide resources for the classroom and *be* resources for particular units of study. Parents can be assistant teachers or teachers' aides working in the classroom with the children. Parents can be used to reach and involve parents who are hard to reach and difficult to work with (Derman-Sparks, 1989). In addition, parent involvement helps parents become effective teachers of their own children and helps them be better informed in many areas (Brigham Young University Press, 1982; Galen, 1990; Swick, 1991). Parents' involvement may be as simple as letting their children know they value education, reading to their children at home, encouraging them with homework, and supporting at-home projects.

It is important for children to be allowed to acquaint their parents with the classroom, teachers, and peers.

Teachers and parents must be sensitive to one another's needs. Teachers must know what each parent in their class or program wants or expects from their child (Gonzalez-Mena, 1992); in effect, teachers must be accountable to parents. They must feel a responsibility to answer parents' questions regarding their children's education and to satisfy parents' wishes and goals for their children.

Another current trend is that of extending the curriculum into the home via the support of parents. Teachers are realizing that school hours pass quickly and that children have an added advantage if their parents can support what is being taught at school by teaching, reinforcing, and extending these same ideas and concepts at home. What parents *do* certainly does make a difference in the child's life (Brigham Young University Press, 1982).

In addition, schools and teachers are realizing that they are one of the best support systems for the family. Realizing that parenting is a difficult task and one in which many persons have had limited training, schools frequently offer parenting classes. These classes allow parents to participate in discussions, lectures, and demonstrations that focus on parenting skills, guidance and discipline, child-rearing practices, home-based learning activities, and family relationships. Teachers can also suggest sources of assistance to parents who are coping with crises. Sometimes teachers can be of great help by listening and demonstrating concern. It is also imperative that teachers remember the diversified nature of the family today and find ways of encompassing and communicating with parents from diverse cultures, working parents, single parents, guardians, and foster parents. Just as each child is unique, so is each child's family situation; therefore, each teacher's method of handling individual circumstances must be unique. Recognizing the diversity of parents, teachers must offer a variety of strategies by which parents can support their child and be involved (Coleman, 1991b). All parents can contribute to the classroom, and parents do not have to be educated to make a difference

in schools (Swick, 1991). Children from low-income and minority families benefit the most from parent involvement (Henderson, 1988).

For clarity and smoothness in writing, *parents* in this chapter includes single parents, guardians, and foster parents. By keeping this in mind, you will be able to adapt the activities and suggestions to the needs of those with whom you associate.

Guidelines for Working Effectively with Parents

The first step in working effectively with parents is to establish a warm and supportive relationship. Frequently there are barriers to overcome. In any job involving human relationships, forming positive and constructive associations is often the most challenging aspect. When extending the curriculum into the home, the most difficult task may not be planning and doing, but establishing and maintaining warm relationships with parents. Because some parents' contacts with schools and teachers have not been positive, teachers often have to work diligently to combat negative attitudes. Some teachers view parents as threats, and some parents develop the same view of teachers. Developing a positive attitude toward working with parents is a major step in developing good relationships with parents. Keep in mind the challenge to serve families and not just children. Remember that children come from families and spend much time within those families; therefore, parents should be viewed as both partners and allies (Bundy, 1991; Coleman, 1991b; Galen, 1990).

Be careful not to appear too strong or too authoritarian. You are a professional, and you do have much skill and expertise. However some teachers give parents the feeling that they "know it all" and that they consider their ways and values to be the best. This attitude almost immediately breaks down relationships with parents.

Social, linguistic, or cultural barriers may interfere with effective communication and work with parents. These barriers often create differences in values, approved child-rearing methods, behavior standards, accepted foods, and many other areas. Complete agreement on everything is unrealistic, but through communication and daily contact, parents and teachers can cooperate, coordinate efforts, and work in harmony as partners in teaching children (Derman-Sparks, 1989).

In working to overcome some of the barriers to effective relationships with parents, teachers' interest and respect frequently assist in achieving positive relationships. Teachers must respect cultural differences and variations in family values, just as these must be respected in children.

As differences in children are accepted, it becomes much easier to understand these differences in their parents; they will sense acceptance or rejection. More time should be spent listening to parents and learning about their feelings, values, and culture. Become effective at cross-cultural communication. Listen and learn about the cultures from which children in your class come, and be careful about misinterpretations and biases (Gonzalez-Mena, 1992).

All parents need to know that they have something to contribute to the classroom, and they need to be encouraged to share these valuable contributions (Swick, 1991). Request the help of parents in singing songs, leading dances, supervising ethnic food preparations, or making costumes or decorations. Invite them to play music, recite poetry, or help portray celebrations or cultural events. Barriers usually disappear when parents sense honesty, sincerity, and a feeling of professionalism.

The importance of listening as a means of building effective teacher–parent relationships was mentioned previously. This cannot be stressed enough. Frequently parents will have insights into the child's behavior that the teacher could not possibly know from associating with the child only in the school setting. The parents may have developed methods for handling the child's behavior challenges at home that would work equally well for the teacher in the classroom. Perhaps the parents have deep concerns, complaints, or irritations that can be resolved through listening and effective communication. Sometimes simply airing concerns helps parents to overcome them if they are heard by sensitive and understanding teachers. Parents should be provided with a constant opportunity to share these feelings, and there are many ways to do this. An open communication line for very young children can be established through daily contact as parents pick up their children from preschool. Teachers should remind parents that their feelings and suggestions are welcomed by making such comments as "How are you feeling about (*child's name's*) school experience? Is there any way I can be more supportive?" At the initial meeting or conference, teachers can indicate a certain time of day when they can be contacted. In addition, teachers should encourage parents with concerns to call them. Parents will sense the sincerity and honesty of the suggestion; they will know whether or not the teacher really meant what he or she said. Some good advice is: "Don't wait passively until the grievances explode. The willingness to examine practices constantly—the little everyday aspects of schooling as well as the major policies—is insurance that the paths of parents and teachers will not drift apart" (Hymes, 1974, p. 43).

To summarize, here are some specific suggestions for working effectively with parents:

1. Listen. Set up a specific open time when parents know that you will be available for listening and communicating. Sense their needs to share and discuss, and find some time—lunchtime, after school, a home visit, an evening telephone conversation—for meeting those needs by being an effective listener.
2. Treat all children and their families with respect and caring concern. Take advantage of the little opportunities that occur almost daily for showing concern and interest in

children and their families. Possibly send home a short note apprising the parents of a particular skill the child mastered that day or telling them something the child said or did that you enjoyed. A quick phone call on the day a child is absent lets the parents and the child know that they are important and cared for. Treat the parents with the kind of respect that conveys the belief that "I see you as an equal partner, having more and superior understanding of the child in some areas than I, the child's teacher."

3. Be sure to know the child well enough to relate specific information about him or her to the parents. Recordkeeping is important, and a list or chart of the items you wish to discuss will be helpful for both you and the parents. Anecdotes or other kinds of dated observation notes can also be supportive. In addition, it is helpful for the parents to see samples of the child's work; over a period of time, progress in specific areas can be observed. For the preschool child, even progress in art stages is easily apparent from selected samples of the child's artwork.

4. Convey to the parents positive and warm feelings regarding their child. Make sure that they know how much you like the child and how interested you are in the child's growth and development.

5. Be objective and realistic about your goals in working with the child. Where necessary, make appropriate referrals for assistance from such professionals as speech therapists, psychologists, and medical doctors.

6. Be a source of help in many parenting areas, and help extend what you are teaching into the home. Parents may need suggestions for age-appropriate good books, meaningful learning activities that can be done at home, toy selection, and where to find helpful materials on guidance. Remember, too, that the school and family alone may not be able to handle the range of children's needs. Schools, with teachers as catalysts, must become "multiple-service brokers for children"

(Edwards & Young, 1992, p. 78). Schools must draw on the full range of community resources to strengthen the child, and they should focus on preventive strategies. What does your local library offer for parents who indicate a particular need? If you have a nearby college or university, what particular services could be recommended to parents? It may be advisable to keep a current file of resources appropriate for the parents of the children you teach.

7. Remember that it will take numerous encounters and meetings to build positive and supportive relationships with parents. Pitcher, Feinburg and Alexander (1989) state:

> Trusting relationships and true dialogues do not happen in semiannual conferences routinely scheduled in November and May. They develop because a teacher takes time to call a parent to say how things went on a child's first day alone in school, or because a teacher realizes that a child seems sad and different on a Monday morning. Such gestures on a teacher's part suggest a way of doing business together. . . . (p. 33)

To work effectively with parents, the same attitudes used in working with children should be applied. Be positive, supportive, interested, caring, objective, friendly, and warm. Work hard, using a variety of techniques to motivate, teach, build, and strengthen.

Extending the Curriculum into the Home

Now that some guidelines for working with parents have been established, we need to focus on the objective of this chapter—to learn how teachers can extend the curriculum into the home. Parent involvement works best when parents are invited to play a variety of roles. It is important "that the involvement is reasonably well-planned, comprehensive, and long-lasting" (Henderson, 1988, p. 150).

How much more effectively children will learn if parents and teachers are partners in the teaching process! Since learning occurs through repetition and many experiences, children will learn more successfully if what is being taught in the classroom is extended into the home. Following are suggested ways for the teacher to extend the curriculum into the home.

Written Communication

Written communications can take many forms, and are a vital link between home and school. Upcoming events and activities, as well as snack assignments or main-course lunch menu items, can be included on a monthly newsletter-calendar.

Teachers can make a list of simple activities

When parents are actively involved in their children's lives, they are better able to assist their children in the learning process.

that parents can do in their homes to be actively involved in their child's learning. For example, activities listed in any chapter in this text could be shared with parents. Or, for each general curriculum area (i.e., math, science, language and literacy, music, art), choose several activities that could easily be done at home and share them with parents. For example, for math:

- Have children sort laundry and match socks. When finished, children can count pairs of socks for each family member and then add them together.
- Make a number lotto game and play it together.
- Circle the numerals in the newspaper beginning with 1 and going to 10, or as far as the child can recognize.
- Ask the child to estimate the weight of several household objects such as a ball, a gallon of milk, and so on. Once the items are weighed, have the child order them from lightest to heaviest.
- Do matching, sorting, and categorizing activities using beans, buttons, groceries, cards, and newspaper pictures or photographs.

Find time each week to send a note or newsletter home with the children in order to tell parents what concepts or ideas are being focused on that week, as well as to provide an overview of planned activities. In addition, write down any individual notes that may be helpful or enjoyed by the parents regarding their child. Parents will be interested in knowing when field trips are being taken; include words to new fingerplays they can teach their child. Children will also enjoy having their parents tell them of the activities planned for the next week or the next day in school; it creates interest, enthusiasm, and eagerness. For example, if parents are aware of the upcoming unit on color, they can add support by reinforcing color concepts at home, even during spontaneous experiences such as eating dinner or going to the grocery store. Also, parents frequently ask children what they did at school, and it is often difficult for young children to remember or to single out the concept being studied. It is helpful to the child for the parent to ask something like "What did you learn about color today?" or "What did the policeman tell you when he visited your classroom at school today?"

A preprimary class at Keene State College (Keene, NH) found "happy-grams" to be particularly effective in home–school relationships during the first few weeks of school. A "happy-gram" is a brief written note such as: "Bill did not cry after he entered the room. He helped pick out a book, which was read to the class," or "Jane was great today. She shared an experience with us about her summer vacation." At the end of the note an invitation is included for the parents to come and visit the classroom anytime. (Wenig & Brown, 1975, p. 374)

Notes are also appropriate when the children have enjoyed a particular food, music, or science experience: "Today the children were amazed with the 'growth' of the chemical gardens we made in class yesterday. You may wish to make them at home. The recipe is . . ." or "Today the children enjoyed the playdough we used. The recipe is. . . ." Parents appreciate these ideas, and knowing that activities will be enjoyed by their children, they will often do them at home.

Notes of appreciation should also be sent to parents. When parents participate in field trips, they have donated several hours of valuable home or work time and should know that their efforts are appreciated. These short notes help to build warm parent–teacher relationships. Also, if a parent sends a snack or assists in the classroom in any way, a short note should be sent. It is helpful to keep thank-you notes and cards readily available so that they can be sent soon after the parent has participated. A "message-sharing board" is an ongoing source of information for parents that might include general school information, lesson or activity schedules, and messages for children and teachers (Levin & Klein, 1988).

Parent Conference or Conversations

As previously mentioned, face-to-face encounters with parents should be planned frequently. It is unrealistic to predetermine the exact number of times per year that these conferences should be held, because some parents may need them every 6 to 8 weeks, while once every 3 or 4 months may be sufficient for others. The important thing to remember is to meet with parents as often as is necessary to maintain close contact, and to be an advocate for the child and his or her best interests. Conferences, to be successful, should also relate to the parents' needs (Swick, 1991).

The teacher should begin and end the parent conference with something positive about the child. Once something positive has been said by the teacher, the parent should be allowed to talk. As a teacher, you gain much knowledge and understanding from parents by listening to them. "Reflective or active listening will encourage information sharing and discourage confrontation between you and the parent" (Bjorklund & Burger, 1987, p. 27). Parents should feel supported, relaxed, comfortable, and wanted. They should be made aware of the child's strengths and needs and of specific ways they can help their child at home.

Teachers must remember that "parents have a strong emotional investment in their child," which may manifest itself as defensiveness, anger, denial, or anxiety (Morgan, 1989, p. 53). Tension during conferences and interfacing with parents can be reduced as teachers use I-messages, seek parents' suggestions, and stress positive aspects. What is best for the child should always be paramount (Bjorklund & Burger, 1987). Be cautious with criticism, and instead of giving advice, give suggestions or guidelines. Never betray a confidence; this applies to children as well as to parents.

The initial conference of the year may consist primarily of questions. Many schools distribute questionnaires with which the parents can become familiar before the first conference. "How does your child feel about himself or herself?" "What expectations do you have for your child during the coming school experience?" "What kinds of learning experiences or activities does your child enjoy most?" "Is the child developing a particular talent or interest?" "How does your child relate to and get along with siblings and/or neighborhood friends?" These questions allow parents to become familiar with some areas of discussion that are often difficult to think about without prior preparation. They generally provide the teacher with much more feedback, and also open the lines of communication, because the parents have had time beforehand to think about something they want to discuss.

As mentioned previously in this chapter, once the child is in school and conferences are scheduled, teachers must be well prepared with ideas and materials to share with the parents. Portfolios are a sampling of the child's work; they can show progress being made in specific curriculum areas. The teacher should be able to discuss the child's progress in a number of areas: socially, emotionally, physically (both large- and small-motor areas), and intellectually. Parents are anxious to know of their child's progress in each of these areas and need to see materials that validate the teachers' appraisals. Anecdotal records can strengthen teachers' evaluations (Abbott & Gold, 1991). Parents are usually anxious to hear about any ideas and activities they can do at home in order to help their child improve. Especially when a child is having difficulties in one or more areas, it is helpful for teachers to give the parents concrete suggestions for helping the child progress.

"The essential ingredients of effective school/parent communication are frequent informal contact and warm, respectful, honest conversation. Omitting key information is a form of dishonesty" (Herrera & Wooden, 1988, p. 80). Again, it is important for the teacher to listen to the parents—to their suggestions for working with the child or about strategies and activities that work in the home. A review of the characteristics of effective communication between parents and teachers concluded the following to be important: concreteness, genuineness, immediacy, and confrontation. The skills found to be important in parent–teacher relationships were

listening, attending, perceiving, and responding (Rotter & Robinson, 1982).

In addition to formal scheduled conferences, teachers should take advantage of informal daily or weekly opportunities for brief but friendly conversations. These may occur when the parent picks the child up from school or when the teacher and parent meet casually in the grocery store. Regardless of how the situation develops, the teacher should make good use of any opportunity for free discussions and for answering any questions the parent may have. These informal conversations are often the building blocks to effective home–school relationships.

Parent Meetings or Parent Education Programs

Parenting classes and workshops have been found to ease parents' tension and anxieties, improve skills, and teach child development concepts. Parent education programs that actively involve parents and require several sessions have been found to be more effective than single sessions, and they have more impact than flyers or dittoed sheets (Coleman, 1991b; Mavrogenes, 1990). These meetings, workshops, or programs are planned by the teachers, by the parents, or by the two in collaboration. Since the focus is on parent education, it is advisable to take a poll of the parents' interests and then strive to meet these needs as meetings are planned. The number of meetings per year will depend on parental support and interest. Various topics for these meetings could include guidance, making home-learning materials, and curriculum topics such as art activities, science at home, or nutritious food activities. There are many commercial parent education programs, and there is no evidence that one particular program is significantly more effective than another (Powell, 1986).

A variation in parental meetings could involve children in both the planning and the presentation. Plan an open house, with the children acting as hosts and hostesses. A display of some of their work and activities would be shown, with the children acting as the chefs for the refreshments. Parent evenings or afternoons could focus on single topics such as "Foods We Like to Make and Eat" or a "Science Fair." The children enjoy the preparation and planning involved in these events, but they especially look forward to sharing their school and activities with their parents. If the majority of parents are single and/or working, addressing these topics as they relate to rearing children could result in provocative and informative meetings. Another excellent topic for a parent meeting is introducing parents to antibias curricula and concepts and helping them understand how they can facilitate antibias development at home (Derman-Sparks, 1989). Parent meetings, workshops, and programs can be very beneficial in enhancing parents' skills, knowledge, and attitudes toward their children.

Technology and Telephone Calls

Technology affords an opportunity for quick and open communication. Parents should feel free to contact teachers, and teachers should contact parents. Telephoning need not be only a means of conveying emergencies or reporting negative behavior and problem situations. It also provides a valuable opportunity to let parents know of positive things that occur in the classroom. Technology now enables some parent barriers to be overcome. For example, the use of electronic mail and telephone answering machines enables parents to leave messages for teachers, and teachers to transmit general class or curriculum information and homework assignments to parents.

If a child has had particular success with a concept or curriculum activity, this information can be conveyed to the parent by telephone. For example, a telephone message conveyed by the teacher might be:

Today we mixed the three primary colors together to make the secondary colors. We used water colored with food coloring, a white Styrofoam egg carton, and an eyedropper. You should have seen how much Christopher enjoyed this activity! For 30 minutes he continued to experiment with mixing the colors, I am sure he would enjoy doing this activity in your home.

Or, if a child is having particular difficulty with a concept presented at school, do not wait until the formal parent–teacher conference to alert the parent. A phone call can suggest, in a warm and positive way, what the difficulty is and how the parent can help. For example, in a first-grade classroom, the children have had their first activity involving concepts related to money. Rachel has difficulty understanding the values of coins and becomes very frustrated with the activity. In a call that day to the home, the teacher might say:

Today we began work with the values of money and coins. Rachel seemed unusually concerned and I plan to give her individual help at school, but you may wish to work with her at home too. You may want to role-play store situations in giving change or develop simple games to match equal values. For example, if you lay down 10 cents, from the change Rachel has at hand she needs to come up with another combination representing 10 cents. You may also want to encourage her in making actual purchases at stores, such as allowing her to purchase a pound of margarine, giving the grocer the dollar bill, and receiving the change.

These kinds of suggestions are usually eagerly welcomed by the parent. It is not as helpful simply to state the learning difficulty, offering no suggestions for action. Technology can and does serve as a bridge between home and school, and it can strengthen the partnership between them.

Home Visits

Through child-centered home visits, a teacher can gain insights about the child that can be obtained in no other way. These visits provide the opportunity to relate to families on their own "ground" and to gain valuable information about the child's needs (Powell, 1990). Home visits build closer ties between parents and teacher (Swick, 1991), strengthen the child's self-esteem, and communicate to the family the child's worth and importance to the teacher (Fox-Barnett &

Meyer, 1992). To be successful at home visits, teachers must be able to accept different homes and the diversity of families (Fox-Barnett & Meyer, 1992). Some particularly enlightening information relating to curriculum planning can occur naturally and spontaneously in a home visit.

One Head Start teacher visited a home where the mother was just preparing dinner. She was preparing peas and happened to mention that she never made Rebecca eat them; as a family, they had learned that the texture of peas made Rebecca sick. The Head Start teacher recalled one lunchtime when peas were being served, and Rebecca had been rather persistently made to taste at least some of them. Reserved Rebecca had sat at the lunch table longer than the other children, and the teacher thought Rebecca was just testing to see if she really must taste at least some of the peas!

A kindergarten teacher was making a home visit and discovered that Stephen, with the help of his geologist father, had assembled a collection of rocks and knew many interesting facts and concepts relating to them. This began a unit on rocks, and Stephen proudly brought his specimens and shared his information with the other children.

When arranging for home visits, teachers need to request a visit to the home. Parent should be informed that the teacher is visiting to learn more about the child, to have an opportunity to spend some time with the child, to meet the family, and to allow the family to become better acquainted with the teacher. Pressure should not be put on the parents to have the teacher in their home. There may be special problems in the home at that time, and the parents may view a teacher's visit as one more problem or pressure to be handled. Most often, teachers can sense whether or not the time is appropriate for a home visit and they are welcome.

When making the home visit, a teacher must be relaxed, friendly, and alert to the needs and responses of the family. The length of the visit should be determined by the needs of both the family and the teacher. Generally, home visits should not be lengthy unless the teacher has been invited for a special occasion such as a family meal or a birthday party.

Home visits also provide an opportunity for the teacher to introduce into the home a game, activity, or book that the child has enjoyed in the classroom, to be shared with the child and perhaps other family members. Depending on the receptiveness of the parent or parents, the visit may be a good time for giving suggestions about learning activities, materials, or equipment appropriate for home use by the child. When making home visits, some teachers prefer to leave a newsletter or handout relating to learning ideas for home use with the parents.

Parent Involvement and Observation in the Classroom

There are many ways of involving parents in the classroom, and probably a great advantage exists in doing so. Research indicates that gains made by children in early childhood education programs are maintained to a greater extent when parents are involved in the program than when they are not (Becher, 1986; Coleman, 1991a; Henderson, 1988; Schaeffer, 1972; Walberg, 1984). When parents take the time to be involved in the classroom, this acts as a teaching experience for the parent, giving new ideas for home activities and guidance principles, and helping the parent observe and learn about the child in the school situation. It is also valuable for the child to know that he or she is important enough for the parent to spend time in the classroom. Parent–teacher rapport is strengthened as the "team" works together in the classroom. Parents become more understanding of the teacher's role as they view the teaching situation from the inside; they have more positive attitudes toward the school and the staff (Becher, 1986).

Many teachers prepare a parent-involvement calendar at the beginning of the year, quarter, or month—based on parents' needs and schedules—inviting all parents who are able into the classroom as volunteers. This is preceded by a parent meeting scheduled at the beginning of the year to help parents understand their responsibilities and opportunities in the classroom. Teachers should convey to the parents the value of their participation, helping parents understand that they have expertise and skills that will contribute greatly to the classroom. Most working parents, if they have adequate advance notice, are able to arrange time to be in the classroom.

Expectations and responsibilities must be very clear when parents are assisting in the classroom; duties assigned to them should not be trivial (Schickedanz, 1977). Parents should view themselves as participators, and not just as cleanup persons; they can become involved with the children in the various activities and experiences. For example, parents could sit at the manipulative table and visit with the children while helping them with the play materials. Parents might also read to children, sing with them, participate in their games, eat with them, build with them, and otherwise interact with them. Where cleanup is necessary, or when assistance in dressing or undressing is needed, do it! In primary-grade classes, teachers should give parents the opportunity of working with their own children, hearing them read, helping them write a story, completing an assignment, or working on a project. Parent volunteers in the primary grades are especially valuable when working with children who have emotional, social, physical, or academic problems.

To interact with parents more, one teacher did a unit titled "What Do Grown-Ups Do All Day? The World of Work" (Nachbar, 1992, p. 6). The unit lasted all year and integrated many curriculum areas. The unit included parent questionnaires; field trips to some parents' workplaces; and activities such as graphing where parents ate lunch, having parent visitors who described what they did, and having children draw their parents at work (Nachbar, 1992).

Parent visits to the classroom may also be for the purpose of observation. Many early childhood programs in colleges and universities have observation booths with one-way viewing mirrors for student and parent observation. In other classrooms, the teachers also encourage the parents to visit and observe their child in action.

Another occasion for parent involvement in the classroom is when extra help is needed. For example, food activities and field trips may require additional help or supervision. Perhaps a parent has a particular skill that lends itself to a unit of study. During a unit on fish, a father who was an avid fisherman visited the class and brought his fishing gear to demonstrate. He showed the children how to prepare the fishing pole, how to use the many different kinds of flies and other gear in his tackle box, and then how to cast out. Slides were brought of a fishing trip he and his son had taken, and pictures were shown of his young son catching a fish. The children watched as he demonstrated how to fillet a fish. Then, with a skillet in the middle of the circle, the fish was cooked and served to the children. Teachers should find out parents' hobbies and learn of special skills or talents they can share with the children. Hymes (1974) states:

Parent help means individualization *and* enrichment. At home in every community are photographers, cabinetmakers, tennis players, trumpeters and cellists, square dancing enthusiasts, storytellers—people with special talents. *And* at home in every community are people with the general talents of good sense, intelligence, reliability, judgment. These "experts" go under the name of *mother* and *father*. When we use these people in the classroom, all children get a better break. (pp. 101–102)

Teachers and staff must recognize that the backgrounds, time, skills, and values of parents are all unique, so the participation of parents must be geared to their individual abilities and needs. The employment needs and schedules of mothers and fathers must also be taken into account. Efforts to involve parents must be done in such a way that teachers respond sensitively to parents (Seefeldt, 1985).

Policy Planning, Decision Making, and Evaluation

Positive effects will also be felt when parents are included as members of policy planning committees or boards involved in decision making and/or evaluations related to the school or center (Becher, 1986). However, parents must have information in order to participate in a meaningful and rational way in policymaking decisions. When parents are invited to be involved, their thinking and suggestions must have merit and be a meaningful part of the decisions made.

Parent Resource Centers

Facilities should be set up to allow parents to visit the classroom and benefit from school resources offering parenting help and methods for extending what is being taught into the home. A parent room or parents' area can be organized to include books on child development; materials, books, and toys that can be checked out for home use; filmstrips; and other resources such as free pamphlets and brochures. Parents must be introduced to this resource and made aware of what is available in order for them to make use of the program. One program prepares parent education bags that include books,materials, games, and resources on particular topics that are packed and ready to go (Witmer, 1991). In another community, the school has put together age-appropriate materials into packets that are given by the hospital when the child is born and then are sent to the family on each child's birthday until the child enters school. This project ties the family to the school before the child even enters school (Spewock, 1991).

Many school districts are now providing parent resource centers, which supply these same kinds of services. Even a small private preschool or a single kindergarten can make available materials and equipment to support parents in teaching their children at home. Parent bulletin boards or displays can be set up, and parents will automatically check for parent education, information, or handouts.

Summary

The teacher's purpose, in part, must be to help parents utilize their potentials, discover their strengths and talents, and then use these for the benefit of the children themselves and their family. In addition, the purpose of any parent–teacher or parent–school activity is to develop school–home relationships, to promote school–community activities, and, most of all, to strengthen the child. It is hoped that any relationship or meeting with the parents will help the child. Rich (1977) believes that parent training can be the "seed" from which more changes and better things can grow in the future. She says:

The parents affected by the programs will be on their jobs for some time to come, just like the teachers. Parent involvement in teacher training will have a growth ripple effect at home on all the children, including those yet to be born. Changes in attitudes and actual behavior between parents and teachers, between parents and their children, offer the greatest potential for this wide-ranging, lasting growing change—this is an investment in people, not in hardware. (p. 309)

Teachers must recognize their responsibility in planning for parent participation and involvement. Teachers are "responsible for initiating contacts"; they must initiate parent participation and request involvement (Becher, 1986, p. 96). One researcher found that the more demanding parent involvement programs may have fewer participants; but over time, they will have greater and more positive effects on those participating (Coleman, 1991a).

Some teachers believe that planning for parent involvement takes too much time. However, "despite the difficulties, the accumulating research on the positive effects of parent participation in educational programs has caused interest in parent involvement to continue to grow. In addition, federal, state, and local requirements for greater parent involvement are expected to expand" (Becher, 1986, pp. 99–100). We must recognize that parents do make valuable contributions to programs and that all parents can make additional contributions (Becher, 1986). We must accept that parents' attitudes toward involvement are important. Often we must begin by developing positive attitudes toward parent involvement, helping parents to understand the benefits that will come from their participation and involvement.

Parents and teachers need to nurture and build one another, drawing on one another's strengths (Swick, 1991). Without parent involvement, programs or schools cannot achieve the ultimate objective of excellence for which both are striving.

Student Learning Activities

1. Find out whether arrangements could be made for you to observe during a professional teacher's home visit of which the purpose is to extend the curriculum into the home environment.

2. Interview an early childhood teacher and find out what methods are being incorporated for extending the curriculum into the home. Ask which methods the teacher feels are most valuable for helping parents carry out learning activities in the home.

3. Visit the home of a child between the ages of 2 and 8 years. It may be a child in your neighborhood, or your instructor may provide a list of parents who would enjoy having you in their home to teach a home-learning activity. Plan a learning activity that would be appropriate for the child's age; there are many suggestions throughout this book. Call the home and arrange for the visit, and then evaluate the visit and the experience. What went well? Were the parents and the child interested in the learning activity you presented? Did the child become involved? What would you do differently on your next visit?

4. Select an early childhood grade level, such as kindergarten, and establish two concepts that would be taught at this age level. For each of these concepts, write three different learning activities that could be suggested or shared with the parents for home use and learning.

5. Read from at least one of the resources suggested at the end of this chapter and make a list of the most meaningful things you learned in working with parents and extending the curriculum into the home.

6. Visit a parent resource center in a local school district and list some of the materials in which you were particularly interested. Discuss how you would use them with parents.

7. Visit your local library and make a list of some of the services it offers parents. Summarize the good parenting material available, and also some of the materials you would suggest to parents for providing meaningful learning activities in the home.

Suggested Resources

Parent Education Books

Becker, W. C. (1971). *Parents are teachers: A child management program.* Champaign, IL: Research Press.

Bellanca, J., Castagna, C. & Archibald Marcus, S. (1990). *Star parents training manual: Skills for effective parenting.* Palatine, IL: Skylight.

Berger, E. H. (1990). *Parents as partners in education: The school and home working together* (3rd ed.). Columbus, OH: Macmillan.

Bettelheim, B. (1988). *A good enough parent.* New York: Knopf.

Brazelton, T. B. (1992). *To listen to a child: Understanding the normal problems of growing up.* Reading, MA: Addison-Wesley.

Brooks, A. A. (1989). *Children of fast-track parents: Raising self-sufficient and confident children in an achievement-oriented world.* New York: Viking.

Brooks, J. B. (1991). *The process of parenting.* (3rd ed.). Palo Alto, CA: Mayfield.

Cataldo, C. Z. (1986). *Parent education for early childhood.* New York: Teachers College Press.

Clark, J. I., Gesme, C., London, M., & Brundage, D. (Eds.). (1986). *Help! For parents of children ages three to six years.* San Francisco: Harper.

Cline, V. (1980). *How to make your child a winner.* New York: Walker.

Dinkmeyer, D., Sr., & Dinkmeyer, D., Jr. (1989). *Parenting young children: Parent's handbook.* Circle Pines, MN: American Guidance Service.

Dobson, J. (1992). *The new dare to discipline.* Wheaton, IL: Tyndale.

Dodson, F. (1971). *How to parent.* New York: New American Library-Dutton.

Dodson, F. (1974). *How to father.* Los Angeles: Nash.

Gordon, T. (1975). *P.E.T.: Parent effectiveness training.* New York: McKay.

Lerman, S. (1985). *Parent awareness: Positive parenting for the 1980's.* San Francisco: Harper.

Olmsted, P. P. (1980). *Parent education: The contributions of Ira J. Gordon.* Washington, DC: Association for Childhood Education International.

Rothenberg, B. A., Hitchcock, S., Harrison, M. L., & Graham, M., et al. (1983). *Parentmaking: A practical handbook for teaching parent classes about babies and toddlers.* Menlo Park, CA: Banster.

Rothenberg, B. A., Dubin, S., Merilo, K., Beacom, R., Hilliard, J., & Sarnat, L., et al. (1992). *Parentmaking: Educators training program.* Menlo Park, CA: Banster.

Szykula, S. A. (1991). *The parenting cookbook: Recipes for raising successful children.* Salt Lake City: Family First.

Taylor, K. W. (1981). *Parents and children learn together* (3rd ed.). New York: Teachers College Press.

Parent Education Videos, Cassettes, and Training Kits

Canfield, J. (1987). *How to build high self-esteem.* Chicago: Nightingale-Conant. (6 cassette tapes)

Coloroso, B. (1989). *Winning at parenting.* Littleton, CO: Barbara Coloroso. (Video)

Dyer, W. (1986). *What do you really want for your children?* Chicago: Nightingale-Conant. (6 cassette tapes)

Father Flanagan's Boys' Home staff. (1988). *Catch 'em being good.* Boys Town, NE: Boys Town Center. (Video)

Father Flanagan's Boys' Home staff. (1989). *It's great to be me: Increasing your child's self-esteem.* Boys Town, NE: Boys Town Center. (Video)

Gordon, T. (1989). *Parent effectiveness training.* Washington, DC: Educational Services. (1 cassette)

Helmstetter, S. (1988). *Predictive parenting.* Studio City, CA: Dove/William Morrow Books on Tape. (2 cassettes)

Johnson, S. (1983). *The one-minute father.* New York: Morrow. (Book and 2 tapes)

Johnson, S. (1983). *The one-minute mother.* New York: Morrow. (Book and 2 tapes)

Popkin, M. (1987). *Active parenting.* Chicago: Nightingale-Conant. (Kit including 6 tapes and booklet: videotapes also available)

Waitley, D. (1987). *How to build your child's self-esteem.* Chicago: Nightingale-Conant. (6 cassette tapes)

APPENDIX A

Teacher-Made Learning Materials

Alphabet Lotto

Alphabet lottos use letters with corresponding lotto cards showing upper-case and lower-case letters. The two sets of cover cards can be used for matching upper-case to upper-case letters and upper-case to lower-case letters. The cover cards are made by putting the letters between two squares of clear plastic and then sealing the edges with transparent tape. The base can be one large board or smaller boards, each with a part of the alphabet.

Alphabet Board

Attach cup hooks or hangers to a wooden base, each hook below an alphabet letter. Key holders (available from stationery stores), circles, or squares cut from index or card stock paper can be used as the base; stickers or small pictures from workbooks are glued to the base. Children match beginning sounds or ending sounds on the alphabet board.

Alphabet Puzzle

A set of commercial alphabet cards are mounted from A to Z in one long strip. Then they are cut apart so that each piece shows half of a picture from one letter, a letter, and half of the next picture. The pieces are cut in puzzle fashion so they fit together only in the correct order.

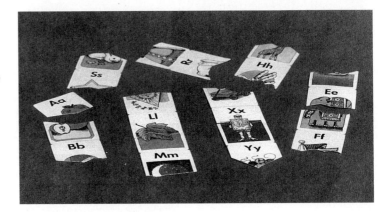

Class/Individual Books

Any number of books can be made by the class or by individual children. They may be based on personal experiences, field trips, families, favorite stories or songs, and so on. Pictures can be cut from magazines or drawn by the children. On the backs or bottoms, a sentence can be written by the children or dictated to a teacher.

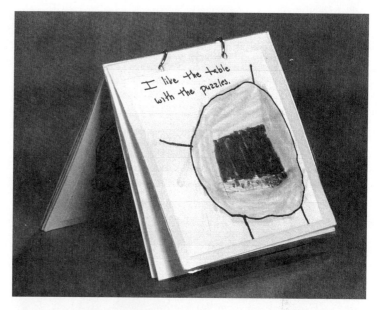

Me Book

Each child takes home pages and, with the help of family members, puts together a book about self. The teacher may send home ideas for pages. Illustrations can be drawn by the child or collaged from magazines, or photographs may be used. Each child should be given an opportunity to share some pages from the book with the class.

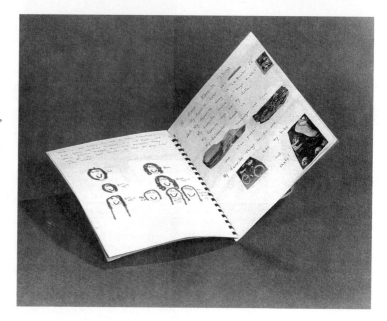

Class Alphabet Book

Each child takes home a page with an alphabet letter on it and, with the help of family members, designs a picture and writes a sentence for the picture that uses alliteration of the assigned letter.

Rhyming Words

Children find and match the pictures that rhyme.

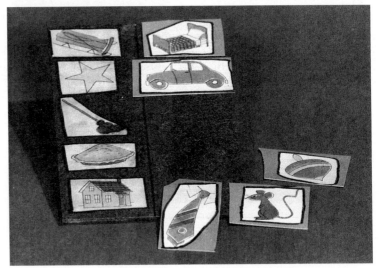

Antonyms (Opposites)

The skill developed by this matching game is an understanding of opposite concepts, such as happy and sad. Similar matching or lotto games can be made for homonyms, synonyms, or other things that go together.

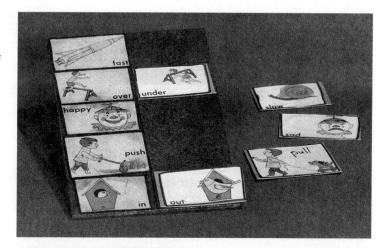

Contraction Match

A lotto matching game where the child matches the contraction with the words represented by the contraction.

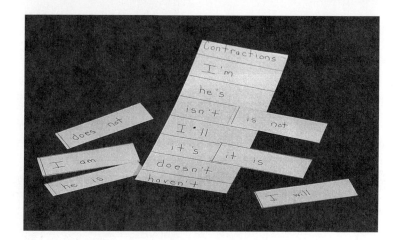

Alphabetizing

Children alphabetize the list of names, either by first name or by last name. This game is made on card stock paper and then laminated.

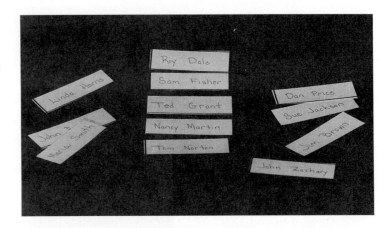

Word Games

Three word games are shown: "Hard C, Soft C," "Rhyming Words," and "Use Your Imagination." There are many word games that can be used to encourage literacy development.

Beginning Sound Baseballs

Baseballs—or anything you wish to use—can be made with word endings on the shape and a sliding strip of various letters to change the beginning sound. This game could also be used for word endings.

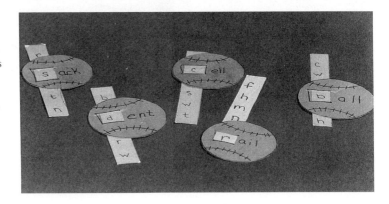

Silent E Game

Words with the silent *E* at the end that make the vowel a long sound can be made in such a way that the child reads the word with the *E* at the end and then folds the strip back and reads it as a three-letter word with a short vowel.

Suffix Flowers

Suffixes are mounted on the inside circle of the flowers, and the letters or words are mounted on the outside circle. The center is rotated to form new words.

Mixed-Up Sentences

Children develop the concept of a complete sentence as they arrange the words in an order that makes a meaningful thought. This requires some foundation in reading.

Sequence Story

"The Three Bears" is made on Pellon so it can be used as a flannel board story.

Matching Pairs

Even very young children enjoy matching pairs of like items. Matching games and materials can be planned to meet the needs of children from ages 2 to 8. The younger the child, the easier the discriminating tasks must be. Vegetable seed packages are shown here. Two of each are provided so they can be matched into pairs. The pictures are mounted on a base (in this case, heavy poster paper) and then covered with clear adhesive-backed paper for durability.

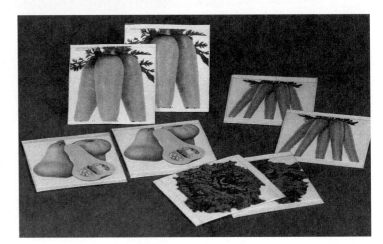

Similar matching materials can be made for numbers, shapes, animals, patterns, colors, textures, objects, and so on. For older children, make the same objects (such as houses), but incorporate finer differences into the pairs, so that more highly developed perception is required for matching.

Position Matching

Place the loose cards of stars on the matching positional star cards mounted on the poster board.

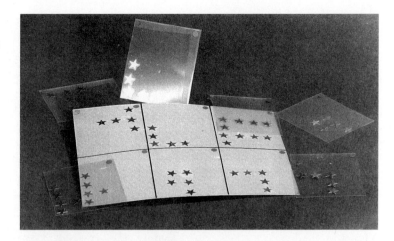

Pattern Copying

Children need many opportunities to practice copying patterns. A variety of letters, numbers, and shapes can be used, with the complexity of the pattern matched to the developmental needs of the children. The cards are laminated and the children use an erasable water-base pen to copy the patterns.

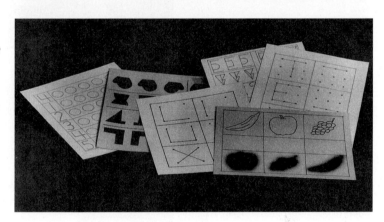

Things That Go Together

Children match two things that go together such as a pair of shoes with a pair of socks. In this game colored golf tees are used to match. For example, there are two red tees, two yellow tees, two blue tees, and so on. Tees of the same color are put on each pair of pictures—shoes and socks, for example. Other tools for matching could be devised.

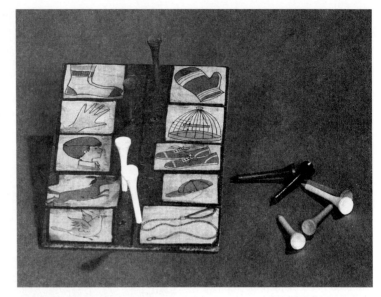

Fraction Pie

Each circle is cut into a different number of pieces; one is left whole; a second is cut into two, or halves; a third, into three, or thirds; another, into fourths, and so on. It is best to make each circle or "pie" a different color. The circles can be made of wood or heavy paper that has been laminated.

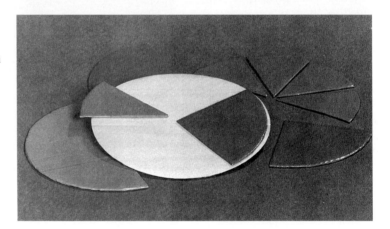

Numeral Matching

Children match the free numerals to the corresponding numeral mounted on card stock or board. Small circles could also be used to develop understanding of "how many."

Box Toss

Connect a series of small boxes by gluing or stapling (cut-off milk cartons or half-pint milk cartons work well). To the inside walls of each box attach items such as shapes, colors, numbers, or objects. Put the numbers on one side of each box, the colors on another side, and so on. When the box is turned a particular way it is a number-box toss game; when turned another way it becomes a color-box toss game; or other variation. Use a small bean bag, Styrofoam ball, or Ping-Pong ball. After the ball or bag is tossed, the child names the number, color, shape, or item.

Number Sticks

The base for the number sticks can be wood, heavy paper, or even tongue depressors. Write or glue numerals on the top of the sticks. Then attach a number of stick-on shapes (available at office-supply stores) or glue beans, buttons, or gummed stars below each numeral equal to the quantity represented by that numeral. The children can use the sticks to order or add (e.g., put two or more sticks together and count how many objects are on the sticks).

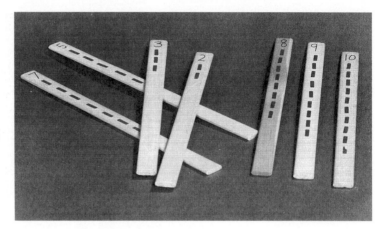

Pegboard Game

Pegboards can be made from scrap pieces of pegboard approximately 10 inches square. One-hundred-hole boards work best. The board can be raised by gluing small blocks or wooden spools under each corner. Be sure to drill through the corner holes so that they can still be used. Purchase wooden pegs or use colored golf tees, as shown here.

The pegboard can be used in many ways, depending on the age and interest of the child: to develop eye-hand coordination and left-right sequencing abilities, as well as to reinforce colors, numbers, or shapes. Cards can be placed vertically to the right of the pegboard to reinforce some of these concepts. For example, make one card with 10 dots the same various colors as the pegs, so that when the card is placed next to

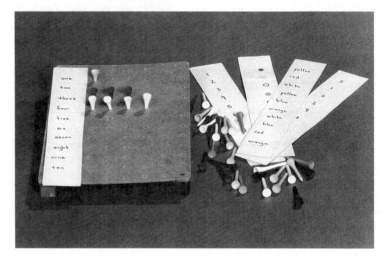

the board, it encourages placement of rows of pegs in various colors. Or write the color names; if the child is just learning to read, the color name may be written in that particular color—red written in red, and so on. Such

cards could also be made up for numbers, with each row indicating to the child how many pegs to put on it. The numbers could be put in order or out of order, could be written as words, or could be arranged in other ways.

Number Pie

Attach the clothespins with dots to the matching numeral on the pie. (Same activity can be made using rectangular mounting boards.) Similar games can be made for color, shape, alphabet, or other concepts.

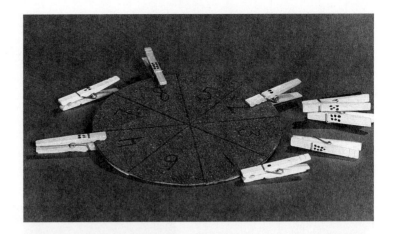

Number Book

This book was made from poster paper covered with clear adhesive-backed paper and bound with rings. It is in three sections: (1) the top section shows numerals in order; (2) the middle section has circles cut from felt, grouped into the various sets but placed out of order; (3) the bottom section contains gummed stickers grouped into the various sets and also placed out of order. Uncut cover sheets, the size of the book, are used for the front and back covers.

Children open to a numeral on the top section, thumb through the shapes in the middle section to find the correct match to the numeral, and then go through the bottom section to find the correct number of objects to match to the numeral at the top.

Add and Subtract Circles

Children spin the pointer on the left-hand circle, determine from the middle circle whether they should add or subtract, then spin the pointer on the right-hand circle and determine the answer.

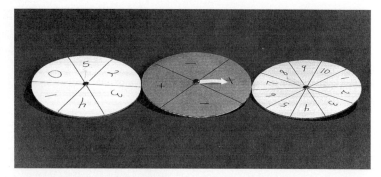

Numeral Puzzles

The puzzle is cut in a self-correcting pattern: only the correct numeral will match the corresponding number of circles. In addition, the strips making up the puzzle will fit together only when they are ordered correctly.

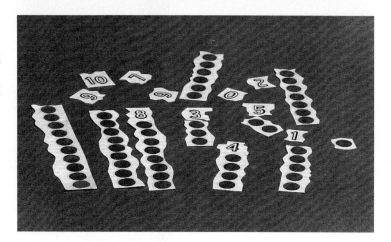

Time Lotto

The base for this lotto, like that of other lottos, may be card stock, poster paper, or a wooden board. Children match the clock faces to the correct digital time.

Time Puzzle

Children match the traditional time reading with the digital time reading in this self-correcting puzzle.

Money Lotto

Pictures of items marked with prices appear on one side, and a combination of coins appears on the other side. The children match priced items with the correct quantity or amount of money.

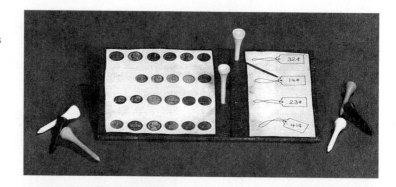

Manipulative Numerals

These numerals cut from wood encourage learning through the senses of sight and touch.

Lacing Match-Ups

These materials provide the opportunity for developing small-muscle skills, as well as practice in matching like items. In the left column of a base, arrange a series of items. In the right column, place identical items in a different arrangement or order. Cover the base with a protective covering such as acetate or clear adhesive-backed paper. The items in the two columns are matched by threading a shoelace or piece of yarn from the item in the left column to the identical match in the right column. If yarn is used, the end should be dipped in paraffin wax or glue to stiffen it and make it easier to thread through the hole without unraveling.

Some of the many ideas for items to match are colors, shapes, numbers, sizes, animals, mother or father animals to baby animals, and patterns.

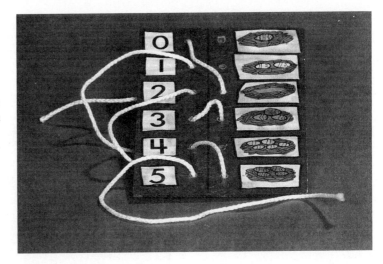

Workbooks purchased from variety stores often contain pages that would be appropriate to use for lacing match-ups. This same idea can be used on a wooden base with holes drilled next to each picture. Use colored pegs or golf tees to match the identical items.

For example, on a number match-up, down the left column use numerals, and down the right column use dots to represent the meaning of each numeral or quantity. A red peg, for example, could then be put by the numeral 3 and another red peg by the three dots.

Shape Matching

This lacing match-up activity uses shoelaces to match the patterns that are the same.

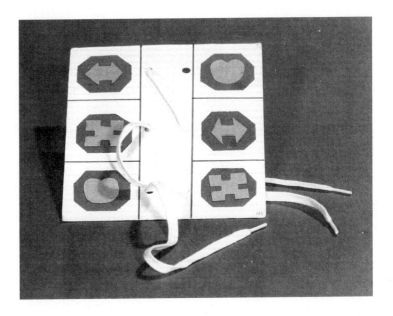

Shape Outlining

Small sticks of varying lengths are used to outline shapes drawn on poster board.

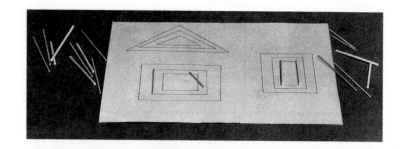

Shape Game

Children take turns moving the spinner to determine which shape to move to next.

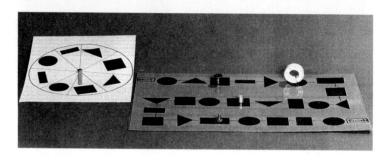

Shape and Color Dominoes

Dominoes are another variation of a matching game. Each domino block shows two items. The item on half of the block is to be matched with an identical item on another domino block. The children place the two blocks so that the ends with the identical items are touching in some way. The blocks may be any size, but should be approximately twice as long as they are wide. For example, a domino that is 4 inches long should be about 2 inches wide. The base material used for the dominoes can vary, but the set pictured is of ply-

wood. On one side are various shapes cut from black adhesive-backed paper. On the other side the background was painted a color—yellow in this case—and then squares of different colors were glued on. Both sides have a polyurethane coating. The yellow

background on the one side makes the two different games easily identifiable. Dominoes can be made for textures, animals, numerals, sets, letters, or objects. Pictures can be obtained from gummed stickers, catalogs, or workbooks.

Muffin-Tin Color Sorter

Glue colored felt circles in the bottom of each muffin hole. Corresponding-colored pom-poms (purchased from craft stores or made from colored yarn) are sorted into the correct spaces. To provide small-muscle coordination practice, tongs can be used to pick up the pom-poms. An alternative, instead of using color, is to put numerals in each space and let the children count out the number of buttons into each space equal to that numeral: four buttons in the space containing the numeral 4, and so on.

Color Words

Children match color/word cards to the corresponding color cards mounted on a board.

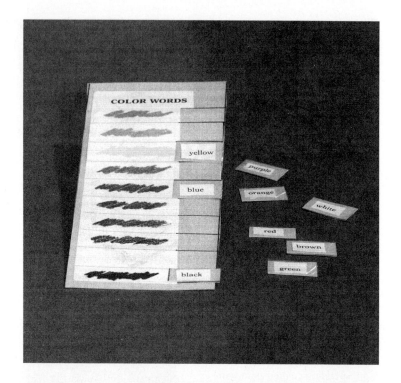

Color Matching

These paint chip samples were obtained from a paint distributor, mounted on pieces of plywood, and then painted over with polyurethane for durability. Colored paper shapes mounted in the same way could be used if the paint samples are not available. Younger children can match them in like pairs. Older children enjoy turning them all over and then taking turns flipping two at a time in an attempt to find matches. This provides excellent memory training.

Dowels in Various Lengths

Cut ¼-inch dowels into different lengths. The children seriate, or order them from the shortest to the tallest, or they match equal lengths.

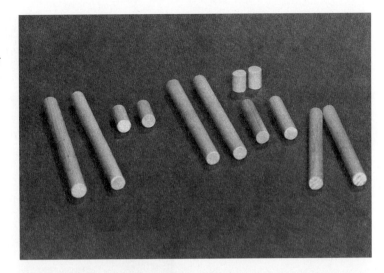

Seriated Shapes

Cut several sizes of one shape from a base material such as plywood or cardboard. Put a sealing or finishing coat such as varnish on each one. The shapes can be seriated, or ordered from smallest to largest, by putting them side by side or on top of each other. If two sets are made, they can be used to match shapes that are the same sizes.

Stacking Cans

The purpose of the stacking cans is to order or stack them by size. Paint all the cans the same color so that color is not an aid in the ordering process. The child arranges them according to size, either by fitting the cans inside each other or by stacking them from largest to smallest. The cans could also be covered with colorful adhesive-backed paper.

Texture Book

Each child is given a different texture and either writes or dictates a description.

Texture Matching

Children match the loose fabric squares to the fabric squares mounted on the board.

Sound Cans

These sound cans are made from empty film containers. They could also be made from small bottles covered so that the contents cannot be seen. Various media such as beans, wheat, paper clips, and salt are put into pairs of the bottles or cans. Care must be taken to put the same amount into each of the pairs. When the lids are on, the children shake the cans and match to like sounds and then match them to the cards with two circle shapes. The children can describe the sounds and guess what might be inside the containers.

Our Town

For exciting dramatic play the children build the town on the mat, and then use miniature cars and people to play. The mat is made of heavy canvas; the street, lake, park, airport runway, and other aspects of the city are cut from felt and glued or sewn onto the canvas. A teacher could design a replica of the children's neighborhood so the children could enjoy finding their own streets and putting their houses on in the appropriate places. Buildings, landscaping, and other selected pieces could be attached with nylon self-gripping fasteners or snaps for easy rearranging.

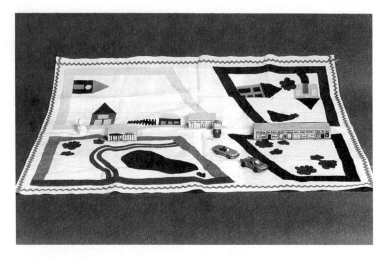

Dress-Me Dolls

These dolls are similar to paper dolls but are much more durable. Outline a boy doll and a girl doll on heavy boards purchased from a craft shop. Glue body parts and facial features to the board; they can be made from felt, yarn, small buttons (for eyes), and other similar scraps. Many different items of clothing can be made from felt. Glue accessories such as buttons, also cut from felt, to the items of clothing.

Stick Puppets

Any variety of pictures may be mounted on card stock and attached to tongue depressors or other sticks.

Fishing Pole

A dowel with screw eyes to hold the cord and an empty wooden spool on bottom representing the reel makes a great fishing pole. A magnet is put on one end of the cord. Fish can be labeled or marked with any concept you wish to work on, such as name recognition, color, shape, number, or words to practice. The fishing pole game is also a good way to pick a song, story, or other activity.

APPENDIX B

Resources and Organizations

A.B. LeCrone Company
819 Northwest 92nd Street
Oklahoma City, Oklahoma 73114

Access Unlimited
9039 Katy Freeway
Suite 414
Houston, Texas 77024

ACT Production
30100 Towncenter Drive
Suite 0–211
Laguna Niguel, California 92677

A&M Records
Hollywood, California 90028

Action for Children's Television
46 Austin Street
Newtonville, Massachusetts 02160

The Administration for Children,
Youth, and Family
Office of Human Development
Services
U.S. Department of Health and
Human Services

P.O. Box 1182
Washington, D.C. 20013

Adventures in Rhythm
1844 North Mohawk Street
Chicago, Illinois 60614

Afro-Am Education Materials
819 South Wabash Avenue
Chicago, Illinois 60605

Alcazar Inc.
P.O. Box 429
Waterbury, Vermont 05676

Alexander Graham Bell
Association for the Deaf
3417 Volta Place, N.W.
Washington, D.C. 20007

Alfred Publishing Company
16380 Roscoe Boulevard
Suite 200
Van Nuys, California 91406–1215

American Academy for Cerebral
Palsy
University Hospital School
Iowa Cita, Iowa 52240

American Academy of Pediatrics
141 Northwest Point Road
P.O. Box 927
Elk Grove Village, Illinois 60007

American Association of
Elementary, Kinder-Nursery
Educators
1201 16th Street, N.W.
Washington, D.C. 20036

American Association for Gifted
Children
15 Gramercy Park
New York, New York 10003

American Association for Health,
Physical Education, and
Recreation
1201 16th Street, N.W.
Washington, D.C. 20036

American Association on Mental
Deficiency
5201 Connecticut Avenue, N.W.
Washington, D.C. 20015

American Association of Workers
for the Blind, Inc.
206 North Washington Street
Alexandria, Virginia 22314

American Brotherhood for the
Blind
Twin Vision Books
18440 Oxnard Street
Tarzana, California 91356

American Education Research
Association
Early Childhood SIG Group
c/o Educational Testing Service
Rosedale Road
Princeton, New Jersey 08541

American Foundation for the
Blind
15 West 16th Street
New York, New York 10011

American Home Economics Association
2010 Massachuetts Avenue, N.W.
Washington, D.C. 20036–1028

American Indian Project
San Francisco Unified School Dis-
trict
135 Van Ness Avenue
Room 19
San Francisco, California 94102

American Indian Resource Center
Huntington Park Library
6518 Miles Avenue
Huntington Park, California
90255

American Library Association
50 East Huron Street
Chicago, Illinois 60611

American Montessori Society
150 Fifth Avenue
Suite 203
New York, New York 10011

American Orthopsychiatric Association, Inc.
1790 Broadway
New York, New York 10019

American Printing House for the
Blind
1839 Frankfort Avenue
Louisville, Kentucky 40206

American Public Health Association, Inc.
1740 Broadway
New York, New York 10019

The American Speech-Language-
Hearing Association
10801 Rockville Pike
Rockville, Maryland 20852

Anti-Defamation League of B'nai
B'rith
823 United Nations Plaza
New York, New York 10017

Appalachia Educational Laboratory
1031 Quarier Street
P.O. Box 1348
Charleston, West Virginia 25325

Argosy Music Corporation
Motivation Records
101 Harbor Road
Westport, Connecticut 06880

Association on American Indian
Affairs
432 Park Avenue South
New York, New York 10016

The Association of Child Advo-
cates
Building 31, Second FLoor
3615 Superior Avenue
Cleveland, Ohio 44114

Association for Childhood
Education International
11141 Georgia Avenue
Suite 200
Wheaton, Maryland 20902

An Association for Children and
Adults with Learning Disabilities, Inc.
5244 Clarwin Avenue
Pittsburgh, Pennsylvania 15229

Association for Children with
Learning Disabilities

4156 Library Road
Pittsburgh, Pennsylvania 15234

Association for Education and
Rehabilitation for the Blind and
Visually Handicapped
206 North Washington Street
Suite 320
Alexandria, Virginia 22314

Association for Education of the
Visually Handicapped
711 14th Street, N.W.
Washington, D.C. 20005

Association Montessori Interna-
tional/USA
780 West Second Avenue
Apartment 4E
New York, New York 10025

Association for Retarded Citizens
2501 Avenue J
P.O. Box 6109
Arlington, Texas 76011

Bank Street College of Education
610 West 112th Street
New York, New York 10025

Bilingual Publications Company
1996 Broadway
New York, New York 10023

Black Child Development Institute
1463 Rhode Island Avenue, N.W.
Washington, D.C. 20005

Bo Peep Productions
P.O. Box 982
Eureka, Montana 59917

Bowmar-Noble Publishers
1901 North Walnut
P.O. Box 25308
Oklahoma City, Oklahoma 73125

Bradford, William K. Publishing
310 School Street
Acton, Massachusetts 01720

Bright Star Technology
1450 114th Avenue
Suite 200
Bellevue, Washington, 98004

Brite Music Enterprises, Inc.
P.O. Box 9191
Salt Lake City, Utah 84109

Broderbund Software
17 Paul Drive
San Rafael, California
94903–2101

Building Blocks
38 West 567 Brindlewood Ln.
Elgin, Illinois 60123

Bureau of Curriculum Innovation
Massachusetts Department of Education
182 Tremont Street
Boston, Massachusetts 02111

Bureau of Education for the
Handicapped
U.S. Office of Education
Department of Health and Human Services
Seventh and D Streets, S.W.
Washington, D.C. 20036

C & C Software
5713 Kentford Circle
Wichita, Kansas 67220

CMS Records, Inc.
226 Washington Street
Mt. Vernon, New York 10553

CRM/McGraw-Hill Films
674 Via de la Valle
P.O. Box 641
Del Mar, California 92014

Caedmon Records and Tapes
1995 Broadway
New York, New York 10023

California Child Care Resource
and Referral Network
809 Lincoln Way
San Francisco, California 94122

Camden-RCA Records
Educational Sales
P.O. Box RCA 1000
Indianapolis, Indiana 46291

Campus Film Distribution Corp.
24 Depot Square
Tuckahoe, New York 10707

Capital Records, Inc.
100 Oak Street
Oakland, California 94607

The Center for the Study of Public Policies for Young Children
High/Scope Educational Research
Foundation
600 North River Street
Ypsilanti, Michigan 48197

Chapel Hill Training Outreach
Project
Merritt Mill Road
Lincoln Center
Chapel Hill, North Carolina
27514

Cheviot Corporation
Rhythms Productions/ Tom
Thumb
Whitney Building
P.O. Box 34485
Los Angeles, California 90034–
0485

The Child Care Action Campaign
P.O. Box 313
New York, New York 10185

Child Care Employee Project
P.O. Box 5603
Berkeley, California 94705

Child Care Information Exchange
P.O. Box 2890
Redmond, Washington 98073

Child Care Information Service
NAEYC
1834 Connecticut Avenue, N.W.
Washington, D.C. 20009–5786

Child Care Law Center
625 Market Street, Suite 815
San Francisco, California 94105

Child Development Associate/
National Credentialing Program
Rep Unit, Suite 802
1341 G Street, N.W.
Washington, D.C. 20005

Child Study Association of America, Inc.
853 Broadway
New York, New York 10028

Child Welfare League of America,
Inc.
67 Irving Place
New York, New York 10003

The Child's World
P.O. Box 989
Elgin, Illinois 60121

Childcraft Education Corporation
20 Kilmer Road
Edison, New Jersey 08817

Children's Book and Music
Center
2500 Santa Monica Boulevard
Santa Monica, California 90406–
1130

The Children's Defense Fund
122 C Street, N.W.
Washington, D.C. 20001

Children's Foundation
815 15th Street
Washington, D.C. 20005

Children's Record Guilde
225 Park Avenue South
New York, New York 10003

Churchill Films
662 North Roberston Boulevard
Los Angeles, California 90069–
9990

Claudia's Caravan
P.O. Box 1582
Alameda, California 94501

Columbia Children's Record Library
CBS, Inc.
15 West 52nd Street
New York, New York 10019

Columbia Records
51 West 52nd Street
New York, New York 10019

Community Change, Inc.
P.O. Box 146
Reading, Massachusetts 01867

Community Playthings and
  Equipment for the Handi-
  capped
Route 213
Rifton, New York 12471

Contemporary Films
(McGraw-Hill Films)
330 West 42nd Street
New York, New York 10036

Coronet Films
65 East South Water Street
Chicago, Illinois 60601

Corporate Child Development
  Fund
1834 Connecticut Avenue, N.W.
Washington, D.C. 20009–5786

Council for Early Childhood Professional Recognition
NAEYC
1834 Connecticut Avenue, N.W.
Washington, D.C. 20009–5786

The Council for Exceptional Chil-
  dren
Division of Early Childhood
Department 651
1920 Association Drive
Reston, Virginia 22091–1589

Council on Interracial Books for
  Children
1841 Broadway
New York, New York 10023

Creative Concepts for Children
P.O. Box 8697
Scottsdale, Arizona 85252–8697

Creative Publications
P.O. Box 10328
Palo Alto, California 94303

Thomas Y. Crowell Company
666 Fifth Avenue
New York, New York 10019

DLM
One DLM Park
Allen, Texas 75002

D.C. Heath & Company
125 Spring Street
Lexington, Massachusetts 02173

David C. Cook Publishing Company
School Products Division
850 North Grove Avenue
Eligin, Illinois 60120

Davidson and Associates
19840 Pioneer Avenue
Torrance, California 90503

Davidson Films, Inc.
165 Tunstead Avenue
San Anselmo, California 94960

Day Care & Child Development
  Council of America
1012 14th Street, N.W.
Washington, D.C. 20005

Day Care and Child Development
  Reports
2814 Pennsylvania Avenue, N.W.
Washington, D.C. 20007

Day Care and Early Education
  (magazine)
75 Fifth Avenue
New York, New York 10011

Developmental Learning Materials
7440 Natchez Avenue
Niles, Illinois 60648

Diabetes Research Institute
University of Miami School of
  Medicine
Foundation Offices
7525 Northwest 74th Avenue
Miami, Florida 33166

Disability Rights Education and
  Defense Fund
2212 Sixth Street
Berkeley, California 94710

Disneyland-Vista Records
350 South Buena Vista Street
Burbank, California 91521

Distribution Sixteen
111 Eighth Avenue
Suite 900
New York, New York 10011

Documentary Films
3217 Trout Gulch Road
Aptos, California 95003

E.C.S. Exceptional Children's
  Software
P.O. Box 487
Hays, Kansas 67601

ERIC Clearinghouse on Elementary and Early Childhood Education
College of Education
University of Illinois
805 West Pennsylvania Avenue
Urbana, Illinois 61801

The Economy Company
Bowmar-Noble Publishers
1901 North Walnut
P.O. Box 25308
Oklahoma City, Oklahoma 73125

Education Development Center,
  Inc.
55 Chapel Street
Newton, Massachusetts 02160

Educational Activities, Inc.
P.O. Box 392
1937 Grand Avenue
Freeport, New York 11520

Educational Equity Concepts
114 East 32nd Street, Third
  Floor, Room 306
New York, New York 10016

Educational Teaching Aids Division
A. Daigger and Co., Inc.
159 West Kinzie Street
Chicago, Illinois 60610

Educational Testing Service
Rosedale Road
Princeton, New Jersey 08541–0001

Eye Gate Media
Division of Carnation Company
3333 Elston Avenue
Chicago, Illinois 60618

Family Resource Coalition
230 North Michigan Avenue
Suite 1625
Chicago, Illinois 60601

Far West Laboratory for Educational Research and Development
1855 Folsom Street
San Francisco, California 94103

Featherstone
P.O. Box 487
Brookings, South Dakota 57006

First Byte
Clauset Center
3100 South Harbor
Suite 150
Santo Ana, California 92704

Folkways Records and Service
Corporation
632 Broadway, Ninth Floor
New York, New York 10012

GAF Corporation
Consumer Photo Products/View-
Master
140 West 51st Street
New York, New York 10020

Ginn & Company
Axerox Publishing Company
191 Spring Street
Lexington, Massachusetts 02173

Great Wave Software
5353 Scotts Valley Drive
Scotts Valley, California 95066

Hap Palmer Record Library
Educational Activities, Inc.
1937 Grand Avenue
P.O. Box 392
Freeport, New York 11520

Happy Time Records
8–16 43rd Avenue
Long Island City, New York
10001

Hartley Courseware
P.O. Box 419
Dimondale, Michigan 48821

Hayes School Publishing Co., Inc.
321 Pennwood Avenue
Wilkinsburg, Pennsylvania 15221

Heartstone Press
P.O. Box 890686
Houston, Texas 77289–0686

Heath Health Communications
1721 Blount Road
Suite 1
Pompano Beach, Florida 33069

High Windy Audio
P.O. Box 553
Fairview, North Carolina 28730

Human Touch
2381 Blue Haven Drive
Rowland Heights, California
91748–3204

IBM Educational Systems
P.O. Box 2150
Atlanta, Georgia 30055

Ideal School Supply Company
11000 South Lavergne Avenue
Oak Lawn, Illinois 60453

Information Center on Children's
Cultures
Administration Offices
331 East 38th Street
New York, New York 10016

Japanese American Curriculum
Project, Inc.
414 East Third Street
P.O. Box 367
San Mateo, California 94401

Joseph P. Kennedy, Jr., Foundation
719 30th Street, N.W.
Suite 510
Washington, D.C. 20005

Judy/Instructo
Educational Materials
4325 Hiawatha Avenue South
Minneapolis, Minnesota 55406

KTAV Publishing House, Inc.
120 East Broadway
New York, New York 10022

Kimbo Educational
P.O. Box 477
10 North Third Avenue
Long Branch, New Jersey 07740

Lawrence Hall of Science
University of California
Berkeley, California 94720

Lawrence Productions
1800 South 35th Street
Galesburg, Michigan 49053

Lifelong Learning
University of California
Extension Media Center
Berkeley, California 94720

Look At Me Productions
P.O. Box 135
Wheeling, Illinois 60090
OR 8 Norbert Drive
Hawthorn Woods, Illinois 60047

Lyons Band
530 Riverview Avenue
Elkhart, Indiana 46514

MCM Record Corporation
7165 West Sunset Boulevard
Los Angeles, California 90046

MTI Teleprograms Inc.
3710 Commercial Avenue
Northbrook, Illinois 60062

Magic Touch Programs
666 North Main Street
Suite 101
Logan, Utah 84321

McGraw-Hill Media
P.O. Box 408
Hightstown, New Jersey 08525–
9377

McGraw-Hill Training Systems
674 Via de la Valle
P.O. Box 641
Del Mar, California 92014

Mead Educational Services
B and T Learning
5315-A Tulane Drive
Atlanta, Georgia 30336

Minnesota Educational Computing Consortium (MECC)
3490 Lexington Avenue North
St. Paul, Minnesota 55126–8097

Melody House Publishing Company
819 Northwest 92nd Street
Oklahoma City, Oklahoma 73114

Mexican American Cultural Center
3019 West French Place
San Antonio, Texas 78228

MindPlay
3130 North Dodge Boulevard
Tucson, Arizona 85716

Mindscape Educational Software
1345 West Diversey Parkway
Chicago, Illinois 60614

Miss Jackie Music Company
10001 El Monte
Overland Park, Kansas 66207–3631

Modern Talking Pictures
2323 New Hyde Park Road
New Hyde Park, New York 11040

Multicultural Resources Center
c/o Margaret S. Nichols or Peggy O'Neill
P.O. Box 2945
Stanford, California 94305

Muscular Dystrophy Association of America, Inc.
1790 Broadway
New York, New York 10019

National Association for the Deaf
814 Thayer Avenue
Silver Spring, Maryland 20910

National Association of the Deaf
2025 Eye Street, N.W.
Suite 321
Washington, D.C. 20006

National Association of Early Childhood Teacher Educators
Family and Child Ecology
Michigan State University
East Lansing, Michigan 48824

National Association for the Education of Young Children
1834 Connecticut Avenue, N.W.
Washington, D.C. 20009

The National Association for Gifted Children
8080 Springnally Drive
Cincinnati, Ohio 45236

National Association for Hearing and Speech Action
10801 Rockville Pike
Rockville, Maryland 20852

The National Association for Mental Health, Inc.
10 Columbus Circle
Suite 1300
New York, New York 10019

National Association of Private Schools for Exceptional Children
P.O. Box 34293
Bethesda, Maryland 20817

National Association for Retarded Children
420 Lexington Avenue
New York, New York 10017

National Audio-Visual Center
National Archives and Records Service
General Services Administration
Washington, D.C. 20409

National Audubon Society
950 Third Avenue
New York, New York 10022

National Black Child Development Institute
1463 Rhode Island Avenue, N.W.
Washington, D.C. 20005

National Center for Clinical Infant Program
733 15th Street, N.W.,
Suite 912
Washington, D.C. 20005

National Committee for Multi-Handicapped Children
239 14th Street
Niagara Falls, New York 14303

National Congress of Parents and Teachers
700 North Rush Street
Chicago, Illinois 60611

National Council of Churches of Chirst in the U.S.A.
475 Riverside Drive
Room 572
New York, New York 10115

National Council for the Gifted
700 Prospect Avenue
West Orange, New Jersey 07052

National Dairy Council
111 North Canal Street
Chicago, Illinois 60606

National Easter Seal Society
2023 West Ogden Avenue
Chicago, Illinois 60612

National Educational Laboratory Publishers, Inc.
P.O. Box 1003
Austin, Texas 78767

National Epilepsy League, Inc.
203 North Wabash Avenue
Room 2200
Chicago, Illinois 60601

National Geographic Society
17th and M Streets, N.W.
Washington, D.C. 20036

National Mental Health Association
1021 Prince Street
Alexandria, Virginia 22314–2932

National Society for Low Vision
    People, Inc.
2346 Clermont
Denver, Colorado 80207

National Wildlife Federation
1412 16th Street, N.W.
Washington, D.C. 20036

Navaho Curriculum Center
Rough Rock Demonstration School
Chinle, Arizona 86503

New York University Film Library
26 Washington Place
New York, New York 10023

Nordic Software
3939 North 48th Street
Lincoln, Nebraska 68504

Orange Cherry Software
P.O. Box 390
Pound Ridge, New York 10576

P.E.A.L. Software
P.O. Box 8188
Calabasas, California 91372

Pearce-Evetts Productions
624 Ridgeview Drive
Pittsburgh, Pennsylvania 15228–
    1706

People Acting for Change To-
    gether (PACT)
163 Madison
Detroit, Michigan 48226

Peter Pan Industries
88 St. Francis Street
Newark, New Jersey 07105

Phoebe James
P.O. Box 475
Oakview, California 93022

Pickwick Records
135 Crossways Park Drive
Woodbury, New York 11797

Play Schools Association
111 East 59th Street
New York, New York 10022

Polymorph Films
118 South Street
Boston, Massachusetts 02111

Practical Drawing Company
P.O. Box 5388
Dallas, Texas 75222

Presbyterian Distribution Service
475 Riverside Drive
New York, New York 10027

Pyramid Film and Video
P.O. Box 1048
Santa Monica, California 90406

Queue
562 Boston Avenue
Bridgeport, Connecticut 06610

R.J. Cooper
24843 Del Prado
Suite 283
Dana Point, California 92629

R and E Research Associates
936 Industrial Avenue
Palo Alto, California 94303

Resource Access Group
Administration for Children,
    Youth and Families (ACYF)
U.S. Department of Health and
    Human Services
Sixth and D Streets, S.W.
Donohue Building
Washington, D.C. 20201

Rhythms Productions
Cheviot Corporation
Whitney Building
P.O. Box 34485
Los Angeles, California 90034–
    0485

Scholastic Book Services
906 Sylvan Avenue
Englewood Cliffs, New Jersey
    07632

Scholastic Early Childhood Cen-
    ter
Englewood Cliffs, New Jersey
    07632

Scholastic, Inc.
P.O. Box 7502
Jefferson City, Missouri 65102

Scholastic, Inc.
P.O. Box 2075
Mahopac, New York 10541

Scholastic Kindle Filmstrips and
    Scholastic Magazine
902 Sylvan Avenue
Englewood Cliffs, New Jersey
    07632

School Age Child Care Project
Center for Research on Women
Wellesley College
Wellesley, Massachusetts 02181

Select Committee on Children,
    Youth and Families
U.S. House of Representatives
House Annex 11, Room 385
Washington, D.C. 20515

Silver Burdett Company
Western Regional Office
1559 Industrial Road
San Carlos, California 94070

Silver Burdett Music Program
250 James Street
Morristown, New Jersey 07906

Social and Rehabilitation Service
Children's Bureau
330 C Street, S.W.
Washington, D.C. 20201

Society for Research in Child De-
    velopment
Institute of Human Development
1209 Tolman Hall
University of California
Berkeley, California 94720

Society for Visual Education, Inc.
1345 West Diversey Parkway
Chicago, Illinois 60614

Southern Association on Children
    Under Six
P.O. Box 5403
Brady Station
Little Rock, Arkansas 72215

Sterling Education Films
Division of the Walter Reede Organization
241 East 34th Street
New York, New York 10016

Sunburst Communications
39 Washington Avenue
Pleasantville, New York 10570

Ta-Dum Productions
P.O. Box 4077
Leucadia, California 92024

Teach Yourself by Computer
Software
349 West Commercial Street
Suite 1
East Rochester, New York 14445

Troubadour Records
Toronto, Ontario
Canada

United Cerebral Palsy Association, Inc.
66 East 34th Street
New York, New York 10016

United Church of Christ
Division of Evangelism, Church Extension and Education
Box 179
St. Louis, Missouri 63166

United States Committee for UNICEF
331 East 38th Street
New York, New York 10016

United States Office of Education
Bureau of Education for the Handicapped
7th and D Streets, S.W.
Washington, D.C. 20202

University of California Extension Media Center
2223 Fulton Street
Berkeley, California 94720

Vanguard Visuals
24266 Thornton Highway
Dallas, Texas 75224

Viking Penguin, Inc.
299 Murray Hill Parkway
East Rutherford, New Jersey 07073

The Viking Press, Inc.
625 Madison Avenue
New York, New York 10022

Weston Woods
Weston, Connecticut 06883

Wings for Learning
1600 Green Hills Road
Scotts Valley, California 95067–0002

Women's Action Alliance
370 Lexington Avenue
New York, New York 10017

World Organization for Early Childhood Education
24000 Lahser Road
Southfield, Michigan 48034

Worldwide Slides
7427 Washburn Avenue, South
Minneapolis, Minnesota 55423

Yale University Media Design Studio
305 Crown Street
New Haven, Connecticut 06511

Young People's Records
225 Park Avenue South
New York, New York 10003

Youngheart Records
2413½ Hyperion Avenue
Los Angeles, California 90027

Early Childhood Education Computer Software Resources

The rapid increase in software for young children makes it imperative that we identify our own attitudes and expectations regarding the place computers and software have in our curricula. Software is being produced so rapidly that we are unable to justify listing particular programs as suggestions to be included in your own plans. The following is a list of distributors and publishers of software appropriate for early childhood education. As expressed through this book, however, the most important guideline for selecting appropriate software is for teachers and caregivers to be familiar with the needs and concerns of the children in order for the software to be developmentally appropriate. Make certain that you preview any programs you are considering, so that you are able to determine whether or not they fulfill the particular goals and directions of your curriculum. The best resource for early childhood education software, without question, is a well-informed, conscientious, selective adult.

Addison-Wesley Publishing Company
2725 Sand Hill Road
Menlo Park, California 94025

Advanced Ideas
2902 San Pablo Avenue
Berkeley, California 94702

AlohaFonts
Box 2661
Fair Oaks, California 95628–2661

American Guidance Service
4201 Woodland Road
Circle Pines, Minnesota 55014–1796

American Peripherals
122 Bangor Street
Lindenhurst, New York 11757

Apple Computer, Inc.
20525 Mariani Avenue
Cupertino, California 94014

Artwork Software
1844 Penfield Road
Penfield, New York 14526

Aquarius
P.O. Box 128
Indian Rocks Beach, Florida
  33535

Automated Simulations
1043 Kiel Court
Sunnyvale, California 94086

Avant-Garde Creations
P.O. Box 30160
Eugene, Oregon 97403

Banana Software
6531 Park Avenue
Kent, Ohio 44240

Bell & Howell
7100 North McCormick Road
Chicago, Illinois 60645

Bertamax, Inc.
3647 Stoneway North
Seattle, Washington 98103

Bolt, Beranek and Newman
50 Mouton Street
Cambridge, Massachusetts 02238

Borg-Warner Educational Systems
600 West University Drive
Arlington Heights, Illinois 60004

Boston Education Computer
78 Dartmouth Street
Boston, Massachusetts 02116

Britannica Software
185 Berry Street
San Francisco, California 94107

Broderbund Software
17 Paul Drive
San Rafael, California 94903–2101

C & C Software
5713 Kentford Circle
Wichita, Kansas 67220

CBS, Inc.
One Fawcett Place
Greenwich, Connecticut 06836

Children's Computer Workshop/
Children's Television Workshop
One Lincoln Plaza
New York, New York 10023

Chipmunk Software
P.O. Box 463
Battleground, Washington 98604

Computer Curriculum Corpora-
tion
P.O. Box 10083
Palo Alto, California 94303

Computer Software Service
2150 Executive Drive
Addison, Illinois 60101

Computing Adventure, Ltd.
9411 North 53rd Avenue
Glendale, Arizona 85302

Conduit
P.O. Box 388
Iowa City, Iowa 52244

Control Data Corp.
8100 34th Avenue South
P.O. Box 0
Minneapolis, Minnesota 55440

Counterpoint Software, Inc.
4005 West 65th Street
Minneapolis, Minnesota 55435

Covox
675 D Conger Street
Eugene, Oregon 97402

D.C. Heath and Company
125 Spring Street
Lexington, Massachusetts 02173

DLM
One DLM Park
200 East Bethany Road
Allen, Texas 75002

DLM
25115 Avenue Standford
Suite 130
Valencia, California 91355

Davidson and Associates
19840 Pioneer Avenue
Torrance, California 90503

Designware
185 Berry Street, Building 3
Suite 118
San Francisco, California 94107

Developmental Learning Materials
P.O. Box 4000
Allen, Texas 75002

Digital Research
160 Central Avenue
P.O. Box 579
Pacific Grove, California 93950

Disk Depot
731 West Colorado Avenue
Colorado Springs, Colorado 80905

Disney Electronics
6153 Fairmont Avenue
San Diego, California 92120

Dr. Daley's Software
Water Street
Darby, Montana 59829

Dynacomp
1427 Monroe Avenue
Rochester, New York 14618

Educational Activities, Inc.
P.O. Box 392
Freeport, New York 11520

Educational Administration Data
  Systems, Inc.
P.O. Box 7005
Springfield, Illinois 62791

Educational Media Assoc.
342 West Robert E. Lee
New Orleans, Louisiana 70124

Educational Progress Corporation
4235 South Memorial Drive
Tulsa, Oklahoma 74145

Educational Teaching Aids
159 West Kinzie Steret
Chicago, Illinois 60610

Edu-Soft
P.O. Box 2560
Berkeley, California 94702

Edutek Corporation
P.O. Box 11354
Palo Alto, California 94036

Edu-Ware Services, Inc.
P.O. Box 22222
Agoura, California 91301

Electronic Arts
1820 Gateway Drive
San Mateo, California 94404

Electronic Courseware Systems,
Inc.
309 Windsor Road
Champaign, Illinois 61820

Encyclopedia Britannica Educational Corporation
425 North Michigan Avenue, Department 10-A
Chicago, Illinois 60611

Evanston Educators
1718 Sherman Avenue
Evanston, Illinois 60201

Floppy Enterprises
716 East Fillmore Avenue
Eau Claire, Wisconsin 54701

Gamco Industries
P.O. Box 1911
Big Spring, Texas 79721

Hammett
Hammett Place
P.O. Box 545
Braintree, Massachusetts 02184

Hartley Courseware, Inc.
P.O. Box 431
Dimondale, Michigan 48821

Harvard Associates, Inc.
250 Beacon Street
Somerville, Massachusetts 02143

Hayden Book Company
50 Essex Street
Rochelle Park, New Jersey 07662

Hayden Software
600 Suffolk Street
Lowell, Massachusetts 01853

Holt, Rinehart & Winston
383 Madison Avenue
New York, New York 10017

I/CT
Taylor Associates
10 Stepar Place
Huntington Station, New York
11746

Intellectual Software
798 North Avenue
Bridgeport, Connecticut 06606

K-12 Micromedia
Box 561
Valley Cottage, New York 10989

Kangaroo
332 South Michigan Avenue
Suite 700
Chicago, Illinois 60604

Krell Software
1320 Stony Brook Road
Stony Brook, New York 11790

Laureate Learning Systems
One Mill Street
Burlington, Vermont 05401

Lawrence Hall of Science
University of California
Berkeley, California 94720

Learning Company
4370 Alpine Road
Portola Valley, California 94015

Learning Systems, Ltd.
P.O. Box 9046
Fort Collins, Colorado 80522

Learning Technologies
13633 Gamma Road
Dallas, Texas 75244

Learning Unlimited Corp.
200 Park Offices Building
Suite 207
Research Triangle Park, North
Carolina 27709

Learning Well
200 South Service Road
Roslyn Heights, New York 11577

Logo Computer Systems
220 Fifth Avenue, Suite 1604
New York, New York 10018

MECC
3490 Lexington Avenue North
St. Paul, Minnesota 55126

Math City
4040 Palos Verdes Drive North
Rolling Hills Estates, California
90274

Mathware
919 14th Street
Hermosa Beach, California 90254

McGraw-Hill, Inc.
1221 Avenue of the Americas
New York, New York 10020

Melcher Software
P.O. Box 213
Midland, Michigan 48640

Mercer Systems
87 Scooter Lane
Hicksville, New York 11801

Merry Bee Communications
815 Crest Drive
Omaha, Nebraska 68046

Micro Learningware
Highway 66 South
P.O. Box 307
Mankato, Minnesota 56002

Micro Power and Light Company
12820 Hillcrest Road
Suite 224
Dallas, Texas 75230

Micro-Ed, Inc.
P.O. Box 24156
Minneapolis, Minnesota 55424

Microgram
P.O. Box 2146
Loves Park, Illinois 61130

Microphys Programs
2048 Ford Street
Brooklyn, New York 11229

Micropi
P.O. Box 5524
Bellingham, Washington 98227

Microsoft Consumer Products
400 108th Avenue, N.E.
Bellevue, Washington 98004

Midwest Software
P.O. Box 214
Farmington, Michigan 48024

Milliken Publishing Co./EduFun
1100 Research Boulevard
St. Louis, Missouri 63132–0579

Minnesota Educational Computing Consortium
2520 Broadway Drive
St. Paul, Minnesota 55113

Modern Education Corporation
P.O. Box 721
Tulsa, Oklahoma 74101

NOVA Software
P.O. Box 545
Alexandria, Minnesota 56308

NTS Software
680 Arrowhead Avenue
Rialto, California 92376

Opportunities for Learning
8950 Lurline Avenue
Chatsworth, California 91311

Orange Cherry Media Software
7 Delano Drive
Bedford Hills, New York 10507

The Other Guys
55 North Main Street
Suite 301-D
P.O. Box H
Logan, Utah 84321

Paperback Software International
2830 Ninth Street
Berkeley, California 94710

Polarware
1055 Paramount Parkway
Suite A
Batavia, Illinois 60510

Polytel
2121 South Columbia
Suite 550
Tulsa, Oklahoma 74114

Prentice-Hall, Inc.
Sylvan Avenue
Englewood Cliffs, New Jersey
07632

Program Design, Inc.
95 East Putnam Avenue
Greenwich, Connecticut 06830

Psydotechnics, Inc.
1900 Pickwick Avenue
Glenview, Illinois 60025

Quality Educational Designs
P.O. Box 12486
Portland, Oregon 97212

Queue
5 Chapelhill Drive
Fairfield, Connecticut 06423

Random House
201 East 50th Street
New York, New York 10022

Reader's Digest Services
Educational Division
Pleasantville, New York 10572

Right On Programs
P.O. Box 977
Huntington, New York 11743

Scarborough Systems
25 North Broadway
Tarrytown, New York 10591

School Office Software Systems
3408 Dover Road
Durham, North Carolina 27707

Scholastic, Inc.
730 Broadway
New York, New York 10003

Scholastic, Inc.
902 Sylvan Avenue
Englewood Cliffs, New Jersey
07632

Science Research Associates
155 Wacker Drive
Chicago, Illinois 60606

Scott, Foresman & Co.
1900 East Lake Avenue
Glenview, Illinois 60025

Sensible Software, Inc.
6619 Perham Drive
West Bloomfield, Michigan 48033

Sierra On-Line
Sierra On-Line Building
Coarsegold, California 93614

Silcon Valley Systems
1652 El Camino Real
Suite 4
Belmont, California 94002

Sirius Software
10364 Rockingham Drive
Sacramento, California 95827

Skillcorp, Inc.
1711 McGaw Avenue
Irvine, California 92714

Society for Visual Education
1345 West Diversey Parkway
Chicago, Illinois 60614

Soft-Kat
16130 Stagg Street
Van Nuys, California 91406

Softswap
San Mateo County Office of Education
333 Main Street
Redwood City, California 94063

Software Arts
27 Mica Lane
Wellesley, Massachusetts 02181

Software Productions
2357 Southway Drive
P.O. Box 21341
Columbus, Ohio 43221

Software Publishing Corp.
1901 Landings Drive
Mountain View, California 94043

South West EdPsych Services
P.O. Box 1870
Phoenix, Arizona 85001

South-Western Publishing Company
5101 Madison Road
Cincinnati, Ohio 45227

Spinnaker Software
215 First Street
Cambridge, Massachusetts 02142

Springboard Software
7808 Creekridge Circle
Minneapolis, Minnesota 55435

Sterling Swift Publishing Company
1600 Fortview Road
Austin, Texas 78704

SubLOGIC Communications
Corporation
713 Edgebrook Drive
Champaign, Illinois 61820

Sunburst Communications, Inc.
39 Washington Avenue, Room YB7
Pleasantville, New York 10570

Tamarack Software
Water Street
P.O. Box 247
Darby, Montana 59829

Teach Yourself by Computer
Software
40 Stuyvesant Manor
Geneseo, New York 14454

Teaching Tools
P.O. Box 12679
Research Triangle Park, North
Carolina 27709

Teaching Tools Microcomputer
Services
P.O. Box 50065
Palo Alto, California 94303

TEKSYM Corporation
145404 County Road 15
Minneapolis, Minnesota 55441

Terrapin, Inc.
380 Green Street
Cambridge, Massachusetts
02139

T.H.E.S.I.S.
P.O. Box 147
Garden City, Michigan 48135

TSC/Houghton Mifflin
Company
One Beacon Street
Boston, Massachusetts 02108

Unicorn Software
2950 East Flamingo Road
Suite B
Las Vegas, Nevada 89121

Universal Systems for Education,
Inc.
2120 Academy Circle
Suite E
Colorado Springs, Colorado 80909

Vocational Education Productions
California Polytechnic State University
San Luis Obispo, California 93407

Weekly Reader Family Software
Xerox Educational Publishing
Company
245 Long Hill Road
Middletown, Connecticut 06457

John Wiley & Sons, Inc.
605 Third Avenue
New York, New York 10158

Zephyr Services
1900 Murray Avenue
Pittsburgh, Pennsylvania 15217

References

Abbott, C. F., & Gold, S. (1991). Conferring with parents when you're concerned that their child needs special services. *Young Children, 46*(4), 10–14.

Allen, J., Freeman, P., & Osborne, S. (1989). Children's political knowledge and attitudes. *Young Children, 44*(2), 55–61.

Almy, M. (1975). *The early childhood educator at work.* New York: McGraw-Hill.

Althouse, R., & Main, C. (1975). *Science experiences for young children: Color.* New York: Teachers College Press.

Andress, B. (1991). From research to practice: Preschool children and their movement response to music. *Young Children, 47*(1), 22–27.

Anselmo, S., & Zinck, R. A. (1987). Computers for young children? Perhaps. *Young Children, 42*(3), 22–27.

Arnstein, H. S. (1975). *The roots of love.* Indianapolis: Bobbs-Merrill.

Atkins, C. (1984). Writing: Doing something constructive. *Young Children, 40,* 3–7.

Bailey, D. B., Jr. & Wolery, M. (1984). *Teaching infants and preschoolers with handicaps,* Columbus, OH: Merrill.

Banks, J. A., & Banks, C. A. M. (1993). *Multicultural education: Issues and perspectives* (2nd ed.). Needham Heights, MA: Allyn and Bacon.

Barclay, K. D, & Walwer, L. (1992). Linking lyrics and literacy through song picture books. *Young Children, 47*(4), 76–85.

Bayless, K. M., & Ramsey, M. E. (1987). *Music: A way of life for the young child* (3rd ed.). Columbus, OH: Merrill.

Beaty, J. J. (1992a). *Preschool: Appropriate practices.* Ft. Worth, TX: Harcourt Brace Jovanovich.

Beaty, J. J. (1992b). *Skills for preschool teachers* (4th ed.). Columbus, OH: Macmillan.

Becher, R. M. (1986). Parent involvement: A review of research and principles of successful practice. In L. B. Katz, (Ed.), *Current topics in early childhood education: Vol. VI* (pp. 85–122). Norwood, NJ: Ablex.

Billman, J. (1992). The Native American curriculum: Attempting alternatives to tepees and headbands. *Young Children, 46*(6), 22–25.

Bjorklund, G., & Burger, C. (1987). Making conferences work for parents, teachers, and children. *Young Children, 42*(2), 26–31.

Blom, G. E., Cheney, B. D., & Snoddy, J. E. (1986). *Stress in childhood: An intervention model for teachers and other professionals.* New York: Teachers College Press.

Bloom, B. (1964). *Stability and change in human characteristics.* New York: Wiley.

Blue is beautiful. (1973, September 17). *Time*, p. 66.

The bluing of America. (1983, July 18). *Time*, p. 62.

Borden, E. J. (1987). The community connection—It works! *Young Children, 42*(4), 14–23.

Bordner, G. A., & Berkley, M. T. (1992). Educational play: Meeting everyone's needs in mainstreamed classrooms. *Childhood Education, 69*(1), 38–40.

Boutte, G. S., & McCormick, C. B. (1992). Authentic multicultural activities: Avoiding pseudomulticulturalism. *Childhood Education, 68*(3), 140–144.

Bradbard, M. R., & Endsely, R. C. (1980). How can teachers develop young children's curiosity? What current research says to teachers. *Young Children, 35*(5), 21–32.

Bredekamp, S. (Ed.). (1986). *Developmentally appropriate practices* (Position Statement). Washington, DC: National Association for the Education of Young Children.

Brigham Young University Press. (1982). *Parental involvement in early childhood education.* Provo, UT: Author.

Broman, B. L. (1989). *The early years in childhood education.* Prospect Heights. II: Waveland.

Brown, R. (1987). Who is accountable for thoughtfulness? *Phi Delta Kappan, 69*(1), 49–52.

Bruner, J. S. (1960). *The process of education.* Cambridge, MA: Harvard University Press.

Buckner, L. M. (1988). On the fast track to . . . ? Is it early childhood education or early adulthood education? *Young Children, 43*(5), 5.

Bundy, B. F. (1991). Fostering communication between parents and preschools. *Young Children, 46*(2), 12–17.

Burns, P. C., & Broman, B. L. (1983). *The language arts in childhood education* (5th ed.). Boston: Houghton Mifflin.

Butler, D., & Clay, M. (1982). *Reading begins at home: Preparing children for reading before they go to school.* Portsmouth, NH: Heinemann.

Caldwell, B. M. (1985). Parent-child play: A playful evaluation. In C. C. Brown & A. W. Gottfried (Eds.), *Play interactions: The role of toys and parental involvement in children's development* (pp. 167–178). Skillman, NJ: Johnson & Johnson.

Caplan, T., & Caplan F. (1983). *The early childhood years: The 2 to 6 year old.* New York: GD/Perigee.

Carr, K. S. (1988). How can we teach critical thinking? *Childhood Education, 65*(2), 69–73.

Carson, R. (1956). *The sense of wonder.* New York: Harper & Row.

Cartwright, S. (1990). Learning with large blocks. *Young Children, 45*(3), 38–41.

Cartwright, S. (1991). Interview at a small Maine school. *Young Children, 46*(3), 7–11.

Casey, M. B., & Lippman, M. (1991). Learning to plan through play. *Young Children, 46*(4), 52–58.

Cazden, C. B. (1970). Children's questions: Their forms, functions, and roles in education. *Young Children, 25*(4), 202–220.

Charlesworth, R., & Lind, K. K. (1990). *Math and science for young children.* Albany, NY: Delmar.

Charron, E., & Jones, T. (1992). Straight to the source. *Science and Children, 30*(3), 36–37.

Chenfeld, M. B. (1990). "My loose is tooth!" Kidding around with kids. *Young Children, 46*(1), 56–60.

Chenfeld, M. B. (1991). Wanna play? *Young Children, 46*(6), 4–6.

Children's Defense Fund. (1990). *Children 1990: A report card, briefing book, and action primer.* Washington, DC: Author.

Children's Defense Fund. (1991). *The state of America's children 1991.* Washington, DC: Author.

Christie, J. F., & Wardle, F. (1992). How much time is needed for play? *Young Children, 47*(3), 28–32.

Clark, L., DeWolf, S., & Clark, C. (1992). Teaching teachers to avoid having culturally assaultive classrooms. *Young Children, 47*(5), 4–9.

Clemens, S. G. (1991). Art in the classroom. *Young Children, 46*(2), 4–11.

Clement, J., Schweinhart, L. J., Barnett, W. S., Epstein, A. S., & Weikart, D. P. (1984). *Changed lives: The effects of the Perry Preschool Program on youths through age 19.* Ypsilanti, MI: High/Scope Educational Research Foundation.

Cohen, S. (1992). Promoting ecological awareness in children. *Childhood Education, 68*(5), 258–259.

Cole, E. (1992). Art and learning. *Childhood Education, 68*(5), 285–289.

Coleman, J. S. (1991a). A federal report on parental involvement in education. *The Education Digest, 57*(3), 3–5.

Coleman, J. S. (1991b). Planning for the changing nature of family life in schools for young children. *Young Children, 46*(4), 15–20.

Combs, A. W. (Ed.). (1962). *Perceiving, behaving, becoming: A new focus for education* (1962 Yearbook). Washington, DC: Association for Supervision and Curriculum Development.

Conlon, A. (1992). Giving Mrs. Jones a hand: Making group story time more pleasurable and meaningful for young children. *Young Children, 47*(3), 14–18.

Connell, D. R (1987). The first thirty years were the fairest: Notes from the kindergarten and ungraded primary (K–1–2). *Young Children, 42*(5), 30–38.

Conroy, M. (1988, February). Sexism in our schools: Training girls for failure. *Better Homes and Gardens*, pp. 44, 46.

Cosgrove, M. S. (1991). Cooking in the classroom. *Young Children, 46*(3), 43–45.

Crosser, S. (1992). Managing the early childhood classroom. *Young Children, 47*(2), 23–29.

Curran, L. (1991). *Cooperative learning lessons for little ones: Literature-based language arts and social skills.* San Juan Capistrano, CA: Resources for Teachers.

Danielson, L. C., & Bellamy, G. T. (1989). State variation in placement of children with handicaps in segregated environments. *Exceptional Children, 55*(5), 448–455.

Davidson, T., & Steely, J. (1978). *Using learning centers with not-yet readers.* Santa Monica, CA: Goodyear.

Davis, A., & Havighurst, R. J. (1947). *Father of the man.* Boston: Houghton Mifflin.

Day, B. (1988). *Early childhood education: Creative learning activities* (3rd ed.). New York: Macmillan.

Derman-Sparks, L., & the A.B.C. Task Force. (1989). *Anti-bias curriculum: Tools for empowering young children.* Washington, DC: National Association for the Education of Young Children.

Dumtschin, J. U. (1987). Music across the curriculum: More than just circle time. *Day Care and Early Education, 15*(2), 22–25.

Dyson, A. H. (1988). Appreciate the drawing and dictating of young children. *Young Children, 43*(3), 25–32.

Dyson, A. H. (1990). Symbol makers, symbol weavers: How children link play, pictures, and print. *Young Children, 45*(2), 50–57.

Edwards, P. A., & Young, L. S. J. (1992). Beyond parents: Family, community, and school involvement. *Phi Delta Kappan, 74*(1), 72–80.

Elkind, D. (1988). *The hurried child* (2nd ed). Reading, MA: Addison-Wesley.

Elkind, D. (1982). Piaget (Article 26). *Annual editions: Human development* (p. 134). Guilford, CT: Dushkin.

Elkind, D. (1986). Formal education and early childhood education: An essential difference. *Phi Delta Kappan, 67.* 631–636.

Elkind, D. (1987). Superbaby syndrome can lead to elementary school burnout. *Young Children, 42*(3), 14.

Ellis, M. (1979). The complexity of objects and peers. In B. Sutton-Smith (Ed.), *Play and learning* (pp. 157–174). New York: Gardner.

Endres, J. B., & Rockwell, R. E. (1990). *Food, nutrition, and the young child* (3rd ed.). Columbus, OH: Macmillan.

Evans, E. D. (1975). *Contemporary influences in early childhood education* (2nd ed.). New York: Holt, Rinehart & Winston.

Fadiman, C. (1984). *The world treasury of children's literature, Book One.* Boston: Little, Brown.

Farina, A. M., Furth, S. H., & Smith, J. M. (1959). *Growth through play.* Englewood Cliffs, NJ: Prentice-Hall.

Feeney, S., & Moravcik, E. (1987). A thing of beauty: Aesthetic development in young children. *Young Children, 42*(6), 6–15.

Fein, G. G. (1979). Play with actions and objects. In B. Sutton-Smith (Ed.), *Play and learning* (pp. 69–82). New York: Gardner.

Fein, G. G. (1982). Pretend play: New perspective. In J. F. Brown (Ed.), *Curriculum planning for young children* (pp. 22–27). Washington, DC: National Association for the Education of Young Children.

Flavell, J. H. (1963). *The developmental psychology of Jean Piaget,* Princeton, NJ: Van Nostrand.

Foley, M. Z. (1988). What? Me teach? *Science and Children, 25*(4), 11–13.

Fowler, W. (1971). On the value of both play and structure in early childhood education. *Young Children, 27,* 24–36.

Fowler, W. (1980). *Curriculum and assessment guides for infant and child care.* Boston: Allyn & Bacon.

Fox-Barnett, M., & Meyer, T. (1992). The teacher's playing at *my* house this week. *Young Children, 47*(5), 45–50.

Francks, O. R. (1979). Scribbles? Yes they are art. *Young Children, 34*(5), 15–22

Freidberg, J. (1989). Helping today's toddlers become tomorrow's readers: A pilot parent participation project offered through a Pittsburgh Health Agency. *Young Children, 44*(2), 13–16.

Galen, H. (1990). Increasing parental involvement in elementary school: The nitty-gritty of one successful program. *Young Children, 46*(2), 18–22.

Gallup Poll. (1984). *Religion in America.* Princeton, NJ: Gallup International.

Gay, G. (1993). Ethnic minorities and educational equality. In J. A. Banks & C. M. Banks (Eds.), *Multicultural education: Issues and perspectives* (2nd ed.), (pp. 171–194). Boston: Allyn and Bacon.

Genishi, C. (1988). Children's language: Learning words from experience. *Young Children, 44*(1), 16–23.

Giffin, H. (1984). The coordination of meaning in the creation of a shared make-believe reality. In I. Bretherton (Ed.), *Symbolic play: The development of social understanding* (pp. 73–100). New York: Academic.

Glasser, W. (1990). *The quality school.* New York: Harper & Row.

Gollnick, D. M., & Chinn, P. C. (1986). *Multicultural education in a pluralistic society.* Columbus, OH: Macmillan.

Gonzalez-Mena, J. (1992). Taking a culturally sensitive approach in infant-toddler programs. *Young Children, 47*(2), 4–9.

Goodlad, J. I. (1984). *A place called school.* New York: McGraw-Hill.

Goodwin, M. T., & Pollen, G. (1980). *Creative food experiences for children.* Washington, DC: Center for Science in the Public Interest.

Gray, S. W., Ramsey, B. K., & Klaus, R. A. (1982). *From 3 to 20: The early training project.* Baltimore: University Park Press.

Greenberg, P. (1989). Parents as partners in young children's development and education: A new American fad? What does it matter? *Young Children, 44*(4), 61–75.

Greenberg, P. (1992). Ideas that work with young children: Teaching about Native Americans? Or teaching about people, including Native Americans? *Young Children, 46*(6), 27–30, 78–81.

Griffing, P. (1983). Encouraging dramatic play in early childhood. *Young Children, 38*(2), 13–22.

Haines, J. E. & Gerber, L. L. (1988). *Leading young children to music: A resource book for teachers* (3rd ed.). Columbus, OH: Merrill.

Hale-Benson, J. (1986). *Black children—Their roots, culture, and learning* (rev. ed.). Baltimore: Johns Hopkins Press.

Hamilton, D. S. (1990). *Resources for creative teaching in early childhood education* (2nd ed.). New York: Harcourt Brace Jovanovich.

Hanson, R. A., & Reynolds, R. (1991). *Child development: Concepts, issues, and readings* (3rd ed.). St. Paul, MN: West.

Hardy, G. R., & Tolman, M. N. (1993). The care and feeding of magnets. *Science and Children, 30*(4), 22–23.

Harlan, J. D. (1991). *Science experiences for the early childhood years* (5th ed.). Columbus, OH: Macmillan.

Harris, V. J. (1991). Research in review: Multicultural curriculum: African American children's literature. *Young Children, 46*(2), 37–44.

Harsh, A. (1987). Teaching mathematics with children's literature. *Young Children, 42*(6), 24–29.

Hatch, J. A. (1992). Improving language instruction in the primary grades: Strategies for teacher-controlled change. *Young Children, 47*(6), 54–59.

Hatoff, S. H., Byram, C. A., & Ayson, M. C., (1981). *Teacher's practical guide for educating young children.* Boston: Allyn and Bacon.

Haugland, S. W., & Shade, D. D. (1988). Developmentally appropriate software for young children. *Young Children, 43*(4), 37–43.

Hayes, L. F. (1990). From scribbling to writing: Smoothing the way. *Young Children, 45*(3), 62–68.

Henderson, A. T. (1988). Parents are a school's best friends. *Phi Delta Kappan, 70*(2), 149–153.

Hendrick, J. (1987). *Why teach: A first look at working with young children.* Washington, DC: National Association for the Education of Young Children.

Hendrick, J. (1988). *The whole child: Developmental education for the early years* (4th ed.). Columbus, OH: Merrill.

Herr, J., & Morse, W. (1982). Food for thought: Nutrition education for young children. *Young Children, 38,* 3–11.

Herrera, J. F., & Wooden, S. L. (1988). Some thoughts about effective parent-school communication. *Young Children, 43*(6), 78–81.

Heward, W. L., & Orlansky, M. D. (1989). Educational equality for exceptional students. In J. A. Banks & C. A. M. Banks (Eds.), *Multicultural education: Issues and perspectives.* Boston: Allyn and Bacon.

High/Scope Educational Research Foundation. (1985). The cost-effectiveness of high quality early childhood programs: A report for the 1982 Southern Governors' Conference, Hilton Head Island, South Carolina. In J. S. McKee (Ed.), *Early childhood education 85/86, annual editions* (pp. 240–241). Guilford, CT: Dushkin.

Hildebrand, V. (1981). *Introduction to early childhood education* (3rd ed.). New York: Macmillan.

Hitz, R. (1987). Creative problem solving through music activities. *Young Children, 42*(2), 12–17.

Holt, B-G. (1989). *Science with young children* (rev. ed.). Washington, DC: National Association for the Education of Young Children.

Holt, B-G., Ives, W., Levedi, B.L., & von Hippel, C. S. (1983). *Getting involved: Your child and science.* (DHHS Publication No. OHDS 83–31143). Washington, DC: U.S. Department of Health and Human Services.

Honig, A. S. (1980). The young child and you—Learning together. *Young Children, 35*(4), 2–10.

Honig, A. S. (1983). Programming for preschoolers with special needs: How child development knowledge can help. *Early Child Development and Care, 11,* 165–196.

Honig, A. S. (1986). Stress and coping in children, part I. *Young Children, 41*(4), 50–63.

Howe, A. C. (1975a). A rationale for science in early childhood education. *Science Education, 59*(1), 95–101.

Howe, A. C. (1975b). Childhood experiences in science. *Instructor, 84*(1), 58.

Hsu, G. V. B. (1981). Movement and dance are child's play. *Music Education Journal, 67,* 42–43.

Hubbard, R. (1990). There's more than black and white in literacy's palette: Children's use of color. *Language Arts, 67*(5), 492–500.

Humphrey, A. L. (1950). *Heaven in my hand.* Richmond, VA: John Knox.

Hungate, H. (1982). Computers in the kindergarten. *The Computing Teacher, 9*(5), 15–18.

Hunt, J. M. (1961). *Intelligence and experience.* New York: Ronald Press.

Hunt, J. M. (1964). The psychological basis for using preschool enrichment as an antidote for cultural deprivation. *Merrill-Palmer Quarterly of Behavior and Development, 10,* 209–248.

Hurlock, E. B. (1977). *Child development* (6th ed.). New York: McGraw-Hill.

Hymes, J. L., Jr. (1974). *Effective home–school relations* (rev. ed.). Sierra Madre, CA: Southern California Association for the Education of Young Children.

Hymes, J. L. (1980). Bulding bridges for children. *Childhood Education, 57*(2), 72–75.

Hyson, M. C., & Eyman, A. (1986). Approaches to computer literacy in early childhood teacher education. *Young Children, 41*(6), 54–59.

Ideas that work with young children. (1988). Positive self-images: More than mirrors. *Young Children, 43*(4), 57–59.

Isenberg, J., & Quisenberry, N. L. (1988). Play—A necessity for all children. *Childhood Education, 64*(3), 138–145.

Jacobson, S. K., & Padua, S. M. (1992). Pupils and parks: Environmental education in national parks of developing countries. *Childhood Education, 68*(5), 290–293.

Jalongo, M. R., & Collins, M. (1985). Singing with young children! Folk singing for nonmusicians. *Young Children, 40,* 17–22.

James, A. (1992). Will it hurt "Shade"? Adopting a tree. *Childhood Education, 68*(5), 262.

Jelks, P. A. (1981). *Much ado about math: Ideas and activities for math.* Palto Alto, CA: R & E Research Associates.

Jenkins, J. R., Odom, S. L., & Speltz, M. L. (1989). Effects of social integration on preschool children with handicaps. *Exceptional Children, 55*(5), 420–428.

Johnson, D. W., Johnson, R. T., Holubec, E. J., & Roy, P. (1986). *Circles of learning.* Alexandria, VA: Association for Supervision and Curriculum Development.

Johnson, N. L. (1983). *How to insure your child's success in school.* Fresno, CA: Mike Murach and Associates.

Johnson, R. T., Johnson, D. W., & Holubec, E. J. (1987). *Structuring cooperative learning: Lesson plans for teachers.* Edina, MN: Interaction.

Juliebö, M., & Edwards, J. (1989). Encouraging meaning making in young writers. *Young Children, 44*(2), 22–27.

Kagan, S. (1992). *Cooperative learning.* San Juan Capistrano, CA: Resources for Teachers.

Kamii, C. (1982). Encouraging thinking in mathematics. *Phi Delta Kappan, 64,* 247–251.

Kamii, C. (Ed.). (1990). *Achievement testing in early childhood education: The games grown-ups play.* Washington, DC: National Association for the Education of Young Children.

Kane, L. (1982). The power of color. *Health, 14,* 36–37.

Karnes, M. B., & Johnson, L. J. (1989). Training for staff, parents, and volunteers working with children, especially those with disabilities and from low-income homes. *Young Children, 44*(3), 49–56.

Katz, L. G. (1983). *Getting involved: Your child and math.* (DHHS Publication No. OHDS 83–31144). Washington, DC: U.S. Department of Health and Human Services.

Katz, L. G. (1984). The professional early childhood teacher. *Young Children, 39,* 3–9.

Katz, L. G. (1985). What is basic for young children? In J. S. McKee (Ed.), *Early childhood education 1985/86* (pp. 12–15). Guilford, CT: Dushkin.

Katz, L. G. (1990). Impressions of Reggio Emilia preschools. *Young Children, 45*(6), 11–12.

Kellogg, R. (1970). *Analyzing children's art.* Palo Alto, CA: Mayfield.

Kellogg, R. (1967). Understanding children's art. *Psychology Today, 1,* 16–25.

Kelman, A. (1990). Choices for children. *Young Children, 45*(3), 42–45.

Klein, A. (1991). All about ants: Discovery learning in the primary grades. *Young Children, 46*(5), 23–27.

Kogan, N. (1983). Stylistic variation in childhood and adolescence: Creativity, metaphor and cognitive sytles. In J. H. Flavell & E. Markman (Eds.), P. H. Mussen (Series Ed.), *Handbook of child psychology: Vol. 3. Cognitive development* (pp. 630–706). New York: Wiley.

Kontos, S. (1986). What preschool children know about reading and how they learn it. *Young Children, 42*(1), 58–66.

Kositsky, V. (1977). What in the world is cooking in class today? Multiethnic recipes for young children. *Young Children, 33*(1), 23–31.

Kostelnik, M. J., Stein, L. C., & Whiren, A. P. (1988). Children's self-esteem: The verbal environment. *Childhood Education, 65*(1), 29–32.

Kotar, M. (1988). Firsthand experience—firsthand knowledge. *Science and Children, 25*(8), 40.

Kuschner, D. S., & Clark, P. Y. (1977.) Children, materials, and adults in early learning settings. In L. H. Golubcheck & B. Persky (Eds.), *Early childhood education.* Wayne, NJ: Avery Publishing Group.

Lamme, L. L. (1982). Handwriting in an early childhood curriculum. In J. F. Brown (Ed.), *Curriculum planning for young children* (pp. 109–116).

Washington, DC: National Association for the Education of Young Children.

Leeper, S. H., Dales, R. J., Skipper, D. S., & Witherspoon, R. L. (1984). *Good schools for young children* (5th ed.). New York: Macmillan.

Lehman, J. R., & Kandl, T. M. (1992). Marvelous marbles. *Science and Children, 30*(2), 38–39.

Levin, D. E., & Klein, A. (1988). What did you do in school today? Using the school environment to foster communication between children and parents. *Day Care and Early Education, 15*(3), 6–10.

Liepmann, L. (1973). *Your child's sensory world.* New York: Dial.

Linehan, M. F. (1992). Children who are homeless: Educational strategies for school personnel. *Phi Delta Kappan, 74*(1), 61–66.

Lowenfeld, V., & Brittain, W. L. (1987). *Creative and mental growth* (8th ed.). New York: Macmillan.

Ludowise, K. D. (1985). Movement to music. *Childhood Education, 62*(1), 40–43.

Lupkowski, A. E., & Lupkowski, E. A. (1985). Meeting the needs of gifted preschoolers. *Children Today, 14*(2), 10–14.

Mandelbaum, J. (1975). Creative dramatics in early childhood. *Young Children, 30,* 84–92.

Margolis, H. (1987). Self-induced relaxation: A practical strategy to improve self-concepts, reduce anxiety, and prevent behavioral problems. *Clearing House, 60*(8), 355–358.

Massachusetts Mutual Insurance Company. (1991). *American Family Values Poll.* Cited in Idaho Falls, Idaho, *Post Register,* 14 October 1992, p. 5.

Matter, D. (1982). Musical development in young children. *Childhood Education, 58,* 305–307.

Mavrogenes, N. A. (1990). Help parents help their children become literate. *Young Children, 45*(4), 4–9.

Maxim, G. (1989). *The very young child: Guiding children from infancy through the early years* (3rd ed.). Columbus, OH: Merrill.

McCaslin, N. (1984). *Creative dramatics in the classroom* (4th ed.). Chicago: Longmans.

McCormick, L., & Holden, R. (1992). Homeless children : A special challenge. *Young Children, 47*(6), 61–67.

McCune, L. (1985). Play-language relationships and symbolic development. In C. C. Brown & A. W. Gottfried (Eds.), *Play interactions: The role of toys and parental involvement in children's development* (pp. 38–45). Skillman, NJ: Johnson & Johnson.

McDonald, D. T. & Ramsey, J. H. (1982). Awakening the artist: Music for young children. In J. F. Brown (Ed.), *Curriculum planning for young children* (pp. 187–193). Washington, DC: National Association for the Education of Young Children.

McMillen, L., (1986). Many professors now start at the beginning by teaching their students how to think. *Chronicle of Higher Education, 32,* 23–25.

Mearns, H. (1958). *Creative power: The education of youth in the creative arts.* New York: Dover.

Miller, J. (1990). Three-year-olds in their reading corner. *Young Children, 46*(1), 51–54.

Mills, H. (1993). Teaching math concepts in a K–1 class doesn't have to be like pulling teeth—But maybe it should be! *Young Children, 48*(2), 17–20.

Mills, H., & Clyde, J. A. (1991). Children's success as readers and writers: It's the teacher's beliefs that make the difference. *Young Children, 46*(2), 54–59.

Misifi, F. L. (1993). A sense of science. *Science and Children, 30*(4), 28–29.

Mitchell, D. (n.d.). *I have feelings.* Carthage, IL: Good Apple.

Modigliani, K., Reiff, M., & Jones, S. (1987). *Opening your door to children: How to start a family day care program.* Washington, DC: National Association for the Education of Young Children.

Mooman, S. (1984). *Discovering music in early childhood.* Boston: Allyn and Bacon.

Morgan, C., & York, M. E. (1981). Ideas for mainstreaming young children. *Young Children, 36*(2), 18–25.

Morgan, E. (1989). Talking with parents when concerns come up. *Young Children, 44*(2), 52–56.

Mugge, D. J. (1976). Taking the routine out of routines. *Young Children, 31*(3), 209–217.

Murphy, L. B., & Leeper, E. M. (1970). *The ways children learn: I—Caring for children.* (DHEW Publication No. OCD 73-1026). Washington, DC: U.S. Department of Health, Education, and Welfare, Office of Child Development.

Nachbar, R. R. (1992). What do grown-ups do all day? The world of work. *Young Children, 47*(3), 6–12.

Napier, G., Kappen, D., & Tuttle, D. (1974). *Handbook for teachers of visually handicapped.* Louisville, KY: American Printing House for the Blind.

National Association for the Education of Young Children (NAEYC). (1988). NAEYC position statement on developmentally appropriate practice in the primary grades, serving 5- through 9-year-olds. *Young Children, 43*(2), 64–84.

National Association for the Education of Young Children (NAEYC) & National Association of Early Childhood Specialists in State Departments of Education (NAECS/SDE). (1991). Guidelines for appropriate curriculum content and assessment in programs serving children ages 3 through 8. (Joint Position Statement). *Young Children, 46*(3), 21–38.

National Commission on Excellence in Education. (1983). *A nation at risk: The imperative for educational reform.* Washington, DC: U.S. Department of Education.

Nebraska State Board of Education. (1986, Winter). What's best for 5-year-olds? *High/Scope Resource, 5*(1), 3–8.

Neugebauer, B. (Ed.). (1992). *Alike and different.* Washington, DC: National Association for the Education of Young Children.

Neuman, D. B. (1992). *Experiences in science for young children.* Prospect Heights, IL: Waveland.

Nielson Media Research. (1990). *1990 Report on television.* Northbrook, IL: A. C Nielsen.

Nourot, P. M., & VanHoorn, J. L. (1991). Symbolic play in preschool and primary settings. *Young Children, 46*(6) 40–50.

Nunnelley, J. C. (1990). Beyond turkeys, Santas, snowmen, and hearts: How to plan innovative curriculum themes. *Young Children, 46*(1), 24–29.

Odom, S. L., & McEvoy, M. A. (1988). Integration of young children with handicaps and normally developing children. In S. L. Odom & M. Karnes (Eds.), *Early intervention for infants and children with handicaps: An empirical base* (pp. 241–267). Baltimore: Paul H. Brookes.

Olmsted, P. P. (1992, Fall). Where did our diversity come from? *High/Scope Resource, 11*(3), 4–13.

Orlick, T. (1982). *The second cooperative sports and games book.* New York: Pantheon .

Osborn, J. D., & Osborn, D. K. (1983). *Cognition in early childhood.* Athens, GA: Education Associates.

Osborn, D. K., & Osborn, J. D. (1991). *Early childhood education in historical perspective* (3rd ed.). Athens, GA: Daye Press.

Parten, M. B. (1932). Social participation among preschool children. *Journal of Abnormal and Social Psychology, 27,* 243–269.

Parten, M. B. (1933). Social play among preschool children. *Journal of Abnormal and Social Psychology,* 28, 136–147.

Pellegrini, A. D., & Perlmutter, J. C. (1988). Rough and tumble play on the elementary playground. *Young Children, 43*(2), 14–17.

Perry, G., & Rivkin, M. (1992). Teachers and science. *Young Children, 47*(4), 9–16.

Phenice, L., & Hildebrand, V. (1988). Multicultural education: A pathway to global harmony. *Day Care and Early Education, 16*(2), 15–17.

Piaget, J. (1952). *The origins of intelligence in children.* New York: International Universities Press.

Piaget, J. (1955). *Language and thought of the child.* (M. Gabian, Trans.). Cleveland: World Publishing.

Piaget, J. (1970a). Piaget's theory. (G. Gellerier & J. Langer, Trans.) In P. H. Mussen (Ed.). *Carmichael's manual of child psychology* (3rd ed.) (Vol. 1, pp. 703–732). New York: Wiley.

Piaget, J. (1970b). *Science of education and psychology of the child.* New York: Viking.

Piaget, J. (1973). *The child and reality.* New York: Viking.

Piaget, J. (1974). *To understand is to invent.* New York: Viking.

Pitcher, E. G., Feinburg, S. G., & Alexander, D. A. (1989). *Helping young children learn* (5th ed.). Columbus, OH: Merrill.

Poest, C. A., Williams, J. R., Witt, D. D., & Atwood, M. E. (1990). Challenge me to move: Large muscle development in young children. *Young Children, 45*(5), 4–10.

Powell, D. R. (1986). Parent education and support programs. *Young Children, 41*(3), 47–53.

Powell, D. R. (1990). Home visiting in the early years: Program design decisions. *Young Children, 45*(6), 65–73.

Raines, S. C., & Isbell, R. (1988). Talking about wordless books into your classroom. *Young Children, 43*(6), 24–25.

Rambusch, N. M. (1962). *Learning how to learn: An American approach to Montessori.* Baltimore: Helicon.

Ramsey, P. G., & Derman-Sparks, L. (1992). Multicultural education reaffirmed. *Young Children, 47*(2), 10–11.

Reutzel, D. R., & Cooter, R. B., Jr. (1992). *Teaching children to read: From basals to books.* New York: Macmillan.

Rich, D. (1977). Family–community involvement in teacher education. In L. H. Golubcheck & B. Persky (Eds.), *Early childhood education* (in cooperation with The American Federation of Teachers). Wayne, NJ: Avery.

Rich, D. (1991). The ABCs of the home–school–community connection. *The Education Digest, 57*(3), 13–15.

Rivkin, M. (Ed.). (1992). Science is a way of life. *Young Children, 47*(4), 4–8.

Roche, R. L. (1977). *The child and science: Wondering, exploring, growing.* Washington, DC: Association for Childhood Education International.

Rogers, C. S., & Morris, S. S. (1986). Reducing sugar in the children's diets: Why? How? *Young Children, 42*(5), 11–16.

Rogers, C. S., & Sawyers, J. K. (1988). *Play in the lives of children.* Washington, DC: National Association for the Education of Young Children.

Rogers, D. L., & Ross, D. D. (1986). Encouraging positive social interaction among young children. *Young Children, 41*(3), 12–17.

Rotter, J. C., & Robinson, E. H. (1982). *Parent–teacher conferencing: What research says to the teacher.* Washington, DC: National Education Association. (ERIC Document Reproduction Service No. ED 222487).

Rounds, S. (1975). *Teaching the young child.* New York: Agathon.

Rubin, K. H., Fein, G. G., & Vandenberg, B. (1983). Play. In E. M. Hetherington (Ed.), P. H. Mussen (Series Ed.). *Handbook of child psychology: Vol. 4. Socialization, personality, and social development* (pp. 693–774). New York: Wiley.

Salinger, T. S. (1988). *Language arts and literacy for young children. Columbus, OH: Merrill.*

Saracho, O. N., & Spodek, B. (1983). *Understanding the multicultural experience in early childhood education.* Washington, DC: National Association for the Education of Young Children.

Saunders, R., & Bingham-Newman, A. M. (1984). *Piagetian perspectives for preschool: A thinking book for teachers.* Englewood Cliffs, NJ: Prentice-Hall.

Schaeffer, E. S. (1972). Parents as educators. *Young Children, 27*(4), 227–239.

Schickedanz, J. A. (1977). Parents, teachers, and early education. In L. H. Golubcheck & B. Persky (Eds.), *Early childhood education* (in cooperation with The American Federation of Teachers). Wayne, NJ: Avery.

Schickedanz, J. A. (1986). *More than ABC's: The early stages of reading and writing.* Washington, DC: National Association for the Education of Young Children.

Schickedanz, J. A., Chay, S., Gopin, P., Sheng, L. L., Song, S-M, & Wild, N. (1990). Perschoolers and academics: Some thoughts. *Young Children* 46(1), 4–13.

Schirrmacher, R. (1986). Talking with young children about their art. *Young Children, 42*(5), 3–7.

Schweinhart, L. J., Berrueta-Clement, J., Barnett, W. S., Epstein, A. S., & Weikart, D. P. (1985). The promise of early childhood education. *Phi Delta Kappan, 68*, 548–553.

Schweinhart, L. J., & Weikart, D. P. (1980). *Young children grow up: The effects of the Perry Preschool Program on youths through age 15.* Ypsilanti, MI: High/Scope Educational Research Foundation.

Seefeldt, C. (1985a). Parent involvement: Support or stress? *Childhood Education, 62*(2) 98–102.

Seefeldt, C. (1985b). Tomorrow's kindergarten: Pleasure or pressure? *Principal, 64*, 12–15.

SEEK Section. (1991). In Ogden, Utah, *Standard-Examiner,* 3 September 1991. pp. 6, 8–9.

Shaver, J. P., & Curtis, C. K. (1981). *Handicappism and equal opportunity: Teaching about the disabled in social studies.* Reston, VA: The Foundation for Exceptional Children.

Sheldon, A. (1990). Kings are royaler than queens: Language and socialization. *Young Children, 45*(2), 4–9.

Sherman, J. L. (1979). Storytelling with young children. *Young Children, 34*(1), 20–27.

Skanchy, G. W. (1993). AEGIS: *Acquiring ethical guidelines for individual self-government.* Salt Lake City, UT: Institute for Research and Evaluation.

Smith, C. A. (1979). Puppetry and problem-solving skills. *Young Children, 34*, 4–11.

Smith, C. A. (1986). Nurturing kindness through storytelling. *Young Children, 41*(6), 46–51.

Smith, R. F. (1981). Early childhood science education: A Piagetian perspective. *Young Children, 36*(2), 3–10.

Smith, R. F. (1987). Theoretical framework for preschool science experiences. *Young Children, 42*(2), 34–40.

Solter, A. (1992). Understanding tears and tantrums. *Young Children, 47*(4), 64–68.

Soto, L. D. (1991). Research in review: Understanding bilingual/bicultural young children. *Young Children, 46*(2), 30–35.

Spencer, M. B., & Markstrom-Adams, C. (1990). Identity processes among racial and ethnic minority children in America. *Child Development, 61*, 290–310.

Spewock, T. S. (1991). Teaching parents of young children through learning packets. *Young Children, 47*(1), 28–30.

Stenmark, J. K., Thompson, V., & Cossex, R. (1986). *Family math.* Berkeley: Regents, University of California.

Stinson, S. W. (1977). Movement as creative interaction with the child. *Young Children, 32*(6), 49–53.

Stone, J. I. (1987). Early childhood math: Make it manipulative! *Young Children, 42*(6), 16–23.

Strother, D. B. (1987). Preschool children in the public schools: Good investment? or bad? *Phi Delta Kappan, 69*, 304–308.

Sutherland, Z., & Arbuthnot, M. H. (1986). *Children and books* (7th ed.). Glenview, IL: Scott Foresman.

Swick, K. J. (1988). Parental efficacy and involvement. *Childhood Education, 65*, 37–42.

Swick, K. J. (1991). *Teacher-parent partnerships to enhance school success in early childhood education.* Washington, DC: National Education Association.

Taylor, C. (1968). Be talent developers. *Today's Education, 57*, 67–79.

Ten Boom, C. (1971). *The hiding place.* New York: Bantam.

Throne, J. (1988). Becoming a kindergarten of readers? *Young Children, 43*(6), 10–16.

Tiedt, P. L., & Tiedt, I. M. (1986). *Multicultural teaching: A handbook of activities, information, and resourses.* Newton, MA: Allyn and Bacon.

Torrance, E. P. (1976). *Guiding creative talent.* Melbourne, FL: Krieger.

Trelease, J. (1985). *The read-aloud handbook.* New York: Viking.

Tye, K. A. (Ed.). (1990). *Global education: From thought to action.* Alexandria, VA: Association for Supervision and Curriculum Development.

Umansky, W. (1983). On families and the re-valuing of childhood. *Childhood Education, 59*(4), 259–266.

U.S. Departments of Agriculture and Health and Human Services. (1980). *Nutrition and your health: Dietary guidelines for Americans.* Washington, DC: U.S. Government Printing Office.

U.S. Department of Commerce. (1991). *Statistical Abstracts of the United States, 1991* (111th ed.). Washington, DC: U.S. Government Printing Office.

Vandenberg, B. (1981). The role of play in the development of insightful tool-using strategies. *Merrill-Palmer Quarterly, 27*, 97–109.

VanKleeck, A., & Schuele, C. M. (1987). Precursors to literacy: Normal development. *Topics in Language Disorders, 7*, 13–31.

VanScoy, I. J., & Fairchild, S. H. (1993). It's about time! *Young Children, 48*(2), 21–24.

Vonde, D. A., & Beck, J. (1980). *Food adventures for children.* Redondo Beach, CA: Plycon.

Vygotsky, L. S.. (1962). *Thought and language* (E. Hanfmann & G. Vakar, Trans.) Cambridge, MA: MIT Press.

Walberg, H. J. (1984). Families as partners in educational productivity. *Phi Delta Kappan, 65*(6), 397–400.

Wardle, F. (1990). Endorsing children's differences: Meeting the needs of adopted minority children. *Young Children, 45*(5), 44–46.

Warner, L. (1982). 37 music ideas for the nonmusical teacher. *Childhood Education, 58*(3), 134–137.

Warner, L. G. (n.d.). *Child Development Center activity/skill checklist.* Richmond: Eastern Kentucky University, Child Development Center.

Warner, L. G. (n.d.). *Specific skill/activity graph.* Richmond: Eastern Kentucky University, Child Development Center.

Warner, L. G. (n.d.). *Weekly activity plan at-a-glance.* Richmond: Eastern Kentucky University, Child Development Center.

Warren, J. (1978). Patterns. *Young Children, 33*(2), 53.

Wayman, J., & Plum, L. (1977). *Secrets and surprises.* Carthage, IL: Good Apple.

Webster, L., & Schroeder, R. M. (1979) *Early childhood education: An overview.* Princeton, NJ: Princeton Book.

Weikart, D. P. (1985). *Movement plus music.* Ypsilanti, MI: High/Scope.

Weikart, D. P. (1986, Winter). What are the *real* basics. Ypsilanti, MI: *High/Scope Resource, 5*(1), 3–8.

Wellman, H. H. (1982). The foundation of knowledge: Concept development in the young child. In S. G. Moore & C. R. Cooper (Eds.), *The young child: Reviews of research, Vol. 3* (pp. 115–134). Washington, DC: National Association for the Education of Young Children.

Wenig, M., & Brown, M. L. (1975). School efforts + parent/teacher communications = happy young children. *Young Children, 30*(5), 373–376.

Werner, E. E. (1984). Resilient children. *Young Children, 40*(1), 68–72.

White House Conference on food, nutrition, and health, 1969: Final report. (1970). Washington, DC: U.S. Government Printing Office.

White, L. D. (1981). Name games. *Music Educators' Journal, 67*(7), 42–44.

Williams, C. K., & Kamii, C. (1986). How do children learn by handling objects? *Young Children, 42*(1), 23–26.

Winn, D. D. (1988). Develop listening skills as a part of the curriculum. *The Reading Teacher, 42*(2), 144–146.

Witmer, J. (1991). Caregivers' Corner: Providing parent education resources. *Young Children, 46*(4), 58.

Wolf, A. P. (1986). Art appreciation for the young. *Day Care and Early Childhood, 14*(1), 18–19.

Wolf, J. (1992). Let's sing it again. *Young Children, 47*(2), 56–61.

Wolter, D. L., (1992). Whole group story reading? *Young Children, 48*(1), 72–75.

Ziemer, M. (1987). Science and the early childhood curriculum: One thing leads to another. *Young Children, 42*(6), 44–51.

Index